The
Additional Insured
Book

For more information on any IRMI® publication call 1-800-827-4242 (in Dallas, 972-960-7693), e-mail info@IRMI.com, or visit our Web site at **www.IRMI.com.**

IRMI® References

International Risk Management Institute, Inc.

Commercial Property Insurance
Analyzes and explains standard commercial property, nonstandard commercial property, inland marine, boiler and machinery, commercial crime, financial institution crime, and businessowners insurance.

Commercial Liability Insurance
Analyzes and explains commercial general liability, owners and contractors protective liability, liquor liability, products-completed operations liability, railroad protective liability, pollution liability, and umbrella liability insurance.

Commercial Auto Insurance
Analyzes and explains state auto insurance laws and regulations as well as business auto, garage, truckers, and motor carrier insurance.

Professional Liability Insurance
Analyzes and explains for-profit D&O, not-for-profit D&O, fiduciary, employment practices, malpractice, professional, and errors and omissions liability insurance.

Personal Risk Management and Insurance
Your source of answers and competitive strategies for homeowners and personal auto insurance. This practitioner's reference annotates the latest policies and all of the countrywide endorsements. Real-life claims and loss examples are used throughout to help you fully understand coverage intent and loss ramifications. You'll know how to tailor better coverage for your clients and when to negotiate claims. Also, an excellent training tool!

IRMI Workers Comp: A Complete Guide to Coverage, Laws, and Cost Containment
Analyzes and explains state workers compensation laws, federal workers compensation and employers liability laws, workers compensation insurance coverage, monopolistic and competitive state funds, employee leasing considerations, and workers compensation cost management strategies.

Risk Financing
Your complete source of guidelines and strategies for retrospective rating, experience rating, large deductibles, paid loss retros, compensating balance plans, pooling, self-insurance, captives, and the alternative market.

Contractual Risk Transfer
Analyzes and explains indemnity provisions, limitation of liability clauses, waivers of subrogation, contract insurance requirements, contractual liability insurance, additional insured issues, owners and contractors protective insurance, certificates of insurance, and contract administration.

Construction Risk Management
Analyzes and explains construction loss exposures and applicable coverages, enables you to provide practical feedback on contract insurance and indemnity requirements/provisions, and helps you control insurance costs and properly structure a more comprehensive risk management and insurance program.

The Risk Report
Special monthly reports on unique loss exposures, important legal trends, significant commercial lines insurance issues and trends, risk financing techniques, contractual risk transfer strategies, and other risk management topics.

Pollution Coverage Issues
This powerful tool gives you every published state and federal appellate court decision forming the current judicial interpretation of commonly litigated issues involving coverage of pollution claims and current and past editions of the CGL policy.

CGL Reporter
This law reporter gives you annotations of the most critical insurance cases involving general liability and other business-related policies. Written by practicing coverage attorneys, the *CGL Reporter* is designed to help you find pertinent case summaries quickly through a unique indexing system.

EPLiC
Employment Practices Liability Consultant (EPLiC) is your quarterly guide to risk control, insurance coverage, and defense strategies.

Strategic RM–Enterprise Risk Management, Finance, and Transfer
A monthly IRMI report addressing important issues within the insurance industry involving all manners of alternative risk finance and transfer techniques from an enterprise risk management perspective.

Captive Insurance Company Reports (CICR)
As the first and most well-known periodical to focus on the alternative market, *CICR* covers reinsurance, tax, and regulatory developments in the captive industry. Additionally, *CICR* provides comprehensive reports and comparisions of new and existing captive domiciles. The publication also contains frequent updates and reports on reinsurance and fronting conditions and their effects on captives.

Levine on California Workers Compensation Premium and Insurance
A comprehensive treatment of practical, technical, and legal issues specifically affecting California workers compensation premiums and insurance.

BOOKS

The MCS-90 Book: Truckers versus Insurers and the Government Makes Three

Terrorism Insurance: What Risk and Insurance Professionals Must Know

Classification Cross-Reference (12th ed.)

The Additional Insured Book (5th ed.)

Glossary of Insurance and Risk Management Terms (9th ed.)

IRMI CGL and Umbrella Insurance Guide (3rd ed.)

IRMI Commercial Auto Insurance Guide (2nd ed.)

IRMI Workers Compensation Insurance Guide (2nd ed.)

IRMI Political Risk Insurance Guide

IRMI Design-Build Risk and Insurance

IRMI Insurance Checklists 2004

The Wrap-Up Guide (3rd ed.)

Insurance for Defective Construction

Exposure Survey Questionnaire (4th ed.)

Guidelines for Insurance Specifications (4th ed.)

Litigation Management

101 Ways To Cut Business Insurance Costs (3rd ed.)

Blueprint for Workers Comp Cost Containment

Captives and the Management of Risk

The Additional Insured Book

Fifth Edition

Donald S. Malecki, CPCU

Pete Ligeros, JD

Jack P. Gibson, CPCU, CLU, ARM

International Risk Management Institute, Inc.
Dallas, Texas

Fifth Edition, July 2004
PRINTED IN THE UNITED STATES OF AMERICA

"This publication is designed to provide accurate and authoritative information in regard to the subject matter covered. It is sold with the understanding that the publisher is not engaged in rendering legal, accounting, or other professional service. If professional advice is required, the services of a competent professional should be sought."

—From a Declaration of Principles jointly adopted by a Committee of the American Bar Association and a Committee of Publishers and Associations.

Edited by W. Jeffrey Woodward, CPCU

ISBN 1–886813–77–9

International Risk Management Institute, Inc.®
12222 Merit Drive
Suite 1450
Dallas, Texas 75251–2276
(972) 960–7693
Fax (972) 371–5120
www.IRMI.com • info@IRMI.com

International Risk Management Institute, Inc.,® and *IRMI*® are registered trademarks.

CONTENTS

ABOUT THE AUTHORS

Donald S. Malecki

Donald S. Malecki, CPCU, is chairman and CEO of Donald S. Malecki & Associates, Inc., an insurance and risk management consulting firm. He is also president of Malecki Communications Company, the publisher of *Malecki on Insurance*, a monthly newsletter on commercial insurance subjects. He is occasionally called on to testify as a consulting expert in insurance litigation cases requiring property and casualty coverage interpretation, or to give testimony about the customs and practices of agents, brokers, and insurance companies. Both his practical experience and the large amount of materials he has accumulated for these cases serve as a basis for this book.

Mr. Malecki is a past president of the Cincinnati Chapter of the Society of Chartered Property Casualty Underwriters and currently serves on the society's Consultants, Legal and Expert Witness Section. He also is on the examination committee of the American Institute for CPCU and is an active member of the Society of Risk Management Consultants. An author of 10 books, including 3 textbooks used in the CPCU curriculum, Mr. Malecki also is contributing author to *The Risk Report, Construction Risk Management,* and *Commercial Liability Insurance,* all of which are published by IRMI. He can be reached at (513) 451–4210.

Pete Ligeros

Pete Ligeros, JD, a California-based lawyer, is president of Ligeros & Associates, an insurance and risk management consulting firm. He is also a principal of Donald S. Malecki & Associates, Inc., and is a writer for *Malecki on Insurance.*

Mr. Ligeros is coauthor of *The Old and New CGL Forms: A Practical Comparison;* "Umbrella and Excess Liability Coverages," supplemental reading for the CPCU curriculum; and *Commercial Liability Insurance and Risk Management*, 3d., a textbook used in the CPCU curriculum. He also was senior editor of *The Umbrella Book* and the *Attorney's Umbrella Book.* Mr. Ligeros speaks frequently on contractual risk transfer and liability insurance topics at industry seminars and symposia, such as the annual RIMS Conference.

Mr. Ligeros currently serves as a consulting expert and expert witness on property and casualty coverage issues and claims handling and risk management practices and procedures. He can be reached at (949) 833–1646.

Jack P. Gibson

Jack P. Gibson, CPCU, CLU, ARM, is president of International Risk Management Institute, Inc. (IRMI). Mr. Gibson majored in risk management at the university of Georgia, where he received a bachelor of business administration, *cum laude,* in 1977 and a master of business administration in 1979.

Mr. Gibson is the coauthor of many reference works on insurance and risk management, all of which have been published by IRMI. Included among these works are *Contractual Risk Transfer* and *Construction Risk Management,* which address subjects related to this book. In addition to his management duties, he continues as editor of *The Risk Report* and currently is editor-in-chief of IRMI.com. A sought-after seminar speaker, Mr. Gibson has been a presenter at meetings of major industry trade associations serving the risk management and insurance communities as well as many construction industry and lawyer seminars. He co-chairs the annual IRMI Construction Risk Conference and has been a highly rated presenter at each of them. Mr. Gibson can be reached at (972) 960–7693.

Chapter 1

EXECUTIVE SUMMARY

This chapter is a brief summary of the entire book. It reviews some of the most important conclusions drawn in the book and includes references to the chapters where these points are discussed in detail. While this chapter summarizes many of the major conclusions presented in the book, it does not present all of the book's conclusions and the rationales for them. In other words, this chapter is not intended as a substitute for reading the book.

Reasons for Requiring Additional Insured Status

There are a variety of valid reasons for one party to require another to add it as an additional insured on the other party's liability policies. For example, doing so reinforces the risk transfer accomplished with indemnity agreements by providing the additional insured with protection in the form of direct rights under the policy. Additional insured status also means that the courts will be less likely to void insurance as being solely for the purpose of funding an indemnity agreement found to be invalid.

Additional insured status provides the additional insured with the right to an immediate defense by the named insured's insurer rather than being indemnified for defense costs at a later date. Further, these defense costs will be paid in addition to policy limits. In contrast, numerous conditions precedent must be met to avoid having defense costs subjected to the policy limit when contractual liability coverage is relied on without additional insured status.

There are also a number of misconceptions about additional insured coverage. For example, additional insured status does not typically secure the right to receive notice of cancellation. Because of exclusions and limitations often included in additional insured endorsements, additional insured status also does not provide the additional insured with coverage for all types of liability it might incur in connection with a project.

The reasons for requiring additional insured status are discussed in detail in **Chapter 4**. Vendors as additional insureds are treated separately in **Chapter 12**. The subjects of cancellation notice and insurance certificates are discussed in **Chapter 20**.

Additional Named Insured Status

There has long been controversy and confusion as to whether it is best to require additional insured status or additional named insured status. This has been so confusing and controversial because there has been no accepted industry definition of additional named insured status. To some in the insurance industry, such status may be achieved with an endorsement containing the same restrictions and limitations as are typically found in additional insured endorsements but calling the additional insured an "additional named insured." To others, only an endorsement containing no restrictions or limitations that do not also apply to the named insured achieves additional named insured status. Still others feel that an additional named insured endorsement is something between these two extremes.

The provisions in standard liability insurance policies carefully differentiate between named insureds and insureds. Some conditions and exclusions apply to insureds, while others apply only to named insureds. Since a named insured is an insured, any provision or exclusion that applies to insureds applies to insureds and named insureds alike. On the other hand, a provision that applies only to named insureds should not be considered when analyzing the coverage or responsibilities of other categories of insureds. Presumably, this concept would carry over to additional insureds and additional named insureds. Thus, an analysis of the differences in how the policy treats these two groups of insureds is helpful in determining which type of insured status a contracting party should seek. In most instances, this analysis leads to the conclusion that it is preferable to require additional insured status— not *named* insured status.

As a result, to avoid potential problems in this area, it is generally preferable to be added as an additional insured and not as an additional named insured. However, this may not be the case in every instance. Because of the increasing use of manuscript policies, some policy wording or exclusions may make additional named insured status preferable. However, making that determination requires careful review of the policy to be used, which is not a practical alternative for most indemnitees. For this reason, it remains preferable to follow the general rule and require additional insured status.

It is also generally preferable to assure that the underlying contract includes a well-written and enforceable indemnity clause and require that this transfer be backed with contractual liability insurance and additional insured status. The additional insured status contract provision generally should require that it be provided by an endorsement that is at least as broad as the appropriate Insurance Services Office, Inc. (ISO), endorsement would provide. Indemnitees should also be careful to arrange their own liability insurance or risk financing program to respond only when the indemnity clause and additional insured status do not apply or their limits are exhausted.

Chapters **2** and **4** discuss in detail the differences between insureds and named insureds as well as the reasons not to require additional named insured status in liability policies.

Additional Insured versus Contractual Liabilty Coverage

Confusion often surrounds the distinction between the protection afforded to indemnitees added as additional insureds to the policy of the indemnitor as opposed to contractual liability coverage available to the indemnitor to fund its contractual obligation to the indemnitee. Once added to the indemnitor's policy as an additional insured, the indemnitee has direct rights under the policy. Those rights are governed by the terms of the policy and not by the terms of the underlying contract.

Generally speaking, only in cases where the policy is ambiguous on a given point will the courts look outside the policy to the contract for guidance in determining the intent of the parties with respect to additional insured status. Any proceeds payable under the policy on behalf of the additional insured are paid directly to or on behalf of the additional insured.

With contractual liability coverage, the insurer has agreed to insure the tort liability of the indemnitee (i.e., the indemnitee's liability to third parties) that has been assumed by the named insured indemnitor in an indemnity provision. The indemnitee is not an insured under the policy and has no direct rights under the policy, absent a court ruling that the indemnitee is an intended third-party beneficiary or establishing such rights under some other legal theory. Contractual liability coverage applies to the named insured indemnitor, and the insurer's obligation to pay runs to the named insured, not to the indemnitee.

This is a critical distinction in cases where the indemnity agreement is held to be invalid, because without a valid indemnity agreement, neither the named insured indemnitor nor its contractual liability coverage has an obligation to pay for injury or damage attributable to the indemnitee. With additional insured status, however, even if the indemnity agreement is invalid, the indemnitee is still entitled to coverage in its own right as an additional insured under the policy.

This issue is addressed in **Chapters 4** and **5.**

Coverage Scope

It is common for indemnity provisions in contracts to transfer liabilities that are not covered by liability insurance. Additional insured status does not change this fact because policy terms, not underlying contract provisions, dictate the scope of additional insured coverage. Furthermore, most additional insured endorsements contain additional restrictions and limitations with respect to the coverage they provide to additional insureds.

Probably the most confusing and controversial area with respect to coverage limitations is sole fault. Indemnitees sometimes require additional insured status in an attempt to circumvent statutes prohibiting the transfer of sole fault in indemnity provisions. This goal may be achieved with additional insured status if the endorsement used to provide additional insured status does not exclude the additional insured's sole fault and if the contract is drafted carefully (with the insurance requirements stated separately from the defense and indemnification provisions).

It also is essential to ensure that the contract does not imply that additional insured status is provided solely to fund the indemnity obligation. Such an implication may transform additional insured status into nothing more than another form of contractual liability coverage. These and other factors will be the basis of a court's interpretation of coverage and its interaction with the relevant indemnification statute.

Until the revision of standard ISO endorsements in 2004, coverage of the additional insured's sole fault was available in a number of additional insured endorsements, including the most widely used endorsement—CG 20 10. The 2004

revision changed that state of affairs. It imposed a new condition on coverage under CG 20 10 and several other standard endorsements used to provide additional insured status in contractual relationships among project owners, contractors, and subcontractors. Under the revised endorsements, an additional insured has coverage only when the injury or damage giving rise to a claim was caused at least partially by an act or omission of the *named* insured. In short, these endorsements now respond only to claims involving the shared liability of the named and additional insureds.

In some circumstances—where it is permitted by law—indemnitors may be obligated to assume liability for their indemnitees' sole fault. Standard additional insured endorsements no longer provide the indemnitee/additional insured with that scope of coverage. Neither, in some cases, will the indemnitor's own contractual liability coverage, when that coverage has been reduced by a contractual liability exclusionary endorsement. One such endorsement was introduced along with the 2004 ISO revision for optional use whenever an additional insured is added to the policy. Indemnitors must be more careful than ever in making certain that their own general liability policies respond as fully as possible to contractually assumed liability. Neither standard additional insured endorsements nor commercial general liability (CGL) contractual liability coverage (if modified by a limiting endorsement) will meet the full range of the named insured's contractual obligations.

The indemnitee should, of course, also maintain insurance for its own benefit to cover such liability exposures, arranging its insurance program to correspond with coverage available to it as an additional insured. Care must also be taken when drafting the contract to clarify that the additional insured's own coverage is intended to apply as excess over that to which it is added as an additional insured.

Chapters 4, 5, 6, and **7** focus on the extent of the coverage provided to additional insureds.

Additional Insured Coverage and Indemnity

When additional insured coverage was typically broader than the protection available to an indemnitee by way of the hold harmless agreement between it and the indemnitor/named insured, the problem of reconciling these two methods of risk transfer created a number of difficulties among contracting parties. The challenge was most often met by modifying the language of the additional insured endorsement, narrowing its scope to match as closely as possible the scope of the underlying indemnity agreement. If only shared liability of the named and additional insureds was addressed by the indemnity agreement, then only shared liability was covered in the modified additional insured endorsement.

With the introduction of new standard additional insured endorsements in 2004, this problem has been largely relegated to history. Additional insured coverage now typically covers only liability of the additional insured for injury or damage caused at least in part by the named insured. In other words, additional insured coverage now closely matches the scope of intermediate indemnity agreements—the broadest indemnity typically found in many kinds of business contract. Nevertheless, claims continue to be asserted under older (broader) additional insured coverage, and such claims still raise questions about the interplay between insurance coverage and contractual indemnity.

Other issues involving the integration of additional insured coverage into a business's overall risk management strategy have become increasingly important in recent years. How can an entity guarantee that the protection it has as an additional insured will respond to a liability claim first—before its own insurance is called on? In the past, many additional insureds have attempted to solve this problem by requiring that the other party endorse its policies to reflect that its coverage is primary. However, this requirement does not fully eliminate conflicting wording when met and, further, was usually resisted by the other party's insurer. Thus, the requirement was often not met.

Another more easily implemented solution becomes evident when the cases involving the "other insurance" additional insured problem are studied. The courts usually examine the other insurance clauses of the two parties' insurance programs very closely when trying to determine payment priority. In most cases, they find identical clauses within the umbrellas as well as the primary CGL policies. For example, both primary policies typically state that they are primary, and all the umbrellas typically state that they are excess. Therefore, it is only logical that the courts would have all of these policies contribute on a pro rata basis (which is exactly what the standard ISO other insurance provision says should happen when two CGL policies apply on a primary basis).

Since the indemnitor's insurance policies will almost always contain generic other insurance clauses, the problems should be avoidable most of the time by attaching a specific other insurance clause to the additional insured's own policies. This endorsement would make it clear that it is the policy's intent to apply in excess of other insurance available to the named insured as an additional insured under another policy. When the courts follow their usual approach of reviewing the other insurance provisions of the two sets of policies, the intent of the parties will be properly communicated; the courts will generally follow the intent.

The real beauty of this solution to the other insurance problem is that it is fairly easy to implement. Instead of requiring another party's insurer to modify its policy in such a way as to increase its exposure to claims, the indemnitee/additional insured is asking its own insurer to modify its policy in a way to decrease the exposure. In other words, the indemnitee is dealing directly with its own insurer in making this request instead of trying to persuade another party's insurer, with which it has no direct relationship, to attach a manuscript endorsement to a policy.

The insurance industry has now revised the other insurance condition of the standard CGL insurance policy to state that it is excess over any other "primary" insurance available to the named insured as an additional insured under another policy. While this has been a much needed clarification of the CGL policy with respect to additional insureds and other insurance, the CGL revision does not address all of the potential problems. For one thing, the excess provision is stated to apply only when the other available insurance is *primary* insurance. This may leave room for the named insured's umbrella/excess insurers to assert that the additional insured's own CGL policy should apply before their policies. Despite this and other drawbacks to the new language, the introduction of a revised other insurance condition is a good first step in resolving this complex problem.

What are the options for an entity (such as a construction project owner) that has insured status under the policies of several of its indemnitors (contractors and subcontractors, for example)? And what is the defense duty of any one of several insurers that all owe a duty of defense to the same indemnitee/additional insured? These questions have moved to the forefront of insurance litigation involving additional insured status. Along with the "other insurance" issue discussed above, they are addressed in **Chapter 5**.

Certificates of Insurance

As a rule, certificates do not amend, extend, or alter the coverage of the insurance policies they document. As with all rules, however, there are exceptions to this one. It is possible to modify the insurance policy so that it works in conjunction with a certificate to define coverage. In such cases, policy wording must be expanded to recognize the certificate as a vehicle for showing what coverage and limits are applicable. Techniques for making such modifications are discussed in **Chapter 20.**

Faced with increasing administrative burdens involving certificates of insurance, some insurers are directing their agents not to forward copies of standard insurance certificates. These insurers indicate that they will no longer accept or maintain standard certificates, so as to save time and the expense of double handling and mailing. What insurers expect

of their agents and how this requirement may affect both parties is also discussed in **Chapter 20.**

Professional Liability and E&O Insurance

Like the CGL policy, most professional liability policies automatically include as insureds the partners, principals, directors, officers, stockholders, managers, and employees of the named insured professional firm. In most cases, they are insured as professionals only while on the job, not for professional activities undertaken on their own time. However, some insurers will provide coverage by endorsement for moonlighting. Persons for whom the named insured is responsible also are granted automatic additional insured status in some policies and by endorsement in others, particularly lawyers professional liability and contractors professional liability coverage, where the use of professional independent contractors is common.

It is possible for the liability of a professional for rendering or failing to render professional services to be imputed to a nonprofessional. For this reason, some organizations request additional insured status on the professional's liability policy. For example, the owner of a construction project might desire to be added to its architect's or engineer's professional liability policy.

However, most professional liability insurers will not provide this coverage because (1) they cannot properly underwrite insureds who are not under the control of the named insured professional and (2) these nonprofessionals usually lack the credentials necessary to qualify for coverage. For these reasons, requirements to add nonprofessionals as additional insureds under professional liability policies should not be included in contracts.

In most cases, the organization's own CGL policy should cover its vicarious liability for its professionals' errors and omissions. When professional liability insurers can be persuaded to add nonprofessionals as additional insureds, the coverage afforded is usually limited to their vicarious liability.

Additional insured status under professional and E&O liability coverage is discussed in **Chapter 17**. **Chapter 8** discusses the scope of liability coverage that architects, engineers, and surveyors have as additional insureds under CGL policies.

Breach of Additional Insured Requirement

Additional insured status can be provided only by a specific grant of such status within the policy's terms or via an endorsement. Since primary liability policies typically do not automatically grant additional insured status to parties that contractually require it, endorsements usually are necessary. As a result, breach of this contractual requirement is common, leaving would-be additional insureds frantically trying to find coverage.

One strategy that has been pursued is to assert that the CGL policy's contractual liability coverage covers such breaches of contract. While few other issues concerning additional insured status have been definitively settled by the courts, case law on this issue is fairly clear. Many courts have agreed that contractual liability insurance does not cover breach of a requirement to add another party as an additional insured.

While the scope of contractual liability coverage is not intended to encompass such breaches of contract, there is a puzzling aspect to these cases. It appears that some of these liability transfers should have been valid and insured under the contractual liability coverage, irrespective of whether the indemnitee was added as an additional insured. Apparently, the courts often did not review the underlying contracts' hold harmless clauses and consider the application of the policies' contractual liability coverage to those provisions. In some cases, it appeared that the parties became so involved with the breach of contract issue that they overlooked valid transfers of liability through hold harmless agreements.

The intent of the contracting parties should be considered when deciphering indemnity and additional insured issues. The two approaches to risk transfer—indemnity under a hold harmless agreement and additional insured status—should be thought of as a belt and suspenders. When one fails, the other should pick up the slack. In many of the breach of contract cases, it appears that this concept was overlooked.

It is difficult to ascertain why the indemnitees were not asking the court to rule that there was an enforceable hold harmless clause covered by valid contractual liability insurance rather than arguing that the contractual liability insurance should cover breach of the requirement to add another party as an additional insured. Lawyers sometimes fail to make the distinction between additional insured status and contractual liability coverage. If this latter argument (i.e., that contractual liability insurance should cover the breach) should be pursued at all, it should be as a last resort after establishing that the hold harmless clause is inadequate or unenforceable.

Two conclusions can be drawn from an analysis of these cases. First, the underlying business contract should clearly set forth the intent of the parties with respect to both indemnification and additional insured status. The contract should address these two issues—indemnification and additional insured status—in separate provisions to avoid the possibility that ambiguity or enforceability problems with one will affect the other. Also, additional insured coverage should not be provided by endorsements linking that coverage to the indemnity agreement.

Second, in the event of a breach of a requirement to provide additional insured status, the other party's contractual liability insurance should not be overlooked as a possible source of indemnification. However, it generally must be through a valid hold harmless agreement that the other party's contractual liability insurance is accessed, not by way of a breach of contract claim.

Chapter 21 discusses the issue of breach of contract and the cases dealing with the application of contractual liability insurance to such breaches. It also discusses two increasingly popular methods of insuring large construction projects: owner-controlled insurance programs (OCIPs) and contractor-controlled insurance programs (CCIPs), commonly referred to as wrap-ups or consolidated insurance programs.

Blanket Additional Insured Endorsements

One way to reduce the possibility of failing to add another party as an additional insured when contractually required to do so is to attach a blanket additional insured endorsement to the named insured's policy. Such endorsements have long been used in the marketplace, but they have historically been on manuscript forms. While these endorsements do reduce the possibility of breaching a requirement to add another as an additional insured, they sometimes present other problems.

For example, one problem that may arise stems from the usual approach of granting additional insured status to another party when the requirement is imposed in *any* written contract. When granting additional insured status, it is advisable to clearly limit the scope of the additional insured's coverage to liability arising from the contracted-for premises, service, or product. To do otherwise could result in a much broader grant of coverage than any of the parties intended when the contract was drafted. Blanket additional insured endorsements that grant automatic additional insured status when the requirement is imposed in any written contract rarely impose limitations that would properly shape coverage for all types of contracts into which a business may enter.

A conservative approach to providing automatic additional insured status is to specifically delineate the types of contracts (e.g., construction contracts or leases) that can effect additional insured status. These endorsements can then be tailored with limitations applicable to the types of activities contemplated by these contracts.

In 1997 ISO introduced the first standard endorsements designed to effect additional insured status when such a requirement is contractually imposed. These two endorsements take the approach of specifying the types of contracts to which they apply.

Over the past decade, a growing number of insurers have been implementing their own versions of blanket and individual additional insured endorsements. However, some of these endorsements look like standard ISO forms and, in fact, stipulate that they include copyrighted ISO material. A close examination reveals that, despite the incorporation of ISO policy language, many of these additional insured endorsements differ significantly from standard coverage. No one should automatically assume that a blanket or automatic additional insured endorsement is necessarily broad in scope. Each must be read carefully.

Chapter 13 discusses the ISO blanket additional insured endorsement.

OCP Policy as an Alternative

With respect to construction projects, an alternative to adding another party (e.g., the owner) as an insured to a contractor's CGL policy is to purchase a separate owners and contractors protective (OCP) policy for that party. The OCP policy is the subject of **Chapter 10.** From the perspective of indemnitees, OCP policies have advantages and disadvantages as compared to additional insured status. For example, OCP policies deal with the other insurance problem and provide a separate set of limits. However, they present the disadvantages of imposing an additional cost and providing a somewhat more restrictive grant of coverage than may be available to an additional insured under a CGL policy.

Coverage available to an additional insured is usually broader for the personal injury perils and liability of the indemnitee arising from its own acts (outside the scope of general supervision and short of the additional insured's sole fault).

When compared to the full scope of an indemnitee's potential liability arising from a construction project, the limitations inherent in OCP coverage may be significant. The general supervision limitation can become less significant if it can be overcome by enforcing a hold harmless agreement and receiving protection from the indemnitor's contractual liability coverage (which does not contain the limitation).

However, other factors still must be considered. In the final analysis, the decision often will depend on weighing the OCP policy's advantage of a separate set of limits against the potentially broader coverage granted to additional insureds in CGL policies, as well as the cost differential. The coverage available through additional insured status becomes increasingly important as the possible unenforceability of the required hold harmless agreement becomes more likely. In those states where intermediate form hold harmless agreements are not permitted by statute, for example, the additional protection of insured status in a CGL policy usually may be desirable.

In states where there is a high probability of the hold harmless agreement being enforced, on the other hand, additional insured status in a CGL becomes less important. In these states, the issue becomes a determination of whether the separate limits provided warrant the additional premium associated with the OCP policy. In many cases, the answer is yes.

In summary, there is no pat answer to the question of whether it is better for an owner or developer to be an additional insured in a contractor's CGL policy or the named insured in an OCP policy purchased on its behalf. Each of these alternatives has advantages and disadvantages that must be weighed with respect to the circumstances of the specific project. However, neither alternative is a substitute for careful attention to the indemnity clause in the relevant construction contract.

In 1997 the American Institute of Architects (AIA) prescribed an alternative to additional insured status under the standard insurance requirements of its General Conditions Form A201. This alternative form of coverage, known originally as the project management protective liability (PMPL) policy and now available under a standard form as a construction project management

protective liability (PMPL) policy, corresponds closely with the standard OCP policy, but there are some significant differences. **Chapter 10** also discusses this form and compares it to the major features of the standard OCP policy.

Marine and Aircraft Liability Insurance

Many of the same indemnity and risk transfer principles that motivate requests for additional insured status under commercial general liability, property, auto, and other widely written coverages also apply to marine and aviation operations. **Chapter 19** discusses additional insured status and the related subjects of indemnity agreements and subrogation, primarily with respect to the most common marine liability form, protection and indemnity (P&I). Comprehensive general liability modified for maritime exposures, marine general liability, and marine excess liability policies also are touched on.

The second part of **Chapter 19** addresses additional insured status with respect to aircraft liability insurance. This subject is somewhat less complicated than marine insurance. In fact, aircraft liability insurance corresponds very closely to insurance written for automobile exposures, particularly with respect to the Who Is an Insured provision of aircraft liability policies.

Summary

Additional insured status should be thought of as a reinforcement of an underlying business contract's hold harmless or indemnity provision. However, this risk transfer technique is not a panacea. Like hold harmless and indemnity clauses, additional insured status has its drawbacks, and a requirement of additional insured status is not a substitute for the careful drafting of hold harmless agreements.

Chapter 2

NAMED INSURED STATUS

Under most circumstances, a person or organization must be an insured in a liability insurance policy to obtain protection under that policy. Generally speaking, one cannot attain insured status under a liability policy without some specific language establishing that status. In many instances, insured status is granted by specifically naming the person or organization in the appropriate place on the policy's declaration page or in an endorsement to the policy. However, there are also policy provisions that effect insured status without specifying the precise person or entity who will qualify as an insured, named insured, or additional insured. This status might arise based on certain facts in a given relationship between the parties involved.

For example, some broad form named insured endorsements provide insured or named insured status for any newly formed entity regardless of whether designated and whether notice is provided to the insurer. Some liability policies, in particular umbrella policies and a growing number of blanket or automatic additional insured endorsements, effect additional insured status where the named insured is contractually obligated to provide such status under the type of insurance found in that policy. In addition, many excess policies include following form provisions that would provide additional insured status to those who are additional insureds in the underlying layers.

Generally speaking, there are three basic categories of insureds.

- Named insureds

- Automatic insureds

- Additional insureds

Named insureds are those individuals or entities to whom the policy is issued. Named insureds typically have more rights and responsibilities than additional insureds and are also subject to more exclusions. *Automatic insureds* are individuals or entities who are automatically provided with insured status in the policy by virtue of being members of a group with close ties to the named insured, such as the named insured's directors, officers, and employees. *Additional insureds* are individuals or entities who require insured status in conjunction with a business relationship. Additional insured status is usually provided either by endorsement or, as previously mentioned, by way of a policy provision that is triggered by a requirement for additional insured status in the underlying contractual agreement.

Additional insured status is the focus of this book. Before the implications of additional insureds can be fully understood, however, it is first necessary to understand the differences and similarities between named insureds and the two other categories of insureds. It is also important to understand the advantages and disadvantages of named insured status. This chapter sets the stage for such an understanding by defining what a named insured is and discussing some of the implications of named insured status. **Chapters 3 and 4** will expand on this base by discussing each of the other two types of insureds.

"Named Insured" Defined

Named insureds are the persons or organizations to whom a liability policy is issued. These may be individuals, partnerships, joint ventures, corporations, limited liability companies, associations, or some other type of legal entity. More than one named insured may be included on a policy, and the various named insureds could consist of a combination of the various types of business entities. For example, a liability policy could be issued to a partnership and a corporation or to a corporation and an individual.

Whenever more than one named insured is included in a liability policy, there is usually a primary named insured—often delineated as the "first named insured." This primary or first named insured is usually named on the declarations page of the policy. Because of space limitations on standard policy declarations (dec) pages, it is often necessary to list the other named insureds on an endorsement. The title "additional named insured endorsement" or "named insureds" is usually typed on the so-called blank endorsement (because it has no printed language on it) to accomplish this.

Regardless of how they are scheduled in the policy, the other named insureds are often referred to in the insurance industry as "additional named insureds." Unfortunately, however, there is no definition of this term in liability insurance policies, and there may be confusion over exactly what an "additional named insured" is. (As will be seen in **Chapter 4,** this has presented significant communication problems with respect to contractual requirements for additional insured status.)

The fact that the standard commercial general liability (CGL) and other liability policies do not define the term "named insured" can create problems. In the case of *Marathon Pipeline Co. v Maryland Casualty Co.*, 5 F Supp 1252 (USDC D Wyo 1998), additional insured proved to be named insureds as well under the same policy. An owner of a pipeline, Platte, retained the services of an oil company, Marathon, to manage its operations. Marathon hired another firm, SSI, to perform work and specifically instructed SSI to hire a certain high school student who was looking for seasonal employment. Under this arrangement, the student would technically be SSI's employee but Marathon agreed to (1) reimburse SSI for all employment costs and (2) assume responsibility for the student's training and any equipment operated by the student.

The student was severely injured while using a mowing tractor. At the time of the accident, SSI maintained general liability and employers liability coverage, with both Platte and Marathon added as insureds. SSI's general liability insurer denied a claim brought by the student on the basis of the policy's workers compensation and employers liability exclusions. The denial did not address whether coverage was available under the employers liability supplement and whether the student was a temporary worker hired on a seasonal basis, which was the subject of an exception to the policy's permanent employee exclusion. After the student settled with SSI, both Platte and Marathon continued to seek coverage as additional insureds.

The insurer did not dispute that the student's employment made him a "temporary worker." However, it did dispute whether Marathon could avail itself of this exception to the employers liability exclusion because of the wording of the definition of "temporary worker," which read as follows.

> "Temporary worker" means a person who is furnished to you to substitute for a permanent "employee" on leave or to meet seasonal or short-term workload conditions.

The insurer argued that use of the phrase "furnished to *you*" (emphasis added) made the definition inapplicable to Marathon, which was only an additional insured under the policy, not a named insured.

The insurer held that the term "named insured" is not defined anywhere in the CGL coverage form and is not limited to parties listed on the declarations page, since it also applies to "any other person or organization qualifying as a named insured under this policy." The court also pointed to the policy's "separation of insureds" condition, which stipulated that the policy applies "as if each named insured were the only named insured" and "separately to each insured against whom claim is made or suit is brought." The court construed reference to a "named insured" in this provision as an allusion to the existence of a "first named insured" so as to distinguish it from other named insureds, which (according to the court) could include additional insureds.

The court also looked to legal precedents interpreting the same CGL language (identifying the term "you" with named insureds) and applying that term to parties added as insureds, as Platte and Marathon had been. Two cases that influenced the court's decision were *Prisco Serena Sturm Architects v Liberty Mutual Insurance Co.*, 126 F3d 886 (7th Cir 1997); and *Wyner v North American Specialty Insurance Co.*, 78 F3d 752 (1st Cir 1996).

The decision in *Marathon* is difficult to reconcile with other sections of the CGL policy that attempt to make a distinction between named insureds and other insured persons and organizations—particularly business risk exclusions, which typically apply only to the named insured.

The 1986 edition of the standard Insurance Services Office, Inc. (ISO), CGL coverage form contains the following wording.

> Throughout this policy, the words "you" and "your" refer to the named insured shown in the Declarations…. The word "insured" means any person or organization qualifying as such under SECTION II—WHO IS AN INSURED.

Contrary to the *Marathon* court's assertions, this wording distinguishes between named insureds and other categories of insureds. Moreover, it does not state or imply that the term "named insured" can include any other form of insured status. Given the sharp distinction drawn by this language between named insureds and other insured persons, the decision in the *Marathon* case is difficult to rationalize.

Beginning in 1990, the CGL introductory language referring to the meaning of "you" and "your" was modified to read as follows.

> Throughout this policy the words "you" and "your" refer to the Named Insured shown in the Declarations *and any other person or organization qualifying as a named insured*…. The word "insured" means any person or organization qualifying as such under WHO IS AN INSURED (SECTION II).

The italicized wording, which has been present in the standard CGL form since 1990, does not contradict the language that follows it, language that continues to draw a distinction between insureds and named insureds.

When more than one party is intended to have named insured status under a CGL policy, care must be taken on this point. The 1986 CGL, as quoted above, states that only named insureds shown in the policy declarations will be considered "you" and thus will become subject to exclusionary language elsewhere in the policy (such as the business risk exclusion) that incorporates references to "you" and "your." Named insureds afforded that status by endorsement under the 1986 CGL wording may not be subject to such exclusions.

Insured-named insured issues like those raised in the *Marathon* case can be especially problematic in owner or contractor controlled construction insurance programs, commonly called "wrap-ups." Instead of multiple policies under which contractors and subcontractors add each other and the project owner as additional insureds, a wrap-up covers all participants in the project under a single policy.

Because a wrap-up policy names all participants as named insureds, confusion can arise in applying business risk exclusions (which apply typically to "you"—that is, the named insured but not other insureds) and in arranging completed operations coverage for the project owner. The definition of the completed operations hazard refers to bodily injury and property damage occurring away from premises the named insured ("you") owns or rents. Since construction operations typically take place on the owner's premises, injury or damage occurring there will not fall within this definition of completed operations under the owner's policy.

On the other hand, as an additional insured under the contractor's policy, the owner is not subject to the coverage limitations imposed by the "completed operations" definition and typically can rely on that other policy for completed operations coverage. When a wrap-up program is utilized, care must be taken to address the problems created when what has traditionally been additional insured status under another party's policy is converted to named insured status under the single wrap-up policy. The contractual obligations of the parties, particularly those related to indemnity, must be reviewed to determine what modifications must be made to the policy to allow coverage to apply in the manner intended.

Named Insureds' Different Roles

As referenced above, since the inception of standard CGL policy forms, the language has carefully distinguished between named insureds and other insureds. As compared to additional insureds, named insureds in general liability policies have certain expanded responsibilities and privileges that are delineated in the conditions. Named insureds also are subject to more exclusions than other insureds. These differences will be explored in more detail in later chapters, but it is important at this point to gain a basic understanding of what they are. In general, they include the following.

- Named insureds have more stringent loss reporting requirements.

- Named insureds' executive officers, directors, and (usually) employees are automatic insureds.

- Named insureds are required to pay premiums.

- Named insureds receive any return premiums.

- Named insureds may cancel the policy.

- Named insureds are subject to the "business risk" exclusions contained in nearly all liability policies.

- Named insureds receive cancellation notice from the insurer.

There are some differences in these responsibilities and privileges as outlined in the commonly used editions of the general liability forms—the 1973 edition comprehensive general liability policy as well as the 1986 and subsequent edition commercial general liability policies.[1] Exhibit 2.1 compares the obligations and privileges of named insureds under these commercial liability forms.

EXHIBIT 2.1
POLICY CONDITIONS AFFECTING NAMED INSUREDS

	1973 CGL	Post-1986 CGL
Duties in event of occurrence, claim, or suit	Insured	Named Insured
Maintenance of records	Named Insured	First Named Insured
Policy representations	Named Insured	Named Insured
Legal representative in event of death of:	Named Insured	Named Insured
Assignment of policy	Silent	Named Insured
Payment of premium	Named Insured	First Named Insured
Authorized policy changes with insurer's consent	Silent	First Named Insured
Cancellation/nonrenewal	Named Insured	First Named Insured

The major difference in the policies' conditions is that the 1973 policy does not make a distinction between named insureds when there happens to be more than one. In the 1986 and later CGL forms, the first named insured bears the responsibility for maintaining records, paying premiums, authorizing changes, and canceling/nonrenewing the policy. This difference between the two editions is significant. Where the 1973 edition form applies all of its conditions equally to all named insureds, some of the 1986 and later form's conditions apply only to the first named insured, i.e., those conditions dealing with the payment of premium, cancellation, policy changes, and maintenance of records. In each of these instances, the *first* named insured has the obligations and privileges as expressed in the policy.

Quite obviously, when there is more than one named insured on the policy, care must be taken in selecting the one to be named first, and all parties must understand the importance of the first named insured's role. An organized system of communication between such named insureds is a necessity if problems are to be avoided.

Impact of Policy Rescission

Disputes sometimes arise concerning the impact of rescission of the named insured's policy on an additional insured's coverage. The purchase of insurance is a contract between the named insured and the insurer. The named insured makes the representations concerning coverage and must pay the premium (part of the consideration). Therefore, it stands to reason that if the named insured voids the policy, coverage also ends for any additional insured. Severability in this instance is not a defense available to an additional insured seeking to enforce its coverage rights under a rescinded policy. The fact that coverage was canceled becomes a matter between the named insured and the additional insured, to the extent that the loss of coverage was a breach of contract between the parties.

A case in point is *First Financial Insurance Co. v Allstate Interior Demolition Corp.,* 14 F Supp 392 (USDC SD NY 1998). The named insured under a liability policy subcontracted with HRH for the re-

moval of two or more elevators at a hotel. As a result of an accident during the removal process, both the subcontractor, HRH, and the hotel filed suit against the named insured for money damages. When the named insured reported the claim to its insurer, the insurer notified all parties that the policy was being rescinded and the premium returned.

The basis of the insurer's action to rescind the policy was, in part, the named insured's alleged misrepresentation of the nature of the work stated in its application. The work was described as "Interior Demolition and Debris Removal Contractor," without reference to elevator removal work. The insurer maintained it would not have issued the policy had it known that the named insured was engaged in elevator removal work. The insurer also based its rescission on the named insured's alleged misrepresentation of payroll. Had it known the true payroll, the insurer argued, the policy would not have been issued.

The court ruled that the facts of the case supported the insurer's right to rescind the policy. The court also held that the additional insured on this policy, HRH, had no basis for its claims of indemnification from the insurer. The court noted that coverage applied only to property damage occurring during the policy period and, since the policy was held to be void from the beginning, it would not have been possible for HRH to obtain coverage under the voided policy as an additional insured.

The court's conclusion that judicial rescission of the policy disqualified HRH from indemnification was buttressed by yet another of the policy's provisions. This provision was the policy's condition stating that no organization had a right to sue the plaintiff pursuant to the policy "unless all of its terms have been fully complied with." The named insured's failure to comply with the terms of the policy, the court explained, extinguished all coverage, including that of the additional insured, HRH.

Premium Obligations

In the 1973 edition CGL form, the obligation to pay premiums is not limited to any particular named insured. Sometimes the question arises as to whether each of multiple *named insureds* added to the policy have the same premium payment obligations as the original or primary named insured. This was one of the arguments in *Hartford Accident & Indemnity Co. v L&T, Inc., Ajax Truck Rentals, Inc., and Beaver Tire Co.,* 455 S2d 1074 (Fla App 1984).

In this case, the insurer filed a complaint against the primary named insured, Lane Lines, seeking to collect premiums on several insurance policies in which the named insureds were Lane Lines; L&T, Inc., Ajax Truck Rentals, Inc., and Beaver Tire Company. When Lane Lines filed for bankruptcy, the insurer sought to collect the premiums from the other three named insureds that were affiliated with the primary named insured. Summary judgment was granted to the three additional named insureds based on a violation of the statute of frauds and an attempt to enforce an unenforceable oral agreement.

On appeal, the three named insureds contended, among other things, that since Lane Lines alone obtained the insurance, it solely was responsible for the payment of the premiums. They also argued that they were never primarily liable to pay the premiums, even though they were included as named insureds on the policies.

The Florida court disagreed. It stated that, as a general rule, a party who accepts the benefits of a contract cannot escape its burdens, so that a named insured included on a policy at the request of another named insured becomes obligated to pay the premiums by accepting coverage under the policy.[2] The court ruled that this and other issues precluded the lower court's grant of summary judgment and left open the parties' opportunity to show who was or was not responsible for the premium.

In *Commercial Union Insurance Co. v A-1 Contracting Co. of Louisiana, Inc.,* 447 S2d 39 (La App 1st Cir 1984), the court also ruled against additional named insureds who attempted to escape premium payment obligations. The policy in question was a combined comprehensive general liability, workers compensation, and auto policy written to include A-1 Contracting Co., Bruce Hunt Contracting Company, and Bruce Hunt, individually. An endorsement was later attached to include Alex J. Hunt Contracting Company as an additional named insured. The court took note of the fact that all of the various entities insured were businesses of Bruce Hunt. Hunt had purchased insurance covering various entities from the same agency over the years and had not designated a specific entity for a specific policy or policy period. When issued, the policy at issue was subject to a deposit premium. After expiration, an audit reflected an additional premium that went unpaid, prompting this suit against the named insureds.

The policy's three original named insureds contended that none of them was liable for the additional premium and argued instead that the named insured added by endorsement was responsible for the premium. The basis for their contention was that A-1 Contracting Company and Bruce Hunt, individually, had no employees or payroll during the policy period and that there was no Bruce Hunt Contracting Company. It was argued that Alex J. Hunt Contracting Company, which was added by endorsement, owed the premium in question because it had employees.

The court ultimately decided that the insurer covered all of the businesses irrespective of the name or names used. Since Bruce Hunt, individually, made application for and purchased insurance for all of the businesses involved—in his individual capacity and as representative of the businesses—all of the defendant named insureds were responsible for the premiums.[3] The court noted that the situation involved in this case arose out of the corporate structures of the insured and the fact that Hunt owned all of them. In this case, like the previous *Hartford* case and a case with similar facts cited by this court, a complex interacting corporate structure did not shield the owner from its responsibility to pay insurance premiums on a policy that would have been looked to in the event of a loss.

The rulings in these cases should not be taken to mean that additional named insureds will be required to pay premiums in every instance. The line of cases discussed here deals with interacting business entities and common ownership. Different fact patterns may yield different results, depending on the jurisdiction.

The 1986 and later edition CGL policies place premium payment responsibilities on only the *first* named insured. This should substantially eliminate disagreements between insurers and the various named insureds on a policy as to who is responsible for paying premiums. Since, however, there have not yet been any cases involving disputes over the responsibility of multiple named insureds to pay premiums, how the courts will interpret the 1986 language remains to be seen. As noted in **Chapter 3,** premium payment responsibilities also have been the subject of controversy between additional insureds.

Notice Requirements

Another significant point with respect to the distinction between the first named insured and all other named insureds in the latest CGL policy forms concerns the condition dealing with duties in the event of occurrence, claim, or suit. Under this condition of the 1986 and later edition CGL forms, it is "you" (the named insured) who is obligated to give notice, as opposed to the first named insured. It therefore does not matter who notifies the insurance company of an occurrence, offense, claim, or suit so long as it is a *named insured.* However, where there are multiple named insureds this could be problematic. In some instances, not all named insureds will be aware of their obligation to provide notice of an occurrence claim or suit. Under the 1986 and later forms, any insured that is sued must provide copies of the claim or suit, but only the named insured is required to provide notice of the suit. Conversely, under the 1973 CGL policy provisions, it is an insured, rather than the named insured, who must give notice.

The stipulation that an insured (as opposed to a named insured) under the 1973 CGL policy provisions has the obligation to provide notice of an occurrence or claim might be of some concern to some entities. In particular, large organizations may experience problems with this since an employee's knowledge of an event or actual loss may not be communicated properly to responsible persons. As a result, an insurer may attempt to deny coverage, alleging it was prejudiced by the late notice. To overcome this potential problem, some insurers have been willing to modify the liability policy with an endorsement stating that, unless certain named persons or designated positions receive notice of an occurrence, offense, claim, or suit, knowledge by someone within the organization will not constitute knowledge of the insured. An example of such an endorsement is shown in Exhibit 2.2.

Insurers that use mutations of standard policies need to be careful to define terms such as "employee" and "executive officer" to avoid problems over the meaning of undefined terms. For example, whether the undefined term "executive officer" was limited to corporate executives who were tied to the corporate charter and bylaws, or whether that undefined term could also encompass a company's branch manager, was a question that had to be litigated in the case of *Industrial Indemnity Co. v Duwe,* 707 P2d 96 (Or App 1985). The court held that that there was adequate indicia of managerial responsibility for affairs of the employer to permit the conclusion that an employer's branch manager was an "executive officer," despite a lack of formal written ties with the corporate charter and corporate bylaws.

**EXHIBIT 2.2
NOTICE MODIFICATION**

It is understood and agreed that knowledge of an "occurrence," offense, claim, or "suit" by the agent, servant, or "employee" of the named insured shall not in itself constitute knowledge by the named insured, unless an "executive officer" or individuals in the following positions shall have received written notice of such "occurrence," offense, claim, or "suit" from the agent, servant or "employee:"

Scheduled Positions: _____

The case of *Royal Insurance Co. of America v The Cato Corp.,* 481 SE2d 383 (NC App 1997), also involved a dispute over notice under a manuscript endorsement. The two provisions of the liability policy that were addressed in this case were (1) Section IV, Condition 2. entitled "Duties In The Event Of Occurrence, Claim Or Suit," and (2) a manuscript (nonstandard) "Knowledge of Occurrence" endorsement modifying part of that policy's notice condition. The pertinent part of the policy condition read as follows.

   2. Duties In The Event Of Occurrence, Claim Or Suit

      a. You must see to it that we are notified as soon as practicable of an "occurrence," or an offense which may result in a claim.

          ...

      b. If a claim is made or "suit" is brought against any insured, you must:

          (1) Immediately record the specifics of the claim or "suit" and the date received; and

          (2) Notify us as soon as practicable.

          You must see to it that we receive written notice of the claim or "suit" as soon as practicable.

      c. You and any other involved insured must:

          Immediately send us copies of any demands, notices, summonses or legal papers received in connection with the claim or "suit";

The manuscript endorsement attached to the policy read as follows.

Knowledge of Occurrence

It is understood and agreed that knowledge of an occurrence by the agent, servant or employee of the Insured shall not in itself constitute knowledge by the Insured unless an executive officer or the insurance department of the Insured Corporation shall have received written notice of such claim from the agent, servant or employee.

The determinative issue in this case was whether the wording of the above manuscript endorsement, dealing with knowledge of an occurrence, modified the notice requirements in Section IV, condition 2(c) of the policy. The insured maintained that it had no duty to send the insurer legal papers filed and served on the insured by a specific claimant until an executive officer or the insurance department had written materials in hand.

The court rejected the insured's argument that the manuscript endorsement modified condition 2(c) of the policy—holding that by its terms, the "Knowledge of Occurrence" endorsement addressed only the insured's duty to provide notice with respect to occurrences. In doing so it designated the insurance department and executive officers as the persons whose knowledge triggers a duty to report occurrences. The court added that the manuscript endorsement made no reference to, and thus did not modify, the insured's obligations to "immediately send" legal documents evidencing commencement of a suit pursuant to condition 2(c). That condition was held to be separate and distinct from the insured's duty under the policy to notify the insurer of an occurrence, offense, or claim. The court therefore concluded that the "Knowledge of Occurrence" endorsement did not modify condition 2(c) of the policy dealing with notice of legal papers in connection with a claim or suit.

Interestingly, the endorsement in this case did not include the following wording: "All other terms of this policy remain unchanged." Without this wording, it can be said that the revised notice condition in the endorsement fully replaced the existing notice provision, as opposed to merely supplementing it. Endorsements take precedence over policy wording, and there was nothing in the endorsement involved in this case to indicate that any portion of the policy's notice provision remained in effect.

Even though the manuscript endorsement failed to state that all other terms of the policy remained unchanged, the court held that it lacked clarity with its reference to claim instead of occurrence. As a result, the endorsement's provisions were held to be limited solely to occurrences and therefore only with respect to policy condition 2(a). Conditions 2(b) and 2(c) involved obligations when a claim or suit is made and therefore were outside the scope of this particular manuscript endorsement.

When the named insured employs a risk manager, the endorsement can be worded so as to make notice contingent on the knowledge of the risk manager or the risk management department. In one unreported case, the risk manager of a company was the last to know about a given suit. In fact, the risk manager did not notify the insurer until the employer had settled the suit. Ordinarily, this type of communication breakdown would lead to a denial of coverage. However, the liability policy in question was endorsed with wording to the effect that notice of an occurrence, claim, or suit to an insurer was not necessary until the risk manager was aware of it. Since such situations are not uncommon, an insurance policy modification concerning the giving of notices might be recommended. Policies that do not contain wording clarifying who must be aware of an occurrence before the notice obligation is triggered may face problems. In the case of a corporate entity, it may be difficult for the insurer to pinpoint precisely when the notice obligation was triggered.

The broad requirement in the 1973 CGL policy provisions that insureds must give notice of a potential claim or suit can be problematic for additional insureds. Since the policy applies separately to each insured against whom claim is made or suit is brought, an additional insured may have an independent duty to notify the insurer of any occurrence, claim, or suit. Failure to provide such notice might be argued to have prejudiced the insurer, and the insurer can then rely on late notice as a defense to deny any protection sought. (However, the courts in some jurisdictions have held that notice to the insurer by the named insured inures to the benefit of all insureds.)

A case in point is *Casualty Insurance Co. v E.W. Corrigan Construction Co.,* 617 NE2d 228 (Ill 1993). The question before the Illinois Appellate Court was whether notice of an occurrence from an employer of an injured party under a workers compensation policy satisfies the notice requirements for an additional insured under a general liability policy issued by the same insurer.

The insurer maintained that if a policy is written or an insured is added to an existing policy, it does not know until notice of an occurrence is sent to it by the insured. In rejecting this argument, the court asked rhetorically, "If this is so, and the insurer does not keep track of who it has insured, how does the insurer determine what its monetary reserves require or even what its projected liability will be over a period?" On its face, the court concluded, "It is nonsensical to contend that Casualty does not know who it has insured, or that, once Casualty receives notice of an occurrence, it would be 'impractical and economically unfeasible' for it to determine if other policies are in force."

Casualty also argued that notice of a workers compensation claim should not be deemed to satisfy the notice requirement of the general liability policy handled by a different department and cited *Mollihan v Stephany,* 368 NE2d 465 (52 Ill App 3d 1034), for the proposition that knowledge of one department of the insurer is not automatically attributable to another department. However, the court in *Casualty* stated that "the better rule of law" is that the department of an insurance company should not be able to "disclaim knowledge of that which is known to another department of the same company." As the additional insured, Corrigan, pointed out in its brief, "a contrary rule would put a premium on ignorance and encourage insurers to conceal their knowledge."

In ruling against Casualty and holding that an insurer is chargeable with knowledge of all policies issued by it to the insured, the court relied on *Duggan v Travelers Indemnity Co.,* 383 F2d 871 (1st Cir 1967), which posed the following question found to be persuasive by this court.

Once a notice of claim is filed, is it too much to ask that an insurer have a reasonable filing system, that its employees check the files for more than one policy covering the same insured for the same risk, and that, if questions arise over coverage, it surface them and, while reserving such rights as it sees fit to assert, proceed both to preserve the rights of its policyholder and itself? We think not. And we are confident that contemporary office systems and management are up to the task.

Since it is the named insured who must provide notice to the insurer, it would still behoove the named insured to notify the insurer of any additional insured involvement. If failure to do so leads to a dispute over whether the additional insured is covered regardless of the outcome of the dispute, the named insured could face a situation where it is in breach of its promise to procure insurance for others. This allegation generally would not be covered under liability insurance (see **Chapter 21**).

Another point in dealing with the 1986 and later CGL forms is that it is "you" (the named insured), rather than the first named insured, whose representations are relied on by the insurance company. Whether the word "you" can be read to mean all named insureds collectively, when there is more than one, is uncertain. In other words, whether an insurer could deny coverage under the policy to all named insureds because of the alleged misrepresentations of the one named insured who signed the application (or its authorized representative) is likely to be vigorously contested.

Insureds generally have no idea that their coverage might be argued to be dependent on the representations made by every other insured under the same policy. Their reliance is based in part on a lack of custom and practice in the insurance and risk management industry, holding all insureds responsible for the representations of another insured under a liability policy.

Insureds also rely on the fact that the liability policy applies separately to each insured and can cite a lack of wording in the policy that clarifies such an application of coverage. This approach of holding all insureds responsible for the representations of another has been limited traditionally to directors and officers and similar liability coverages. In those policies, that position is clearly stated in the application that is made a part of the policy.

Cross-Liability Exclusions

Most types of liability policies, including the CGL forms drafted by ISO, contain severability of interests clauses making the policy applicable to claims made by one insured against another insured. However, so-called cross-liability or insured versus insured exclusions are sometimes added to these policies. This subject is discussed more fully in **Chapter 6,** but it is important to note here that such an exclusion could preclude coverage if one named insured were to sue another named insured.

This type of exclusion is also used when there is an intercompany products liability exposure, but the insured does not desire to pay for coverage for this exposure. An example is when two or more subsidiaries produce components of a product that is assembled and sold by another subsidiary or the parent company. If there is a chance for cross-suits between the insureds, it would be best to avoid the cross-liability exclusion. However, coverage is not without its cost. If coverage does not appear to be necessary, an exclusion may be attached to the policy in return for a reduced premium. The appropriate ISO endorsement is CG 21 41, Exclusion—Intercompany Products Suits. This endorsement is shown in Exhibit 2.3.

**EXHIBIT 2.3
EXCLUSION—INTERCOMPANY
PRODUCTS SUITS**

This insurance does not apply to any claim for damages by any Named Insured against another Named Insured because of "bodily injury" or "property damage" arising out of "your products" and included within the "products-completed operations hazard."

Copyright, Insurance Services Office, Inc., 1984

It should be noted that the Intercompany Products Suits Exclusion endorsement does not designate an area on the form for a premium reduction. The reason is that the premium reduction results from the use of a lower exposure base instead of a lower rate. When the endorsement is attached, the dollar amount of the intercompany sales is subtracted from total sales, thus reducing the exposure base used to determine the premium. It is important that the exclusion endorsement be pointed out to premium auditors so that there is no possibility that intercompany sales will be included in the exposure base when the final premium is calculated.

Under no circumstances should a general cross-liability exclusion be attached to the policy when the intent is to preclude only intercompany suits involving products. If an insurer makes a cross-liability exclusion a condition of insurance, the insured or producer should ensure that there is a commensurate reduction in premium. In addition, other steps must be taken to address this risk.

Deductibles

The application of deductibles is another possible source of problems that can confront multiple named insureds under liability policies. A case in point is *Northbrook Insurance Co. v Kuljian Corp.,* 690 F2d 368 (3d Cir 1982). This case involved two corporate entities with common ownership. The Kuljian Corporation was in the construction business, and H.A. Kuljian & Company was in the business of architecture and engineering. The insurer issued a professional liability policy covering both entities as named insureds. In fact, both corporations were listed on the policy without differentiating between their nature. This policy was subject to a deductible of $25,000, an obligation inuring to the insured.

Suit was brought against H.A. Kuljian & Company by a school district that alleged negligent design and construction of a school building. The Kuljian Corporation was not a party named in this action.

Eventually, the school district agreed to a $25,000 settlement. Unfortunately, however, it turned out that H.A. Kuljian & Company, against whom suit was filed, was insolvent and therefore was unable to pay the deductible amount. When the suit was finally settled, the insurer paid the named insured's share, amounting to $25,000, and an additional $12,153 for legal costs. The insurer then filed suit against the Kuljian Corporation for the deductible amount.

Following trial, the district court ruled that the remaining named insured on the policy, the Kuljian Corporation, was obligated to pay the insurer the amount sought. In so holding, the court stated that in accepting the policy, both named insureds likewise accepted the policy's terms that obligated the insured—consisting of both Kuljian entities—to pay whatever deductible might be necessary following payment of claim by the insurer.

Both named insureds argued that the correct interpretation of the policy would only require the named insured on whose behalf claim payment was made to pay the deductible. However, neither named insured was able to point to any specific policy provision that reinforced their argument, and the court stated that it was not in the position to rewrite the terms of the policy, which applied to the deductible obligation to the insured a term defined to include the named insured. One justice dissented on the basis of policy ambiguity. Nonetheless, the Kuljian Corporation, which had no responsibility for the underlying legal action, still had an obligation to pay on behalf of H.A. Kuljian Company, which was responsible for the deductible amount under the policy.

Sometimes the question raised is whether it is the named insured or an additional insured that is responsible for the deductible. In fact, this is sometimes a concern to contract drafters, and they often try to deal with the issue in various ways within the underlying business contract (e.g., by specifying that it is the named insured's responsibility to pay any deductibles or by prohibiting deductibles altogether). However, this would not be necessary if the policy were to include the standard CGL deductible endorsement. The ISO Deductible Liability Insurance (CG 03 00) endorsement clearly makes it the named insured's responsibility to reimburse the deductible to the insurer. The applicable provision is shown in Exhibit 2.4. When reviewing this reimbursement provision, it is important to remember that the term "you" is defined in the policy to be the "named insured."

EXHIBIT 2.4
DEDUCTIBLE LIABILITY INSURANCE REIMBURSEMENT PROVISION

D. We may pay any part or all of the deductible amount to effect settlement of any claim or "suit" and, upon notification of the action taken, *you* shall promptly reimburse us for such part of the deductible amount as has been paid by us. [Emphasis added.]

This was one of the issues in *Hartford Accident and Indemnity Co. v U.S. Natural Resources, Inc.,* 897 F Supp 466 (D Ore 1995). The named insured argued that its insurer's payment toward the settlement on behalf of additional insureds satisfied the named insured's obligation to reimburse the insurer for the deductible. The named insured's theory appeared to be that if an entity is an insured under its policy, then the additional insured should be obligated to pay the deductible.

However, the court agreed with the insurer that the plain language of the policy defeated the named insured's arguments because (1) the policy was a contract between the named insured and the insurer that the policy preamble makes clear, and (2) the deductible provision obligated the named insured to promptly reimburse the insurance company for such part of the deductible amount as has been paid by the insurer.

In the case of *Continental Casualty Co. v Campbell Design Group,* 914 SW2d 43 (Mo App ED

1996), the insurer of professional liability coverage brought a suit against the named insured and two of its corporate officers to recover the deductible in the amount of $75,000. The court held that the corporation was answerable for repayment of the deductible, but not the corporate officers and additional insureds who were not parties to the contract (policy).

Of course, the fact that the standard deductible endorsement requires the named insured, rather than the additional insured, to reimburse the insurer for amounts within the deductible does not give complete assurance that a problem will not arise in this regard. Nonstandard policy forms or endorsements could certainly impose the requirement on the insured rather than the name insured. This was exactly the case in *Northbrook v Kuljian,* discussed previously. In that case, because the term "insured" included the named insureds, each named insured was independently liable for the deductible.

In addition, self-insured retention (SIR) endorsements, usually manuscript in nature, can also be prepared in such a way as to impose the obligations of assuming the SIR amount on any insured, which might be interpreted, depending on the entire endorsement, to include additional insureds.

Summary

There are some differences in the rights and duties of named insureds and insureds under liability policies. However, as will be made even clearer in the next two chapters, there are probably not as many advantages to named insured status as many insurance and legal professionals seem to believe. On the other hand, there are some significant additional obligations associated with named insured status—such as requirements to notify the insurer of potential claims or suits and to pay premiums and deductibles—that are not imposed on other insureds.

Chapter 2 Notes

1. The 1973 CGL policy still is used by some insurers for competitive reasons. Other insurers offer a prototype of this policy. This means that some of the provisions correspond to the 1973 policy provisions but may include some of the broader exclusionary provisions of later forms. Reference to the 1986 CGL forms includes subsequent revisions unless otherwise stated. See **Appendix A** for more information about the different forms.

2. On the other hand, it has been said that it is not a condition of being an insured that the latter pay any premiums (*Couch on Insurance 2d,* Sec. 31:135). But as noted later, this statement may be more appropriate to additional insureds.

3. An earlier Louisiana case that ruled the same way as the *Commercial Union* case is *Liberty Mutual Insurance Co. v Petroleum Venture Capital Corp.,* 216 S2d 925 (La 1968). Here, the insurer instituted an action to recover insurance premiums. The court ruled that the insured corporation—which made application for and had purchased, in its individual capacity, policies covering it and other corporations having common ownership—was responsible for the payment of premiums.

Chapter 3

AUTOMATIC INSURED STATUS

As noted in **Chapter 2,** there are two categories of additional insureds: (1) those persons or organizations who are *automatically* included as insureds within the Persons Insured or other provisions of the policy because they belong to a group with close ties to the named insured and (2) those persons or organizations who are provided insured status in response to a provision contained in a business contract. This chapter will discuss automatic insured status under primary liability policies. **Chapters 4 and 5** will address insured status provided to comply with contractual agreements.

Automatic Insureds

The policy provisions that effect automatic additional insured status on behalf of various parties are the Who Is an Insured provisions (Section II) in the 1986 and later edition commercial general liability (CGL) policies or the Persons Insured provisions in the 1973 edition comprehensive general liability policy. Those who are provided automatic additional insured status by standard policy wording generally have a close relationship to the named insured(s), such as spouses, stockholders, directors, and employees of the named insured. Exhibit 3.1 depicts the Who Is an Insured section of the standard CGL form, and Exhibit 3.2 schematically depicts the automatic insureds of the 1986 and later edition forms. With two differences, Exhibit 3.2 also reflects the additional insureds of the 1973 CGL policy provisions. The two differences, as explained more fully later, concern employees and newly acquired or formed organizations.

Careful review of the Who Is an Insured provision of the 1986 or 1973 CGL policy provisions will reveal that most automatic insureds are related in some special way to the named insured. For example, if Construction Company A, as the policy's named insured, is a sole proprietorship, the owner and the company will be one and the same.[1] The owner's spouse is an automatic additional insured but only with respect to the conduct of the named insured's business. If, on the other hand, Construction Company A is a corporation, the automatic additional insureds will include the entity's executive officers, employees, directors, and stockholders, subject to certain specific limitations or extensions.[2]

Stockholders

Stockholders have been considered automatic insureds for years. As a matter of fact, the comprehensive general liability policy used in the 1940s included stockholders under the definition of "insured."

Historically, the condition of stockholders' coverage under liability policies was contingent on their acting within the scope of their duties as such. However, with the introduction of the 1986 commercial general liability policy provisions, the phrase "while acting within the scope of his duties as such" was eliminated. While some commentators have speculated that this phrase may have been eliminated primarily for editorial purposes, the more likely reason is insurers' realization that the courts were beginning to regard this phrase as ambiguous. A case in point is *Turner & Newall, PLC v American Mutual Liability Insurance Co.*, 1985 WL 8056 (D DC 1985 applying Pennsylvania law).

This complex case involved an English corporation, Turner & Newell (T&N), with its principal

EXHIBIT 3.1
CGL WHO IS AN INSURED PROVISION

SECTION II—WHO IS AN INSURED

1. If you are designated in the Declarations as:

    a. An individual, you and your spouse are insureds, but only with respect to the conduct of a business of which you are the sole owner.

    b. A partnership or joint venture, you are an insured. Your members, your partners, and their spouses are also insureds, but only with respect to the conduct of your business.

    c. A limited liability company, you are an insured. Your members also are insureds, but only with respect to the conduct of your business. Your managers are insureds, but only with respect to their duties as your managers.

    d. An organization other than a partnership, joint venture or limited liability company, you are an insured. Your "executive officers" and directors are insureds, but only with respect to their duties as your officers or directors. Your stockholders also are insureds, but only with respect to their liability as stockholders.

2. Each of the following is also an insured

    a. Your "volunteer workers" only while performing duties related to the conduct of your business, or your "employees", other than either your "executive officers" (if you are an organization other than a partnership, joint venture or limited liability company) or your managers (if you are a limited liability company), but only for acts within the scope of their employment by you or while performing duties related to the conduct of your business. However, none of these "employees" or "volunteer workers" are insureds for:

        (1) "Bodily injury" or "personal injury":

            (a) To you, to your partners or members (if you are a partnership or joint venture), to your members (if you are a limited liability company), to a co-"employee" while in the course of his or her employment or performing duties related to the conduct of your business, or to your other "volunteer workers" while performing duties related to the conduct of your business;

            (b) To the spouse, child, parent, brother or sister of that co-"employee" or "volunteer worker" as a consequence of paragraph (1)(a) above;

            (c) For which there is any obligation to share damages with or repay someone else who must pay damages because of the injury described in paragraphs (1)(a) or (b) above; or

            (d) Arising out of his or her providing or failing to provide professional health care services.

        (2) "Property damage" to property:

            (a) Owned, occupied or used by,

            (b) Rented to, in the care, custody or control of, or over which physical control is being exercised for any purpose by

            you, any of your "employees", "volunteer workers", any partner or member (if you are a partnership or joint venture), or any member (if you are a limited liability company).

continued

EXHIBIT 3.1
CGL WHO IS AN INSURED PROVISION (cont.)

b. Any person (other than your "employee" or "volunteer worker") or any organization while acting as your real estate manager.

c. Any person or organization having proper temporary custody of your property if you die, but only:

  (1) With respect to liability arising out of the maintenance or use of that property; and

  (2) Until your legal representative has been appointed.

d. Your legal representative if you die, but only with respect to duties as such. That representative will have all your rights and duties under this Coverage Part.

3. With respect to "mobile equipment" registered in your name under any motor vehicle registration law, any person is an insured while driving such equipment along a public highway with your permission. Any other person or organization responsible for the conduct of such person is also an insured, but only with respect to liability arising out of the operation of the equipment, and only if no other insurance of any kind is available to that person or organization for this liability. However, no person or organization is an insured with respect to:

a. "Bodily injury" to a co-"employee" of the person driving the equipment; or

b. "Property damage" to property owned by, rented to, in the charge of or occupied by you or the employer of any person who is an insured under this provision.

4. Any organization you newly acquire or form, other than a partnership or joint venture, or limited liability company, and over which you maintain ownership or majority interest, will qualify as a Named Insured if there is no other similar insurance available to that organization. However:

a. Coverage under this provision is afforded only until the 90th day after you acquire or form the organization or the end of the policy period, whichever is earlier;

b. Coverage A does not apply to "bodily injury" or "property damage" that occurred before you acquired or formed the organization; and

c. Coverage B does not apply to "personal injury" or "advertising injury" arising out of an offense committed before you acquired or formed the organization.

No person or organization is an insured with respect to the conduct of any current or past partnership or joint venture or limited liability company that is not shown as a Named Insured in the Declarations.

place of business in England, and an American company, Keasbey & Mattison (K&M), which was a Pennsylvania corporation engaged in the manufacture and sale of a wide variety of asbestos-containing cement, textile, and insulation products.

From 1934 to 1938, T&N owned and directly held *a majority* of K&M's common stock. From 1938 to 1951, T&N owned and held directly *all* of K&M's common stock. From 1951 to 1967, K&M's common stock was held by T&N's wholly owned subsidiary, Turner and Newell Overseas (T&NO). T&NO was a holding company formed to enable T&N to raise capital. T&NO owned no factories, manufactured nothing, and sold nothing. The officers and directors of T&N and T&NO were virtually identical. In 1962 K&M sold its assets to a number of different concerns and filed for dissolution, which became final in 1967.

With the dissolution of K&M, tort claimants who otherwise would have filed claims against K&M sought others against whom claims could be brought. One of the issues in this case was whether T&N was entitled to defense by the former insurer of K&M, American Mutual. The language at the center of this dispute concerned the definition of "insured" and whether T&N was a stockholder of K&M for the several years during which T&NO— and not T&N—held the K&M stock directly. T&N, through its officers and directors, who were the same as T&NO, exercised control over K&M that the court found incident to stock ownership. Because the court found no separate identity between T&N and T&NO, it held that T&N was a stockholder of K&M, even for the period that T&N held the stock of K&M through T&NO.

Another major question before the court was whether the phrase "while acting within the scope of his duties as such" created a duty on the part of American Mutual to defend T&N when it was being sued following the dissolution of K&M due to T&N's status as K&M's owner. Among the issues to be decided by the court in making this determination was whether the term "stockholder" and the phrase "while acting within the scope of his duties as such" were ambiguous. The court, in ruling that

the insurer had an obligation to provide defense for T&N, held that the phrase "while acting within the scope of his duties as such" was ambiguous. The insurer argued that the phrase was meant to apply in situations in which the actions of stockholders gave rise to liability on the part of the named insured and not in situations in which the actions of the named insured were claimed to give rise to liability on the part of the additional insured.

In any event, such questions as were before the court in the preceding case are now moot because the phrase "while acting within the scope of his duties as such" has been eliminated. It also is interesting to note that the court in this case applied, in reverse, the same concept and principle used by the courts to determine liability of various entities for insurance premiums. In the cases involving premiums, discussed in **Chapter 2,** complex corporate structures were not allowed to defeat the obligation of the various entities (usually owned in one way or another by the same person or entity) to pay premiums on insurance they would look to in the event of a loss.

In *Turner & Newall,* the courts did not allow complex corporate structure and interaction between the various entities to defeat the right of coverage since these same entities would likely be jointly and severally liable to pay the premiums.

In *CertainTeed Corp. v Federal Insurance Co.,* 913 F Supp 351 (ED Pa 1995), the issue was whether CertainTeed was an insured under policies of insurance issued by Federal to Bay Mills. A complex (so-called Perringer) release was negotiated in the underlying claim whereby only Bay Mills, the settling defendant, was released. Federal refused to defend or indemnify CertainTeed, alleging it was neither a named insured nor an additional insured under the policy and that the settlement nullified any claims for contribution or indemnity brought against Bay Mills by nonsettling defendants.

Bay Mills was owned by CertainTeed through two intermediary holding companies. CertainTeed Ltd. held all stock of Bay Mills. CertainTeed Ltd. was owned by CRT Inc. All of the stock of CRT Inc., in turn, was owned by CertainTeed Corporation.

EXHIBIT 3.2
WHO IS AN INSURED

The following is a simplified diagram illustrating those individuals and organizations that are automatically covered as insureds. Refer to the text and the policy for qualifications and limitations.

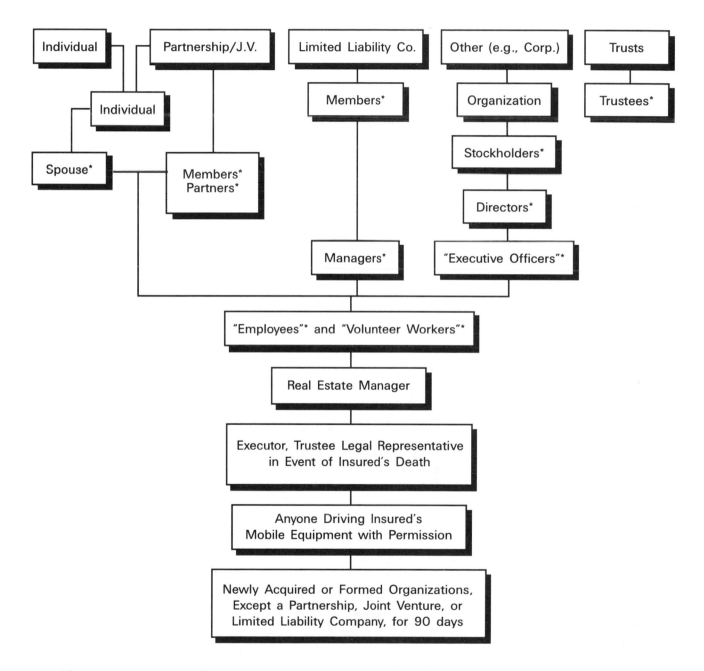

*As respects conduct of the business or their duties for the organization.

CertainTeed sought coverage on two theories. First, CertainTeed contended that as the "ultimate parent" with two nonoperating companies between it and Bay Mills, it was a stockholder of Bay Mills. Second, CertainTeed argued that because the complaint against it alleged that Bay Mills and CertainTeed constituted a joint venture, it was entitled to a defense along with Bay Mills.

The Who Is an Insured provision of the primary liability policy issued by Federal Insurance Company held that executive officers and directors were insureds but only with respect to their duties as officers and directors. Stockholders were insureds but only with respect to their liability as stockholders. The policy also stated that no one was insured for the conduct of any current or past partnership or joint venture that was not shown as a named insured in the Declarations.

Federal also issued an umbrella excess policy to Bay Mills that provided that any officer, director, stockholder, or employer of the named insured was an insured "while acting within the scope of his duties as such." The Who Is an Insured provisions of the umbrella policy did not contain the wording precluding coverage for unnamed partnerships or joint ventures.

In holding that CertainTeed Corporation could not be described as stockholder, the court held that the term "shareholders" applies to the holder of the legal title to the stock. The court found reinforcement for this view in policy wording stating that stockholders are insured "only" with respect to their liability as stockholders. The court pointed out that the claims made against CertainTeed Corporation in the underlying case were not as alter ego or as stockholder but, rather, as an independent act charged with the same conduct on its own and together with Bay Mills. Therefore, CertainTeed Corporation was not being held liable because of its status as stockholder as required by the policy wording.

By raising the issue of CertainTeed's status in the pleadings (alter ego versus independent liability), the court appears to have left unresolved another issue. What if those pleadings had alleged that CertainTeed Corporation was the alter ego of Bay Mills? In this instance, it could be argued, particularly for purposes of defense coverage, that CertainTeed Corporation was being held liable solely because it was perceived to be a stockholder. This portion of the court's ruling raises troubling questions. The possibility that CertainTeed Corporation was being sued because it was perceived to be a stockholder could be argued to exist under the present facts, though not specifically plead in the underlying complaint. Since artful drafting of a complaint is not a prerequisite to coverage, that possibility should be sufficient to trigger a defense obligation.

The court also found that there was no coverage for unnamed joint ventures under the primary policy because it contained a specific exception of coverage to that effect. However, the court also ruled that, despite omission of that specific exception to the definition of Who Is an Insured in the umbrella policy, coverage was not intended to apply to an unnamed joint venture. This also is controversial, particularly as regards the defense obligation, since the absence of such wording has been found to allow coverage in many instances. In fact, the definition of Who Is an Insured in standard ISO commercial general liability forms was modified in 1985 to specifically preclude coverage for unnamed partnerships and joint ventures so as to avoid allegations of ambiguity in this area. The fact that the umbrella policy did not include such wording appears to have been adequate to trigger defense coverage.

Proprietorships

Many entrepreneurs, particularly contractors, begin their businesses as sole proprietors. As their businesses progress and expand, they often join forces with others as partners, joint ventures, or limited liability companies, or they incorporate their businesses. When a contractor or other service performs work as a sole proprietor and then incorporates, a coverage gap may occur unless the contractor maintains liability insurance for both legal entities. The proprietorship would have a continuing completed operations liability exposure for which it would need a policy in effect at the time bodily injury or property damage occurs (e.g., after the proprietorship has been converted to a corporation of some other legal entity). Much depends on how the allegations are pled. If suit is filed against a contractor at the time the contractor is, say, incorporated, but the damages sustained are for work performed when that contractor was a sole proprietor, the contractor may be without liability insurance unless the sole proprietor (individual) also is listed as a named insured.

The reason is that the preamble to the Who Is an Insured provision of the CGL policy states: "If you are designated in the Declarations as:" Thus, if the Declarations lists the named insured as an individual, the named insured and his or her spouse are considered to be insureds "but only with respect to the conduct of a business of which you are the sole owner." On the other hand, if the named insured is designated as an organization other than a partnership or joint venture, the named insured is an insured along with its executive officers and directors "but only with respect to their duties as your officers or directors." Whether coverage applies, therefore, hinges on how the Declarations lists the entity involved. If a contractor begins business as a sole proprietorship or partnership and later incorporates, it would be wise to list both businesses on all liability policies.

Although not construction-related, a case that exemplifies this caveat about listing as named insureds all the different legal entities in which the named insured has been involved on liability policies is *Georgakopoulos v Century Surety Co.,* 588 NE2d 143 (Ohio App 1990). In 1986 an insurer issued a CGL policy to John and Dena Georgakopoulos, doing business as the Dena Lounge. A year later, the Dena Lounge was incorporated under the name 128 Main Street, Inc. The two individuals became 50 percent joint owners, and two other individuals each became 25 percent shareholders in the corporation.

Later that year, a suit was filed against one of the individuals who owned a 25 percent share of the corporation. The plaintiff alleged that he was assaulted and beaten by three unknown patrons of

the Dena Lounge and that the owner had negligently failed to remove these individuals from the premises. That original suit was dismissed and later refiled to name the individual shareholders who owned 25 percent of the stock along with John and Dena Georgakopoulos, individually and as agents of 128 Main Street, Inc.

At the time of the alleged assault, the Dena Lounge was no longer owned and operated as a sole proprietorship but instead as a corporation. None of the individuals against whom suit was filed, therefore, was an insured pursuant to the terms of the liability policy. The individuals against whom suit was filed maintained that (1) the transfer of the business from individual to corporate ownership without the insurer's approval did not preclude coverage where the individual was not divested entirely of his or her ownership in the business, (2) the liability policy had no applicable exclusions as to corporations but only to situations involving partnerships and joint ventures, and (3) notice of incorporation was given by telephone to the insurance agency.

The trial court ruled that no coverage applied. The court of appeals of Ohio affirmed that decision, basing its rationale on the policy's Persons Insured provision and certain policy conditions dealing with statements in the Declarations and policy changes.

The court ruled that John and Dena Georgakopoulos were covered under the terms of the liability policy only as individuals *and only while they were conducting business as a sole proprietorship.* The court also held that the policy was not modified based on the alleged telephone call to the insurance agency because of the policy condition dealing with changes. This condition states that any modification of the policy can only be effected by written endorsement by an authorized representative of the insurer, and no such endorsement was ever produced.

Partnerships and Joint Ventures

The need to properly designate the insured is similar when it comes to partnerships and joint ventures under the 1986 and 1973 policy provisions. When, for example, Construction Company A and Construction Company B agree to form a joint venture (a partnership created for a limited purpose) and purchase a policy for that venture, the members or partners and spouses of each such entity are deemed to be insureds under both policy editions. Under the 1986 and later edition CGL forms, employees are also afforded insured status.

However, it is important to note here that for protection to apply to insureds associated with a partnership or joint venture, the entity must be designated as the named insured on the policy. If a partnership is dissolved, a joint venture fulfills its limited purpose, or the property of a partnership or joint venture is sold and reference to the partnership or joint venture is deleted from liability coverage, problems might arise under such circumstances when insurance is terminated. No protection will apply in policies subsequently purchased by the former partners or joint venturers unless the former entity is designated in the policy. This can cause a significant gap in liability insurance protection, particularly with respect to the products-completed operations exposure.

The language of the 1986 CGL policy and subsequent revisions makes this clear, stating that:

> No person or organization is an insured with respect to the conduct of any *current* or *past* partnership or joint venture that is not shown as the Named Insured in the Declarations.

The corresponding partnership and joint venture provision of the 1973 CGL policy is less clear. It states simply that:

> This insurance does not apply to bodily injury or property damage arising out of the conduct of any partnership or joint venture of which the insured is a partner or member and which is not designated in this policy as a named insured.

When this language was introduced in 1966, ISO explained that its purpose was to serve as a control measure, allowing insurers to be notified of joint venture or partnership exposures that developed during the policy period. This provision also allowed insurers to charge for these exposures—assuming, of course, that they desired to provide the coverage at all.

This 1973 language led to the obvious conclusion that coverage was precluded only for active, ongoing joint ventures not designated in the 1973 CGL form. By implied exception, liability arising from the products or completed operations of a past joint venture was believed to be covered. Some insurance professionals—relying on what they perceived as clear policy wording for this exposure—took no affirmative action to cover it. However, this reasoning and policy wording was ignored by at least one court.

That case, *Austin P. Keller Construction Co. v Commercial Union Insurance Co.,* 379 NW2d 533 (Minn 1986), rudely alerted insurance professionals to a potential coverage gap, given the diversity of court rulings by jurisdiction. Insurance Services Office, Inc. (ISO), more clearly excluded past joint ventures when it revised the CGL forms in 1986. However, since the case clearly demonstrates the nature of the liability exposure arising from past joint ventures, it is worthy of discussion despite the fact that the ruling is contrary to the wording of the policy.

Two construction companies, Keller Construction and Montgomery Construction, formed a joint venture in 1970 to construct water and sewer lines for a city. Alan Montgomery supervised the work. The joint venture was dissolved shortly after completion of the project in 1972. Ten years later, a gas explosion occurred in the city, causing bodily injury and property damage. The utility that owned the gas lines was sued. Alan Montgomery individually and the two parties that made up the joint venture were joined as defendants on the theory that the explosion resulted from the negligence of the joint venture in backfilling the sewer and water trenches. At the time of the explosion, one of the construction firms, Austin P. Keller Construction, was insured for its current exposures under a 1973 edition CGL policy. However, this policy did not specifically name the joint venture as an insured.

Keller's CGL insurer denied any coverage based on the joint venture exclusion. Focusing on the words "joint venture of which the insured is a member," Keller Construction asserted that it was unnecessary to name the old joint venture as a named insured in the policy so as to obtain the policy's completed operations liability coverage. The court of appeals agreed with this contention, stating that:

> [I]f the insurer intended to exclude claims arising out of work by a terminated joint venture, they could have specified "joint venture of which the insured *is* or *was* a partner or member."

However, one justice dissented. He maintained that the joint venture exclusion was clear and unambiguous and should be valid and enforceable. The court of appeals decision was itself appealed and reversed by the Minnesota Supreme Court. In doing so, the court explained that had Keller's argument that its current insurance policy's exclusion applied solely to current joint ventures been validated, the exclusion would be meaningless.

It is interesting to note that even though the insurer ultimately prevailed in its denial of coverage to Keller, the insurance industry heeded the advice of the court of appeals when it revised the CGL form in the early 1980s. Current policy forms specifically exclude coverage with respect to liability arising from any current or past joint venture not specifically scheduled in the policy as an insured.

The fact that a joint venture is listed in the policy as a named insured, or adjudicated to be so, does not necessarily mean that the insurer is obligated to automatically list such entity on every renewal. Such was the case in *Liberty Mutual Insurance Co. v York Hunter, Inc.,* 945 F Supp 742 (USDC SD NY 1996), where a construction management firm involved in a joint venture found itself without protection when the joint venture was not listed as a named insured on the policy renewal. Based on the complex fact pattern of this case, the court held that any contractual obligation of an insurer to list a joint venture as a named insured on a CGL policy did not carry over from an expiring policy to a renewal policy that excluded coverage for unnamed joint ventures.

Divisions

The term "division," unlike "subsidiary," is not defined with clarity in the law, because "division" is a generic term. *Merriam-Webster's Collegiate Dictionary* (10th ed, 1999) defines "division" as "an administrative or operating unit of a governmental, business, or educational organization." A division, therefore, could be a total separate entity or of the type described in *Miller v United States,* 307 F Supp 932 (ED Va 1969).

In *Miller,* the plaintiffs were employed by the Installation Division, Painter's Department, of the defendant's shipyard. They sustained injuries when an elevator fell on them and sued the Design Division for faulty work. The court ruled that the suit was barred under the workers compensation statutes' exclusive remedy limitation. While the two divisions had separate officers, both divisions were part of the same shipyard and ultimately subject to the same president and board of directors. In essence, the two divisions were integral parts of a larger whole.[3]

The fact that a division can be part and parcel of a corporate entity, and sometimes a separate and distinct entity, can lead to confusion and problems. Unless separately incorporated and maintained as such, divisions are generally encompassed by a corporation's liability policies and generally obligated for policy premiums jointly and severally.

Take, for example, *Argonaut Southwest Insurance Co. v American Home Assurance Co.,* 483 F Supp 724 (USDC ND Tex 1980), where the insurer of a corporation brought an action against the insurers of a division of that corporation seeking judgment that it was not obligated to provide liability coverage for an accident involving a machine manufactured by the division. At the time the corporation acquired the division, the division, even though not a separate legal entity, operated in much the same way and at the same location as it did prior to its purchase. It even continued to maintain its own insurance through a long-standing relationship with an agent.

The division designed and manufactured a large industrial pipe grinder. The purchaser of this grinder cut pipe to meet customers' specifications. The dispute arose following an accident in which the purchaser's employee was seriously injured while using the grinder. The employee filed suit against the corporate owner and later against the division because liability apparently rested with the division. A dispute between the insurers of the corporation and the division eventually arose over the obligation to pay for the damages sought.

The named insured provision of the corporation's policy had been modified to preclude coverage for the division. The court followed the intent conveyed by this provision. It ruled that the corporation's insurance did not apply, not only for the reason that the named insured provision specifically precluded the division, but also because the division maintained its own separate insurance portfolio.

In this case, the corporation's insurance representatives had the foresight to convey an intent in the policy not to cover the division's liability. In all likelihood, the result would have been entirely different had this modification not been made. The court, in noting that the division had been specifically omitted as an insured under the policies at issue, also emphasized that the designation of who was to be an insured was a material part of a coverage decision and was held to be important in calculating the risk to be insured.

This analogy, however, while applicable to situations where the insurer conducts an underwriting investigation into the risks it is willing to insure, is not always relevant to the issue of additional insureds. Underwriters seldom calculate each individual risk brought about by providing additional insured status. Rather, they rely on the premium generated by underwriting the named insured's exposure at the outset.

Premiums for additional insured endorsements vary widely among insurers. Some impose only an administrative charge. Since general liability premiums include a component for contractual liability exposures, there is no rationale for making any other charge for additional insured status, unless the insurer is willing to give the additional insured completed operations coverage.

When it comes to listing all named insureds on the policy, there is some question whether it is necessary to also list wholly owned divisions of corporations. In one case, the insurer refused to defend such a division because it was not specifically identified on the general liability policy. In *Container Supply Co. v Fireman's Fund Insurance Co.*, 715 F Supp 326 (DC Kan 1989), the court ruled against the insurance company, stating that despite the absence of case law as to whether wholly owned divisions of corporations are insureds under liability insurance, the "common sense of corporate liability under the circumstances should have led the defendant [insurer] to the conclusion that it had a duty to defend the plaintiff [division]."

Executive Officers

Executive officers of named insured corporations have benefited from automatic insured status in CGL policies since the 1940s. The coverage available to executive officers applies only as respects their duties as such.

Employees as insureds is an issue that has relevance here and merits a brief discussion. It was not until the 1970s that it became commonplace to provide insured status for other employees. However, instances where employees are not provided insured status under their employer's general liability policies are now certainly the exception rather than the rule. To eliminate their insured status under the post-1973 edition CGL forms, the Exclusion—Employees as Insureds (CG 21 37) endorsement, must be attached to the policy. Likewise, the Broad Form CGL endorsement could not be attached to the 1973 edition CGL form if employees were not to be provided insured status, and rarely were CGL policies written on the 1973 CGL form without this endorsement. However, if coverage were ever written without including employees as insureds, it could become important for a person to establish insured status as an executive officer.

Indicative of this potential problem of determining who qualifies as an executive officer is the case of *Guillory v Aetna Insurance Co.,* 415 F2d 650 (5th Cir La 1969). This was an action brought by an employee who was injured at a construction job site, allegedly by the negligence of that employee's supervisor. The supervisor maintained that he was protected as an insured within the provision of the liability policy, which provided coverage to "any executive officer, director, or stockholder while acting within the scope of his duties as such." The insurer argued that an individual can become an officer of a corporation only if formally designated as such by the corporation, and since the supervisor was not designated as an officer by the corporation's charter, bylaws, or resolutions, the question of whether the supervisor was an executive officer should not have gone before the jury.

In rejecting the insurer's argument, the Louisiana court pointed out that the insured was a "thinly capitalized corporation which issued no capital stock, owned no property, kept no minutes, had no bylaws, and had only one job contract at the time of the accident." Although the supervisor was not formally elected, appointed, or designated as an officer of the corporation by action of the board of directors or stockholders, the court explained, the supervisor assisted in negotiating the contract, had general authorization to represent the entity in matters concerning contracts, and could hire and fire employees, among other responsibilities.

An unusual scenario is when one executive officer injures another executive and then turns to the CGL policy for protection. Such was the case in *Fontana v Zurich Insurance Co.,* 430 S2d 718 (La App 1983). The insured's president was working on the underside of a suspended truck belonging to the corporation when his brother, the vice president, negligently caused the truck to fall and injure him. The vice president sought protection under the corporation's general, auto, and excess liability policies.

The Persons Insured provision of the liability policy included as an insured "any executive officer while acting within the scope of his duties as such." (Both executives were eligible for workers compensation benefits but elected not to come within the statutory coverage. However, that fact did not have any impact on the court's decision to bar recovery under the policy.)

The court ruled that both brothers, even as executives of the corporation, were "employees" of the corporation, and they were both performing manual operations when the accident occurred. As a result, they were eligible for workers compensation benefits, and the exclusive remedy doctrine prohibited one employee from suing another. Thus, the Persons Insured provision dealing with executive officers had no application in this case.

It is important to note that insured status is provided to executive officers separately from the provision effecting insured status for the named insured's employees. As a result, the limitations on the coverage available to employees do not apply to executive officers. The most important limitation that applies to employees but not to executive officers is the fellow employee exclusion. Some states currently permit an employee to sue and collect from an allegedly negligent fellow employee even though their injuries are covered under workers compensation. Thus, employees in one of these states may have a need for the coverage available to executive officers.

Representative of the kind of case that can arise in a state that permits fellow employees suits is *Young v New Hampshire Indemnity Co.,* 424 A2d 205 (NH 1980). Here, the employee was injured while operating a hydraulic press. After collecting workers compensation benefits, she brought an action against a fellow employee, alleging that he was in charge of plant safety and that he breached that duty by failing to provide a safe place for her to work.

The alleged tortfeasor was the plant manager whose responsibility was to supervise three foremen and four other employees. He also was head of a safety committee and responsible for compliance with Occupational Safety and Health Administration (OSHA) regulations. He sought coverage as an executive officer under the CGL policy to avoid application of the fellow employee exclusion. The insurer denied protection, and the parties went to court to determine the application of coverage. Ultimately, the court ruled that the negligent employee was an executive officer and was entitled to coverage.

Both the retired treasurer and the president of the named insured company were under the impression that the supervisor was an executive officer. What affected the adverse ruling against the insurer was that the term "executive officer" was not defined by the policy. Referring to a dictionary, the term "executive" was defined as "one who holds a position of administrative or managerial responsibility in a business or other organization." The term "corporate officer," on the other hand, carried a more precise and narrow meaning tied to the corporate charter and bylaws.

The court rationalized that the term "executive officer" encompassed something more than an employee but was not restricted to a corporate officer; otherwise, the insurer could have been more explicit in intent. In any event, the court ruled against the insurer based on the lack of clarity over the meaning of the term "executive officer."

In response to cases such as *Young v New Hampshire,* a definition of "executive officer" was added as part of 1993 revisions to the CGL forms. The new definition, shown in Exhibit 3.3, should significantly reduce disputes of this type.

EXHIBIT 3.3
1993 "EXECUTIVE OFFICER" DEFINITION

"Executive officer" means a person holding any of the officer positions created by your charter, constitution, bylaws or any other similar governing document.

Copyright, Insurance Services Office, Inc., 1992

The 1993 policy definition is similar to that contained in the Alabama and Louisiana Changes— Who Is an Insured (CG 01 08) endorsement for use in the two states where the problem of employees seeking executive status to avoid application of the fellow employee exclusion has been especially prevalent. The definition attempts to clarify that if insureds expect protection as executive officers, they must meet one of the criteria stipulated in the policy. This new definition may also serve to mitigate the affects of decisions by some courts that have held the absence of a definition for the term "executive officer" makes the policy ambiguous.

On the other hand, the fact that "executive officer" is now a defined term could cause problems for insureds and insurers in certain circumstances. For example, it is not uncommon for an executive officer also to be an employee of a corporation. Thus, the same individual could be acting as an executive officer in some cases and simply as an employee in others. In either case, such a person would have been insured (as an executive officer or employee) under earlier policy editions where the terms "executive officer" and "employee" were not defined.

Under newer policy language that assigns specific meanings to those terms, things could be different. If the corporate charter, constitution, bylaws, or other similar governing document clearly designates an individual as an executive officer, there could be problems in maintaining that he or she also is an employee or was acting in that capacity. Under the revised wording, unless an executive officer is acting within the scope of his or her duties, there may not be coverage. If the conduct leading up to the injury or damage was an employee-related task, it would not always fall within the parameters of coverage for an executive officer.

A case that illustrates the potential problems created by these policy definitions is *Creel v Louisiana Pest Control Insurance,* 723 S2d (La App 1998). In this case, Roy Slay, president of a pest control company, was operating a vehicle in the course and scope of his employment and collided with a vehicle driven by Linda Creel. Slay was insured under a CGL policy issued by Louisiana Pest Control Insurance (LPCI). Creel sued LPCI under a direct action statute, alleging that Slay was an insured under the LPCI policy.

LPCI countered that the policy excluded damages arising from an insured's use of his or her own automobile and that the vehicle driven by Slay at the time of the accident was owned by him. The exclusion in question applied to the following.

> "Bodily injury" or "property damage" arising out of the ownership, maintenance, use, or entrustment to others of any ... auto ... owned or operated by or rented or loaned to any insured ....

The trial court agreed with the insurer, holding that the automobile use exclusion applied to Slay, who was an insured, as defined by the policy, either as an executive officer or as an employee. Creel appealed, arguing that the trial court erred in interpreting the term "insured" to include Slay as an executive officer, because he was performing duties as an employee, and that the policy excluded all coverage for officers acting as employees.

The appellate court concurred with this argument and ruled the exclusion inapplicable. It noted that the legal precedent relied on by the trial court—i.e., that an individual could be both an employee and an executive officer of a corporation—was premised on facts involving cross-employee exclusions and entitlement to workers compensation coverage. The case at hand, the appellate court noted, did not involve facts where the injured parties had recourse to workers compensation insurance.

The appellate court then pointed out that the policy wording at issue specifically precluded an executive officer from being an employee. The Who Is an Insured provision of the policy at issue stated as follows.

> 1. If you are designated in the Declarations as:
>
>   c. An organization other than a partnership or joint venture, you are an insured. Your executive officers and directors are insureds, but only with respect to their duties as your officers or directors ....

The appellate court held that under this wording, an executive officer could be an insured only when performing his or her executive duties. At the time of the accident, Slay was en route to spray a house for insects, which the appellate court found not to fall within the duties of an executive officer. As a result, the appellate court held that Slay was not an insured and thus not subject to the automobile exclusion.

The importance of this ruling and the coverage issues it raises should not be underestimated. A finding that an executive officer is not an insured because of his or her activities at the time of injury or damage can be helpful to corporate officers seeking CGL coverage. However, the same principle may also be the basis of a finding of no coverage in other fact patterns. Careful consideration should be given to the wording of corporate charters, constitutions, bylaws, and other similar documents, as those documents define or describe the functions of executive officers. Such definitions and descriptions may have an impact on the applicability either of coverage or of a policy exclusion to officers as "insureds."

Employees as Insureds

Employees are often included as insureds in liability policies purchased by employers for two basic reasons. The first is to satisfy management's perceived corporate responsibility in protecting employees from loss arising from their activities on behalf of their employer. The second is to help secure the employees' cooperation in defending claims made against the employer.

Absent additional insured status for employees, plaintiffs could name employees of the named insured as codefendants in lawsuits. Then the plaintiff could offer to drop the suit against the uninsured employee if the employee would cooperate with the plaintiff in its suit against the named insured. Even if the employee refused to help the plaintiff, he or she would certainly be hostile toward the employer who refused to assist with his or her defense. If, on the other hand, the employee is assured of a defense in the employer's policy, the employee's loyalty would be much more difficult to sway.

Under the 1973 edition CGL policy, employees are automatic insureds with respect to liability arising from the operation of mobile equipment registered under any motor vehicle registration law for purposes of locomotion on public highways. Other than for this specific exposure, it took an endorsement to add employees as additional insureds to the 1973 edition CGL policy. The endorsement can be one designed solely to add employees to the policy, or the Broad Form CGL (GL 04 04) endorsement, which provides insured status to employees as one of many coverage extensions, can be used instead.

The ISO endorsement designed solely to add employees to the 1973 edition CGL form did so only with respect to bodily injury and property damage coverage. It did not afford them additional insured status under personal injury coverage if that was provided by the policy. The Broad Form CGL endorsement, on the other hand, provided employees with additional insured status under all the policy's coverages.

Under the 1986 CGL and later edition forms, employees are automatic insureds with respect to liability arising from acts within their scope of employment for the named insured. The 1986 and later edition forms also provide employees the same protection for liability arising from the operation of mobile equipment, except that these later edition policies, unlike the 1973 edition, appear to require that the mobile equipment be registered in the name of the named insured.

If, for some reason, employee coverage is not desired and the Exclusion—Employees as Insureds (CG 21 37) endorsement were to be added to the 1986 CGL policy, employees would still be viewed as insureds against the exposure dealing with mobile equipment, just as employees would be protected under the 1973 CGL policy.

The problem with the exclusionary endorsement CG 21 37 insofar as an insurer is concerned is that coverage still applies despite this endorsement, by exception to exclusion g., to an employer's vicarious liability stemming from an employee's use of his or her automobile even though an employee is not covered. Such coverage, however, applies only on an excess basis. (Coverage likewise applies to an employer's vicarious liability stemming from the use of an independent contractor's motor vehicle.) To eliminate this vicarious liability coverage exposure of automobiles, insofar as employees are concerned, ISO introduced a revised exclusionary endorsement CG 21 37 that became effective in most states in March 1997, which amends exclusion g. of the CGL forms.

The Who Is an Insured section of the 1986 and later editions of the CGL forms contains an exclusion for liability of employees arising from the providing of professional health care services. The apparent intent is to require such medical professionals to purchase professional liability insurance. By inference, however, any liability imputed to the named insured because of the professional acts or omissions of employed medical professionals would be covered by the policy. This is often referred to as "incidental medical malpractice coverage."

The 1973 CGL policy does not contain a medical malpractice exclusion with respect to employees because employees are not automatic insureds under the form (except for the mobile equipment exposure noted previously). However, when an insured purchases the Broad Form CGL endorsement, employees become automatic insureds for other exposures, and it becomes necessary for the policy to incorporate an exclusion dealing with employees who are medical professionals. This exclusion is contained in the "incidental medical malpractice liability coverage" provisions of that endorsement.[4]

Volunteer Workers

Under the 1986 ISO CGL, two endorsements were available to extend insured status to persons working as volunteers for the named insured One of these endorsements was Additional Insured—Volunteer Workers (CG 20 21). The other was endorsement Additional Insured—Church Members, Officers and Volunteer Workers (CG 20 22).

Eventually, it became so commonplace for entities to employ the services of volunteers, and the demand for insured status for these volunteers on the same basis became so widespread, that the use of endorsements simply became too burdensome for insurers. ISO revised the Who Is An Insured provision of the CGL coverage form in 2001 to include volunteers automatically as insureds—in the same section of the policy that gives the named insured's employees insured status. The use of a separate additional insured endorsement thus became unnecessary. Endorsement CG 20 21 was withdrawn from use, and endorsement CG 20 22 was revised to eliminate references to church volunteers. Volunteers can be excluded from insured status under the CGL policy by means of the Exclusion—Volunteer Workers (CG 21 66) endorsement.

Leased Workers

It has become increasingly common in recent years for businesses to meet some of their personnel needs by using the services of employee leasing firms. Workers who remain technically the employees of the leasing firm go to work on a long-term basis for the company that has contracted with the leasing firm for their services. The arrangement is similar, except as regards term of employment, to the temporary help offered by employment contractors that provide clerical, bookkeeping, light industrial, and similar services on a short-term basis.

The insurance implications for a business that hires the services of leased workers have taken a long time to resolve. The first issue demanding an answer was where responsibility for workers compensation coverage on leased workers rested. Answers to this question must be found on a state-by-state basis by looking either to common law or to specific state legislation that defines the responsibilities of employee leasing firms and their client businesses for providing coverage.

Where common law prevails, the majority position is that the business for which the leased worker actually performs work is the employer of that worker and assumes an employer's legally defined responsibility for providing workers compensation coverage. Some individual states have made different allocations of this responsibility, imposing either sole responsibility for workers compensation coverage on the leasing firm or shared responsibility on both the leasing firm and its client business.

While the "employee" status of leased workers has been addressed in the context of workers compensation coverage, this issue was not addressed in relation to general liability insurance until 1993 when the ISO multistate revisions resolved the question. It introduced a policy definition of "employee" that includes within that term a "leased worker" but not a "temporary worker." The 1993 CGL policy definitions of these three terms are shown in Exhibit 3.4.

EXHIBIT 3.4
1993 "EMPLOYEE" AND "WORKER" DEFINITIONS

"Employee" includes a "leased worker." "Employee" does not include a "temporary worker."

"Leased worker" means a person leased to you by a labor leasing firm under an agreement between you and the labor leasing firm, to perform duties related to the conduct of your business. "Leased worker" does not include a "temporary worker."

"Temporary worker" means a person who is furnished to you to substitute for a permanent "employee" on leave or to meet seasonal or short-term workload conditions.

Copyright, Insurance Services Office, Inc., 1992

Because there are mutations of standard CGL policies in existence that may not include the definition of "employee," as now found in the ISO standard CGL forms, it is important to mention a case where a temporary worker was considered to be an employee and, therefore, subject to the so-called employers liability exclusion of the policy. The case is *Western World Insurance Co. v Spevco,* 671 NE2d 1100 (Ohio App 1996).

In that case, Spevco, which was in the business of sports marketing and promotion, was engaged to perform services and, therefore, contracted with Snelling Personnel Services to provide workers to erect tents and do other work. While performing such work, one worker was killed and another injured. Both the estate of the decedent and the injured worker filed suit against Spevco, and Spevco sought coverage under its liability policy. However, the policy included an Injury to Employee and Volunteer exclusion, which stated in part that this insurance did not apply:

> 1.   to bodily injury to any employee or volunteer of the insured arising out of and in the course of his employment by or service to the insured for which the insured may be held liable as an employer or in any other capacity…

The insurer filed a declaratory judgment action maintaining that since the decedent was an employee (undefined term) within the meaning of the above exclusion, the insurer was not obligated to pay damages on its insured's behalf. The trial court held that the undefined term "employee" was ambiguous and that the employee exclusion of the policy, therefore, had to be construed in the insured's favor.

The higher court reversed the decision because Spevco controlled and directed the decedent in the material details of how the work was to be performed. Furthermore, no Snelling employee was on the work site to supervise the work, and both Snelling's account manager and president and chief executive officer testified that Snelling provided no work supervision. The court, therefore, ruled the exclusion of Spevco's liability policy to be applicable because the decedent was considered to be its employee, though temporary.

The fact that the word "includes" is used in the definition of "employee" in lieu of the word "means" avoids limiting the definition of "employee" solely to a "leased worker." Under this definition, "employee" means any person employed by the insured other than an excluded person, such as a temporary worker.

Defining the named insured's leased workers as "employees" under the CGL policy has a number of ramifications. As employees, they automatically become insureds under their employer's policy and thus have liability coverage for acts within the scope of their employment. This represents a broadening of coverage, since there was nothing in previous CGL editions that specifically extended insured status to workers leased to the named insured by an employee leasing firm.

Of course, defining the term "employee" to include leased workers also causes the fellow employee exclusion of the Who Is an Insured provision to apply to any liability a regular employee may have to an injured leased employee or vice versa. In other words, such suits are precluded from coverage in the same manner as are suits brought by one regular employee against another.

By far the most important ramification of considering leased workers as employees under the CGL policy, however, is that it makes the policy's employers liability exclusion—exclusion e.—applicable to leased workers when they are injured on the job. As a result of this exclusion, an employer has no CGL coverage with respect to injury to an "employee" if the injury arises out of and in connection with the injured person's employment by the named insured.

This exclusion usually does not create a coverage gap for the employer as long as workers compensation/employers liability coverage is in place. With respect to employee leasing situations, however, the exclusion may create a problem in any jurisdiction where the CGL insured is not legally defined as the leased worker's employer and where its workers compensation/employers liability coverage therefore does not extend to the leased worker (refer to **Chapter 16** for a discussion of this topic). In such circumstances, the employer leasing employees from another party would have no coverage for an action brought by the injured leased worker in either the CGL policy or a workers compensation policy.

Recognizing this potential coverage gap, ISO also introduced, as part of the 1993 multistate revisions, an endorsement—CG 04 24—that effectively buys back general liability coverage for injury to leased workers by defining such workers out of the CGL employers liability exclusion. Businesses covered under a 1993 edition CGL form should investigate thoroughly their workers compensation status as employers of leased workers, perhaps seeking competent legal advice on the subject. If they do not have workers compensation/employers liability coverage in place for their leased workers, these businesses should seriously consider purchasing the Coverage for Injury to Leased Workers (CG 04 24) endorsement to fill the coverage gap.

Real Estate Managers

Historically, real estate managers were often individuals who lived on the premises. These individuals faced a liability exposure as a result of their responsibilities that would not be covered under their personal liability insurance. For this reason, it became desirable to provide them with protection under the building owner's liability insurance.

It was with the 1955 CGL policy provisions that this category of automatic insureds was introduced. At that time, the definition of insured section of the CGL policy provided coverage on behalf of "any organization or proprietor with respect to real estate management for the named insured." Current CGL policy provisions refer to this class of insureds as "any person (other than your employee) or any organization while acting as your real estate manager."

The current provision limits automatic insured status for real estate managers to those times when such a person or organization is acting as a real estate manager. The earlier policy did not contain the same "while clause."

One problem with this category of automatic insureds is that the term "real estate manager" is not defined in the policy. Therefore, what the term encompasses may be a question for a court to decide. In making that determination, courts should construe the meaning broadly and with the insureds' expectations of coverage in mind. However, not all courts do so, and the rulings in this regard vary depending on the facts.

For example, while not involving a CGL policy, the case of *Bewig v State Farm Fire & Casualty Insurance Co.,* 848 SW2d 521 (Mo App ED 1993), provides a sense of direction as to the meaning of "real estate manager." Briefly, this case dealt with a mail carrier who was bitten by a dog owned by a woman who lived in a dwelling owned by her father, mother, aunt, and uncle. These owners maintained a dwelling policy that also consisted of liability insurance. Since the dog owner did not maintain liability insurance, she sought protection under the policy of her relatives, which included as an insured "any person or organization while acting as real estate manager for the named insured." The defendant's father attested that the dog owner was responsible for obtaining additional tenants besides herself, paying the utility bills, and either maintaining the premises or advising the owners of the need for repairs. Her role was characterized as a resident manager.

The plaintiff contended that the dog owner was a "real estate manager" and, therefore, an insured. The court, however, stated that the insurance was intended to protect the landlord and those acting on his or her behalf in regard to the property. The insurance was not intended to protect employees or agents in their individual capacities unrelated to the landlord's interests. Since the record was totally silent as to when the bite occurred or the circumstances involved, the court ruled against coverage, because the plaintiff had the burden to establish facts, proving she was a real estate manager and that the injury occurred while she was acting in that capacity, which she failed to do.

Another case where a real estate manager relationship was found not to exist is *Savoy v Action Prod-*

ucts Co., 324 S2d 921 (La App 1975). The plaintiff filed for injury sustained in a restaurant when the chair in which the plaintiff was sitting collapsed. Among the defendants named were the lessors-owners of the restaurant, their insurer, and lessees-operators of the restaurant. The plaintiff contended that one of the lessees was an insured because she was a "real estate manager" for the lessors.

In concluding that the lessee in question did not fit that description, the court stated as follows.

> While a real estate manager may also be a lessee, not all lessees are real estate managers. It is true that a lessee possesses for his lessor and not for himself. ... It is likewise true that the lessee must act as a good administrator of his lessor's property ..and that certain repairs must be made by the lessee and that the lessee may call upon the lessor to make certain others ... But though a person who performs these acts may be said to have the "conduct or direction of a thing," he does not as a result of that performance become a real estate manager, for these acts are merely affirmative duties required of every lessee.

Yet another case involving an entity seeking "real estate manager" status under the liability policy of another is *Insurance Company of North America v Hilton Hotels U.S.A.,* 908 F Supp 809 (US-DC D Nev 1995). This case arose from the Tailhook convention held for naval aviators at the Las Vegas Hilton Hotel in 1990 and 1991. Twelve actions were filed against the hotel and the Tailhook association alleging sexual assaults against women during those conventions. The claimants alleged that some or all of the hotel defendants were liable for failing to exercise due care in providing reasonable precautions and/or adequate security.

Insurance Company of North America (INA) issued a liability policy to the Tailhook Association that defined an "insured" as including "Any person (other than your employee), or any organization while acting as your real estate manager." The sole issue before the court was whether Hilton qualified as an insured under the INA policy.

The court looked to other cases where the term "real estate manager" was held not to be ambiguous and ruled against Hilton. Among them were the following:

- *Jackson v East Baton Rouge Parish School Board,* 348 S2d 739 (La App 1977), where the Department of Public Safety was a lessee and not a real estate manager for the school board, even though the Department managed real estate in some manner, because it did so to serve its own purposes and not on behalf of the school board

- *Parr v Head,* 442 S2d 1234 (La App 1983), finding that a tenant was not a real estate manager for the owner's house, even though the tenant agreed to make all repairs to the house, since the landlord agreed not to increase rent in return

- *Olympic v Providence Washington Insurance Co.,* 648 P2d 1008 (Alaska 1982), where a construction company (lessor) did not qualify as a real estate manager because the rights and obligations required under the lease were not substantially different from those required of every lessor

- *California Union Insurance Co. v City of Walnut Grove, Miss.,* 857 F Supp 515 (SD Miss 1994), where a city that leased a building to a clothing manufacturer did not qualify as a real estate manager since maintenance and repairs were undertaken for the city's own benefit and incidental benefit to the manufacturer was not conclusive

Hilton maintained that it undertook obligations toward Tailhook that were independent of its duties as a hotel-casino operator. These obligations included the provision of security for the hospitality suites, the maintenance of separate suites for separate squadrons, and the allowance for Tailhook's provision of its own beverages in common areas of the hotel. The court, however, in ruling against Hilton, held that these obligations were consistent with the obligations imposed on hotel operators in light of the number in attendance and the size of the convention space.

The court summed up its position by stating that a person or organization cannot qualify as a real estate manager if that person's or entity's rights or obligations do not differ from the duties imposed on it by operations of law or if that person or entity undertook such operations for its own benefit. However, the last portion of this summation is contrary to the application of coverage generally and the expectations of insureds. Precluding real estate manager status because a person or entity undertook an operation for its own benefit will be overly restrictive in most instances. Nearly all commercial activity can be labeled as undertaken for the benefit of the entity involved, thus potentially precluding all coverage for this exposure.

In another case, *Fireman's Fund Insurance Co. v Vordemeier,* 415 S2d 1347 (Fla App 1982), a court-appointed receiver sought protection as a real estate manager under a liability policy issued to the property owners. The case arose when a minor fell from the fifth floor of the building and sustained permanent injuries. The property owners' insurer denied the receiver protection for several reasons. One was that the receiver was not acting for the named insureds.

The court disagreed with the insurance company, explaining that when a receiver in bankruptcy takes over the management of real estate during the pendency of legal proceedings, the ownership of the property remains with the title owners. It stated further, "There can be no question that a court-appointed receiver, as a matter of law, manages property as the representative of the court for all interested parties, including the owners and named insureds."

The court went on to say, "The mere fact that a receiver may manage the real property for creditors or other interested parties in addition to the named insureds is not sufficient to defeat coverage." The court added that the Persons Insured provision in question did not restrict coverage to those acting as real estate managers *exclusively* for the named insured.

In affirming the trial court's decision against the insurer, the higher court explained that an insurer,

as drafter of a policy, has an obligation to spell out clearly who is and is not intended to be covered by the policy. Also, any ambiguity will be interpreted against the insurer. The court also stated that, as a matter of public policy and absent policy language to the contrary, insurance coverage should be extended to court-appointed receivers in situations such as those in this case. Interestingly, ISO introduced a new endorsement in 1986 to take care of this situation under current liability policies, the Additional Insured—Mortgagee, Assignee, or Receiver (CG 20 18) endorsement.

In *Hartford Insurance Co. of the Southeast v State Farm Fire & Casualty,* 630 S2d 652 (Fla App 1994), a Florida appellate court held that employing common usage to interpret the meaning of the phrase "real estate manager" to determine whether coverage existed under a liability policy issued to the owner of real estate development was an error given the clear definition of the manager's responsibilities in a contract with the owner. In so holding, the court afforded a construction manager additional insured status in the liability insurance policy of the project owner even though the two parties had not agreed that this should be done.

The developer, Chapel Trail Associates, and the construction manager, Zimmerman and Associates, entered into a 10-year contract. Under the contract, Zimmerman was responsible for managing the construction of the project and for managing it for a number of years after its completion. Zimmerman would be paid a management fee plus a percentage of the profits from the project.

During the course of construction, a motorist was killed in an automobile accident when she struck some debris that had fallen from a truck hauling mud from the property. Her estate brought suit against both Zimmerman and Chapel Trail, subsequently reaching a settlement under which each paid $250,000.

Zimmerman's insurer, the Hartford, then brought a declaratory action, claiming that Zimmerman was also an insured (as real estate manager) under Chapel Trail's policy, which was written by State Farm. Recognizing the existence of the two other insurance clauses, the Hartford's suit sought to recover a pro rata share ($125,000) of the settlement it paid on behalf of its insured.

The trial court focused on evidence as to the common usage meaning of the term "real estate manager" presented by the conflicting parties. In so doing, it ruled that Zimmerman was not a real estate manager and, therefore, not an insured under Chapel Trail's policy. The appellate court, on the other hand, carefully examined the contract between the two organizations and held that it "clearly established Zimmerman to be something considerably different than a 'construction manager' as determined by the trial court." Therefore, the court held that Zimmerman was an insured under Chapel Trail's State Farm policy, reversing the lower court's decision.

Parties entering into construction and real estate ventures should be cognizant of this when they draft the contract documents. If there is a chance that one organization could secure additional insured status even though not intended by the parties when the contract was executed, it may be prudent to modify the appropriate policy to clarify that the contractual relationship was not intended to effect additional insured status.

Because the term "real estate manager" is not defined, additional insured status "as a real estate manager" has been sought under an extraordinary variety of fact situations. In one unreported case, for example, a general contractor claimed to be a real estate manager of a construction project because, in a sense, it was managing the property as it was being constructed.

In another case—*First National Bank of Palmerton v Motor Club of America Insurance Co.,* 708 A2d 69 (NJ 1997), insurance coverage as a real estate manager was sought by a mortgagee. A corporation, its president, and the president's spouse, as mortgagors, entered into a mortgage and security agreement with a bank, as mortgagee, on property consisting of apartments. The agreement provided that in the event of a default, the bank could take possession and assume operation of the property, including leasing, collecting rent, repairing, and

maintaining the property. The mortgagors had given their consent for the bank to act in their place in the event of default and were in essence the beneficiaries of the continued operation of the property if default occurred.

The mortgagor was required to maintain insurance on the property, which it did. The liability coverage procured encompassed any organization acting as "your [the named insured mortgagor's] real estate manager." The bank eventually assumed control of the property as the result of default. During this period of control, a person fell on the premises and filed suit against the bank and others. When the bank sought protection under the policies procured by the former mortgagors, coverage was denied. The bank filed suit against the insurers, maintaining that, as a real estate manager, it was an additional insured and entitled to coverage.

The court viewed the duties and responsibilities of a mortgagee in possession to be so similar to those of a real estate manager "that any reasonable interpretation of the insurance policy would include a mortgagee in possession as a manager of real estate." In arriving at this decision, the court rejected a number of arguments advanced by the insurers, who had contended (1) that the bank was not a real estate manager because it seized and operated the apartments only to protect its own interests; and (2) that the word "your" in the phrase "your real estate manager" was defined as the named insured shown in the declarations. The court found both of these arguments to be without merit.

In another case, a manager of an apartment complex swimming pool unsuccessfully claimed insured status as a real estate manager—*Gilbert v B.D.O.W.S.,* 711 S2d 765 (La 1998). A guest of an apartment complex resident was injured in the pool and filed suit against the owners of the complex; the owner of an adjoining apartment complex who had been hired and paid on an hourly basis to oversee, clean, and maintain the pool; and the owners of two other nearby complexes who also paid the pool owner for pool use privileges for their residents. The case centered on the pool maintenance person's status as a "real estate manager" under the liability policies of these two other apartment complex owners. The court ruled that the maintenance person had no insured status, since there was no evidence to show that the two insured apartment owners, paying to use the pool, exercised any control over the pool maintenance person or that the maintenance person took any directions from them.

The lack of a definition for the term "real estate manager" in the CGL policy is likely to lead to additional disputes and cases in the future. It will be interesting to see if the insurance industry responds to these cases by including a definition in the CGL policy at some future date or deletes reference to real estate manager as an automatic insured. In the meantime, potential additional insureds will continue to anticipate that the undefined term "real estate manager" will be applied broadly when coverage is sought.

When a real estate manager is an automatic insured on another's liability policy and also maintains its own policy, it is likely that the issue of "other insurance" will be raised. In these kinds of events, the insurer of the policy that automatically includes the real estate manager will maintain that its policy and the real estate manager's policy should contribute pursuant to a formula designed for the occasion and pursuant to the law of the venue involved, whereas the insurer of the real estate manager's policy will maintain that its coverage applies on an excess basis.

Such was the argument in the case of *Nationwide Mutual Insurance Co. v Hall,* 643 S2d 551 (Ala 1994). This case arose out of a wrongful death action brought as a result of a fire in an apartment building owned by Hall and managed by Friedlander. In the issue concerning other insurance, the real estate manager's insurer, Nationwide, maintained that its policy applied on an excess basis. The owner's insurer, Alfa Mutual, argued that its policy was primary only to its named insured, Hall, and excess insofar as the additional insured, Friedlander, was concerned. However, the lower court concluded that both policies applied on a primary basis and, therefore, were required to prorate. The higher court agreed.

The insurer of a liability policy issued to a real estate manager in *Woodson v A&M Investments,* 591 S2d 1345 (La App 1991), had attached the Real Estate Property Managed (CG 22 70) endorsement to its policy to address this issue. That endorsement is shown in Exhibit 3.5.

EXHIBIT 3.5
REAL ESTATE PROPERTY
MANAGED ENDORSEMENT

This insurance does not apply to "property damage" to property you operate or manage or as to which you act as an agent for the collection of rents or in any other supervisory capacity.

With respect to your liability arising out of your management of property for which you are acting as real estate manager this insurance is excess over any other valid and collectible insurance available to you.

Copyright, Insurance Services Office, Inc., 1984

The court held that the intent to provide only excess insurance was clearly expressed by the endorsement to the real estate manager's own policy and ruled that the policy to which the real estate manager was an additional insured applied as primary coverage.

Not all CGL policies are standard, and even those that are may be modified by endorsement to tailor or limit coverage to the particular needs of the insureds or insurers. While real estate managers may rightfully assume they are insureds under the property owner's policy, they cannot or should not make any assumptions as to the scope of coverage provided to them. Only an examination of the actual policy language in force can answer the question of what is and is not covered.

An illustration of this point is provided in *U.S. Fire Insurance Co. v Aetna Casualty & Surety Co.,* USDC ED Pa. #95–5861 (1998). The case arose following a 1991 fire in a Philadelphia high-rise office building. The building was owned by a general partnership, E/R Associates. However, 65 percent of E/R Associates was in turn owned by another general partnership, USA One Associates. In early 1989, Rodin Investment Administration Company (RIAC) contracted with USA to perform certain services related to the building. RIAC agreed, among other things, to act as the agent of USA in supervising the property management services provided by Richard I. Rubin & Co., Inc. (Rubin), with respect to the operation and management of the building. In late 1990, RIAC also contracted with E/R Associates to perform certain services dealing with the execution, amendment, termination, and other administrative duties related to tenant leases.

Since RIAC provided property management services for both USA and E/R Associates, RIAC considered itself to be an insured under the primary liability policy issued to E/R Associates. However, this insurer denied defense of RIAC alleging RIAC was not an insured under the liability policy, and even if RIAC were to be an insured, the policy was subject to a professional services exclusion. This exclusion read as follows.

> With respect to any professional services shown in the Schedule, this insurance does not apply to "bodily injury," "property damage," "personal injury," or "advertising injury" due to the rendering or failure to render any professional service.

> Schedule

> Description of Professional Services:
> Real Estate Management

As a result of the fire, RIAC was named as a defendant in at least 30 suits, with one complaint alleging that in at least one instance, RIAC's liability was premised on its alleged role as a real estate manager. A lower court held that, to the extent the underlying actions involved claims for conduct as a real estate manager for E/R Associates, RIAC was not entitled to coverage because of the professional services exclusion.

A complicating feature of the insurance policy in this case is that it also contained an endorsement, which read as follows.

> It is agreed that managing agents of locations covered by this policy are included as additional named insureds.

The court stated that if the allegations in the other 29 underlying actions did not involve RIAC's role as an alleged real estate manager (which exposure the court had held to be specifically excluded), it might qualify for coverage as a "managing agent" of the building, a term not defined in the policy.

On appeal, this issue was decided by the U. S. District Court for the Eastern District of Pennsylvania. After examining the relevant contracts, documents, and the nature of RIAC's activities, the district court concluded that RIAC was acting as a managing agent. The court pointed out that the term "managing agents" as used in the endorsement was plural, which acknowledged the possibility that the building could have more than one managing agent. It stated further that Aetna's policy, which did not define "managing agents," clearly provided that managing agents of covered locations were insureds.

Professional Services Exclusion

Professional services exclusions are a common feature of general liability policies. Generally, the use of these exclusions is required by the manual rules for classifying and determining the insurance premium, but in some cases these exclusions are added with no particular underwriting purpose and regardless of the classification of the risk.

Whatever the reason for its use, a professional services exclusion on a liability policy intended to encompass real estate management activities can indicate a misunderstanding of the distinction between general liability and errors and omissions exposures. Coverage of these exposures under CGL and professional liability policies is supposed to dovetail so as to reduce the chance of a coverage gap. E&O policies insuring real estate agents, brokers, managers, and kindred operations typically will limit their coverage to negligent acts, errors, or omissions that result in damages *not* based on bodily injury, property damage, personal injury, or advertising injury. The only way to close the gap created by an E&O policy exclusion of this kind—that is, to cover liability arising from bodily injury, property damage, personal injury, or advertising injury—is to purchase a CGL policy.

When CGL coverage is written for a person or organization involved in real estate sales, service, or management, any professional liability exclusion attached to the CGL policy should contain an exception. That exception should state that the exclusion does not apply to liability for bodily injury, property damage, personal injury, or advertising injury (assuming the policy included the latter two coverages).

A CGL policy written with a professional services exclusion applicable to bodily injury, property damage, or personal and advertising injury for real estate businesses (or other unrelated businesses that are candidates for a separate E&O policy) virtually nullifies any hope for undisputed coverage. Complicating this matter is the fact that, as automatic insureds on the CGL policies of others, real estate managers frequently do not have the opportunity to see coverage provisions of those policies until after something happens.

A professional services exclusion on a property management company's liability policy was held to be inapplicable in *Bonnie Owen Realty v Cincinnati Insurance Co.,* 670 NE2d 1182 (Ill 1996). This case arose following a fire at an apartment managed by the insured. Some of the victims filed suit against the insured, alleging negligence in (1) failing to provide proper security at the apartment building, which allowed an arsonist to enter the premises and start the fire, (2) failing to provide a sufficient number of proper and working smoke alarms, (3) failing to properly equip the property with fire escapes, and (4) failing to warn of the hazards associated with the property.

The insurer denied coverage to the apartment manager based on the following exclusions found in two policies issued to the insured.

This insurance does not apply to "bodily injury" or "property damage" arising out of: The rendering or failure to render professional services if such injury or damage arises out of any claim for Professional Liability or Malpractice made against an insured caused by any negligent act, error, omission of an insured or any other person for whose acts you are legally responsible in the conduct of any business, trade, or profession.

It is agreed that such insurance as is provided by this policy for bodily injury, personal injury, or property damage does not apply if such injury or damage arises out of any claim for Professional Liability or Malpractice made against an insured caused by any negligent act, error, or omission of an insured or any person for whose acts an insured is legally liable in the conduct of any business, trade, profession, municipal service, such as, but not limited to, law enforcement departments, fire departments, (including volunteers), health departments, ambulance services, paramedics, lawyers, or judges.

A lower court ruled in favor of coverage and the insurer appealed, arguing that the exclusions for professional services were applicable to the claims. The higher court affirmed the lower court's decision in part because the underlying complaints did not allege conduct of a professional nature but, instead, simple negligence. The court also said that the exclusions did not apply to all negligence in the conduct of the plaintiff's (insured's) business but only to negligence based on the rendering of or failure to render professional services. In so ruling, the court went on to assign a definition of professional services, as follows.

…[T]he term is not limited to services performed by persons who must be licensed by a governmental authority in order to practice their professions but refers to any business activity conducted by the insured which involves specialized knowledge, labor, or skill and is predominantly mental or intellectual as opposed to physical in nature.

Given this court's expansive view of the meaning of professional services for purposes of excluding coverage, professional service exclusions should be carefully scrutinized when added to a policy.

Other Automatic Insureds

In the event of the named insured's death, the post-1986 and 1973 CGL policies specifically provide that the named insured's rights and duties under the policy are automatically transferred to such insured's legal representative. These stipulations are found within the conditions section of the respective policy editions. Until a legal representative is officially selected, the policies protect anyone who has proper, temporary custody of such property, but protection is limited solely with respect to the property in question.

Also deemed to be automatic insureds are other persons with respect to the operation of certain mobile equipment of the kind and scope as applies to employees of the named insured. By automatically including as insureds any persons driving registered mobile equipment on a public road, the CGL policy's coverage of liability arising from mobile equipment tracks with the business auto policy's coverage of automobile liability.

It should be noted that persons or organizations responsible for the actions of the person operating the equipment are also automatically included as insureds. Thus, for example, if an employer was held vicariously liable for its employee's negligent operation of mobile equipment borrowed from another organization, it would be covered as an insured under the equipment owner's CGL policy.

Newly acquired or formed organizations also are automatic insureds in the 1986 and later editions of the CGL policy, subject to certain conditions. Protection of a newly acquired organization is automatic until the ninetieth day of the acquisition or formation, or the end of the policy period, which-

ever is earlier. If continued coverage is desired, the insurer must be notified before the expiration of that grace period.

However, no coverage applies to such newly acquired or formed organizations with respect to (1) bodily injury or property damage that occurred before such acquisition or formation, or (2) personal injury or advertising injury arising out of an offense committed before such acquisition or formation. In addition, no coverage applies if other insurance is available to the newly acquired organization. If any amount of insurance is available, this protection does not apply.

Under the 1973 policy provisions, it is necessary to purchase the Broad Form CGL endorsement to obtain insured status for newly acquired organizations. However, the scope of protection and conditions under which insured status applies are otherwise identical to the 1986 and subsequent edition policy forms.

"Doing Business As"

For various business reasons, organizations or individuals sometimes conduct business under a name other than their official or legal name. For example, the individual, Richard Roe, might decide to operate his sole proprietorship under the name of Roe Construction Company. When this is done, the organization is required by law to file, in the county where it does business, a "fictitious name" or "fictitious business name" statement. This statement shows the true name and address of the organization or individual(s) and states that those listed are "doing business as" whatever the chosen name is. In essence, it provides an official public record linking the fictitious name to the legal name and address.

By providing such a record, those interacting with the business are given the opportunity to determine exactly with whom they are dealing. This helps to prevent fraudulent activities and provides clear reference of all parties that must be involved in any legal action against the organization or individual.

The abbreviation for the phrase "doing business as," i.e., "d/b/a," is commonly used in the Declarations pages of insurance policies under the section that identifies the named insured(s). Continuing the example stated previously, this would give rise to a named insured of "Richard Roe d/b/a Roe Construction Company."

As simple as its application may appear, this designation is the source of many insurance disputes. The apparent root of these problems is that insureds and their insured representatives, along with insurers, do not always understand the composition of business organizations such as sole proprietorships, partnerships and joint ventures, corporations, and unincorporated associations.

Adding to this complication is that when applications and Declarations pages for insurance policies are prepared, sometimes very little thought is given to designating the appropriate nature of the business (although, admittedly, there are instances when the structure of business enterprises is so complicated as to be difficult to comprehend and describe). Yet, determining the proper organizational structure is important because there is a direct relationship between the nature of the business and the Who Is an Insured provision of liability policies.

Individually Owned Businesses

By far the greatest number of problems associated with the term "d/b/a" deal with individuals who own and operate businesses under trade names. Sometimes individuals select trade names that utilize the word "Company" (such as R. Roe d/b/a ABC Company), giving the impression that the business is a corporation. Since an individual cannot do business as a corporation without complying with certain legal requirements, this designation in the policy declarations can create a problem for the insured and insurer alike.

The involvement of a single individual in more than one entity sometimes can create complications for the unwary. In one such case, the sole proprietor of two businesses was left uninsured when one of his entities was not listed on the poli-

cy. In this case, *Consolidated American Insurance Co. v Landry,* 525 S2d 567 (La 1988), the policy was issued to a "Lersey Landry d/b/a Landry's Apartments." However, an action against the insured involved another business not listed on the policy as "Lersey Landry d/b/a Landry Lumber Yard." The insurer denied coverage because the latter business entity was not specifically listed on the policy. The insured argued that coverage should apply because the term "insured," as contained in the liability policy, extended coverage to any business of which Lersey Landry was the sole proprietor. Also, unless the policy contained an exclusion of all other sole proprietorships, the policy should apply.

The court disagreed with the insured and held that the policy clearly applied solely to the apartment business, because the lumberyard was a separate and distinct business pursuit even though operated by the same sole proprietor.

Partnerships and Joint Ventures

When a partnership or joint venture is designated in the policy declarations, the Who Is an Insured provision extends coverage to the partnership or joint venture, along with its members, partners, and their spouses, but only with respect to the conduct of such business. The question often arises as to whether it is preferable to name the partners or members individually, since they are already covered as to their partnership liability.

Under some fact patterns, specifically naming the partners or members individually can lead to problems. A case in point is *Bryan v Continental Casualty Co.,* 587 F2d 441 (DC Ariz 1978). The policy declarations listed the following as the named insured: "K.L. Engebretson & T. Townsend d/b/a: Engebretson-Grupe Co." The box in the Declarations also designated an individual and a partnership as the named insureds. The question was whether the policy, which applied to K.L. Engebretson, individually, likewise applied to T. Townsend, individually.

The person who prepared the policy testified that it was his intent to insure only two persons and entities: Engebretson-Grupe Co., as a partnership, and K.L. Engebretson, as an individual. He further testified that he checked both the "individual" and "partnership" boxes on the declarations to distinguish between two separate operations (one which was individually owned by K.L. Engebretson and the other as a partnership owned by both Engebretson and Townsend). He went on to say that there was nothing in the policy that expressed an intent to insure Townsend as an individual. However, an employee of the named insured testified that it was her understanding the policy was to cover both individuals and the partnership. The court held that the policy also applied to Townsend, individually.

Based on this case, one could conclude that the proper way to designate a partnership or joint venture is to mention solely the entity's name as the named insured on the policy declarations. To also mention the individual partners' names with the descriptive d/b/a could lead to the conclusion that the partners so named also are covered for their individual liability wholly apart from the liability of the partnership.

One case, however, that does not agree with this conclusion is *Milazo v Gulf Insurance Co.,* 224 Cal App 3d 1528 (1990). This was a dispute between the general partners (Pringle) and one of the limited partners (Milazo) who sought protection as a partner as well as in his individual capacity. Two CGL policies were at issue. The first, issued for the period ending 1983, designated the named insured as "M.H. Pringle, M. Miloza [sic] & Millard Ellis d/b/a Alexander's Choice Meats." The second policy issued for the year ending 1986 listed the named insured as: "Duncan Howie, Michael Milaza [sic] and Millard Ellis, *partners,* d/b/a Alexanders [sic] Choice Meats." The box in the policy declarations also designated that the entity was a partnership.

The suit was filed because of certain wrongful acts of the partner in question in misappropriating assets and other misdeeds that also resulted in some personal injury offenses. The court held that the partner qualified as an insured under the liability policy but only with respect to his liability as a partner of the firm, because it was only the part-

nership that was the named insured. But the court also ruled that his wrongful acts could not be considered to have been committed *while acting in his capacity as a partner.* The court's rationale was that there could be no partnership liability for the conduct involved and so no coverage under the liability policy. The partner accused of the wrongdoing sought coverage for his liability in his individual capacity but was overruled by the court in each of the instances as follows.

> The second policy for the period ending 1986 referred specifically to the term "partners" following the listing of the partners' names. The earlier policy, it was maintained, likewise should have included that term so as to include the partners, individually, under the policy. The partner therefore maintained that he was protected in his individual capacity under the policy.

The court saw no significance to that term's reference in the policy, because each such policy was issued to a business entity in which the named individuals were, in fact, partners and that the partnership nature of the entity was understood by the partners. Both the partners and the partnership were listed as named insureds on the policy Declarations. The partner therefore maintained that he was protected in his individual capacity under the policy.

The court stated that the partners were listed as "d/b/a"; that is, they were an integral part of the business entity that admittedly was a partnership. Also, the policy Declarations specifically stated that the named insured is a partnership thus precluding the partner as a named insured in his individual capacity.

Parenthetically, the court also stated that where the named insured is three people who are designated as "d/b/a" and where the policy specifically states that the named insured is a partnership (rather than three individuals or three individuals and the partnership), it would be unreasonable to say that those three people are insured as individuals separate and apart from their coverage as partners. The partner accused of wrongful conduct would have been covered for liability arising out of its conduct outside of the partnership had the members of the partnership been named individually as well as under the partnership name.

In conclusion, from the insurer's perspective it is preferable to name only the partnership, since naming the partners individually increases the insurer's exposure. However, insureds and their agents and brokers may prefer naming the partners individually as well. It is not unusual for individual members of a partnership to be sued only as individuals instead of as a partnership. If the individual partners are not named as insureds, coverage may not apply.

Corporations

Most of the problems involving insured corporations' use of the "doing business as" designations appear to involve solely owned or closely held corporations and commercial auto policies. Some of these problems are discussed in **Chapter 15,** dealing with insureds under commercial auto policies.

However, as a general rule, the designation of an insured as an individual "doing business as" a corporation is an invitation to controversy and disputes. In most cases, the named insured should be the corporation, and the individual owner will be afforded automatic additional insured status under the provisions previously discussed in this chapter. If there is a further reason to specifically name the individual in the policy (e.g., to extend coverage to some business venture beyond that of the corporation), either the individual should be named without reference to the d/b/a or the other business entity should be named.

Impact of Endorsements

Up to this point, the discussion of "doing business as" has dealt with insurance policy issues limited to the named insured designations on the policy Declarations page. However, it is also important to consider the impact endorsements have on policies when the endorsements are issued for purposes of listing insureds. It is quite common for entities to be involved in a variety of business relationships past and present. Since space on the policy Declarations page is limited, a notation commonly is made on the Declarations page to refer to the named insured endorsement as designated.

The people who prepare these endorsements must be extremely careful in this regard because of the effect an endorsement can have on the policy. Use of the descriptive term "individually" following a person's name on an endorsement as the named insured should be pondered carefully. The reason is the insurer might have the obligation to protect the individual so identified for liability stemming from both nonbusiness and business activities, regardless of whether the business liability involves a sole proprietorship, partnership, or other organization. This approach may be preferable for insureds, since individuals not only get sued as owners of businesses but also in their individual capacity.

Tailoring the Persons Insured Provision

While the basic structure of the Who Is an Insured provision may meet the needs of most insureds, it is sometimes necessary to modify the provision so that the nomenclature of persons or entities to be insured more closely corresponds to the nature and structure of the organization. For example, the Who Is an Insured provision of all editions of ISO CGL forms issued prior to the 1996 edition omit reference to limited liability companies, a very common form of business entity in today's market. Likewise, the Who Is an Insured provision of the 1986 CGL form is inappropriate for governmental subdivisions, charitable institutions, churches, or schools, to name a few. Thus, for coverage to apply properly and without raising issues of ambiguity that can adversely affect the insurer and the insured alike, endorsements may be necessary to amend the Persons Insured provision.

For many years, there was no standard endorsement to amend the basic Persons Insured provision of the CGL policy when the subject of the policy's coverage was a governmental subdivision. This caused some problems because governmental entities consist of elected and appointed officials and do not have executive officers, directors, and stockholders, as those terms are used in the policies.

A case in point is *Holm v Mutual Service Casualty Insurance Co.,* 261 NW2d 598 (Minn 1977). The insurer here issued a general liability policy containing the standard Persons Insured provision drafted with private sector named insureds in mind. The case was prompted when a law enforcement officer sought protection under the policy as an "executive officer" of the municipality.

The court ruled that the meaning of the term "executive officers," insofar as a governmental entity was concerned, would encompass those persons who would be responsible for high-level governmental policy making. This would include the mayor, manager, members of the council, administrative board members, and department heads but would not include employees whose duties were largely ministerial, such as law enforcement officers.

However, in the case of *Ohio Casualty Co. v Gray,* 746 F2d 381 (7th Cir 1984), the court ruled in favor of a law enforcement officer who sought protection. The insurer here issued a general liability policy to a town in Indiana, with the town designated as the named insured on the declarations. The policy contained the standard Persons Insured provision providing coverage for "executive officers, directors, and stockholders" when acting within the scope of their duties. The insurer brought this action on the question of whether it was obligated to defend or indemnify the town marshal under the terms of the liability policy.

The district court granted judgment for the insurer by holding that police officers and, consequently, town marshals were not executive officers of the municipality. On appeal, however, the judgment was reversed since the policy's Persons Insured provision did not clearly fit the nomenclature of the positions commonly associated with municipalities.

Under the 1986 and later edition CGL forms, a special endorsement is available when the named insured is a governmental entity. The endorsement, CG 24 09, Governmental Subdivisions, introduces two amendments, one dealing with the

Who Is an Insured provision. The endorsement is shown in Exhibit 3.6.

EXHIBIT 3.6
GOVERNMENTAL SUBDIVISIONS
ENDORSEMENT (CG 24 09)

WHO IS AN INSURED (Section II) is amended to include as an insured any elective or appointive officer or member of any board or agency of yours while acting within the scope of their duties as such.

Copyright, Insurance Services Office, Inc., 1992

Similar endorsements have been introduced for churches: the Additional Insured—Church Members and Officers (CG 20 22) endorsement; clubs: the Additional Insured—Club Members (CG 20 02) endorsement; and charitable institutions: the Additional Insured—Charitable Institutions (CG 20 20) endorsement. These endorsements are included in **Appendix B.**

While standard endorsements are available for the purpose of adding certain volunteers as additional insureds, none is available for companies that desire to employ their retired employees as consultants. Currently, only manuscript endorsements are used to clarify the intent and scope of coverage for this exposure.

Policy Conditions: Insured versus Named Insured

As noted in **Chapter 2,** there are two types of named insureds: the first named insured and all other named insureds. Likewise, there are two general types of insureds: automatic insureds and additional insureds. To determine whether there are any meaningful differences between these general categories of insureds, it is necessary to compare their respective rights and obligations under the liability policy. The fact that the scope of an additional insured's coverage may vary under the policy is no bar to considering policy conditions or the so-called ground rules that insurers and insureds must observe.

EXHIBIT 3.7
INSURED AND NAMED INSURED POLICY CONDITIONS DIFFERENCES

	1973 CGL	Post-1986 CGL
Occurrence and Claim Reporting Requirements	Insured	First Named Insured
Premium Payment Requirements	Named Insured	First Named Insured
Return Premium Privileges	Named Insured	First Named Insured
Policy Cancellation Rights	Named Insured	First Named Insured
Notice of Cancellation Rights	Named Insured	First Named Insured
Insurer's Right To Examine Books	Named Insured	Named Insured
Transfer of Policy Rights	Named Insured	Named Insured

Exhibit 3.7 lists most of the differences in policy conditions as they exist between named insureds and automatic insureds or additional insureds under the 1973 and 1986 CGL policies. As Exhibit 3.7 depicts, most of the obligations made in the policy conditions of the 1986 and 1973 liability policies fall on the shoulders of named insureds. In fact, the only obligation imposed on insureds is to report occurrences and claims to the insurer, and this requirement is only imposed on insureds in the 1973 policy.

This could be viewed as a disadvantage because failure of the insured to provide notice could prejudice coverage under the policy. On the other hand, since insureds are not subject to this provision under the 1986 and later edition policies, there is a much reduced risk that delayed notice of an occurrence will result in a claim denial.

Not addressed here are the various exclusions that apply to the named insured (You) and not to insureds or additional insureds.

Cancellation Problems

A condition that might be viewed as unfavorable to insureds under 1973 and later edition policies concerns notice of cancellation. This is especially true since additional insureds generally seek some assurances that their protection will be continued, especially since they do not receive a copy of the policy. The approaches taken by additional insureds to obtain assurances of notice are discussed in **Chapter 20** under the subject of insurance certificates.

However, one case of interest on this subject is *Jefferson Insurance Co. of New York v Curle,* 771 SW2d 424 (Tenn App 1989). This involved a liability policy issued to two partners of a roofing company. Three months after the policy was issued, the partnership was dissolved. One of the partners agreed to finish one project and left the other partner to wind up the other partnership affairs. The latter partner then signed a cancellation request/policy release and collected the unearned premium.

While working on one of the buildings on which this partnership had performed roofing work, a painting contractor fell through a hole allegedly covered by the former roofing firm with tar paper or felt. The injured painting contractor filed suit against the roofing partnership and its two partners who, in turn, sought protection from their former general liability insurer. The insurer then filed a declaratory judgment action, contending that the policy was totally canceled, even though only one partner of the partnership canceled the policy.

The court in this case ruled that the insurer was under no obligation to provide coverage. The court explained in part that the policy as issued covered the individual partners only in their capacity as partners. Thus, when one of the partners canceled the partnership's insurance, any coverage applicable to both of the partners, individually, ceased.

The court also found that failure of the partner who canceled coverage to follow the cancellation provisions in the policy was not adequate to defeat the cancellation notice submitted. The court ruled that the wording in the cancellation provision was permissive and did not preclude other forms of cancellation.

The only way to obligate another party's insurer to provide notice of cancellation is to have that party convince its insurer to endorse the policy to include the requirement. Unfortunately, there is no standard endorsement available to effect this requirement, and it is usually very difficult (or impossible) to convince underwriters to make it.

When such an endorsement is required by contractual agreements, a beach of contract often results.

Summary

A number of individuals with close ties to the named insured enjoy automatic insured status under modern liability insurance forms. For the most part, this practice benefits both the named insured and the automatic insureds. The areas where coverage gaps or disputes are most likely to occur involve the named insured's liability arising from products or completed operations of past, unscheduled, partnerships or joint ventures, one employee's liability for bodily injury to another employee, and the named insured's liability to an injured leased employee. Each of these potential coverage gaps can be handled through specific modification of the CGL policy, by either a standard or manuscript endorsement, or through proper arrangement of other types of insurance (e.g., workers compensation insurance).

Chapter 3 Notes

1. The case of *Jones v United States Auto Assn.,* 299 S2d 894 (La App 1974), surrounded a policy that designated an individual as named insured. An employee sought protection by maintaining he was an executive officer, but the court ruled against coverage, stating that neither the individual nor the sole proprietorship was deemed to have officers within its business structure.

2. In the case of *DiTullo v Hawaiian Insurance & Guarantee Co.,* 616 P2d 221 (Haw 1980), the court ruled that a policy that designated an insured corporation's stockholders as insureds was ambiguous in regard to a nonprofit corporation because the latter had no such stockholders.

3. The content of this paragraph is based on wording taken from the case of *Gigax v Ralston Purina Co.,* 186 Cal Rptr 395 (Cal App 1982).

4. The addition of incidental medical malpractice liability coverage to the Broad Form CGL endorsement has been viewed as a limitation on protection rather than an extension. At best, it clarifies a restriction. The reason, as advocated by some, is that without this provision, medical professional liability coverage would apply without restriction in the absence of a professional services exclusion. But one of the advantages of the Broad Form CGL endorsement insofar as employees are concerned, in addition to being included as automatic additional insureds, is protection under personal injury and advertising injury liability coverages. Some insurers still prefer to provide the various coverages—as normally provided by a Broad Form CGL endorsement—on a piecemeal basis.

    When, for example, an earlier CGL policy was endorsed to include employees as additional insureds, their protection was limited to bodily injury and property damage. If an endorsement were added to provide personal injury and advertising injury liability coverages, it would have been necessary to amend the latter coverages by an additional endorsement to add employees as insureds for those coverages as well. Unfortunately, this was often overlooked until it was too late. While employees under current liability policies need not be as concerned, care must be exercised with respect to the 1973 CGL or a prototype policy that is still being offered by some insurers for competitive reasons.

Chapter 4

ADDITIONAL INSURED STATUS

This chapter is devoted solely to discussing nonautomatic additional insured status with respect to liability insurance. The reasons persons and organizations seek additional insured status are explored as well as the importance of contractual agreements as a complement to such status. Subsequent chapters look into the many problems that confront named insureds and additional insureds and explore ways to overcome those problems.

"Additional Insured" Defined

The term "additional insured," as used in this book, is intended to signify those insureds that generally are not automatically included as insureds under the liability policy of another but for whom the named insured desires or is required to provide a certain degree of protection under its liability policies. An endorsement usually is used to effect additional insured status for these parties.[1]

Why should the named insured provide others with additional insured status? One reason is to protect the other party because of a close relationship with that party; another is to comply with a contractual agreement to do so. This first group of additional insureds is typically made up of individuals—rather than business entities—who have an ownership, membership, employee, or similar relationship with the named insured. Examples of this first group of additional insureds include the following.

- Employees of the named insured organization[2]

- Members of a named insured club or church

- Volunteers working on behalf of a named insured charity or government entity

- Unit owners of a named insured condominium association

The second group of additional insureds comprises people or, more frequently, organizations with whom the named insured has a business relationship. These additional insureds are often either the named insured's customers or the owners of property the named insured rents or leases. To protect these customers or property owners from liability arising out of the named insured's activities, they are included as additional insureds on the named insured's liability policy—often to satisfy a requirement of the underlying business contract (e.g., rental or lease agreement or construction contract). Examples of these types of additional insureds include the following.

- Project owners on the policies of general contractors

- General contractors on the policies of subcontractors

- Owners or lessors of real estate on the policies of lessees or tenants

- Lessors of leased equipment on the policies of lessees

- Retailers and distributors on the policies of manufacturers

Much of the controversy surrounding and the problems resulting from additional insured status arises from this group of contractually required additional insureds. Therefore, this book is primarily concerned with these types of additional insureds.

Reasons for Requiring Additional Insured Status

Contractual risk transfer (or noninsurance risk transfer) has long been considered a valid technique for treating risks. Simply stated, contractual risk transfer involves an attempt to allocate potential legal liabilities that could arise in connection with the performance of a contract between the parties to the contract. These liability risks are often allocated in a manner that would not have occurred under common law in the absence of the contract.[3]

In theory, the rationale behind many of these transfers is to make the party with the most control over the risk responsible for suffering the financial loss should it fail to prevent losses from occurring. Of course, the relative bargaining positions of the contracting parties also play a key role in determining the extent of any such transfers. The contractual provisions used to effect such noninsurance risk transfers are hold harmless or indemnity provisions and insurance provisions.

Hold harmless or indemnity provisions are agreements whereby one party (the indemnitor) assumes the other party's (the indemnitee's) legal liability to whatever extent delineated in the provision. For example, contractors usually agree to indemnify and hold harmless project owners for liability arising out of their construction operations. If the project owner is held vicariously liable for injury or damage that the contractor causes, the contractor must pay the owner's loss.[4]

Indemnity provisions operate independently from the indemnitor's insurance, which may or may not cover the risks assumed by the indemnitor. Where a named insured (e.g., a contractor) is obligated to indemnify another party (e.g., the project owner), the named insured's contractual liability coverage will respond to this obligation if coverage for the claim is not otherwise precluded by the terms of the policy (e.g., the claim must involve liability for bodily injury or property damage and none of the exclusions may be applicable). However, if the indemnity agreement is not enforceable for some reason, the contractual liability coverage will not respond.

Additional insured status achieves a similar end without relying on the terms of an indemnity clause. It makes the other party (e.g., the owner) an insured in the named insured's (e.g., the contractor's) liability policies, subject to the terms and conditions of the policy and the additional insured endorsement.

The primary motives for requiring additional insured status on the liability policy of another are listed below and are discussed in detail in the pages that follow.

- It may reinforce risk transfers otherwise accomplished through indemnity agreements that could be invalidated by the courts or by statute.

- It may make it more difficult for a court that finds an indemnity agreement to be void to find that the insurance required in an agreement is solely for purposes of indemnifying the indemnitee (additional insured) and thus inextricably tied to the invalid indemnity provision.

- It may allow one party to transfer liability arising from its sole negligence to the other party's insurer, even in those states that prohibit broad form indemnity clauses.

- It may give those who attempt to transfer risk to others direct rights under the other party's insurance, particularly with respect to defense coverage.

- It provides the additional insured with direct defense coverage that applies in addition to limits without requiring that a host of conditions precedent be met, as is the case under contractual liability coverage.

- It may prohibit the indemnitor's insurer from subrogating against the indemnitee when a loss is caused by the indemnitee's acts or omissions.

- It may provide the indemnitee with personal injury liability coverage.

- It may avoid having losses impact the loss history of the additional insured, thus avoiding increased insurance premiums for the additional insured in future years.

- It may substantially increase the limits of insurance available to the additional insured for a given operation or project.

- It may lessen the chance that the additional insured will be forced to sue the indemnitor directly to be made whole following a claim or suit.

- It may increase the chances of cooperation between the indemnitor and indemnitee in the event of a claim or suit.

Reinforcement of Risk Transfer by Contract

Indemnity clauses are included in contracts to transfer the liability risk of one of the contracting parties (the indemnitee) to the other party (the indemnitor). Typically, the financial consequences of potential legal liability to a third party are the risk being transferred. The contract does not absolve the liable party from its legal obligation to an injured third party; it merely makes the indemnitor responsible for meeting the legal (financial) obligation on the liable party's behalf. If the indemnitor does not have the financial resources to meet the legal obligation, it remains the obligation of the liable party.

For example, a contract between the owner of a waste site and a contractor retained to clean it up might specify that the contractor indemnify the owner for any liability claims arising from the project. The contractor (the indemnitor) would therefore be required by the contract to respond to any claims made against the owner (the indemnitee) by third parties injured by the contractor. However, the owner would be obligated under the law to respond directly to claims made against it if the contractor failed to do so for any reason, such as financial shortcomings.

To reduce the possibility that an indemnitor will be unable to respond to its contractual obligation, it is common to require liability insurance to reinforce the legal liabilities transferred in hold harmless agreements. While the contract may actually transfer to the indemnitor some uninsured liabilities, such as pollution liability, the existence of the insurance policy helps guarantee that resources will be available to respond to many types of claims.

The scope of an indemnity agreement can vary dramatically depending on the intent and the skill with which it is drafted. As a rule, the scope of the indemnity agreement has no effect on the scope of coverage provided to an additional insured. The exceptions to this rule are cases alleging ambiguous policy wording or additional insured endorsements that limit coverage to that status required in the contract. In instances where ambiguity is alleged, courts may look outside the four corners of the policy to the indemnity agreement for assistance in determining the intent of the parties. Absent allegations of ambiguity, however, the scope of the indemnity obligation impacts the scope of contractual liability coverage, the purpose of which is to insure liability the named insured has assumed under an indemnity obligation. It also has relevence where, as referenced above, the additional insured endorsement provides coverage only to the extent required by contract. Otherwise, additional insured status allows the additional insured direct coverage under the named insured's policy and, thus, only the terms of the policy can affect coverage.

Commercial general liability (CGL) and umbrella liability insurance is usually required in the underlying contracts to cover the risks transferred in indemnification agreements. One of the drawbacks to relying solely on the contractual liability coverage feature of these liability policies is that this coverage relies on the enforceability of the indemnity provision. Many states have enacted anti-indemnity statutes that limit the enforceability of some types of hold harmless provisions, especially those that attempt to transfer the sole liability (as opposed to joint liability) of one party to another in a construction contract.[5]

States with anti-indemnity statutes applying to construction and other contracts are listed in Exhibit 4.1. Such statutes are one of the reasons it is common to require that the indemnitee be included as an additional insured on the indemnitor's liability insurance. Doing so means that the indemnitee has some protection to fall back on in the event there is a problem with the enforceability of the hold harmless agreement.

This, in effect, is what is known as the "belt and suspenders" concept. Thus, if contractual liability insurance applies, there is no need to rely on additional insured status. Conversely, if contractual liability coverage does not apply for some reason, additional insured status can be relied on for the protection of the indemnitee.

The "Inextricably Tied" Issue

Caution must be exercised in wording when drafting contracts containing an indemnification provision and requirements for insurance. Insurance and indemnification requirements should not be combined in the same provision. Even addressing those issues in separate provisions is inadequate if they are or appear to be interdependent. An example is a contract requiring the assumption of liability (indemnity) in one provision and the specific requirement in another provision that contractual liability insurance be procured to cover the same indemnification requirement previously addressed.

The wording for insurance requirements should clearly state that the insurance required is in addition to and separate from any other obligations contained in the contract. Also important is a requirement that the indemnitee be added as an additional insured to the policy. Contracts that merely require the indemnitor to procure insurance (not adding the indemnitee as an additional insured) run a greater risk that courts will find the indemnity and insurance requirements to be inextricably tied.

An agreement to provide insurance without additional insured requirements can be construed to mean that the insurance is intended only to fund the indemnity obligation in the same contract. Therefore, if the indemnity agreement is held to be invalid so, too, might the coverage under the policy as it relates or applies to the party being indemnified.

EXHIBIT 4.1
STATES WITH ANTI-INDEMNITY STATUTES

The following states have enacted anti-indemnity legislation precluding indemnification for the sole fault of another in a construction contract. These statutes vary in scope and type of contracts to which they apply. However, a common thread is the prohibition against indemnifying for the sole fault of another. Those states without anti-indemnity statutes generally hold that this form of indemnity is valid provided certain requirements are met in the contracts.

Alaska	Hawaii	Minnesota	New York	South Dakota
Arizona	Idaho	Mississippi	North Carolina	Tennessee
California	Illinois	Montana	North Dakota	Texas
Colorado	Indiana	Nebraska	Ohio	Utah
Connecticut	Louisiana	Nevada	Oregon	Vermont
Delaware	Maryland	New Hampshire	Pennsylvania	Virginia
Florida	Massachusetts	New Jersey	Rhode Island	Washington
Georgia	Michigan	New Mexico	South Carolina	West Virginia

In some jurisdictions, if the indemnification requirement is deemed to be unenforceable, that finding *may* also nullify insurance requirements pertaining or applicable to the nullified indemnity wording. In the words of some courts, the two provisions are so "inextricably tied" that the voiding of one inevitably makes the other unenforceable. This is said to occur where, as referenced above, the insurance required in the contract is determined to be solely for the purpose of funding the indemnitor's obligation to indemnify.

An inextricably tied case where coverage was ruled out and many of the issues discussed here were addressed is *Transcontinental Insurance Co. v National Union Insurance Co.,* 662 NE2d 500 (Ill App 1996). The contract in this case required that the subcontractor procure insurance; however, it did not require that the general contractor be added as an additional insured. The indemnity provision required that the subcontractor indemnify the general contractor for all liability arising out of the project, which the court concluded encompassed the general contractor's sole fault. As a result, the indemnity contract was held to be void.

To make matters worse, the closing paragraph of the insurance section of the contract stated as follows:

> The insurance provided to the foregoing shall include Contractual Liability coverage in accordance with Contractor's obligations under paragraph 14 above.

Paragraph 14 was the indemnification obligation.

Because the two sections were held to be interdependent, they were inextricably tied. As a result, when the indemnity provision was held to be invalid so, too, were the insurance requirements to the extent they applied to the party to be indemnified.

There was a blanket additional insured endorsement attached to the policy that stated as follows:

> 1. Who Is Insured (Section II) is amended to include as an insured anyone for whom

you have agreed prior to a loss to provide insurance, but only as respects liability arising out of your premises or your work.

However, the wording in the underlying contract requiring that the insurance to be provided apply to the indemnitor's obligation to indemnify the indemnitee had been declared unenforceable by the court. As a result, this endorsement could not operate to make the indemnitee an additional insured. It could do so only if there were an *enforceable* contract provision requiring the indemnitor to provide insurance.

One of the cases where the "inextricably tied" issue was held not to be applicable by a court is *Juretic v USX Corp.,* 596 NE2d 810 (Ill App 1992). The contract in question, imposed by a project owner on a contractor, contained an indemnity agreement and a separate insurance provision. The insurance provision required coverage in three parts.

(1) The insurance would cover the contractor's obligations to the owner under the indemnification clause of the contract.

(2) Said policies of insurance were to provide that the owner be named as an additional insured ....

(3) The contractor was to carry insurance covering the contractor's and owner's liability to pay for any and all loss, damage, any injury to property of any and all persons ... connected with or growing out of the contractor's performance of the work covered by the agreement.

The parties, for purposes of appeal, conceded that the indemnity provision was void pursuant to state statute. Therefore, the focus of the case was on the insurance provision, because if the insurance provision were to be found "inextricably tied" to the indemnity provision, the insurance provision would also be void. In fact, the insurance provision in (1) above was held to be "inextricably tied" to the void indemnity provision and, therefore, was also held to be void.

The court of appeals, in reversing the trial court's decision denying the applicability of insurance, held that the indemnity and insurance provisions were not "inextricably tied" so as to void the insurance requirements because they were concerned with more than just the obligations under the voided indemnity provision. The court stated that these kinds of agreements to obtain insurance are consistent with public policy—assuring compensation for injured workers. The insurance provision, therefore, was held to be enforceable to the extent of parts (2) and (3) of the above contract.

One important provision included in the insurance provision referenced for this case was a requirement that the owner be named as an additional insured. By inserting this requirement, the obligation to indemnify was not solely tied to the indemnitor's insurance coverage. The indemnitee now had its own independent right to the insurance coverage, which made it more difficult to argue that the insurance required was solely for purposes of indemnifying the indemnitee and, thus, inextricably tied to that obligation.

This case shows that even though one insurance provision is held to be "inextricably tied" to an indemnity provision, it is possible to overcome the potential voidance of coverage by careful wording and even by inserting an additional insured provision that has no dependency on the indemnity agreement.

In *Getty Oil Co. and Texaco v Insurance Co. of North America,* 845 SW2d 794 (Tex 1992), for example, the court held that while it expressed no opinion about the plaintiff's status as an additional insured, the indemnity provision was supported by an insurance provision separate from the requirements of additional insured status provision. The last sentence of the indemnity provision provided that "insurance covering this indemnity agreement shall be provided by the seller [indemnitor]." This provision's preamble, moreover, which began, "All insurance coverage carried by the Seller ... shall extend to and protect the Purchaser," became tied to the indemnity agreement. However, the additional insured provision required the seller (the indemnitor) to extend insurance coverage to the purchaser "whether or not required [by other provisions of the contract]." The court, therefore, stated that the additional insured provision of the contract was not there solely to support the indemnity agreement but, rather, was a separate obligation. It also said that, "[T]he additional insured provision, which does not support an indemnity agreement, is not prohibited by the language of the Anti-Indemnity Statute."

Covering Sole Fault Indemnification

As stated previously, some states have statutes voiding indemnification agreements that attempt to transfer the sole fault of one party to another in a construction contract. However, a number of states allow the parties to, in essence, indemnify against sole fault by providing additional insured status to the indemnitee in the indemnitor's policy or procuring some other form of liability insurance for the indemnitee.

Even where it is permissible to require another party to provide insurance covering the first party's sole negligence, caution must be exercised in the implementation of the insurance purchase because some of the statutes providing an insurance exception for sole fault require that the insurance be provided by an admitted, authorized, or licensed insurer. It therefore is necessary to determine whether the insurer to be utilized complies with the statutory requirements. For example, if the insurer is considered not to be an admitted, licensed, or authorized insurance company, the anti-indemnity statute may be used to make the additional insured's coverage void and unenforceable. The result might be that those who are contractually obligated to provide the insurance may be in breach of their contractual obligation in not using an admitted, authorized, or licensed insurer.

Another important issue involving anti-indemnity statutes is the use of self-insurance, which has become a popular method of handling risk, especially among many large commercial and public entities. However, in relation to anti-indemnity statutes, self-insurance, fronting arrangements, captives, and risk retention groups pose a special problem.

When an insurance exception is included in an anti-indemnity statute, it is presumed that any loss will be paid by an insurer, not the indemnitor. Thus, there is no apparent violation of the prohibition against the indemnitor paying for this exposure. But when self-insurance is the funding method to be employed, the indemnitor, in fact, is actually paying for the indemnitee's sole fault. This is a violation of the spirit and intent behind anti-indemnity legislation.

In *Transport Insurance v Insurance Co. of N. America*, 59 Cal Rptr 2d 126 (Cal App 1996), the court discussed a fronting policy. In this case, an insured had a policy with limits of $2 million and a deductible in the same amount. In describing this arrangement, the court concluded that the policy was a "noninsurance risk transfer" or "fronting arrangement," distinguishing a fronting arrangement from classic insurance. With insurance, the court noted, it is the insurer who is the primary party liable upon the occurrence of a contingency and who must bear the ultimate loss.

This perspective precisely sums up the problem insureds face when a front is involved and the insured seeks to insure another's sole fault. A fronting arrangement may present the same problem self-insurance does, because the named insured under such an arrangement actually funds the payment. The insurer in a fronting arrangement simply is the guarantor of the policy proceeds; however, the indemnitor ultimately guarantees the insurer reimbursement through a bond or letter of credit. Captives and risk retention groups may also be confronted with this problem in relation to the issue of indemnity statutes that include insurance exceptions.

Furthermore, as previously stated, many of the anti-indemnity statutes that allow indemnitors to insure against the indemnitee's sole fault require that the insurance be provided by an admitted or licensed insurer, which, in most cases, will not include self-insurance. Even the anti-indemnity statutes that do not mandate an admitted or licensed insurer make no reference to self-insurance. Whether self-insurance qualifies as insurance for purposes of allowing an indemnitor to indemnify

the indemnitee for the latter's sole fault may therefore be a question for the courts to decide.

A case in point is *USX Corp. v Liberty Mutual Insurance Co. and Turner Construction Co.,* 645 NE2d 396 (Ill App 1994). USX was to act as the subcontractor and Turner as the general contractor. Turner submitted a standard form agreement obligating USX to provide workers compensation and liability insurance and to name Turner as an additional insured. USX responded with a letter stating that USX was providing certificates attesting to their authority to act as self-insurers in the state of Illinois.

Following an injury, a USX employee filed suit against Turner. Turner, in turn, sought to obtain indemnity from USX based on the underlying contractual obligation of USX to indemnify Turner. USX insisted it had no obligation to indemnify Turner, as the cause of the loss was the sole fault of Turner. As a result, USX argued, it would be a violation of the Illinois anti-indemnity statute to require or allow USX to indemnify for the loss involved.

USX argued that the anti-indemnity statute applied equally to a promise to indemnify and an agreement to include the indemnitee/promisee in the indemnitor's/promisor's self-insurance program, which, according to USX, was not the same as insurance. The Illinois statute involved *does* contain an insurance exception to the anti-indemnity statute that allows the indemnitor to insure against the sole fault of the indemnitee. That exception does not require the insurance to be provided by an admitted insurer. The Illinois court sided with USX, holding that:

> ... while the contract compelling a subcontractor to procure insurance would be valid as a logical extension of section three of the indemnity act, compelling a subcontractor to itself become an insurer is not ... no such rationale for the allowance of self-insurance is provided under the Indemnity Act to allow for the substitution of self-insurance in the place of actual insurance. Moreover, there is no provision to allow for state certification or to invest any

state agency including the director of insurance with power to certify any self-insurance plan for that purpose.

The importance of this ruling and others like it cannot be overstated. Those entities that enter into construction agreements as indemnitors, with promises to insure the indemnitee, may find themselves in breach of contract if they use self-insurance. Because a true insurance policy can cover the sole fault of the indemnitee, whether added as an additional insured or automatically for liability assumed by the named insured by contract, the failure of self-insurance to apply similarly will leave the indemnitor in breach of its promise to the contrary. The indemnitee also may find itself in a financially impaired situation after having relied on the indemnitor's promise of indemnity only to find that the indemnitor cannot or does not have the resources to fulfill its promise.

Not all states view self-insurance in the same manner as the court in the preceding case. Some states hold that self-insurance can be considered insurance for purposes of determining whether it is "other insurance" within the meaning of that provision in insurance policies. However, whether those states will allow self-insurance to apply under an anti-indemnity statute is another matter. Finding self-insurance to be insurance for purposes of the other insurance condition found in liability policies is one thing. Finding that self-insurance does not violate the legislative intent behind anti-indemnity statutes is another matter.[6]

Contractual Agreement without Additional Insured Status

Where the indemnitee is not provided with additional insured status under the indemnitor's policy and the indemnitor or its insurer successfully challenges an indemnity provision, the insurer can avoid the financial obligation of responding to the indemnitee's liability.[7] *Allianz Insurance Co. v GoldCoast Partners,* 684 S2d 336 (Fla App 1996), is a case in point. Here, a patron sued GoldCoast, a Burger King franchisee, based on injuries the patron sustained because a chair he sat in had not been repaired properly. Décor Concepts Inc., which was insured by Allianz, had supplied the chair. The Allianz policy provided coverage to Décor for bodily injury assumed by Décor through contracts. In fact, Décor did assume the liability of Burger King to some extent. However, the injured party had alleged that GoldCoast was negligent in failing to repair a chair that it knew was in need of repair. As a result, the court viewed this as a matter in which GoldCoast sought coverage for its own sole fault. Because the contract to indemnify GoldCoast did not clearly express this intent, the court refused to enforce it.

Another case in point is *Gotro v The Town of Melville,* 527 S2d 568 (La App 1988), where a motorist sued the town for bodily injury sustained when his pickup struck a rut that extended the full width of a street. Prior to the accident, the town had contracted with a firm to perform sewer line construction. The contract provided that the sewer contractor would indemnify and hold harmless the town from and against all claims, damages, losses, and expenses arising out of or resulting from the performance of the sewer contract. The motorist and the town sought contribution and indemnity from the contractor and its insurer.

The town argued that since it entered into an incidental contract with the contractor, the contractor's insurer should protect the town even though the town was not listed as an additional insured on the policy. The town's argument failed since it was unable to establish that the accident arose out of or resulted from the contractor's performance of sewer work.

A similar case but with an unusual twist is *DiPietro v City of Philadelphia,* 496 A2d 407 (Pa Super 1985). Here, the city contracted with an elevator company to perform some work. The contract required the elevator company to obtain liability insurance endorsed to include the hold harmless agreement between the city and the elevator company; evidence of insurance was required before work could begin. However, the elevator company did not purchase a liability policy endorsed with the hold harmless clause in the city's favor. (The consequences of the failure of a party to fulfill insurance obligations as required by contract is discussed in **Chapter 21.**)

An elevator company employee fell to his death in the elevator shaft, and suit was brought against the city. The court held that the elevator company was not accountable for failing to obtain the insurance as specified—contrary to the general rule that one who enters into an agreement to obtain insurance and fails to do so becomes the insurer. Instead, the court held that even if a liability policy had been procured and had included by reference the hold harmless agreement, the policy still would have been inapplicable because, under Pennsylvania law at that time, indemnity was disallowed if the indemnitee was actively negligent, and the court did find such active negligence by the city.

The city argued that it was protected since the cost of the insurance was included in the contract price and thus was paid for by the city. The city cited some cases to reinforce its argument, but the cases cited involved policies modified with additional insured endorsements and, for that reason, did not apply. In addition, the indemnification provision of the contract revealed that it did not provide for indemnity against injury caused by the city. Thus, the purpose of the insurance that the elevator company was supposed to have procured was to fund the elevator company's own liability and not the city's. The court explained that for the city to have protection, the city would have had to require that it be named as an additional insured on the elevator company's policy or that the elevator company specifically agree to hold the city harmless from its own negligence.

It is interesting to note that in this case, the parties actually chose to have the insurance policy reference the hold harmless agreement. This is not good practice overall for reasons previously discussed, particularly in relation to the party seeking indemnity. If the indemnity agreement is held to be invalid and found to be inextricably tied to the insurance coverage, both forms of protection might be lost. The result could be no protection for the indemnitee.

In this case, part of the problem was that the city was to be an indemnitee under the policy as opposed to an additional insured. Had the city been an additional insured, it may have been covered. However, the city here merely contracted to be indemnified under the policy of another instead of spelling out the elevator company's assumption of the city's liability. As a result, it ran afoul of case law requiring that assumption of another's tort liability be clear and unequivocal, which was not the case. Because the contractual transfer of the city's liability to another was held invalid, there was no hope of coverage for the indemnification obligation, which could not be enforced.

Void Hold Harmless Agreement Nullifies Insurance Protection

The question arises whether insurance protection mandated by an indemnity provision is always nullified when the contractual agreement to indemnify is deemed unenforceable by a court. In one commonly cited case, a contract requiring that the subcontractor provide the general contractor with insurance was held to be unenforceable. The insurance clause in the contract required that the subcontractor maintain insurance "insuring all the subcontractor's indemnity obligations." The court in *Shaheed v Chicago Transit Authority,* 484 NE2d 542 (Ill App 1985), ruled this insurance provision unenforceable because it sought insurance against a void agreement to indemnify.

In a case involving Tennessee law, *Posey v Union Carbide Corp.,* 507 F Supp 39 (MD Tenn 1980), a project owner expected protection but received none. Here, the contractor agreed to indemnify the owner from any claims for bodily injury sustained on premises resulting from the construction work. The indemnity agreement also required that the contractor secure insurance to this effect, including the project owner as an insured. The contractual agreement was deemed unenforceable because it attempted to transfer the project owner's (the indemnitee's) sole liability to the contractor (the indemnitor). In light of this unenforceability, the indemnitor was not liable to the indemnitee and, hence, not obligated by virtue of the written contract to provide the insurance.

Despite these cases, a growing number of states have allowed protection for an additional insured even though the contractual agreement is unenforceable. Courts in some states will enforce insurance provisions even if the hold harmless agreement is void. But for coverage to apply, it must be clear that the insurance is intended to apply for all claims *arising from the performance of the contract* rather than insurance *limited solely to the indemnity obligation.* If it is the former, insurance coverage may be permitted.

Also of importance in making a determination of coverage in this context is the endorsement or policy provision effecting additional insured status. Where additional insured status is not granted, only contractual liability coverage applies, and the indemnity provision will govern the extent of the risk being transferred. If the indemnity agreement is held to be unenforceable, the insurer's obligation to indemnify pursuant to contractual liability coverage will not be activated. There may be liability imposed upon the insured indemnitor on some other basis, and in that event, coverage would still apply to the insured separate and apart from any contractual obligation to indemnify.

If additional insured status is provided, the additional insured's coverage will apply based on the terms of the policy or endorsement rather than on the terms of the underlying contract. Therefore, the validity of the indemnity agreement will have no effect on coverage determinations. It is in cases involving broad additional insured endorsements where disputes arise involving the contract and its relation to additional insured status. Normally, the underlying contract has no bearing on additional insured coverage.

However, this can change where policy wording confers additional insured status on a blanket basis to those for whom the named insured is required by contract to provide insurance. In those instances, additional insured status is dependent on the existence of a contract provision requiring that insurance be provided. In those scenarios, disputes might arise over whether wording requiring "indemnity" constitutes or equates to "requiring insurance," for purposes of finding additional insured status pursuant to a contractual requirement to provide insurance.

Void Hold Harmless Agreement and Valid Insurance Coverage

If a hold harmless agreement is ruled unenforceable by law, it does not necessarily mean that coverage of an additional insured likewise is nullified. To the contrary, insurance is viewed by some jurisdictions as a valid alternative to unenforceable contractual transfers. As stated under "The Inextricably Tied Issue," many states allow for the transfer of sole fault if it is accomplished through the use of insurance. The insurance also is being handled by a professional risk bearer rather than a person or organization that would otherwise be required to assume such risk.

Because the coverage provided to an additional insured is not dependent on the terms of a contract but, rather, on the terms of the policy, there is no valid reason to preclude insurance coverage if the indemnity agreement is invalid. It is only in situations where the two obligations (to provide insurance and to indemnify) become inextricably tied that the courts will void insurance coverage because of a void indemnity agreement.

However, this too is subject to the caveat that not all states make an exception for insurance relating to anti-indemnity statutes that preclude sole fault indemnification. *Breczek v Standard Oil Co.,* 447 NE2d 760 (Ohio App 1982), explained the rationale behind allowing the use of insurance despite the fact that it amounted to allowing one entity to indemnify the sole fault of another. In that case, an employee of a tank company was injured while working at the premises of an oil refinery. In his suit he alleged that his injury was the result of the refinery's negligence, including that of its employees and agents. Pursuant to a contractual agreement, the refinery requested that the tank company defend the action and hold the refinery harmless. The contractual agreement between the parties provided that the tank company, as an independent contractor, would clean and remove sludge from the refinery's tanks. The contract contained an indemnity clause that read as follows.

Indemnification: (a) In General—Contractor hereby indemnifies and agrees to defend and save Owner and its affiliated Corporations, their agents, servants and employees harmless from all liabilities and claims for loss, damage, or injury to or death of persons or property, including property of Owner, in any manner arising out of or in connection with the work, *unless initiated or proximately caused or resulting from the negligence of Owner,* its other independent contractors, agents, employees or indemnitees, and to pay all damages, costs and expenses, including attorney's fees arising in connection therewith .... [Emphasis added.]

Another part of the contract required that the tank company obtain liability insurance and name the refinery as an additional insured. The tank company provided an insurance certificate signifying that the insurer was providing such coverage.[8] After the tank company refused to defend this action on behalf of the refinery, the refinery instituted an action against the tank company and its insurer alleging breach of both the indemnity provision and the insurance policy.

The lower Ohio court ruled against the refinery, citing the state statute that renders null and void any contract that attempts to transfer the sole liability of the indemnitee to the indemnitor. Specifically, the trial court found that this statute prohibited the tank company from purchasing insurance for the refinery's protection against the refinery's own negligence. The court, therefore, concluded that the refinery could not benefit from any insurance obtained by the tank company.[9]

However, the trial court's decision was based on the state's statute dealing with enforceability of contractual transfers and the section of the contract between the two parties dealing with insurance. This insurance section, which was said by the trial court to be nullified by the state statute cited previously, reads as follows.

Prior to the commencement of any work, Contractor [tank company] shall obtain and maintain in force at its sole cost and expense, the following insurance coverages ... Comprehensive General and Automobile Liability Insurance (covering use of owned, nonowned or hired vehicles) with limits of: Bodily injury—$300,000/occurrence, Property damage—$100,000/occurrence. Such liability insurance shall contain provisions insuring the contractual liability assumed hereunder, naming Owner [refinery] as an additional insured with respect to the work under this contract and *providing that such insurance is primary to any liability insurances carried by the Owner.* [Emphasis added.]

The trial court then analyzed the second sentence of the Ohio Revised Code 2305.31, which reads as follows.

Nothing in this section shall prohibit any person from purchasing insurance from an insurance company authorized to do business in the state of Ohio for his own protection or from purchasing a construction bond.

The trial court found that this sentence permitted the purchase of insurance solely for one's own benefit and that the purchase of insurance for another's protection would violate the purpose of the statute. However, the trial court's decision was reversed on appeal. The higher court stated that it did not read the statute as voiding the insurance policy as obtained by the tank company wherein the refinery was listed as an additional insured. The trial court's interpretation, the higher court explained, would preclude the naming of more than one insured per insurance policy. Such a restriction, it said further, was not the intent of the legislature. It also is common practice to name several parties as insureds in a policy, each having different liabilities. The court based the foregoing comment on a legal text that reads as follows.

Where several persons are insured under one policy, the rights and obligations of one insured are not necessarily dependent upon those of another insured, and the insurance company may undertake separate and distinct obligations to the various insureds. Insurance policies may name additional insureds by their definition of the term "insured." This is particularly true in liability policies.[10]

The higher court held that the insurance provision requiring the refinery to be named as an additional insured on the liability policy of the tank company was not null and void due to the application of the state statute and was not contrary to public policy.

What was interesting about the insurance requirements, however, was the stipulation that the insurance as provided for the additional insured was to be primary over the insurance carried by such insured under its own policy. Insurance companies are typically reluctant to fulfill those kinds of stipulations. Part of the reason is the self-serving position taken by some insurers that the only protection provided to additional insureds is vicarious in nature. To that extent, the additional insured may receive primary protection from the other party's insurer. But in many cases, the allegation is that the additional insured is the culpable party, and in this case, the insurer prefers not to defend or pay on behalf of an additional insured if it has its own liability insurance. Most of these points are discussed in later chapters along with the ways to combat the problems.

Many of other state courts have ruled that additional insured requirements do not conflict with statutes regulating contractual transfers. One such case is *Bosio v Branigar Organization,* 506 NE2d 996 (Ill App 1987), which involved an Illinois statute dealing with contractual risk transfers. The court held that a construction contract provision requiring public liability insurance for the owner's benefit did not violate this state's anti-indemnity statute prohibiting "broad form" hold harmless agreements, i.e., those agreements that indemnify another person or organization against its sole liability. Part of the rationale for this decision was that such liability insurance provides injured persons with an alternative source of compensation.

In *McAbee Construction Co. v Georgia Kraft Co.,* 343 SE2d 513 (Ga App 1986), a Georgia court held that an indemnification provision holding a property owner harmless for its own negligence was enforceable when construed together with an insurance clause. It has been recognized by numerous authorities, the court said, that where parties to a business transaction mutually agree that insurance will be provided as part of the bargain, such agreement must be construed as providing mutual exculpation to the bargaining parties that must be deemed to have agreed to look solely to the insurance in the event of loss and not to the liability on the part of the opposing party.

Another decision that adds to this trend is the California case of *Chevron U.S.A. Inc. v Bragg Crane and Rigging Co.,* 225 Cal App 742 (1986). The contract between the refinery and the crane company required the crane company to hold harmless and indemnify the refinery for damages resulting from its sole and active liability. The crane company also was required to maintain certain liability insurance as specified and to name the refinery as an additional insured.

Two employees of the crane company subsequently suffered injuries that the refinery admitted were its sole fault. When the refinery was sued, it looked to the crane company for protection. However, its claim was denied because the crane company held the understanding that insurance for the refinery was not to apply to its sole fault.

The court disagreed with the crane company's argument, even though the state's statute on indemnity makes sole liability transfers unenforceable. The reason was that while there is a limit to the amount of risk that can be transferred under indemnity contracts, there is no similar limit on obtaining insurance. In fact, such a limit on insurance, it was said, would be contrary to a fundamental purpose of insurance, i.e., to protect against liability for one's own negligence. Thus, the refinery did not contract to exculpate itself from liability but, instead, contracted for the procurement of insurance.

Likewise, a New York court in the case of *Long Island Lighting Co. v American Employers Insurance Co.,* 517 NYS2d 44 (NY 1987), ruled that a utility, as an additional insured under another entity's liability policy, was to be protected by the policyholder's insurer even if the indemnity provision were to be void as being against public policy. Protection, therefore, was applicable whether the liability was due to the utility's own negligence or to that of the named insured.

Finally, a Maryland court ruled in the case of *Heat & Power Corp. v Air Products & Chemical, Inc.,* 578 A2d 1202 (Md App 1990), that an indemnitee that is an additional insured on the indemnitor's liability policy can obtain protection against its sole fault, even though there is a Maryland law that holds sole negligence transfers of indemnitees to be void and unenforceable.

Whether a given contractual transfer is enforceable hinges on the circumstances and, of course, on the wording of the contract. The requirement of one party adding another as an additional insured to its liability insurance is made, in part, as a backup to risk transfers normally accomplished through hold harmless agreements. It should be noted that the additional insured requirement is usually made in addition to, rather than in place of, hold harmless agreements. The reason for this is that hold harmless agreements often transfer more risks than are insured by liability policies. Indemnitees often transfer these risks to other parties and simply rely on the other parties' existing financial resources to fund any losses that are not covered by insurance.

Additional Insured Status in Absence of Contractual Agreement

Sometimes persons and organizations require additional insured status under the insurance of others but do not also complement coverage with a hold harmless agreement. As stated previously, once additional insured status is afforded, coverage applies to the full extent of the policy, subject to any coverage limitations imposed by the additional insured endorsement or a policy provision. The intent of the parties and the wording of the underlying contract no longer play a role in determining the scope of coverage being provided. Therefore, the absence of a contractual agreement is not a factor for the coverage.

In most cases, however, it is not advisable to rely solely on additional insured status to transfer liability risks. An indemnity provision provides the indemnitee with a vehicle for recovering from the

indemnitor that is not dependent on the existence of insurance coverage. This could be important if the insurance is canceled or not renewed, or if the insurer becomes insolvent. Indemnity agreements may also transfer types of risks that would not be covered under liability insurance. An example of this is liability arising from a release of pollutants. Thus, most contractual risk transfers generally involve using both an indemnity clause and additional insured status to work hand-in-hand.

Contractual Agreement Corresponding to Additional Insured Status

As previously stated, to increase the certainty that a risk transfer will be successful, most contracts include both an indemnification agreement and a requirement of additional insured status. Relying only on an indemnification agreement or only on a requirement to procure insurance to effect a risk transfer is much less certain. If the indemnity agreement is unenforceable for some reason, or if it is unclear or ambiguous, the indemnitee has a second chance for recovery as an additional insured. Likewise, if insurance is not applicable, the indemnitee can look to the hold harmless agreement.

Even when this approach is taken, there can be instances where liability risks associated with the activity or project are not transferred. For example, the indemnity agreement often will not be broad enough to encompass all the inherent liability risks. Likewise, some additional insured endorsements, particularly nonstandard endorsements, impose restrictions on the scope of coverage provided to additional insureds. A worthwhile objective when arranging additional insured status often will be to structure the coverage such that it corresponds with the risk transfer contemplated under the indemnity agreement without making coverage subject to the indemnity agreement.

A case that exemplifies this point is *Travelers Indemnity Co. v Hanover Insurance Co.,* 470 F Supp 630 (USDC Va 1979). A city leased some of the premises it owned to a concert promoter. Under the lease agreement, the promoter (the lessee) agreed to hold harmless and indemnify the city (the lessor) for any claims made against the city *occasioned by the negligence of the promoter* in connection with use of the city's premises for purposes of the concert. A certificate of insurance was issued, showing the city as an additional insured as respects the promoter's activities. The additional insured endorsement included a provision that specifically limited coverage to the additional insured's vicarious liability for the acts of the insured promoter.

When a concert patron died in an accident, suit was filed against both the promoter and the city. However, there were no allegations that fell within the hold harmless agreement, i.e., no allegations were made accusing the city (the lessor) of being accountable due to the promoter's (the lessee's) negligence. Thus, when the city sought protection as an additional insured under the promoter's liability policy, the insurer denied coverage. The court ruled that the lease agreement and the specific wording of the additional insured endorsement only protected the city for its liability arising from the promoter's negligence. Since the allegations involved the city's negligence—not the promoter's negligence—they did not correspond to the liability assumed, and the promoter's (the lessee's) insurer was not obligated to defend nor indemnify the city (the lessor).

Another case where additional insured coverage corresponded with limited form indemnity agreement is *Consolidation Coal Co. v Liberty Mutual Insurance Co.*, 406 F Supp 1292 (WD Pa 1976). A trucker was hired to haul products for a fuel company. Under the contract, the trucker agreed to hold harmless and indemnify the fuel company against all claims, liabilities, losses, and suits caused by or in any manner resulting from the actions of the trucker, its agents, or employees. An employee of the trucker, while in the course of his employment driving a truck on the fuel company's property, was struck by one of the fuel company's owned railroad cars. The trucker's employee filed suit against the fuel company, claiming that the negligence of the fuel company's employees was the sole and proximate cause of the accident.

The fuel company was added as an additional insured to the trucker's liability policy using a non-

standard endorsement. The additional insured endorsement read as follows.

> It is agreed that the "Persons Insured" provision is amended to include as an insured the person or organization named below, *but only with respect to acts or omissions of the named insured* in connection with the named insured's operations at the applicable location designated below. [Emphasis added.]

The fuel company's insurer asked the trucker's insurer to defend the lawsuit and to provide the fuel company, as an additional insured, with protection. The trucker's insurer refused, maintaining that the intent and plain meaning of the words "acts or omissions of the insured," as they appeared in the additional insured endorsement, were designed to restrict coverage to those accidents caused by the negligence of the trucker while acting pursuant to its contract with the fuel company. The trucker's insurer also argued that the only reasonable interpretation of the additional insured endorsement—when read in conjunction with the indemnity agreement—was that the trucker agreed to indemnify the fuel company only for liability incurred as a result of the trucker's negligence or that of its employees in the performance of the contract.

The court sided with the trucker and its insurer. In doing so, the court stated that the fuel company was to be an additional insured under the trucker's policy only when the negligent acts or omissions of the trucker directly caused the fuel company's loss. The court also stated that it may be inferred that the additional insured endorsement was intended to provide the fuel company with coverage as required by the indemnity provision. This statement of the court is, absent additional clarification, technically incorrect, since the wording of the endorsement and not that of the indemnity clause governs the coverage provided to an additional insured. It must be assumed that the court's inference referred to the fact that the coverage provided by the endorsement happened to correspond with the scope of the indemnity agreement and not to a finding that the scope of coverage could or would be dictated by the indemnity agreement.

The *Travelers* and *Consolidated Coal* cases illustrate how additional insured endorsements may be drafted in a manner that corresponds with the scope of the risk transfer contemplated under indemnity provisions. However, such coordination of coverage provided under an additional insured endorsement with the scope of the indemnity clause is very rare. Most of the standard additional insured endorsements in use today cover the additional insured for liability arising from its sole fault. In other words, they correspond with the scope of risk transferred under a broad form hold harmless agreement. Thus, when they are used to effect additional insured status, most standard additional insured endorsements essentially override indemnity agreements that attempt to transfer a lesser degree of risk.

Insurers often argue that additional insureds are covered only for their vicarious liability or that the scope of additional insured coverage is dictated by the intent expressed in the indemnity agreement of the underlying contract. However, the fact remains that only when contractual liability coverage is being utilized does the indemnity agreement dictate the extent of coverage. Even then, coverage will not be broader than the policy terms allow.

This independent operation of additional insured status and the indemnity provision can be problematic. Consider, for example, two parties that painstakingly negotiate an indemnity clause that transfers to the indemnitor the joint negligence of the two parties but not the indemnitee's sole negligence. To assure that it is protected, the indemnitee also requires additional insured status in the indemnitor's liability insurance. The indemnitee is then added using a standard endorsement containing no limitations on coverage with respect to liability arising from the sole fault of the additional insured. This very common occurrence, in essence, negates all the work done by the parties in negotiating the indemnity clause!

At first blush this might not seem so bad, since it is the insurer and not the indemnitor that will pay any losses covered under the additional insured endorsement. However, these losses ultimately will be paid by the indemnitor, whether immedi-

ately through deductibles or retrospective rating adjustments, or later through higher future insurance premiums. Payments on behalf of the additional insured will also erode the named insured's limits available to cover other claims.

Nevertheless, it is rare for two parties to contractually agree to a limited scope of indemnity and to arrange corresponding additional insured status. When this is achieved, it is generally done by way of manuscript endorsement, as was the case in *Travelers* and *Consolidated Coal.*

Additional Insured Coverage Broader than Contractual Assumption

Obviously, standard additional insured endorsements must be drafted with the general needs of insureds in mind. As mentioned previously, most of them provide coverage broad enough to encompass liability arising from the sole fault of the additional insured. Thus, they often cover a broader scope of liability than is transferred in indemnity clauses.

Because the endorsement and policy wording, not the underlying business contract, dictate the scope of coverage, the courts generally hold that it is permissible for additional insured status to cover the sole fault of an additional insured (indemnitee) even where the indemnity agreement does not transfer liability arising from the sole fault of the indemnitee. A case in point is *Shell Oil Co. v National Union Fire Insurance Co. of Pittsburgh, Penn.,* 52 Cal Rptr 2d 580 (Ct App 2d Dist 1996). This case addresses a number of legal issues, including the relationship of additional insured status and indemnity provisions.

In 1985 Shell entered into a contract with S.I.P. Engineering, Inc., for the performance of engineering work on Shell's oil refinery in the state of Washington. Paragraph 6 of the contract obligated S.I.P. to defend and indemnify Shell up to $5 million for any claims, liabilities, or expenses on account of personal injury or property damage arising out of S.I.P.'s or its subcontractors' work, except when any injury or damage was caused by the sole negligence of a party otherwise indemnified, i.e., Shell.

Paragraph 7.1 of the contract provided that during the term, S.I.P. would maintain comprehensive general liability insurance including products/completed operations coverage and contractual liability coverage for S.I.P.'s obligations to defend and/or indemnify Shell with a combined single limit of $1 million for bodily/personal injury and property damage. In addition, paragraph 7.2 of the contract provided that:

> To the fullest extent permitted by law, all insurance policies maintained by S.I.P. in accordance with paragraph 7.1 above and any other insurance maintained applicable to S.I.P.'s performance hereunder shall include Shell and any parties in joint operation with Shell as additional insureds....

In fulfillment of its insurance obligations under paragraphs 7.1 and 7.2 of the contract, S.I.P. provided a CGL policy with $1 million limits from National Union Insurance Company. In its definitions of whom it insured, the policy provided that:

> if specifically required to be included as a named insured, this policy shall include as a named insured any person or organization to whom the named insured [i.e., S.I.P.] is obligated by virtue of a contract, entered into before loss, to provide insurance such as is afforded by this policy, but only to the extent required by said contract and not to exceed the coverages and the limits of liability afforded by this policy.

Three other insurers provided excess limits of $5 million covering the same insureds as the National Union underlying policy.

In 1986 an employee of one of S.I.P.'s subcontractors was injured at Shell's refinery in connection with work subject to the contract. Shell was sued for negligence and was also sued in subrogation by the subcontractor's workers compensation insurer.

One of the key issues before the court was whether insurance extended to claims arising out of Shell's sole negligence. Paragraph 6.2 of the contract provided for indemnity of Shell by S.I.P. but excluded claims or liabilities for injury caused by Shell's

sole negligence. The primary insurer (National Union) pointed out that a sole negligence transfer would be void and unenforceable under Washington's statute. The court pointed out, however, that paragraph 6.2 of Shell's contract concerned itself with indemnity by S.I.P., not with the scope of Shell's insurance under the contract; this latter subject of insurance was dealt with under paragraphs 7.1 and 7.2 of the contract.

The court then went on to examine paragraph 7.1(d) of the contract, which required S.I.P. to carry:

> Comprehensive General Liability Insurance (hereinafter CGL), including products/completed operations coverage and contractual liability coverage *for Contractors' obligations hereunder to defend and/or indemnify Shell,* with a limit of $1 million each occurrence. (Emphasis added by the court.)

National Union contended that the italicized language did not simply modify "contractual liability coverage" but, rather, applied to and defined "Comprehensive General Liability Insurance" as a whole, with the result that S.I.P was to maintain CGL coverage only for S.I.P.'s indemnity obligations and not for liabilities occasioned by Shell's sole negligence. Shell, on the other hand, contended that the italicized wording modified a particular species of CGL, namely contractual liability coverage and, thus, the CGL policy required by the contract was otherwise not limited to S.I.P.'s indemnity obligations.

The court found Shell's interpretation to be more reasonable than that of National Union. In explaining its rationale, the court stated as follows.

> Textually, paragraph 7.1(d) first requires CGL, without limitation. There follows a parenthetical, modifying phrase, set off by commas, that begins with the illustrative word "including," and in turn contains the italicized "indemnity" language. Moreover, that language immediately follows and is attached to, without intervening punctuation, "contractual liability coverage," which is the particular type of liability insurance that would cover liabilities assumed by contract

(e.g., an agreement to indemnify...) Thus, it appears both syntactically and substantively appropriate to read the italicized language as relating to and modifying that coverage, rather than CGL as a whole.

The court then explained that National Union's construction of the italicized indemnity wording poses several anomalies, as follows.

First, had that been the intent of the parties, the italicized language more naturally would have appeared immediately after "Comprehensive General Liability Insurance," rather than in the parenthetical phrase following it. Moreover, CGL does not normally cover indemnity obligations; that is the office of the special contractual liability coverage endorsement... And similarly, the other special coverage called for by paragraph 7.1(d)—product/completed operations coverage"—provides coverage for injuries from products, construction, services after their completion ... not for the insured's obligation to indemnify another. Yet, National insists that the contract meant to provide for this coverage too solely for S.I.P.'s indemnity obligations.

The court also stated that National Union's construction of paragraph 7.1(d) as limiting the CGL policy to coverage for S.I.P.'s indemnity obligation also did not make sense in the larger context of the contract. As explained by the court:

Paragraph 7.1 as a whole required S.I.P. to maintain a varied package of insurance ... covering the general range of risks S.I.P. could encounter in performing this contract. The apparent purpose of this requirement extended beyond insuring S.I.P.'s indemnity obligation, to providing S.I.P.—as well as Shell, under paragraph 7.2 (discussed below)—protection from out-of-pocket liability and dislocation. To construe paragraph 7.1(d) to limit the broad CGL coverage to insuring "Contractors' obligations hereunder to defend and/or indemnify" would slight both S.I.P.'s and Shell's business interests. Moreover, insofar as Shell was to be a direct beneficiary of the contract's insurance

requirements, restricting the CGL to indemnifiable claims, and thus excluding from it those involving Shell's sole negligence, would have left Shell unprotected for those claims for which it most needed insurance.

However, National Union contended further that its interpretation of paragraph 7.1(d) and the consequent lack of coverage for Shell's sole negligence were confirmed by paragraph 7.2 of the contract, which required Shell's inclusion as an additional insured in S.I.P.'s insurance (or alternatively a "waiver of subrogation," which was not given). To this argument of the insurer, the court answered as follows.

That requirement (additional insured status) applied to "all insurance policies maintained by S.I.P. in accordance with paragraph 7.1 and any other insurance maintained *applicable to S.I.P.'s performance hereunder....*" [Emphasis added by the court.] The reference to paragraph 7.1 of course begs the issue of paragraph 7.1(d)'s meaning. But National appears to argue that the language italicized above limited the insurance to "S.I.P.'s performance" of its indemnity obligations. We do not so read it. Like the rest of paragraphs 7.1 and 7.2, this language plainly appears to refer to S.I.P.'s performance of the contract as a whole. Once again, there is no textual or practical reason to perceive the broad, plain language of these insurance provisions of the contract as requiring coverage only for S.I.P.'s indemnity obligations.

National Union also argued at great length that an agreement to procure insurance for the indemnitee's sole negligence should be either against public policy or at least subject to strict construction. However, the insurer did admit that no Washington court has so held. Furthermore, neither the foreign decisions cited by National Union nor the Washington statute that invalidates construction contract indemnity agreements for the indemnitee's own negligence convinced this court that the state of Washington either outlaws or imposes a strict rule of construction on insurance policies or procurement contracts.

The court, therefore, concluded that paragraphs 7.1 and 7.2 of Shell's contract required S.I.P. to provide insurance coverage for Shell, including its sole negligence. Those provisions, the court explained, rendered Shell an insured under National Union's policy.

Limited Additional Insured Coverage

Another variation of an additional insured endorsement that was intended to limit the scope of coverage was discussed in *Department of Social Services v Aetna Casualty & Surety Co.,* 443 NW2d 420 (Mich App 1989). The Department of Social Services (DOSS) leased office space from the property owner. As part of the lease agreement, the property owner agreed to purchase liability insurance naming the DOSS as an additional insured, which it did. However, coverage for DOSS as an additional insured was subject to the following limitation.

> This insurance does not apply or shall not be construed as being applicable to liability for damages arising out of bodily injury to any person or damage to property of others resulting from the sole negligence of the state, its officers, employees, or agents.

Subsequently, a woman slipped and fell at the leased office. She sued both the property owner and DOSS, alleging that her cause of injury was due to a wet substance on the waiting room's floor. The court found no cause of action against the property owner but did find DOSS liable for failing to warn visitors of slippery floors. The property owner's insurer refused to defend DOSS in light of the above provision precluding insurance against the sole negligence of DOSS.

However, on appeal, the court held that judgment in favor of the property owner's insurer was improper because the insurer failed to show that the sole negligence exclusion was applicable, that is, that DOSS was "solely negligent" or 100 percent at fault. Having failed to prove such sole negligence on the part of DOSS, the property owner's insurer was obligated to protect DOSS.

It is important to note that coverage restrictions in additional insured endorsements, such as in this case, are not at all uncommon. This case is silent about any hold harmless agreement, but indemnitors must be careful to ensure that the insurance they obtain is at least as broad as the contractual assumption. Otherwise, the indemnitor could be accountable for the difference—given the fact that the contractual assumption is otherwise enforceable.

In another case, a subcontractor agreed to hold harmless and indemnify a general contractor for the latter's sole fault and to add it as an additional insured. When the general contractor sought protection under its indemnification agreement, it was held to be unenforceable. The general contractor, as an additional insured, then looked to the subcontractor's insurance for primary protection. While a blanket additional insured endorsement was issued by the subcontractor's liability insurer, it excluded any negligent acts committed by the additional insured. The effect of this endorsement was to drastically limit the protection of the general contractor.

Indemnification Statutes for Oil and Gas Production Contracts

The rationale for anti-indemnity statutes that are enacted for construction-related projects also applies to oil and gas production operations. Prior to the enactment of these laws, some oil companies and oil well operators required broad hold harmless agreements from oil well drilling and servicing contractors. These contracts not only made the contractors accountable for their own acts of negligence but also for the liability of the oil companies and operators. Since these indemnification agreements were perceived by some as placing an undue financial burden on the contractors who generally had no bargaining power to negotiate the contracts, the only alternative was to pass laws to protect the contractors.

While a number of oil and gas producing states, such as Alaska, Arizona, California, and South Dakota, have anti-indemnity statutes that deal with construction contracts, only Louisiana, New Mexico, Texas, and Wyoming have anti-indemnity statutes directed at oil and gas operations. However, the fact that a state has an anti-indemnity statute does not categorically mean that shifting the burden through additional insured status would likewise be prohibited. Unless an anti-indemnity statute, such as the one in Louisiana, expressly prohibits the shifting of the insurance burden through additional insured status or a court expresses doubt that such additional insured status would be valid, there is the prospect that the shifting of the insurance burden through additional insured status will be permitted so long as the insurance requirements are an obligation separate and distinct from the indemnification agreement. However, case law in the state involved should be reviewed carefully in this area.

Securing Direct Rights in the Policy

When another party is entitled to indemnification that may be covered by the named insured's contractual liability insurance, some insurers refuse to step in and indemnify the other party. Instead, they prefer to wait until the underlying action is settled and then reimburse the indemnitee or challenge the validity of the indemnification clause. In the meantime, someone else, such as the indemnitee, must fund the defense costs and pay any settlements or judgments.[11] Therefore, one of the most important reasons for seeking additional insured status in addition to contractual indemnification is to secure direct rights in the indemnitor's insurance policy. This will allow the indemnitee to pursue its right to coverage directly with the indemnitor's insurer rather than rely solely on the rights outlined in the indemnification clause of the underlying business contract.

Generally, when a person or organization contracts with another entity and part of the bargain is to include the payment of legal costs of the former party as such costs are incurred, the contract must be explicit. Take, for example, the American Institute of Architects Document A201, 1997 edition, under section 3.18 on indemnification. This states, in part, as follows.

3.18 Indemnification

3.18.1 To the fullest extent permitted by law, the Contractor shall indemnify and hold harmless the Owner ....

What is conspicuous by its absence is some clear agreement that the contractor will pay legal costs as they are incurred. The word "indemnify" connotes reimbursement and not pay-as-you-go. There are two ways that an indemnitee can change this approach to indemnification: (1) change the indemnification clause to require the indemnitee to pay on behalf of the owner or (2) secure additional insured status.

The Insurer's Direct Defense Obligation to Indemnitees

It is quite common for indemnity agreements to require the indemnitor to pay not only liability settlements or judgments on behalf of indemnitees, but also the costs incurred to defend indemnitees. Of course, indemnitors expect their liability insurance policies to cover their contractual responsibility to pay these defense costs. However, in 1992 Insurance Services Office, Inc. (ISO), proclaimed in a circular that the standard CGL forms do not cover defense costs of parties whom the insured agrees to hold harmless and filed an endorsement to the policy form, the Changes in Commercial General Liability Coverage Form (CG 00 43) endorsement, to provide this coverage.

However, ISO did not adopt this position in its standard policy forms until 1996, and even then it did so in a different way than originally contemplated. The circular ISO issued was not publicly proclaimed and evidenced little more than an undisclosed attempt to rewrite history rather than a material change in policy coverage at that time. While the endorsement ISO issued was made available, its use was not widespread given the competitive problems insurers faced in using it.

Objections to ISO's course of action in addressing this issue of indemnitees' defense costs under the contractual liability portion of the policy came from a number of directions within the insurance industry. Some argued that the CGL policy already covered these defense costs, within the policy limits, since an indemnitee could recover from its indemnitor both the amount of damages awarded against it and its defense costs by enforcing the hold harmless agreement. Others worried that coverage of indemnitees' defense costs as damages, and therefore within the policy limits, represented a step backward from actual industry practice, which had always been to defend both the insured and the insured's indemnitee outside the policy limits.

As noted throughout this book, coverage for contractual liability is distinguished from additional insured status primarily by the way in which coverage applies. Coverage for an additional insured runs directly to the additional insured that is entitled to direct rights under the policy. The underlying contract does not determine the additional insured's scope of coverage, though a court may review the contract to determine intent if the policy is deemed ambiguous. Unlike additional insured status, contractual liability coverage usually is dictated by the terms of the contract and applies directly to the insured, which in turn is obligated by applicable indemnity provisions of the contract to reimburse the party being indemnified. The insurer has no direct obligation to indemnify the indemnitee, but as a matter of practice, payments on behalf of the insured typically are made directly to the indemnitee. Contractual liability coverage then is said to pass through the insured, as opposed to directly to the indemnitee.

For example, assume that the manufacturer of a product, seeking to have it marketed, agrees to indemnify and hold harmless the distributor. The manufacturer has a liability policy that includes contractual liability coverage. Additional insured status (vendors coverage) is not requested by the distributor and therefore is not provided. Following a product-related loss, the distributor is sued and a judgment is rendered against it. If the obligation of the manufacturer to indemnify the distributor is upheld, the responsibility of the manufacturer's insurer to pay is based upon contractual liability coverage, which in turn is based on the manufacturer's obligation to indemnify the distributor. Because the distributor is not an additional insured, the distributor cannot make a direct claim to the insurer except as a third-party beneficiary and then depending on applicable law. Instead, the distributor must obtain reimbursement from the manufacturer, who in turn obtains the

funds from the insurer, assuming that the damages are covered. The judgment is paid by the manufacturer's insurer, but the sums due are paid (passed through) the manufacturer. Even where the insurer pays the distributor directly, the money technically is paid on behalf of the insured manufacturer, not the distributor. All this is subject to potential legal issues pertaining to third-party beneficiary status.

Often overlooked by the indemnitee when requiring indemnification is the importance of including wording that also requires the indemnitor to provide a defense. If that obligation is not clearly stated, the indemnitor's insurer may decline to defend the indemnitee when the claim is tendered. While it generally is presumed that obligations to indemnify and hold harmless encompass a defense obligation, that area often is subject to dispute and better clarified. It is often presumed that because the insurer's obligation to indemnify runs through the insured (indemnitor), the defense obligation applies in a like manner. However, this is not true in every instance, particularly under the theory accepted in most jurisdictions that the duty to defend is broader than the duty to indemnify. Policy wording, coupled with the conduct of insurers traditionally in undertaking to directly defend indemnitees, can result in a finding that the insurer's defense obligation runs directly to the indemnity. Once an insurer initiates a defense on behalf of an indemnity, retaining and paying for defense counsel, it cannot be logically argued that the defense is being provided vicariously through the insured.

Policy wording reinforces the premise that an insurer's defense obligation for an indemnitee is a direct one. For example, consider the common pay-on-behalf approach of a primary liability policy. Under the format utilized by standard CGL forms, defense costs must be paid on behalf of the insured as they are incurred. If the insurer undertakes to defend the indemnitee, it must pay defense costs directly to legal counsel on behalf of the indemnitee. While the insurer might argue it has the option of reimbursing such costs, industry practice has demonstrated otherwise through the years. Original policy wording and revisions to that wording beginning with the 1996 ISO CGL forms also reinforce that insurers obligated to defend indemnitees must do so directly.

For example, consider the following relevant wording contained in the insuring agreements of standard ISO forms prior to the 1996 edition.

> We will pay those sums that the insured becomes legally obligated to pay as damages .... We will have the right and duty to defend any "suit" seeking those damages ....

The relevant wording contained in the Supplementary Payments—Coverages A and B section of the ISO forms states as follows.

> We will pay, with respect to any claim or "suit" we defend:

Relevant wording contained in standard commercial liability forms promulgated by the American Association of Insurance Services (AAIS) reads as follows.

> We have the right and duty to defend a suit seeking damages which may be covered under the Commercial Liability Coverage ....

Note that this wording does not limit the insurer's obligation such that it is required to defend only suits against an insured. The policy obligates the insurer to defend suits (any suits, including those against the indemnitee) seeking damages covered by the policy. This wording encompasses suits against an indemnitee that are otherwise covered by the policy because of the insured's obligation to indemnify the indemnitee.

In 1996 ISO revised the basic policy text as regards the insurer's obligation to defend indemnitees. The relevant wording of the insuring agreement contained in the 1996 and subsequent editions of ISO forms now reads as follows.

> We will pay those sums that the insured becomes legally obligated to pay as damages .... We will have the right and duty to defend *the insured* against any "suit" seeking those damages .... [Emphasis added.]

The relevant Supplementary Payments—Coverage A and B wording of these forms reads as follows.

> We will pay, with respect to any claim we investigate or settle, or any "suit" against *an insured* we defend ....

If we defend an insured against a "suit" and an indemnitee of the insured is also named as a party to the "suit", we will defend the indemnitee if all of the following conditions are met: [Emphasis added.]

(1) The suit also names an indemnitee of the insured as a party to a suit

(2) The suit against the indemnitee seeks damages for which the insured has assumed liability of the indemnitee in an insured contract

(3) The insurance provided under the policy applies to such liability assumed by the insured

(4) The obligation to defend, or the cost of the defense of, the indemnitee has also been assumed by the insured in the same contract

(5) The allegations in the suit and information known about the occurrence are such that no conflict appears to exist between the insured's interests and the indemnitee's interests

(6) The indemnitee agrees in writing to:

  a. cooperate with the insurer in the investigation, settlement, or defense of the suit;

  b. immediately send the insurer copies of any demands, notices, summonses, or legal papers received in connection with the suit;

  c. notify any other insurer whose coverage is available to the indemnitee;

  d. cooperate with the insurer in coordinating other applicable insurance available to the indemnitee; and

e. provide the insurer with written authorization to: (i) obtain records and other information related to the suit; and (ii) conduct and control the defense of the indemnitee in such suit.

Note that whenever a suit only names the indemnitee, such as in a third-party-over action, the defense costs supplementary payments coverage will not be activated. The reason is that (1) above requires that the suit "also" name the indemnitee, meaning that the indemnitee and indemnitor must both be named.

As a matter of practice, many insurers do pay defense costs on behalf of the indemnitees of their insureds. The sudden revelation by ISO that this coverage was not included in the standard ISO form was contradicted by policy wording in the minds of many. Since there have been no cases dealing precisely with this issue, the applicability of coverage in pre-1996 forms may remain uncertain indefinitely, at least in the minds of those insurers unwilling to defend in a manner consistent with policy wording prior to the 1996 revisions made to the ISO forms. What is important for purposes of this discussion are the changes implemented by ISO in 1996 and first evidenced in the 1992 endorsement. That revised wording makes it obvious that under the earlier wording of ISO forms, and AAIS forms and policies that are not endorsed to the contrary, policy wording is clear in creating a direct obligation to defend indemnitees. Even under the revised wording of the 1996 ISO commercial general liability forms, the obligation to defend indemnitees remains if all of the conditions imposed are met.

This uncertainty over the applicability of contractual liability coverage to defense costs establishes one of the most compelling reasons for indemnitees to require indemnitors to provide additional insured status. As an additional insured in the indemnitor's liability policies, an indemnitee's defense costs are covered without question and in addition to the policy's limits of liability.

Additional Insured Status

The insuring agreements of primary liability policies specifically cover the "insured" rather than the "named insured" because generally more than one person or organization is protected by the policy. Also, the policy preamble commonly indicates that the word "insured" means any person or organization *qualifying* as such under the Persons Insured or Who Is an Insured provision of the policy. Whenever an additional insured endorsement is used to add an insured, the endorsement will commonly state that the Who Is an Insured provision is amended to include as an insured the person or organization designated in the endorsement. As a result, those provisions that apply to "insureds," in general, apply to additional insureds unless there is a contradictory provision in the endorsement itself. Therefore, when an indemnitee, such as a construction project owner, is also an additional insured on the policy of the indemnitor, and the loss is not clearly excluded by the policy, the defense costs should be paid by the insurer as they are incurred.[12]

The case of *Shell Oil Co. v National Union Fire Ins., supra,* discussed beginning on page 69, illustrates just how important this direct right under the policy can be. Shell was an additional insured on a policy written by National Union for S.I.P. Engineering. An employee of one of S.I.P.'s subcontractors was injured due to Shell's negligence and brought suit against both S.I.P. and Shell. National Union essentially ignored Shell's request for coverage for 6 months, in the meantime exhausting the $1 million policy limit in settling the claim against the named insured (S.I.P.). Shell ultimately settled for $2 million with the claimant and brought suit against National Union.

The court held that, while the policy limit was $1 million, National Union was separately obligated to both Shell and S.I.P.—referring to the severability of interest provision—and that National Union was not entitled to choose between two insureds in the payment of its policy benefits. This, the court said, was particularly true "where no detriment is demonstrated by providing equal treatment to both insureds." Thus, the court awarded Shell $500,000, half the policy limit. Note that, as a result, National Union ultimately paid out $1.5 million, even though the policy limit was only $1 million.

Despite the advantages of having another party's insurer pay defense costs, there are times when an organization would rather have those legal costs reimbursed later. This may occur when a large entity would rather control its own destiny in terms of defense than have such defense controlled by legal counsel of the insurer's choice. An organization with such a philosophy should think twice about seeking additional insured status. Even though insurers sometimes attempt to avoid providing additional insureds with defense, the insurance policy clearly provides them with the right to control the defense of their insureds. (But the insurer-retained counsel is still the *insured's* lawyer and must represent the best interests of its client.) Large organizations that desire to have full control over their defense of lawsuits should probably rely solely on contractual indemnification clauses or appoint their own lawyer to monitor the conduct of insurance defense counsel.

Unless the additional insured endorsement contains other conditions applicable to the additional insured, then the insured in question must assume that the policy provisions apply without change. In effect, this gives the additional insured the same rights and obligations as all other insureds, except named insureds. In addition to assuring the applicability of defense coverage in the indemnitor's policy, there may be other advantages for securing direct rights in the named insured's policy. If, for example, the insurer contends that coverage for a particular loss is precluded by an exclusion, an additional insured would be able to argue its case directly with the insurer whereas a contractual indemnitee would have more difficulty obtaining a forum.

Preventing Subrogation

Another motive for requesting additional insured status is to prevent the named insured's insurer from instituting a suit against the additional insured in subrogation. It has been said that "no right of subrogation arises against a person who holds the status of an additional insured, whether by the terms of the policy or the operation of a statute."[13]

One of the most frequently cited cases disallowing subrogation by the insurer against an additional in-

sured on its policy, *Pennsylvania General Insurance Co. v Austin Powder Co.,* 502 NE2d 982 (NY 1986), involved automobile insurance. In that case, Austin Powder rented a truck from Bison Ford. Under the rental contract, Bison Ford agreed to obtain primary insurance coverage, and Austin Powder agreed to indemnify Bison Ford for liability arising out of Austin Powder's use of the vehicle. Bison Ford insured the vehicle with both a basic auto policy and a comprehensive automobile excess policy issued by Liberty Mutual. Austin Powder maintained a policy providing excess liability coverage for nonowned business vehicles and a CGL policy providing contractual liability coverage. The need for adequate coverage was obvious when the rental truck exploded while loaded with dynamite and blasting caps outside of a quarry, causing nearly $1 million in property damage. It was alleged that the accident occurred because an Austin Powder employee overloaded the truck, causing the wheels and wheel wells to overheat from friction.

Liberty Mutual paid various claims arising out of the explosion and then sought recovery from Austin Powder based on the indemnification provisions contained in the truck rental agreement. In support of its position, Bison Ford (on behalf of Liberty Mutual) argued that the antisubrogation rule was inapplicable because, although Austin Powder was an additional insured under the Liberty Mutual policy, it was Bison Ford rather than Austin Powder that paid for the coverage. The court stated that this argument was unrealistic in that it overlooked the very likely possibility that Bison Ford's insurance costs were passed along to Austin Powder in the form of an increased vehicle rental price. More importantly, the argument was unpersuasive because it ignored the fact that the rule against allowing subrogation claims against an insured is based, in part, on the potential for conflicts of interest that is inherent in such situations. In that regard, the court stated the following.

> Here, for example, the interests of the insured indemnitor, Austin Powder, can only be fully protected through the rigorous defense of the indemnitee, Bison Ford. Yet, if indemnification from Austin Powder could be had for losses

sustained on Bison Ford's behalf, Liberty Mutual would have less incentive to defend Bison Ford from claims made against it. As a consequence, allowing indemnification might sanction an indirect breach of the insurer's obligation to defend its insured Austin Powder. Furthermore, it would sanction a direct breach of the primary obligation the insurer undertook—the obligation to indemnify Austin Powder from loss.

Since allowing Liberty Mutual to claim indemnification here would, directly or indirectly, place the insurer's own interest at variance with those of its insured, we are not persuaded by Bison Ford's argument that an exception to the rule should be created, because of the mere fortuity that Austin Powder had separate insurance covering the same loss and had expressly agreed to indemnify. Indeed, the public interest in assuring integrity of insurers' relations with their insureds in averting even the potential for conflict of interest in those situations must take precedence over the parties' private contractual arrangements.

Similar sentiments were expressed by the court in *Briseno v Chicago Union Station Co.,* 557 NE2d 196 (Ill App 1990). This case involved the demolition of the old Union Station in Chicago in preparation for the construction of a new office complex to be owned by Chicago Union. The contract between Chicago Union and the demolition contractor, NWC, required NWC to purchase $30 million of general liability and excess liability insurance. Bituminous provided the coverage, and NWC paid all premiums due under it. NWC was the named insured, with Chicago Union as an additional insured. During construction, an employee of NWC was killed, and the employee's estate brought a wrongful death and Structural Work Act lawsuit against Chicago Union. Bituminous defended Chicago Union, but Chicago Union, through Bituminous, filed a third-party action for contribution against NWC, seeking to shift part of the loss from Bituminous to NWC. The underlying action was settled prior to trial, and the trial court later granted NWC's motion to dismiss Chicago Union's third-party contribution claim.

That judgment was affirmed on appeal. The court took a dim view of the subrogation attempt against NWC by Bituminous through Chicago Union. The court noted the novel situation in which Bituminous, through Chicago Union, the additional insured, was attempting to shift onto NWC, the named insured and the purchaser of the policy, the liability for the third-party claim. The court took a strong position on this issue, stating that "Bituminous' actions in this matter are unconscionable and will not be allowed." The agreement between the parties provided that they were to be protected against bodily injury claims arising from NWC's demolition work by a comprehensive general liability policy to be purchased by NWC. That agreement was thereafter fulfilled in all respects. To allow Bituminous to seek an additional recovery from NWC would allow Chicago Union to recover twice for the same loss and allow Bituminous to manipulate the lawsuit so that the party who purchased the policy and paid the premium suffered the loss. Therefore, the court struck down the insurer's attempt at subrogation.

Additional insured status on liability policies will generally provide a "safe haven" against insurer attempts to seek repayment from tortfeasors. However, this principle does not necessarily apply to other kinds of insurance or in all circumstances.[14] In particular, there have been cases where insurers successfully subrogated against insureds on builders risk and certain other property insurance policies. Rather than relying on additional insured status to avoid the possibility of subrogation against one of the parties to a contract (e.g., a lease or construction contract) by the other party's insurer, an explicit waiver of subrogation may be inserted into the contract itself. Most insurance policies allow such waivers if entered before the occurrence of loss, but the applicable policy provisions should be reviewed to verify that a condition is not being violated by the waiver.

Because subrogation is an equitable (as opposed to a legal) remedy, concepts of fairness as opposed to pure legal precedent can often be relied on by the court in fashioning relief. In light of this, the facts of a specific case will often dictate the court's ruling regarding subrogation. As a result, there is a slight potential for a court to disallow a waiver of subrogation included in a contract if the policy does not specifically allow the waiver. To avoid potential problems, it is preferable to specifically endorse the policy to allow pre-loss waivers of subrogation.

Obtaining Personal Injury Coverage

Another reason why a person or entity may desire additional insured status on the policy of another is to obtain personal injury liability coverage (Coverage B of the 1986 and subsequent CGL forms). Personal injury coverage applies to such intentional torts as libel, slander, defamation, and false arrest. Advertising injury coverage—which applies to libel, slander, defamation, and such in the insured's advertising—is provided by the same insuring agreement in the CGL forms. Generally, Coverage B does not apply to personal injury and advertising injury for which an insured has assumed liability in a contract.

The main exception to this coverage involves independently filed forms. The contractual liability coverage of some independently filed liability policies of insurers does cover personal injury offenses. Of course, the standard form may also be modified by endorsement. The contractual liability exclusion is sometimes deleted from the personal injury coverage section of the policy by manuscript endorsement. Also, there is an ISO endorsement available for use with the CGL policy—the Amendment of Contractual Liability Exclusion for Personal Injury Limited to False Arrest, Detention or Imprisonment for Designated Contracts or Agreements (CG 22 74) endorsement—that provides contractual liability coverage for some of the personal injury liability offenses, i.e., false arrest, detention, or imprisonment.[15] However, this coverage does not apply to many of the personal injury offenses, such as libel, slander, and defamation, and the contract to which it applies must be designated in the endorsement.

On the other hand, when an organization is designated as an additional insured in another's liability policy, the additional insured status usually applies to the personal injury and advertising injury liability

coverage (Coverage B) in addition to the bodily injury and property damage liability coverage (Coverage A). Therefore, obtaining additional insured status in another party's insurance is a way to secure personal injury and advertising injury coverage in the other party's policy without necessitating the removal of the contractual liability exclusion from that party's personal injury coverage (which can be difficult to obtain from underwriters).

While additional insured status would typically apply to the policy's personal injury and advertising injury coverage, it should be noted that the coverage is limited to offenses arising out of the named insured's business or the named insured's advertising activities. The reason for this is that the personal and advertising injury liability insuring agreement contains this limitation. Thus, liability arising from activities or advertising conducted solely by and on behalf of the additional insured would not be covered by the indemnitor's/named insured's policy.

For example, assume that a contractor adds a real estate developer as an additional insured to its CGL policy. If a suit is subsequently brought against the developer alleging false arrest by a security guard hired by the contractor to protect the developer's project, the developer should be protected because the offense arose out of the contractor's business. If, on the other hand, the security guard was an employee of the developer rather than the contractor, the contractor's policy probably would not protect the developer because the loss did not arise out of the contractor's business.

Scope of Coverage

Securing additional insured status does not necessarily guarantee that coverage will apply to all types of liability the indemnitee (the additional insured) may incur. When a party is included as an additional insured on the CGL policy of another, all of the provisions of that policy that apply to insureds also apply to additional insureds. However, if the endorsement makes certain stipulations, then the endorsement takes precedence over the policy to the extent of those stipulations.

Apart from the foregoing situations, the policy is to be read as though nothing else is changed. In fact, the phrase commonly found at the bottom of endorsements that reads, "All other terms and conditions remain unchanged," is intended to bolster that intent. Omission of this statement should not alter the fact that the policy, in some circumstances, is to be read as though nothing else has changed. However, in many other situations, depending on the wording of the endorsement involved, the policy becomes hopelessly ambiguous where this wording is omitted.

While it does not specifically address the additional insured's rights under a policy, a case that demonstrates the applicability of all policy provisions to additional insureds is *Oakland Stadium v Underwriters at Lloyd's, London,* 313 P2d 602 (Cal 1957). The stadium owner was added to a racing association's liability policy as an additional insured. The argument was whether the additional insured was subject to the same policy exclusions as the named insured. The court relied on the phrase "all other terms and conditions remain unchanged" in holding that the policy exclusions that applied to the named insured also applied to the additional insured.

It is important to point out that these exclusions were worded such that they applied to the activities of the named insured and the additional insured. These were not the type of exclusions subject to the concept of severability where an exclusion specifically applicable only to a named insured will not be applicable to other insureds. The concept of severability is discussed in **Chapter 6.**

As discussed previously, the coverage provided to additional insureds does not always correspond to the contractual undertaking involved. The cases discussed on pages 67 and 68 illustrate the effect of protection when the insurance corresponds to the contractual obligations. However, it is probably the exception rather than the rule that the scope of an additional insured's protection will correspond exactly to the contractual agreement.

For example, the contractual transfer may only involve an "intermediate form" hold harmless agreement (e.g., transferring liability for joint negligence but not sole negligence), whereas the additional insured endorsement may not be specifically limited to liability arising from joint negligence. In this case, the endorsement may cover the additional insured for liability arising from its sole negligence even though the transfer initiated in the contract's indemnity provision was not this broad. In this situation, the endorsement—rather than the hold harmless agreement—should govern the amount of protection provided to the additional insured.

A case that exemplifies this point is *Shell Oil Co. v National Union Fire Insurance*, discussed earlier in this chapter, where the additional insured endorsement was broad enough to cover the additional insured's (indemnitee's) sole fault, despite the fact that the indemnity clause did not encompass sole fault.

This result is not accidental. The objective of many contract drafters is to transfer all potential liability possible. One purpose underlying additional insured status is to broaden the scope of protection under the policy, not limit it to what is already available for the exposures of the contract.

Employment Exclusion Application

As previously mentioned, most exclusions in the CGL policy also apply to additional insureds. In determining their application, however, it is important to consider the exclusions in the context of the additional insured's situation. One of the leading problem areas involving CGL policy provisions has been with respect to the workers compensation and employers liability exclusions. There have been numerous cases on this subject, although they are not as frequent as they once were. Part of the reason may be that there is now a better understanding of how the principle of severability of interests applies in liability insurance.

The scenario could involve as few as three parties—for example, a general contractor, a subcontractor, and the subcontractor's employee. Following an injury, the subcontractor's employee files suit against the general contractor, alleging that the general contractor's fault was the primary cause of the injury. The general contractor then looks to the subcontractor's CGL insurer for protection because it is listed as an additional insured on the subcontractor's liability policy. The insurer denies the protection because the policy excludes coverage for "bodily injury to any employee of the insured arising out of and in the course of his employment by the insured." In other words, the insurer maintains that the additional insured is not covered because the bodily injury as sustained by the worker arose out of and in the course of his employment by the insured, i.e., the additional insured.

The question boils down to this: Does the employers liability exclusion apply when the injured employee is not in the employ of the additional insured at the time of the injury? The answer is no. The intent of the employers liability exclusion is to preclude those claims involving employer-employee relationships that are or should be covered by the workers compensation policy. Thus, if an employee of the named insured is injured at the hands of an additional insured that is deemed not to be the employer of such injured employee, the employers liability exclusion does not apply to the additional insured. This subject is more fully discussed in **Chapter 6.**

Vicarious versus Direct Liability

Some insurance and risk management professionals believe that the protection afforded to additional insureds is limited to their vicarious or derivative liability. With such a limitation, the additional insured would have no insurance protection wholly separate from that of the named insured, such as would be necessary to cover liability arising from the additional insured's sole negligence. So, the argument goes, the policy does not have to respond to the additional insured unless the policy's named insured was also at fault. Whether this interpretation of coverage scope is a legitimate one should be resolved not on what insurers believe the additional insured endorsement should do but on what the endorsement actually says. In fact, most of the standard ISO additional insured endorsements contain no restrictions on coverage for

liability arising from an additional insured's sole negligence.

This is not to say that endorsements are never issued to limit coverage to the vicarious liability of additional insureds. But if it is the intent of an insurer to limit coverage of an additional insured to its vicarious liability, the endorsement should be worded clearly to that effect. And, in the event of any lack of clarity, the additional insured should be given the benefit of the doubt.

There are cases that have involved nonstandard endorsements that are clearly worded to limit coverage to the vicarious liability of additional insureds. It is cases of this kind that can bolster the mistaken notion that *all* additional insured endorsements are intended to convey the same purpose of providing the same protection limited solely to the vicarious liability of additional insureds.

One such case is *Harbor Insurance Co. v Lewis,* 562 F Supp 800 (ED Pa 1983). This case was prompted by an accident in which a youth was run over by a train. The parents of the youth subsequently brought suit against the railroad, which, in turn, joined the city as an additional defendant. The jury found both the railroad and the city jointly and severally liable and rendered a verdict of more than $3 million.

The city then looked to the liability insurance of the railroad for the payment of damages rendered against it, since the city was added to the railroad's liability policy as an additional insured. The city maintained that since the accident was an occurrence that arose out of the negligence of the railroad, the city was covered for any liability resulting from that occurrence.

However, the insurer argued that the endorsement in question only provided additional insureds with coverage for their vicarious liability or, in other words, where the additional insured's liability arose from the negligence of the named insured. In this case, the insurer argued, the city's liability was held to be contributing and concurrent with that of the railroad and, therefore, not vicarious. The question there centered on whether the additional insured endorsement provided the city with coverage for its own liability. The endorsement in question reads, in part, as follows.

> It is agreed that the insurance afforded by this policy shall apply to the following additional insureds but only to the extent of liability resulting from occurrences arising out of the negligence of Reading Company and/or its wholly owned subsidiaries.

The insurer called an attorney as an expert witness to testify about the customary practices of the insurance industry with regard to additional insured endorsements. It was stated, and the court so held, that additional insured provisions are intended to protect parties that are *not* named insureds from exposure to vicarious liability for acts of the named insured.

These provisions, it was said, are designed for countless situations, including such simple circumstances as those involving landlord and tenant relations. The insurance industry, it was stated further, places this meaning on additional insured provisions because insurers will not increase and alter the kind of risks insured against without charging additional premiums.[16]

However, it was explained further that with this kind of provision, i.e., the additional insured endorsement, the risks are not increased or altered since the insurer is only protecting the additional insured against its vicarious liability. It was held by the court that, "in the customary practices of the industry," the endorsement in question "would be viewed as a typical additional insured provision, which protects the additional insured against vicarious liability for acts of the named insured."

What should not be overlooked about this case, and the expert's opinion regarding the application of coverage involved, is that the additional insured endorsement in question was in manuscript form and therefore not typical. It clearly limited the additional insured's protection to its vicarious liability and therefore should not have applied in the manner that the additional insured (the city) had maintained. In fact, in *McIntosh v Scottsdale Insurance Co.,* 992

F2d 251 (10th Cir 1993), which is discussed more fully in **Chapter 9,** the court rejected the insurer's reliance on the *Harbor Insurance* case for precisely this reason; that is, the additional insured endorsement clearly limited the additional insured's protection to its vicarious liability. However, many additional insured endorsements in use today are not so clear on the subject of direct versus vicarious liability insurance protection.

In the case of *Anaconda Co. v General Accident, Fire & Life Assurance Corp.,* 616 P2d 363 (Mont 1980), the Montana court attempted to make the additional insured's protection contingent on the liability of the named insured, even though the contract wording did not justify it. This case involved a contractor installing environmental controls on a manufacturer's premises. Part of the contract between the two parties related to insurance coverages, requiring the contracting firm and any subcontractors to name the manufacturer as an additional insured under their policies, and "insuring risks of any kind relating to the construction" pursuant to the contract.

The contractor complied with the contract by naming the manufacturer as an additional insured under its auto and general liability policies. Some of the work also was undertaken by a subsidiary of the contractor. In accordance with the contract, the subsidiary also named the manufacturer as an additional insured.

An employee of the contractor's subsidiary was injured by the manufacturer's employees, and suit ultimately was filed by the injured worker against the manufacturer. By formal demand, the manufacturer sought protection under the subsidiary's liability policy as an additional insured. The insurer denied protection because the incident did not fall within "the description of operations" as covered by the policy. However, the court sided with the manufacturer's motion for summary judgment.

The primary question for the court to decide on appeal was on the matter of focus; that is, both the subsidiary and its insurer maintained that to determine liability, the focus must be on the actions of the manufacturer's employees who caused the accident. The manufacturer, on the other hand, argued that the focus should be on the injured worker. Both parties based their arguments on varying interpretations of the contract provisions. One of the more important provisions reads as follows.

> Article 10. Insurance ... (d) Contractor agrees to cause owner to be made an additional insured under all of the contractor's liability policies insuring risks of any kind relating to the construction and to arrange, in terms approved in advance by owner, that such policies will constitute primary coverage in the event of any claims against owner that are insurable under any of such policies.

The endorsement that made the manufacturer an additional insured on the subsidiary contracting firm's policy reads as follows.

> ... the Anaconda Company, Anaconda, Montana, is an additional insured under this policy in accordance with provisions of contract number 2081 with Arthur McKee & Company and dated May 15, 1971.

Both parties focused their arguments on the part of the contract that read, "... insuring risks of any kind relating to the construction...." No mention was made by either party of any provision in the insurance policies that would exclude coverage. In fact, a review of the insurance policies did not bring any such exclusions to the surface.

The court stated that the real issue dealt with the nature of the risks the parties intended to cover under the insurance provisions of this contract, which was specifically designated by number. Complicating the issue was controverted evidence as to whether the work being performed by the manufacturer's employees at the time of the accident was undertaken pursuant to this specific contract.

The court stated that, in determining the relationship between the parties, it is necessary to look at the employment contract that created the risk and the work to be done pursuant to the contract. The court explained further that had the focus been placed entirely on the activities of the injured work-

er rather than on the activities of the named insured (contractor), the application of the contract would have been overly broad and would have made the insurer responsible for all of the manufacturer's activities, regardless of control and benefit. The court decided that this would overly burden the insurer. The case, therefore, was remanded for trial.

Two justices dissented. They stated that in determining whether the insurer was obligated to protect the manufacturer, one should look to the terms of the insurance policy. Under the contract in question, the justices explained, the contractor agreed to make the manufacturer an additional insured in the contractor's policies to the extent of "insuring risks of any kind relating to the construction" and that such protection would be viewed as primary coverage in the event of any claim against the manufacturer.

If this policy had been purchased by the manufacturer in its own right, the justices explained, there would be no doubt as to the policy's application. Thus, the justices said, it made no difference that the policy was purchased by the subsidiary contracting firm and that the manufacturer was listed as an additional insured. By reason of the severability of interests clause, the manufacturer and subsidiary were two separate firms except with respect to the policy's limits of liability.[17]

The message imparted by these kinds of cases is that the meaning to be conveyed by an endorsement depends on the actual wording of the endorsement, not on the general understanding of the insurance industry. The other point to be made here is that in construing coverage under additional insured endorsements, the intent of the parties is of no relevance for purposes of determining the scope of coverage once the endorsement is issued. At that point, the additional insured is protected to the full extent allowed by the policy, which includes limitations imposed by the endorsement used. If the endorsement wording allows coverage for a given loss, the wording of the underlying contract should not be used to modify the coverage wording. It is only where contractual liability coverage is being applied that the underlying contract can limit the scope of coverage provided by the policy.

Additional Insured versus Additional Named Insured

A controversy has long raged in the risk management and insurance communities concerning the differences between additional named insured status and additional insured status and the advantages and disadvantages of each approach. Insurers generally resist adding additional named insureds, and there is no standard industry endorsement to accomplish this. On the other hand, some risk managers and risk management consultants are adamant about receiving additional named insured status for their employers or clients.

A close examination, however, reveals that there is one meaningful distinction between the two types of additional insured status. The primary distinction is in the application of exclusions that apply solely to the named insured. Indemnitees should avoid these debates by requesting only additional insured status. The reasons for this conclusion are discussed in the following sections.

"Additional Named Insured" Defined

A major cause of the confusion and controversy concerning "additional named insured" status is that there is no formal definition of what the term means that has been accepted by the insurance industry and risk management community. There is no standard "additional named insured endorsement," and liability insurance policies offer no definition of the term. There are as many definitions of this term as there are insurance and legal professionals to dream them up. Since additional named insured endorsements are manuscripted on a case-by-case basis, these varying definitions result in substantially different scopes of coverage being provided to additional named insureds.

In **Chapter 2** of this book, a definition of "additional named insured" is proposed. Basically, this encompasses the various scheduled named insureds other than the primary or first named insured. These named insureds are typically related in some man-

ner—usually through ownership—to the primary named insured, and the policy applies to each named insured as if it is the only named insured (with a few exceptions). Importantly, the operations and resultant liability exposures of all of these named insureds are revealed to and considered by underwriters when determining the acceptability of writing the policy and the premium that will be charged.

For example, if two of three named insureds on a policy are manufacturers and the third is a contractor, the total sales for both manufacturers and the total payroll for the contractor will be used as the rating basis for the liability policy's premium. The policy will also cover liability arising from all of the operations, products, and completed operations of these named insureds.

Of course, this type of arrangement is not normally the intent when one party to a contract (the indemnitee) requires another party (the indemnitor) to add it as an additional named insured. As evidenced by the fact that there is little or no premium charged to add additional insureds to liability policies, insurers do not intend to cover all of the indemnitee's liability exposures, and indemnitors certainly do not desire to expose their insurance program to all of the additional insured's activities. Instead, the indemnitee is seeking some degree of liability protection arising out of the operations or premises that are the subject of the contract. The degree of this protection is undefined.

Some would argue that the most common differentiation between additional insureds and additional named insureds is that an additional named insured is covered for liability arising from its own sole negligence, while an additional insured is covered only for its vicarious liability. However, this is merely a distinction made by some; it is not a widely agreed upon rule or guideline, nor is that perspective supported by policy wording. Since additional named insured endorsements are manuscripted, limitations applying coverage only to vicarious liability can certainly be included in them, and it is also possible to specifically cover the additional insured's sole negligence in an additional insured endorsement. The difference is that while limiting coverage to vicarious liability must be spelled out, allowing the additional insured access to all coverage under the policy does not, if the policy otherwise applies. As discussed previously, policy wording dictates the scope and application of coverage.

Since there is no widely accepted definition of "additional named insured," it can be concluded that such a contractual requirement is ambiguous and that the scope of coverage being requested is not really defined by mere mention of this term. Further, the "additional named insured" endorsement that is attached to a policy may provide overly broad or extremely narrow coverage to the indemnitee. Again, the policy wording determines the scope of coverage.

For example, what many would consider overly broad coverage would result if the indemnitee is merely listed as a named insured without limiting coverage in any manner to the operations or premises dealt with in the underlying contractual agreement (or including any of the other limitations suggested in **Chapter 21**). On the other hand, an indemnitor's insurer could draft an exceedingly restrictive additional named insured endorsement that provided very little protection to the indemnitee. In either case, merely naming the endorsement an "additional named insured endorsement" and calling the indemnitee an additional named insured in the endorsement is probably sufficient to comply with a vague requirement of additional named insured status since there is no acknowledged true meaning of this term. What will ultimately control is the wording of the endorsement.

Distinctions between Insureds and Named Insureds

If the preceding discussion is accepted, the general distinction between additional insured status and additional named insured status is that the indemnitee is called a "named insured" instead of an "insured." Beyond this, any distinctions arise from the unique provisions of the endorsements effecting additional insured (or additional named insured) status.

Only those policy provisions that apply to "insureds" apply to the coverage provided to additional insureds. On the other hand, the provisions applying exclusively to named insureds would also apply to the coverage afforded additional named insureds. Therefore, it is appropriate to review the application of the various policy provisions to both classes of insureds in comparing additional insured status and additional named insured status. Exhibit 4.2 shows the basic differences between insureds and named insureds in the 1986 and subsequent editions of the CGL forms.

EXHIBIT 4.2
INSURED AND NAMED INSURED DIFFERENCES

1. The named insured (NI) has more stringent occurrence reporting requirements.

2. The NI's employees, executive officers, and directors are insureds.

3. Certain exclusions apply only to the NI (e.g., property damage).

4. The NI must reimburse the amount of any deductible paid by the insurer.

5. The *First* NI is required to pay premium.

6. The *First* NI receives any premium return.

7. The *First* NI may cancel policy.

8. The *First* NI receives cancellation notice.

Notice that there are two types of named insureds in the 1986 and all subsequent editions of the CGL forms: the "first named insured" and all other named insureds. Since many insureds actually constitute several entities, each of which should be a named insured, the insurance industry has assigned to one of these entities—the first named insured—certain exclusive rights and responsibilities involving communications and financial obligations. The other named insureds do not share these rights and responsibilities. *The most important conclusion drawn from this is that a party added to another's policy as an additional named insured has not by doing so secured the right to receive notice of cancellation from the insurer.*

In contrast to the current CGL policy, the 1973 edition did not differentiate between named insureds. As a result, insurers were obligated to notify all named insureds when cancelling coverage. One of the reasons the practice of requiring additional named insured status probably originated was to secure the right to cancellation notice (issuance of a mere certificate of insurance usually does not accomplish this). This previous advantage of additional named insured status no longer exists except with respect to those indemnitors that are still obtaining coverage on the old form.

The distinction between the first named insured and all other named insureds also eliminates a disadvantage of being an additional named insured that previously existed: a potential liability to pay premiums to the insurer. Under the previous CGL form, all named insureds were responsible for paying premiums. There were a few instances where insurers successfully required additional named insureds to pay premiums on behalf of bankrupt named insureds. With the premium payment obligation now limited to only the first named insured, this should no longer be a possibility.

Because of the distinction between the first named insured and all other named insureds, the first three differences between insureds and named insureds listed in Exhibit 4.2 determine which should be preferred by contracting parties. Numbers 1 and 3 make additional insured status advantageous, and number 2 makes additional named insured status advantageous. Employees of an insured do not automatically receive insured status in the CGL policy. On the other hand, the CGL policy automatically includes as insureds the employees and executive officers of all named insureds. This is the main advantage of additional named insured status over additional insured status.

Being included as an additional insured on another party's liability insurance does not secure insured status for the additional insured's employees in the other party's insurance (employees and executive officers would, however, still be protected by the additional insured's own liability insurance). The primary reasons that employees and executive officers are included as insureds are to help secure their cooperation in the defense of suits and to live up to management's perceived corporate responsibility to protect employees. As a practical matter, however, employees and executive officers are not typically named as individual defendants in the types of tort liability actions covered by general liability policies. Because of this and because employees would be covered by the additional insured's own liability insurance, this advantage of additional named insured status does not seem that important.

An important disadvantage of additional named insured status comes from the application of the CGL policy condition concerning duties in the event of occurrence, claim, or suit. This condition requires named insureds to promptly notify the insurer of an occurrence that may result in a claim. Failure of the named insured to do so may prejudice coverage under the policy. Since insureds are not subject to this provision, there is a much reduced risk that delayed notice of an occurrence on the part of an additional insured will result in a claim denial.[18]

The second difference that presents a disadvantage of additional named insured status is that some exclusions apply only to named insureds and not to insureds. While on the surface this appears quite compelling, it may not be as important as it first appears. The reason is that those few exclusions that do not apply to insureds may not be relevant to the additional insured's exposures being covered under the policy or are otherwise dealt with by the additional insured endorsements themselves. However, this cannot be taken for granted in every instance. Each contract and each additional insured must take this factor into consideration before reaching any conclusions in this regard.

Exhibit 4.3 shows the differences in the application of various exclusions to insureds and named insureds under current CGL policies, and Exhibit 4.4 does the same with the 1973 edition CGL policy exclusive of the Broad Form CGL endorsement.

An important point to take into consideration in reading Exhibits 4.3 and 4.4 is that an "insured" is commonly defined to include the "named insured." However, the reverse is not true. If an exclusion applies to the "named insured," it does not apply to an "insured." But what is intended to be precluded by

EXHIBIT 4.3
CGL POLICY PROVISIONS
NAMED INSURED VERSUS INSURED

Named Insured	Insured	Policy Provisions
		Insuring Agreement
	✔	Pay on behalf of
		Exclusions
	✔	Intentional injury from the standpoint of
	✔	Obligation to pay damages by reason of contractual liability[a]
	✔	Liquor liability[b]
	✔	Obligations under workers compensation and other laws
	✔	Employers liability
	✔	Except for liability assumed under contract by[c]
✔	✔	Environmental pollution by
	✔	Watercraft, aircraft and autos[d]
	✔	Transportation of mobile equipment by auto of
✔		Property damage to owned, rented or occupied property of
✔		Property sold, given away or abandoned of
✔		Property loaned to
	✔	Personal property in care, custody or control of[e]
✔		That particular part of any real property being worked on by
✔		That particular part of property to be restored because of the work of
✔		Property damage to product of
✔		Property damage to work of
✔		Property damage to impaired property dealing with:
✔		a product of
✔		a delay or failure to perform a contract by
		Damages incurred for the:
✔		recall of products of
✔		work of

[a] The exception to this exclusion is an "insured contract" as defined. However, part f. of "insured contract" specifically applies to contracts pertaining to the named insured's (your) business under which the named insured (you) assumes the tort liability of another.

[b] The CGL policy makes the exclusion application to any insured, but the exception to the exclusion only applies if the named insured (you) manufactures, sells, serves, etc., alcoholic beverages.

[c] The employers liability exclusion provides an exception for liability assumed by the *insured* under any contract or agreement. However, contractual liability coverage subpart f., as provided by the policy, is specifically limited to liability assumed by the *named insured* (you). (See (b) above.) This presents a possible ambiguity.

[d] Three of the five exceptions to this exclusion apply specifically to the named insured (you).

[e] The 1986 CGL policy excluded personal property in the named insured's (your) care, custody, or control.

EXHIBIT 4.4
1973 CGL POLICY PROVISIONS
NAMED INSURED VERSUS INSURED

Named Insured	Insured	Policy Provisions
		Insuring Agreement
	✔	Pay on behalf of
		Exclusions
	✔	Liability assumed under any contract by[a]
	✔	Aircraft and autos[b]
	✔	Transportation of mobile equipment on auto of
✔		Watercraft owned, operated by, rented or loaned to
	✔	Any other watercraft operated by any person in the course of his employment by
	✔	War with respect to liability assumed by
	✔	Liquor liability[c]
	✔	Obligations under workers compensation and other laws
	✔	Employers liability except for liability assumed under an incidental contract by[d]
		Property damage to:[e]
	✔	property owned, occupied or rented to
	✔	property used by
	✔	property in the care, custody, or control of
✔		Premises alienated by:
		Loss of use of tangible property not physically injured from:
✔		a delay or lack of performance by or on behalf of
✔		failure of the products or work of
✔		Property damage to the product of
✔		Property damage to work performed by or on behalf of
		Damages incurred for the:
✔		recall of products of
✔		work of

[a] An exception is made for any incidental contract as defined. But the definition is silent on who can make such an assumption, i.e., named insured and/or insured. When the Broad Form CGL Endorsement is purchased, coverage is extended to include any oral or written contract relating to the *named insured's* business.

[b] Only one exception applies and that is for the parking of autos on premises of the named insured or ways immediately adjoining such premises.

[c] This exclusion refers to the insured, which gives the inference that what is excluded and excepted by the exclusion applies to an insured as well.

[d] This exclusion does not apply to a liability assumed by the *insured* under an incidental contract; when Broad Form CGL Endorsement is purchased, the term "incidental contract" is extended to include any oral or written contract relating to the *named insured's* business, but there is no restriction on who can make such contractual assumptions.

[e] When this exclusion is modified by the Broad Form CGL Endorsement, it takes into consideration broad form property damage coverage.

exclusions that apply only to named insureds is coverage that, in their absence, would be provided solely to the named insured in the first place.

For example, the current CGL policy excludes coverage for property damage to the named insured's products. The reason is that what products liability coverage probably is intended to be provided within the basic policy provisions is limited to the named insured's products (which can include the component products of others). However, this intent can be defeated, depending on the circumstances, with the addition of an unrestricted additional insured endorsement that does not in some way preclude coverage for liability arising from the products of the additional insured.

A third potential disadvantage of additional named insured status is the possible obligation to reimburse deductibles paid by the insurer or to pay a self-insured retention. For example, the standard Deductible (CG 03 00) endorsement developed by ISO for use with CGL policies requires the named insured (i.e., "you") to reimburse any deductibles paid by the insurer. Thus, an additional insured would have no such obligation. The operative provision from this endorsement is shown in Exhibit 4.5.

EXHIBIT 4.5
CGL DEDUCTIBLE ENDORSEMENT
REIMBURSEMENT PROVISION

We may pay any part or all of the deductible amount to effect settlement of any claim or "suit" and, upon notification of the action taken, you shall promptly reimburse us for such part of the deductible amount as has been paid by us.

Copyright, Insurance Services Office, Inc., 1994

Application of Contractual Liability Coverage

Another area where the distinction between named insured and insured is significant is with respect to contractual liability coverage. Of importance is not only who is covered by such insurance but also who is permitted by the policy to assume liability under contracts. Exclusion b. of the 1988 and subsequent CGL forms eliminates coverage for liability assumed under all but insured contracts. Both the exclusion and the definition of insured contract are shown in Exhibit 4.6. Note that both the contractual liability exclusion and the exception to it refer to the "insured." As a result, they apply to both "named insureds" and insureds.

The contracts itemized in parts a. through e. do not qualify who—the insured or the named insured—can make such contractual assumptions. However, part f., which applies to any other contract (e.g., a construction contract), is restricted to the assumption of another's tort liability by the *named insured* (you). If it were the intent to restrict all contractual assumptions to those by the named insured, the definition of "insured contract" could have been worded to say so.

In those cases where the named insured is a corporation, the "you" would be interpreted to mean those insureds within the corporation who have such authority. Likewise, it would be the partners of a partnership and members of a joint venture who would be qualified insureds. But, because reference to part f. of "insured contract" specifically mentions "you," it would not include nonautomatic insureds.

Having established who is permitted to assume liability under contracts, the next step is to determine to what extent insureds are protected. This will depend on the nature of the claim or subject of concern. Refer, for example, to the exception of employers liability exclusion (e), which reads: "This exclusion does not apply to liability assumed by the insured under an insured contract." Based on the preceding analysis, one cannot conclude categorically that the exception to the employers liability exclusion applies to any or all insureds. The exception, of course, would apply to the named insured, but whether some other insured would qualify hinges on the nature of the "insured contract." If the "insured contract" concerns parts a. through e., a nonautomatic insured could conceivably be protected. It would depend on the nature of the additional insured endorsement.

For example, endorsement CG 20 10, Additional Insured—Owners, Lessees, or Contractors, contains no exclusion (as some nonstandard endorsements do) of liability assumed in a contract. So, an insured under CG 20 10 might be covered by the exception to employers liability exclusion (e) but only with respect to parts a. through e. of "insured contract."

This same conclusion is made with respect to the definition of "incidental contract" in the 1973 CGL, including the Broad Form CGL endorsement. As defined in the policy, "incidental contract" does not refer or restrict the contractual as sumptions to anyone in particular. It therefore can encompass the named insured and all other insureds. However, when the Broad Form CGL endorsement is attached, the term "incidental contract" is extended to include any oral or written contract or agreement relating to the conduct of the named insured's business. Thus, the contractual undertaking would be limited to the named insured or its authorized representatives.

EXHIBIT 4.6
CONTRACTUAL LIABILITY COVERAGE PROVISIONS

Exclusion

This insurance does not apply to … b. "Bodily injury" or "property damage" for which the insured is obligated to pay damages by reason of the assumption of liability in a contract or agreement. This exclusion does not apply to liability for damages:

(1) Assumed in a contract or agreement that is an "insured contract" provided the "bodily injury" or "property damage" occurs subsequent to the execution of the contract or agreement.

(2) That the insured would have in the absence of the contract or agreement.

Definition

"Insured contract" means:

a. A lease of premises;

b. A sidetrack agreement;

c. Any easement or license agreement, except in connection with construction or demolition operations on or within 50 feet of a railroad;

d. An obligation as required by ordinance to indemnify a municipality except in connection with work for a municipality;

e. An elevator maintenance agreement; or

f. That part of any other contract or agreement pertaining to your business (including an indemnification of a municipality in connection with work performed for a municipality) under which you assume the tort liability of another to pay damages because of "bodily injury" or "property damage" to a third person or organization. Tort liability means a liability that would be imposed by law in absence of any contract or agreement.

Additional Insured Status Preferred

Contrary to what many risk management and insurance professionals would have guessed without performing a detailed analysis, additional insured status is preferable over named insured status. By requiring that additional insured be provided on a form equivalent to one of the standard industry endorsements, an indemnitee obtains a relatively known scope of protection. Certainly this is preferable to making a vague requirement for a type of coverage that has no accepted meaning within the industry and for which there is no standard endorsement form.

Fronting Arrangements and Additional Insureds

While prevalent for years, the use of large deductibles, self-insured retentions, and self-insurance has taken on added significance with the use of additional insured endorsements and contract provisions imposing more specific insurance requirements. In some jurisdictions, self-insurance, large self-insured retentions, and deductibles are deemed not to be insurance because the insured is solely responsible for the payment of claims. A method of risk transfer utilized more often than many insurance and risk management professionals realize is what is known as a "fronting arrangement" or, simply, "fronting."

Fronting typically involves an insurer issuing a policy to the insured and then, by way of a separate claims servicing contract, agreeing to pay claims on behalf of the insured or passing that obligation to pay claims under the fronting policy to another insurer, to the insured, or elsewhere. This approach allows the insured, utilizing the front, to show proof of insurance and to issue certificates of insurance and additional insured endorsements acceptable to lenders, regulators, and others requiring evidence of insurance for various reasons. It also helps the insured to avoid having to qualify as a self-insurer or obtaining licensing as a captive in all states.

The reason insurers front for others, in a nutshell, is profit. The fronting insurer charges a fee for its service. While the fee typically is a percentage of the insurance premium, this amount varies depending on the services the fronting insurer is to provide. Where the fronting insurer obtains adequate guarantees of being reimbursed, a fronting arrangement takes on the appearance of a lucrative profit center for the fronting insurer, one relatively free of risk in many cases. However, in many fronting arrangements the fronting insurer must stand tall for any claims in the event the party utilizing the front is unable or unwilling to reimburse it.

While fronting arrangements are similar to deductibles and self-insured retentions in that the insured ultimately pays for the claims, some versions of fronting arrangements are more susceptible to characterization as insurance for a number of reasons, as will be discussed.

Fronting Generally

From an insurance and risk management standpoint, fronting has to come to mean the use of an insurer to provide coverage, the cost of which will fall upon the insured. The cost includes not only the pure insurance provided but also the claim and other expenses associated with it. A number of terms have described fronting arrangements, including "reinsurance agreements," "indemnity agreements," and others, but "fronts," "fronting policies," and "fronting arrangements" remain the terms most widely used.

Fronting arrangements are utilized for various reasons. Self-insured entities utilize fronting arrangements to comply with financial responsibility laws and contractually imposed insurance requirements requiring evidence of insurance and, to a lesser extent, to obtain claims and loss-prevention services offered by some insurers. (Self-insured layers of coverage provided by self-insured retention endorsements might also provide this latter feature.) Captive insurance companies sometimes utilize a fronting arrangement to write business in a state requiring admitted insurers and to comply with financial responsibility and other laws.

For example, fronting arrangements can involve the purchase of a liability policy (with the insured fronting up to 100 percent of policy limits) to provide evidence of insurance to governmental entities for regulation or certification purposes. The purchase of traditional insurance may be impractical for a variety of reasons, including loss history, the exposure to the insured, or the fact that the entity is self-insured. The insured in these arrangements agrees to reimburse the insurer for any claims paid, up to the amount agreed to in the contract between them. That amount may or may not be reflected in the policy as a deductible and is the subject of a hold harmless or similar agreement between the parties. In many fronting arrangements, defense costs are reimbursed pursuant to a separate claims servicing agreement.

Another fronting scenario involves two insurers. Consider for example, a nonadmitted insurer (one not licensed to do business in a particular state) who contracts with a licensed or admitted insurer to issue a policy for a specific risk the nonadmitted insurer seeks to underwrite in a state that requires admitted insurers. In this instance, the nonadmitted insurer, in agreeing to reimburse or pay directly all claims charged against the fronting insurer, is also utilizing a fronting arrangement. Another example involves an insurer with a B+ rating that seeks to underwrite a specific exposure involving contract requirements calling for insurance provided by an insurer with an A+ rating. The B+ rated insurer might have the higher-rated insurer actually issue the policy, but with a side agreement obligating the B+ rated insurer to bear the burden of claims made against the fronting policy. That agreement would likely call for the B+ rated insurer to assume all claim- and defense-related obligations associated with the risk.

As these examples illustrate, fronting arrangements can be utilized by insureds and insurers in a variety of ways. A characteristic common to fronting arrangements is that the fronting insurer takes on the appearance of providing coverage when in reality the party utilizing the front ultimately bears responsibility for obligations incurred by the fronting policy. How that obligation is paid varies depending on the agreement between the parties

and will ultimately be a major factor in how courts interpret the coverage being provided.

Fronting Arrangements as Insurance

When one insurer fronts for another, it is common for the fronting insurer to contractually abdicate *any* responsibility for the damages paid in any claims or costs and expenses incurred in providing a defense. Where business entities utilize a fronting insurer, however, the method of paying claims is often different and takes on the characteristics of insurance, despite the fact that the insured reimburses the fronting insurer. These situations are the emphasis of this chapter. As discussed earlier, self-insureds utilizing fronting arrangements to provide an appearance of insurance often do so to comply with contractual requirements or regulations.

As a result, a fronting arrangement has all the trappings of true insurance. It also is viewed as such by third parties relying on the fronting policy to provide insurance and by additional insureds added to the coverage. In most cases, the fronting insurer handles the defense and indemnity as any insurer would, appearing to function under an insurance policy, complete with coverage document. In fronting arrangements of this type, whereby the party utilizing the front provides certificates of insurance, additional insured status, and other amenities associated with insurance coverage, there is no way for anyone other than the named insured to distinguish between traditional insurance coverage and the fronting policy. The fronting policy is usually a typical liability policy for which certificates of insurance and additional insured endorsements are routinely issued. When claims arise under a fronting arrangement, they are handled in a manner similar to that involved in a standard policy of insurance. Outward appearances then are of a standard insurance program.

The difference here is that the insured has agreed by way of a separate agreement to pay for claims as if it had a deductible or to reimburse the fronting insurer for any claims paid. However, in a classic insurance sense, the *insurer* is still the primary party liable and who must bear the risk of loss. The fronting insurer often bears the risk of the insured's inability to reimburse it and must take steps to ensure that it is paid. The fronting insurer is a risk-taker, providing the services typically expected of an insurance policy. The fact that the insured reimburses the fronting insurer does not, in and of itself, alter that fact. Some go so far as to characterize the reimbursable sums as an exorbitant premium to get this point across.

Consider for example a situation where the party utilizing the fronting arrangement is temporarily unable to pay, refuses to do so, or files bankruptcy. In those cases, the fronting insurer becomes the responsible party and the one that pays the claim. Some of the many insurance company failures in the 1970s and 1980s involved fronting insurers who could not meet unexpected obligations to pay claims, often because they failed to secure adequate capitalization from the entity utilizing the front. The result was a more conservative approach by fronting insurers. Current practice dictates that fronting insurers require the entity utilizing the front to provide adequate security for the payment of defense obligations and claims. A common form of security utilized for this purpose is a letter of credit from a bank with financial stability.

Obviously, there can be exceptions to the general notion that the fronting insurer functions as a typical insurer and is later reimbursed. An example is where the party utilizing the front and the fronting insurer contractually agree that the insured will pay all costs of indemnity and defense directly. In these situations, additional problems must be considered, and the fronting arrangement might become problematic.

If additional insured endorsements or certificates of insurance evidencing compliance with insurance or regulatory requirements or other laws are issued, the question is whether the representation of available insurance coverage made by the insured and the fronting insurer is legitimate. Insureds utilizing fronting arrangements and insurers providing the coverage should carefully consider the implications of their underlying agreement regarding how defense and indemnity will be addressed, particularly where others will rely on the existence of available insurance. If a court finds that coverage under the fronting arrangement will not be applied as traditional insurance, the net result may be to eliminate the coverage that was represented to have been available.

For example, consider a situation where a fronting insurer disavows any obligations under its policy in a separate contract with the insured. If that same insurer issues, or allows to be issued, certificates of insurance, additional insured endorsements, or both, what are the implications if coverage is ruled not to be insurance? Those relying on additional insured status or certificates of insurance as evidence of available coverage may argue that they have been misled. A fronting policy without obligations may pose problems for those relying on it for insurance.

If a fronting policy—which provides a defense, pays claims, and later seeks reimbursement—is considered not to be insurance, the party utilizing the front should not be deemed to have misled those relying on the fronting policy. This is because such arrangements are, in custom and practice, viewed as insurance, and a court ruling to the contrary should not be viewed as foreseeable, given the widespread use of fronting arrangements and their perception as insurance. However, where the fronting insurer has no obligations at all, both the insured and the insurer have less justification for reliance on such an arrangement as insurance. As a result, representations to the contrary made by one or both to third parties may lead to legal complications for all involved.

An issue often lost on those utilizing fronting arrangements is when the fronting insurer, as opposed to the insured, becomes insolvent. Because fronting arrangements are often characterized as insurance, the state guarantee fund may take over the handling of claims, while the insured remains liable to reimburse sums paid to defend and settle claims. Under this scenario, the insured might lose all control of the claims handling process and may likely find itself involved in protracted litigation until all claims are ultimately concluded. Therefore, it is important for those contemplating the use of a fronting arrangement to choose the fronting insurer carefully.

Fronting Arrangements in Relation to Self-Insurance

Often, an entity chooses a fronting arrangement in lieu of providing evidence of self-insurance because third parties requiring proof of insurance will not accept self-insurance as compliant with insurance requirements. Also, with self-insurance, there is often no coverage document to evidence, clarify, or limit the scope of coverage being provided by a self-insured. Some self-insureds turn to a fronting arrangement because it provides the necessary comfort of knowing there is a specific level of insurance to those requiring it. Third parties dealing with the insured receive certificates or other evidence of insurance available to the insured. The insured in turn gets the benefit of complying with third-party insurance requirements and a coverage document clarifying and limiting the scope of coverage being provided.

While some courts addressing fronting arrangements utilize nomenclature associated with self-insurance, they vary in their treatment of fronting arrangements when applying the coverage provided. Some courts view fronts as self-insurance, despite the fact that they exhibit the characteristics of insurance and are viewed and relied on as insurance by most insureds. However, even some of the courts that view a fronting arrangement as self-insurance apply the coverage under a fronting policy as they would under a traditional insurance program.

A case in point is *Chicago Insurance Co. v Travelers Insurance Co.*, 967 SW2d 35 (1998). Travelers Insurance and Chicago Insurance both issued policies covering a pharmacist employed by Walgreen Company. Chicago's policy provided professional liability coverage, while the Travelers policy provided CGL coverage. The court described the coverage provided by Travelers as a fronting policy in which Walgreen's policy limits of $1 million were subject to a deductible of the same amount. The court characterized the fronting arrangement as

one that "effectively provides the terms of Walgreen's plan to be self-insured for $1 million." Walgreen had admitted to having the policy issued for the purpose of providing certificates of insurance to municipalities and vendors and for utilizing the insurance industry's claims handling experience and expertise provided by Travelers.

The Travelers policy stated it was primary, while the Chicago policy stated it was excess if: "there is other valid insurance, (whether primary, excess, contingent *or self-insurance*) which may apply against a loss or claim covered by this policy ...." The circuit court ruled that if both policies applied, Chicago's coverage would be excess. However, it held that the Travelers policy did not apply to an employee's liability in rendering professional services and that the Chicago policy was primary under the facts at issue. However, that ruling contradicted a prior admission that the Travelers policy did cover the claim. A subsequent ruling held that, based on that admission, both policies applied. It also held that to the extent the Travelers policy had an applicable deductible, it was not insurance, and the provision in the Chicago policy making it excess was inapplicable.

On appeal, Chicago argued that its policy was excess over the self-insurance coverage governed by the Travelers policy. The appellate court agreed, in large part, because the fronting policy was in fact a policy of insurance, complete with policy provisions that were to be given effect. The court held that the Traveler's policy "unequivocally states that it is primary ..." and "the Chicago policy specifically says that it shall be deemed excess insurance over and above the applicable limit of all other insurance *or self insurance* ...." (Emphasis added.)

The court did not premise its holding solely on the fact that the Chicago policy was excess even above self-insurance. In again pointing up the significance of a policy document, the court added:

> Even if the terms of these policies had not contemplated a situation involving self-insurance or the existence of *another policy* with an extremely high deductible, the Travelers cover-

age would still be primary. Walgreen elected to be self-insured and bargained with Travelers on the terms of *its policy* …. Opting to be self-insured does not equate to being uninsured. (Emphasis added.)

This ruling points out the significance of a fronting arrangement providing coverage utilizing a policy of insurance. The *Chicago* court did not address whether Travelers was to be reimbursed, whether Travelers bore the risk of Walgreen's insolvency or unwillingness to pay, and other issues discussed above regarding fronts. However, the court was swayed by the fact that the fronting policy had the characteristics of traditional insurance and applied coverage accordingly.

The Allocation Issue

There are jurisdictions holding that periods during which an insured is self-insured cannot be allocated a percentage of defense costs for claims involving multiple policy periods and progressive damages. The court in the case of *Keen Corp. v Insurance Company of North America,* 667 F2d 1034 (DC Cir 1981), for example, said that:

> We have no authority upon which to pretend that Keene also has a "self-insurance" policy that is triggered for periods in which no other policy was purchased. Even if we had the authority, what would we pretend the policy provides? What would its limits be? There are no self-insurance policies ….

Reference here to the fact that the scope or limits of coverage under self-insurance cannot be described and the fact that there is no coverage document with self-insurance further reinforces the notion that coverage under a fronting policy should be applied as insurance. As stated throughout this discussion, the utilization and reliance on fronting policies as insurance makes it difficult to justify applying the coverage provided by fronting policies as something other than insurance. Unlike the self-insurance described by the *Keen* court, fronting arrangements provide a coverage document, policy period, limits, and a defined scope of coverage, and they do pay claims. It is only when self-insurance is provided

without a coverage document that it can be classified as true self-insurance.

Judicial doctrine varies as to how self-insurance is treated and applied. The issue of defense coverage, because it is addressed differently by law, must be addressed separately when analyzing and applying coverage under a fronting policy. Where defense is involved, it may be more difficult to argue that coverage under a fronting policy must be viewed as insurance, though the fact that the insurer first pays defense costs should weigh heavily, as it does in the case of indemnity payments. The fact that the insured reimburses the fronting insurer should not preclude a finding that coverage under a fronting policy is not insurance. However, as the discussion below points out, some courts will view it as such.

The Fronting Insurer's Defense Obligation

Generally speaking, an insurer's defense obligation under a fronting policy is the same as with a nonfronting policy. That is to say, the insurer is obligated to defend suits seeking damages covered by the policy. The fact that a fronting policy is involved does not alter this principle, with one possible exception. The contract between the insured and the fronting insurer absolves the insurer of any obligations to pay claims or defense costs on behalf of the insured and, instead, calls for the insured to pay all such costs directly.

As noted, one purpose of a fronting policy is to create an insuring arrangement as opposed to self-insurance. As a result, insurers providing coverage in these instances typically defend and pay claims before seeking reimbursement from the insured. The insurer functions as it would in any other scenario under which its policy had been asked to defend. In these instances, the fronting insurer later seeks reimbursement from the insured. Its vehicle for doing so is usually the contract provisions imposed on the insured in a claims servicing or other agreement.

However, applying traditional legal doctrines related to the defense obligations under a fronting arrangement gets more complicated. In some situations, as discussed previously, defense coverage under a fronting policy can be viewed as insurance. One of the problems that might arise is whether the fronting policy is other insurance for purposes of allocating defense costs among insurers where injury or damage is progressive over a period of time. A case viewing and applying defense coverage under a fronting policy and pointing out some of the legal dilemmas involves *Aerojet-General Corp. v Transport Ind.,* 948 P2d 909 (Cal 1997). The issue was whether insurers who were obligated to defend against progressive damages occurring over time could allocate a portion of the defense costs to periods when the entity was insured under a fronting arrangement. The court in this matter referred to the fronting period as one during which the insured was effectively self-insured.

While the insured, Aerojet, was obligated to reimburse the fronting insurer for indemnity payments made by it, that insurer had no obligation to defend Aerojet. Rather, the insured was obligated to handle and pay for its own defense directly. The court ultimately ruled that while insurers may be required to make equitable contributions to defense costs among themselves, an insured is not required to make such a contribution together with insurers. At this juncture, one can only speculate as to how the court would rule were the facts such that the fronting insurer did in fact have a defense obligation for which it was entitled to indemnity from the insured. In that instance, it could be argued that the insurer literally made the payment and that other insurers could seek equitable contribution from the fronting insurer, who in turn would recover such sums from the insured.

Claims Servicing Agreements

The defense of claims often involves a claims servicing agreement similar to those used with self-insurance. Fronting insurers often, in addition to extracting a fee for the service they provide, derive additional income by providing claims management services to the party utilizing the fronting arrangement. Fronting arrangements, like many large deductibles or self-insured retentions, typically involve the use of a claims services agreement pursuant to which claims under the front are han-

dled. Such agreements are separate from the wording of the policy itself, which typically contains wording obligating the insurer to provide a defense.

A separate claims servicing agreement is often entered into, defining the obligations of the insurer providing the claims services and those of the insured to reimburse the costs of doing so. However, the claims servicing agreement does not modify the insurer's obligation to provide a defense to the insured or to additional insureds pursuant to policy wording and in accordance with accepted principles of insurance and risk management. These agreements are the insurer's way of contractually obligating the insured to reimburse the insurer for defense and related costs and to clarify the parties' respective obligations. Claims servicing serves as a profit center from which the fronting insurer or other party providing the service derives a substantial income for its service, with little accompanying risk, depending on the collateral provided by the insured. As discussed previously, the fronting insurer's principal risk is in the solvency of the insured and the insured's continuing ability to reimburse the costs incurred by the fronting insurer.

In addition to administrative and claims service fees, claims servicing agreements also might call for the insured to be charged a separate fee to compensate the insurer for the loss of use of its funds when paying the insured's claim payments and allocated claim expenses prior to receiving reimbursement. This is not always the case, however, and the terms of these agreements often vary, depending on the amount of income to be derived by the party providing the claims service. These agreements usually make clear that the obligation to defend and pay claims rests with the fronting insurer, reinforcing the premise that coverage under a fronting arrangement is viewed, and should be treated, as insurance in such cases. A related problem here concerns who ultimately is to control the claims management process. The interests of the insured and the party providing the claims service sometimes are at odds for obvious reasons.

The claims administrator is charged with viewing the claim as an insurer. The insured, on the other hand, as the party who reimburses all such costs and indemnity payments, becomes concerned with mitigating its exposure. This practical reality creates a breeding ground for collusion between the insured and the insurer or claims administrator. It is not uncommon to find third parties, seeking redress against the insured under a fronting arrangement, embroiled in a coverage dispute. The insured might encourage the claims administrator to dispute coverage and delay payment of a claim to the extent possible. The irony of such a development is that the insured comes full circle, behaving in a manner it would label bad faith were it seeking coverage under a policy it does not have to reimburse. In these situations, an understanding of the fronting arrangement best serves the interests of a third-party claimant. Knowing that it is to the insured's advantage to dispute to avoid paying claims might lead to an early resolution of such disputes. Insureds inclined to behave in this manner may lose their incentive for doing so once their rationale is disclosed and made an issue in any pending litigation.

Reserving sums to pay defense costs (a form of collateral) also might become a point of contention under the claims servicing agreement. Insureds want to deposit minimal sums for this contingency, while the fronting insurer or claims administrator wants as much as possible on hand at all times. Proper claims management, auditing, and forecasting usually can address these problems. Doing so should provide a comfort level for the insurer or claims administrator as to the insured's ability and willingness to promptly reimburse all sums exceeding reserves.

Who Pays under a Fronting Arrangement?

It is generally understood that in many fronting arrangements, as discussed previously, the fronting insurer pays any sums due under the policy and then seeks reimbursement from the insured. If the insured for any reason refuses or is unable to pay the fronting amount, the burden is expected to fall to the insurer who contracted to provide the fronting policy. In some cases, the contract between the fronting insurer and the insured might require that

the insured directly pay claims made against the fronting policy. As noted, this could be construed by some courts to constitute self-insurance. On the other hand, where the fronting insurer pays and later seeks reimbursement from the insured, the arrangement is viewed by insureds as one involving an insurance policy, with the fronting insurer bearing the risk that the insured will be able to reimburse it. However, when the insured directly pays sums normally paid by an insurer, the chances of coverage being applied by the courts as self-insurance increases.

Such was case in *Transport Insurance Co. v Insurance Co. of North America,* 59 Cal Rptr 2d 126 (Cal App 2 Dist 1996). Here, an employee of Spreader Specialists was injured while unloading a tractor-trailer. Spreader owned the tractor and Koch Materials owned the trailer. Spreader's motor vehicle policy, issued by Transport Insurance, covered both the tractor and trailer and included Koch as an additional insured. Koch was insured by Insurance Company of North America (INA). Koch's policy limits of $2 million were matched by a deductible of the same amount, and the policy provided that INA had the right to pay, "in its sole discretion, any damages within the amount of the $2 million." At issue was the order in which coverage would apply under an applicable Insurance Code section 11580.9, which held as follows.

> [W]here two (or more) policies apply to the same loss arising out of the loading or unloading of a motor vehicle, and one policy insures the owner of the premises and the other insures the vehicle, the policy covering the premises owner shall be primary and the vehicle policy shall be excess.

The court was charged with deciding whether this statute applied when the owner's policy was a so-called fronting policy. In doing so, the court noted that for section 11580.9 subdivision (c) to apply, there must be two or more policies that are applicable to the same loss. The court held that the Transport policy would be excess "only if there is 'other valid and collectable insurance applicable to the same loss.'" The court concluded that the INA policy was not "collectable" because it was not an indemnity policy. There was no obligation for the insurer to indemnify the insured (and seek reimbursement later) because *the insurer's obligation to pay was purely discretionary*. The court phrased its decision as follows.

> Where, as here, a fronting policy provides no right of coverage under any circumstances except at the insurer's discretion, there is no "collectable insurance" within the meaning of section 11580.9, subdivision (c).

Because of this *discretionary obligation to pay* on the part of the fronting insurer in conjunction with the deductible amount, the court found Koch to be uninsured, noting that at least one published decision addressing fronting arrangements had indicated that the holders of such policies were self-insured to the extent of their policy limits. However, despite this, Koch was not deemed to be self-insured because self-insurers were required to be issued a certificate of self-insurance before they could be considered as such under the statute.

Technically then, Koch was not self-insured even though it was in practicality, given the deductible, which the insurer did not have to pay, according to the court. In rendering this opinion, the court was careful to point out that it was not excluding other policies with large deductibles from section 11580.9. Nor, said the court, was it providing an opinion as to whether other types of fronting policies were covered by this statute or as to the validity of fronting policies in general. The court narrowed its focus on the issue of fronting to discretionary payment obligation. In doing so, it pointed out the perils of a fronting arrangement that does not function as an insurance arrangement.

In its concluding remarks, the court noted that Transport, the insurer being required to bear the brunt of coverage because the front was not insurance for purposes of applying the statute, was in a Catch-22. Transport had argued that it was unfair to allow the fronting policy to be deemed insurance for regulatory purposes but not for purposes of applying the insurance code. While the court could not deny the logic of that assertion, it merely stated that it was not being asked to address the validity of a fronting policy for regulatory purposes. Ultimately the court ruled that the insurer's was a primary policy, despite the fact that this may not have been the result had the fronting policy qualified under the applicable statute as "other collectable insurance."

Fronting Arrangements and Insurance Requirements

Fronting policies are relied on as compliant with insurance requirements. Because a fronting arrangement provides coverage in the same manner as a nonfronting policy, other than the fact that the insured reimburses the insurer, fronting policies are perceived to be insurance. The insurance and risk management industries have long accepted their use, view them as compliant with insurance requirements, and distinguish them from self-insured programs. If this were not so, fronting arrangements would be viewed no differently than self-insurance and could be viewed as a misrepresentation by the insured and insurer alike regarding the existence of insurance coverage. Third parties requiring insurance are told by contract wording or certificates of insurance that such coverage is being provided and, in many cases, that additional insured status is being provided as well.

Certificates of Insurance

Standard form certificates of insurance generally are intended to convey only broad information regarding the policy of insurance at issue. It is well known in the insurance and risk management industry that standard form certificates of insurance do not, for example, provide options for a specific additional insured endorsement to be provided. Standard form certificates of insurance do not provide for the identification of fronting arrangements or large deductibles in the primary layer of coverage, nor do they provide information on available policy limits or the extent to which those policy limits may have been depleted on other projects. The 1999 edition of the standard ACORD certificate includes a box to check when a deductible or retention is involved. But it does so only in relation to excess coverage. Since most fronting and self-insurance are used in the primary layer of coverage, this addition will be of little use in many cases.

Insureds typically accept and rely on standard certificates and the limited information contained therein as proof of insurance. Even with a more detailed manuscripted certificate, most insureds providing proof of coverage or additional insured status do not think to point out fronting arrangements, self-insurance, deductible amounts, or available policy limits for a given project. This is the case particularly with fronting because it is commonplace and viewed as insurance in the risk management and insurance industries.

Additional Insured Status

Because fronting policies take on the outward appearance of insurance, those requiring additional insured status seldom know the difference between fronts and traditional insurance. That is consistently the case, except where those seeking additional insured status or evidence of insurance address the issue in the underlying contract. It is not until a loss occurs for which the additional insured seeks protection that problems might arise.

For example, if a fronting policy is not deemed to be insurance, what is the additional insured's legal status? How does the additional insured's own coverage apply in relation to the fronting policy if the front is found to be self-insurance? Is the additional insured's policy (other insurance) in line to pay first, given that the policy to which it was added may be held not to be insurance? If a front is found not to be insurance and the entity insured thereunder is deemed to be self-insured, the self-insured entity may have no obligations to other insurers. How will this impact the rights of the additional insured in varying fact patterns where the self-insured entity owes no duty to insurance layers above the self-insured layer? The answers to these questions and others are not settled under the laws of many jurisdictions.

Generally speaking, those who must look to such policies for protection view fronts as insurance. However, in complex situations involving multiple insurers and conflicting interests, the outcome

for additional insureds under a fronting policy may not be satisfactory. There is a governing insurance document with policy provisions to rely on. However, because the person or entity that procures the fronting policy is responsible for any injuries or damages claimed under such a policy, courts may not agree with custom and practice that views fronts as providing insurance coverage. If underlying contract provisions do not address these contingencies, the additional insured may find itself facing serious legal complications.

Addressing the Issue of Fronts Contractually

One overriding question that arises when a fronting policy is involved is whether the use of such a policy is in compliance with the insurance requirements of the underlying contract. The answer, of course, depends on the wording of those requirements. If the party seeking evidence of insurance or additional insured status does not specifically preclude the use of fronts or self-insurance, there is no reason to believe that the party providing a fronting policy is not in compliance with requirements to provide insurance. That, of course, presumes that the fronting arrangement is such that the insurer pays and later seeks reimbursement. This is because most insureds view a fronting policy as insurance and are unaware of the distinctions between fronting and actual insurance. The problem is more complex where self-insurance is involved.

If no policy is issued by an insurer with provisions to handle defense and claims, it becomes difficult to argue that insurance, as required by insurance requirements, is being provided. Where the fronting arrangement is such that the insurer does not pay and later seek reimbursement from the insured, the fronting coverage might be interpreted by the courts as pure self-insurance. Resolution of disputes as to whether these scenarios will result in allegations that the party providing a fronting policy breached contract requirements to provide insurance will require a review of the contract language. Absent specific contract language addressing this issue, courts may be reluctant to find a breach of any obligation to provide insurance, particularly where the fronting arrangement is one that pays and later seeks reimbursement.

In many cases, those requiring additional insured status do not concern themselves with this issue when reviewing certificates of insurance evidencing coverage or when drafting insurance requirements. This is the case despite the fact that neither custom and practice in the insurance and risk management industry nor standard certificates of insurance require disclosure of fronting arrangements or deductible amounts. Ultimately, precluding the use of a fronting arrangement is the responsibility of the party requiring the coverage. Those requiring additional insured status may get some help here from the courts, depending on the jurisdiction. The problem is that case law in this area is unsettled, particularly in relation to balancing the equities of qualifying a front or self-insurance as insurance and a contracting party's failure to preclude their use absent disclosure and compliance with specific guidelines.

If the person or entity requiring coverage does not preclude, control, or otherwise address its issue contractually, when the insurance requirements of the underlying contract are negotiated, it must take what it gets. If a fronting policy or, for that matter, self-insurance is not acceptable to an entity requiring proof of insurance or additional insured status, the issue should be addressed in writing to avoid problems. It would be wise to specify in insurance requirements whether additional insured requirements can be complied with using self-insurance or fronting arrangements and that any applicable deductibles will be the responsibility of the named insured only. Such provisions might require written disclosure of a front and provide an opportunity for the party seeking additional insured status to assess the situation.

Responsibility for Paying Fronting Deductible Amounts

Many fronting policies ultimately have the named insured pay the cost of defense and indemnity utilizing a claims servicing agreement and a deductible endorsement. In some cases, these are reinforced by a hold harmless agreement. A hold harmless agreement might, for example, state that the named insured will report no losses under the policy and that, if it does, it agrees to reimburse the fronting insurer for all sums paid on the insured's behalf. In many instances, policy wording makes clear that only the named insured utilizing the fronting arrangement is obligated to pay the deductible amount. Standard endorsements and many manuscripted ones refer to the party obligated to pay the deductible as "you" and "your," which are defined to mean the named insured. The distinction between a named insured and other insureds (including additional insureds) is made throughout most policies.

The named insured, for example, is subject to what are referred to as business risk exclusions, whereas insureds automatically included in policies and additional insureds added by endorsement are not. The named insured is obligated to provide notice of an occurrence and pay premiums; has the ability, with the insurer's permission, to transfer policy rights; and receives notice of cancellation and premium refunds. None of these benefits, exclusions, or obligations applies to an insured or additional insured under the wording of a standard ISO CGL policy, some independently filed policies, or manuscript policies.

When the policy states that the named insured is obligated to pay the deductible or self-insured retention, that wording means what it says. The premise that only the named insured is responsible for paying a deductible or self-insured retention is also consistent with insurance and risk management industry custom and practice. Despite this, however, some insurers persist in asserting that additional insureds also must pay the deductible amount. It is contrary to generally accepted principles and the expectations of insureds that anyone other than a named insured will be charged with the deductible amount, absent specific notification to that effect.

Problems are exacerbated where a deductible endorsement is silent on who pays. While industry practice and the expectations of insureds hold that the named insured bears this obligation, insurers often persist in attempts to have the deductible applied to the named insured and any additional insureds. This can cause the named insured considerable problems where it has also agreed to indemnify the additional insured who is being charged with paying the deductible. The argument that an additional insured must pay the deductible under a fronting policy is unusual and would cause many insureds obligated to provide additional insured status to be in breach of their contractual obligations to do so. If all of the coverage contractually required by an additional insured is subjected to a deductible or self-insured retention (as in a fronting arrangement), the very thing bargained for and agreed to (additional insured coverage) is eliminated from the outset. The net result is to defeat one of the principal reasons for requiring additional insured status in the first place.

Lack of clarity in the wording of deductible endorsements may also hinder the insurer. Consider the case of *Columbia Cas. Co. v Northwest National Insurance Co.,* 282 Cal Rptr 389 (Cal App 4 Dist 1991). In this case, a fronting insurer provided limits of $1 million with a deductible of the same amount. The court ultimately found a lack of clarity in the deductible endorsement in relation to other policy provisions. The lower court had granted the fronting insurer's motion for a judgment on the pleadings, holding that it merely stood behind or guaranteed the insured's obligation to pay the first million dollars of any covered loss.

On appeal, the umbrella insurer argued that the fronting insurer should pay $1 million above the $1 million deductible. The fronting insurer, in turn, argued that it was a pure fronting policy, clear and unambiguous on its face. The appellate court, in reviewing the propriety of the lower court's granting a motion for a judgment on the pleadings, said that the fronting policy was:

> … by no means unambiguous …. More a vehicle for Jesuitical or Talmudic debate than a definition of the rights and obligations of the parties to the contract, the policy crosses one's eyes and boggles one's mind.

The court pointed to the wording of a combined single limits endorsement attached to the policy that purported to indemnify against "ultimate net loss" while imposing a total liability on the fronting insurer of $1 million as the result of any one occurrence.

The court also noted an "indemnification endorsement" obligating the insurer to reimburse the insured for "ultimate net loss," defined in an "ultimate net loss" endorsement as the total sum the insured may pay as a consequence of an occurrence. The court then contrasted this wording with that of the deductible endorsement, which provided that $1 million was to be deducted from any loss. The insurer, the court held, read the deductible endorsement as taking away what it gave in the combined single limit endorsement. The fronting insurer sought to blunt the ambiguity allegations by arguing that its policy, labeled as one of indemnity, was merely a surety instrument. The court had problems with this position in relation to the standard required to sustain a motion for a judgment on the pleadings and ruled against the fronting insurer, reinstating it as a defendant and remanding the case back to the lower court.

Pay-on-Behalf versus Indemnity

The *Columbia* case, discussed above, is a complex case that raises more than merely the issue of clarity in the deductible endorsement. It also seeks to make a distinction between "pay-on-behalf" and "indemnity" policies in relation to a fronting policy. In doing so, the fronting insurer alleges that, because it utilizes an indemnity format, it is nothing more than a surety. That argument trivializes the complex mechanics of a fronting policy and virtually abolishes the notion of liability coverage being provided by indemnity and pay-on-behalf formats. While both are considered to be liability policies, there is a distinction between a pay-on-behalf form and an indemnity policy. It can be argued that an indemnity policy reimburses the insured after the insured first pays a loss.[19]

Some policies include what is known as a loss payable clause, which defines precisely when a policy is obligated to pay. However, in practical application, there is seldom a distinction made by insurers providing liability coverage. Claims generally are paid once the insured is legally obligated to pay, regardless of whether the insured has first paid the sums owed. Requiring that the insured first pay the loss would, in essence, force many small entities into bankruptcy. The net result would be that even after bankrupting the insured by insisting it pay first, the insurer would still end up paying on the insured's behalf because insolvency of the insured will not, in most cases, eliminate the insurer's obligation to pay. Otherwise, insurers utilizing indemnity insuring agreements, as opposed to those stating that they pay on behalf, could simply force their insureds into bankruptcy by insisting they pay large losses before being reimbursed by the insurer. Were such conduct allowed, the insurer could then seek to avoid its bargained-for obligation. While some insurers argue that "indemnity" means they have no obligation until the insured has first paid, this typically is discretionary with the insurer.

The assertion that an indemnity insuring agreement in a fronting arrangement is nothing more than a surety arrangement cannot be sustained in the eyes of insureds and pursuant to insurance and risk management industry custom and practice. As this chapter repeatedly points out, fronting arrangements involve the issuance of a policy that is represented to and relied on by third parties, including additional insureds, as an insurance policy. It is not logical to argue that the insurer is a surety for additional insureds any more than it is to argue that it is a surety for a named insured when a fronting policy has been issued. The insurer pays for defense and indemnity and is reimbursed by the insured.

In many cases, side agreements obligate the insured to reimburse the insurer, in addition to deductible endorsements, all of which points to an intent that the insurer will pay and the insured will later reimburse it. Absent a contractual agreement that the fronting insurer has no obligations other than to induce others to rely on the existence of its policy (inherently problematic in its own right), the insurer assumes the risk of the insureds insolvency or unwillingness to pay. Given that a fronting arrangement functions as insurance—that many courts interpret and apply the coverage provided under a fronting policy in the same manner

as traditional insurance—the argument that fronting is merely a surety creates an incredible contradiction. It also places the named insured in a precarious situation in relation to its contractual obligations under a fronting policy.

Summary

Whatever the additional insured's motive is for wanting to be covered by the liability policy of another, protection is shaped by what the parties intended only for contractual liability coverage, along with what is otherwise legal and what the insurer is willing to give. While there may be some overly selfish reasons behind an additional insured's request for protection at another's expense, it is probably safe to say that most such insureds want the insurance to fund insurable risks, especially in cases when the contractual transfer may be unenforceable, and to prevent suits in subrogation. To impose a contractual risk transfer without an insurance backup can invite trouble if the contract turns out to be null and void.

The nature of contractual risk transfer is changing. At one time, all an indemnitee may have desired was protection against its vicarious liability. An example is a landowner who hires a contractor to perform some work. If the contractor causes injury to a third party, the landowner wants to be protected by the tortfeasor. Currently, however, the third party is commonly the contractor's employee who files suit against the landowner. But to get into the landowner's "deep pocket," it must be alleged that it is the landowner who is the tortfeasor or who is the party primarily liable. Whether the allegations are true or not, the landowner is now confronted with an action that, "but for" this job by the contractor, would not have arisen. It is for these kinds of legal actions that broader contractual agreements and additional insured endorsements are sought.

Yet, there is no guarantee that the insurance as prescribed for the additional insured necessarily will respond in time of need. Coverage not only is based on the provisions of the liability policy but also on how the additional insured endorsement is worded.

It does make good sense, however, to remember that a contract of indemnity ought to be viewed separately from a contract of insurance. Contracts of indemnity trigger contractual liability insurance. The coverage then is determined by the indemnity agreement, assuming otherwise encompassed by the policy. In insurance, it is the policy wording that dictates coverage. So whether the underlying contract is valid or not, with additional insured status, the resulting risks of loss can be handled by professional risk takers who are better equipped financially to do so than the ones who initially accepted such risks.

Chapter 4 Notes

1. As discussed in **Chapter 13,** this additional insured endorsement may specifically name the additional insured or it may provide blanket additional insured status to entities with whom the named insured agrees in a contract to provide additional insured status. Of course, it also is possible for a provision providing such blanket additional insured status to be incorporated directly into a nonstandard or manuscript liability insurance form, eliminating the need for an endorsement.

2. Employees are automatic insureds under 1986 and later edition commercial general liability policy forms.

3. This is not to be confused with common law indemnity where one who seeks to be indemnified in the absence of an express agreement must prove freedom from fault. This usually involves a court distinguishing between the active and passive fault of the parties. The one who is found to be passively at fault wins.

4. Technically speaking, an indemnity provision involves the obligation to reimburse, with one party (the indemnitor) agreeing to indemnify another upon the occurrence of a loss. A hold harmless agreement is similar in that the indemnitor assumes the liability inherent in a situation, relieving the other party of responsibility.

5. For a current status of hold harmless laws by jurisdiction, see Wielinski, Patrick J., "Hold Harmless Agreements in Construction Industry," *Construction Risk Management,* Vol. 2, X.D.1, Dallas, TX: International Risk Management Institute, Inc., May 1994; Wielinski, Patrick J., Woodward, W. Jeffrey, and Gibson, Jack, "Indemnity Provisions," *Contractual Risk Transfer,* Vol. I, Section II, Dallas, TX: International Risk Management Institute, Inc.; or Parkerson, G. Bruce, "The Enforceability of Broad Form Hold Harmless Clauses," *The Risk Report,* Vol. XVI, No. 7, Dallas, TX: International Risk Management Institute, Inc., March 1994.

6. See *46 American Law Reports 4th and Supp.* for a discussion of the seminal case of *American Nurses Association v Passaic General Hospital,* 484 A2d 670 (Sup Ct NJ 1984), and subsequent cases of other jurisdictions dealing with the question of whether self-insurance is considered to be other insurance for purposes of a liability insurance policy. See also "Insuring Sole Fault Indemnity," *Malecki on Insurance,* Vol. 4, No. 11, Sept. 1995.

7. Usually contracts that contain hold harmless agreements are prepared in such a way that indemnity is wholly separate from the indemnitor's obligation to obtain insurance. So, for example, if insurance does not cover the claim, the indemnitor may still be accountable. It therefore might be in the best interests of the indemnitor to get the other party to agree that any insurance obtained is intended to satisfy any obligation to indemnify.

8. Insurance certificates are discussed more fully in **Chapter 20.**

9. A corollary point of interest is that some courts will enforce an otherwise void hold harmless agreement to the extent that at least part of it is lawfully enforceable. Thus, for example, if the law voids the indemnitee's attempted sole liability transfer, and the ultimate liability between the indemnitor and indemnitee is concurrent or joint, the indemnity agreement may still be enforced to the extent permitted by law. See the cases of *Chrysler Corp. v Brencal Contractors, Inc.,* 381 NW2d 814 (Mich 1985); and *Texaco, Inc., v East Coast Management,* 719 F Supp 319 (D NJ 1989).

10. *43 American Jurisprudence 2d 312,* Insurance, Sec. 253.

11. Insurers assume they can approach coverage in this manner when contractual liability coverage is involved because this coverage essentially applies to the named insured. The coverage applies to the named insured's assumption of another's tort liability. However, this approach to coverage is not without risk to the insurer. Because the named insured has agreed to indemnify (and usually defend) another party, the insurer's conduct in delaying payment may result in allegations of breach of contract against the named insured.

12. There is still one potential argument that an insurer could make in attempting to avoid providing a defense for an additional insured: It is not obligated to defend because the additional insured has its own insurance. Often, the result of this tactic is for the additional insured's own insurer to provide the defense and then seek reimbursement of costs and damages from the other insurer. As was the case with insurers that delay providing protection to indemnitees of the named insured, this can lead to problems for the insured and the insurer. A refusal by the insurer to defend could lead to allegations of breach of contract against the named insured. One of the reasons additional insured status is sought is to avoid the necessity for the indemnitee to use its own policy. If the indem-

nitee is forced to have its own insurance defend a suit, the very purpose underlying additional insured status has been thwarted. This subject of other insurance is discussed more fully in **Chapter 5.**

13. Couch, George J., *Couch on Insurance 2nd,* Sec. 61:134, Rochester, NY: The Lawyers Co-operative Publishing Co., 1968.

14. Builders risk policies often are the source of subrogation attempts by insurers against co-insureds. See, for example, "Builders Risk Subrogation," *Construction Risk Management,* Dallas, TX: International Risk Management Institute, Inc.

15. The Amendment of Contractual Liability Exclusion for the Personal Injury endorsement was revised in 1992 as part of the contractually assumed defense within limits filing discussed previously in this chapter. The new endorsement was introduced for used in 1997.

16. The payment of premium is not always a criterion to be an additional insured. See, for example, the case of *City of Northglenn, Colo., v Chevron U.S.A.,* 634 F Supp 217 (DC Colo 1986).

17. See **Chapter 6** for a discussion of "severability of interests."

18. Another issue that arises when there are multiple insureds on a policy is whether notice of an occurrence by one insured satisfies the notice requirement for another insured. This was particularly important under the pre-1986 policies because they required notice from insureds, not just named insureds. There is some common law precedent that holds that notice by the named insured inures to the benefit of all insureds. This means that under policies that still require insureds to give notice of an occurrence, the notice requirement may be considered as having been fulfilled with notification to the insurer by the named insured.

19. Perhaps the purest example of the "indemnity contract" concept is found in reinsurance; the reinsurer's assumption of risk constitutes a contract of indemnity because the reinsurer's obligation, if there is coverage, is to indemnify only the ceding company. In the reinsurance context, a primary insurance policy (i.e., between a policyholder and an insurer) is referred to as a contract of liability, presumably because the insurer pays damages on behalf of, rather than indemnifying, the insured. Outside of the context of reinsurance terminology, however, assertions that only primary insurance may be viewed as a contract of liability create confusion, because reinsurance placed on a liability risk is as much liability insurance as is a primary liability policy.

Chapter 5

PROBLEMS WITH ADDITIONAL INSURED STATUS

A variety of potential coverage problems confronts both additional insureds and named insureds, some of which have been discussed in previous chapters. It is the party that adds another to its policy (the indemnitor or named insured) that faces most of the problems rather than the party being added (the indemnitee or additional insured). However, there are also disadvantages for the additional insured. Some of the most important problems of named insureds and additional insureds are listed in Exhibit 5.1. These problems are the focus of this chapter.

Dilution of Limits

One of the more commonly voiced disadvantages to named insureds that add others as insureds on their policies is the possible dilution of the named insured's limits of insurance. This is made clear in severability of interest provisions where the policy is said to apply separately to each insured against whom a claim is made or suit is brought *except* with respect to the policy's limits. When other insureds have access to a named insured's policy, all must share the limits applicable to any occurrences that result in claims against one or more of such insureds. While this is indeed a disadvantage to the named insured, it is not unique to additional insured status.

The problem also exists when another party has access to the named insured's limits through an enforceable hold harmless clause, i.e., when the named insured's contractual liability insurance protects the other party.

Under a standard commercial general liability (CGL) insurance policy, the limits may reduce even more quickly under these circumstances, because covered defense costs are within policy limits, unless the 12 conditions imposed by the Supplementary Payments provision applicable to Coverage A and B can be met. (Refer to the discussion of these conditions on page 75.) The problem, from the standpoint of hold harmless clauses in construction contracts, is that the first of the Supplementary Payments conditions requires that an indemnitee be named in the suit in which the insurer also is defending its named insured.

**EXHIBIT 5.1
ADDITIONAL INSURED
STATUS PROBLEMS**

Named Insured's Problems

- Dilution of policy limits

- Defense conflicts

- Providing unintended coverage

- Overriding the indemnity provision

Additional Insured's Problems

- Loss of defense control

- Increased likelihood of coverage disputes

- Other insurance conflicts

- Possible loss of governmental immunity

In most, if not all, third-party-over actions, however, the only party named in a suit will be the named insured's indemnitee. The common scenario involves a subcontractor (indemnitor) who agrees to hold harmless and indemnify a general contractor (indemnitee). An employee of the subcontractor is injured, collects workers compensation benefits, and then files suit against the general contractor (the indemnitee) for having caused the injuries. Considering that workers compensation is the exclusive remedy against the employer (subcontractor), only the general contractor will be named in the suit. In such cases, the first of the 12 conditions for CGL defense of the indemnitee outside policy limits cannot be met. Any reimbursement of the indemnitee's defense costs will be made as covered "damages" and will be paid from the policy's applicable limit of insurance.

Thus, dilution of limits poses the same problems absent additional insured status that it does with it, where the named insured has agreed to indemnify another. Either way, the limits of the named insured will be diluted to pay for the claim or suit. As a matter of fact, in some instances the problem of dilution can arise without additional insured status or an indemnity obligation.

If the named insured causes a loss, the obligation to reimburse for its percentage of fault for that loss will likely arise via a suit for negligence, common law indemnity, or some other legal theory. While dilution, therefore, may be more of a problem with additional insured status, it is by no means a problem that arises solely because the named insured has provided additional insured status to others. However, while there are few court cases on this subject, one should not conclude that the dilution of policy limits might not be a problem. One of the cases dealing with the dilution of limits issue is *Hartford Accident & Indemnity Co. v Firemen's Insurance Co. of Newark, NJ,* 536 NYS2d 260 (NY 1989). An agreement was drawn up between a county and a city over the sponsorship of a federally funded work program. This agreement contained a hold harmless clause in the county's favor that reads in part as follows.

The operator [City] shall hold and save the Government, the sponsor [County], their offic-ers, agents, and employees, harmless from liability of any nature or kind, including costs and expenses, for or on account of any or all suits or damages sustained by any persons or property resulting in whole or in part, from the negligent performance or omission of any employee, agent, representative of the operator *by endorsement of an insurance policy naming the Government and Prime Sponsor and* [sic] *additional insured.* [Emphasis added.]

A child was subsequently injured, and suit was brought against the city and county. The city had failed to name the county as an additional insured on the city's policy, and the city's insurer refused to defend the county. Accordingly, the county's insurer had to provide defense for its insured. The case was eventually settled for $570,000, with the city's insurer paying $300,000 for the city's liability, the county's insurer paying $250,000 for the county's liability, and a third party paying $20,000. The county's insurer then commenced an action against the city and its insurer to recoup what it had paid on behalf of the county.

Despite the city's negligence in failing to obtain the necessary additional insured endorsement, the court held that the county, having been protected by its insurer, was not damaged and therefore was not entitled to recover the amounts expended. The evidence revealed that the city intended to have the county added to its policy but failed to do so. However, the city's policy was subject to a limit of $300,000 per occurrence and aggregate. Since the total policy limit was paid on the city's behalf, no further coverage was available. The court explained that even if the insurance policy of the city had been endorsed properly, no greater amount than the policy limit would have been paid.

The court also pointed out that the indemnity clause of the policy was poorly drafted and vague. It did not state which policy was to be endorsed to cover the additional insured or mention the amount for which the county was to be held harmless. As a result, the city could have procured coverage for an insignificant amount and still been in compliance with the hold harmless clause.

The county also argued to no avail that in light of the hold harmless agreement between the two parties and the contractual liability insurance that was provided, there was an additional $300,000 available for this coverage. This point, likewise, was overruled by the court in consideration of the policy's aggregate limit.

A related problem—which causes the named insured's limits to be diluted even more than it may at first appear—is that amount of coverage provided to an additional insured is not usually capped by the limits that are contractually required of the named insured. As with other legal liability exposures, it is virtually impossible for an indemnitee to quantify what the maximum liability might be in a given instance arising out of the contracted-for work or services. For this reason, most contract drafters word insurance requirements such that they specify a minimum amount of liability insurance to carry rather than the exact amount to carry. For example, such a provision might require the indemnitor to purchase "commercial general and umbrella or excess liability insurance with a total each occurrence limit of not less than $X,000,000."

As discussed in more detail in **Chapter 14,** many umbrella and excess liability policies are structured such that an additional insured in an underlying policy is automatically provided additional insured status in the umbrella or excess policy. Therefore, it is common for additional insured status to apply above the contractually required limits.

It is possible to mitigate this problem by modifying the named insured's policies to cap the amount of insurance provided to an additional insured to the limits required in the underlying contract. Such policy provisions are standard features in the umbrella policies of some insurers and are sometimes added by endorsement to CGL policies. This measure could present some different problems, however. First, unless the indemnity agreement is also subject to the same dollar limitation, a dispute may arise with the insurer as to whether coverage is being provided under the contractual liability coverage in response to the indemnity provision or under the additional insured provisions, which are subject to the lower limit of liability. Second, if the

contract's insurance requirement specifies a minimum limit of liability rather than an exact amount, there would still be room for dispute between the parties as to whether the limitation should apply. Third, this could result in allegations that the insurance and indemnity contract are interdependent and thus inextricably tied.

To effectively cap the amount of coverage being provided to an indemnitee that is also an additional insured, the following actions would be prudent.

1. Contractually cap the indemnitor's liability under the indemnity agreement to the same dollar amount as the limits of liability insurance being required.

2. The contract's insurance requirements should clearly indicate that the limits being required are the exact amount expected by the indemnitee.

3. Endorse the named insured's liability policies to apply a sublimit on the liability coverage provided to the additional insured equal to the amount of insurance required in the contract.

Defense Conflicts

Another problem with additional insured status, particularly for the named insured's insurer, involves the possibility of conflicts of interest in defending claims. When a lawsuit is brought against both a named insured and an additional insured, often the best defense for one of the parties involves condemnation of the actions of the other party. This can present an insurer charged with defending both parties with severe conflicts of interest. Under the laws of most states, this conflict is resolved by retention of separate counsel at the insurer's expense.

It is important to note that this additional legal expense also can have the effect of diluting the policy's protection when the legal costs are within, rather than in addition to, the limits. While the standard Insurance Services Office, Inc. (ISO), commercial general liability (CGL) forms and most umbrella forms provide defense coverage in addition to policy limits, this could be a problem for named insureds that must buy coverage on more restrictive forms.

In addition, liability policies usually state that the insurer's right and duty to defend ends when it has used up the applicable limit of insurance in the payment of judgments or settlements. Thus, further defense protection may be in jeopardy when the policy includes additional insureds, particularly when the claim or suit is filed against a named insured and one or more additional insureds.

When the named insured (indemnitor) has a layered insurance program, and the limits of any primary policy are exhausted, the first dollar of protection available to the additional insured should come from the next policy in the indemnitor's excess layer, which may be the umbrella policy or an excess liability policy.

Providing Unintended Coverage

Another possible problem that named insureds face when they provide insured status to others involves providing coverage for liability exposures the named insured does not intend to cover. This often is the case when the endorsement used to grant additional insured status is poorly worded. Without clearly defined limitations on the coverage provided, it is possible that an additional insured can be given general insured status and coverage could extend beyond the activities covered by the underlying contract. This should not be taken to mean that steps necessarily must be taken in every instance to impose limitations, since the intent may occasionally be to provide the additional insured with protection as broad as that provided to the named insured.[1] However, this is not generally the intent when an otherwise unrelated party is added to the policy in compliance with a contractual requirement. Therefore, it is usually necessary to make sure that the coverage constraints are made clear to all parties and that the policy is endorsed accordingly. Absent a policy limitation, coverage for additional insureds applies as broadly as the policy wording allows.

Part of the current problem as perceived by some is that ISO endorsements are standardized forms, so-called shelf forms, because they are designed for general use without regard to the respective desires of the parties to a particular agreement. In reality, most standard endorsements do limit the protection an additional insured receives. For example, the additional insured does not receive protection unless its liability is related to the named insured's work or operations for the additional insured. Many times, additional insureds incur liability arising solely out of their own conduct or the work of other additional insureds that is unrelated to the work of the named insured. To provide exactly the right scope of coverage for specific situations, manuscript endorsements must often be used. Unfortunately, the problem here is that many underwriters are not willing to draft, or may be prohibited from drafting, endorsements even though they may more closely fit the needs of the insured.

In addition, it must be remembered that additional insureds play no role in procuring the policy and usually never receive a copy. As noted in **Chapters 4 and 6,** it is therefore possible for courts to hold that the policy's limitations do not apply to the coverage afforded an additional insured. From a practical and competitive standpoint, utilization of manuscript endorsements requires numerous other changes, including probable use of standard contract provisions. Because such an approach would be nearly impossible to implement, monitor, and control, it is not a practical option for most insurers to apply across the board. There are numerous manuscript endorsements in use, but many of these endorsements come with their own sets of problems.

Overriding the Indemnity Provision

As discussed in **Chapter 4,** additional insured status and indemnification under a contract's hold harmless clause operate independently of each other. And, since contractual liability insurance responds only to the named insured's obligations under the indemnity agreement, additional insured status and contractual liability coverage are likewise independent of each other. As a result, the coverage provided to an additional insured often does not correspond with the scope of liability transferred under the indemnity agreement. In some respects, an additional insured enjoys broader coverage as an additional insured than the protection intended under the contract's indemnity clause.

Consider, for example, the common situation where the contract transfers liability only for joint negligence of the two parties to the indemnitor but also requires the indemnitor to add the indemnitee as an additional insured. The indemnitor would not be contractually obligated to indemnify the indemnitee for liability arising from the indemnitee's sole negligence.

When the named insured's indemnitee also has additional insured status under the named insured's CGL policy, it has traditionally been the case that the indemnitee had more protection for claims against it *as an insured* than it did by invoking the indemnity agreement. The reason for this disparity was that standard additional insured endorsements were historically broad enough to cover the additional insured's sole negligence, while in most circumstances the indemnity agreement between the named and additional insured would respond, at most, to claims involving shared negligence of the two parties—so-called intermediate form indemnity.

This became a critical problem when the intermediate form indemnity provision was the result of bargaining between the parties. The indemnitee who desired the belt-and-suspenders approach of both indemnification and additional insured status could essentially override the negotiated indemnity provision if a standard endorsement had been used to effect additional insured status for the indemnitee. This often occurred unintentionally because the parties negotiating the contract terms did not have a thorough understanding of the independent operation of these two contractual risk transfer tools. On the other hand, the disparity between the scope of the indemnity agreement and the scope

of required additional insured status was sometimes an *intended* result, particularly given the growing awareness of a need for the belt-and-suspenders approach and the superior bargaining power of many additional insureds.

For indemnitors who were reluctant to provide their indemnitees with more coverage as additional insureds than the indemnitees were requiring in the hold harmless agreement, two courses of action were available. One was simply to resist the request for additional insured status, relying on the indemnity provision backed up with contractual liability insurance. The other was to manuscript an additional insured endorsement that matched in coverage the limited scope of risk transfer accomplished in an intermediate form indemnity agreement.

As it turned out, some insurers in the mid-1990s began to cut back the scope of additional insured coverage regardless of the indemnity arrangement between the named and additional insureds. These insurers amended a standard additional insured endorsement to exclude coverage for any fault attributed to the additional insured. The result was "pure vicarious" liability coverage—coverage only for liability attributed to the additional insured because of its relationship to the named insured. Some other insurers that offered blanket additional insured endorsements were more accommodating by providing broad coverages, if specifically requested in a written contract or agreement.

In July 2004, ISO revised a number of its additional insured endorsements—primarily those used in connection with contracting operations—to eliminate coverage for the additional insured's sole fault. The revised endorsements apply only to claims against the additional insured when injury or damage arises at least partially from the acts or omissions of the named insured. In theory, this more limited approach to providing additional insured coverage keeps the named insured's policy from having to provide a defense to additional insureds that it would not have to provide to the same named insured's indemnitee.

In 13 states, however, construction-related hold harmless agreements are not restricted to intermediate form indemnity as long as the transfer of broader liability is "clear and unequivocal." In these states, when a hold harmless agreement transferring the indemnitee's sole fault is coupled with a standard additional insured endorsement, the additional insured-indemnitee's defense will come as part of the policy's contractual liability coverage. That defense coverage, as already pointed out, will reduce the policy's limits of insurance in many cases (i.e., unless the Supplementary Payments conditions are all met).

Much will depend on the scope of the applicable contractual liability coverage. The broad form contractual liability coverage of the standard CGL policy—encompassing assumption by the named insured of the sole fault of the indemnitee—can be narrowed by attachment of the Contractual Limitation (CG 21 39) endorsement or the Amendment of Insured Contract Definition (CG 24 26) endorsement.

In light of the 2004 revisions, it is uncertain what the future holds for additional insured status as a risk transfer device. While many insurers are likely to use the standard endorsements, others issuing their own independently filed CGL policies may continue to offer blanket additional insured coverage—at an appropriate premium—particularly for better risks. Still others may continue to provide additional insured status to the extent required by the underlying contract, or to manuscript endorsements that match contractual obligations more precisely.

Loss of Defense Control

A disadvantage to some indemnitees that want to require others to name them as additional insureds is the possible loss of control of the defense of claims made against them. Many large organizations—particularly those that are heavily self-insured—take very active roles in managing litigation. In most CGL and umbrella liability policies, however, insurers are provided with the exclusive right to control the defense of claims that they

cover. Therefore, an organization included as an insured in another party's policy may benefit from the insurance protection but lose control over the defense of claims made against it.

On the other hand, hold harmless provisions in contracts can be worded in a manner that allows the indemnitee to defend itself and then seek reimbursement for its costs. As noted earlier, this is the approach taken by standard CGL forms, unless the 12 Supplementary Payments conditions can be met (see page 75). Of course, the disadvantage of this approach is that the indemnitee must rely exclusively on the enforceability of the hold harmless clause and the application of the indemnitor's contractual liability insurance to fund the transferred losses. The more practical and cost-effective approach for firms that would normally defend their own interests is to provide their own defense counsel to monitor what insurance defense counsel is doing.

Increased Likelihood of Coverage Disputes

Becoming an additional insured in another's liability policy, as opposed to relying solely on the enforceability of a hold harmless clause and the indemnitor's contractual liability insurance, may increase the possibility of coverage disputes with the indemnitor's insurer to some extent. One area for possible coverage disputes concerns the policy's treatment of cross-liability claims—claims by one insured against another insured. This topic is discussed at length in the next chapter.

Another possible problem area concerns the application of the policy's exclusions. Policy exclusions that specifically do not apply to the contractual liability coverage—such as the aircraft and watercraft exclusion and the employee injury exclusion—may be interpreted to apply to the coverage provided to an additional insured. Take, for example, the aircraft and watercraft exclusion. It specifically does not apply to liability the named insured assumes under an insured contract. Therefore, a contractor's contractual liability coverage would protect the owner of a construction project that is an indemnitee but not an additional insured for a suit against the owner for bodily injury sustained by a third party resulting from the contractor's use of an aircraft or watercraft. If, on the other hand, the owner was an insured in the contractor's policy, an insurer could attempt to deny the claim since the exclusion applies to "aircraft or watercraft owned or operated by or rented or loaned to any insured."

In addition, other exclusions may be applied differently to that of an additional insured's coverage than they would to that of an indemnitee that is held harmless. A good example of this is the exclusion in the 1988 and subsequent editions of the CGL forms that precludes coverage for "property damage to personal property in the care, custody, or control of the insured." Assume, for example, that an organization is constructing a second building on its premises and allows the contractors to store their equipment in its existing building during off-hours. Further assume that a fire occurs due to the joint negligence of the project owner and the general contractor, and that equipment owned by the various subcontractors is damaged or destroyed.

If the owner had an enforceable hold harmless clause with the general contractor but was not an additional insured in the general contractor's policy, the contractor/indemnitor's contractual liability insurance would cover claims made against the owner by the various subcontractors. The care, custody, or control exclusion would not apply, because the equipment was not in the care, custody, or control of the contractor (the insured) and the owner was not an insured under the policy. If, however, the owner were also an additional insured in the contractor's policy, an insurer could assert that the care, custody, or control exclusion applied to the loss and attempt to deny the owner coverage. In this particular situation, the severability of interest provision, discussed in **Chapter 6,** would probably cause the exclusion to remain inapplicable.

Another way of avoiding the dilemma is to ensure that an enforceable indemnity agreement accom-

panies additional insured status. As previously stated, the belt-and-suspenders concept of both forms of protection is important to retain. In the preceding example, if coverage were excluded for the additional insured, the named insured could invoke the contractual liability coverage to get the job done. However, the possibility of a dispute cannot be ignored.

Additional Insured versus Contractual Liability Coverage

A commonly asked question is, "When both additional insured and contractual liability coverages are available, which coverage applies to the claim or suit?" The answer is whichever one covers the loss. Insurers cannot pick and choose which coverage they want to invoke so as to eliminate coverage. If both forms of protection are available, the insurer must provide all of the protection possible.

If a portion of the loss is excluded for an additional insured, then the named insured has the option of invoking the contractual liability coverage. This can be an effective alternative as long as the named insured's policy has not been endorsed to restrict the scope of contractual liability coverage. (Two such restrictive endorsements are the Contractual Limitation (CG 21 39) endorsement and the Amendment of Insured Contract Definition (CG 24 26) endorsement.) Unless modified in this way, the CGL policy will respond to the named insured's obligation under any insured contract—even one that transfers the indemnitee's sole negligence. However, the use of endorsements limiting contractual liability coverage has become more widespread in recent years. It should not automatically be assumed, therefore, that status as an indemnitee represents broader protection than a standard additional insured endorsement.

If the insurer refuses to provide this alternate form of protection, the named insured will be forced to pay the loss on its own. That, in turn, would be breach of the insurer's duty to the named insured and could lead to a bad faith allegation.

The Other Insurance Problem

Probably the most significant problem for both additional insureds and named insureds is the conflict between other insurance clauses. For many liability claims, an additional insured is covered by both its own liability policies and those on which it is an additional insured. Usually these policies will have identical other insurance clauses. Worse yet, these policies will sometimes have conflicting other insurance clauses. The result is often litigation to determine which policies pay and how.

When the reasons for requiring additional insured status are considered, disputes over other insurance seem unfair to additional insureds. After all, one of the reasons for requesting additional insured status is to obtain a certain amount of *primary* protection as the first recourse under the liability policy of the named insured. However, when the named insured's insurer raises the other insurance issue, it has the tendency to defeat one of the very purposes for being an additional insured.

The number of cases on this issue is growing, and the courts have not been consistent in their findings. Some of these cases are discussed in the sections that follow. The discussion is divided into two groups of cases: those with holdings that did not follow the intent of additional insureds/indemnitees and those with holdings that did follow this intent.

Cases That Departed from the Indemnitee's Intent

In these cases, the courts took each party's own liability insurance into consideration and decided that either the indemnitor's liability policy was considered excess (rather than primary) or the policies of both were to be prorated. With either outcome, the solution of the court clearly was contrary to the intent of the additional insured. However, as previously discussed, where additional insured status is involved, it is policy wording that should control and not external (parol) evidence of an intent not recognized by policy wording.

The first such case is *Deerfield Management Co. v Ohio Farmers Insurance Co.,* 529 NE2d 243 (Ill App 1988). Legal and equitable title to a hotel was held by a bank, as land trustee, but cared for by a real estate management firm/lessor as the bank's agent. One of the ground floor tenants of the building was a dry cleaner/lessee. A fire that originated in the dry cleaner's portion of the premises resulted in several injuries and deaths, and subsequent suit was brought against the real estate management firm. The lease with the dry cleaner reads in part as follows.

> Lessee hereby indemnifies and holds Lessor and its agents and employees harmless for all claims and any costs, including attorneys' fees, related thereto, made by any person arising out of Lessee's use and operation of the leased premises. Lessee shall carry comprehensive public liability insurance with a policy limit of at least $500,000 per individual or occurrence. Such insurance shall be carried with a financially sound carrier and shall name Lessor as an additional insured. Lessor shall be furnished with a certificate of insurance requiring at least 10 days' prior written notice to Lessor of the cancellation of such insurance.

In compliance with the above provision, the dry cleaner/lessee carried liability insurance with itself as the named insured and the real estate management firm/lessor as an additional insured. The parties agreed that both the policy purchased by the real estate management firm on its own behalf and the dry cleaner's policy, under which it was an additional insured, would cover the real estate management firm. However, the parties disagreed over which policy should be primary and which should apply in excess.

The other insurance provision of the dry cleaner's liability policy reads as follows.

> This insurance shall apply only as excess insurance over any other valid and collectible insurance which would apply in the absence of this policy, except insurance written specifically to cover as excess over the limit of liability applicable to Section II of the policy.

In contrast, the other insurance provision of the real estate management firm's liability policy reads as follows.

> The insurance afforded by this policy is primary insurance, except when stated to apply in excess of or contingent upon the absence of other insurance. When this insurance is primary and the insured has other insurance which is stated to be applicable to the loss on an excess or contingent basis, the amount of the insurer's liability under this policy shall not be reduced by the existence of such other insurance.

Based on these provisions, the court concluded that the real estate management firm/lessor's liability policy was primary. The real estate management firm argued that the terms of the lease indicated that the parties' intent was for the dry cleaner's policy to apply as primary. The court disagreed for two reasons. First, there was no indication that the dry cleaner's insurer ever considered the provisions of the lease in its dealings with its named insured prior to the execution of the policy. Second, the lease did not require primary insurance and did not indicate an intent that the insurance must be primary in all instances. All the lease indicated was that the dry cleaner carry liability insurance for a certain minimum and include the real estate management firm as an additional insured.

In addition, the court made two additional and critical observations in deciding this case. First, there was no issue as to contractual liability coverage being involved. As a result, the intent of the parties could not be decided nor was it determinative in this case dealing with additional insured status. Second, the court noted the obvious. The policy of the real estate agent was worded to be an excess policy and as such applied excess of the dry cleaner's liability policy, which clearly stated it was a primary policy.

In giving full effect to the policy wording involved, the court also noted that the interests of the real estate manager were covered as an additional insured under the policy of the dry cleaner and under the real estate manager's own policy. Therefore, policy wording denoting which policy

was primary and which was excess made the order of application clear and unambiguous.

This case also illustrates the concept of the policy wording controlling the application of coverage for insureds, absent an ambiguity or other problem requiring the court to look outside the policy. If there had been an ambiguity involved or the other insurance clauses had been mutually repugnant in the eyes of the law, then the court would have been free to look outside the four corners of the policy to resolve the dispute.

Obviously, the real estate manager's policy should have been endorsed to clearly state it would apply as excess insurance over that of any party adding it as an additional insured. The policy of the dry cleaner should also have been endorsed to state it would apply on a primary basis in relation to any additional insureds under the policy. Since this was not done, the policy wording that was in place determined the application of coverage.

In another case involving a real estate transaction, the insurers of both the lessor and lessee were required to prorate their respective policy limits. *Hausman v Royal Insurance Co.,* 544 NYS2d 605 (NY 1989), was an action brought by the lessor against the lessee of the premises and its insurer following an action by a claimant who fell and sustained injuries on the premises. While the lessee's insurer admitted its obligation to provide coverage on behalf of the lessor, it contended that there was concurrent coverage due to the lessor's insurance on the property.

The lease agreement contained a clause that stated that the lessee would hold harmless the lessor from any damage resulting from bodily injury on the premises. The lease further provided that the lessee would obtain liability insurance for the benefit of the lessor. The lessee did keep its promise by adding the lessor as an additional insured. As is usually the case, the lessor also maintained its own liability insurance. Both liability policies contained clauses stating that they were excess over any other valid and collectible insurance. The court ultimately ruled that both insurers were to prorate their limits based on the general rule that where multiple policies cover the same risk and each generally purports to be excess to the other, the excess coverage clauses are held to cancel out each other and each insurer contributes in proportion to its limit amount of insurance.

Another case where the application of liability policy limits was contrary to the expectations of the lessor is *Sacharko v Center Equities Limited Partnership,* 479 A2d 1219 (Conn App 1984). Here, the property owner, as lessor, leased certain premises to a restaurant owner as lessee. As a condition of the lease, the lessee agreed to carry liability insurance at its expense and to include the lessor as an additional insured.

The action was brought against the lessor by an employee of the lessee for injuries she sustained in a fall on icy pavement at the rear of the premises. When the lessor submitted this claim to the lessee's insurer, coverage was denied. The lessor's insurer therefore defended the action and ultimately paid damages to the injured party.

The lessee's insurer raised a number of issues to avoid having to pay on behalf of the additional insured. However, the important question for purposes of this discussion concerned which of two insurance policies—one issued to the lessee and the other to the lessor—was to provide primary coverage for the liability of the lessor.

In this case, the other insurance clauses of the two policies were the same, with each policy stipulating that it was primary. Therefore, the court applied the general rule "that all insurers providing primary coverage to an insured are duty bound to defend the insured and will be required to contribute their pro rata share of the cost of defense." Had the policies been endorsed to clarify which applied primary and excess as the named insured and additional insured, this apportionment of damages between the two policies likely would not have been the finding of the court.

One of the more complex cases dealing with a variety of liability and insurance issues, including the other insurance clauses of numerous primary and liability policies, is *Crown Center Re-development Corp. v Occidental Fire & Casualty Co. of NC,* 716 SW2d 348 (Mo App 1986). This case followed the collapse of two elevated skywalks in the lobby of the Hyatt Regency Hotel in Kansas City, Missouri, that killed more than 100 people and injured more than 200 others.

What complicated matters was that each contracting party included the other as an additional insured on its primary and excess liability policies. One set of policies was procured by the owner that designed, constructed, and financed the hotel. The hotel management company, Hyatt, was added as an additional insured on these policies. The second set of insurance policies was maintained by the hotel management company. The hotel owner, Crown Center, was included as an additional insured under this set of insurance policies. Thus, the hotel owner was an additional insured on the hotel management company's set of insurance policies, and the hotel management company was an additional insured on the hotel owner's set of insurance policies.

There was no clear and consistent indication of intent in the policies as to which set should be primary and which excess. Finding that the additional insureds were protected against their direct and vicarious liability under the policies of others and that the other insurance clauses of both insurance lines were the same, the court ruled that the other insurance clauses were mutually repugnant. As a result, the court disregarded all such other insurance clauses and held both sets of insurance to be concurrently applicable. Neither set of insurance policies, in other words, was primary or excess of the other.

Perhaps the most important lesson to be learned from the *Crown Center* case is that it usually is not advisable for two contracting parties to each add the other to their policies as additional insureds. There are no standard additional insured endorsements designed for this purpose, and in almost every case, proper application of the policy terms would lead to a pro rata sharing between the parties' insurers on every claim. This often leads to unequitable results, particularly if one of the parties purchases broader coverage or higher limits than the other. In those situations where the two contracting parties have equal bargaining positions, it generally is preferable for neither party to add the other as an additional insured. They can then each look to the indemnity agreement in the contract to define the extent of each party's liability and rely on their own insurance programs for protection against any liability imposed on them.

Another case that worked to the disadvantage of the additional insured is *Honeywell d/b/a Micro Switch v American Motorists Insurance Co.,* 441 NE2d 348 (Ill App 1982). A food vending company and a manufacturer entered into an agreement whereby the manufacturer gave the vendor the right to install and maintain automatic food vending devices on the manufacturer's premises. Five years later, a separate paragraph was added to this agreement that provided that the vendor would make the manufacturer an additional insured under its policy with minimum limits of $50,000 per person and $100,000 per accident. The agreement did not specify that such insurance adding the manufacturer as an additional insured was to apply on a primary basis as to the manufacturer's already existing policy or that its policy was to apply on an excess basis. The certificate as issued showed that the vendor was maintaining insurance of $1 million, even though the agreement required minimum limits of $50,000/$100,000.

While an employee of the vendor was on the manufacturer's premises servicing food dispensing machines, he slipped and fell. The vendor's employee brought suit against the manufacturer for his injuries, alleging that the dangerous conditions that caused his fall were caused by the manufacturer's employees. When the manufacturer tendered its defense to the vendor's insurer, coverage was declined. In consideration of an indemnity agreement between the two parties, the manufacturer attempted to seek arbitration on the claim. However, the arbitration was denied because the indemnity agreement between the two parties did not relieve the manufacturer from the consequences of its own negligence.

When the underlying tort liability case went to trial, the manufacturer lost. Its insurer paid the damages to the injured person and then instituted a suit in subrogation against the vendor's insurer. The manufacturer's insurer maintained that the certificate of insurance issued by the vendor's insurer made the latter insurer the primary insurer rather than the manufacturer's insurer. However, the lower court ruled in favor of the vendor's insurer in light of the fact that the manufacturer's CGL policy acknowledged that it was primary insurance. Its provision reads as follows.

> When this insurance is primary and the insured has other insurance which is stated to be applicable to the loss on an excess or contingent basis, the amount of the company's liability under this policy shall not be reduced by the existence of such other insurance.

The other insurance clause of the vendor's CGL policy reads as follows.

> The insurance afforded by the policy is primary insurance, except that when this insurance and any other valid and collectible insurance apply to the loss on the same basis, this insurance shall be excess of such other insurance and shall not contribute with such other insurance.

On appeal, the manufacturer's insurer contended that the trial court should have concentrated on the indemnity agreement between the two parties. This showed an intention between the parties for the vendor to insure the manufacturer against any and all claims that might arise out of the vendor's operations on the manufacturer's premises. The manufacturer's insurer argued that, even conceding that its policy made it the primary insurer, the insurance certificate issued on behalf of the vendor showed an intention to make the vendor primarily liable for any injury arising out of the food vending operations. The manufacturer's insurer, in other words, maintained that the intention of the parties should govern over the other insurance clauses of the respective policies.

The Illinois Appellate Court, however, ruled against the manufacturer's insurer, affirming the lower court's decision. In doing so, the court held that it was not necessary to disregard the other insurance clauses and to rely instead on the intention of the parties. In fact, the other insurance clauses were not to be disregarded to make loss payable on a pro rata basis either, the higher court said. On the matter of intent, the court explained that it probably was not the intent of the vendor to furnish insurance relieving the manufacturer from its tort liability for an injury sustained by the vendor's employee on the manufacturer's premises by reason of the manufacturer's negligence. Had the vendor's employee been negligent and caused injury to a third party by his negligent conduct in the course of his operations on the manufacturer's premises, the court explained, the vendor clearly would have been obligated to protect the manufacturer, but this was not the case.

Here again, the court expressly refused to consider the parties' intent in determining coverage when policy wording is clear and unambiguous. Had the two other insurance clauses been the same or mutually repugnant, the court could have opted for a pro rata apportionment or even looked outside the policy for the intent of the parties. However, absent such an ambiguity or other problem, the terms of the policy controlled. Those terms made it clear that one policy was primary and one excess, which is how the court applied coverage.

Cases That Followed the Indemnitee's Intent

Not all cases that go before the courts for resolution on other insurance issues end the way the aforementioned cases did. A number of courts have encountered coordinated other insurance provisions that clearly communicated an intent for the indemnitee's policies to apply in excess of the indemnitor's insurance. A few other courts have reasoned that to decide the issue on the basis of the other insurance provisions alone would abrogate the intent of the contract's indemnity provision, and these courts were remiss to do that. And, finally, in one important decision, the court affirmed the right of an additional insured to choose which policy it desires to have provide its coverage.

Until recently, there were only two endorsements designed to coordinate coverage such that the indemnitee's coverage would apply in excess of the indemnitor's insurance. One was used to make a

vendor's insurance excess of products liability coverage provided for it by its manufacturer; the other accomplishes this goal for real estate managers. The courts have generally upheld the intent of both endorsements.

For example, in *Woodson v A&M Investments,* 591 S2d 1345 (La App 1991), a real estate manager's insurer had attached the Real Estate Property Managed (CG 22 70) endorsement to the named insured's policy. The endorsement includes the following provision.

> With respect to your liability arising out of your management of property for which you are acting as real estate manager this insurance is excess over any other valid and collectible insurance available to you.

As a real estate manager, Woodson was, of course, an automatic additional insured in the policy of A&M. The court held that the intent to provide only excess insurance was clearly expressed by the endorsement to the real estate manager's own policy and ruled that the policy to which the real estate manager was an additional insured applied as primary coverage.

Until 1997, there were no standard endorsements available for use in connection with construction activities to stipulate an intent for the indemnitee's insurance to apply in excess of the indemnitor's insurance. However, manuscript endorsements have been used for this purpose. The courts in most instances have also followed the intent of these endorsements.

A construction case where the named insured's liability policy applied as primary and the additional insured's liability policy applied as excess because of a nonstandard endorsement is *Northbrook Property & Casualty Co. v U.S. Fidelity & Guaranty Co.,* 501 NE2d 817 (Ill App 1986). This case involved a construction manager and two subcontractors whose insurance policies listed the construction manager as an additional insured. The additional insured endorsement of the respective liability policies agreed to cover the additional insured but only with respect to liability arising out of operations performed for the additional insured (construction manager) by or on behalf of the named insured (the subcontractor).

This action arose when two employees, each employed by separate subcontractors, were injured on the job and filed suit against the construction manager, alleging violations under the Illinois Structural Work Act. When the construction manager sought primary protection as an additional insured under the liability policies of the two subcontractors (who had the same insurance company but separate policies), the insurer denied such protection, maintaining that no coverage was afforded to the construction manager under the additional insured endorsement. No further rationale for denying the coverage was given.

The lower court held that: (1) the construction manager was an additional insured under the respective liability policies of the subcontractors, (2) the subcontractor's policies were valid and collectible, as well as primary, (3) the additional insured's liability insurance was excess, and (4) there was no reference in the additional insured endorsement requiring the fault of the respective subcontractors as a condition precedent for coverage under their policies. However, the court did rule that the cost of the additional insured's defense was to be borne equally by its own insurer and the subcontractor's insurer. But on appeal, this latter decision was reversed, and the defense costs of the additional insured construction manager had to be borne solely by the subcontractors' insurer.

The basis of the court's decision was policy wording in the construction manager's policy that made it apply excess of other valid and collectible insurance. Since the court found the subcontractor's insurance to be valid and collectible, the logical conclusion was that the construction manager's policy applied excess of the subcontractor's policy. Again, policy wording dictated coverage between insureds under the policies involved.

Another case where an additional insured was found to have primary protection under the liability policy of another is *Rossmoor Sanitation v Pylon,* 119 Cal Rptr 449 (Cal 1975). The property owner employed a contractor to construct a sewage pump station and certain sewer lines according to plans prepared by an engineering firm retained by the owner. Under the contract, the contractor agreed to indemnify the owner against all claims for damages arising out of the work and for legal costs that might be incurred in the event of a suit for damages. The contractor also agreed to obtain insurance for itself, naming the owner as an additional insured. The contractor did include the owner as an additional insured on its policy, and the owner also purchased liability insurance for its own benefit. The contract reads, in part, as follows.

The Owner, the Engineer, or their authorized assistants shall not be answerable for or accountable in any manner for any loss or damage that may happen to the work or any part thereof, or for any material or equipment used in performing the work, or for injury or damage to any person or persons, either workmen or the public, or for damage to adjoining property from any cause whatsoever during the progress of the work, or any time before final acceptance of the work.

Contractor shall indemnify and save Owner, the Engineer or other authorized assistants harmless against all claims for damages to persons or property arising out of Contractor's execution of the work covered by this contract and any and all costs, expenses, attorneys fees and liability incurred by the Owner, the Engineer, or said assistants, in defending against such claims, whether the same proceed to judgment or not and Contractor at his own expense agrees upon written request of the Owner, to defend any such suit or action brought against the Owner, said Engineer or assistants ....

The Contractor shall not commence work under this contract until he has obtained all insurance required hereunder in a company or companies acceptable to the Owner, nor shall the Contractor allow any subcontractor to commence work on his subcontract until all insurance required of the subcontractor has been obtained. The Contractor shall take out and maintain at all times during the life of this contract the following policies of insurance.

... (2) Public liability and property damage; on account of bodily injuries including death resulting therefrom, in the sum of not less than $500,000 for one person and $1,000,000 for more than one person and property damage in the sum of $1,000,000 resulting from any one accident which may arise from the operations of the Contractor in performing the work provided herein.

Each of the policies of insurance provided for in subparagraphs (1), (2) and (3) shall name Owner as an additional assured.

This case arose following a cave-in that killed one worker and injured another. In a tort action brought by the estate of the decedent and the injured worker, the owner's liability insurer paid certain damages as assessed against the owner, including legal costs. A suit was then filed against the contractor and its insurer, which sought indemnification of the sums paid. However, the contractor's insurer filed a cross-complaint that sought an apportionment of the sums between both insurers pursuant to the other insurance clauses of the respective liability policies.

The lower court reasoned that inasmuch as the contractor's liability policy was part of the consideration for the job, it provided primary coverage to the owner as an additional insured and that the owner's policy applied as excess. The contractor and its insurer, on the other hand, argued that the limits of both policies should be apportioned based on the other insurance clauses of the policies, which both read as follows.

If the insured has other insurance against a loss covered by this policy, the company shall not be liable under this policy for a greater proportion of such loss than the applicable limit of liability stated in the declarations bears to the total applicable limit of all valid and collectible insurance against such loss; ....

The limit of the contractor's policy was $500,000 per occurrence, while the owner's liability policy limit was $1 million per occurrence. The court, nonetheless, ruled that the contractor's liability policy applied on a primary basis. In doing so, the court stated that both insurers calculated and ac-

cepted premiums with knowledge that they might be called on to satisfy a full judgment.

Furthermore, there was no evidence that either insurer knew there was or would be other insurance when they issued the policies. The fact that there was other insurance, the court said, was "a mere fortuitous circumstance." One additional reason given by the court for requiring the contractor's insurer to be primary is that "to apportion the loss ... pursuant to the other insurance clauses would effectively negate the indemnity agreement." It also would impose liability on the owner's insurer, the court added, even though the owner bargained with the contractor to avoid that very result as part of the consideration for the construction agreement.

The court further declared that the indemnity agreement was sufficiently explicit to cover the accident and found that any negligence on the part of the owner that led to the cave-in was merely of a passive nature, i.e., in failing to discover that the contractor's employees intended to enter an unshored trench. On appeal by the contractor and its insurer, the lower court's decision for the owner and its insurer *was affirmed.* In this case, the other insurance clauses both called for proration. While not expressly saying so, this allowed the court to look outside the four corners of the policy to resolve the matter. In doing so, it looked to the underlying intent behind the contracts and the indemnity obligations involved.

Another case where the court considered the contract's indemnification clause in applying coverage is *J. Walters Construction v Gilman Paper Co.,* 620 S2d 219 (Fla App 1993). A construction company (Walters) contracted with a manufacturer (Gilman) to perform construction work at the manufacturer's premises. One of Walters' employees was injured on the job and filed suit against Gilman. The contract between Walters and Gilman included an indemnity clause in favor of Gilman and required Walters to provide Gilman with additional insured status under its liability policies. Thus, Gilman filed an action against Walters and its insurer, CNA, seeking contractual indemnification.

Gilman was added as an additional insured to Walters' policy. However, both Walters and CNA argued that CNA should be responsible for only half of the settlement amount because Gilman had its own insurance with Liberty Mutual that also covered the claim.

The court, however, disagreed with CNA. In doing so, it stated that:

> to apply the "other insurance" provisions to reduce CNA's liability would serve to abrogate the indemnity agreement and that there was no such authority under Georgia law… Only one insurer, CNA, has provided insurance to cover the contractor's "contracted-for liability;" thus, there is no occasion to look to the insurance coverage that Gilman might have obtained independent of its agreement with Walters.

In essence, the court chose to find coverage under Walters' contractual liability insurance rather than under the additional insured endorsement. In doing so, the court was able to fashion relief consistent with the indemnity obligations of the contract as opposed to additional insured status. This approach is logical since Gilman received the same degree of protection that would have been available had it not been included as an additional insured on Walters' policy. To have proceeded otherwise would have penalized Gilman for reinforcing its indemnity provision with the additional insured status. When both contractual liability coverage and coverage as an additional insured apply, the coverage necessary to cover the loss should be applied. Here the court did so in a manner that gave effect to the parties' intent as expressed in the indemnity agreement.[2]

There probably has been no other additional insured case in which a court so specifically followed the intentions of an indemnitee as in *Institute of London Underwriters v Hartford Fire Insurance Co.,* 599 NE2d 1311 (Ill App 1992). Great Lakes Towing retained Thatcher Engineering to repair a damaged dockwall. The agreement between Thatcher and Great Lakes required Thatcher to have Great Lakes named as an additional insured on Thatcher's liability insurance policy, which it did. Thatcher's liability insurer was the Institute of London Underwriters (ILU),

and Great Lakes was insured by Hartford Fire Insurance Co.

When the widow of one of Thatcher's employees killed on the project brought suit against Great Lakes, Great Lakes tendered the defense of the action to Thatcher, requesting coverage under Thatcher's policy with ILU. Great Lakes also notified Hartford of the action but never asked Hartford to defend or indemnify it with respect to the suit. The suit was subsequently settled by ILU for $75,000, and the attorney who had been retained by ILU to defend the underlying action wrote to Hartford requesting it to contribute half of the settlement. Hartford denied any liability for paying half of the claim. This resulted in this declaratory judgment action to determine if an insured may elect which of its insurers under two policies is to defend and indemnify the claim by tendering its defense to one and not the other.

ILU based its claim on the doctrine of equitable contribution (under which one who has paid the entire loss is to be reimbursed from other insurers who are also liable for the loss) and on the Hartford policy's other insurance clause, which indicated that the policy would pay pro rata when it and another policy both applied on a primary basis. The court, however, carefully considered the fact that the insured, Great Lakes, never asked Hartford to defend and indemnify it and had specifically indicated that Hartford should not become involved. The court reviewed the substantial body of legal precedent holding that coverage under a liability policy is not triggered until a tender of defense is made by the insured. It then held that since the insured, Great Lakes, never tendered its defense to Hartford, the Hartford policy was never triggered and, thus, Hartford could not be called on to contribute under either the doctrine of equitable contribution or the other insurance clause.

In this case, the court did not feel compelled to rule on the issue of other insurance or the actual intent of the parties. It based its ruling on the fact that Hartford was never asked to respond to the claim by its insured. It also noted that the demand made by ILU was not made to Hartford until 14 months after the underlying litigation had commenced, something that was deemed to be inadequate to trigger Hartford's obligation.

The CGL Other Insurance Clause

Many of the cases discussed on the preceding pages dealt with other insurance clauses that are identical to or very similar to that included in the standard CGL forms in use prior to 1997. The 1973, 1986, 1988, 1993, and 1996 CGL other insurance clauses are very similar and have the same basic intent. (These clauses are included in Exhibits 5.2 and 5.3.) They establish that the CGL policy is intended to provide the named insured with primary liability insurance protection in all but the very rarest circumstances. It is important for the policy to establish this intent to avoid confusion in determining the application of liability insurance written specifically to provide limits in excess of those provided by the CGL policy (e.g., umbrella liability policies).

These other insurance clauses do not specifically address the issue of coverage available to the named insured as an additional insured under the insurance policy of another party. This is the reason there are so many cases seeking to interpret the application of coverage to additional insureds. Such disputes could be reduced or eliminated simply by specifically addressing this issue in the insurance policies.

One of the key observations to make here is that, at least when the standard CGL form is involved, the policy causing the problem is not that of the indemnitor (named insured). The indemnitor's CGL policy clearly states that it is primary insurance, as is usually the intent of the contracting parties. It is the additional insured's own CGL policy that causes the ambiguity because it also states that it is the primary policy. Since the courts typically look at both other insurance clauses when trying to determine the application of other insurance, the ambiguity can usually be eliminated by adding a provision to the additional insured's own policy stating that it is excess over coverage available under another party's insurance program by virtue of contractually required additional insured status.

EXHIBIT 5.2
1973 CGL OTHER INSURANCE CLAUSE

6. **Other Insurance.** The insurance afforded by this policy is primary insurance, except when stated to apply in excess of or contingent upon the absence of other insurance. When this insurance is primary and the insured has other insurance which is stated to be applicable to the loss on an excess or contingent basis, the amount of the company's liability under this policy shall not be reduced by the existence of such other insurance.

When both this insurance and other insurance apply to the loss on the same basis, whether primary, excess, or contingent, the company shall not be liable under this policy for a greater proportion of the loss than that stated in the applicable contribution provision below:

(a) Contribution by Equal Shares. If all of such other valid and collectible insurance provides for contribution by equal shares, the company shall not be liable for a greater proportion of such loss than would be payable if each insurer contributes an equal share until the share of each insurer equals the lowest applicable limit of liability under any one policy or the full amount of the loss is paid, and with respect to any amount of loss not so paid the remaining insurers then continue to contribute equal shares of the remaining amount of the loss until each such insurer has paid its limit in full or the full amount of the loss is paid.

(b) Contribution by Limits. If any of such other insurance does not provide for contribution by equal shares, the company shall not be liable for a greater proportion of such loss than the applicable limit of liability under this policy for such loss bears to the total applicable limit of liability of all valid and collectible insurance against such loss.

EXHIBIT 5.3
1986-1996 CGL OTHER INSURANCE CLAUSE

4. Other Insurance.

If other valid and collectible insurance is available to the insured for a loss we cover under Coverages A or B of this Coverage Part, our obligations are limited as follows:

a. Primary Insurance

This insurance is primary except when b. below applies. If this insurance is primary, our obligations are not affected unless any of the other insurance is also primary. Then, we will share with all that other insurance by the method described in c. below.

b. Excess Insurance

This insurance is excess over any of the other insurance, whether primary, excess, contingent or on any other basis:

(1) That is Fire, Extended Coverage, Builders Risk, Installation Risk or similar coverage for "your work;"

(2) That is Fire insurance for premises rented to you; or

(3) If the loss arises out of the maintenance or use of aircraft, "autos" or watercraft to the extent not subject to Exclusion g. of Coverage A (Section I)

When this insurance is excess, we will have no duty under Coverages A or B to defend any claim or "suit" that any other insurer has a duty to defend. If no other insurer defends, we will undertake to do so, but we will be entitled to the insured's rights against all those other insurers.

When this insurance is excess over other insurance, we will pay only our share of the amount of the loss, if any, that exceeds the sum of:

(1) The total amount that all such other insurance would pay for the loss in the absence of this insurance; and

(2) The total of all deductible and self-insured amounts under all that other insurance.

We will share the remaining loss, if any, with any other insurance that is not described in this Excess Insurance provision and was not bought specifically to apply in excess of the Limits of Insurance shown in the Declarations of this Coverage Part.

c. Method of Sharing

If all the other insurance permits contribution by equal shares, we will follow this method also. Under this approach each insurer contributes equal amounts until it has paid its applicable limit of insurance or none of the loss remains, whichever comes first.

If any of the other insurance does not permit contribution by equal shares, we will contribute by limits. Under this method, each insurer's share is based on the ratio of its applicable limit of insurance to the total applicable limits of insurance of all insurers.

The case of *Transamerica Insurance Co. v Turner Construction Co.*, 601 NE2d 473 (Mass App 1992), illustrates just how effective this policy modification can be. Turner had required and received additional insured status on the CGL policy of its subcontractor. One of the subcontractor's employees was injured while working on the project and filed suit against Turner. Turner tendered the claim to the subcontractor's insurer, Transamerica; the insurer defended Turner and ultimately paid a settlement to the injured employee. Transamerica then brought suit seeking to collect all or part of the damages it paid on behalf of Turner from Turner's liability insurer, Liberty Mutual Insurance Company.

One of Transamerica's arguments was that Liberty Mutual was obligated to share equally with Transamerica the settlement costs and legal expenses involved with the claim. The court indicated that "this might be the result in cases of overlapping essentially identical coverage." In this case, however, the other insurance provisions were not identical. The Liberty Mutual policy issued to Turner included an endorsement stating that it did not apply to losses for which Turner had coverage as an additional insured on policies purchased by its subcontractors. The endorsement reads as follows.

> It is agreed that this policy does not apply to that portion of the loss for which the Insured has other valid and collectible insurance, as an Additional Insured on a Liability Insurance policy issued to a subcontractor of the Named Insured whether such policy is on a primary, excess or contingent basis.

Commenting on this endorsement, the court said:

> Liberty's policy, thus, was tailored to fit the allocation of risk made by the subcontract. There is a happy—and perhaps uncommon—coincidence of plain language with plain purpose.

Needless to say, the court followed the intent as expressed in the endorsement and did not require Liberty Mutual to share in the settlement costs and legal expenses.

This same modification did not function as intended in *Home Insurance Co. v Liberty Mutual Insurance Co. and Turner Construction Co.*, 641 NE2d 855 (Ill 1994), however. The underlying facts of this Illinois case are very similar to *Transamerica v Turner*. An employee of Turner's subcontractor was injured and filed suit against Turner. One distinguishing fact of this case is that the suit alleged both negligence and a violation of the Illinois Structural Work Act against Turner.

Turner's liability insurer was Liberty Mutual, and Turner was also included as an additional insured in the subcontractor's liability insurance, which was written by Home. The endorsement used by Home to effect Turner's additional insured status was essentially the same as the now-withdrawn ISO endorsement CG 20 09—Form A. This particular additional insured endorsement excluded from coverage liability arising from the acts or omissions of the additional insured other than the additional insured's general supervision of the work. This exclusion played an important role in circumventing the intent of the Liberty policy to coordinate with the insurance available to Turner as an additional insured. The operative wording, as cited by the court, is as follows.

> It is agreed that:
>
> 1. The "persons insured" provision is amended to include as an insured the person or organization named above [Turner], but only with respect to liability arising out of (1) operations performed for [Turner] by the named insured at the location designated above or (2) acts or admissions [sic] of [Turner] in connection with his general supervision of such operations…
>
> 3. Additional exclusions. This insurance shall not apply: …
>
>   (b) To bodily injury or property damage arising out of any act or omission of [Turner] or any of his employees, other than general supervision of work performed for [Turner] by the named insured; …

The other insurance provision of the Home policy was similar to the provision of ISO standard CGL forms and reads as follows.

> Other Insurance. The insurance afforded by this policy is primary, except when stated to apply in excess or contingent upon the absence of other insurance. When this insurance is primary and the Insured has other insurance which is stated to be applicable to the loss on an excess basis or contingent basis, the amount of the company's liability under this policy shall not be reduced by the existence of such other insurance.

> When both this insurance and other insurance apply to the loss on the same basis, whether primary, excess or contingent, the company shall not be liable under this policy for a greater proportion of the loss than that stated in the applicable contribution provision below.

The only provision of the Liberty policy issued to Turner that was pertinent to this case was Endorsement 21. This endorsement added to Turner's policy the same other insurance provision as the court had relied upon in *Transamerica v Turner.*

> It is agreed that this policy does not apply to that portion of the loss for which [Turner] has other valid and collectible insurance, as an additional insured on a liability insurance policy issued to a subcontractor of [Turner] whether such policy is on a primary, excess or contingent basis.

Liberty's primary argument was that it was not obliged to defend because of the language of Endorsement 21. According to the court, the primary area of contention between the parties was whether the endorsement was an "escape clause," which holds the policy null and void to the extent that any other insurance applies, or an "excess clause," which allows coverage only "over and above" other insurance. Home insisted Endorsement 21 was an escape clause. Liberty, on the other hand, insisted its provision was an excess clause and admitted that it would be obliged to contribute on a pro rata basis if its endorsement were an escape clause.

The court stated that Endorsement 21 "does not apply to that portion of the loss for which [Turner] has other valid and collectible insurance" with subcontractors. The only "portion of the loss" for which Turner had other valid and collectible insurance with Home, the court concluded, was for loss caused by Turner's negligence in failing to supervise. Endorsement 21 did not exclude coverage for the other acts alleged in the complaint. Therefore the court reversed the decision of the trial court. It held that Endorsement 21 was an escape clause, that the coverage available to Turner as an additional insured did not cover all the allegations against Turner, and that the insurance provided to Turner was therefore not "collectible" as required by Endorsement 21. Thus, the court held that both Home and Liberty were primary insurers and both were obliged to defend the complaint pro rata.

Liberty had cited *Transamerica v Turner*, pointing out to the court that the very same endorsement was at issue and that the court in that case held the endorsement to apply coverage on an excess basis. However, this court distinguished *Transamerica* from this case because the subcontractor in *Transamerica* had agreed to indemnify Turner "for all claims arising out of or occurring in connection with the execution of the work." "If it was the intent of Turner to require its subcontractors to provide the same coverage that existed in Transamerica, it could have done so," said the court.

Several lessons can be learned from these two cases. First, using an escape clause rather than an excess clause in an other insurance provision to coordinate coverage between the named insured's own policy and that in which it is an additional insured can be problematic. Had Liberty's policy clearly applied coverage on an excess basis above the coverage available to Turner as an additional insured, the outcome might have been completely different.[3] Second, merely requiring "additional insured status" without specifying the extent of coverage to be provided may not be specific enough to avoid the use of restrictive standard or nonstandard additional insured endorsements.[4] Third, it is prudent to assure that the underlying contract clearly conveys the intent of the contracting parties as to whose policy should be primary.[5]

The 1997 Other Insurance Clause

Prior to ISO's 1997 revisions to the CGL forms, there were only two endorsements available in the standard forms portfolio to modify the other insurance clause to make the policy excess when the insured had coverage as an additional insured under another's policy. One of these endorsements, Excess Provision—Vendors (CG 24 10), was designed for use solely in those instances where the additional insured is a vendor covered under the Additional Insured—Vendors (CG 20 15) endorsement attached to its supplier's CGL policy. The other endorsement, the Real Estate Property Managed (CG 22 70) endorsement, is attached to the policy of real estate managers (who are automatic additional insureds in the policies of the owners of the real estate properties they manage, as discussed in **Chapter 3**). There was no standard endorsement for use in other situations, such as when the insured is a contractor or project owner added as an insured to another contractor's policy or when the insured is a lessor added to the policy of its lessee.

Previous editions of this book suggested that manuscript endorsements be used for this purpose, and such endorsements were widely used in the mid-1990s. In 1996 ISO filed "mandatory" endorsements for use with the occurrence and claims-made versions of the CGL policy. These endorsements were approved for use during 1997 in most states. One was an occurrence version (CG 00 55) and the other (CG 00 56) was designed for use with claims-made policies. The endorsements modified paragraph 4.b. of the Other Insurance condition (see Exhibit 5.3). The pertinent addition to the other insurance condition is reproduced in Exhibit 5.4.

While the other insurance clause will help avoid disputes over the application of coverage when a named insured in one liability insurance program is also an additional insured under the liability insurance program(s) of another party(ies), there are some potential problems with the clause.

EXHIBIT 5.4
1997 OTHER INSURANCE CLAUSE AMENDMENT

4. Other Insurance

   b. Excess Insurance

   This insurance is excess over:

   (1) ...

   (2) Any other *primary* insurance available to you covering liability for damages arising out of the *premises or operations* for which you have been added as an additional insured by *attachment of an endorsement.* [Emphasis added.]

Copyright, Insurance Services Office, Inc., 1996

First, note that the excess provision applies only when the other insurance is primary insurance. This leaves open the question of how coverage will coordinate with the other party's umbrella/excess liability program. The additional insured/indemnitee will usually intend for the other party's entire liability insurance limits (or, at minimum, the contractually required limit of liability) to apply first with its own liability insurance program held in reserve. However, this other insurance clause leaves room for the other party's umbrella/excess insurers to argue that, since their policies apply on an excess basis (i.e., they are not primary insurance), the additional insured's own CGL and umbrella/excess policies should either pay first or contribute according to the various policies' other insurance clauses.

Having the excess provision apply only when the other insurance is primary insurance may also cause problems for additional insureds when the other party's policy does not include the standard other insurance clause stating that it is primary. Most CGL policies will include this standard clause, but it can be modified either by endorsement to the standard ISO form or simply by changing the wording used in a policy form drafted by the insurer and either filed with the applicable state or used on an excess and surplus lines basis.

These two problems could be significant for organizations that are often included as additional insureds on the policies of others. To reduce the possibility of their occurring, consideration should be given to striking the term "primary" from the clause.

Another potentially problematic part of the other insurance provision is its dependency on additional insured status being effected by an endorsement. Read literally, this would make it inapplicable when additional insured status is granted automatically by the policy rather than via some endorsement attached to the policy. For example, real estate managers are automatic additional insureds under the standard ISO CGL form (see **Chapter 3**). Similarly, some insurer-drafted primary liability forms and many umbrella/excess liability forms grant additional insured status to any person or organization with whom the insured agrees in a written contract to provide that status. It is hard to imagine an insurer arguing that the obvious intent of the parties should not be carried through based on such a minor technical point, but nevertheless it could occur. For this reason, it may be prudent to request that insurers reword this provision to apply whenever the named insured is an additional insured in another party's policy in compliance with a contractual requirement.[6]

One concern some risk management professionals expressed about modifying their own insurance to be excess when their firms were covered as additional insureds in the policies of others was that their own insurer would require exhaustion of all avenues before stepping in to defend and pay damages (if necessary). To overcome this potential problem, the CGL policy's other insurance clause requires the insurer to defend the named insured in the event the other insurer refuses to do so. The named insured's insurer will then be entitled to the insured's rights against the other insurers for failure to defend.

The other insurance clause's application to other insurance covering "liability for damages arising out of premises or operations" does not preclude it from applying to insurance covering the products and completed operations hazard. The term "operations" in insurance parlance has broad connotations, encompassing both operations in progress and completed operations. Thus, it is no longer necessary to add the Excess Provision—Vendors (CG 24 10) endorsement to the policies of vendors that have been added as additional insureds for the purpose of providing products liability coverage on the policies of manufacturers or distributors, as long as the Amendment of Other Insurance Condition endorsement has been attached to the vendor's policy. It will only be necessary to use the Excess Provision—Vendors (CG 24 10) endorsement if the same result is desired when products/completed operations coverage is being provided by way of the Products/Completed Operations Coverage part. ISO even changed the title of the endorsement, and the *Commercial Lines Manual* rule (#36) governing its use, to reflect this fact.

Mitigating the Other Insurance Problem

The *Institute of London Underwriters v Hartford Fire Insurance Co., supra,* case (see page 121) gives a prescription for overcoming the other insurance problem in the way the claim is submitted to the applicable insurers. Recall that the additional insured, Great Lakes, tendered the claim to its contractor's insurer (ILU), specifically telling its own insurer (Hartford) not to get involved. The court ultimately ruled that Hartford's policy was never triggered because the insured had never tendered the claim to it and, thus, ILU could not recover any of its costs from Hartford. One of the key factors relied on by the court was that Great Lakes was a sophisticated insured with the ability to determine its own best interest in choosing the insurer to which it would tender its claim.

Another case, *Hartford Accident & Indemnity Co. v Gulf Insurance Co.*, 776 F2d 1380 (7th Cir 1985), had previously come to a similar conclusion. The *Hartford* court held that mere knowledge that an insured is sued does not constitute tender of a claim where a sophisticated insured is involved. What was required was knowledge by the insurer that the suit was potentially within the policy's coverage coupled with knowledge that the insurer's assistance was desired.

A subsequent case, *Federated Mutual Insurance v State Farm,* 688 NE2d 627 (Ill App 1996), discussed many of these same issues and made a contrary ruling with respect to some of the findings in *ILU* and *Hartford.* The *Federated* court rejected the distinction between sophisticated and unsophisticated insureds and stated emphatically that requiring a formal tender when the insurer has actual notice is of no benefit to the insurer, except as a loophole through which the insurer might escape a lawful contractual obligation.

However, there is an important factual difference between *Federated* and *ILU. Federated* involved one insurer trying to avoid coverage by asserting that the claim was never submitted to it, rather than an election by the insured. There was no evidence that the insured in *Federated* (a driver of an auto owned by a car dealership) was aware of the second insurance policy, that she conducted an investigation, or that she made an election of insurers to defend her. As a result, the *Federated* court refused to rule that the driver had made an election of insurers. Thus, the ruling leaves unchallenged the right of the insured to select which insurer will defend it. The *Federated* court even recognized this when it summarized "for the foregoing reasons, we hold that an insurer's duty to defend claims potentially falling within the terms of a policy is triggered by actual notice of a lawsuit, regardless of whether the insured is sophisticated or unsophisticated—*provided the insured has not selected one insurer to provide an exclusive defense and there is no prejudice to the insurer."* [Emphasis added.]

The question then becomes, how does an additional insured tender its claim for defense to the insurer(s) without involving its own insurance? First, the additional insured should inform the insurer to whom it is tendering that it does so as an additional insured. Second, the additional insured should point out that it has made an election as to which insurer it wants to defend it and that the election is based on factors the additional insured deems important to protecting its overall interests. Third, the additional insured should indicate that its insurance has been endorsed to apply as excess of other insurance in which it is an additional insured. Fourth, when possible, point out those areas of the complaint that trigger coverage and the policy wording involved. Fifth, the additional insured should inform the insurer that the additional insured is relying on that insurer to protect all of its interests and does not want its own insurer contacted for payment of any portion of the defense or indemnity. Sixth, the insured should tender the claim immediately to avoid incurring expenses prior to notifying the insurer.

Some jurisdictions, as seen in the *Towne Realty* case discussed below, hold that the insurer has no obligation to pay for defense costs incurred before a claim is tendered. While this rule may be tempered where the insured is forced to respond to legal proceedings before the insurer is notified or responds, an immediate tender once the insured is sued could avoid disputes in this area.

In *Towne Realty v Zurich Insurance Co.,* 548 NW2d 64 (Wis 1996), the insured did not follow any of these guidelines in tendering its claim, and litigation became necessary to determine if an actual tender was made. The insured, 11 days after receiving suit papers, sent notice to the insurer, but it did not clarify at the time that this notification was in fact the tender of a claim. Instead, the insured wrote:

> I am sending it to your attention for review and discussion. As it is an unusual and complicated situation, we would first like to see Zurich's insight into potential position on extent of coverage.

The insurer denied a defense in the case 7 months later. Following a declaratory action to determine coverage, it was held that the policy did cover the allegations made against the insured. The court was asked to decide two issues. First, did the insured's statement when the complaint was sent to the insurer constitute a tender? If the insured's correspondence were found to constitute a tender, the insurer would have breached its duty to defend. The insurer argued that the plain meaning of the insured's words were that there was no tender. Unfortunately for the insurer, the court disagreed, holding that a tender occurs *once an insurer is put on notice of a claim against the insured.* Had the insured properly submitted the claim in the first place, it could have avoided lengthy litigation on the tender issue. The insurer's obligation to defend would have been determined by the ruling in the underlying declaratory action to determine the applicability of coverage.

The other issue before the court was whether the insurer was obligated to pay for the substantial defense costs incurred during the 11-day period preceding the tender. The court ruled in favor of the insurer on this issue, holding that it had no obligation to pay for costs incurred before the claim was tendered.

Of course, the additional insured should also notify its own insurers of the claim. However, it should request that they only monitor the claim without getting involved unless the insured requests otherwise. Taking this approach, the insurer can stay apprised of the situation without getting involved. If the other insurer denies the claim or it will exceed the limits of liability, the additional insured's own insurer can then become more actively involved.

One complication in this regard arises where the party demanding additional insured status also requires that its own coverage apply excess of the additional insured coverage. In those situations, currently commonplace, how does the additional insured preserve defense coverage under its own policy? Consider, for example, a contractor's requirement that all subcontractors add the contractor as an insured to their policies and that such coverage be provided on a primary and noncontributing basis in relation to any insurance the contractor may have. When the contractor is sued, it may be advisable to tender to all applicable insurers, including the contractor's own CGL insurer, to preserve the contractor's defense rights under each of those policies and avoid the implications of the selective tender rule. Could such an action

come into conflict with the contractor's intention that its own insurance apply only as excess coverage above the policies to which the contractor has been added as an insured?

Generally speaking, a tender must be made to trigger a defense obligation. Not doing so means running the risk of waiving a right to a defense from the insurer(s) to which no tender was made. As discussed in the preceding pages, many jurisdictions adhere to what is referred to as the selective tender rule. If the insured does not tender to a given insurer, that insurer may assume the insured did not wish to trigger defense or coverage under that policy and thus might be relieved of any defense obligation. What is required to trigger and or preserve a defense obligation is some notice to the insurer that the insured wants to be defended.

A minority rule holds that if the insurer is aware of the action against its insured there is no need for a formal tender. The insurer is obligated to notify an additional insured and learn if it wants a defense in the case. The rule is expressed in *Cincinnati Cos. v West American Insurance Co.,* 701 NE2d 499 (Ill 1998). In that decision, the Illinois Supreme Court stated:

> It is true that an insured may choose to forgo an insurer's assistance for various reasons, such as the insured's fear that premiums would be increased, or the policy canceled, in the future and that an insured's ability to forgo that assistance should be protected.

Insurers counter that this rule would require them to defend every suit that ever involved any insured under their policies. Technical compliance with the rule, however, would merely obligate the insurer, upon becoming aware that its insured is involved in litigation, to contact the insured and ask if it wants a defense. In some cases, an additional insured might not even know it has defense coverage available. The question then is whether it is equitable to allow the insurer to walk away from a defense obligation or one where its contribution might benefit the insured, because of the insured's lack of knowledge as to the availability of defense coverage.

While the *Cincinnati v West American* rule may be the better one from an insured's standpoint, it remains the minority view. Absent a tender, most insureds run the risk of losing contribution from an insurer to which no tender had been made. Because of the majority rule, it is not a conflict to notify all potentially applicable insurers, including umbrella insurers, since *not* doing so could result in a loss of defense coverage. As pointed out earlier, to mitigate the possible impact on its loss history, the insured might notify its own insurer of a *potential* need for defense, asking that the insurer not undertake action unless other applicable insurance does not respond. This would satisfy the notice obligation while at the same time letting the insurer know the insured is attempting to avoid its involvement. The intent of insurers whose named insured has additional insured status elsewhere is to respond only on an excess basis, and many forms—including the standard ISO CGL—say so.

Allocating Defense Costs

One problem faced by insureds and insurers alike is how defense costs will be allocated among those insurers to whom a defense has been tendered. Typically, where a tender to multiple insurers is made, many if not all of those insurers agree among themselves to fund a percentage of the defense, which arrangement is to the insured's benefit. In some cases, one or more insurers will refuse to participate in such an allocation, leading to litigation seeking to enforce the insured's right to a defense. A related issue is the insurer's right to allocate back to the insured the cost of defending suits alleging injury or damage not covered by the policy.

Generally speaking, the insurer's defense obligation is determined from the face of the complaint. In the past, most states have held that if even one cause of action is potentially covered, the insurer is required to defend the entire action. While the concept of allocating defense costs between covered and noncovered claims has been around for many years, the reasonable expectation of insureds, as well as custom and practice in the insurance and risk management industries, has been

that defense costs would not be allocated back to the insured.

Beginning with the 1996 revisions to the ISO CGL coverage form, defense wording was revised to state that the insurer has no obligation to defend suits alleging injury or damage not covered by the policy. While this wording on its own did not alter the defense obligation, subsequent case law indicated ways in which it might, combined with other factors. The pivotal case in this area is *Jerry H. Buss et al. v The Superior Court of Los Angeles County (Transamerica),* 16 Cal 4th 35 (1997). The insured, Buss, was sued in a complaint alleging 27 causes of action, of which only one had the potential of being covered. The insurer, Transamerica, reserved its right to allocate back to Buss the cost of defending the 26 causes of action determined not to be covered. It is important to note that the insurer included in this reservation a statement that the insurer expressly reserved its rights to be reimbursed if it was determined that there was no coverage. In addition, the attorney defending the case was instructed by the insurer to keep specific records of time allocable to the covered and noncovered elements of the claim respectively.

When Transamerica later sought to recover the costs associated with defending the 26 causes of action determined not to be covered, Buss sought judicial protection relying on existing precedent that imposed a heavy burden of evidence on an insurer seeking allocate such costs. In issuing its ruling, the court addressed four specific questions. Before answering those questions; the court set forth specific standards to be used as future guidelines. First the court made it clear that the insurer's duty to defend is not unlimited. "It extends to claims that are actually covered and to those that are merely potentially so—but no further." The court's rational here is that when insureds pay premiums, they expect a defense for claims that are covered and for those that are potentially covered. However, there is no expectation that claims not covered by the policy will be defended. The court made clear, however, that the insurer could not reserve its right to allocate back to the insured the cost of defending claims *potentially covered* by the policy, because of the expectation such claims would be defended and the fact that the insured had paid a premium for its expectation. The court then when on to pose the following hypothetical questions.

1. In a mixed action (i.e., a combination of covered and noncovered claims), may the insurer seek reimbursement from the insured for defense costs? The court's answer was that, as to claims that are at least potentially covered, the insurer could not seek reimbursement for the reasons discussed earlier. However, as to claims *not even potentially covered,* the insurer could seek reimbursement for the reasons set forth above.

2. In a mixed action, for what specific defense costs may the insurer obtain reimbursement from the insured? Again, the court held that the insurer could seek reimbursement for defense costs that could be allocated solely to claims not even potentially covered.

3. When an insurer seeks reimbursement for defense costs from the insured, which party must carry the burden of proof? The court placed this burden on the insurer.

4. What burden of proof must the insurer carry to obtain reimbursement from the insured? The court set the burden of proof as a preponderance of evidence, which is a much lower standard than previously existed and one which insurers can meet in most cases if defense counsel properly documents costs.

The court's ruling places a heavy onus on lawyers. Because defense counsel must represent the interests of the insured, allocation will pose a serious obstacle to representing clients in insurance-related matters. On one side is the lawyer's duty to its client; on the other, the reality that a failure to allocate properly will result in a loss of future business from the insurer. Defense counsel must understand coverage sufficiently to allocate as much of the cost as possible to time expended defending covered claims. However, this in turn must be balanced with the need *not* to ignore claims that are not covered by the policy, since doing so would be a disservice to the client. The one factor consistent

throughout this debate, however, is the need for legal counsel knowledgeable in the application of coverage.

The allocation doctrine does not limit the scope of an insurer's duty to defend. Even after *Buss,* if one allegation is potentially covered, the insurer must defend the entire action and reserve its rights to allocate back to the insured those costs attributable to allegations with no potential for coverage. This aspect of the issue was addressed in *Presley Homes v American States Insurance Co.,* 90 Cal App 4th 571, 108 Cal Rptr 2d 686 (2001). In this case, the insured, Presley Homes, was an additional insured under two policies issued by American States. One of the additional insured endorsements provided additional insured status only for Presley's vicarious liability. When Presley was sued for construction defects, American States agreed to share in the defense costs but denied a duty to defend against all of the allegations.

The trial court held that the insurer did not have a duty to provide Presley with a full and complete defense as to all claims. On appeal, the court held that the insurer had a duty to defend the entire action if even one cause of action was potentially covered. The appellate court also held that, while the insurer may have limited its indemnity obligation, the additional insured endorsements did not limit the defense obligation of the policy in any way.

The insurer argued that there were no facts supporting a finding that the insured reasonably expected a defense for the entire action. The appellate court, citing the *Buss* decision, ruled that the duty to defend the entire action was based on public policy, not the terms of the policy. To defend meaningfully, the court held, means to defend immediately. To defend immediately, the insurer must defend entirely. An insurer cannot parse the claims, dividing those that are potentially covered from those that are not. To do so, the court said, would be time-consuming and potentially futile.

The court also dismissed the argument that Presley had not paid a premium for its insured status. The court properly noted that, if an additional premium had been contemplated, it could have been collected as a matter of contract between the insurer and the subcontractors that had agreed to add Presley to their policies as an additional insured.

The *Presley* decision's holding that the additional insured endorsements, while potentially limiting the indemnity coverage, did nothing to limit the defense obligation. This does not bode well for insurers under the current language of standard additional insured endorsements. The additional insured endorsement at issue in *Presley* limited coverage to acts or omissions of the named insured, excluding coverage for the sole negligence of the additional insured. Despite that limitation, the court held there was no comparable limitation on the defense obligation.

This same problem will exist under the additional insured endorsements introduced in 2004. Under those endorsements, coverage for additional insureds is limited to injury or damage caused in whole or in part by the acts or omissions of the named insured or those acting on the named insured's behalf. This wording is similar to that used to provide additional insured status in the *Presley* case. Moreover, where the additional insured is found to have been acting on the named insured's behalf, as may be the case where a contractor overseeing a project is added to the policies of subcontractors, the additional insured may still have coverage for what might be termed its sole fault.

Given that an insurer providing additional insured coverage remains obligated to defend the entire action against its insured, complications will arise when multiple insurers are called on to meet that obligation. In such a situation, it is possible for the additional insured to play the insurers against one another, arguing that what one insurer excludes is covered by the others. Since each insurer obligated to defend a potentially covered claim is obligated to defend the entire action, the insured can ask that the multiple insurers involved seek contribution from each other as to defense costs each alleges is attributable to causes of action with *no* potential for coverage.

In addition, the insured retains the right to choose which of the insurers obligated to provide a defense

will be called on to do so. This can be particularly beneficial where one policy provides more favorable coverage than others. However, if the insured makes such a selection, it should do so with the previously discussed precautions in mind to avoid losing coverage under any of the applicable policies.

Loss of Governmental Immunity

Many states, cities, counties, school districts, and other political subdivisions benefit from a tort claims act limiting their liability for negligent acts or even providing absolute immunity. However, these acts often include provisions waiving the liability limitation when the public entity purchases liability insurance. In such a state, a political subdivision obtaining coverage by way of additional insured status in another liability policy may find it has waived its liability limitation otherwise provided under the state Tort Claims Act. This possibility should be carefully considered and explored with legal counsel before additional insured status is sought on the liability policies of others by public entities.

Breach of Contract as a Basis for Excluding Coverage

A problem relevant to additional insureds—and to anyone with insured status under a general liability or umbrella liability policy—is a trend over the past 10 years for insurers to deny claims on the basis that the alleged injury or damage arose out of a breach of contract. The doctrine that breach of contract is not the subject of liability insurance is a judicial creation. It holds basically that a liability policy applies only to third-party tort liability and has no application to actions against an insured that sound in or are based on contract. Application of this doctrine confuses insureds and, in many jurisdictions, has become one of the most abused legal doctrines governing liability coverage. In most business settings, and particularly in construction projects where many additional insured issues arise, nearly all rights and obligations between the parties derive from contracts. Given that reality, the question becomes: When, if ever, will coverage apply to such business relationships if all injury or damage arising out of a contract is deemed to be excluded?

For example, when a general contractor agrees under contract with the project owner to perform certain work, would the general contractor be covered (assuming no applicable exclusions) under its liability policy if the work of one of its subcontractors causes property damage? Or, would the general contractor's coverage be inapplicable because the failure of the subcontractor caused the general contractor to be in breach of contract with the owner? Based on insurance and risk management custom and practice (as well as policy drafting history) nearly all insureds would rightfully assume that the contractor's coverage applies to such exposures.

However, despite clear policy wording to the contrary, insurers have successfully argued in some instances that such exposures are *not* covered because they arise out of a contractual relationship; that is, if there would be no liability but for the existence of a contract, there is no covered liability exposure. The problem with this reading of general liability policies is that, in construction and nearly every other business activity, the relationships of the parties are contract-derivative. Under the position often advocated by insurers, the contractor in the above scenario would have no liability had it not entered into a contract to build a building. As such, resulting liability had its origin in contract and is not the subject of general liability coverage.

Generally speaking, liability coverage does not apply to damages for pure breach of contract resulting in only economic loss. An example is the retailer who purchases equipment and refuses to pay for it. The seller has suffered a monetary loss caused by the "purchaser's" breach of contract. If, however, breach of contract (1) results in injury or damage to a third party, (2) is the result of an occurrence or offense, and (3) is not otherwise excluded, general liability and umbrella coverage should apply.

The principal source of confusion in resolving this coverage issue has been the use of the CGL phrase

"legally obligated to pay." Insurers argue that this wording is applicable only to tort—not to contractual—liability. This view would not necessarily lead to inequities if insurers were to confine its application to situations like the one described above, involving a pure breach of contract and resulting economic loss rather than bodily injury or property damage. But insurers have invoked the doctrine to exclude coverage in a variety of settings that involve more than simple breach of contract or economic loss, on the basis that one can be *contractually* obligated to pay damages without being "legally obligated to pay."

When general liability policies were introduced in 1941, the insuring clause referred to coverage for damages "by reason of liability imposed upon [the insured] by law or assumed by [the insured] under contract, as defined herein." With the 1947 liability changes, the insuring clause was amended to read as it does today, referring to sums the insured is "legally obligated to pay." The opinion of many at that time was that the term "legally obligated to pay" would broaden the scope of the insuring clause.

There are a number of areas in a standard CGL policy where liability arising out of a breach of contract is specifically excluded. Those exclusions clarify that, absent a specific exclusion regarding breach of contract, liability arising out of contract should be covered, as long as there has been an occurrence or an offense and the resulting injury or damage is otherwise covered by the policy. The "impaired property" exclusion is one such example. It is targeted at property damage to impaired property or property that has not been physically injured. The exclusion applies to damage arising out of a defect in the named insured's work or a "delay or failure by the named insured or anyone acting on its behalf to perform a contract or agreement in accordance with its terms."

Here, liability for injury or damage otherwise covered by the policy is specifically excluded *if that liability arises out of a breach of contract.* The predecessor to this exclusion, the so-called failure to perform exclusion, also referenced a breach of contract. Coverage was excluded under that earlier language for loss of use of tangible property because of a delay in contract or the failure of the named insured's work or product to meet the level of performance or quality as warranted or represented. Liability arising out of a breach of contract is also specifically excluded under CGL advertising injury coverage.

The wording found in liability policies does not alert even the most sophisticated insured to the potential elimination of coverage for injury or damage otherwise covered by the policy but emanating from a breach of contract. How, then, did the premise that there is no coverage for injury or damage arising from a breach of contract become so widely recognized by the courts? From an analytical standpoint, the problem in large part is attributable to the fact that legal counsel for insureds have all too often been willing to concede to insurers on this point.

The doctrine grew out of a series of California cases seeking to apply the legal notion that liability arising out of contract *(ex contractu)* as opposed to tort *(ex delicto)* is not a proper subject of general liability insurance. Insurers argued in case after case that the term "legally obligated to pay" refers to liability arising in tort only, and they were successful in a long line of court decisions on this issue. The net result, however, was widespread confusion, particularly in the construction industry, as to the scope of CGL coverage for standard business operations. In case after case, damages otherwise covered by a liability policy were held to be excluded because they were alleged to have had their source in a contract. But for the existence of a contract, the insurers would argue, there could be no liability. If tort liability was involved, insurers argued that such liability did not arise separately and independently from the contract, but rather because the contract existed. In essence, these rulings made typical construction industry exposures (and those associated with other industries as well) virtually uninsurable.

Additional insureds were among the biggest losers in these coverage denials. Denials of coverage based on allegations that the injury or damage arose from a contract were not limited to the named insured's coverage. The breach of contract defense was not avoidable based on arguments of severability. The additional insured's coverage rights allegedly were grounded in a contractual obligation imposed on the named insured to add them to the policy. Likewise, the liability of the additional insured was said to have its origins in the same underlying contractual arrangements that precluded coverage for the named insured.

Fortunately, the California Supreme Court intervened in August 1999, rendering a decision that clarifies the application of coverage and summarily dismisses the tortured logic underlying the long line of cases that had previously ruled against coverage. That case is *Vandenberg v Superior Court of Sacramento County v Centennial Insurance Co.,* 982 P2d 229 (Cal 1999). In its decision, the California Supreme Court summarily dismissed the argument that the "phrase *legally obligated to pay as damages* describes liability based upon a breach of duty imposed by law, i.e., tort, rather than by contract."

In doing so, the court enunciated another important principle, holding that the artful drafting of a complaint is not and should not be a prerequisite to finding coverage. "The legal theory asserted by the claimant is immaterial to the determination of whether the risk is covered. ... The nature of the damage and the risk involved, in light of particular policy provisions, control coverage," according to the court.

Summary

A number of potential problems can be encountered by both indemnitees and indemnitors when the latter adds the former as an insured to its liability policies. In fact, the entire goal of risk transfer to another party can be defeated if care is not taken in drafting the underlying contract and arranging insurance programs that reflect the contract's intent.

One of the most substantial problems encountered by indemnitees concerns the possibility of its insurer being called on to participate with the indemnitor's insurance as a result of the other insurance clause. This problem can be largely eliminated by amending the CGL policy's other insurance clause to apply in excess of other insurance under which the named insured is an additional insured. There are now standard endorsements available to accomplish this goal in most states. Of course, some insureds and insurers will also choose to draft their own endorsements tailored to their particular goals and circumstances.

The cases discussed in this chapter point to a three-pronged approach to avoiding this problem.

- The underlying contract should clearly spell out the intent of the parties as to whose policies will apply as primary insurance. Generally the intent will be for the indemnitee's policy to apply as primary insurance with the additional inured's own insurance as excess.

When this is the case, no endorsement generally will be needed on the indemnitor's insurance.

- The indemnitee (additional insured) should have its own policy endorsed to apply in excess of coverage available to it as an additional insured on the policy of another.

- When presented with a claim that should be covered by the indemnitor's policy, the additional insured should clearly and unequivocally tender defense to the indemnitor's insurer. It should also notify its own insurer of the claim, asking it to monitor the situation but to not become involved unless requested to do so.

Chapter 5 Notes

1. In the case of *Allegheny Airlines v Forth Corp.,* 663 F2d 751 (7th Cir 1981), a subsidiary was identified as an additional insured under the excess policy of its parent company. However, it turned out that the actual intent was to give the subsidiary the same named insured status as its parent. Once that intent was established, the subsidiary, like its parent, was found to be without coverage under an excess policy because of an exclusion of liability for any aircraft owned by the named insured.

2. An interesting sidelight to this case is that at the trial level, the contractor and its insurer conceded that the contractor had agreed to indemnify the manufacturer but argued that because the manufacturer's negligence was sole or at least contributory, the indemnification was inappropriate. On appeal, both of these parties also presented the "inextricably tied" issue to the court because of the way the required insurance and the indemnification agreement were combined in one provision. The idea was that if there were no indemnification agreement (it being null and void under the law), the insurance likewise would have been inapplicable. The court in

this case, however, saw no merit to this particular issue.

3. Courts in many states have a long track record of frowning on escape clauses. Excess clauses, on the other hand, are generally viewed more favorably since they are attempts to coordinate coverage rather than completely escape providing it.

4. The additional insured endorsement in *Home* appears to be one of two standard ISO endorsements that were available to add a contractor as an additional insured to the policy of another contractor. However, it is the more restrictive of the two endorsements (see **Chapter 9**). For an example of a case where a similar situation arose as a result of a nonstandard endorsement, see *National Union Fire Insurance v Glenview Park District,* 594 NE2d 1300 (Ill App 1992).

5. The court specifically commented on and speculated about the intent of Home, Turner, and the subcontractor in *Home v Liberty.* A clear indication in the subcontract agreement of the intent of the parties may have gone far to answer these questions.

6.   Barring this modification, real estate managers may want to continue obtaining the modification to the other insurance clause provided by the Real Estate Property Managed (CG 22 70) endorsement.

Chapter 6

SEVERABILITY OF INTERESTS AND CROSS-LIABILITY

One question that often arises when one party adds another as an insured to its liability policy is how the policy will respond when one insured brings a suit against another insured. For example, this would be a concern when an additional insured (the indemnitee) brings an action against the named insured (the indemnitor). It is not the intent of an indemnitee to jeopardize the coverage of the indemnitor by requiring additional insured status. An indemnitee certainly desires for policies purchased by the indemnitor to respond to claims made against the indemnitor by the indemnitee. Such a claim—where one insured sues another insured—is often called a "cross-liability claim"; the concept of severability of interests requires liability insurers to defend such suits.

To eliminate the insurers' obligation to defend cross-liability claims, it would be necessary to subject the policy to a cross-liability exclusion. These exclusions typically preclude coverage for claims and suits between all insureds or between just named insureds.

Excluding coverage only for claims between named insureds is more limited in scope and applies only when one named insured makes a claim or sues another named insured. Cross-liability exclusions that preclude coverage for claims or suits between insureds are broader and would apply to all insureds under the policy.

It is relatively uncommon to see a cross-liability exclusion in a primary liability policy other than with respect to employees as insureds. For example, the standard Insurance Services Office, Inc. (ISO), commercial general liability (CGL), business auto, garage, motor carrier, and business owners coverage forms contain no such exclusion, and there is no endorsement in the ISO forms portfolio to add one (except as respects products liability). Even most manuscript primary liability policies do not contain such exclusions. But the same cannot be said of umbrella policies, where cross-liability exclusions are somewhat more common.

It is important to note that the concept of severability is not totally defeated when these exclusions are applied. Coverage still applies separately to each insured for third-party claims made against them. Only coverage for claims and suits between insureds or named insureds is affected by these exclusions.

Severability of Interests

It has been said that an additional insured should receive no broader coverage than the protection provided to the named insured. Because of the severability of interests provision, however, it is possible for a liability policy to apply to an additional insured even though coverage for the named insured is excluded. The purpose of the severability of interests provision of insurance policies is to clarify that the word "insured," as it appears within various parts of a policy, applies severally and not collectively. Thus, a policy provision that refers to "the insured" is not limited in its application to the named insured. (In fact, as noted in **Chapter 4,** the term "insured" includes the named insured, but the reverse is not true.) Instead, when there is more than one insured, the effect is as though a separate policy is issued to each insured against whom claim is made or suit is brought.

The one exception to this is that the policy limits are not cumulative; that is, one set of limits applies to all insureds collectively.

The severability of interests provision—though it was always intended that the concept apply—was first introduced in 1955 for use with automobile and general liability policies. It has been said that the provision was necessary to eliminate the confusion prompted by conflicting court decisions, to strengthen the intent of policies that the obligations of the named insured and any other insureds be treated separately, and to discourage insureds from requesting separate policies or endorsements that had the effect of incorporating wording that signified that the policy was several and not collective.

This clause was not necessary with pre-1955 general liability policy provisions because coverage was commonly limited to the named insured, directors, officers, stockholders, or partners of the named insured while acting within their duties. However, there was an ever-increasing demand by others for additional insured status. In fact, automatic insured status for real estate managers also was added with the 1955 comprehensive general liability policy. This latter addition has been viewed as somewhat significant because it gave real estate management primary protection under policies of others even though these entities might have been independent contractors that had maintained liability insurance of their own. In subsequent CGL policy editions, the severability of interests provision was moved around within the policy and even revised slightly, but the overall intent has not changed. Exhibit 6.1 shows the severability of interests clauses from the 1955 through the current edition CGL policies.

Since there is no standard umbrella or excess liability policy in use by the insurance industry, the wording of these policies varies considerably from one insurer to another. Most, but by no means all, umbrella forms contain severability of interests provisions such as those cited in Exhibit 6.1. When umbrella policies contain these provisions, they are usually either included in the definition of "insured" or in a specific "separation of insureds" provision in the policy conditions.

EXHIBIT 6.1
SEVERABILITY OF INTERESTS PROVISIONS

1955 Edition Auto and General Liability Policies

Severability of Interests. The term "the insured" is used severally and not collectively, but the inclusion herein of more than one insured, shall not operate to increase the limits of the company's liability.

1966 and 1973 Edition CGL Policies

"Insured" means any person or organization qualifying as an insured in the "Persons Insured" provision of the applicable insurance coverage. The insurance afforded applies separately to each insured against whom claim is made or suit is brought, except with respect to the limits of the company's liability.

Post-1986 Edition CGL Policies

Except with respect to the Limits of Insurance, and any rights or duties specifically assigned in this Coverage Part to the first Named Insured, this insurance applies:

a. As if each Named Insured were the only Named Insured; and

b. Separately to each insured against whom claim is made or "suit" is brought.

Includes copyrighted material of Insurance Services Office, Inc., with its permission. Copyright, Insurance Services Office, Inc., 1982, 1984, 1988, 1992, 1994, 1997.

Copyright, ISO Properties, Inc., 2000

The concept of severability is not always spelled out in liability policies. However, coverage becomes ambiguous or even unintelligible if this concept is not applied. Insurers obviously intend that this concept apply to most forms of liability coverage, given the manner in which coverage applies to various insureds. As a result, the concept of severability is applicable to nearly all liability coverages regardless of whether it is specifically set out in policy wording. While it is preferable to have policy wording that clearly sets forth this coverage application in the policy, it is not a prerequisite to applying this concept.

Cross-Liability

A requirement for a "cross-liability endorsement" is often included in contract provisions detailing required insurance coverages. There is no standard "cross-liability endorsement" available for use with liability policies, and, therefore, an endorsement with this moniker could either exclude or grant coverage for claims made by one insured against another. In fact, early cross-liability endorsements were exclusions of coverage, since cross-liability coverage has long been included in standard forms.

When the severability of interests provision was first introduced to quell arguments over the application of insurance policies written for more than one insured, the provision also made clear that the policy provided cross-liability coverage. This means that if one insured were to sue another insured, the policy will protect the alleged tortfeasor (an insured) and pay damages on its behalf to the injured party (also an insured). The reason is that when there is more than one insured, the policy is viewed as though a separate insurance policy is issued to each such insured.

Because it is not necessary to attach an endorsement specifically adding cross-liability coverage to policies that contain a severability of interests clause, requirements in leases and other contracts to require such endorsements are usually unnecessary. However, the possibility that a nonstandard form may be used (particularly for excess coverage) or that a cross-liability exclusion can be attached to standard forms must be considered. Therefore, it is probably a good idea to stipulate that the required liability policies provide cross-liability coverage. This type of contractual requirement should make it clear that coverage for a suit brought by the additional insured against the named insured or another insured is desired without confusing matters by requiring an unneeded manuscript endorsement.

The Employee Injury Exclusion and Severability

Virtually all general and umbrella liability policies contain an exclusion precluding coverage for injury to the insured's employees. An example of this exclusion from the 1988 and 1993 CGL forms is provided in Exhibit 6.2. The purpose for this exclusion is to avoid duplication of coverage with an employer's workers compensation and employers liability coverage. However, it is not unusual, particularly in construction-related work, for there to be circumstances whereby an employee of the named insured (employer) is injured due to the negligence of an additional insured. The employee collects workers compensation benefits and then files an action against the additional insured. The additional insured, in turn, seeks protection under the named insured's liability policy. (This type of claim is commonly referred to as a "third-party-over action.") Neither the workers compensation

---

EXHIBIT 6.2
EXAMPLE EMPLOYEE INJURY EXCLUSION

This insurance does not apply to ... e. "Bodily injury" to:

    (1) An employee of the insured arising out of and in the course of employment by the insured; or

    (2) The spouse, child, parent, brother or sister of that employee as a consequence of (1) above.

This exclusion applies:

    (1) Whether the insured may be liable as an employer or in any other capacity; and

    (2) To any obligation to share damages with or repay someone who must pay damages because of the injury.

This exclusion does not apply to liability assumed by the insured under an "insured contract."

Copyright, Insurance Services Office, Inc., 1988

---

exclusion nor the employers liability exclusion is applicable to the additional insured assuming that (1) there are no special limitations applicable to the additional insured endorsement, (2) the policy is not subject to any cross-liability exclusion, and (3) the injured person is an employee of the named insured rather than the additional insured.

When these exclusions are read, one must keep in mind that the policy is several in nature; it applies separately to each insured against whom claim is made or suit is brought. Thus, when referring to the workers compensation and employers liability exclusions, the following question should be asked: Which insured—the named insured or the additional insured—is considered to be the employer of the employee who was injured? If the additional insured is the employer, then the exclusion applies to the additional insured. Conversely, if the policy's named insured is the employer, then the exclusion has no application to the additional insured.

As simple as this analysis appears, sometimes insurers attempt to stretch the exclusion's application to encompass all insureds despite the policy's application with respect to severability of interest. As a result, this issue has been the subject of a number of legal disputes, and the majority opinion of the courts is that additional insureds are covered when they are liable for injuries to the employees of other insureds. This school of thought is demonstrated in *Erdo v Torcon Construction Co.*, 645 A2d 806 (NJ Super 1994).

In this case, a subcontractor agreed to name the general contractor as an additional insured. After work commenced, an employee of the subcontractor was injured and filed suit against the general contractor. However, the subcontractor's insurer refused to provide the general contractor with a defense, relying on the employers liability exclusion. The insurer maintained that the term "insured" was intended to include any insured listed in the policy, whether the named insured or additional insured. Thus, neither the general contractor nor the subcontractor would be entitled to coverage for any suit brought by an employee of either

for employment-related injuries. The general contractor (additional insured) argued that the exclusion precluded coverage only for the insured that was the actual employer of the person injured on the job.

The court of appeals ruled against the insurer based on the policy's severability of interests provision. In doing so, the court stated that the severability clause creates multiple policies with identical terms but different insureds. The clause also requires that the policy be read as if each insured were the only insured.

If the additional insured were deemed to have been the employer by statute (commonly referred to as statutory employer) instead, the outcome would have been different. Likewise, had the named insured and additional insured been held to be coemployers of a leased employee and had both been entitled to immunity under exclusive remedy provisions of a workers compensation act, the outcome would have been different. Any cross-liability exclusion also should be taken as an important caveat because this exclusion, as noted previously, could nullify the severability of interests concept to the detriment of any additional insured or named insured where the litigation is between those parties.

A project owner that was an additional insured found itself without protection because of the employers liability exclusion of a nonstandard liability policy even though the injured persons were not its employees in *Stearns-Roger Corp. v Hartford Accident and Indemnity Co.*, 571 P2d 659 (Ariz 1979). Stearns-Roger, an engineering construction firm, entered into a long-term agreement with a project owner. Under the contract, Stearns-Roger agreed to procure a CGL policy along with other forms of insurance. Though not expressly named, the project owner was considered an additional insured under the policy provision, which read as follows.

The unqualified word "Insured" includes:

> Any person, organization, trustee, estate, or governmental entity to whom or to

which the Named Insured is obligated, by virtue of a written contract or by the issuance or existence of a permit, to provide insurance such as is afforded by this policy, but only with respect to operations by or on behalf of the Named Insured or to facilities of, or facilities used by the Named Insured and then only for the limits of liability specified in such contract, but in no event for limits of liability in excess of the applicable limits of liability for this policy ....

During the course of construction, two Stearns-Roger employees were injured and filed suit against the project owner. When the owner sought protection from Stearns-Roger's liability insurer, it was denied because of the workers compensation and employers liability exclusions. The latter, which actually served to the disadvantage of the project owner, read as follows.

... to personal injury to any employee of the Named Insured arising out of and in the course of his employment by the insured.

It was Stearns-Roger's (the named insured's) position that for the above exclusion to apply, the injured party must be the employee of the insured that was seeking coverage. In this case, since the employees who were injured were not employees of the insured claiming coverage (the project owner), the exclusion was inapplicable, and the insurer was required to provide defense. Stearns-Roger also maintained that the word "insured," as it appeared in the above exclusion, was ambiguous because it could mean either the named insured or the additional insured. The court, however, saw no ambiguity, stating that the exclusion could have used the word "named insured" in place of "insured," but it would have strained the English language to interpret the exclusion any other way.

Exclusions worded in this manner may not appear to be ambiguous at first glance. However, when viewing them from a perspective of risk management and insurance custom, their application to anyone other than the named insured is not what insureds would anticipate and is contrary to the intent behind the original drafting of this type of exclusion. If it is the intent of insurers to exclude coverage for insureds who are not the employers of injured employees, that intent should be clarified in a manner that will be understood by all insureds under the policy rather than buried in an innocuous editorial change.

Another interesting observation about this case, particularly with respect to this nonstandard policy, is that it appears that the exclusion is an expanded version of insured versus insured exclusions, which are probably more prevalent today than at the time of this case. Also, it is doubtful that the additional insured would have known about the broad scope of this exclusion even if a certificate of insurance had been issued. The intricacies of certificates are discussed in **Chapter 20.**

One source explains the effect of the severability of interests provision on employee exclusions of policies as follows.

The presence of a severability clause has been held to work a liberalizing effect in that an additional insured who injures one of the named insured's employees may have coverage in spite of the exclusion.[1]

In another case involving a nonstandard employers liability exclusion, coverage was applied to the additional insured on the basis of the exclusion's ambiguity. The case is *Cyprus Plateau Mining Corp. v Commonwealth Insurance Co.*, 972 F Supp 1379 (Utah 1997). A mining company hired a contractor to excavate mine tunnels. The contractor agreed to name the mining company as an insured under the contractor's CGL and umbrella liability policies. An employee of the contractor was injured while working at the site and brought a claim against the mining company. The mining company notified the contractor's insurer of the claim and, as an additional insured, sought coverage under the contractor's policies. The insurer denied coverage based on the following exclusionary language.

This policy does not cover personal injury, including bodily injury, to any employee of any insured under this policy for which the insured or his indemnitee may be liable.

The insurer argued that this exclusion meant no coverage for any claim brought by an employee of one insured (e.g., the contractor) against another insured (e.g., the mining company). The additional insured mining company, on the other hand, asserted that a "fair and reasonable" reading of the exclusion was that it applied only to claims against the named insured brought by its own employees.

As precedent, the mining company relied heavily on *Transport Indemnity Co. v Wyatt,* 417 S2d 568 (Ala 1982), discussed on page 148. In that case, the Alabama Supreme Court had been asked to interpret an exclusion of "any occurrence which causes bodily injury to any employee of any insured" and had found the exclusion to be ambiguous. Similar rulings were cited by the mining company in *Pacific Indemnity Co. v Transport Indemnity Co.,* 146 Cal Rptr 648 (1978); and *U.S. Steel Corp. v Transport Indemnity Co.,* 50 Cal Rptr 576 (1966).

For its part, the insurer pointed to several court rulings in which similar exclusions were found not to be ambiguous and applied to similar claims:

- *Allen v Prudential Property and Casualty Insurance Co.,* 839 P2d 798 (Utah 1992)

- *Spezialetti v Pacific Employers Insurance Co.,* 759 F2d 1139 (3d Cir 1985)

- *Michael Carbone, Inc. v General Accident Insurance Co.,* 937 F Supp 413 (Penn 1996)

The court in *Cyprus Plateau* found the additional insured mining company's argument and precedents to be most persuasive. It held the employers liability exclusion to be ambiguous and cited specifically the exclusionary clause that referred to an employee "of any insured ... for which the insured or his indemnitee may be held liable." The use of the collective term "any insured" in conjunction with the singular and restrictive term "the insured" along with the singular pronoun "his" led the court to recognize at least two reasonable interpretations of the exclusion.

Since one of those interpretations was the additional insured's, the court found the exclusion inapplicable to the mining company's claim.

When arranging general liability coverage under nonstandard forms, the employers liability exclusion should be carefully examined to make sure that it does not eliminate coverage for contractual assumptions. CGL and umbrella policies are the customary source of coverage for third-party-over actions based on a named insured's assumption of an additional insured's liability for injury to the named insured's employee. Employers liability coverage like that provided under standard workers compensation policies typically excludes this very contractual exposure. Indemnitees who also have additional insured status under their indemnitors' liability policies expect to have coverage under those policies for third-party-over actions. The *Cyprus Plateau* decision discussed above was a recognition of the drafting intent behind the CGL employers liability exclusion and of custom and practice in the insurance, construction, and risk management industries.

Parent and Subsidiary Company Issues

What can be somewhat complex insofar as the employee injury exclusion and severability of interests provisions are concerned are situations where liability policies cover parent and subsidiary companies. The intricacies of parent and subsidiary company relationships are far too complex to discuss here. Suffice it to say that subsidiary companies are established for many reasons, including to limit liability, and that a parent company generally is not responsible for the liability of its subsidiaries.

One of the problem areas of parent and subsidiary companies is where the employee of a subsidiary collects workers compensation benefits under the subsidiary's policy and then attempts to circumvent the workers compensation law's exclusive remedy doctrine by looking to the parent, as a third party, for additional damages. Whether these types of actions are successful hinges in part on which entity is found to be the actual employer of the injured employee. This task is often complicated by the fact that the parent company may actually be one that has directly or indirectly paid for the workers compensation insurance. Also, these kinds of actions arise whether the insurance program encompasses the parent and its subsidiary companies or the insurance is written separately for each of them. It is an exposure inherent in the risks associated with parent and subsidiary relationships that needs to be recognized.

In many situations where a tort action is filed by an injured employee against the parent company (or against the subsidiary), the company against whom suit is brought will seek protection under the liability insurance program, asserting that the employer's liability exclusion is not applicable. If, in fact, it turns out that a parent company and its subsidiary are separate, legal entities, the severability of interests concept should apply to allow coverage.

In any event, it is not unusual for parent companies, subsidiaries, and joint subsidiaries, by the nature of their close relationships, to encounter all kinds of scenarios that raise severability issues. In *St. Katherine Insurance Co. v Insurance Co. of North America,* 11 F3d 707 (7th Cir 1993), the issue was between an umbrella insurer and a primary liability insurer. It concerned whether a sulfur pit constructed by a subsidiary on the parent company's property could be considered a completed operations hazard, given that injury or damage must occur away from premises of the named insured to qualify. This question was crucial, because if the loss were to be classified as falling within the completed operations hazard, the aggregate limit would be exhausted and would require the umbrella policy to drop down and pay part of the damages.

The case arose following injury by an employee of the parent company. The employee fell into the pit and filed a claim against both the parent and subsidiary company. There was no question that the sulphur pit was completed and that the subsidiary company relinquished all control upon completion. Even so, the umbrella insurer maintained that the loss was not within the completed operations hazard of the primary policy for two reasons. First, the primary policy's definition of "completed operations hazard" required two criteria: (1) that bodily injury or property damage occur after operations are completed or abandoned, and (2) that the injury or damage occur *away* from the premises owned by or rented to the *named insured.* Second, looking to the policy definition of "insured," the umbrella insurer argued that since the named insured is the parent and its subsidiaries, the loss cannot be categorized as a completed operations hazard because the accident occurred on the property of the named insured.

The court stated that the umbrella insurer's interpretation would be correct if the named insured were a single, nonseverable entity under the policy. But, said the court, the severability of interests provision, which formed a part of the definition of "insured," worked to sever the parent from the subsidiary for purposes of the policy. The court also stated that the purpose of the severability of interests provision is to treat each entity covered under the policy as if each were insured separately. The court added that to maintain that there was only one named insured encompassing the parent and its subsidiary companies was inconsistent with the severability clause.

As a matter of interest, in support of its arguments the umbrella insurer relied on *American Cast Iron Pipe Co. v Commerce & Industry Insurance Co.,* 481 S2d 892 (Ala 1985), which involved a liability policy that excluded completed operations coverage. The court held that injury to an employee of a subsidiary that occurred on the premises of the subsidiary, as a result of a defectively designed conveyor belt installed by the parent, was not within the completed operations hazard because the injury happened on the premises of the "named insured." The court held that, even though there was a severability clause in the policy, the premises of the subsidiary were considered to be the premises of the parent, because under that state's law, the parent was the owner of the subsidiary's premises. Its rationale for doing so was partly because Alabama law treated shareholders as equitable owners of corporate assets, including real estate, which had the effect of disregarding the corporate form of the entities and thus holding that the premises of the subsidiary were the premises of the parent.

The court in *St. Katherine Insurance,* however, viewed the *American Cast Iron* case to be distinguishable because this latter case involved a situation in which the parent's defective product was located on the premises of the subsidiary, thus leading to the conclusion that the accident occurred on premises "owned by" the parent. Also, unlike *St. Katherine Insurance,* the insurer did not argue that the subsidiary controlled or owned the premises of its parent company.

The court in *St. Katherine Insurance* stated that an entity's corporate existence cannot be so casually disregarded as was done in *American Cast Iron,* explaining:

> [A] corporation is an entity separate and distinct from its shareholders and from other corporate entities with which it may be connected.... Unless there is evidence to suggest that the separate existence of the subsidiary and parent company is illusory and that the entities are not dealing at arms length, but are, in effect, abusing the corporate form, we ought not disregard the corporate form.

The court concluded that there was nothing in the record to suggest that the subsidiary and parent companies disregarded their separate corporate entities. The fact that the injured employee could bring a suit against the subsidiary company and was not prohibited from doing so under the exclusivity of the workers compensation law was evidence that separate corporate entities existed.

The case of *McGurran v DiCanio Planned Development Corp.,* 251 AD2d 467 (NY App Div 1998), involved a dispute between two subsidiary companies. An employee of one subsidiary, DRC, was injured while working at the job site of another subsidiary, DPD. Both subsidiaries were included as insureds under the liability policy of their parent company. The injured employee sued DPD, the subsidiary that owned the job site. After the in-

surer settled the claim on behalf of DPD, it sought indemnification from DRC, the subsidiary that employed the injured employee. DRC also maintained a workers compensation policy from the state fund that defended DRC throughout this litigation.

After this action was settled, DRC moved to dismiss the action by DPD's insurer for indemnification on the grounds that the antisubrogation rule precluded the CGL insurer, the true party in interest, from subrogating to a claim against its own insured. The trial court granted DRC's motion, holding that there were public policy considerations underlying the antisubrogation rule.

The critical issue on appeal in ascertaining whether the antisubrogation rule applied to preclude the insurer from subrogating against its own insured was to determine whether the liability policy in question covered both subsidiaries, DRC and DPD, for damages arising out of the accident. On this score, despite the fact that the insurer covered both parties, the higher court permitted subrogation against DRC because the insurer did not provide each of the subsidiaries with coverage for the same risks. The basis for the conclusion that the risks were said to be different between the two subsidiaries was the policy's employer's liability exclusion. That exclusion stated that coverage did not apply:

> (j) to bodily injury to any employee of the insured arising out of and in the course of his employment by the insured or to any obligation of the insured to indemnify another because of damages arising out of such injury.

In light of this exclusion, DRC, the employer, was not covered for the claim of its employee that arose out of and during the course of his employment. The court held that by virtue of the fact that DRC had obtained a separate workers compensation policy to cover that risk, its liability insurer was not seeking indemnity from DPD for a risk covered by its policy. Finally, since the liability insurer was not obligated to defend DRC, there also was no conflict of interest between it and DPD.

Fellow Employee Cross-Liability Exclusion

Even though the standard CGL policy provides cross-liability coverage in most instances, it does contain one cross-liability exclusion. Virtually all primary and umbrella liability policies have a built-in cross-liability exclusion precluding coverage for suits brought against insured employees by injured fellow employees. While these exclusions are sometimes modified during insurance placement negotiations, they have a legitimate purpose. Under most state workers compensation laws, injured employees have as their sole remedy the mandated workers compensation benefits. These exclusions are included in liability policies to reinforce this intent. They are intended to avoid opening the door to possible circumvention of the exclusive remedy doctrine by showing courts and juries that fellow employees do not have available a third-party funding mechanism (their employer's liability insurance) for such claims.

The need for this exclusion—in addition to the employee injury exclusion previously discussed—was clearly explained in one case as follows.

> The logical theory for the employee exclusion is to prevent the employee of the tortfeasor from suing his employer for injuries received thru his employer's negligence. A reason for this is that employees are usually covered by workers compensation and can recover from the employer, with or without negligence. When negligence is committed by other than his employer, the logic for the exclusion disappears. If the insurer wishes to further exclude its liability, it could clearly so state in its contract and its failure to do so should be strictly construed. Especially is this true when the policy contains a severability of interests clause, for there it can be implied that the insurer actually is recognizing a separate obligation to others, distinct and apart from the obligation it owes to the named insured.[2]

Fellow employee cross-liability exclusions were not generally needed in the early years of general liability insurance because employees were seldom provided insured status. However, as pointed out in **Chapter 3,** the Persons Insured provision of earlier CGL policies provided some automatic insured protection to employees while operating mobile equipment. When this protection first became available in 1966, it made necessary the inclusion of a fellow employee cross-liability exclusion. Selected portions of the 1966 CGL provision are included in Exhibit 6.3.

EXHIBIT 6.3
MOBILE EQUIPMENT OPERATORS AS INSUREDS PROVISION

Each of the following is an insured under this insurance to the extent set forth below:

... (e) with respect to the operation, for the purpose of locomotion upon a public highway, of mobile equipment registered under any motor vehicle registration law, (i) an employee of the named insured while operating any such equipment in the course of his employment provided that no person or organization shall be insured under this paragraph (e) with respect to (I) bodily injury to any fellow employee of such person injured in the course of his employment ....

Except for any claim or suit involving this provision, the cross-liability exclusion dealing with fellow employee suits was not the subject of much litigation. However, employees (and spouses) were routinely provided with insured status following the introduction of the Broad Form CGL endorsement by ISO in 1976. When employees were added as insureds, such as by this endorsement, it was again necessary to include an employee injury cross-liability limitation to avoid providing coverage by way of the severability of interests provision. It is worth noting the employee injury cross-liability exclusion in the Broad Form CGL endorsement because of subsequent cases involving it and the fact that the corresponding provision of the post-1973 CGL forms offers less protection. Selected portions of this provision are included in Exhibit 6.4.

EXHIBIT 6.4
BROAD FORM CGL ADDITIONAL PERSONS INSURED PROVISION

As respects bodily injury, property damage and personal injury and advertising injury coverages, under the provision "Persons Insured," the following are added as insureds:

A. Spouse—Partnership ...

B. Employee—Any employee of the named insured while acting within the scope of his duties as such, but the insurance afforded to such employee does not apply:

   (1) to bodily injury or personal injury to another employee of the named insured arising out of or in the course of his employment;

   (2) to personal injury or advertising injury to the named insured or, if the named insured is a partnership or joint venture, any partner or member thereof, or the spouse of any of the foregoing; ....

One case that involved this provision is *Commercial Union Insurance Co. v Rose's Stores,* 411 S2d 122 (Ala 1982). The insurer sought a declaration that it was not obligated to defend as additional insureds under a CGL policy two employees of the store against claims for bodily injury brought by another employee of the store. The insurer was ordered to defend the action. However, on appeal, the decision was reversed.

The action arose out of an accident allegedly caused by the two employees. In reviewing the provisions of the policy and endorsement granting employees insured status, the higher Alabama court could find no ambiguity in the policy language. The court stated instead that the additional insured provision at issue clearly communicated that the insurance as provided to employees does not apply to injury to another employee arising out of or in the course of his employment.

One case that involved a partnership is *Kelley v Royal Globe Insurance Co.,* 349 S2d 561 (Ala 1977). A minor employee sustained serious injuries while operating a meat grinder at a store. Because the store employed only three persons, application of the workers compensation statute was not compulsory, and the owner had elected not to purchase coverage. Therefore, the injured employee filed suit against the store owner.

The lower court reformed the liability policy so that its named insured was a partnership composed of the owner and his spouse. It also found the minor to be an employee and further found the employers liability exclusion of the policy applicable to the partnership. The minor maintained that the store's liability was covered under its liability policy because his suit was against the owner individually. The employers liability exclusion, the minor explained, did not apply because he was employed by the partnership.

The court referred to three provisions of the partnership's liability policy. Two provisions had to do with partnerships under the Persons Insured provision and the other dealt with the employers liability exclusion. The court then decided that the partners and partnership, together, were an insured within the meaning of the severability of interests provision. The court concluded that the policy clearly excluded coverage because of the court's finding that the minor, at the time of the accident, was an employee of the insured acting within the line and scope of his employment.

Although workers compensation benefits are the exclusive remedy available to injured employees in most states, some firms still request that the fellow employee exclusion be deleted to provide employees with defense of these actions. Underwriters who are thinking of accommodating these requests should determine the geographic scope of the insured's operation to determine if it reaches any jurisdictions where fellow employee suits are still recognized.

It is important to note that CGL policies distinguish between employees and executive officers of corporations when granting insured status to them. As a result, the fellow employee exclusions in CGL policies do not apply to suits made against executive officers by employees alleging injuries due to the executive officers' negligence. This, of course, has led to disputes concerning whether particular employees are executive officers and, ultimately, to the inclusion of a definition of the term "executive officer" when the CGL policy was revised in 1993. This issue, as well as some illustrative cases, is discussed in **Chapter 3.**

Post-1973 Employee Cross-Liability Exclusion

The post-1973 edition CGL forms are subject to a more restrictive employee injury cross-liability exclusion than was the case with the 1973 policy provisions. The pertinent part of the Who Is an Insured provision is reproduced in Exhibit 6.5.

The significance of the provision in Exhibit 6.5 compared to the previous liability policy provisions is that the 1986 and later edition policies preclude coverage if the named insured is injured at the hands of an employee and the latter is sued under the policy by the named insured. A case in which claim covered under an older edition policy that probably would have been excluded had the policy provision corresponded to the one of the latest CGL forms is *Evans v General Insurance Co.,* 390 SW2d 818 (Tex 1965).

A company president was injured when a company truck, while being operated by a company employee within the business premises, struck him. Since the president was not an "employee" within the meaning of the fellow employee exclusion, the policy provided the employee with protection for the suit brought by the president. The Texas court stated that although a person might be an officer or an employee of a corporation, or both, the mere fact he was an officer of a corporation did not mean that he also should be regarded as an employee.

EXHIBIT 6.5
POST-1973 EMPLOYEE INJURY
CROSS-LIABILITY EXCLUSION

2. Each of the following is also an insured:

a. Your employees, other than your executive officers, but only for acts within the scope of their employment by you. However, none of these employees is an insured for:

(1) "Bodily injury" or "personal injury" to you or to a co-employee while in the course of his or her employment; ....

Also, the fellow employee exclusion of the 1973 policy was held not to apply in a situation where the named insured filed suit against an employee who caused the injury. In *LaRiviere v New Hampshire Insurance Group,* 413 A2d 309 (NH 1980), the named insured was in the house-moving business. As the business owner was cutting some tree branches while in the bucket of a cherry picker, the employee operating the unit backed it up suddenly. This caused the owner to fall out of the bucket and sustain injuries. When the business owner filed suit against the employee and the employee looked to the owner's liability policy for protection, the insurer denied coverage based on the fellow employee exclusion, which read, "... to 'bodily injury' to any fellow employee of such person injured in the course of his employment ...."

The insurer's rationale for denying coverage was that since the owner of the business at the time of the accident was engaged in work that could have been performed by a common laborer, he was, for purposes of the exclusion, a fellow employee of the one who allegedly caused his injury. The court, however, disagreed with the "strained" interpretation of the insurer and held that the owner was an executive officer rather than a fellow employee.

Diluting the Severability Provision

Some insurers feel that with the multitude of insureds that can be added to liability policies, the severability of interests provision creates a complex situation that is difficult to deal with. An example is in determining what policy provisions, particularly exclusions, are meant to apply severally as opposed to collectively and vice versa. As a result, some insurers have attempted to eliminate the severability of interest provision by a more subtle way than with a cross-liability exclusion. The approach instead has been to substitute reference to "the insured" (which connotes severability) with the words "an insured" or "any insured."

If an insurer uses the words "any insured" in an exclusion, the courts of some states hold that the concept of severability is defeated and the exclusion in question is applicable to all insureds whether directly or vicariously liable. Take, for example, reference to "any insured" as used in the following manuscript employers' liability exclusion.

> This insurance does not apply to bodily injury" to an "employee" of any Insured arising out of and in the course of employment by "the insured.

Such a construction is contrary to both the intent of the employers' liability exclusion and insurance and risk management custom and practice. One case illustrative of this subject is *Transport Indemnity Co. v Wyatt,* 417 S2d 568 (Ala 1982). An employee who was injured in the scope of his employment filed suit against the executive officers of the employer. The executive officers sought protection under the employer's CGL policy as insureds. However, coverage was denied by the insurer based on the employer's liability and fellow employee exclusions.

The employer's liability exclusion read in part:

> This insurance does not apply ... [t]o any OCCURRENCE which caused BODILY INJURY to any employee of any INSURED arising out of or in the course of his employment by any INSURED....

The court, in looking at the policy's severability of interests provision, stated that the term "any INSURED," as used in the policy, was ambiguous on its face in that a fair construction thereof could be that it referred to "any one of the insureds." It also held that the word "insured," as used in the policy, meant only the person claiming coverage and, as such, "the term was used severally and not collectively." Thus, each insured had coverage except with respect to its own employees.

Use of the one word "any" throughout a policy cannot and should not be considered to defeat the concept of severability that is inherent and runs throughout the liability policy. This kind of construction will lead to an illogical gap in coverage for one of the more predominant risks sought to be covered. Furthermore, such an exclusion would require clear and obvious notice to the insureds, because a party who has contractually required additional insured status will expect that third-party-over actions will be covered as is common industry practice. Failure of the named insured to procure the insurance as required by contract may result in a breach of contract claim (and such breach of contract claims are generally not covered by insurance).

Although *Transport Indemnity* illustrates this point, another example is exclusion j.(4) of CGL forms, which applies to property damage "to personal property in the care, custody or control of the insured." While there may be some disagreement, the words "the insured" in this exclusion have the effect of barring protection only to the person who has possession of the personal property at the time of its loss or damage and not to all insureds who may be drawn into a case. Thus, if the personal property were in the possession of an employee (insured) at the time of loss or damage, coverage would still apply to the employer (named insured) for its vicarious liability. However, assume exclusion j.(4) were to preclude coverage for property damage to "personal property in the care, custody or control of any insured." This exclusion *could be* interpreted as precluding coverage for even the employer's vicarious fault.

As previously noted, to limit the scope of the severability of interests provision of liability policies, some insurers have substituted the phrase "an insured" or "any insured" in place of "the insured" in some exclusions. While that substitution may in and of itself initially give the effect of narrowing coverage, the overall effect may be to create an ambiguity, unless the separation of insureds condition is removed from the policy or the policy is endorsed with a cross-liability exclusion.[3]

The legal precedent most violated by this very subtle attempt to eliminate coverage is that which gives effect to the insured's reasonable expectation of coverage. The concept and application of severability of interests are well ingrained in the minds of insureds and are custom and practice in the insurance and risk management industry. Insureds have no expectation that this vital and anticipated coverage concept is being subtly eliminated in select exclusions merely by substituting the word "any" for the word "the."

Cross-Liability Exclusion Endorsements

The practice by insurers of adding cross-liability exclusion endorsements to umbrella policies seems to be increasingly common. The genesis of cross-liability exclusions varies with the insurance policy. Questions were raised years ago about whether an automobile liability policy should apply to a suit involving one spouse against another. The answer hinged on both prevailing common law and statute by jurisdiction. Some states did not permit interspousal tort suits; others did. The abrogation of intrafamily immunity in the majority of states opened the door to many such suits under automobile and homeowners package policies. Insurance companies eventually added exclusions to their automobile, homeowners, and apartment dwellers package policies to eliminate such cross-suits.[4]

There is substantial variation between cross-liability exclusion endorsements used with CGL and umbrella liability policies. Some restrict coverage only with respect to suits brought by one named insured against another named insured, while others apply across the board to all types of insureds. Examples of these types of cross-liability exclusion endorsements are provided in Exhibit 6.6.

**EXHIBIT 6.6
EXAMPLE CROSS-LIABILITY
EXCLUSION ENDORSEMENTS**

Named Insured Cross-Liability Only

It is hereby understood and agreed that the coverage afforded by this policy does not apply to a claim for damages arising out of personal injury, property damage, or advertising injury, as defined, initiated, alleged, or caused to be brought about by a Named Insured or Additional Named Insured covered by the policy against any other Named Insured or Additional Named Insured covered by this policy.

Any Insured Cross-Liability

This policy does not apply ... to liability for bodily injury, personal injury, or property damage caused by an insured covered by this policy against any other insured.

Named insured versus named insured cross-liability exclusion endorsements may be justified in some cases, such as when a business organization desires to eliminate coverage for intercompany products. But it would be advisable that this be accomplished with the ISO Exclusion—Intercompany Products Suits (CG 21 41) endorsement, described in **Chapter 2.** Otherwise the exclusion may be broader in scope than intended.

Also, such exclusions should reflect a reduction of premium since they are reducing coverage that otherwise would apply. The more restrictive insured versus insured endorsements should be avoided if at all possible, particularly if the named insured is in a business where it is common to include others as additional insureds. If there is a valid reason for attaching such an endorsement, it should be carefully drafted to exclude precisely the types of claims for which there is a concern, leaving coverage for other types of cross-liability suits.

While they have not been commonly used in CGL and umbrella policies in the past, cross-liability exclusions are quite common in directors and officers (D&O) liability policies. The inclusion of these exclusions was prompted by suits filed against directors and officers by their financial institution employers. Since they have been frequently included in policies, D&O liability policy cross-liability exclusions—commonly labeled "insured versus insured" exclusions—have been tested in at least two cases, one being *American Casualty Co. of Reading, Penn. v Federal Deposit Insurance Corp.,* 677 F Supp 600 (USDC ND Iowa 1987). The court held here that the insured versus insured exclusion was not ambiguous and applied to the Federal Deposit Insurance Corporation, which was acting as a receiver for a failed bank when it filed suit against the directors and officers of the bank. However, in another bank case, *Continental Casualty Co. v Allen,* 710 F Supp 1088 (DC Tex 1989), the insured versus insured exclusion was ruled to be ambiguous and inapplicable.

Summary

The severability of interests clause (or separation of insureds condition) was introduced in liability policies to give every insured the same coverage it would have had if a separate policy had been issued (except with respect to the limits). Thus the effect of the severability of interests clause is to clarify that the term "insured" applies separately and not collectively, except with respect to the policy's limits. By achieving this, the severability of interests provision also clarifies the existence of cross-liability coverage. If one insured sues another insured, the insurer is obligated to protect the alleged tortfeasor (the insured) and pay damages to the injured person (the other insured) just as if the injured person were not an insured in the policy.

Further proof of the availability of cross-liability coverage in liability policies is the inclusion of the so-called fellow employee exclusion. The fellow employee exclusion is a limited form of a cross-liability exclusion that pertains solely to fellow employees, and it would not be needed if the policy did not generally cover claims made by one insured against another insured. In other words, the presence of a fellow employee exclusion implies that cross-liability coverage applies for claims and suits between other insureds.

Since liability policies cover cross-liability suits between additional insureds and named insureds, there are no standard "cross-liability endorsements" available for attachment to CGL policies. For this reason, contractual insurance provisions requiring cross-liability endorsements often create unnecessary negotiations and paperwork. It is probably a better approach to simply include a requirement in contract insurance provisions that the liability policies provide cross-liability coverage. In most situations, this will be provided by the named insured's basic policy form without modification.

Some insurers currently view the severability of interests provision of liability policies as being especially troublesome when a policy encompasses a variety of insureds, as well as in determining whether a policy provision applies severally or collectively. Instead of adding cross-liability exclusions, however, some insurers are taking the more subtle approach of substituting the words "an insured" or "any insured" in place of the words "the insured." While this approach may work to their advantage, it also may create an ambiguity, particularly if the separation of insureds condition is left intact. It also defeats the insured's reasonable expectation of coverage.

Chapter 6 Notes

1. *Couch on Insurance 2d,* Sec. 45:549, as cited in *Barnette v Hartford Insurance Group,* 653 P2d 1375, 1383 (SC Wyo 1982).

2. *General Aviation Supply Co. v Insurance Co. of North America,* 181 F Supp 380 (ED Mo 1960).

3. As a point of interest, though not involving a CGL policy, a Massachusetts court in the case of *Worchester Mutual Insurance Co. v Marnell,* 496 NE2d 158 (Mass 1986), ruled that the severability of interests provision was to take precedence over an exclusion that referred to the words "any insured."

4. Intrafamily cross-liability exclusions are permitted in only slightly more than half the states.

Chapter 7

STANDARD ADDITIONAL INSURED ENDORSEMENTS

As discussed in previous chapters, endorsements are used to effect additional insured status in commercial general liability (CGL) policies. There are a number of standard endorsements that have been drafted by Insurance Services Office, Inc. (ISO), for this purpose. While they are very useful tools, these endorsements do not address all the issues that may arise when one party is added to the liability policy of another as an additional insured. To address some issues, it is necessary to manuscript specialized endorsement forms.

Endorsements are not typically needed to effect additional insured status in umbrella liability policies. Most of these policies automatically include as additional insureds: (1) any organization qualifying as an insured in the scheduled underlying insurance, and (2) any organization with whom the named insured contractually agrees to include as an additional insured. While this practice minimizes the occurrence of breaches of contractual agreements to add others as insureds, it also leads to other problems (see **Chapter 14**). These problems can also be addressed with nonstandard manuscript endorsements.

However, the use of manuscript endorsements can lead to other problems. While standard ISO endorsements do not meet all needs of all additional insureds, they have been carefully drafted and subjected to industry review and, in many cases, judicial review. Additionally, since they are not drafted by the additional insured, they will usually be interpreted in favor of the additional insured, depending, of course, on the facts of the case involved.

Also, if manuscript endorsements are required by the indemnitee or utilized by the indemnitor and submitted to the insurer, other problems arise. For example, the administrative burden of monitoring compliance with requirements calling for manuscript endorsements or simply ensuring that the insurer adopts them becomes extremely difficult. In many cases, insurers reject manuscript endorsements. When they do, the party requiring them must monitor, analyze, and report on what was substituted. All too often, what is offered as a replacement falls short of contract requirements.

In addition, despite the automatic additional insured provisions found in most umbrella policies, it may actually be preferable to utilize standard ISO endorsements with umbrella policies, with slight modifications in wording to reflect use in an excess layer. The reason is that automatic additional insured provisions often limit coverage to what is required in the underlying contract. This leads to the interdependency/inextricably tied issue discussed in **Chapter 4.** It will also lead to complications and coverage disputes in applying all available layers of coverage when a loss exceeds the minimum amount required in the contract, as discussed in **Chapter 14** on umbrella policies.

Of course, limiting additional insured coverage to what the contract requires essentially converts the coverage to contractual liability coverage rather than providing the broader coverage additional insureds have become accustomed to. This means that there may be a gap in the coverage provided by the primary layer utilizing a standard additional insured endorsement and the umbrella policy that limits additional insured status to what the contract calls for.

Because of the distinction between the coverage afforded to additional insureds and the way coverage applies to additional insureds that are indemnitees under contractual liability coverage, there may be gaps in coverage, uninsured additional insured losses in the excess layer, and allegations of breach of contract. In some cases, the loss will be paid on behalf of the named insured if sued by the additional insured, but this may not always be the case. As discussed previously, there are losses that would be covered for the additional insured but excluded for the named insured. In those instances, the named insured that is the indemnitor faces a problem.

This chapter takes a general look at the ISO endorsements used to effect additional insured status in CGL policies. It also examines the *Commercial Lines Manual (CLM)* rule that governs their use. Later chapters look more closely at some of the most commonly used endorsements.

Historical Development

The authors have been unable to ascertain when standard additional insured endorsements were first introduced for use by member and subscriber companies of the ISO's predecessor organizations. It might have been in 1966, when the comprehensive general liability policy forms were revamped extensively. One indication of this is that the *Manual of Liability Insurance,* commonly referred to in earlier years as the *"Liability Manual,"* did not contain an extensive additional interests rule dealing with the addition of insureds and premium charges.[1]

The first standard general liability policy (referred to then as "public liability insurance") provisions were introduced in 1941. An attorney for the National Bureau of Casualty and Surety Underwriters, one of ISO's predecessor bureaus, had written a series of articles between September 1941 and January 1943 about the new standard insurance policies, endorsements, and manual rules, which eventually were compiled into a book entitled *Comprehensive Liability Insurance.*[2]

The subject of additional insured status (referred to as "additional interests" in the *Liability Manu-*

al as well as in the current ISO *Commercial Lines Manual)* was viewed as cautiously then as it is today. The confusion over additional named insureds also existed even in those early days. This is what E.W. Sawyer had to say in *Comprehensive Liability Insurance* about additional named insureds.

> … [I]t is important to keep constantly in mind that, because the insuring language blankets the activities of the insured named in the declarations, the addition of additional named insureds extends the coverage of the policy to the activities of each of the named insureds. Therefore, if it is intended to endorse a policy to cover the liability which B may have because of the activities of A, it is not proper to use an endorsement the effect of which is to make B a named insured, because to do so would extend the coverage to all activities of B. The endorsement should extend the coverage of the policy to cover only the liability of B arising from the activities of A. But, if it is intended that the policy shall cover not only A's activities but also B's activities, it would be proper to use an endorsement the effect of which is to make B an additional named insured.

Some interesting observations can be made based on the foregoing. First of all, it is not certain whether the author is referring to an additional insured to be named in the policy or to an additional named insured. It would appear he intended the former. It is not unusual for people even today to refer to additional insureds as additional named insureds. This is probably the reason many people today ask for additional named insured status. It appears to have been a source of confusion right from the beginning.

The liability policies of the 1940s contained a definition of insured that was concise compared to today's policies:

> The unqualified word "insured" includes the named insured and also includes any partner, executive officer, director or stockholder thereof while acting within the scope of his duties as such.[3]

Since these policies were designed for corporations and partnerships, it was necessary to add an "individual as named insured" endorsement whenever a sole proprietor was to be the named insured. However, since an individual can be involved in nonbusiness pursuits, insurers recognized that the policy had to be limited solely to the individual's business activities. For this reason, the Individual as Named Insured (L 6370) endorsement read, in part:

> It is agreed that the policy does not apply except in connection with the conduct of a business of which the named insured is the sole owner.[4]

The above endorsement, which was available for use from the 1940s until the introduction of the 1966 general liability policy provisions, had the effect of not only excluding nonbusiness pursuits of the individual (named insured) but also limiting coverage to the business in which the individual was the sole owner; that is, no coverage applied where the individual was a part owner. This endorsement became unnecessary with the introduction of the 1966 standard general liability forms by the National Bureau of Casualty Underwriters.[5]

In the earlier years, the additional insured endorsements were prepared to fit the needs of nonautomatic insureds as they arose. An example of one such endorsement used in the early 1950s was the Additional Interest (L 6959) endorsement and read, in part: "It is agreed that such insurance as is afforded by the policy under [insert coverages] of the policy shall apply to each interest named herein; but such inclusion of additional interest or interests shall not operate to increase the limits of the company's liability."

It is interesting to note that this endorsement was used during the period before the severability of interests provision was added to general liability policies. Prior to this time, severability was almost always inferred instead of being specifically stated in the policy. Also, reference in the endorsement to the effect that additional interests did not operate to increase the limits substantiates that the concept of severability existed as it does today, even though not specifically mentioned in the policy.

This also was a broad form endorsement because it added the additional interest without limitation. However, the additional interest was not specifically referred to as an "insured." This created the potential for ambiguity because it did not clearly direct the reader to assume that the term "insured" wherever used in the policy also was to include the additional interest as named in the endorsement.

Another approach sometimes used prior to 1966 was for the endorsement to simply state that in consideration of an additional premium, the person or entity listed is an additional insured, "as their interests may appear" but only with respect to operations conducted by the named insured as described therein. The problem with this type of endorsement is reference to the phrase in quotes. This phraseology should be avoided in liability policies because it is a relatively indefinable term. Other endorsements simply listed a person or organization as an additional insured without restriction, other than mentioning the project, contract, or other reason for having named such person or entity.

Employers who desired or were required to cover their employees as insureds needed to have an endorsement added to the policy. In 1966 a standard endorsement was introduced, the Additional Insured (Employees) (L 9106, G 106) endorsement. It covered employees while acting within the scope of their duties, subject to exclusions for injury to fellow employees and damage to property the employee owned, occupied, rented, or was otherwise in his or her care, custody, or control. It was not until the introduction of the Broad Form CGL (GL 04 04) endorsement by ISO in 1976 that the separate employee as additional insured endorsement became unnecessary. The advantage of the broad form endorsement, from the employees' perspective, was that it covered them not only for bodily injury and property damage, which were the two coverages of the basic policy, but also personal injury and advertising injury, which were also added by the Broad Form CGL endorsement.

A variety of other endorsements also became standardized in 1966 when the National Bureau of Casualty Underwriters introduced a new set of liability policies with a unique format consisting of a policy jacket and coverage part.

By 1986, when the 1973 edition comprehensive general liability program was replaced by the commercial general liability program, there were 14 standard additional insured endorsements. All but one of these endorsements (the limited form vendors endorsement) were rolled into the 1986 CGL program with only minor editorial changes to make them compatible with the new "plain language" policy forms. Of course, the endorsement numbers were also changed to correspond to the new numbering system. The 1986 CGL program also introduced 14 new additional insured endorsements.

Throughout the 1990s, a number of the standard endorsements were modified in various ways, and several new additional insured endorsements were introduced. Exhibit 7.2 outlines the changes made to standard additional insured endorsements.

Current ISO Endorsements

Within the 2004 CGL edition ISO portfolio, there are 28 endorsements that can be used to extend insured status to one party (or class of people, such as church or club members) under another entity's CGL policy. These endorsements are listed in Exhibit 7.1. One endorsement listed in the exhibit, Additional Insured—Owners, Lessees or Contractors—Scheduled Person or Organization (for Use When Contractual Liability Coverage Is Not Provided To You Under This Policy) (CG 20 09) endorsement, is no longer part of the ISO portfolio. This endorsement, as its name indicates, was intended for use only on policies that did not provide contractual liability coverage. It provided coverage for additional insureds comparable to that of an owners and contractors protective (OCP) liability policy. Since CGL coverage for contractors virtually always includes contractual liability coverage, the circumstances under which CG 20 09 could appropriately be used have become all but nonexistent, and ISO decided to withdraw the endorsement as part of the 2004 revision.

The *CLM* is published by ISO to provide guidance on the use of standard policy forms and in determining the appropriate premium to charge for including the endorsements on a policy. In most states the rules delineated in this manual are submitted to and approved by regulators and must be followed by insurers. General Rules Section I deals with general liability insurance issues. In this section, Division Six Rule 16, "Additional Interests," addresses the use of the additional insured endorsements. The most current version (2004) of this rule is reproduced in Exhibit 7.2.

Many of the ISO additional insured endorsements are designed for use in situations other than those which are the focus of this book. For example, endorsements are available to add as insureds persons with special relationships with the named insured, such as church members and club members, and to modify the persons insured provision to more closely fit the needs of certain types of organizations, such as condominium associations and governmental entities. Since they typically do not involve the complexity and problems dealt with in this book, these endorsements are not treated in detail in this book.

The focus of this book is on additional insureds that are not directly related to the named insured but that have a business relationship with the named insured. Further, this business relationship is delineated in a contract or agreement that, among other things, requires the named insured to include the other party as an additional insured in its liability policy(ies). Examples include the following.

- Contracts between manufacturers and vendors

- Contracts between lessors of real or personal property and their lessees

- Contracts between project owners and contractors

- Contracts between contractors and their subcontractors

- Contracts between project owners and architects, engineers, or surveyors

EXHIBIT 7.1
CGL ADDITIONAL INSURED ENDORSEMENTS

Additional Insured Endorsements, Category 20

Endorsement Number	Title
CG 20 02	Additional Insured—Club Members
CG 20 03	Additional Insured—Concessionaires Trading under Your Name
CG 20 04	Additional Insured—Condominium Unit Owners
CG 20 05	Additional Insured—Controlling Interest
CG 20 07	*Additional Insured—Engineers, Architects or Surveyors (CGL)
CG 20 31	Additional Insured—Engineers, Architects or Surveyors (OCP)
CG 20 08	Additional Insured—Users of Golfmobiles
CG 20 09	*Additional Insured—Owners, Lessees, or Contractors—Scheduled Person or Organization (for Use When Contractual Liability Coverage Is Not Provided to You under this Policy)
CG 20 10	*Additional Insured—Owners, Lessees, or Contractors—Scheduled Person or Organization
CG 20 11	*Additional Insured—Managers or Lessors of Premises
CG 20 12	Additional Insured—State or Political Subdivisions—Permits
CG 20 13	Additional Insured—State or Political Subdivisions—Permits Relating to Premises
CG 20 14	Additional Insured—Users of Teams, Draft or Saddle Animals
CG 20 15	*Additional Insured—Vendors
CG 20 17	Additional Insured—Townhouse Associations
CG 20 32	*Additional Insured—Engineers, Architects or Surveyors Not Engaged by the Named Insured
CG 20 33	*Additional Insured—Owners, Lessees or Contractors—Automatic Status When Required in Construction Agreement with You
CG 20 34	*Additional Insured—Lessor of Leased Equipment—Automatic Status When Required in Lease Agreement with You
CG 20 18	Additional Insured—Mortgagee, Assignee or Receiver
CG 20 20	Additional Insured—Charitable Institutions
CG 20 21	Additional Insured—Volunteers
CG 20 22	Additional Insured—Church Members, Officers and Volunteer Workers
CG 20 23	Additional Insured—Executors, Administrators, Trustees or Beneficiaries
CG 20 24	*Additional Insured—Owners or Other Interests from Whom Land Has Been Leased
CG 20 25	Additional Insured—Elective, Appointive Executive Officers of Public Corporations
CG 20 26	*Additional Insured—Designated Person or Organization
CG 20 27	Additional Insured—Co-owner of Insured Premises
CG 20 28	*Additional Insured—Lessor of Leased Equipment
CG 20 29	Additional Insured—Grantor of Franchise
CG 20 30	Oil or Gas Operations—Nonoperating, Working Interest
CG 20 37	*Additional Insured—Owners, Lessees or Contractors—Completed Operations

*These endorsements are discussed in this book.

EXHIBIT 7.2
CLM ADDITIONAL INTERESTS RULE 16

Policies may be written to cover additional interests. Refer to each endorsement to determine the applicable Coverage Parts.

A. No Additional Charge

1. For architects, engineers or surveyors engaged by the insured, use Additional Insured—Engineers, Architects Or Surveyors Endorsement **CG 20 07** with the Commercial General Liability Coverage Part; use Additional Insured—Architects, Engineers Or Surveyors Endorsement **CG 20 31** with the Owners And Contractors Protective Liability Coverage Form.

2. For churches—members, trustees, officials, members of the board of governors, clergy or volunteers—on policies covering churches, use Additional Insured—Church Members, Officers And Volunteer Workers Endorsement **CG 20 22**.

3. For co-owners of premises only with respect to their liability as such, use Additional Insured—Co-Owner Of Insured Premises Endorsement **CG 20 27**.

4. For controlling interests, use Additional Insured—Controlling Interests Endorsement **CG 20 05**.

5. For elective or appointive executive officers of public and municipal corporations—including members of boards, corporations or commissions of such bodies on policies covering such boards, corporations or commissions, use Additional Insured—Elective Or Appointive Executive Officers Of Public Corporations Endorsement **CG 20 25**.

6. For executors, administrators, trustees or beneficiaries on policies covering estates of deceased persons or living trusts, use Additional Insured—Executors, Administrators, Trustees Or Beneficiaries Endorsement **CG 20 23**.

7. For grantor of licenses:

    a. When automatic status is required by licensor, use Endorsement **CG 20 35**.

    b. To add a grantor of the license on a Schedule basis, use Endorsement **CG 20 36**.

8. For members of clubs or unincorpo1rated associations—on policies covering such clubs or unincorporated associations, use Additional Insured—Club Members Endorsement **CG 20 02**.

9. For mortgagees, assignees or receivers—on policies covering owners or general lessees, use Additional Insured—Mortgagee, Assignee, Or Receiver Endorsement **CG 20 18**.

10. For oil or gas operations—co-owners, joint ventures or mining partners with nonoperating working interests with the insured in oil or gas leases—on policies covering the operators of such leases, use Oil Or Gas Operations—Nonoperating, Working Interests Endorsement **CG 20 30**.

11. For owners or other interests from whom land has been leased, use Additional Insured—Owners Or Other Interests From Whom Land Has Been Leased Endorsement **CG 20 24**.

12. For states, counties, cities or other governmental units—permits issued to:

    a. Owners or lessees, use Additional Insured—State Or Political Subdivisions—Permits Relating To Premises Endorsement **CG 20 13**.

    b. Contractors, use Additional Insured—State Or Political Subdivisions—Permits Endorsement **CG 20 12**; use Additional Insured—State Or Political Subdivisions—Permits Endorsement **CG 29 35** with the Owners And Contractors Protective Liability Coverage Form.

This rule does not apply to operations performed for such governmental units.

13. For trustees, members of boards of governors—on policies covering charitable institutions, use Additional Insured—Charitable Institutions Endorsement **CG 20 20**.

continued

EXHIBIT 7.2
CLM ADDITIONAL INTERESTS RULE 16 (cont.)

B. Additional Charge—Refer To Company

1. For concessionaires, use Additional Insured—Concessionaires Trading Under Your Name Endorsement **CG 20 03**.

   Those who are physically separated and who operate under their own name cannot be added as additional interests.

2. For grantors of franchises, use Additional Insured—Grantor Of Franchise Endorsement **CG 20 29**.

3. For lessors of leased equipment who have signed a contract or agreement that requires them to be added as an additional insured on a policy covering a lessee, with respect to liability arising out of the named insured's maintenance, operation or use of such leased equipment, use Additional Insured—Lessor Of Leased Equipment—Automatic Status When Required In Lease Agreement With You Endorsement **CG 20 34**.

   For all other lessors of leased equipment, use Additional Insured—Lessor Of Leased Equipment Endorsement **CG 20 28**.

4. For owners, lessees or contractors—Owners or Lessees on policies covering contractors or contractors on policies covering subcontractors, but only as respects liability for operations performed for those owners, lessees or contractors by or on behalf of the insured contractor or subcontractor, use Additional Insured—Owners, Lessees Or Contractors—Scheduled Person Or Organization Endorsement **CG 20 10**. In addition, this endorsement is to be used when requests for additional insured status are not in writing.

   If the policy covering the insured contractor or subcontractor does not provide contractual liability coverage, use Additional Insured—Owners, Lessees Or Contractors—Scheduled Person Or Organization (For Use When Contractual Liability Coverage Is Not Provided To You In This Policy) Endorsement **CG 20 09**. Attach this endorsement whenever such additional insured coverage is requested and Contractual Liability Limitation Endorsement **CG 21 39** is also attached to the same policy.

5. For managers or operators of premises or interests from whom premises have been rented or leased on policies covering lessees or tenants, use Additional Insured—Managers Or Lessors Of Premises Endorsement **CG 20 11**.

6. For vendors' product liability on policies covering manufacturers or distributors, use Additional Insured—Vendors Endorsement **CG 20 15**.

7. For all others, use Additional Insured—Designated Person Or Organization Endorsement **CG 20 26**.

8. For architects, engineers or surveyors not engaged by the named insured but contractually required to be added as an additional insured to the named insured's policy, use Additional Insured—Engineers, Architects Or Surveyors Not Engaged By The Named Insured Endorsement **CG 20 32** with the Commercial General Liability Coverage Part.

9. For owners or lessees, or contractors who have signed a contract or agreement that requires them to be added as an additional insured on a policy covering a contractor or a subcontractor, with respect to liability arising out of the named insured's ongoing operations performed for that additional insured, use Additional Insured—Owners, Lessees Or Contractors—Automatic Status When Required In Construction Agreement With You Endorsement **CG 20 33**. Do not attach this endorsement if Contractual Liability Limitation Endorsement **CG 21 39** is also attached to the same policy.

10. For owners, lessees or contractors—Completed operations coverage for owners or lessees on policies covering contractors, or contractors on policies covering subcontractors is available. Use Additional Insured—Owners, Lessees Or Contractors—Completed Operations Endorsement **CG 20 37**.

EXHIBIT 7.3
AAIS ADDITIONAL INSURED ENDORSEMENTS

Title	Form Number	Corresponding ISO Endorsement
Additional Insured—Church Members, Officers, and Volunteer Workers	GL-107	CG 20 22
Additional Insureds—Co-Owner of Insured Premises; Controlling Interest; or Mortgage, Assignee, or Receiver	GL-108	CG 20 05, CG 20 18, and CG 20 27
Additional Insured—Landlord	GL-109	CG 20 11
Additional Insured (State or Political Subdivision Permits)	GL-110	CG 20 12
Additional Insured (State or Political Subdivisions—Premises Permits)	GL-111	CG 20 13
Additional Insured—Grantor of Franchise; Lessor of Leased Equipment; Owners, Lessees or Contractors	GL-112	CG 20 10, CG 20 28 and CG 20 29
Additional Insured—Owners, Lessees or Contractors	GL-113	CG 20 09 and CG 20 10
Boats	GL-114	No ISO equivalent; insures a person or organization legally responsible for the use of a scheduled watercraft that the named insured does not own, but is used with the named insured's permission
Colleges or Schools	GL-116	No ISO equivalent; insures the named insured's trustees or members of its Board of Governors; the named insured's board members or commissioners; and student teachers teaching as part of their educational requirements
Additional Insured—Engineers, Architects, or Surveyors	GL-117	CG 20 07
Additional Insured—Condominiums	GL-160	CG 20 04
Additional Insured—Officers and Board Members—Public Corporations	GL-837	CG 20 25
Additional Insured—Designated Party	GL-841	CG 20 26
Additional Insured—Lessors	GL-842	CG 20 24
Additional Insured—Vendors	GL-843	CG 20 15
Additional Insured—Club Members	GL-844	CG 20 02
Additional Insured—Concessionaires Trading Under Your Name	GL-845	CG 20 03
Additional Insured—Golfmobiles	GL-874	CG 20 08
Additional Insured—Nonprofit Organizations—Members, Officials and Volunteer Workers	GL-887	CG 20 20

EXHIBIT 7.4
KEEPING UP WITH ISO ENDORSEMENT CHANGES

The following list summarizes the most significant changes to standard additional insured endorsements—either revision of existing language or the introduction of new endorsements—since 1985.

Additional Insured—Engineers, Architects or Surveyors CG 20 07 <u>01 87</u>

The <u>10 93</u> edition substituted reference to "ongoing operations" in place of "your work."

The <u>07 98</u> edition reflected some editorial changes only, e.g., changing reference to personal injury and advertising injury to personal and advertising injury.

The <u>07 04</u> edition attempts to eliminate the additional insured's sole negligence.

Additional Insured—Owners, Lessees or Contractors (Form A) CG 20 09 <u>11 85</u>

The <u>10 93</u> edition substituted reference to "ongoing operations" in place of "your work."

The <u>03 97</u> edition dropped reference to (Form A) and was retitled as Additional Insured—Owners, Lessees or Contractors—Scheduled Person or Organization (For Use When Contractual Liability Coverage Is Not Provided To You In This Policy)

This endorsement was withdrawn as part of the 2004 revision.

Additional Insured—Owners, Lessees or Contractors (Form B) CG 20 10 <u>11 85</u>

The <u>10 93</u> edition substituted reference to "ongoing operations" in place of "your work."

The <u>03 97</u> edition dropped the reference (Form B) from its title.

The <u>10 01</u> edition added two provisions to eliminate ambiguity allowing coverage for completed work in some fact patterns.

The <u>07 04</u> edition attempts to eliminate the additional insured's sole negligence.

Additional Insured—Vendors CG 20 15 <u>11 88</u>. This endorsement incorporated the wording of the broad form and limited form vendors endorsements that were available prior to its introduction.

The <u>07 04</u> edition attempts to eliminate the vendor's sole negligence coverage, with certain exceptions.

Additional Insured—Volunteers CG 20 21 <u>11 85</u>.

The <u>10 93</u> edition amended the endorsement's title to Additional Insured—Volunteer Workers and made some other editorial changes.

The <u>07 98</u> edition made some editorial changes only.

This endorsement was withdrawn with the <u>10 01</u> changes and its extension of insured status to volunteers was incorporated into the CGL provisions.

continued

EXHIBIT 7.4
KEEPING UP WITH ISO ENDORSEMENT CHANGES (cont.)

Additional Insured—Church Members, Officers and Volunteer Workers CG 20 22 11 88.

The 10 93 edition added an exclusion for medical payments and a co-volunteer exclusion encompassing family members. It also added an exclusion for any obligation to share damages.

The 07 98 edition made some editorial changes only.

The 10 01 edition dropped reference to volunteers, who were granted insured status in the standard CGL policy provisions.

Additional Insured—Executors, Administrators, Trustees or Beneficiaries CG 20 23 11 85.

The 10 93 edition added living trusts.

Additional Insured—Designated Person or Organization CG 20 26 11 85.

The 07 04 edition replaces the reference to the named insured's "work" with "ongoing operations" and attempts to eliminate the additional insured's sole negligence.

Additional Insured—Lessor of Leased Equipment CG 20 28 11 85.

The 07 04 edition attempts to eliminate the additional insured's sole negligence.

Additional Insured—Engineers, Architects or Surveyors CG 20 31 01 96.

This endorsement is used with the OCP policy only, in circumstances when the professional is engaged by the named insured.

The 07 04 edition attempts to eliminate the additional insured's sole negligence.

Additional Insured—Engineers, Architects or Surveyors CG 20 32 01 96.

This endorsement is used when the professional is not engaged by the named insured.

The 07 98 made some editorial changes only.

The 07 04 edition attempts to eliminate the additional insured's sole negligence.

Additional Insured—Owners, Lessees or Contractors CG 20 33 03 97. This endorsement was introduced in 1997 to provide coverage on a blanket basis and only for ongoing operations, i.e., excluding completed operations.

The 07 98 edition made some editorial changes only.

The 10 01 edition added a more explicit exclusion of completed operations.

The 07 04 edition attempts to eliminate coverage of the additional insured's sole negligence.

Additional Insured—Lessor of Leased Equipment—Automatic Status When Required In Lease Agreement With You CG 20 34 03 97. This endorsement was introduced in 1997 to provide coverage on a blanket basis.

The 07 04 edition attempts to eliminate the additional insured's sole negligence.

Additional Insured—Owners, Lessees or Contractors—Completed Operations CG 20 37 10 01. Introduced to provide completed operations for insureds at scheduled locations.

The 07 04 edition attempts to eliminate the additional insured's sole negligence.

The standard additional insured endorsements most often used in this context are marked with an asterisk (*) in Exhibit 7.1 and are discussed in the chapters that follow.

AAIS Additional Insured Endorsements

The American Association of Insurance Services (AAIS) is a licensed rating organization providing advisory information and technical support to its affiliated property and casualty insurance companies. While the majority of these insurers are regional insurers, the growth of this organization and its product lines has resulted in a diverse membership, including midsized and larger commercial insurers. AAIS is licensed to provide services in all states, the District of Columbia, and Puerto Rico.

The origin of AAIS dates back to 1936 with the formation of the Mutual Marine Conference. In 1946 the name was changed to Transportation Insurance Rating Bureau (TIRB). As the name TIRB suggests, AAIS originally specialized in providing services for transportation insurance. It was in 1975 that TIRB became the American Association of Insurance Services.

AAIS has developed a general liability program for commercial insureds similar to ISO's. Many of the additional insured endorsements for use with this program correspond to those of ISO. Exhibit 7.3 lists the most widely used AAIS additional insured endorsements and indicates the ISO endorsement to which each most closely corresponds.

Summary

Standard ISO and AAIS additional insured endorsements have been available for use with CGL policies for many years. The endorsements were changed little from 1973 until the early 1990s, when some new or revised endorsements modified coverage for contractors, lessors, and professional liability exposures. The ISO *Commercial Lines Manual* Rule 16 gives underwriters guidance on when to add additional insureds and what, if any, premium to charge.

Chapter 7 Notes

1. The following manuals were contained within the *Liability Manual* binder: *Contractual Liability Manual; Elevator Manual; Manufacturers and Contractors Manual; Owners, Landlords and Tenants Liability Manual; Owners or Contractors Protective Manual;* and *Product Liability Manual.* The following could also be combined into that same binder: *Druggists Liability Manual; Hospital Professional Liability Manual; Miscellaneous Medical Professional Liability Manual;* and *Physicians, Surgeons, and Dentists Professional Liability Manual.*

2. E. W. Sawyer, *Comprehensive Liability Insurance,* New York: The Underwriter Printing and Publishing Company.

3. The specific 1941, 1947, and 1955 edition policies in question were the owners, landlords, and tenants (OL&T) policy, the manufacturers and contractors (M&C) policy, and the standard comprehensive general liability policy. It was with the 1955 editions that the definition of insured also included any organization or proprietor with respect to real estate management for the named insured. The standard comprehensive auto-general liability policy was first introduced in 1943. This latter policy also included an "omnibus clause" that specified the persons or organizations considered to be automatic insureds.

4. Davis Tyree Ratcliffe, *General Liability Insurance Handbook,* 1959, pp. 164–165.

5. The National Bureau of Casualty Underwriters became the Insurance Rating Board in 1968 and Insurance Services Office, Inc., in 1971.

Chapter 8

ENGINEERS, ARCHITECTS, OR SURVEYORS AS ADDITIONAL INSUREDS

Design professionals—engineers, architects, surveyors—often include requirements in their agreements with project owners to be provided with additional insured status on the liability policies of general contractors or, in some cases, the policies of the project owner or subcontractors that will be involved in the project. The protection sought by the design professional under the policy of others is not for liability stemming from any professional acts or omissions but, instead, from liability emanating from the *general* negligence of the design professional outside the realm of what could be labeled as a professional act or omission. A very limited form of protection is being sought by the design professional under the additional insured endorsement of a commercial general liability (CGL) insurance policy because most of the services to be performed by a design professional are professional in nature and, therefore, require professional liability insurance. Yet there are instances when the nature of the professional's fault could be outside the scope of professional services, and it is this exposure that is targeted by the design professional as an additional insured under the liability policies of others.

Probably the most important exposure being targeted by design professionals who require additional insured status in the CGL policy of the general contractor is that arising from suits by injured employees of the contractor. These suits often allege that the design professional had an obligation to provide a safe job site or monitor the contractors' safety programs. Being an additional insured in the general contractor's CGL policy will also prohibit the contractor's insurer from subrogating in the event of a claim against the contractor for a construction defect or other damage or injury that may have been partly attributable to the design professional.

The problem is that when claim is made or suit is brought in a situation where there is injury or damage during or following the completion of work or services at a construction project, it is not unusual for the insurer of the project owner or contractor to deny protection to the design professional as an additional insured. The common reason given is that what the design professional did or failed to do was professional in nature and outside the scope of any protection under the additional insured endorsement. This kind of situation has happened so often that the protection being relied on by these professionals sometimes warrants the label "illusory."

Prisco Serena Sturm Architects v Liberty Mutual Insurance Co., 126 F3d 886 (7th Cir 1997), is an example. The insurer denying coverage in that claim offered the following two examples of coverage an additional insured design professional might have. If someone entering the architect's trailer at the construction site were to slip and fall and then file an injury claim against the architect, the named insured's CGL policy would provide coverage. Likewise, if the architect's employee were to leave a coffee pot on after departing for the day, resulting in a fire that caused damage to the construction project, claims based on that occurrence would be covered by the CGL policy.

These are not the only problems that confront design professionals under general (nonprofessional) liability policies. Another issue is the extent to which protection *automatically* applies to such professionals under the contractual liability coverage of an indemnitor's CGL policy. It is a coverage feature that is overlooked and misunderstood. The fact that there is disagreement over the meaning of "professional services" also is a source of dispute between insureds and insurers.

Additional Insured Status

In recent years, there have been a number developments with respect to additional insured endorsements for design professionals. The endorsement used prior to 1993 not only encompassed the completed operations hazard, but also was used whether the professional was engaged by the named insured or by someone else. This endorsement has since been amended to limit coverage to ongoing operations. In 1993 two additional endorsements were introduced. The first, the Additional Insured—Engineers, Architects or Surveyors Not Engaged by the Named Insured (CG 20 32) endorsement, is intended to take care of those situations where the professional is not engaged by the named insured but is still required to be named as an additional insured on the named insured's CGL policy. The other, the Additional Insured—Engineers, Architects or Surveyors (CG 20 31) endorsement, is intended to provide additional insured status to these same professionals but in an OCP policy. In light of these changes, this discussion first addresses the pre-1993 edition of this endorsement, followed by the trials and tribulations of these professionals as additional insureds, and then addresses recent amendments, including endorsement CG 20 31, which is designed solely for use with owners and contractors protective (OCP) liability coverage.

Although from time to time a court will hold an architect, engineer, or surveyor to be covered as an additional insured for his or her general negligence, it is rare for such a professional either to do or fail to do something in a business setting that will amount to general negligence. In those cases where these professionals have been fortunate enough to obtain coverage as an additional insured

under the Additional Insured—Engineers, Architects or Surveyors (CG 20 07) endorsement, their protection for liability arising out of ongoing operations has applied even when they have been solely at fault. The reason for this goes back to the meaning of the endorsement's phraseology "arising out of," which, as understood in custom and practice and as interpreted by the majority of courts, connotes coverage encompassing the additional insured's sole fault.

Stating that sole fault coverage was contrary to the original intent of the additional insured endorsements, Insurance Services Office, Inc. (ISO), introduced changes in 2004 that amend additional insured endorsements to limit coverage of additional insureds to their partial fault. The language of CG 20 07, as amended to effect this coverage intent, is shown in Exhibit 8.1.

One potential problem with this new version of the endorsement, a problem that it shares with other endorsements revised in 2004, is that it does not specify the *extent* to which an act or omission of the named insured causes the injury or damage for which the additional insured is liable. All that is required to trigger coverage is an allegation that at least 1 percent of the cause of the injury or damage can be attributed to the named insured's actions. The additional insured has no coverage with respect to its *sole* fault under the current version of the endorsement, but if it is only 99 percent at fault—and the named insured's fault is set at as little as 1 percent—then coverage will apply. How insurers can avoid this type of predicament is explained in **Chapter 9**.

Apart from the foregoing, the current (2004) endorsement is like the 1998 edition of the endorsement which it replaced in that it is not necessary to schedule the name of the professional being given insured status. The endorsement applies on a blanket basis—to "any architect, engineer or surveyor engaged by [the named insured]." One subtle difference between the current and earlier edition of the endorsement is that the current version refers to the professional as an "additional insured." Earlier editions of this endorsement referred simply to "insureds."

**EXHIBIT 8.1
ENDORSEMENT CG 20 07
(2004 Edition)**

A. **Section II—Who Is An Insured** is amended to include as an additional insured any architect, engineer, or surveyor engaged by you but only with respect to liability for "bodily injury", "property damage" or "personal and advertising injury" caused, in whole or in part, by your acts or omissions or the acts or omissions of those acting on your behalf:

   1. In connection with your premises; or

   2. In the performance of your ongoing operations.

B. With respect to the insurance afforded to these additional insureds, the following additional exclusion applies:

   This insurance does not apply to "bodily injury", "property damage" or "personal and advertising injury" arising out of the rendering of or the failure to render any professional services by or for you, including:

   1. The preparing, approving, or failing to prepare or approve, maps, shop drawings, opinions, reports, surveys, field orders, change orders or drawings and specifications; or

   2. Supervisory, inspection, architectural or engineering activities.

   © ISO Properties, Inc., 2004

The change does not appear to make any difference, since wherever the word "insured" appears throughout the policy, one needs to insert the additional insured who is seeking coverage. Moreover, the additional insured is as much an insured as anyone else, whether referred to as an insured or as an additional insured. The revised language does, however, make it clearer that the person or organization being added to the policy is an insured in addition to those automatically included within the policy provisions.

This new endorsement is unlike all earlier editions in that no coverage applies to an additional insured unless the injury or damage has been caused at least in part by an act or omission of the named insured. Earlier versions of standard additional insured endorsements like CG 20 07 required only that the injury or damage arise out of the named insured's operations. That language has consistently been interpreted to apply even to the additional insured's sole negligence as long as the claim had some causal connection to the work the named insured was hired to do. Under the current language of the endorsement, if the named insured is not at fault, then no coverage applies to the additional insured. If, however, the named insured is found to be 1 percent at fault, the insurer would owe the additional insured both defense and indemnity. Since CG 20 07 (like other similarly worded endorsements revised in 2004) does not address the matter of percentages, it could be an issue of controversy.

The nature of the protection given to the professional, as described in the first paragraph of this endorsement, is limited to the *named insured's premises or ongoing operations*. The term "premises" is not defined in the CGL policy insofar as liability coverage is concerned. But the apparent rationale for this stipulation is to clarify that the source of liability must have some relationship to the named insured's premises, *unless the named insured also is involved in performing some or all of the work.* If this latter circumstance applies, it does not matter where the work is being performed so long as it is the work project of the named insured.

Furthermore, what can happen as the result of professional error is not limited to bodily injury, property damage, personal injury, or advertising injury, as those terms are commonly defined in liability policies. An architect, for example, can make a mistake in judgment that results in economic damages because work has to be rectified. This kind of an exposure is not specifically addressed under the second paragraph of this additional insured endorsement because the insuring agreement of the policy to which the endorsement is attached is limited solely to resulting "bodily injury," "property damage," "personal injury," and "advertising injury." However, if there is an otherwise covered claim involving bodily injury or property damage, any economic damages that follow as a result should likewise be covered.

It also is a condition of the second paragraph of the additional insured endorsement that the injury or damage not arise out of the "rendering or failure to render any professional services ...."

This quoted language applies to both intentional and unintentional *acts*. The point is that the CGL policy covers liability arising from intentional acts, except with respect to the intentional acts of a professional nature by the design professional for whom the additional insured endorsement is issued. Thus, by inference from the provisions of the additional insured endorsement, coverage should apply to the liability of the design professional because of injury or damage, as defined in the CGL policy, arising from the performance of services outside of what are considered to be the professional services of such insured.

Whether the professional will be protected under this additional insured endorsement should depend on the nature of the allegations and on whether what led to the resulting bodily injury or property damage could be labeled as a breach of *general duty* rather than a professional duty. When a claim is too close to call, the insurer may file a declaratory judgment action to enlist the court's opinion on whether coverage should apply.

Relevant Case Law

One of the cases that has ruled against coverage for the professional under a general liability policy is *U.S. Fidelity & Guaranty Co. v Continental Casualty Co.,* 505 NE2d 1072 (Ill App 1987), as a result of a professional services exclusion endorsement. In this case, an architectural firm maintained both general and professional liability policies. When an injured construction worker brought an action against the architectural firm, it sought protection under its general liability policy. Coverage ultimately was held by the court to be inapplicable

because the architectural firm was in charge of the construction project, and it failed to perform certain acts in that capacity that were the proximate cause of the construction worker's injury.

Other cases with similar results are *Wheeler v Aetna Casualty & Surety Co.,* 298 NE2d 329 (Ill App 1973), and *Sheppard, Morgan, and Schwab v U.S. Fidelity & Guaranty Co.,* 358 NE2d (Ill App 1977). Neither of these cases dealt with an additional insured endorsement. Instead, they involved the standard ISO design professionals professional services exclusion endorsement. This endorsement contains exclusionary language identical to that of the additional insured endorsement. In other words, the forms are designed such that these professionals have essentially the same coverage under a CGL policy whether they are additional insureds or named insureds. Therefore, cases interpreting the application of the standard ISO professional services exclusion in a policy purchased by an architect or engineer also should generally be applicable to the professional services limitation in the additional insured endorsement.

Despite the previously stated decisions rendered against coverage of professionals under general liability policies, the courts in other cases have ruled for coverage even though the policies were endorsed with professional liability exclusions. One such case is *U.S. Fidelity & Guaranty Co. v Armstrong,* 479 S2d 1164 (Ala 1985). This case dealt with the design and construction of a municipal sewage system. During construction, raw sewage flowed onto adjacent land.

Among the reasons coverage was denied by the insurer were the pollution exclusion and the professional services exclusion that, the insurer maintained, applied to the engineering firm that had been added to the city's general liability policy as an additional insured. The engineering firm maintained that while some of its functions were considered to be services of a professional nature, other functions were nonprofessional in nature, such as providing liaison between the city and the contractor. In upholding coverage for the engineering firm under the city's general liability policy, the court held that by matching the allegations of the complaint with the terms of the policy, no allegation fell obviously within the terms of the phrase "the rendering or failure to render professional services" as it appeared in the additional insured endorsement.

Camp Dresser & McKee v Home Insurance Co., 568 NE2d 631 (Mass App 1991), involved an engineering firm that provided services in connection with a city's water pollution control system. The suit arose when one of the city's employees was injured and filed suit against the engineering firm. The firm then sought protection under its professional liability policy, which carried a deductible of $150,000 per claim, and under its CGL policy, which had no deductible. The CGL insurer denied coverage, relying on the standard ISO professional services exclusion.

The Massachusetts court rationalized that coverage applied under the engineering firm's CGL policy for a number of reasons, including the following.

- The obligation of the insurer to provide a defense was based not only on the facts alleged in the complaint but also on facts known or readily known to the insurer. In this regard, the insurer was found to have been aware of the fact that the underlying case involved a claim of *negligence* based on the engineering firm's failure to warn properly of the hazards associated with the mechanism that gave rise to the claimant's injury.

- In determining whether an activity falls within the professional services exclusion, it was stated that courts generally look to the nature of the conduct in question rather than to the title or position of the person involved. The fact that work for the city was performed by engineers or professionals did not mean all work necessarily called for professional services. "Such an interpretation," the court said, "would have the exclusion swallow the policy."

- In looking at the professional liability exclusion in question, the court held that "claims of ordinary negligence or negligent management or control are not expressly precluded." The court also stated that the phrase "supervisory,

inspection or engineering services" is reasonably susceptible of ambiguous interpretation. In other words, the court explained, that term can be interpreted narrowly as describing "supervision of purely professional activities" or broadly as describing "management or control of aspects of a project involving both professional and nonprofessional activities."

A number of other cases have dealt with the professional services exclusion with mixed results. In the case of *Aetna Fire Underwriters Ins. Co. v Southwestern Engineering Co.,* 626 SW2d 99 (Tex App 1981), the court ruled for coverage holding that the term "engineering services," as it appeared in the professional services exclusion, was ambiguous. Coverage, therefore, applied under a CGL policy for damages stemming from the activity of locating underground piping.

Coverage likewise applied under a CGL policy of an engineering firm despite a professional services exclusion in the case of *Gregoire v AFB Construction,* 478 S2d 538 (La App 1985). One allegation of the professional entity was that it knew of the danger but still allowed the project to proceed. The court stated that "such a duty to warn could be found to be outside the scope of the 'professional' or 'supervisory' services."

On the other hand, the professional services exclusion in a CGL policy was held to bar coverage in the case of *Natural Gas Pipeline Co. of America v Odom Offshore Surveys,* 889 F2d 633 (5th Cir 1989). The U.S. Court of Appeals held that the professional liability exclusion barred coverage for damage to a natural gas pipeline caused by the negligence of the insured's employees in misdirecting the placement of a boat's anchor.

Contractual Liability Coverage

No discussion of design professionals liability would be complete without also addressing contractual liability insurance. Several points about contractual liability insurance for design professional liability exposures are sometimes are misunderstood or at least overlooked. These points should be considered to gain a fuller perspective of the entire subject.

Insurers that write general liability insurance are, of course, quite reluctant to cover the assumed liability of professionals. Separate professional liability insurance exists to address that exposure. As a matter of fact, a number of anti-indemnity statutes specifically preclude these professionals from transferring the financial consequences of their conduct to contractors. In fact, the CGL policy excludes most such contractual assumptions. Keep in mind that the CGL policy provides contractual liability coverage by making two exceptions to the contractual liability exclusion. One exception to the exclusion makes it clear that coverage applies when the insured would have still been liable in the absence of the contract. The other exception effects contractual liability coverage with respect to certain specified types of "insured contracts." It is the policy's definition of "insured contract" that excludes coverage for assumed design professionals professional liability. The portion of the current definition that imposes this limitation is shown in Exhibit 8.2.

It is important to note that the term "insured contract" does not specifically encompass the following.

- Liability of the insured (indemnitor) who is not a professional but nonetheless agrees to indemnify a professional (indemnitee)

- Liability of the insured (indemnitor) who is a professional and agrees to indemnify someone else (indemnitee) for his or her professional acts or omissions

This does not necessarily mean that contractually assumed liability coverage for the professional liability exposure under the CGL policy is flatly excluded, absent a professional liability exclusion. Much will depend on the nature of the contractual assumption and how the policy is written. Some illustrations may be helpful.

Assume a CGL policy written for an engineer has *no* professional liability exclusion attached. The insured firm agrees to hold harmless and indemnify a project owner for any bodily injury or property damage sustained by a third party caused solely by the professional's rendering or failure to render professional services. The fact that the insured is a professional does not necessarily mean that this contractual assumption is flatly excluded by the CGL policy. What must be determined, to establish contractual liability coverage under the policy, is the nature of the contractual assumption.

Thus, if the insured engineer promises nothing more than to be accountable for his or her own professional acts or omissions, contractual liability coverage should apply for resulting bodily injury or property damage because this type of liability would have applied (in the absence of a professional liability exclusion) even without the contractual assumption.

EXHIBIT 8.2
CONTRACTUAL LIABILITY COVERAGE LIMITATION FOR DESIGN PROFESSIONALS

An "insured contract" does not include that part of any contract or agreement:

(2) That indemnifies an architect, engineer or surveyor for injury or damage arising out of:

   (a) Preparing, approving or failing to prepare or approve maps, shop drawings, opinions, reports, surveys, field orders, change orders, drawings and specifications; or

   (b) Giving directions or instructions, or failing to give them, if that is the primary cause of the injury or damage;

(3) Under which the insured, if an architect, engineer, or surveyor assumes liability for an injury or damage arising out of the insured's rendering or failure to render professional services, including those listed in b. above and supervisory, inspection or engineering services;....

On the other hand, if the assumed liability for which the insured engineer is accountable would not have applied except for such specific contractual assumption, the test for coverage will hinge on the meaning of "insured contract." In this light, the exclusion in the definition of "insured contract" of that part of any contract or agreement "(3) under which the insured, if an architect, engineer or surveyor, assumes liability for an injury or damage arising out of the insured's rendering or failure to render professional services" should preclude coverage.

Assume now that the standard design professionals professional liability exclusion *is* attached to the engineer's CGL policy. It does not matter in this case what the nature of the professional's contractual assumption is, no contractual liability coverage is likely to apply to any professional liability. The reason is that the exception to the CGL policy's contractual liability exclusion dealing with liability that the insured would have in the absence of the contract or agreement is offset by the policy's professional liability exclusion. Or, to say it another way, what professional liability coverage might apply for liability the insured would have in the absence of a contractual assumption is nullified by the professional liability exclusion. Likewise, the design professionals professional liability limitation in the definition of "insured contract" also will preclude coverage. These illustrations of coverage apply equally well to the design professional who is added to the CGL policy by way of an additional insured endorsement.

Up to this point, the discussion of the contractual liability coverage's application under the CGL policy has dealt solely with the assumption of liability stemming from the rendering of or failure to render professional services. Another area that requires explanation is the extent to which contractual liability coverage applies to the *general negligence* of the design professional if the cause of the liability falls outside the scope of professional services. (As previously noted, the CGL policy covers the general negligence of the design professional outside the realm of what could be labeled a professional act or omission.)

Assume an architect is included as an additional insured on the CGL policy of a project owner,

using the standard ISO Additional Insured—Engineers, Architects or Surveyors (CG 20 07) endorsement. (This endorsement is intended only to be used when the named insured engages the professional who is to be an additional insured on the named insured's policy. When the named insured engages the professional but requires additional insured status on the policy of another, endorsement CG 20 32, discussed later, should be attached.) Part of the rationale for use of this endorsement is the project owner's promise to hold harmless and indemnify the architect against liability of a nonprofessional nature that could emanate from the work project. An important question is whether the project owner's CGL policy to which this additional insured endorsement is attached will protect the architect for injury or damage that is caused solely by the architect.

Barring some otherwise applicable policy exclusion, contractual liability coverage should apply to the architect's general negligence wholly apart from such additional insured endorsement. General negligence of the indemnitee (or professional in this case) is the primary object of contractual liability coverage. In this illustration, the project owner's contractual assumption can be labeled as dealing with a nonprofessional liability exposure and therefore within the meaning of the term "insured contract."

One reason that the indemnitee under a contractual agreement should require that it be named as an additional insured on the indemnitor's liability policy is to reinforce the attempt to transfer the risk. If, for whatever reason, the contractual assumption or liability is deemed to be unenforceable, the indemnitee can rely on its status as an additional insured under the indemnitor's policy. It is important to note that there often is very little correlation between the contractual requirements and the provisions of an additional insured endorsement unless the endorsement is written to follow the contractual provisions. Generally, more accountability is transferred than can possibly be covered by insurance. But it also is true that an additional insured endorsement often can provide more protection to the indemnitee than what might otherwise be expected, depending on the scope of the liability policy to which the additional insured endorsement is attached.

As sometimes happens, however, the indemnitee erroneously assumes that contractual agreement between the parties is the equivalent of being an additional insured. Unfortunately it is not until litigation arises that this kind of thinking is found to be false. One such case is *Alex Robertson Co. v Imperial Casualty & Indemnity Co.,* 10 Cal Rptr 2d 165 (Cal App 1992). This is an unusual case in that it was the contractor that was seeking to transfer certain risks to the architect rather than the reverse, which is the more common scenario. In any event, the general contractor (indemnitee) entered into a contract with an architectural firm (indemnitor). At the time the professional services agreement was executed, the architect did not carry professional liability insurance. The contractor demanded that such insurance be purchased and also agreed to pay the premiums.

The contract between the contractor and the architectural firm was submitted to the professional liability insurer. It contained a clause under which the architectural firm agreed to indemnify and hold harmless the general contractor from liability, suits, claims, demands, judgments, or penalties arising out of the architectural firm's negligent acts, errors, or omissions. When the professional liability policy was issued, a contractual liability endorsement was attached, recognizing the contractor as an indemnitee and agreeing to protect the contractor for its *vicarious liability* resulting from the negligent acts, errors, or omissions of the architectural firm. (In insurance parlance, the contractual agreement in question would have been labeled by the underwriter as the "limited type" assumption.)

During the time the policy was in effect, the contractor was sued for breach of contract and negligence in connection with the construction for which the insurance was procured. The contractor tendered its defense to the professional liability insurer, but the tender was denied on the basis that the contractor was not an insured under the policy. Following the trial, the contractor demanded that the architectural firm's professional liability insur-

er pay part of the damages. The insurer would not capitulate because the architect denied any negligence in connection with the design work and was not a party to the underlying action. The contractor then filed an action against the professional liability insurer alleging various breaches. The insurer continued to maintain that it had no duty to indemnify nor defend the contractor.

The insurer's argument was upheld by the trial court and affirmed on appeal. In so ruling, the courts held that a contractual liability coverage endorsement does not make the person whose liability is assumed (the indemnitee) an insured on the policy of the indemnitor. Instead, as the endorsement so states, it expands coverage under the policy to encompass contractually assumed liability of the named insured. The effect of the endorsement, therefore, was to expand the insured's coverage—subject to policy limits—to the liability assumed by the architectural firm (the indemnitor) and not to insure the indemnitee.

The court explained as follows.

> [P]rofessional liability policies often exclude indemnification agreements with third parties because such agreements may expand the professional's liability beyond the traditional malpractice concept.

Thus, the court went on to say, the contractor was a potential indemnitee of the architectural firm under the indemnification clause of the contract, but the contractor was *not an insured under the professional liability policy.* (The questions of whether the architectural firm owed a duty to defend the contractor, whether that firm breached that duty, and whether any resulting liability of the firm was covered by the professional liability policy were not before the court and therefore were not ruled upon.)[1]

The Completed Operations Hazard and 1993 Revisions

The products-completed operations exposure was not addressed in the pre-1993 design professionals additional insured endorsement. Rather than incorporate an exclusion in the endorsement, it was expected that no endorsement effecting additional insured status for the design professional would be added to the renewal policies issued once the project was completed. Thus, a design professional could have coverage for liability arising from a completed project in the interim between completion of the project and expiration of the policy on which it was an additional insured. In those instances where design professionals had contractually required that additional insured status be maintained for a period of time (e.g., 2 or 3 years) following completion of the project, the endorsement could also be attached to renewal policies to provide such status. ISO sought to change this when the Additional Insured—Engineers, Architects or Surveyors (CG 20 07) endorsement was revised along with the CGL coverage form and a number of other endorsements in 1993.

Despite the revised reference to "liability arising out of your ... ongoing operations," it remained possible in some fact patterns to obtain completed operations coverage. In circumstances where a project owner provided additional insured status to its architect or engineer, the completed project usually becomes the owner's premises (e.g., a building) or ongoing operation (e.g., an assembly line). Thus, an additional insured architect or engineer may still have enjoyed liability coverage as an additional insured under the project owner's policy in these circumstances. Of course, the coverage a design professional got by way of this endorsement was limited by the endorsement's professional liability exclusion, and that exclusion is even more central to completed operations than to work in progress. It is unlikely that a design professional will be held liable for bodily injury or property damage arising from a completed building other than as a result of its professional services.

All of this changed when the 2001 edition of these endorsements was introduced. An extended exclusion of liability arising from the named insured's completed work shut the door on any such arguments. The latest 2004 edition continues that trend by limiting coverage to injury or damage caused in

whole or in part by the acts or omissions of the named insured in the performance of the named insured's ongoing operations.

In any case, it is not extremely common for owners to agree to add design professionals to their liability policies as additional insureds. It is more common for this requirement to be made of the general contractor of the project. Since the completed project would not normally become the premises or ongoing operation of the contractor that builds it, the intended exclusion of coverage for the completed operations hazard will probably be effective. (As noted below, however, this endorsement is not really appropriate for adding an architect as an insured to a contractor's policy in most situations.)

It is probably unreasonable for an architect or engineer to expect an owner or contractor to provide it with additional insured status in liability policies purchased long after the work has been completed. But such contractual requirements are nonetheless still imposed on occasion, and it is important to understand that this endorsement will not generally effect coverage for an additional insured architect or engineer with respect to the completed operations exposure. If, therefore, a named insured agrees to provide such coverage on behalf of an architect or engineer, the pre-1993 endorsement should be used. The ramifications of noncompliance are discussed in **Chapter 21.**

Additional Insureds in Contractors' Policies

A potential problem with the design professionals as additional insureds endorsements used with the 1993 and earlier CGL programs is created by the requirement that the design professional be *engaged* by the named insured. A literal application of this requirement would limit the endorsement's use solely to those entities that engage the professional, making it inappropriate for use in adding a design professional to the policy of a contractor in most cases. This is unfortunate, because the common industry practice is for the project owner (who engaged the design professional) to include a requirement in the construction contract for the contractor (who did not engage the design professional) to provide additional insured status to the design professional in the contractor's liability policies.

While it was technically inappropriate to use endorsement CG 20 07 to provide additional insured status to the design professional in this situation, it was for several years a common insurance industry practice to do so because there was no other standard endorsement designed for this purpose. When a named insured is required to provide insured status for any one or more of these professionals engaged by *someone else* (e.g., a contractor who must make the project owner's architect an additional insured), the language of CG 20 07 will not convey the appropriate coverage terms.

Under such circumstances, the Additional Insured—Engineers, Architects or Surveyors Not Engaged by the Named Insured (CG 20 32) endorsement, should be used instead. The endorsement, which was introduced for use in 1996, is essentially the equivalent of CG 20 07, except that it provides insured status to the professional who is specifically identified in the schedule. The insuring agreement of the endorsement further identifies the named professional as "contractually required to be added as an additional insured to your policy," although "not engaged by you." Endorsement CG 20 32 imposes on its coverage the same exclusion relative to professional liability exposures that is found in CG 20 07.

One case in which an architect argued that endorsement CG 20 07, attached to a contractor's CGL policy, was inapplicable to preclude a professional liability claim because the architect was not "engaged by" the contractor was the *Prisco Serena Strum* case referred to earlier. (See page 165.) Complicating the coverage issues in that case was the fact that the attached CG 20 07 endorsement had been modified with an additional three paragraphs reading as follows.

> Any person or organization to whom the Named Insured is obligated by an agreement to

provide insurance such as that afforded by this endorsement.

Limits of Liability

> It is further agreed that the Limits of Liability with respect to the insurance afforded by this endorsement are not greater than the Limits of Liability required by the terms of any such agreement, but in no event greater than the Limits of Liability stated in Item 3 of the Declarations.

> Professional Liability is specifically excluded.

The fact that the architect was engaged by the project owner did not matter from the court's perspective because the project owner, as an additional insured, was considered to be a "you" (named insured) for purposes of the professional liability exclusion as well as the rest of the CGL policy. The court ruled, therefore, that the architect was "engaged by" an insured party. The court also stated that:

> both the specific language of endorsement CG 20 07 01 87 para. 2, and the typed addendum to that endorsement, make it clear that professional liability coverage is excluded for the kind of architectural service described in the complaint.

The court's upholding of the typed addendum to endorsement CG 20 07 appears to open the door for professionals added as additional insureds to question the endorsement's clarity in the absence of that addendum. The court's finding that an additional insured is also a named insured "you" for purposes of the CGL policy is puzzling. Perhaps the court was caught up in the same confusion that confronts others who use the terms additional insured and additional named insured interchangeably. Ironically, the court best summarized the coverage issues before it in its opening remarks.

> Torn between the desire to use common forms, which ought to lead to consistent results, and the need to tailor coverage to particular situations, the insurance industry often ends up with policies that are, to put it charitably, convoluted.

The Additional Insured—Engineers, Architects or Surveyors (CG 20 31) endorsement was introduced for use in 1993 and applies solely with the OCP policy. Its provisions are identical to those contained in endorsement CG 20 07.

Summary

Design professionals often require additional insured status in the policies of contractors working on their projects and occasionally on the policies of project owners. Two endorsements are available for accomplishing this, one to add the design professional to a contractor's policy and one to add it to the client's policy. The coverage provided is limited in scope but should be sufficient to cover the most important exposure design professionals are targeting with the requirement (i.e., claims by the contractor's injured employees) under most circumstances.

Chapter 8 Notes

1. A similar case where the indemnitee was under the mistaken impression that it was an insured under the contractual liability coverage of a CGL policy issued to an indemnitor is *Jefferson v Sinclair Refining Co.,* 223 NYS2d 863 (1962).

OWNERS AND CONTRACTORS AS ADDITIONAL INSUREDS

It is typical for project owners to require additional insured status from general contractors, for general contractors to require it from subcontractors, and so on. The provision of additional insured status with respect to construction projects is probably the most complex of all the circumstances in which this practice is common. As such, it has become controversial at times, and there has been a substantial amount of change not only with standard Insurance Services Office, Inc. (ISO) endorsements, but also with independently filed forms and endorsements.

Changes to standard additional insured endorsement language over the last 15 years have been frequent and major. While the most recent set of revisions—implemented in the summer of 2004—is expected to be in widespread use throughout the country almost immediately upon approval by state regulators, policies modified on the basis of older endorsement language will continue in effect for some time. The multiplicity of standard form editions still available in the marketplace makes it essential to note carefully which version of an endorsement is being used on a particular policy. Compounding the problem still further are the many independently filed and manuscript additional insured endorsements relied on by some insurers. These nonstandard endorsements are discussed in **Appendix C.**

This chapter addresses the application of standard construction-related additional insured endorsements. Broad coverage issues involving such endorsements will be discussed within the context of standard endorsement language as revised by ISO in 2004. Earlier revisions of construction-related endorsements have also produced important

changes in coverage, and that evolution will also be examined in this chapter. Chief among these earlier changes was the 1993 revision that attempted to limit the additional insured's coverage to losses arising out of the named insured's "ongoing operations" and eliminate coverage in connection with completed work. Standard and nonstandard automatic (blanket) additional insured endorsements are discussed in **Chapter 13.**

Endorsement CG 20 10

The most common circumstance under which one participant in a construction project is called on to add another participant as an insured under its policy is the contractual relationship between indemnitors and indemnitees. A project owner will typically require that the contractor(s) it hires to perform the work will also hold the project owner harmless—i.e., agree to pay liability claims made against the owner—when injury or damage to a third party occurs because of the contractor's work. In this situation, the contractor becomes the indemnitor (the party that assumes the other party's liability) and the owner becomes the indemnitee (the party that has transferred its own liability to the indemnitor). The same contractual relationship will typically exist between contractors and their subcontractors, with the contractor being the indemnitee and the subcontractor being the indemnitor.

As a corollary to the agreement to hold harmless or indemnify another party, indemnitors may also be required to arrange insured status for their indemnitees under the indemnitors' liability policies. This arrangement makes it possible, as explained in

Chapter 4, for the additional insured indemnitee to submit a claim directly to the indemnitor's insurer, rather than having to channel the claim through the indemnitor itself. When a project owner requests insured status under its contractor's commercial general liability (CGL) insurance policy—or a contractor requests insured status under its subcontractor's policy—that insured status will most often be effected by using standard additional insured endorsement CG 20 10.

Endorsement CG 20 10, currently titled Additional Insured—Owners, Lessees or Contractors—Scheduled Person or Organization, was introduced as part of the ISO CGL program in 1986. In the intervening years it has undergone a number of revisions, most of which will be reflected in this chapter's discussion of the endorsement's coverage. The most recent edition of CG 20 10 was promulgated in July 2004. As the endorsement's title suggests, the name of the person or organization being given insured status is listed in the endorsement's schedule, along with the locations of the operations to which coverage will apply.[1] The persons or organizations so listed then become insureds with respect to injury or damage that is covered by the policy, but only when the injury or damage is caused, in whole or in part, by an act or omission of the named insured. The actual language of the CG 20 10 insuring agreement is shown in Exhibit 9.1.

EXHIBIT 9.1
CG 20 10 INSURING AGREEMENT

Section II—Who Is An Insured is amended to include as an additional insured the person(s) or organization(s) shown in the Schedule, but only with respect to liability for "bodily injury", "property damage" or "personal and advertising injury" caused, in whole or in part, by:

1. Your acts or omissions; or

2. The acts or omissions of those acting on your behalf;

in the performance of your ongoing operations for the additional insured(s) at the location(s) designated above.

Copyright, ISO Properties, Inc., 2004

The language quoted in Exhibit 9.1 establishes a number of important features of the coverage available to additional insureds under endorsement CG 20 10.

1. Insured status exists under the endorsement with respect to both of the major coverages of the CGL policy—Coverage A (Bodily Injury and Property Damage), and Coverage B (Personal and Advertising Injury).

2. Coverage exists for the additional insured only when the injury or damage has been caused at least partially by some act or omission of the named insured, or those acting on the named insured's behalf. A claim involving the sole negligence of the additional insured will, therefore, virtually never be covered. (This elimination of coverage for the additional insured's sole negligence could represent a significant diminution in coverage compared to earlier editions of CG 20 10.) This, of course, depends on the ability of the insurer to establish that the named insured is not responsible—"in whole or in part"—for the alleged injury or damage. In many cases, the additional insured may be able to demonstrate at least 1-percent fault on the part of the named insured and therefore potentially trigger coverage, even where the additional insured is arguably 99 percent at fault.

3. The relationship between the named insured and additional insured must be one in which the named insured is performing operations for the additional insured. Such relationships exist between a named insured contractor and additional insured project owner, or a named insured subcontractor and additional insured general contractor.

4. The operations of the named insured that give rise to the claim against the additional insured must be "ongoing." This is the language that has been used in standard additional insured endorsements since 1993 to eliminate coverage the additional insured might have—and did have prior to 1993—for claims arising from the named insured's completed operations. (As explained on page 177, the term "ongoing" in and

of itself may not in all instances limit coverage to injury or damage that occurs while work is in progress. Endorsement CG 20 10 also contains additional exclusionary language that effectively eliminates completed operations coverage.)

5. The job site at which the operations are being performed by the named insured must be listed in the endorsement's schedule in order for coverage to apply.

The "Sole Negligence" Issue

Versions of endorsement CG 20 10 that preceded the 2004 revision imposed no requirements as to the cause of covered injury or damage. The only requirement of these older endorsements was that the additional insured's liability had to "arise out of" the named insured's work or operations. Courts repeatedly interpreted the phrase "arising out of" to require only an indirect causal connection between the named insured's operations and the injury or damage. (In cases involving the injured employee of a named insured contractor, for example, who brings a claim against the additional insured project owner, courts often viewed the mere presence of the named insured's employees on the additional insured's premises performing their work as a sufficient connection to prove that the injury "arose out of" the named insured's work or operations. Under such a reading of the endorsement, the additional insured would have coverage even when its own negligence was determined to be the sole cause of the injury.) See the discussion later in this chapter of the interpretation that has historically been given the phrase "arising out of."

ISO eventually stated that this broad interpretation of "arising out of" contradicted its own understanding of the intended scope of additional insured coverage and prompted the revision of endorsement CG 20 10 in 2004. The phrase "arising out of" was removed, to be replaced by "caused, in whole or in part, by," which the ISO drafters believe expresses a stronger causal relationship. And instead of the open-ended phrase "your ongoing operations," the 2004 edition ties the claim to "your acts or omissions." Under this new language, it will not be sufficient for the additional insured to show that injury or damage would not have occurred *but for the fact*

that the named insured was performing operations. It will be necessary to show that some act or omission of the named insured *actually caused the injury or damage.* The named insured's act or omission need not, however, be the only cause; an act or omission of the additional insured may be a contributing cause as well.

In addition, use of the term "caused by," rather than previous editions' "arising out of," may prove to be more limiting. "Caused by" typically denotes a more direct causal relationship to the injury or damage than "arising out of," which has been interpreted by the courts as requiring only a minimal causal nexus. This change in the 2004 edition of the endorsement is analogous to the use by some insurers of the term "resulting from." As discussed on page 191, "resulting from" has also been viewed by some insurers and some courts as expressing a more direct causal connection.

The practical result of these changes in wording is the elimination of coverage for liability attributable to the additional insured's sole negligence. A preliminary filing of the 2004 revision actually contained an exclusion of injury or damage arising out of the sole negligence of the additional insured, but that provision was dropped in the final revision. Having already specified in the endorsement's insuring agreement that injury or damage must be caused at least partly by the named insured, an exclusion of sole negligence on the part of the additional insured was considered superfluous by ISO. In fact, a specific mention of the additional insured's sole negligence—as the single excluded alternative to loss caused "in whole or in part" by the named insured—might have created the impression that only three possible "negligence scenarios" exist in a construction accident:

1. sole negligence of the additional insured

2. sole negligence of the named insured

3. shared negligence of the named and additional insureds

But injury or damage on a construction project can be caused by the negligence of persons and organizations that are not insureds under the policy at all. ISO wanted the key to coverage for an additional insured to be not just the partial or sole negligence of *someone else* besides the additional insured, but rather the partial or sole negligence of *the named insured*. The language finally settled on for the endorsement conveys that point. A "sole negligence of the additional insured" exclusion could conceivably have obscured the point.

To illustrate the potential confusion that might be created by excluding *only* the sole negligence of the additional insured, imagine an injury caused by a parcel delivery driver bringing a shipment to a construction site. Negligence is attributed 50 percent to the driver and 50 percent to the general contractor, who failed to take precautions that would have prevented the accident. Language suggesting that the additional insured general contractor has coverage—*except for injury or damage arising out of its sole negligence*—could be used to make a case for coverage in this instance, since the additional insured was not solely negligent. Removal of the sole negligence exclusion focuses attention more clearly on the other prescribed condition of coverage in the endorsement: injury or damage must be caused in whole or in part *by the named insured*.

"Caused in Whole or in Part"

Under endorsement CG 20 10, an additional insured has coverage only with respect to injury or damage that is "caused, in whole or in part," by the named insured's acts or omissions. (Note that the acts or omissions of the named insured that cause the injury or damage need not be *negligent* acts or omissions.[2]) In other words, the endorsement responds only in the event of injury or damage for which the named insured and additional insured share the responsibility (if not necessarily the legal liability). The proportion of this shared responsibility is not specified in the endorsement, nor is the method of determining or measuring the named insured's required share. If as little as 1 percent of the cause of a claimant's injury or damage is some act or omission of the named insured, the requirements of the endorsement have been met.

For a number of years prior to the 2004 revision of endorsement CG 20 10 that contains the "caused in whole or in part" language, individual insurers were developing their own endorsements that sought to eliminate coverage of the additional insured's sole liability by requiring some level of contributory negligence on the named insured's part. In actual claims practice, these insurers soon found that additional insureds often had little difficulty attributing at least a minimal level of negligence to the named insured—even if that level was the hypothetical 1 percent mentioned above.

A possible solution to this problem that was adopted by some insurers is shown in Exhibit 9.2. The exhibit shows a nonstandard additional insured endorsement that defines "sole fault" to require a finding of more than 10 percent fault on the part of the named insured to circumvent the limitation. In the example clause, if the additional insured is 90 percent at fault or more (i.e., the named insured is 10 percent at fault or less), the sole fault exclusion applies.

Experience under the "caused in whole or in part" language of CG 20 10 may parallel that of insurers that used the sole-fault-exclusion approach. In fact, the challenge for additional insureds seeking to establish coverage under CG 20 10 may be even easier, since they will need only to establish some act or omission of the named insured as a contributing cause of the injury or damage; they need not prove or quantify any degree of actual negligence on the part of the named insured. If that turns out to be the case, some future effort may be seen by policy drafters to define "in whole or in part" more precisely.

Third-Party-Over Claims

The additional insured's access to a defense under the named insured's policy, as explained in **Chapter 4**, is one of the principal benefits of additional insured status. The insurer's duty to provide a defense is triggered when the allegations being made against the insured match—at least potentially—the coverage provisions of the policy. Under the current edition of CG 20 10, therefore, the additional insured's right to a defense will depend on its ability to demonstrate a causal connection between (1) the injury or damage being alleged in the suit or claim

---

**EXHIBIT 9.2
DEFINING SOLE FAULT**

WHO IS AN INSURED Section (II) is amended to include as an insured the person or organization shown in the Schedule, but only with respect to liability arising out of your operations, and those done on your behalf, performed for that insured. Coverage under this endorsement does not apply to sums that the insured shown above is legally obligated to pay because of that insured's sole fault.

For purposes of applying coverage under this endorsement, sole fault is defined to mean:

A finding establishing the respective parties' percentage of liability, based upon a decree or order issued by a court of competent jurisdiction, or an arbitration or mediation proceeding conducted by an association approved by the state bar in the state hosting the proceeding, or an agreement, stipulation, stipulated judgment or other form of written agreement between the parties and litigants, that 90% or more of the legal obligation to pay incurred by the insured shown above is attributable to the conduct of that insured or its members, managers, officers, directors, employees, or stockholders acting on its behalf in their capacity as such.

---

and (2) an act or omission of the named insured. When the named insured and additional insured are both being sued in connection with the same injury or damage, this connection will be self-evident.

It is possible, however, for a claim to be brought against the additional insured alone—without any related allegations being made against the named insured. The most common example of such a suit is, in fact, one of the most common kinds of suit to arise in the context of a construction project—a third-party claim by an employee of one insured against another insured. When a construction worker is injured on the job, workers compensation statutes prohibit that worker from bringing suit against the employer, to the extent to which the injury comes within the state's workers compensation system. It is sometimes possible, however, for the injured employee to sue another party for the injury.

Circumstances in which such a third-party claim are permitted vary from jurisdiction to jurisdiction. Where they are permitted, however, they will typically constitute a suit against an additional insured (a project owner, for example) brought by an employee of the named insured (the owner's general contractor). The named insured itself will be immune from the suit by virtue of its status as an employer—*even if that named insured's act or omission was a cause of the employee's injury.*

Can an additional insured establish its right to a defense in a third-party action of this kind, when no allegations of negligence are being made—or, by law, even *can be* made—against the named insured employer? How can the additional insured demonstrate that the injury for which it is being sued was "caused, in whole or in part, by [the named insured's] acts or omissions" so as to bring the claim potentially within the scope of additional insured coverage and trigger defense?

The revised language of CG 20 10 that raises this issue is too new to have generated any case law. Insurers must be guided by reasonable interpretations of the endorsement language itself, and the legal principles that govern the duty to defend in various jurisdictions. Here are some considerations that will be pertinent to a resolution of the question.

- **Coverage under CG 20 10 is not dependent on alleging *negligence* of the named insured.** A suggested argument against coverage for an additional insured in third-party-over actions is that the named insured employer cannot technically be negligent for injury to its employee within the workers compensation system. But the additional insured under CG 20 10 has coverage with respect to injury that is caused by "acts or omissions" of the named insured. The acts or omissions need not be negligent acts or omissions to comply with the endorsement language. (For purposes of defense, this argument of "no employer negligence" will also be difficult to sustain, since some responsibility of the employer can typically be asserted for the manner in which work was performed at the job site. The named insured employer thus can be said to have contributed in some way to the employee's injury, even if that allegation is not directly stated in the pleadings.)

- **Allegations of negligence against one party imply nothing necessarily about the possibility of other concurrent causes of injury resulting from that negligence.** If an injured employee of XYZ Subcontracting brings suit for his injuries against ABC General Contractor (for whom XYZ was performing work), the fact that the employee is not also suing XYZ is not a declaration or even an implication that no act or omission of XYZ contributed to the injury. Allegations of *sole* negligence on the part of the additional insured would clearly put those allegations outside the scope of potential coverage under CG 20 10 and would not, therefore, trigger a defense. But it is not clear that allegations of negligence on the part of the additional insured—*and silence as to any other cause of the injuries being alleged*—would automatically excuse the insurer from a duty to defend.

- **The coverage intent of CG 20 10 does not seem to encompass a blanket exclusion of third-party-over suits.** The 2004 revision of CG 20 10 was undertaken to address what ISO considered overly liberal interpretations of the scope of the endorsement's coverage in one particular set of circumstances—imposition of sole liability on the additional insured for injury or damage because the named insured is not involved in any direct way in causing that injury or damage. Third-party-over suits involve quite a different set of circumstances: imposition of sole liability on the additional insured because the named insured is statutorily immune to liability, regardless of its involvement in causing the injury.

Whether they weigh these considerations or not, some insurers are likely to conclude that a third-party-over suit against an additional insured does not trigger a duty to defend if the suit does not specifically cite acts or omissions of the named insured. (And such suits will virtually never do so.) Since the exposure to liability from third-party-over actions is one of the primary concerns of indemnitees under construction contracts, widespread denials of defense would be extremely disruptive to the effective allocation of construction risks. Only time will tell how much of a disruption the new language produces.

"Those Acting on Your Behalf"

The cause, or at least one cause, of injury or damage that constitutes the claim against the additional insured under CG 20 10 must be an act or omission of the named insured *or an act or omission of "those acting on [the named insured's] behalf."* Who would such persons be?

In the case of an additional insured project owner and a named insured general contractor, the most obvious example of such a person would be the general's subcontractor. If an action of the subcontractor results in a claim against the project owner, the additional insured endorsement to the general contractor's CGL policy will provide the owner with coverage. The same would be true of an additional insured general contractor, a named insured subcontractor, and an act or omission of the subcontractor's sub-subcontractor. Other examples would be the named insured's employees, material suppliers, consultants, and other agents.

Conventional risk transfer sees both indemnification and additional insured status flowing up through the tiers of a project—subcontractors indemnify and extend insured status to contractors, contractors indemnify and extend insured status to project owners. In exceptional circumstances, the negotiating positions of parties to a construction contract may make it possible for a contractor to demand indemnification and additional insured status from the project owner; or for a subcontractor to impose the same requirements on a general contractor. In rare cases like these, the coverage of endorsement CG 20 10 would effectively revert to the sole negligence scope of earlier editions—the additional insured would be "acting on the named insured's behalf" in such circumstances, and any act or omission of the additional insured would therefore trigger the endorsement's coverage.

Some risk management professionals have suggested that the phrase "those acting on your behalf" may constitute an argument for CG 20 10 coverage in third-party-over actions as well. The allegation that an additional insured third party (a project owner, for example, or a general contractor) failed to maintain a safe workplace could be viewed as an allegation that the additional insured was or should have been acting "on behalf of" the employer and its employees.

For example, consider a situation in which a contractor overseeing a project is added to the policies of subcontractors. The contractor's responsibility for work site condition is arguably one that it exercises on behalf of all those working at the site. When a subcontractor or its employees actually allege that the contractor failed to maintain a safe work environment, inherent in that allegation is an implied duty on the part of the contractor to do so. As a result, coverage applicable to injury or damage caused in whole or in part by the named insured's acts or omissions, *or the acts or omissions of those acting on the named insured's behalf,* could be triggered.

Additional Insureds and Completed Operations

As has been discussed, an indemnitee/additional insured in a construction project will want coverage for liability associated with the indemnitor's work in progress (a project owner for the work being performed by the general contractor, or a general contractor for the work being performed by a subcontractor). But the indemnitee/additional insured also faces a continuing liability exposure from the indemnitor's work even after that work is completed. Damage to the project itself (or to contents) from faulty construction and bodily injury to occupants of a building from defects or dangerous conditions associated with the construction can occur any time after the project ends and is turned over to the owner. Additional insured coverage for this so-called completed operations exposure is one of the most troublesome issues in construction risk management.

When they were introduced in 1986, standard construction-industry additional insured endorsements like CG 20 10 provided coverage to the additional insured in connection with the named insured's "work." The CGL policy defines the named insured's work—"your work"—in such a way as to include work that had been completed. In other words, additional insured endorsements originally included completed operations coverage. In 1993, however, CG 20 10 was revised in an

---

EXHIBIT 9.3
THE 1993 "ONGOING OPERATIONS" LIMITATION

CG 20 10 (1986 Version)

WHO IS AN INSURED (Section II) is amended to include as an insured the person or organization shown in the Schedule, but only with respect to liability arising out of "your work" for that insured by or for you.

CG 20 10 (1993 Version)

WHO IS AN INSURED (Section II) is amended to include as an insured the person or organization shown in the Schedule, but only with respect to liability arising out of your ongoing operations performed for that insured.

effort to remove completed operations coverage from the endorsement. The revised language, alongside the original language it replaced, is shown in Exhibit 9.3.

The difference between "your work" and "your ongoing operations" is that "your work," within the parameters of the CGL definition, can be either work in progress or work that has been completed; "ongoing operations" is not a defined CGL term, but suggests work only for as long as it is actually being performed. In short, coverage for the additional insured with respect to the named insured's completed operations was clearly present in the original edition of CG 20 10. The insurance industry sought to remove that component of coverage by insuring only liability arising out of the named insured's ongoing operations—or work in progress—beginning with the 1993 version of the endorsement.

The restriction of coverage to only ongoing operations attempts to clarify that additional insureds would have no coverage under the named insured's policy for liability arising out of the products-completed operations exposure. Despite ISO's attempts to clarify its intent to exclude completed operations coverage for additional insureds under its standard endorsements, that intent was not clearly applicable in every fact pattern. A true completed operations exclusion can be thought of as one that limits coverage to "bodily injury" or "property damage" *that occurs during ongoing operations.* However, the revised wording of the 1993 and 1997 editions of ISO endorsement CG 20 10 addresses only the type of operation (ongoing) out of which the additional insured's *liability* for injury or damage must arise. This distinction can have important coverage consequences.

Black's Law Dictionary (6th ed.) defines "liability" in part as "responsibility for torts." The term "liability," then, as used in the wording under discussion, relates to the additional insured's legal obligation to pay. That, in turn, corresponds to the insuring agreement of the standard ISO CGL and many other liability forms, which agree to pay sums the insured (including an additional insured) is legally obligated to pay.

The insuring agreement of standard ISO forms and many other liability forms constitutes promises to pay sums the insured (including any additional insured) is legally obligated to pay. That obligation to pay may be understood as the liability covered by insurance.

To seek completed operations coverage under the revised wording of the 1993 and 1997 editions of CG 20 10, the additional insured need only demonstrate that its legal obligation to pay (its "liability") for injury or damage *arose out of* activity while operations were in progress. This is often the case in claims involving property damage, where the source of the damage is ordinarily some conduct that occurs while operations are "ongoing."

The broad meaning given by the courts to the term "arising out of" is discussed subsequently. Applying that broad meaning, it can be argued that standard policy references to liability "arising out of" ongoing operations do not limit coverage to injury or damage *that occurs* during such operations. Rather, those references require only that the additional insured's legal obligation to pay must "arise out of"—originate from or be causally connected to—ongoing operations. The body of law discussed later in this chapter holds that the "arising out of" wording refers only to a claim growing out of or having its origin in the subject matter, which in this case is ongoing operations.

Apparently realizing that completed operations coverage might still be found to apply despite the 1993 revision that introduced the concept of "ongoing operations," ISO amended endorsement CG 20 10 again in 2001 by adding to the endorsement's existing language the further exclusionary provision shown in Exhibit 9.4.

With the addition of the exclusionary language shown in Exhibit 9.4, the insurance industry eliminated the ambiguity inherent in previous editions of CG 20 10, which had relied exclusively on the phrase "ongoing operations" to eliminate coverage of completed work.

For some time after completed operations coverage was effectively removed from CG 20 10, addi-

---

EXHIBIT 9.4
THE CG 20 10 "COMPLETED WORK"
EXCLUSION

With respect to the insurance afforded to these additional insureds, the following exclusion is added:

2. Exclusions

This insurance does not apply to "bodily injury" or "property damage" occurring after:

(1) All work, including materials, parts or equipment furnished in connection with such work, on the project (other than service, maintenance or repairs) to be performed by or on behalf of the additional insured(s) at the site of the covered operations has been completed; or

(2) That portion of "your work" out of which the injury or damage arises has been put to its intended use by any person or organization other than another contractor or subcontractor engaged in performing operations for a principal as a part of the same project.

---

tional insureds were often able to obtain completed operations coverage by insisting on a manuscript endorsement; or on the original CG 20 10 (often referred to as the "11 85" version because of its edition date); or on an alternative standard additional insured endorsement, Additional Insured—Designated Person or Organization (CG 20 26) endorsement, which had never been revised to refer to "ongoing operations" only. But with the explosion of construction defect litigation in the late 1990s, most of which claims involved completed operations, the availability of alternative additional insured language to cover completed operations all but ended.

In the 2004 ISO revision of standard additional insured endorsements, even CG 20 26 was rewritten to apply to the named insured's "ongoing operations" rather than "operations." Interestingly, however, ISO did not add to the 2004 edition of CG 20 26 the "completed work" exclusion that is shown in Exhibit 9.4 and that is contained in other endorsements that apply only to "ongoing operations." As was previously the case with CG 20 10, then, the wording of the 2004 edition of CG 20 26 seems ambiguous enough to leave some possibility of completed operations coverage, as explained above in reference to the 1993 edition of CG 20 10.

Insurers will certainly argue that this is not their intent, but the difference in the wording of CG 20 10 and CG 20 26 with respect to completed operations—the absence in CG 20 26 of the explicit completed work exclusion—can be argued to evidence broader coverage under CG 20 26. Clearly, insureds will believe that is the case, absent a change in wording. It would be imprudent to rely on this ambiguity as a means of obtaining completed operations coverage—or of meeting a contractual obligation to provide it to an additional insured. But in many construction projects, no other hope of arranging completed operations coverage for an indemnitee exists. One thing is clear, there will be litigation on the issue. Additional insureds, therefore, are well advised to make clear their expectations of coverage. Insurers, too, should seriously consider revising the wording to clarify that such coverage will not be provided.

In 2001 ISO promulgated an endorsement designed specifically to insure an additional insured's liability in connection with the named insured's completed operations. The Additional Insured—Owners, Lessees or Contractors—Completed Operations (CG 20 37) endorsement applies only to work of the named insured that falls within the products-completed operations hazard of the CGL policy. It is designed to be used in conjunction with endorsement CG 20 10, and requires a scheduling of both the additional insured and the completed operations to be covered. Since its introduction came at a time when many insurers were seeking to minimize their exposure construction defect claims, endorsement CG 20 37 has not been widely used.

Faced with the reality of obligations to provide additional insured status for a period of years following completion of a project, indemnitors have at least four basic options to consider.

- Require the attachment of endorsement CG 20 37 or its equivalent in addition to the standard endorsement providing "ongoing operations" coverage. This completed operations endorsement is not widely issued by insurers; where it is available, it is carefully underwritten on a project-by-project basis, and may be expensive.

- Amend the insurance requirements of the underlying contract to state that any and all coverage available to the named insured is applicable to the additional insured. This would assist in efforts to demonstrate intent of both the named insured and the additional insured to provide the additional insured with the same completed operations coverage available to the named insured. (For their part, insurers can endorse coverage to clarify that coverage for additional insureds is limited in scope to a specific project.)

- Insist that the additional insured endorsements attached to their policies use language like that of the pre-1993 forms, with reference to "your work" or equivalent language that encompasses the completed operations exposure. Some insurers will accommodate their insureds by using the pre-1993 edition of CG 20 10 even though they are also using later editions of additional insured endorsements for other clients.

- Resist the additional insured's demand for completed operations coverage. This is not always a practical option, given the reality of stringent insurance requirements imposed in many contracts.

There are legitimate arguments in favor of eliminating such demands from contract insurance requirements. As an insured under the contractor's CGL policy with respect to the contractor's completed operations, a project owner is afforded a basis for submitting to the contractor's insurer virtually any premises liability claim brought against it; even slip-and-fall cases can be said to arise out of the contractor's completed operations, that is, the building itself. Of course, none of the parties in such a situation intends for the contractor's insurer to become responsible for such premises liability claims unless the liability arose from the contractor's negligence. Nevertheless, coverage this broad may be provided when an additional insured endorsement covers liability arising out of "your work."

The strongest rationale for requiring contractors to provide project owners with coverage under the contractors' policies lies in the perceived fairness of making the contractor responsible for the increased exposure to loss created for the owner by the contractor's operations. It is certainly true that a property owner can incur premises liability because of the negligence of the contractor that built, installed, or repaired the property. (For example, people may be injured or the property of others damaged when an inadequately supported ceiling collapses, faulty air-conditioning causes sick building syndrome, or substandard electrical wiring starts a fire.) But even without additional insured coverage, property owners will still have recourse against their negligent contractors in situations like these, either by virtue of the indemnity agreement in which they are held harmless by the contractor for such losses or simply in tort. Indeed, any building owner held liable for such a loss would have grounds for recovery against the negligent contractor regardless of whether a contractual relationship ever existed between the two. That such recourse may at some time prove necessary is not automatically viewed as justification for requiring the builder of any given property to purchase liability insurance for the owner of those premises.

From the perspective of the project owner, a number of concerns are not addressed by these potential contractual and noncontractual remedies. First, the reality of litigation is that with countersuits, allegations of contributory/comparative fault, excessive demand for production of documents that invade privacy, and other maneuvers, the owner often will be forced to compromise its claim. Where there is a possible contract-based remedy, there is still the possibility of protracted litigation as well as the possibility that the contractual agreement will be held invalid.

Securing additional insured status with respect to completed operations is no panacea for these problems; there is still substantial potential for disputes as to the application of coverage. However, it will put the project owner in a much better position to obtain coverage under the contractor's liability insurance. For this reason, many project owners will choose to require additional insured status when they have the negotiating clout to do so. However, all parties must keep in mind the realities of the insurance marketplace and the fact that the coverage may not always be obtainable.

An issue that sometimes causes confusion when analyzing the need for additional insured status with respect to completed operations coverage is that of defective work claims. If the project owner is going to own the completed premises for some period of time after completion of the project, securing additional insured status under the contractor's completed operations coverage does not improve the owner's chance of successfully recovering on a defective work claim against the contractor. Such a defective work claim is an action in tort directly against the contractor, and the fact that the owner is an insured under the contractor's liability insurance may have a bearing on the coverage provided to the contractor. Being an additional insured does not give the owner an ability to submit its claim directly to the liability insurer as if it were a first-party policy. However, when the owner can allege that damage to its owned property was caused by the contractor, there may be coverage. Under standard CGL forms, the exclusion for damage to owned property applies only to the named insured's (contractor's) property. Damage to the additional insured's (owner's) property would be covered if caused by the contractor.

The fact that both the owner and the contractor are insureds under the same policy may provide comfort in some fact patterns. For example, the insurer who takes a coverage stance that may be improper is jeopardizing the interests of two of its insureds.

Also, where counterclaims are generated, the same insurer is obligated to defend both sides, which may encourage the insurer to take a position favorable to settling the case.

If an indemnitor is unsuccessful in negotiating out of providing completed operations coverage for its additional insured, it must be careful that the endorsement used to effect additional insured status does not limit coverage to "ongoing operations." The indemnitor breaching such an agreement may be required to provide the financial protection on behalf of the other party without insurance coverage. The reason is that breach of contract in failing to procure insurance as required is not covered by current standard CGL policy provisions.

Arising Out Of

In various endorsements and policy provisions used to effect additional insured coverage, the phrase "arising out of" is found repeatedly. In some nonstandard endorsements, it is the operative wording in the insuring agreement, defining the causational relationship between the named insured's actions and the additional insured's liability. In others, it is used in attempts to limit coverage, often with mixed results, as will be discussed later. In pre-2004 editions of ISO additional insured endorsements, it was the foundation of those endorsements' very broad coverage—broad enough to encompass the additional insured's sole fault.

"Arising out of" is but one of a number of phrases that additional insured endorsements may use to characterize the central condition of coverage—the relationship between (1) the liability for which the additional insured is seeking coverage and (2) the actions or operations of the named insured. The 2004 edition of endorsement CG 20 10 employs a phrase that the insurance industry regards as a very narrow characterization of that relationship; injury or damage for which the additional insured seeks coverage must be "caused by" the acts or omissions of the named insured, either completely or partially. Whether the "caused by" language will be interpreted as narrowly as the policy drafters intend remains to be seen. But case law is extensive on the way in which courts have interpreted other causative restrictions on additional insured coverage. This section of the chapter will examine that case law.

Causation versus Nexus

A number of cases have reached consistent conclusions as to the meaning of additional insured coverage grants that apply with respect to injury or damage "arising out of" the named insured's work. The consensus emerging from these court decisions is that "arising out of" does not require a direct causal relationship between the named insured's conduct, work, or operations and the additional insured's liability. A case exemplifying broad application of coverage based on claims "arising out of" the named insured's conduct is *Merchants Insurance Company of New Hampshire, Inc. v U.S. Fidelity & Guaranty Co.,* 143 F3d 5 (1st Cir 1998).

In this case, D'Agostino, the general contractor on a project involving the removal and replacement of a bridge, required additional insured status under the policy of Great Eastern Marine Service Inc., a subcontractor. An employee of the subcontractor was injured by one of the general contractor's workers. The injured employee subsequently sued the general contractor, alleging his injuries were the direct and proximate result of the general contractor's negligence. The subcontractor's insurer refused to defend the general contractor, arguing that the policy's additional insured endorsement did not afford the general contractor coverage for its own direct negligence. The additional insured endorsement at issue read as follows.

> WHO IS INSURED (Section II) is amended to include as an insured the person or organization in this Schedule [in this instance, the general contractor], but only with respect to liability arising out of "your work" [in this instance, work of the subcontractor] for that insured by or for you.

The court ruled that the insurer had a duty to defend the general contractor. It pointed out that at the time of the injury, the injured employee was within the course and scope of his employment for the subcontractor, who in turn was working for the general contractor pursuant to the subcontract. The injury was a consequence of work the subcontractor was performing. This finding was applied to the court's interpretation of the "arising out of" wording, which the court addressed as follows:

> Beyond question, under Massachusetts law the phrase "arising out of" denotes a level of causation that lies between proximate and actual causation. As recently as 1996 that state's intermediate appellate court said in *New England Mutual Life v Liberty Mutual Insurance Co.,* 667 NE2d 295 (1996):
>
> > The usual meaning ascribed to the phrase "arising out of" is much broader than "caused by"; the former phrase is considered synonymous with "originate" or "come into being".

> And later in the same year the Massachusetts Supreme Judicial Court confirmed in *Rischitelli v Safety Insurance Co.,* 423 Mass 703, 671 NE2d 1243 (1996):
>
> > The expression "arising out of" indicates a wider range of causation than the concept of proximate causation in tort law.

McIntosh v Scottsdale Insurance Co., 992 F2d 251 (10th Cir 1993), is a leading case in the history of judicial interpretations of "arising out of" within the context of an additional insured endorsement. The case involved a spectator's injury on city property at an affair sponsored by a nonprofit organization. The city was sued because of its failure to warn of a dangerous condition. When it tendered its defense as an additional insured to the sponsor's liability insurer, coverage was denied on the basis that the injury was caused by the city's premises, not the named insured's operations.

The endorsement language in question made the city an additional insured "only with respect to liability arising out of the named insured's operations." The court of appeals stated that this phrase "is ambiguous as to whose negligence is excluded from coverage" and therefore had to be construed in favor of the insured. The court also concluded that the city's liability did arise out of the sponsor's operations, stating that the phrase "arising out of" related to causation, "but its terms are both broad and vague."

The court also stated that the additional insured endorsement did not limit the policy's coverage to claims in which the city was held to be vicariously liable for the sponsor's negligence. In support of this statement, the court cited *Philadelphia Electric Co. v Nationwide Mutual Insurance Co.,* 721 F Supp 740 (ED Pa 1989), where additional insureds that were added "for any work performed by the named insured on their behalf" were held to be covered for their own negligence related to the work of the named insured. The court also cited *Dayton Beach Park No. 1 Corp. v National Union Fire Insurance Co.,* 573 NYS2d 700 (1991), holding that the phrase "... arising out of ... operations performed for the additional insured ... by the named insured" covered the additional insured for its own negligence.

Transamerica Insurance Co. v Turner Construction Co., 601 NE2d 473 (Mass App 1992), also illustrates the broad scope of the "arising out of" language. A subcontractor agreed to hold harmless and indemnify a general contractor and also to name the latter on its liability policy as an additional insured. The general contractor was sued in a third-party-over action and sought primary coverage as an additional insured under the contractor's policy.

The general contractor was added to the subcontractor's policy by way of a pre-2004 edition of CG 20 10. In denying coverage to the general contractor, the insurer argued that the words "arising out of" had the effect of requiring that the named insured (the subcontractor) be the proximate cause of the incident. The court disagreed with the insurer because there was a causal connection between the subcontractor's work and the resulting injury, even though there was some evidence that the general contractor was partially at fault.

In *Admiral Insurance Co. v Trident NGL,* 988 SW2d 451 (Tex 1999), the court of appeals for the First District of Texas addressed the "arising out of" wording. In this case, K-D Oilfield Services (KD) provided crews and equipment to service oil and gas facilities owned by other companies. Trident and KD entered into a contract calling for KD to service facilities owned by Trident. A KD employee was assisting Trident in performing preventive maintenance on a compressor by unloading Trident's tools from Trident's truck when the compressor exploded, injuring him.

In compliance with contract requirements, KD had added Trident as an additional insured to the KD policy. The additional insured endorsement read as follows.

> In consideration of the premium charged, the persons or entities insured provision is amended to include as an insured the organizations designated below, but only with respect to liability arising out of the named insured's [KD's] operations.

When the injured employee sued Trident, Trident tendered the claim to KD's insurer, which promptly denied any coverage obligation. Among the reasons asserted by the insurer for the denial was the argument that Trident's liability did not arise out of KD's operations. According to the insurer, wording providing coverage for liability "arising out of" the named insured's operations was intended to provide coverage only if KD's performance was a cause of the explosion.

The court sided with Trident, which had cited a number of cases from around the country construing almost identical additional insured language. The court stated that:

> ... the majority view of these cases is that for liability to "arise out of" operations of a named insured, it is not necessary for the named insured's acts to have "caused" the accident; rather, it is sufficient that the named insured's employee was injured while present at the scene in connection with performing the named

insured's business, even if the cause of the injury was the negligence of the additional insured.

The case of *Aetna Casualty and Surety Co. v Ocean Accident & Guaranty Corp.,* 386 F2d 413 (3d Cir 1967), echoed that same rationale, with that court stating as follows.

> The policy language "arising out of" is very broad and vague.... [It] means causally connected with, not proximately caused by. "But for" causation, i.e., a cause and result relationship, is enough to satisfy this provision of the policy.

In referencing "but for" causation, the court indicated that coverage should apply broadly in circumstances where the additional insured's liability would not have arisen but for its engagement of or association with the named insured.

In the case of *Franklin Mutual Insurance Co. v Security Indemnity Insurance Co.,* 646 A2d 443 (NJ 1994), discussed in **Chapter 11**, a tenant leased space in a building to operate a restaurant. Additional insured status was provided to the building owner under the following wording.

> It is agreed that the "Persons Insured" provision is amended to include as an insured the person or organization designated below but only with respect to liability arising out of the ownership, maintenance or use of that part of the premises designated below leased to the named insured....

A patron of the restaurant who slipped and fell on the exterior steps leading into the restaurant sued the building owner and the restaurant. When the building owner sought coverage as an additional insured under the restaurant owner's policy, the insurer denied coverage. It justified its denial by arguing that the wording of the additional insured endorsement shown above did not provide coverage because the accident took place on the exterior steps, which were not part of the premises leased to the restaurant as required by the endorsement's "arising out of" language.

In ruling that coverage applied, the court held as follows.

> That phrase must be interpreted or construed in a broad and comprehensive sense to mean originating from the use of or growing out of the use of the premises.... Thus there need be shown only a substantial nexus between the occurrence and the use of the leased premises in order for coverage to attach. The inquiry, therefore, is whether the occurrence which caused the injury, although not foreseen or expected, was in the contemplation of the parties to the insurance contract, a natural and reasonable incident or consequence of the leased premises, and, thus, a risk against which they may reasonably expect those insured under the policy would be protected.

In the case of *Harrah's Atlantic City v Harleysville Insurance Co.,* 671 A2d 1122 (NJ 1996), also discussed in **Chapter 11,** the court referenced these conclusions of the *Franklin Mutual* case. As in that case, the issue in *Harrah's* was whether the additional insured's liability arose out of the use of the leased premises when the injury occurred off those premises. In addressing this issue, the court stated as follows.

> [In] negotiating for such an endorsement in a lease, the landlord is simply attempting to insure against the risk of liability generated by the business to be conducted by the tenant... Consequently, where the landlord can trace the risk creating its liability directly to the tenant's business premises, it is not unreasonable for the landlord to expect coverage, inasmuch as it can be truly said that the accident originated from or grew out of the use of the leased premises.

In both the *Franklin Mutual* and *Harrah's* cases, the court looked to the reasonable expectation of coverage created by a broad interpretation of the "arising out of" wording.

Unless and until insurers modify the "arising out of" wording or limit the coverage it provides by additional provisions, courts are unlikely to alter their approach to interpreting the phrase broadly.

The words of the court in *Merchants Insurance Co. of New Hampshire, Inc. v U.S. Fidelity and Guaranty Co.,* discussed on page 188, are representative.

> After all, if USF&G had really intended to limit coverage under the additional insured endorsement to those situations in which an added insured such as D'Agostino was to be held vicariously liable only for the negligence of a principal insured such as Great Eastern, USF&G was free to draft a policy with qualifying language that expressly implemented that intention. [See, e.g., *Consolidation Coal Co. v Liberty Mutual Insurance Co.,* 406 F Supp 1292 (WD Pa 1976).]

In fact, that is precisely what ISO has attempted to do in its 2004 revisions to the standard construction-related additional insured endorsements. Instead of providing coverage to the additional insured for liability "arising out of" the named insureds operation's, work, ongoing operations, etc., ISO's stated goal is to eliminate coverage for the additional insured's sole fault, which courts have consistently interpreted the older "arising out of" language to provide in many instances.

"Arising Out of" versus "Resulting from"

Recognizing the broad defense and indemnity obligations created by additional insured coverage for liability "arising out of" the named insured's conduct or out of certain premises, some insurers—even before the introduction of the 2004 ISO revisions—have opted for a different approach. In some forms, additional insureds are covered for their liability "resulting from" the named insured's work for them. According to these insurers, use of the "resulting from" wording in the insuring agreement is intended to limit coverage to a narrower scope of liability—liability for injury or damage with a stronger causational link to the named insured.

The notion that there is a distinction between "arising out of" and "resulting from" was the issue in *Vitty v D.C.P. Corp., J.C. Towing v The New*

Jersey Highway Authority, 633 A2d 1040 (NJ App Div 1993). In this case, the New Jersey Highway Authority (NJHA) engaged J.C. Towing, Inc., to perform towing services. J.C. agreed to defend and indemnify liability claims "arising out of" the license contract.

Vitty (an employee of J.C.) was killed when a drunken driver struck his tow truck while it was parked at an official U-turn. Although Vitty was not engaged in wrecking or towing activities, he was on duty. Vitty's estate sued J.C. and NJHA. The suit against NJHA was predicated on the notion that the highway median was defective because it lacked a guardrail and sloped upward, causing the drunken driver's car to become airborne, crashing into Vitty's tow truck. The trial court dismissed all claims against J.C. except that of NJHA relating to the indemnification agreement. The court found that J.C. was obligated to defend and indemnify NJHA.

J.C. argued that Vitty's death resulted not from the towing and wrecking contract, but from the actions of the drunken driver. J.C. argued that its indemnity obligation applied only to claims "arising out of" the license contract, language that (it contended) connotes causality. J.C. therefore argued that its obligation to indemnify NJHA was triggered only where a claimant's injuries were *the result of* J.C.'s towing services.

Consistent with the case law discussed earlier, the appellate court hearing this case rejected the notion that "arising out of" required that the damage sustained be directly and proximately caused by the operation of the tow truck. The court held that the "arising out of" wording referred only to a claim growing out of or having its origin in the subject matter. As such, only a substantial nexus—not a direct causal connection—was required to bring the injuries involved within the parameters of the indemnity obligation.

The court contrasted obligations under the "arising out of" wording with indemnity obligations applicable to liability "resulting from" the subject matter. In doing so, it referenced the case of *McCabe v Great Pacific Century Corp.,* 566 A2d 234 (NJ

App Div 1989). There, an electrical contractor had agreed to indemnify the general contractor for all claims "resulting from" any act or omission of the subcontractor related to the subject matter of the subcontract. In contrasting the obligations under the "arising out of" wording before it with those under the "resulting from" wording in the *McCabe* case, the court stated as follows.

> The indemnification agreement here is quite different. Unlike *McCabe,* it does not require that the claim pertain to "an act or omission resulting from" the towing agreement. The cause of the claim need not relate to an act or omission in carrying out the duties of the license. Instead, all that is required is that the injury or property damage grow out of or have its origin in, or be connected to the subject matter of the towing agreement. *Unlike McCabe ... Garage's obligation does not depend on causality.* [Emphasis added.]

A case addressing this issue in the context of an additional insured endorsement is *Continental Heller Corp. v St. Paul Fire and Marine Insurance,* 47 Cal App 4th 291, 54 Cal Rptr 2d 621 (1996). Continental Heller was a general contractor. An employee of a subcontractor was injured at the job site when he slipped while fetching tools for his day's labor. The injured employee later sued Continental Heller, which was an additional insured under the subcontractor's CGL policy.

In refusing to defend the general contractor, the subcontractor's insurer argued that its additional insured endorsement covered Continental Heller only for damage that "results from" the named insured's—that is, the subcontractor's—work. The insurer's position was that because the employee's injuries were sustained while fetching tools in preparation for work, they did not result from the work. This wording, the insurer argued, was clear and unambiguous and created no duty to defend.

The insurer acknowledged that a duty to defend would have existed under the broader "arising out of" wording. In fact, part of the insurer's argument was based upon a comparison between standard ISO "arising out of" wording and what the insurer

represented to be its manuscript "resulting from" wording.

The court resolved the case by finding it reasonable that injuries sustained while fetching tools necessary to perform certain work results from that work and therefore fell within the policy's definition of "your work" so as to trigger coverage for the additional insured. The *Heller* case was overturned for reasons unrelated to the "resulting from" issue. It nonetheless remains an important case, because it represents the insurer's position, regarding the "resulting from" wording. What is important to note for purposes of this discussion is the distinction drawn between "arising out of" and "resulting from."

Insurers' concerns regarding the broader scope of coverage provided by the "arising out of" wording were reinforced by a large body of case law reflecting the opinions set forth in the *Vitty* case and others, some of which are discussed in this chapter. On the other hand, some courts that have not been exposed to industry practice in this regard have viewed the terms "arising out of" and "resulting from" as meaning the same thing, though their value as precedent is questionable given the facts of each case in relation to the wording at issue. For example, the court in *Pension Trust Fund for Operating Engineers v Federal Insurance Co.,* 307 F3d 944 (9th Cir 2002), addressed the distinction between "arising out of" and "as a result of" as opposed to "resulting from" in the context of a fiduciary responsibility policy. In doing so, the court held that it would be "doubtful that the California Supreme Court would view *as a result of* significantly differently from *arising out of.* In another California case, *State Farm Mutual Auto. Insurance Co. v Davis,* 937 F2d 1415 (9th Cir 1991), dealing with auto insurance, the court held that:

> a slight causal connection would be required between an insured vehicle and a shooting injury before the injury may be held to arise out of the use of the insured vehicle…. This slight causal connection in our view is also what reasonable men and women would understand the phrase 'resulting from the use of' an insured vehicle to mean.

Neither of these cases addresses the "arising out of/resulting from" distinction in the context of CGL insurance, or the custom and practice of the insurance and risk management industries that acknowledges a distinction between the two phrases. Despite that, however, these cases will be relied on by those seeking to blur or abolish what has been viewed as a longstanding distinction between the two phrases by the insurance and risk management industries and by many insureds. Given that many insureds have lost coverage based on this distinction, it is likely that eventually the California Supreme Court and others will continue to uphold the distinction that has long distinguished these two phrases. In any event, insureds should pay close attention to nonstandard wording in additional insured endorsements and be aware of the judicial meaning ascribed to it.

Summary

The issues that arise with respect to additional insured status on the policies of contractors are perhaps the most complex of all additional insured issues. Recent developments in the evolution of policy language for this purpose have consistently been in the direction of reducing coverage. The most significant of these developments have been the elimination of completed operations coverage beginning in 1993; and the elimination of coverage for the additional insured's sole fault arising out of the construction operations, in 2004.

These changes to standard endorsements have come at a time when many insurers have introduced their own independently filed additional insured endorsements, primarily applying on a blanket basis. A review of these endorsements reveals that some are more limited than standard endorsements, while others are quite broad. Presumably, some insurers who are willing to compete for the better risk are willing to provide broader coverage for an additional cost.

How the most recent changes to additional insured status will affect the insurance and construction industries remains to be seen. Likely to complicate matters is the fact that the CGL policy's contractual liability coverage can now be amended either to eliminate coverage for the assumption of another's tort liability in a business contract (such as a construction contract); or to cover only limited and intermediate indemnity obligations and eliminate coverage for the insured's assumption of another party's sole fault.

A number of states still permit the assumption of another's sole fault, provided the contract is clear and unequivocal on the point; an even larger number of states permit contractual requirements of additional insured coverage broader in scope than the permissible scope of indemnity. Current versions of standard additional insured endorsements are at odds with the contractual risk transfer "climate" of these states. Those who must read contracts and verify that required insurance is in place have to be more alert than ever in paying attention to existing laws, contract provisions, and available coverages.

Chapter 9 Notes

1. These scheduling requirements could become burdensome when a contractor or subcontractor must add many parties as insureds in connection with many different projects. Of course, insurers could issue the automatic status or so-called blanket endorsement CG 20 33 instead, which provides the same coverage as CG 20 10. The criterion for eligibility of CG 20 33, however, is that the additional insured status be required in a written contract. Some underwriters are willing to transform scheduled additional insured endorsements into automatic endorsements simply by inserting the word "blanket" where the additional insured's name and described operations are to be shown.

Scheduling of the location of insured operations is also required under CG 20 37, the separate standard endorsement designated to provide additional insureds with completed operations coverage. Similar location scheduling may be required in many blanket additional insured endorsements that have been issued in recent years. Such requirements are imposed in order to prevent an additional insured from obtaining coverage on a blanket basis for work being done at other locations.

2. The reference simply to *acts* rather than *negligent acts* of the named insured is necessary because endorsement CG 20 10 applies to personal and advertising injury as well as bodily injury and property damage. Personal and advertising injury offenses may constitute volitional or intentional conduct where no negligence is involved. For the same reason, coverage exists for the additional insured with respect to bodily injury and property damage, even if that injury or damage results from the named insured's intentional (rather than negligent) act.

Chapter 10

OCP VERSUS ADDITIONAL INSURED STATUS

Construction projects are inherently risky operations in which numerous unaffiliated organizations—property owners, architects, and contractors—must work closely together. Contracts are used to define the responsibilities of the various parties. These contracts include many clauses and requirements relating to indemnification and insurance. The typical scenario is for the project owner to require indemnification from the general contractor, who then passes the same requirement to its subcontractors. Of course, similar requirements are made concerning liability insurance.

These persons and organizations are not generally included as insureds on the liability policies of the other parties unless endorsement is added to the policy to effect coverage. One of three standard Insurance Services Office, Inc. (ISO), additional insured endorsements may be used to accomplish this. These endorsements are:

- Owners, Lessees or Contractors (CG 20 10)

- Additional Insured—Designated Person or Organization (CG 20 26)

- Additional Insured—Owners, Lessees or Contractors—Automatic Status When Required In Construction Agreement With You (CG 20 33)

Endorsement CG 20 10 is the most commonly used additional insured endorsement in connection with construction projects and is discussed in detail in **Chapter 9.** Endorsement CG 20 33 provides similar coverage on an automatic basis when

the named insured is required in a contract to provide such coverage. It was introduced with ISO forms in 1997.

Endorsement CG 20 26 was originally developed as a generic tool for adding insureds who did not fit neatly into another category. Until it was revised in 2004 to apply only with respect to ongoing operations, it was widely regarded as an option to pre-1993 CG 20 10, which provided the additional insured with completed operations coverage. A fourth endorsement, the Additional Insured—Owners, Lessees or Contractors–Scheduled Person Or Organization (For Use When Contractual Liability Coverage Is Not Provided To You In This Policy) (CG 20 09) endorsement, was long available as an alternative to the owners and contractors protective (OCP) liability policy, which is the subject of this chapter. However, it was withdrawn by ISO in 2004 because of the availability of the OCP policy and the infrequency with which contractors' commercial general liability (CGL) insurance policies are written without contractual liability coverage.

This chapter discusses the coverage provided by an OCP policy and compares it to additional insured status in a CGL policy. It shows that OCP coverage does not insure against all of the types of liabilities that may be incurred by a project owner—a CGL policy is also needed to cover some exposures. It also shows that while coverage under an OCP has certain advantages as compared to additional insured status in a CGL policy, particularly with respect to the provision of a separate limit, it provides a more narrow grant of coverage.

Also discussed in this chapter is the project management protective liability (PMPL) policy. It was prescribed by the American Institute of Architects (AIA) in 1997 as an alternative to additional insured status within the context of construction contract insurance requirements. A form providing coverage as envisioned in the AIA contract documents was briefly marketed but later withdrawn by the insurer that developed it. In 2001, however, ISO introduced its own construction project management protective liability (CPMPL) endorsement, which is designed to be attached to an OCP policy. Both the PMPL policy and the CPMPL endorsement will be analyzed in this chapter as their coverages compare to that of the OCP policy.

OCP Policy Coverage

The OCP liability policy was introduced for use at the turn of the century, and its use became increasingly common as the potential for principals to be held liable for the actions of their independent contractors increased.[1] (At one time there were as many as 21 recognized exceptions to the general rule that a party is not vicariously liable for the torts of its independent contractor.[2])

The OCP policy is designed to provide the named insured (a project owner having construction work done, for example) with liability protection that is limited with respect to both duration and exposures covered. There is a standard OCP coverage form (CG 00 09) that was promulgated by ISO. This form is used extensively; however, some insurers have also developed their own versions. This discussion applies to the 1986, 1988, 1993, 1996, and 2001 editions of the ISO form.

While OCP policies are generally issued for the entire period of a construction project—a period that can span a number of years—their coverage terminates once the operations are completed.[3] Said another way, the policy is intended to cover liability arising from injuries or damages that occur while operations are in progress. Once the job is completed, the insurance protection ends.[4] The OCP policy contains an exclusion, shown in Exhibit 10.1, to effect this intent.

EXHIBIT 10.1
COMPLETED PROJECT
EXCLUSION

This insurance does not apply to:

c. Work Completed or Put to Intended Use

"Bodily injury" or "property damage" which occurs after the earliest of the following times:

(1) When all "work" on the project (other than service, maintenance or repairs) to be performed for you by the "contractor" at the site of the covered operations has been completed; or

(2) When that portion of the "contractor's" "work", out of which the injury or damage arises, has been put to its intended use by any person or organization, other than another contractor or subcontractor working directly or indirectly for the "contractor" as part of the same project.

The completed project exclusion was the point of contention in the case of *James v Hyatt Corp. of Delaware,* 981 F2d 810 (5th Cir 1993), where the court held that an escalator maintenance contractor and its insurer had no duty to defend the hotel from a suit by a patron injured while using an escalator. The OCP policy issued to the hotel covered injury or damage arising from the contractor's performance of duties under the service agreement or arising from the negligence of the hotel in connection with its general supervision of the contractor's work. It also contained an earlier version of the exclusion shown in Exhibit 10.1, which read as follows.

This insurance does not apply:

(b) to bodily injury or property damage occurring after

(1) all work on the project (other than service, maintenance, or repairs) to be

performed by or on behalf of the named insured at the site of the covered operations have been completed; or

(2) that portion of the designated contractor's work out of which the injury arises has been put to its intended use by any person or organization.

The OCP insurer maintained that the claimant's injuries fell within exclusion (b)(2), arguing that the OCP policy covered only damage that occurs while service or maintenance work is in progress. In effect, the policy treats each act of servicing or maintenance as a discreet insurance event. The hotel argued that the exclusions (b)(1) and (b)(2) should be read together and that, per (b)(1), "service, maintenance, or repairs," are exempt from the exclusion. This argument, the court said, is not persuasive because sections (b)(1) and (b)(2) are joined in the disjunctive; the exclusions, therefore, must be treated separately. Furthermore, the contractor was not servicing or maintaining the escalator, and it was being put to its intended use when the injury occurred. Accordingly, the occurrence, the court held, fell with the (b)(2) exclusion, which was similar to the completed operations exclusion found in some CGL policies.

As discussed in **Chapter 9** and demonstrated by the problems encountered by the insurer in the *Hyatt* case discussed above, the wording shown in Exhibit 10.1 is clearer in attempts to eliminate coverage for completed operations. The reason is that this exclusion specifically applies to the occurrence of bodily injury or property damage *after operations have been completed.* Wording that attempts to accomplish the same limitation by referring to "ongoing operations" will not be clearly applicable in a number of completed operations scenarios.

Insurers may also encounter problems attempting to limit coverage to ongoing operations by using the following or similar wording.

We won't cover bodily injury or property damage that results from completed work.

The problem with this exclusionary language of this kind is addressed at length in **Chapter 9,** which discusses the distinction between "arising out of" and "resulting from." As discussed there, the phrase "resulting from" may be considered in some jurisdictions to require a direct causal connection. In many cases involving the "resulting from" wording of the completed operations exclusion quoted above, insurers might be forced to demonstrate a direct causal connection between completed work and the injury or damage that produces a claim. Demonstrating such a connection often proves to be a difficult undertaking in cases involving property damage. In many such cases it can be argued that the damage resulted from something that was done while operations were in progress, though not discovered or manifested until operations were complete.

Demonstrating that the property damage "resulted from" the *completed* work rather than from operations while they were in progress makes application of this exclusion complex. It may also require addressing applicable law in each jurisdiction regarding the manifestation of damage as opposed to the date of discovery, injury in fact, and other coverage trigger theories.

Like the duration of coverage, the exposures covered by the OCP policy are also quite limited. (Relevant portions of the 2001 OCP policy insuring agreement are included in Exhibit 10.2.) The first covered exposure is the named insured's (i.e., the property owner's) liability imputed to it because of acts or omissions of the person or organization who has the obligation: (1) to perform work for the owner and (2) to purchase the OCP policy. The second covered exposure is the owner's direct liability arising out of its "general supervision" of the work performed by the contractor.

It is also important to note that for either of these covered exposures, coverage is limited only to liability for bodily injury or property damage. The policy does not apply to the so-called personal injury or advertising injury perils (e.g., libel, slander, defamation, false arrest, etc.). However, coverage for false arrest, detention, or imprisonment is sometimes added by endorsement (CG 28 05).

EXHIBIT 10.2
EXCERPTS FROM THE 2001 OCP POLICY INSURING AGREEMENT

a. We will pay those sums that the insured becomes legally obligated to pay as damages because of "bodily injury" or "property damage" to which this insurance applies. We will have the right and duty to defend the insured against any "suit" seeking those damages. However, we will have no duty to defend the insured against any "suit" seeking damages for "bodily injury" or "property damage" to which this insurance does not apply. We may, at our discretion, investigate any "occurrence" and settle any claim or "suit" that may result. But:

(1) The amount we will pay for damages is limited as described in Section III—Limits Of Insurance; and

(2) Our right and duty to defend ends when we have used up the applicable limit of insurance in the payment of judgments or settlements.

No other obligation or liability to pay sums or perform acts or services is covered unless explicitly provided for under Supplementary Payments.

b. This insurance applies to "bodily injury" and "property damage" only if:

(1) The "bodily injury" or "property damage" is caused by an "occurrence" and arises out of:

(a) Operations performed for you by the "contractor" at the location specified in the Declarations; or

(b) Your acts or omissions in connection with the general supervision of such operations;

(2) The "bodily injury" or "property damage" occurs during the policy period....

Copyright, ISO Properties, Inc., 2000

A significant case that examined the overall purpose and scope of the OCP policy was *County of Monroe v The Travelers Insurance Cos.,* 419 NYS2d 410 (1979). An OCP policy was purchased by a contractor on behalf of a county government for which the contractor was performing some work. It was explained in the trial proceedings that the OCP policy was written to provide only a "narrow range" of liability protection. The court found that, as its name suggests, the policy is generally intended to protect the named insured from having to pay on account of the negligence of the contractor it has hired. Such insurance by its terms, the court added, is not intended to and does not constitute general coverage (as a CGL policy does).

As a coverage form, the OCP policy not only has its own insuring agreement, as previously noted, but also its own exclusions and conditions. While the exclusions of this coverage form correspond closely to the CGL form, there are three notable exceptions.

First, the form's definition of "insured contract" includes such contracts as lease of premises, side-track agreements, elevator maintenance agreements, or easement agreements, but it does not include the equivalent of the last category of CGL "insured contract"—any other contract or agreement pertaining to the named insured's business in which the named insured assumes the tort liability of another party. Therefore, the OCP policy's named insured is not covered, for example, with respect to a construction contract hold harmless agreement it executes in favor of another entity involved in the project. For coverage of this exposure, the named insured must look to its own CGL policy. This is the equivalent of what an insured receives when the 1988 or subsequent CGL forms are modified with the Contractual Liability Limitation (CG 21 39) endorsement. The result also is the equivalent of "incidental contract" as defined in the 1973 CGL policy provisions.

What all of this means is that the OCP policy should not be relied on to cover liabilities of others assumed in construction contracts. When the named insured is the project owner, as is usually the case, this probably is not a significant limitation—because project owners typically transfer liabilities *to* others; they do not normally assume the liabilities of others. If, on the other hand, the named insured is a contractor, the OCP policy should not be relied on to cover the contractor's assumption of liabilities from the owner. The contractor needs a CGL policy to provide broad form contractual liability coverage.

EXHIBIT 10.3
OCP GENERAL SUPERVISION LIMITATION

This insurance does not apply to: ... "bodily injury" or "property damage" arising out of your, or your "employees,'" acts or omissions other than general supervision of "work" performed for you by the "contractor."

Copyright, ISO Properties, Inc., 2001

Second, there is a specific exclusion, shown in Exhibit 10.3, of any liability that results from acts or omissions of the named insured or its employees—other than "general supervision" of work performed for the named insured by the designated contractor. This exclusion reinforces the intent of the policy, as defined in the form's insuring agreement, to cover only liability incurred by the named insured as a result of the negligence of the contractor designated in the policy declarations. It does not completely insulate the named insured from liability associated with a construction project and should not be thought of as a complete replacement for a CGL policy.

Third, this form, unlike the CGL policy, does not exclude property damage to work performed by the named insured. This kind of an exclusion is not necessary because the work to be performed for the OCP policy's named insured is performed by the designated contractor. However, the OCP policy does exclude damage to work performed for the named insured by the contractor. Otherwise, the insurer of the OCP policy (which generally is the same one that provides the contractor's CGL insurance) would, in some cases, duplicate that provided by the broad form property damage coverage (i.e., by exception to CGL policy exclusions j. and l.) under the contractor's policy, or

more coverage could be provided by the OCP policy at the hands of the contractor than what coverage the contractor actually has purchased under its own CGL policy.

A potentially dangerous limitation found in OCP policies—and as was the case with additional insured endorsement CG 20 09—is the exclusion of damage to property the insured owns, rents, or occupies. The effect of this exclusion will depend in part on legal principles determining when title to property under construction actually passes to the owner. Contract wording addressing the same question will also bear on the application of the exclusion. Many construction contracts specifically identify the point at which title is deemed to pass in this regard. Such provisions should be closely monitored to determine when the owned property exclusion would apply in a given case.

Actual transfer of title provisions vary widely from one construction contract to another, ranging from total silence on the question to provisions stating that title will pass to the owner no later than the time of payment or upon incorporation of the materials into the work. In some cases, the owner may benefit by having title pass as soon as possible (e.g., by avoiding problems if the contractor goes bankrupt). These and other business considerations must be balanced against the application of the owned property exclusion under a policy purchased in large part to protect the owner against property damage caused by contractors and subcontractors.

EXHIBIT 10.4
OCP OTHER INSURANCE PROVISION

The insurance afforded by this coverage part is primary insurance and we will not seek contribution from any other insurance available to you unless the other insurance is provided by a contractor other than the designated "contractor" for the same operation and job location designated in the Declarations. Then we will share with that other insurance by the method described below....

Copyright, ISO Properties, Inc., 2001

The OCP policy has two notable conditions. First and most importantly, the insurance as provided by this form is considered to be primary to any other insurance that may be available to the named insured. Not only does this condition, which is shown in Exhibit 10.4, state that the insurance is primary, but it also delineates the circumstances under which the insurer will seek contribution from other insurance. This is important in the common situation wherein the project owner has in force a CGL policy, which covers the so-called independent contractor's exposure, and requires the general contractor to purchase an OCP policy, in which the owner is the named insured. In the event of a loss arising from the contractor's operations, both policies would be triggered. However, because of this OCP policy condition, the OCP policy would apply on a primary basis. Thus, the OCP policy is designed to serve as a buffer against the use of the named insured's own CGL policy.[5]

A second noteworthy condition in the OCP policy is the cancellation provision. It requires the insurer to provide both the first named insured (the indemnitee) and the designated contractor with 30 days' advance notice of an intent to cancel coverage for any reason other than nonpayment of premium. The usual 10 days' notice must be given to both parties when cancellation is predicated on the failure to pay premium.

The General Supervision Limitation

A potential problem for owners, developers, and others seeking recovery under their OCP policies, particularly for claims involving an injury to the contractor's employee, is the limitation of coverage for liability arising from the named insured's negligence to only that involving its general supervision of the designated contractor. There is a considerable amount of uncertainty surrounding the meaning of the term "general supervision." For liability arising out of its general supervision of the independent contractor's work, exactly how much coverage does the project owner have? The meaning of "general supervision," a term left undefined in the OCP coverage form and the ISO Construction Project Management Protective Liability (CPMPL) (CG 31 15) endorsement, hinges on the circumstances in each case, leaving the scope of OCP coverage a question of fact for each individual court to decide.

While parties over the years have turned to the courts for assistance in defining "general supervision," there is no pat answer on which litigants can rely. Representative of a growing list of court decisions on this subject is *Continental Casualty Co. v Florida Power & Light Co.,* 222 S2d 58 (Fla 1969). The action against Florida Power & Light (FPL), which the insurer refused to defend, was brought by an employee of an independent contractor. The employee charged FPL with failure to have its lines in such a condition that they could be safely worked on at the time and place of the injury.

Among other allegations, it was alleged that FPL negligently failed to (1) provide the employee with a safe place to work and (2) make reasonable inspection of the work site and equipment on which the contractor was to perform work.

The OCP policy issued to FPL covered liability for operations performed for FPL but excluded coverage for acts or omissions of FPL other than liability for general supervision of the work. The insurer denied coverage because it was alleged that FPL's negligence was what gave rise to the claimant's injury. The court, however, ruled in favor of coverage. In doing so, it held that all of the allegations against FPL could, in their implications, be construed to constitute omission of "general supervision" under the broad language of the policy. Cases that reached similar conclusions follow.

- In *Union Electric Co. v Pacific Indemnity Co.,* 422 SW2d 87 (Mo App 1967), the term "general supervision" meant the kind of supervision that an owner-insured customarily undertakes with respect to work performed by an independent contractor.

- In *Western Casualty & Surety Co. v Southwestern Bell Telephone Co.,* 396 F2d 351 (8th Cir 1968), the court held that supplying specifications and plats of work to be done and reserving the right to inspect constituted general supervision.

- In *Citizens Mutual v Employers Mutual Insurance Co.,* 212 NW2d 724 (Mich App 1973), the general supervision of the actions of an independent contractor digging a sewer line did not extend to keeping a hydrant key available for use in a possible emergency.

- In *Casualty Insurance Co. v Northbrook Property & Casualty Co.,* 501 NE2d 812 (Ill App 1986), the term "general supervision" was held to encompass a construction manager's role in coordinating, scheduling work, and inspecting the work of another, as well as in stopping the work and issuing change orders.

- In *Ohio Casualty Insurance Co. v Flanagin,* 210 A2d 221 (NJ 1965), general supervision was said to mean that the prime contractor supervises the work of the subcontractor only to the extent necessary to see that the work is done in accordance with the contract and specifications. The court further said that it does not connote control of the means to accomplish the required result.

The term "general supervision" was declared to be ambiguous by the court in the case of *City of Detroit Board of Water Commissioners v Maryland Casualty Co.,* 1974 CCH (Fire and Casualty) 49 (Mich App 1974). The Michigan court stated that the term "general supervision," as contained in the policy, was not defined therein or by cases and custom. Under the general rules of construction of insurance contracts, therefore, the term in question presented an uncertainty and ambiguity as to its meaning that had to be construed in favor of the insured, the court said.

The problem with the uncertainty over the definition of the term "general supervision" is that, unless it is defined very broadly, the coverage limitations imposed on an OCP policy's coverage cause the OCP policy to be more restrictive than the extent of liability that can be transferred by an indemnity clause. In other words, an OCP policy

may not cover all of the liabilities transferred in a legitimate and acceptable hold harmless agreement. The reason is that liability under contractual liability coverage of a CGL policy is determined by the degree of fault.

For example, the indemnitor may be solely at fault, or the indemnitee may be solely at fault, or both the indemnitor and indemnitee may be at fault, 50–50, 60–40, or some other combination. However, the degree of fault does not establish liability and coverage under the OCP policy. Instead, the liability of the policy's named insured must be translated as liability stemming from acts or omissions in connection with the "general supervision" of the operations. For example, if the sole fault alleged against the policy's named insured is failure to provide a safe place to work, can that allegation be equated as an act or omission in connection with the general supervision of the operations? Unless the answer is yes, no coverage applies for the OCP policy's named insured.

There are also other types of fault not involving general supervision that may be imposed on the indemnitee and would not be encompassed by an OCP policy.

A case in point is *First Insurance Co. of Hawaii Limited, v State of Hawaii,* 665 P2d 648 (Haw 1983). A CGL policy was obtained by the contractor pursuant to a contract with the state for the construction of a highway. The endorsement, added to the policy listing the state as an additional insured, provided the equivalent of OCP coverage under additional insured endorsement CG 20 09.

One day after the road was open to traffic, an accident occurred, resulting in the death of a motorist. Suit was subsequently filed against the contractor, the state, and the county. The contractor's insurer acknowledged coverage for the state as an insured to the extent any judgment was rendered against the state because of the contractor's negligence, but it disavowed any duty to defend the state for its own negligence and liability resulting therefrom. The insurer contended that any duty it may have had to defend the state depended on the state's construction contract with the contractor and then on the contractor's insurance policy that named the state as an additional insured.

A review of the contractor's policy and additional insured endorsement revealed that the insurer was obligated to defend the state for any liability the state incurred as a result of the contractor's negligence or as a result of the state's own negligence in supervising the contractor's work. The policy did not cover liability of the state arising from its own acts of negligence. The court stated that the insurer's argument was partly flawed because the insurer attempted to define its duty to defend on the basis of the relationship between its policy provisions and the ultimate outcome of the case. On this point the court stated that the insurer's duty to defend arises whenever an action raises the potential for liability of the insurer to indemnify the insured.

Thus, the lawsuit involving the deceased motorist raised the possibility that the state could be held liable (1) for its own negligence, (2) for negligence in connection with its general supervision of the contractor's operations, or (3) from the contractor's negligence.

The primary question before the court was whether the contractor's CGL policy obligated the insurer to indemnify the state. The provisions of the additional insured endorsement provided coverage, "but only with respect to liability arising out of (1) operations performed for the additional insured (the state) by the named insured (the contractor) at the location designated, or (2) acts or omissions of the additional insured (the state) in connection with its general supervision of such operations."

The state contended that provision (1) provided coverage to the state with respect to any liability "arising out of" the contractor's operations, irrespective of whether the contractor was negligent. The state cited *Retherford v Kama,* 470 P2d 517 (Haw 1970), for the proposition that the phrase "arising out of" should not be read as necessitating a causal relationship between the state's liability and fault on the part of the contractor.

The fallacy of this argument, the court explained, was that the state overlooked exclusion 3.(b) of

the endorsement. This exclusion explicitly provided as follows.

> This insurance does not apply: ... (b) to bodily injury or property damage arising out of any act or omission of the additional insured or any of his employees, other than general supervision of work performed for the named insured by the additional insured.

Thus, the exclusion limited coverage of the policy to liability incurred by the state that resulted from the contractor's negligence. Since the jury in the underlying lawsuit found the contractor not to be negligent, provision (1) of the additional insured endorsement did not afford the state with protection.

The state then argued that provision (2) of the endorsement was applicable by contending that the jury verdict did not determine conclusively that the state's negligence was not the result of the state's failure to supervise the contractor's operations. The court disagreed here as well. When the jury verdict absolved the contractor and the county of any negligence on their parts, the court explained, it was determined that the state was negligent in failing to warn the public adequately, and such negligence of the state did not hinge on the failure to supervise the contractor.

A later case, *Liberty Mutual Insurance Co. v Capeletti Bros, Inc.*, 699 S2d 736 (Fla App 1997), is discussed in **Chapter 9** because the issue involved additional insured endorsement CG 20 09. That case is important to note here because coverage for liability arising from the acts or omissions of the named insured is limited to liability arising out of the general supervision of the work. In the case in question, the court ruled that the general contractor's liability did not arise from its supervision of the subcontractor's work, so coverage did not apply.

In another general supervision case, apparently where insurance coverage was not an issue, a subcontractor's employee was injured when he fell into an open trench. The worker brought suit against the project's general contractor, claiming that the latter maintained sufficient control over safety at the site to have the duty to provide a safe place to work. The general contractor maintained it had no duty to the employee. Both the trial and appellate courts agreed, holding that a general contractor is not liable for a subcontractor's negligence, unless the general contractor retained control over the subcontractor's work. In examining the kind of control necessary to hold the contractor accountable, the court found that: (1) the general contractor did not exert any control over the excavation, (2) there was no evidence to suggest that the subcontractor was not entirely free to perform the work on its own, (3) the general contractor never directed the "operative details" of the work performed by the subcontractor, and (4) the subcontractor supplied all of the equipment used. The case is *Bieruta v Klein Creek Corp.,* 770 NE2d 1175 (Ill App 2002).

The point should be clear that whenever the named insured of an OCP policy is negligent independent of the contractor's fault, it is necessary that such negligence can be labeled as an error or omission in the general supervision of the designated contractor. This limitation to liability arising from general supervision may preclude coverage even when the designated contractor was also partly at fault if the named insured is liable because of its acts outside the scope of general supervision.

For example, assume that as a condition precedent to performing work on a developer's premises, a contractor agrees to do two things. The first is to hold harmless and indemnify the developer for the latter's joint or comparative liability to other parties. The second is to purchase an OCP policy with the developer as named insured.

Recall that the OCP policy provides protection in two contexts: (1) when liability is imputed to the named insured because of acts or omissions of the contractor, and (2) when the developer becomes liable because of its general supervision of the work.

Assume next that an employee of the contractor is injured in the course of the project, collects workers compensation benefits, and then files suit against the developer, alleging that the developer's sole fault contributed to the injury. (This is commonly referred to as a third-party-over action. Workers compensation insurers that pay statutory benefits usually file liens so that the injured employee must repay the insurer if the employee is successful against the third party. The employee in these cases will usually allege sole fault of the third party, since 100 percent recovery may be available from such party. If the employee alleges only partial fault of the third party, acknowledging that the employer was also at fault, the recovery from the third party may not be sufficient to make it worthwhile for the employee to file suit for damages.) The developer's OCP policy will not apply unless the developer's liability can be connected to acts of general supervision. Making such a connection, as has already been noted, could be a problem. In any event, if the OCP policy does not apply, then the contractual liability insurance of the contractor should apply for the benefit of the developer (because of the hold harmless agreement).

As a rule, then, whenever an indemnitee (such as a project owner hiring an independent contractor) imposes an indemnification agreement encompassing its sole or even partial fault, it should be recognized that an OCP policy does not cover all of the potential liabilities transferred in the hold harmless agreement. On the other hand, blanket contractual liability insurance, which does not typically include any restrictions as to the degree of fault, should cover these liabilities if the clause is enforceable. Likewise, coverage provided through additional insured status in the indemnitor's CGL would also cover these liabilities if additional insured endorsement CG 20 10 is used. (Endorsement CG 20 10 does not restrict coverage to general supervision.)

Advocates of the OCP policy will, nevertheless, often recommend its purchase *in addition to* a Hold harmless agreement (and an appropriate insurance requirement). The rationale for doing so is threefold. First, if the indemnification agreement with the contractor turns out to be unenforceable, the owner can fall back on its OCP policy for at least partial recovery. Second, an additional set of limits applies to the OCP coverage. Third, the

OCP policy specifically applies on a primary basis.

On the surface, this first reason appears to make sense. But closer scrutiny reveals that an indemnification agreement (in which the owner transfers all or part of its own tort liability to the contractor) and an OCP policy do not always complement each other.

For purposes of illustration, consider a case where a developer imposes a hold harmless and indemnity clause that attempts to transfer the developer's sole fault to the contractor along with the requirement that the contractor purchase an OCP policy in the developer's name. It is subsequently alleged by one of the contractor's employees that the developer's failure to provide a safe place to work was the *sole* cause of injury suffered by the employee. The attempted contractual transfer of the developer's sole fault is held to be unenforceable by law because the jurisdiction in question permits no more than joint negligence of the parties. Since the contractor's CGL insurer does not have to hold harmless and indemnify the developer, an important question is whether the developer has any secondary recourse under its OCP policy.

The answer, as always, hinges on whether the circumstances that gave rise to the sole liability of the developer can be successfully labeled "general supervision." Any other liability arising out of an act or omission by the developer is excluded. Unless the link to general supervision can be made successfully, the developer will be no better off with the OCP policy than it was with the nullified hold harmless agreement.

Now assume that the employee's injury is held to result from the joint negligence of the developer and contractor, and the contract includes a hold harmless agreement that is deemed to be ambiguous and unenforceable. Again, the contractor's CGL insurer would not have to respond under the contractual liability coverage. In this case, the OCP policy would cover the developer's vicarious liability arising from the operations of the contractor, subject to a separate set of insurance limits. But whether the OCP policy also will protect the developer against its own separate liability arising from its negligence depends on whether that liability can be categorized as arising from the developer's general supervision of the contractor.

Had the fault in the previous circumstances been attributable on a comparative basis to both the developer and the contractor (and thus transferable by means of an indemnity agreement), the only benefit of having an OCP policy in place is the separate set of policy limits. Any transfer of liability short of what is unenforceable by law would also be covered by the contractual liability insurance of the contractor's CGL policy. On the other hand, had the fault been solely that of the developer, neither a hold harmless agreement nor an OCP policy would have protected the developer.

Another point to keep in mind is that, while the standard ISO CGL policy automatically includes built-in contractual liability coverage encompassing broad form indemnity, insurers now use with some regularity the Contractual Liability Limitation (CG 21 39) endorsement, which excludes the assumption of an indemnitee's tort liability in business contracts. Insurers can now also eliminate contractual liability coverage for an indemnitee's sole negligence through the use of Amendment of Insured Contract Definition (CG 24 26) endorsement, which was introduced by ISO with its 2004 endorsement amendments.

The principal loss exposure insured under the OCP policy is the named insured's vicarious liability arising out of the activities of independent contractors. Except in connection with the named insured's supervisory function, OCP coverage does not apply when the named insured's own negligence is the cause—or partial cause—of a claim. The allegations of any direct negligence on the part of the policy's named insured have been held to defeat coverage under the provisions of the OCP policy, even when the injury or damage was partly attributable to acts of the contractor as well.

An illustration of this point is *Baltimore Gas & Electric Co. v Commercial Union Insurance Co.*, 688 A2d 496 (Md App 1997). (While this case was based on disputed coverage under an additional insured endorsement (i.e., CG 20 09), the relevant policy language was identical to that of the standard OCP policy.) A utility company hired an excavation contractor to dig a hole alongside the utility's underground cables to allow access to the cable. The contractor dug the hole as specified in the contract and was paid. Several months later, a motorist drove his car into the still-open hole and was injured. The motorist sued the utility, the excavation contractor, operators of the cable company that used the cable for which the hole was dug, and a number of other parties. The basis of the suit against all of the defendants was "the negligent, careless and reckless construction activities of the defendants, their agents, servants and employees."

The utility company was an additional insured under the CGL policy of the excavation contractor (as required in the contract between them) and sought a defense against the suit from the contractor's insurer. The additional insured endorsement in question, like the OCP coverage form, excluded:

> bodily injury or property damage arising out of any act or omission of the [utility company] or any of their employees, other than the general supervision of work performed for the [utility company] by [the contractor].

After suit was filed, the injured motorist amended the complaint, dropping his allegations against every party except the utility company, which in effect dismissed those other parties from the suit. In taking this action, the motorist implicitly accepted the argument of the excavation contractor that it had no contractual obligation to fill the hole it had dug and that the failure to fill the hole was the utility company's own sole negligence. With the utility company remaining as the only defendant in the suit, the contractor's insurance company denied any duty to defend, arguing that the utility company's coverage as an additional insured did not extend to liability for its own negligent acts.

The resulting case before the Maryland Court of Special Appeals presented the following question: If original allegations against an OCP insured are broad enough to encompass negligent general supervision (or purely vicarious liability arising out

of a third-party contractor's own negligence), does the resulting duty to defend disappear when the allegations are amended to apply exclusively to the insured? In its simplest terms, the issue was whether an OCP policy can ever provide coverage to the insured as a sole defendant.

The Maryland court ruled that it was the insurer's duty to defend the utility company against the *original* allegations (which were broad enough to imply vicarious or supervisory liability on the utility company's part). When the complaint was dismissed against all but one defendant, the court held that the allegations that dictated the insurer's defense obligation had been altered. But the court held that, as a sole defendant, the utility company was clearly being sued for direct negligence on its own part and that the nature of such suit triggered the exclusion pertaining to any "act or omission" of the insured. In the court's words:

> By its contract, the insurer is obligated to provide a defense to a covered claim, even if the claim will ultimately fail. The converse is also true, however. The insurer is not obligated to provide a defense to a suit that does not assert a covered claim. Therefore, as a matter of contract interpretation, the insurer is entitled to refuse to defend a suit for which it has no obligation under the contract.

Thus, the court held, the allegations in the complaint, following modification by virtue of a dismissal of all but one defendant, were no longer encompassed by the policy. The utility company had disputed the excavation contractor's denial of any obligation to fill the hole it had dug and argued that it was being sued essentially for the contractor's actions, thereby making its alleged liability vicarious in nature (and hence covered). The court rejected this line of reasoning.

> In an attempt to bring the [injured motorist's] claim within the policy, [the utility company] argues that its liability arose out of [the excavation contractor's] work, because [the contractor] was responsible for filling in the splicing pit, and since the policy covers [the utility company] for claims based on that theory of negligence, [the

insurer] should have a duty to defend. This argument misses the point, however. [The insurer's] duty depends upon whether the *allegations* raised by [the injured motorist] are within the scope of the policy. In this case, [the motorist] chose to revise their allegations, to sue [the utility company] on a theory that [the utility company] was responsible for the ... injuries directly, entirely because of its own negligence. This claim is simply not covered by [the] policy.

Overcoming the Problem of Subrogation

In most cases, parties to a contract requiring the purchase of an OCP policy for another party attempt to purchase the policy from their own general liability insurers. In fact, there is often no other alternative. When this is done, the danger of subrogation against the purchaser of the OCP policy is potentially eliminated. The amount the insurer would be entitled to recover from the contractor in subrogation (as the OCP insurer) would be an amount it would be obligated to pay on behalf of the contractor (as the contractor's general liability insurer).

However, there are instances when contractors are unable to purchase OCP coverage from their own CGL policy insurers. Moreover, the circumstances of a loss may be such that it is covered by the OCP policy but not under the contractor's CGL policy. (Pollution losses sometimes fall into this category, especially when the contractor's CGL policy has been endorsed with a total pollution exclusion.) Or, the loss may be covered by the OCP policy and another policy of the contractor (e.g., employers liability) that has been issued by a different insurer. In any of these circumstances—when the OCP insurer will not be obligated to pay out as a general liability insurer what it gains in subrogation—some attempt at recovery against the contractor/OCP-purchaser by the OCP insurer can be expected.

Contractors understandably balk at having to turn to their own CGL policies to cover a subrogated claim with respect to which they have already purchased insurance protection for another party. For this rea-

son, it is important for any contractor purchasing an OCP policy to make certain that the policy contains a waiver of subrogation. The OCP policy subrogation waiver endorsement CG 29 88 (formally titled the Waiver of Transfer of Rights of Recovery Against Others to Us (CG 29 88) endorsement) specifically eliminates the right of the OCP insurer to recover from the contractor named in the endorsement any amounts paid out for covered losses under the OCP policy. As explained previously, use of this endorsement is most obviously necessary to protect the designated contractor in cases when the OCP insurer is not also the contractor's CGL insurer. But as a matter of practice, CG 29 88 should always be made a part of the OCP policy to avert any possible disputes over the OCP insurer's right to recover paid losses for which the designated contractor may be legally liable.

One of the earlier cases to uphold subrogation of the OCP insurer against the contractor that purchased the policy is *Rome v Commonwealth Edison Co.,* 401 NE2d 1032 (Ill 1980). The contractor in this case, Walsh Construction Company, agreed to perform work for the project owner, Commonwealth Edison. As conditions precedent, the contractor agreed to purchase an OCP policy at its own expense for the project owner's benefit.

The case arose when an employee of the contractor was injured and filed claim against the project owner. The project owner, in turn, filed an action against the contractor based on both common law indemnity and an express indemnity agreement of the two parties. The latter agreement was subsequently dismissed because of the statute making such contracts unenforceable. The contractor sought to dismiss the complaint of common law indemnity because the liability policy it obtained for the project owner satisfied any right of indemnity that might have existed, whether contractual or implied. On the other hand, the project owner maintained that (1) the obligations to purchase insurance and to indemnify were separate, and (2) the parties did not agree that the insurance would satisfy the obligation to indemnify.

In reviewing the insurance and contract specifications, the court found that the insurance provisions did not refer to the indemnity provision nor did the contract say, pursuant to the express indemnity agreement, that the insurance would satisfy any obligation to indemnify the owner. An affidavit taken from an employee of the insurer and presented at trial stated that the insurer, which provided OCP coverage for a $3 million limit, could subrogate against the contractor in an amount of $250,000 and could seek common law indemnity for an additional $250,000. As noted by the court, however, there was nothing in the policy that referred to these amounts.

The appellate court of Illinois, in reversing the decision of the lower court, upheld the owner's action of common law indemnity. It also held that the contractor's purchase of OCP insurance for the project owner did not appear to relieve the contractor from its liability to indemnify the owner.[6]

A more recent attempt by an OCP insurer, which was thwarted despite the absence of a waiver of subrogation but illustrates that attempts are possible, is *North Star Reinsurance v Continental Insurance Co.,* 624 NE2d 647 (NY 1993). The case arose out of a construction accident in which the contractor's employee was injured and then sued the project owner. A judgment was awarded against the project owner and paid for by the OCP policy purchased for the project owner by the contractor. The OCP insurer (which also was the contractor's CGL insurer) then brought an action against the contractor. (The OCP insurer would, of course, be responsible for paying this subrogated claim in its role as the contractor's CGL insurer, but it pursued subrogation anyway so as to trigger contribution in the loss on the part of the contractor's employers liability policy.)

The New York Court of Appeals involved the principle that an insurer may not subrogate against its own insured. That principle is well established when a loss is paid under a policy and the insurer then seeks to subrogate against another party that is insured by the same policy. The court expanded that principle to apply with respect to two separate policies when the policy under which the loss was paid is an OCP policy purchased by the named insured under the other policy. The court stated as follows.

Application of the [no-subrogation principle] is warranted because the two policies [i.e., the OCP policy and the contractor's CGL policy] are integrally related and indistinguishable from a single policy in any relevant way. Plainly, a potential conflict of interest arises where the insurer that issued both policies seeks indemnification against the contractor. As is apparent in the present cases, the mutual insurer, as subrogee of the owner, can fashion the litigation so as to minimize its liability under the CGL. By failing to assert a contractual indemnification claim on the owner's behalf, the insurer can trigger coverage under other insurance policies held by the contractor, such as workers compensation or excess policy.

In a related action, the court allowed subrogation by the OCP insurer against a designated contractor when the contractor's CGL policy did not provide contractual coverage for the loss, because of an exclusion in the definition of "insured contract." In such a case, the court reasoned, the OCP and CGL policies are distinguishable and do not function as a single coverage mechanism, since the CGL policy does not respond to the loss already paid under the OCP policy.

ISO Additional Insured Endorsements

As was noted in **Chapter 7,** there are three ISO endorsements for use in adding additional insureds to CGL policies in connection with construction contracts. They are:

- **CG 20 10, Additional Insured—Owners, Lessees or Contractors.** This endorsement is the primary form to use when adding a project owner or contractor as an insured under another party's CGL policy. The additional insured is specifically scheduled (named) in the endorsement. The current (2004) edition of CG 20 10 specifically does not apply to the additional insured's sole negligence, departing from the broader coverage that courts consistently found in earlier editions of the endorsement. Policies endorsed with CG 20 10 may also be modified with Amendment of Insured Contract Definition (CG 24 26) endorsement so as to not give a contracting party broader protection as the named insured's indemnitee than it has as an additional insured. Contractual liability coverage could be restricted even further when a contractual liability limitation endorsement, such as CG 21 39, is issued instead.

- **CG 20 26, Additional Insured—Designated Person or Organization.** This endorsement at one time was viewed as a superior alternative to CG 20 10, since it continued to apply to liability arising out of the named insured's "work" rather than "ongoing operations" and therefore provided completed operations coverage. With the 2004 ISO amendments, however, this endorsement loses any coverage advantage it previously had over CG 20 10, in that it too now applies in connection with the named insured's ongoing operations and does not encompass the additional insured's sole negligence.

- **CG 20 33, Additional Insured—Owners, Lessees or Contractors—Automatic Status When Required In Construction Agreement With You.** This endorsement is prescribed when additional insureds are to be covered on a blanket basis. Coverage is the equivalent of endorsement CG 20 10, except that coverage must be requested in a written contract, and it automatically includes a professional services exclusion.

Another endorsement, the Additional Insured—Engineers, Architects or Surveyors (CG 20 31) endorsement, is intended to provide additional insured status to these professionals in an OCP policy. All of these endorsements are included in **Appendix B.**

Regardless of which endorsement is used to effect additional insured status, the following are the primary differences between additional insured status and coverage under an OCP policy.

- *A separate set of limits is not provided.* Unlike the OCP policy, additional insured status does not provide the additional insured with a separate set of limits. Since the CGL policy limits are shared by all insureds, there is a general dilution of protection.

- *Access to named insured's umbrella is provided.* As discussed in **Chapter 14,** additional insured status in a CGL policy usually flows through all layers of an umbrella or excess liability program. OCP policies, on the other hand, are not typically listed as underlying insurance in umbrella policies, and OCP insureds therefore do not obtain additional insured status in the indemnitor's umbrella program. Keep in mind, however, that an indemnitee would still have access to these layers through the insured's contractual liability insurance with an enforceable hold harmless clause.

- *Losses adversely affect the named insured's experience.* Losses paid on behalf of an additional insured become part of the named insured's (e.g., contractor's) CGL loss experience. If the named insured's CGL is in a loss-sensitive rating plan, there will be an immediate cost imposed. If coverage is on a guaranteed cost basis, losses will be considered in underwriting and rating future policies. This does not usually occur when losses are covered under an OCP policy.

- *There is little or no premium charge.* When, as is usually the case, a CGL policy provides contractual liability coverage, there should be little or no additional premium charged to add another party as an additional insured to the policy. Of course, this is nullified somewhat, as discussed previously, if losses are incurred on behalf of the additional insured. While the premiums charged for OCP policies typically are not substantial, premiums are charged for this coverage nevertheless.

- *There is an enhanced chance of other insurance problems.* Additional insured status brings with it the possibility of conflicting other insurance clauses and accompanying disputes discussed in **Chapter 5.** The OCP policy is explicit in stating that it provides primary coverage and how other insurance is to be treated.

- *There is a lack of cancellation notice.* Additional insured status does not provide a contractual right to notice of cancellation from the insurer. Named insured status in an OCP policy does obligate the insurer to provide such notification.

- *No general supervision exclusion applies.* Additional insured status is not usually subject to the general supervision limitation because additional insured endorsement CG 20 10 is typically used to effect additional insured status. When that form is used, the coverage provided will more closely correspond to the liabilities transferred in intermediate hold harmless agreements.

Deciding between the Alternatives

Coverage under an OCP policy and additional insured status are generally considered alternatives to each other. Each approach has its advantages and disadvantages. Before considering these, however, it is important to emphasize that these alternatives do not replace the need for an indemnity provision. Their purpose, instead, is to secure immediate defense coverage from an insurer and to reinforce risk transfers effected through such indemnity provisions.[7]

Therefore, it follows that the first step in implementing an effective risk transfer program with respect to construction projects should be to make a concerted effort to assure that the indemnity provisions in the related contracts are clearly written and in conformance with the laws of the states in which they will be used. If this task is done properly, the reinforcements—either named insured status in an OCP or additional insured status in a CGL—will rarely be called on.

With this caveat in mind, the two alternatives can be weighed. However, there is no pat answer to the question of which approach is best. The final decision as to which alternative should be used will vary from project to project, depending on the goals of the various parties. The advantages and disadvantages of OCP protection as compared to additional insured status are shown in Exhibit 10.5. Most have already been discussed in this chapter or in **Chapter 5.**

In reviewing the exhibit, it is important to keep in mind that some of the disadvantages of either approach, such as the other insurance problem with the CGL, can be alleviated through other techniques discussed in this book. Both approaches give the indemnitee direct access to an insurance policy to secure immediate defense coverage. OCP protection has the further advantages of applying specifically on a primary basis, requiring the insurer to give the named insured (the indemnitee) notice of its intent to cancel, and by providing a separate set of limits. Additional insured status is typically less costly and provides somewhat broader coverage. Additional insured status also usually gives access to the indemnitor's umbrella or excess insurance program, but this will be important only when such access is unavailable through the indemnitor's contractual liability insurance because the hold harmless agreement is not enforceable.

In the final analysis, the decision will often depend on weighing the OCP policy's advantage of a separate set of limits against the broader coverage granted to additional insureds in CGL policies as well as the cost differential. Coverage available to an additional insured is broader with respect to the personal injury perils and to liability of the indemnitee arising from its own acts (outside the scope of general supervision). When compared to the full scope of an indemnitee's potential liability arising from a construction project, these limitations may not seem extremely significant.

The general supervision limitation becomes even less significant if it can be overcome by enforcing a hold harmless agreement and relying on the indemnitor's contractual liability coverage that does not contain the limitation.

EXHIBIT 10.5
OCP PROTECTION VERSUS ADDITIONAL INSURED STATUS

The following shows how named insured status in an OCP policy compares to additional insured status under Form CG 20 10 of a CGL policy. **Bold** type indicates which approach is advantageous for each item.

Comparison Point	OCP Protection	AI Status
Cost	Moderate	**Inexpensive**
Limits	**Apply separately for named insured (NI)**	Included with Contractor and other AIs
Excess or umbrella limits	Not a scheduled underlying policy	**Usually provided**
Effects of losses	**Minimal**	Affects current loss-sensitive plans and affects future CGL costs
Other insurance	**Specifically applies as primary**	Clauses often conflict
Notice of cancellation	**Contractor and NI receive notice**	Only contractor receives notice
Coverage for indemnitee's (owner's) negligence	Limited to general supervision only	**Must only be in connection with contractor's work but excludes the additional insured's sole fault**
Personal injury perils	Not usually covered	Covered
Effects on contractor's coverage	**None**	May cause problems with respect to certain exclusions
Evidence that contractor has complied with requirement	Copy of policy received	Certificate of insurance

Therefore, the broad coverage available through additional insured status becomes increasingly important as the possibility of the hold harmless agreement of the type desired by the indemnitee (e.g., intermediate form) being deemed unenforceable increases. In those states where intermediate form hold harmless agreements are not permitted by statute, for example, the protection of additional insured status under a CGL would be desirable.

However, in states where there is a high probability of the hold harmless agreement being enforced, the broad coverage of additional insured status in a CGL becomes less important. In these states, the issue becomes determining whether the separate limits provided warrant the additional premium associated with the OCP policy. In many cases, the answer is yes.

Project Management Protective Liability

The project management protective liability (PMPL) policy was, until withdrawn in 2003, an optional coverage prescribed by the American Institute of Architects (AIA). Language under which the policy may be required was introduced into the

1997 edition of AIA Document A201, "General Conditions of the Contract for Construction," under Article 11 of the Insurance and Bonds section. The policy, developed by CNA Insurance Company and Victor O. Schinnerer & Company, is remarkably similar to the standard OCP policy. In fact, except for some defined terms, a broadened Who Is an Insured provision, and modification to the limits of insurance section, coverage is the same as that provided by the standard OCP policy. Exhibit 10.6 provides a comparison of important features of these two policies and the Construction Project Management Protective Liability (CPMPL) (CG 31 15) endorsement, which has largely replaced it.

The stated rationale underlying formulation of the PMPL policy was to minimize total litigation costs, a difficult goal to achieve in construction projects involving sometimes elaborate combinations of hold harmless agreements and additional insured endorsements. With primary coverage applying to the owner, contractor, and architect, savings were to be expected for defense costs incurred by insurers required to defend more than one of the policy's named insureds.

It is uncertain why the PMPL policy was withdrawn, but the popularity and demand for additional insured endorsements certainly must have had an impact. The PMPL policy also was not approved for use in all states. The Construction Project Management Protective Liability (CPMPL) (CG 31 15) endorsement of ISO may fill the gap created by withdrawal of the PMPL policy, particularly since this endorsement is approved for use in more states than was the PMPL policy. Whether the ISO endorsement will achieve more widespread use than the PMPL policy, however, remains to be seen, since it has the same disadvantages as the OCP policy.

"General Supervision" Defined

One important difference between the PMPL policy and the OCP policy and CPMPL endorsement was that the PMPL policy defined the term "general supervision" as follows:

> "General supervision" includes all activity except preparing designs, drawings, specifica-

tions, or taking charge of or control over the means and methods of the "named contractor's" operations, or in the case of the "named contractor", taking charge of or control over the means and methods of the subcontractor's operations. In this context, subcontractor means anyone having a contract with the "named contractor" to perform a portion of the "work" at the site.

One of the first questions that might have been addressed in connection with that definition was whether reference to "all activity" encompassed allegations of an owner's failure to provide a safe place to work. When an injured contractor's employee files a third-party-over action against the project owner, the allegation commonly made is that the owner failed to make the premises a safe place to work. If "all activity" did not encompass this allegation, project owners purchasing the PMPL policy may have been disappointed.

The exception to the definition of general supervision dealing with "taking charge of or control over the means and methods of the ... operations" served as a reminder to project owners and general contractors of potential problems in this area. If they take charge of or control over the means and methods of another's operations, the legal relationships involved may change. For example, the relationship between the general contractor and subcontractor might be transformed from one of a principal/agent to some other legal status, even to an employer/employee relationship in some jurisdictions and under some fact patterns.

It is unclear why Document A201 describes the PMPL policy as coverage for the owner's, contractor's, and architect's vicarious liability. The coverage actually provided in the policy went well beyond vicarious liability, encompassing also liability for sole fault arising out of the named insured's general supervision of a project. The AIA document's characterization, however, may be used in some cases to argue that there was no expectation of coverage for anything but vicarious liability. If other insurers decide to develop their own PMPL product and offer coverage under the same name but limit it to vicarious liability, coverage likely will be deficient and insureds under such policies will have problems arguing that they expected anything more. This is a serious problem, given that coverage limited to an insured's vicarious liability often falls short of what is needed in the type of third-party-over action discussed earlier.

EXHIBIT 10.6
OCP POLICY, PMPL POLICY, AND CPMPL ENDORSEMENT COMPARISON

OCP Policy (ISO)	PMPL Policy (CAN)	CPMPL Endorsement (ISO)
Coverage applies only while operations are in progress and also on a site- specific basis	Same	Same
Named Insured: The owner or contractor for whom work is being done (1)	Owner, contractor, architect/engineer, and construction manager	Same as PMPL policy
Coverage for the sole fault of the named insured is limited to "general supervision" of the work performed by others (2)	Same, except the term "general supervision" is a defined term	Same as the ISO OCP policy (2)
Does not apply to contractual liability, except "insured contract" as defined (3)	Same	Same
A professional services exclusion does no form a part of this policy	Same, but a mandatory endorsement excluding professional services is required (4)	A professional services exclusion is built-into this endorsement
Coverage does not apply to completed operations	Same	Same
A separate set of limits applies to the named insured and is applicable to each consecutive 12-month period (5)	Limit applies to the entire policy period, which is the duration of the project (6)	Same as the OCP policy
Policy applies as primary over other insurance available to the named insured	Same	Same
Does not include a waiver of subrogation against the contractor purchasing this policy (7)	Subrogation in this instance is not permitted	Same as OCP, except subrogation is waived for a "you"

continued

EXHIBIT 10.6
OCP POLICY, PMPL POLICY, AND CPMPL ENDORSEMENT COMPARISON (cont.)

Notes

(1) This policy is used when an owner or contractor requires a contractor or subcontractor to furnish this specific policy. Sometimes the owner or contractor may require to be listed as an additional insured but offer the OCP policy as an alternative. Whatever the case may be, this policy does not apply to the subcontractor or contractor who purchases it for the benefit of others.

(2) One of the more controversial areas of the OCP policy is over the meaning of "general supervision," a term not defined in the OCP policy or the ISO CPMPL coverage endorsement. The meaning of this term is important, because named insureds obtain coverage for their independent (sole) fault so long as the act, error, or omission arises out of their general supervision of the work.

(3) Both policies and the endorsement exclude liability assumed under contract, except an "insured contract," as defined to include the five types of following agreements, whether written or not: (a) lease of premises, (b) easement or license agreement, except in connection with construction or demolition operations within 50 feet of a railroad, (c) agreement required by ordinance to indemnify a municipality, except in connection with work for such municipality, (d) sidetrack agreement, or (e) elevator maintenance agreement.

(4) The definition of "general supervision" does not include liability for professional services relating to the preparing of designs, drawings, specifications, or taking charge of, or control over the means and methods of the contractor's operations.

(5) According to the latest edition (2001) of the policy, the limits apply separately to each consecutive annual period and to any remaining period of less than 12 months starting with the beginning of the policy period. However, if the policy is extended after issuance for an additional period of less than 12 months, the additional period is considered to be part of the preceding period for purposes of determining limits. Also, if more than one project is designated in the policy, the aggregate limit is applicable to each such project.

(6) Since the policy period is determined to be the anticipated duration of the project, it does not apply to each consecutive 12-month period. However, if it turns out that the anticipated duration of the project is longer and the policy period needs to be extended, no additional limits are available. Instead, the additional period is considered to be part of the original period for purposes of determining limits. However, like the ISO policy, if the PMPL policy designated more than one project, the aggregate limit applied separately to each project.

(7) It is probably safe to say that contractors who furnish an OCP policy for the benefit of others will obtain it from the same insurer that writes that contractor's CGL policy. However, in those cases where some other insurer were to issue the OCP policy, it would behoove the contractor to obtain a waiver of subrogation endorsement, CG 29 88. Otherwise, the insurer of the OCP policy can subrogate against the contractor who actually purchased such policy for the benefit of others.

Subrogation Possibilities

Another important difference between the OCP policy, the CPMPL endorsement, and the PMPL policy is that contractors who purchase the ISO policy or endorsement for others are subject to subrogation action by the insurer. If the OCP or CPMPL insurer pays damages for liability assessed against its named insured, and that liability is attributable to the contractor who purchased the policy or endorsement, the insurer will look to the contractor. In cases where the contractor did not purchase the OCP or CPMPL endorsement from its own insurer, which is sometimes the case, the insurer of the OCP or CPMPL endorsement will likely be in a position to enforce its subrogation rights. To be safe, the contractor should request that Waiver of Transfer of Rights of Recovery Against Others to Us (CG 29 88) endorsement be issued with the OCP or CPMPL endorsement when it is purchased.

Subrogation against the contractor was not possible under the PMPL policy because the contractor was a named insured, along with the project owner and architect or engineer. Under the OCP policy and CPMPL endorsement, the project owner is the named insured and the architect or engineer is an additional insured. Coverage for the contractor, on the other hand, is not available.

Summary

There is no simple answer to the question of whether it is better for an owner or developer to be an additional insured in a contractor's CGL policy or the named insured in an OCP policy purchased on its behalf. Each of these alternatives has its own advantages and disadvantages that must be weighed with respect to the circumstances of the specific project. However, no alternative is a substitute for careful attention to the indemnity clause in the relevant construction contract.

Chapter 10 Notes

1. Michelbacher, G.F., *Casualty Insurance Principles,* 2nd Edition, New York, NY: McGraw-Hill Book Company, Inc., 1942, p. 10.

2. Malecki, Donald S.; Donaldson, James H.; and Horn, Ronald C., *Commercial Liability Risk Management and Insurance,* Volume I, Malvern, PA: American Institute for Property and Liability Underwriters, 1978, p. 344.

3. All insurance policies should be viewed as encompassing the entire period of construction even though they need to be reissued annually. In other words, the obligation of the insurance company is dictated by the underlying construction agreement as agreed to in part by its named insured.

4. Since the OCP policy is written on an occurrence basis, it does not matter if a claim is made or suit is brought after the policy expires, so long as the alleged bodily injury or property damage took place during the policy period.

5. However, it has not been unusual for indemnitees to request both an OCP policy and additional insured status. In such a situation, other

insurance should not be an issue because the OCP policy should activate first due to this OCP provision. Nevertheless, other insurance issues are likely to arise because three different primary policies potentially apply on behalf of the indemnitee: the indemnitee's own CGL, the OCP policy, and the contractor's CGL policy. The indemnitee should, of course, modify its own CGL policy's other insurance clause as discussed in **Chapter 5** to reduce the possibility of this problem.

6. For a discussion of some of the older cases that have attempted subrogation by the OCP insurer against the contractor who purchased that coverage, see Donald S. Malecki, "Non-Insurance Transfer: Double Loss," *The National Underwriter*, P/C Edition, March 27, 1981, p. 33.

7. Hold harmless agreements often do not require the indemnitor to defend the indemnitee. Additional insured status is one method by which an indemnitee can obtain a defense under an indemnitor's policies. Of course, hold harmless agreements can also be written to include an explicit defense obligation. This alternative should be strongly considered.

Chapter 11

REAL PROPERTY LESSORS AS ADDITIONAL INSUREDS

The Additional Insured—Managers or Lessors of Premises (CG 20 11) endorsement is the primary form used to add as an additional insured the owner of premises from whom the named insured leases property. It can also be used to provide insured status to the owner's real estate manager. The earlier edition, for use with the 1973 CGL policy provisions, is entitled "Additional Insured (Premises Leased to the Named Insured)." The provisions of both endorsements are identical. A number of problematic areas with these endorsements are discussed in this chapter.

Designation of the Premises

Whenever this endorsement is issued to include a manager or landlord (or lessor) as an additional insured to the policy of the tenant (or lessee), the Who Is an Insured provision of the tenant's commercial general liability (CGL) insurance policy is amended to include the person or organization so specified in the schedule of this endorsement as an additional insured to the following extent:

> ... but only with respect to liability arising out of the ownership, maintenance or use of that part of the premises leased to you and shown in the Schedule and subject to the following additional exclusions ....

The description of "that part of the premises leased to you" that must be added to the schedule of the endorsement may be the source of significant problems with respect to delineating the scope of coverage provided. It is important for this description to be specific and accurate if problems are to be avoided when the additional insured seeks protection under this endorsement.

This means that the description of the part of the premises to be leased to the named insured should not be left blank or completed without first reviewing a copy of the lease or rental agreement. Unfortunately, these contracts are not always available, and when they are, they are not always clear as to the parties' intentions. Nonetheless, without this kind of information, problems can be expected.

Problems also can be expected when the standard Insurance Services Office, Inc. (ISO), endorsement is modified for use as a blanket form of coverage. For example, this can be done by inserting an asterisk in the schedule where the designation of premises is to be typed and then adding the following provision:

> *Any lessor providing written terms and conditions of the lease between lessors and the named insured specifying that liability insurance be maintained for the benefit of both the lessee and the lessor or that the lessor be included as an insured under the lessee's policy or policies of liability insurance.

It is not only these kinds of provisions that can complicate matters but also carelessness in manuscripting wording that should be clear and unambiguous, since ambiguities are commonly construed against the drafter.

The designation of premises (describing the leased premises) is particularly important when injuries take place outside the described or designated area where the actual business operations of the tenant are conducted. This issue leads to most litigation in this area.

One such case in which injury occurred off the landlord's premises but was still covered under a tenant's liability policy is *Harrah's Atlantic City, v Harleysville Insurance Co.,* 671 A2d 1122 (NJ App Div 1996). The tenant was a store owner who leased space within a hotel. The lease required the tenant to obtain a CGL policy to cover the hotel as an additional insured, which was done. The wrong additional insured endorsement was attached to the policy but was later reformed by the court to provide "managers or lessors of premises" coverage as intended in the lease.

The injured parties were an employee of the tenant and her friend who had driven to the hotel and parked her car in its garage, a detached building across the street. The employee and friend then entered the hotel, ate lunch at a restaurant within the hotel, and shopped at the store. When they left the store, they walked through the hotel onto the sidewalk in front of the hotel and were in the process of crossing the street to enter the hotel's garage when they were struck by a vehicle driven by one of the hotel's parking valets. The hotel, as an additional insured, requested coverage from the tenant's insurer, but the claim was denied.

The lower court denied coverage to the hotel on the grounds that the injury in question did not arise out of the use of the leased premises, as required by the language of the additional insured endorsement. On appeal, the court said that the words in the endorsement, "arising out of the … use of" the leased premises, are not capable of precise definition. What is not clear from the language used in the endorsement, the court said, is to what extent the parties anticipated coverage for accidents occurring outside the leased premises, i.e., the "landscape of risk as contemplated by the policy." In ruling that the hotel had coverage, the court stated that the requirement that there be a causal link between the accident and the leased premises does not mean that there must be any degree of physical proximity between the leased premises and the scene of the accident.

The court added that where the landlord can trace the risk creating its liability directly to the tenant's business presence, it is not unreasonable for the landlord to expect coverage when the accident originated from or grew out of the use of the leased premises. The court stated further that the hotel had the duty to provide a safe means of ingress and egress to the store owner's business visitors and employees. That duty, it said, arises solely from the store owner's use of the leased premises and is not discharged until such visitors and employees leave the premises safely. Inasmuch as the hotel's liability in this case arose out of a breach of that duty, the court added, the hotel's liability fell within the "landscape of risk" the hotel reasonably could expect to be insured against.

In rendering this decision, the court relied generally on the reasoning in *Franklin Mutual Insurance Co. v Security Indemnity Insurance Co.,* 646 A2d 443 (NJ App Div 1994), which dealt with an additional insured provision virtually identical to that in *Harrah's v Harleysville.*

This case involved a luncheonette that was a tenant within an office building. The tenant's liability policy covered the landlord as an additional insured "but only with respect to liability arising out of the ownership, maintenance or use" of the premises leased to the tenant. The accident occurred on the exterior stairs leading away from the luncheonette and involved a fall by a customer who had just left the luncheonette. When the fall victim sued the landlord as well as the tenant luncheonette, the landlord asserted coverage as an additional insured under the tenant's policy. The trial court ruled for the insurer, but the decision was reversed on appeal.

The higher court explained that the additional insured coverage was not limited to an occurrence *within* the leased premises. Instead, coverage was defined by the significantly broader phrase, "arising out of the use" of premises. The court interpreted that crucial phrase as follows.

> That phrase must be interpreted or construed in a broad and comprehensive sense to mean "originating from the use of" or "growing out

of the use of" the premises leased to [the luncheonette]. Thus, there need be shown only a substantial nexus between the occurrence and the use of the leased premises in order for the coverage to attach. The inquiry, therefore, is whether the occurrence which caused the injury, although not foreseen or expected, was in the contemplation of the parties to the insurance contract a natural and reasonable incident or consequence of the use of leased premises and, thus, a risk against which they may reasonably expect those insured under the policy would be protected.

This court concluded that the accident in question was a risk against which the tenant's insurer had provided protection. It found that there was a "relationship, a substantial nexus," between the fall on the exterior steps and the use of the premises leased to the luncheonette. Therefore, the accident was said to have arisen out of the use of the premises leased to the luncheonette "in the broadest and most comprehensive sense."

In *General Accident Fire & Life Assurance v Travelers Insurance Co.,* 162 AD2d 130 (NY 1990), the tenant's liability policy did not protect the landlord, as an additional insured, for a claim made by the tenant's employee against the landlord even though the additional insured endorsement (identical to the one described earlier) designated the landlord's entire premises as leased to the tenant. In contrast, *J.P. Realty Trust v Public Service,* 102 AD2d 68 (NY 1984), held that the tenant's liability policy did protect the landlord as an additional insured against a claim made by an employee of the tenant while using the freight elevator. The lease encompassed only two floors of a building, including the use of a freight elevator for those two floors. The additional insured endorsement described the entire building as that part leased to the insured (the tenant). The court looked to the lease to determine the intentions of the parties and decided that the landlord should be protected by the tenant's policy.

In *Northbrook Insurance Co. v American States Insurance Co.,* 495 NW2d 450 (Minn App 1993), a shopping center tenant's liability policy was held not to cover the landlord as an additional insured for an injury sustained by the tenant's employee in a common area of the shopping center. The insurer's policy described the insured premises as the 3,200 square feet the bakery occupied in the shopping center. The premium charged was based on insuring the bakery, not the common areas of the shopping center. The court held that the endorsement's coverage for the additional insured was limited to its negligence *in the bakery* and not the rest of the shopping center. This court also looked to the lease and noted that the landlord was required to maintain the alley where the injury occurred.

Another shopping center case, *Liberty Village Associates v West American Insurance Co.,* 706 A2d 206 (NJ 1998), concerned an insurance policy of a tenant that added the landlord as an additional insured, but only with respect to incidents arising "out of the use of" the tenant's premises. The question presented to the court was the applicability of that language to an accident that occurred off the tenant's premises, but close to those premises, involving a prospective customer who was approaching the tenant's store.

The landlord, a shopping center, argued that two of the cases discussed earlier, *Harrah's v Harleysville* and *Franklin Mutual v Security Indemnity,* should be taken as precedent. The tenant's insurer, on the other hand, maintained that the issue was critically different from the *Franklin* and *Harrah's* cases.

The facts of the case were simple. The shopping center consisted of 88 stores, one of which was owned by Carter and another operated by Gourmet. An invitee, while shopping, visited the store of Carter and then crossed an open cobblestone street and sidewalk to visit Gourmet, located in a different building. Just before she reached a covered entrance to Gourmet, the shopper apparently slipped on some ice and fell with her feet landing under the covered entranceway. She filed suit against the shopping center and Gourmet.

There was no question that the fall occurred outside the premises leased to Gourmet and that the fall took place within very close proximity to those premises, in an area where Gourmet employees normally provided maintenance and snow and ice removal. No such functions had been performed on the day in question.

Under the lease between the shopping center and Gourmet, it was mandated that "the tenant's liability insurance will indemnify and save the landlord harmless from and against any and all claims, actions, damages, liability and expenses in connection with loss of life, personal injury and/or damaged property arising from or out of any occurrence in, upon or at the premises, or any part thereof." Pursuant to that lease, Gourmet obtained liability insurance naming the shopping center as an additional insured. However, the relevant policy language stipulated that the shopping center had that additional insured status "only with respect to liability arising out of the ownership, maintenance or use" of the premises leased to Gourmet.

The court ruled that injury fell within the scope of protection provided the shopping center as an additional insured under the policy of Gourmet. Other questions—e.g., precisely where the fall took place and the lease provisions dealing with maintenance and snow and ice removal—were not dispositive from the court's perspective. As in the *Harrah's* case, insurance coverage for the landlord was not contingent on a finding of the tenant's liability, the court added. Indeed, the court said, "the very premise of the need for the policy is the actual or potential liability of the landlord—not the tenant."

When the injury takes place in a common area of a shopping center or other place of business, protection for the landlord as an additional insured under a tenant's liability policy could be more difficult. Parking areas are a common example of how such difficulties arise. In one case that settled out of court, a woman was using a telephone booth, which was positioned on the sidewalk between the entrance to a convenience store and a laundromat, both tenants of the property owner. A motorist lost control of his auto while parking it and hit the telephone booth, injuring the woman, who filed suit against the landlord and convenience store. The landlord sought coverage under the store owner's liability policy as an additional insured. However, the store owner's insurer denied defense and coverage because the parking space in front of the store was considered a common area outside the control of the store owner even though the description of the additional insured endorsement listed the address of the store.

Insurers are likely to balk at providing defense coverage to additional insureds for injuries sustained in parking lots provided for the use of named insured commercial enterprises. Denials in such cases are often on shaky ground unless the endorsement or the lease specifically precludes such areas. Absent such clarification, one would look to the conduct to determine if it would fall within the scope of the "arising out of" wording discussed above and in **Chapter 9.**

A case where no coverage was held to apply *is U.S. Fidelity & Guaranty Co. v Drazic,* 877 SW2d 140 (Mo App 1994). The tenant's insurer brought an action against the landlord and its insurer seeking a declaratory judgment as to its liability on a claim by another tenant's employee who fell in the parking lot of the landlord's commercial building. The trial court ruled that no coverage applied to the additional insured. On appeal, the judgment was affirmed.

The additional insured endorsement naming the landlord was identical to the standard Additional Insured—Managers or Lessors of Premises (CG 20 11) endorsement. The appeals court stated that there were two contracts to analyze, the lease and the tenant's liability policy. The lease described the premises leased as "designated portion of a commercial building known and numbered as … plus the area adjacent to the entrance of the tenant's place of business." The landlord argued that coverage of the additional insured endorsement encompassed the ways immediately adjoining the building, such as parking areas and walkways. To buttress its argument, the landlord pointed to the policy definition of "insured premises," which included the "ways immediately adjoining such premises on land." However, the additional insured endorsement does not contain the term "insured premises." The endorsement instead refers only to "premises designated below leased to the named insured." The court held that the land on which the victim was injured was not a part of the premises "leased to the named insured."

In citing the *Northbrook Ins. Co.* case discussed earlier, the court in *Drazic* also said that the purpose of an additional insured endorsement is to provide landlords protection from vicarious liability due to a tenant's action that takes place on the leased premises. While that may sometimes be the intent, it is not what the standard endorsement says, nor is it in every case what the contract between the two parties stipulates.

Another parking lot case finding no coverage for an additional insured landlord is *Pennsville Shopping Center v American Motorists Insurance Co.,* 719 A2d 182 (NJ 1998). This case arose following a patron's fall in a shopping center parking lot when her shopping cart rolled into a pothole.

In the lease agreement, the tenant agreed to indemnify the landlord from loss or liability for damages "occurring on the demised premises except [for those] due to Landlord's negligence." The tenant also agreed to name the landlord as an additional insured for limits of $1 million. The lease went on to say that the landlord would indemnify the tenant from loss or liability for damages "resulting from Landlord's failure to carry out repairs or maintenance of the common areas required of it by this lease." The lease also stated that this obligation of the landlord was absolute and would not depend on receipt of notice by the landlord of the existence of defects or failure to make such repairs. Another provision of the lease required payment by the tenant of its pro rata share (with all other tenants) of the costs of maintaining the common areas of the shopping center, including the parking lot.

In ruling against additional insured coverage for the landlord under the tenant's liability policy, the court acknowledged that the case did not directly involve the application of the lease agreement, but rather interpretation of a separate insurance contract. However, the court had difficulty in finding any causal nexus to establish a basis for coverage

of liability "arising out of" the leased premises when the claim in fact arose out of conditions in the parking lot.

The court explained that, irrespective of the language of the tenant's policy covering the landlord as an additional insured, the tenant could not be seen providing any indemnification to the landlord for damages sustained because of a condition for which the tenant bore no responsibility. To the contrary, it added, the parties had expressly agreed in their lease that the condition of the parking lot was the landlord's responsibility. Therefore, the court concluded, the tenant's undertaking to name the landlord as an additional insured had to be understood as coextensive with the scope of the tenant's liability.

Given the broad interpretation of the term "arising out of" in other cases discussed above and in **Chapter 9,** the *Pennsville* decision may be too fact-specific to be regarded as an important precedent. The causal nexus is as strong as in many cases in which courts found the "arising out of" language sufficient to establish coverage. Emphasis in *Pennsville* appears to have been placed on the specific contractual obligations of the parties.

Based on these mixed court decisions, it is important that the parties' respective responsibilities under a lease be clearly stated. Where a court has problems applying specific policy wording, on the basis of ambiguity, for example, it will look to the contract and other extrinsic evidence to determine the intent of the parties. Especially troublesome in this regard are leases involving common areas, shopping centers, and parking lots. While additional insured endorsements employing the phrase "arising out of" will ordinarily be interpreted broadly when an argument arises, it is uncertain what the outcome will be when the argument turns to determining the intent of the parties in an underlying lease agreement.

Extent of Covered Liability

As with any additional insured endorsement, an important issue concerns the extent of the additional insured's liability that is encompassed by the coverage provided. In the *Northbrook* case, the comment was made that one of the primary functions of the additional insured endorsement, in general, is to protect the additional insured from vicarious liability for acts of the named insured. However, this is not the sole function of the additional insured endorsement.

The case commonly cited to support a contention that coverage applies only to vicarious liability is *Harbor Insurance Co. v Lewis,* 562 F Supp 800 (ED Pa 1983). However, the endorsement in *Harbor* was not a standard ISO form, and it specifically and clearly limited the additional insured's protection to its vicarious fault. The endorsement's terms should rule the scope of coverage, and there is nothing within the terms of the ISO Additional Insured—Managers or Lessors of Premises endorsement to limit coverage to vicarious liability.

Ownership, Maintenance, or Use Limitation

The part of the additional insured endorsement for managers or lessors of premises that reads "but only with respect to liability arising out of the ownership, maintenance or use of that part of the premises leased to you" is subject to various interpretations. It has been maintained that the phrase "ownership, maintenance or use" refers to the tenant's (the named insured's) exposures rather than that of the additional insured (the landlord). One of the problems with this interpretation is that a tenant is not the owner of the premises.

Another possible interpretation is that the term "ownership, maintenance or use" refers to the landlord's (the additional insured's) interests or exposures. However, the insurer is likely to balk at protecting the landlord if coverage is sought for the landlord's failure to maintain the premises unless the designation of the endorsement encompasses the common ways.

Yet another way to interpret this endorsement is to say that the word "ownership" refers to the landlord's liability exposure (which would be vicarious

in nature) and the words "maintenance or use" refer to the tenant's liability for exposures within its control. It would be preferable, in the interest of clarity, for the endorsement to separate the reference to "ownership" from "maintenance or use."

The fact that a landlord and tenant relationship was arranged under a management contract rather than a lease agreement worked to the disadvantage of the lessee and its insurer in *ZKZ Associates LP v CNA Insurance Co.,* 224 AD2d 174 (NY 1996). ZKZ was the owner of premises that contained a garage managed by Guardian. The management contract between the parties provided that Guardian was required to obtain and maintain garage liability insurance and to include the owner as an additional insured. Pursuant to this contract, Guardian obtained the insurance and the additional insured endorsement. This case arose out of an accident that occurred on the sidewalk abutting the garage. ZKZ maintained that in addition to its own insurance policy, the policy of Guardian also owed it a defense as an additional insured.

In the Guardian policy, ZKZ was named as an additional insured "only for liability arising out of the ownership, maintenance and use of the described premises which is leased to [Guardian]." However, contrary to the policy terminology, there was no lease but, rather, a management contract. Since use of the term "leased" in the endorsement was not congruent with reality, that incongruence, to the extent of any ambiguity, must be construed against the insurer, the court said.

The court continued by saying that in that context, the perimeters of the coverage afforded under the policy had to be viewed not in strictly territorial terms but, rather, in operational terms covering the extent of control over the premises that the management agreement vested in Guardian.

The court noted that it was not relevant that the management contract between ZKZ and Guardian may have assigned maintenance of the sidewalks to ZKZ. At issue was the extent of insurance coverage provided by the policy—which the court said clearly extended to ZKZ's protection for liability arising out of the use of the premises, defined not on the basis of who was obligated to maintain them but, rather, by the consequences stemming from their use.

One justice dissented. His opinion, in part, was that the relationship between both parties for purposes of coverage under Guardian's liability policy had been treated by both parties as a lease. The plain fact was that if the agreement between ZKZ and Guardian were not, for purposes of the endorsement, regarded as a lease, the justice said, then ZKZ would not be covered at all as an additional insured under the policy at issue. "ZKZ cannot, on one hand, claim a status as an additional insured with respect to garage operations under an endorsement limiting the endorsement's application to demised premises and then, on the other, claim that it is not bound by the endorsement's limitation because there was no lease in effect," said the dissenting justice.

Concluding his dissenting opinion, the judge added that, for purposes of determining the scope of coverage, it was of no consequence whether the premises were "leased" or "managed" by Guardian; the majority, he said, provided no rationale as to why its view of the agreement would broaden the scope of coverage to include any part of the premises that Guardian might use rather than limit coverage to that part of the premises that Guardian was obligated to maintain.

This case did not mention the title of the additional insured endorsement. Since the standard ISO endorsement refers to "Managers or Lessors of Premises," it might be prudent for insurers to modify the endorsement to take into account management contracts such as in the *ZKZ* case. All that would be necessary would be to insert the phrase "or premises managed by you" in the appropriate parts of the endorsement.

Influence of Other Facts on Coverage Interpretation

In determining the proper application of this additional insured endorsement, the parties may refer to other evidence to prove their cases if the lease is silent on the parties' intent. One approach advocated by insurers is to look at the way the premium was calculated for the liability insurance.

For example, in the *J.P. Realty Trust* case referred to previously, the landlord's insurer pointed to the premium charged by the tenant's insurer pertaining to the elevator, alleging that this constituted recognition that the elevator was to be included in the coverage. This approach is not always practical because there usually is no separate charge shown for elevators. In the *Northbrook Insurance* case, the tenant's insurer relied on the square footage of the interior of the premises to argue that the common ways were not encompassed by the policy. However, this approach also is not available when the premium is on a gross sales/receipts basis, as is the case with many liability policies.

Sometimes courts will view additional insured coverage as being very limited because of the nominal premium charged for an additional insured endorsement compared to the cost of the policy to which it is attached. Premiums are not good indicators of the scope of additional insured coverage because the charges often are discretionary among underwriters and soft market conditions can influence the extent to which a premium, if any, is charged.

Owners of Land as Additional Insureds

The Additional Insured—Owners or Other Interests from Whom Land Has Been Leased (CG 20 24) endorsement is virtually identical to the Additional Insured—Managers or Lessors of Premises (CG 20 11) endorsement of the 1988 CGL policy and Additional Insured—Premises Leased to the Named Insured endorsement as used with the 1973 CGL policy. The only difference is that CG 20 24 is intended for use when land, rather than a building or structure, is being leased, whereas CG 20 11 applies to the latter as "premises." Also, endorsement CG 20 24 requires the designation of the premises that are leased to the named insured. Since this endorsement is intended for use only when the additional insured is leasing land to the named insured, it would be clearer if it required a designation of land *rather than* premises.

Although special standard endorsements are available for the protection of lessors as additional insureds, other endorsements are sometimes used. In the case of *Township of Springfield v Ersek d/b/a The Pro Shop,* 660 A2d 672 (Pa 1995), the township that leased its pro shop to a lessee required additional insured status. The endorsement obtained by the lessee on its policy read as follows.

> The "persons insured" provision is amended to include as an insured the person or organization named below but only with respect to liability arising out of the operations performed by the named insured.

The dispute arose following injury sustained by one of the pro shop operator's employees who slipped and fell on the steps leading from the front door of the pro shop to the parking lot. The insurer did not dispute that it issued a policy to the lessee and named the township as an additional insured. The insurer took the position that liability was governed by the lessee's potential liability to the township under the lease agreement and/or employment agreement with the township. However, the court held that neither of these agreements controlled the legal relationship or obligations between the lessor and lessee. What was at issue, instead, was the insurance contract.

The court also held that the policy clearly provided coverage to the township where injury occurred on the pro shop's premises as a result of the pro shop's operations, regardless of whether the negligence that gave rise to the claim rested with the lessor or lessee. Had the insurer sought to restrict coverage to only claims arising from the negligence of the lessee, it could have clearly so stated in the additional insured endorsement language, the court said, rather than stating that the township was insured "with respect to liability arising out of [Ersek's] operations."

The court also stated that the phrase in the additional insured endorsement, "arising out of," has been defined as "causally connected with, not proximately caused by," citing the *McIntosh v Scottsdale Insurance Co.,* 992 F2d 251 (10th Cir 1993), case discussed in **Chapter 9.** The court said that jurisdictions other than Pennsylvania have interpreted similar insurance provisions such as the one in question to require the insurer to provide a defense and indemnity for the additional insured's negligence that occurred on the covered premises.

On the other hand, the case of *Maryland Casualty Co. v Chicago & North Western Transportation Co.,* 466 NE2d 1091 (Ill App 1984), held that the endorsement's phrase "arising out of" was ambiguous. As a result, a railroad terminal owner was held to be covered as an additional insured on a tenant's liability policy. The endorsement designated the street location as that part of the premises leased to the named insured (tenant).

Summary

To avoid disputes over the scope of insurance protection under the Additional Insured—Managers or Lessors of Premises endorsement, it is important that the designation of premises (or part leased to the named insured tenant) fits the description agreed to by the respective parties under the lease—if a lease is available and it contains such an agreement.

If the designation of premises encompasses the entire premises or the common ways, the additional insured endorsement should provide coverage for the landlord's liability arising out of the ownership, maintenance, or use of the premises leased to the tenant and so designated. Conversely, if the designation of premises is restricted to the interior of the premises, the landlord's protection is limited to its liability arising from its ownership, maintenance, or use of the interior of such premises.

Chapter 12

VENDORS AS INSUREDS

One of the ways a manufacturer can induce retailers, distributors, wholesalers, and others (vendors) to sell its products is to provide vendors with additional insured status under the products liability coverage of the manufacturer's commercial general liability (CGL) insurance. A similar situation arises with respect to distributors or "wholesalers" that seek to establish a system of independent retailers dedicated to handling their products. Like the manufacturer, the distributor may find the vendor's endorsement to be a useful tool in inducing retailers to carry its product line.

This additional insured status is usually provided by attaching a "vendors endorsement" to the manufacturer's or distributor's policy.[1] It provides the vendor with products liability coverage with respect to claims arising from the named insured manufacturer's or distributor's products. Vendors rightfully view additional insured status as being advantageous because their protection comes at the expense of another, and it is not unusual for everyone in the stream of commerce to become involved in a claim or suit following injury or damage caused by a product.

Perhaps the primary reason manufacturers and distributors are sometimes reluctant to provide vendors with this protection is that it can be costly, particularly when a manufacturer has a high self-insured retention, a loss-sensitive rating plan, or a fronted program. Even when first-dollar protection is available, including others as insureds will also dilute the policy limits in the event of claims.

Yet, the manufacturer or distributor may have no other choice but to offer the coverage to its vendors. This is particularly so where the vendor is a large national chain or otherwise can offer substantial marketing wherewithal to the manufacturer. The vendors endorsement may not be the only concession. The manufacturer or distributor may also be required to indemnify the vendor. The extent of the manufacturer's or distributor's concessions in this regard will, of course, hinge on the bargaining power of the respective parties.

In light of the various editions and formats of CGL insurance in existence, ranging from standard to independently filed and manuscript policies, and the importance underwriters assign to the vendors endorsement, it is difficult to discuss in general the precise scope of coverage it provides. At one time, insurers utilizing standard forms offered by the predecessors of Insurance Services Office, Inc. (ISO), had two vendor endorsements from which to choose. One was referred to as the broad form vendors endorsement and the other the limited form. Currently, there is only one standard ISO vendors endorsement, the Additional Insured—Vendors (CG 20 15) endorsement, which corresponds to the older broad form. It is also not unusual to find insurers using the older vendors endorsements (broad and limited forms) or their own versions.

One school of thought about the application of these vendors endorsements is that the vendor is merely the "conduit" of the product and not the "instrumentality" that causes bodily injury or property damage. This means that coverage applies only to liability that attaches to the vendor because of the vendor's position in the stream of commerce, i.e., as the seller of the product and very little, if anything, else. One of the cases commonly cited to support this view of the coverage is *American White Cross Laboratories v Con-*

tinental Ins. Co., 495 A2d 152 (NJ App Div 1985), where the court said:

> When a manufacturer produces a product which contains a defect in design or one caused by faulty workmanship and it is sold to a distributor who in turn sells it to a retailer, the latter two links in the chain to the ultimate consumer are merely conduits in the stream of commerce which ends at the ultimate consumer. The manufacturing or design defect, as to which they had no creative role, was in existence when each of them received the product and each is merely a nonculpable accessory in the eventual sale. Nevertheless, each, in that role, is strictly liable to the injured ultimate consumer ... The nonculpable distributor or retailer is not, however, without remedy and has "an action over against the manufacturer who should bear the primary responsibility for putting the defective products in the stream of trade." It is in this complex [sic] of the facts of merchandising life and the imposition of strict liability at law that the vendor's endorsement has its natural role and serves specific purpose. Since, in the ordinary case, the liability trail eventually leads back to the manufacturer, and consequently to his insurer, it is a matter of common sense and fair dealing that the coverage of the manufacturer should be extended to the distributor and the insurance of the distributor in turn cover the retailer... *This insurance is clearly designed to cover the vendor when he is only a conduit of the product in the stream of commerce but not when he is the instrumentality causing bodily injury (or property damage) to another.* [Emphasis added.]

The last sentence in this quoted passage is emphasized because it addresses the common thread and underlying role of the vendors endorsement discussed in that case. The reasoning behind this decision is often relied on by insurers seeking to buttress their position regarding the scope of coverage provided by a vendors endorsement. However, there is a problem in relying on this case to establish that vendors liability coverage is purely *vicarious* liability coverage in every instance. In fact, the language of the vendors endorsement in the *American White Cross* case is more restrictive than the current standard ISO vendors endorse-

ment. The American White Cross endorsement defined persons insured to include a vendor "but only with respect to the distribution or sale of the named insured's products...." Those who use the standard ISO endorsement will note that vendors are covered "... with respect to 'bodily injury' or 'property damage' *arising out of*" the named insured's products. The key distinction between the two clauses is use of the phrase "arising out of," which is consistently held by the courts to include a broad range of degrees of causality.

A case in point is *Pep Boys v Cigna Indemnity Insurance,* 692 A2d 546 (NJ 1997). This case arose following the death of a minor from inhalation of Freon used for automobile air-conditioning systems. The complaint alleged negligence in the sale of Freon to a minor in violation of a state statute and negligence in training store personnel; the claim did not assert any claims under products liability for a manufacturing defect, a design defect, or a warning defect. At the time of the sale, the manufacturer maintained a liability policy that applied to "All Vendors of the Insured," and "All Products of the Insured." The insurer of the manufacturer denied coverage to the vendor on the grounds that the youth's death was caused by the vendor's independent act of negligence—in effect, that the injury did not "arise out of" Freon. The lower court adopted the insurer's reasoning when it determined that the cause of the injury was not a product but rather its sale to a minor. In so ruling, the court relied on the *American White Cross* case, as well as the narrow meaning that courts have assigned to the phrase "arising out of."

The court distinguished the *American White Cross* case, noting that that decision had ruled against coverage on the basis of applicable exclusions and because the vendors endorsement applied only with respect to the distribution or sale of the named insured's products. In *Pep Boys*, by contrast, there were no applicable exclusions and coverage applied with respect to bodily injury "arising out of" the manufacturer's product, a broader grant of coverage.

The lower court's decision was reversed on appeal. The appellate court held that a vendor's coverage for bodily injury arising out of a manufacturer's product was applicable to a suit alleging the vendor's negligence in selling the product.

A similar conclusion was reached in *Sportmart v Daisy Manufacturing Co.,* 645 NE2d 360 (Ill App 1994). Through its subsidiary, a retail sporting goods chain contracted with the manufacturer of BB guns and pellets. As part of the contract, a certificate was issued to the subsidiary on the manufacturer's behalf reflecting that a liability policy was in effect for the manufacturer, including an additional insured vendors endorsement. The endorsement provided coverage for vendors of products "but only with respect to 'bodily injury' or 'property damage' arising out of the products ... which are distributed or sold in the regular course of the vendor's business...."

The endorsement also contained the following exclusion.

> The insurance afforded [the vendor] does not apply to: ...
>
> e.   Any failure to make such inspections, adjustments, tests or servicing as [the vendor] has agreed to make or normally undertakes to make in the usual course of business, in connection with the distribution or sale of the products....

The claim in question arose following a young boy's injury caused by a BB gun firing pellets that the boy had purchased from the vendor. The complaint alleged that the vendor and its employees were negligent in that they (1) sold ammunition to the minor, who was under the age of 21 years and in violation of a state statute, (2) sold the ammunition to a minor under age 16 in contravention of established store policy, (3) sold the ammunition to the minor when it knew or should have known that his use of ammunition could result in injury, and (4) failed to determine the minor's age prior to selling the ammunition to him. There were no allegations of product liability.

The retail sporting goods chain tendered defense of the complaint to the manufacturer under the terms of the vendors endorsement. The manufacturer's in-

surer denied defense on the basis that the complaint alleged negligence on the part of the vendor, rather than any defect in the product itself. The lower court sided with the manufacturer and its insurer.

The primary issue on appeal turned upon the meaning of the phrase "arising out of" in the vendors endorsement. The retail sporting goods chain argued that this language unambiguously required the insurer to defend it in all bodily injury claims growing out of or resulting from the manufacturer's products. As to the quoted phrase "arising out of," the court stated this phrase repeatedly has been recognized as being both broad and vague. Contrary to the position taken by the manufacturer's insurers in this case, the court found nothing in the insurer's policy limiting coverage to claims alleging a product defect. The court added that, provided the product was sold in the same condition as when it left the manufacturer's control, there was no exclusion for injuries directly caused by the product, even if such injuries were also attributable to the negligence of another party. In deciding in favor of coverage for the vendor, the appellate court held that the minor's injury would not have occurred but for his use of the pellets.

In the case of *Hulsey v Sears, Roebuck and Co.,* 705 S2d 1173 (La App 1997), the coverage question was whether injuries sustained by a prospective purchaser during a sales demonstration of a treadmill were encompassed by the coverage afforded under a vendors endorsement, where the cause of the injuries was not shown to be any defect in the product.

The retailer maintained that it was covered by the vendors endorsement of the manufacturer in part because the endorsement, while it excluded liability for "the demonstration, installation, servicing or repair operations," made an exception for such operations performed at the vendor's premises in connection with the sale of the product. The manufacturer countered that its contract with the retailer only required it to obtain products liability coverage, not insurance sufficient to protect the retailer from the negligence of its own employees. The court agreed, saying that the exception to the exclusion would apply if the customer were injured during a sales demonstration on the vendor's premises as a result of a defect in the product itself. However, there was no evidence that the treadmill performed other than as intended.

It is important to note that the endorsement wording at issue in *Hulsey* did not specify the "arising out of" causal connection. Vendors insured status applied with respect to the distribution or sale, in the regular course of the vendor's business, of the named insured's products. Had the insurer utilized the "arising out of" wording, the court's ruling may have been different, given that the injury arose out of the product.

EXHIBIT 12.1
ADDITIONAL INSURED—VENDORS ENDORSEMENT (CG 20 15)

A. **Section II—Who Is An Insured** is amended to include as an additional insured any person(s) or organization(s) (referred to below as vendor) shown in the Schedule, but only with respect to "bodily injury" or "property damage" arising out of "your products" shown in the Schedule which are distributed or sold in the regular course of the vendor's business, subject to the following additional exclusions:

1. The insurance afforded the vendor does not apply to:

    a. "Bodily injury" or "property damage" for which the vendor is obligated to pay damages by reason of the assumption of liability in a contract or agreement. This exclusion does not apply to liability for damages that the vendor would have in the absence of the contract or agreement;

    b. Any express warranty unauthorized by you;

    c. Any physical or chemical change in the product made intentionally by the vendor;

    d. Repackaging, except when unpacked solely for the purpose of inspection, demonstration, testing, or the substitution of parts under instructions from the manufacturer, and then repackaged in the original container;

    e. Any failure to make such inspections, adjustments, tests or servicing as the vendor has agreed to make or normally undertakes to make in the usual course of business, in connection with the distribution or sale of the products;

    f. Demonstration, installation, servicing or repair operations, except such operations performed at the vendor's premises in connection with the sale of the product;

    g. Products which, after distribution or sale by you, have been labeled or relabeled or used as a container, part or ingredient of any other thing or substance by or for the vendor; or

    h. "Bodily injury" or "property damage" arising out of the sole negligence of the vendor for its own acts or omissions or those of its employees or anyone else acting on its behalf. However, this exclusion does not apply to:

        (1) The exceptions contained in Subparagraphs **d.** or **f.**; or

        (2) Such inspections, adjustments, tests or servicing as the vendor has agreed to make or normally undertakes to make in the usual course of business, in connection with the distribution or sale of the products.

2. This insurance does not apply to any insured person or organization, from whom you have acquired such products, or any ingredient, part or container, entering into, accompanying or containing such products.

The scope of the phrase "arising out of" as a defining term of additional insured coverage is discussed in more depth in **Chapters 9.**

Who the Endorsement Covers—Problems

The relevant provisions from the standard ISO Additional Insured—Vendors (CG 20 15) endorsement are shown in Exhibit 12.1. The endorsement gives insured status under the named insured's CGL policy to scheduled persons or organizations with respect to their distribution or sale of the products specifically identified in the endorsement.

Endorsement CG 20 15 was revised in 2004 for the specific purpose of eliminating coverage of the vendor's sole negligence, or the sole negligence of its employees or anyone else acting on its behalf, with certain exceptions as noted later under Coverage Limitations. It would, however, be difficult to interpret earlier versions of CG 20 15 as having applied to the sole fault of the vendor. Coverage for the vendor's *partial* fault in certain instances was made explicit by exceptions to the endorsement's exclusions. An example is exclusion b., which precludes coverage for any express warranty unauthorized by the named insured. If the named insured were to permit a vendor to make certain express warranties and a claim were to arise, the vendor would be covered for a bodily injury or property damage claim as a result of that authorized express warranty.

Some insurers have taken a different approach in excluding the sole fault of vendors. One direct writer's vendors endorsement excludes the vendor's sole fault succinctly by stating: "This insurance does not apply to the negligence of any person or organization other than the named insured."

Endorsement CG 20 15 requires that the vendor be specifically named, and that the named insured's products handled by the vendor also be listed. When there are numerous requests for vendors coverage, it is not unusual for underwriters to in-

sert the words "all vendors" or "blanket all vendors" in lieu of a specific vendor's name. This cuts down on the time and expense of the underwriter and producer having to issue and verify an individual endorsement for each vendor.

Sometimes the words "as per schedule on file with the company" are inserted in the space of the additional insured endorsement reserved for scheduling the person or entity for which coverage applies. One of the problems with this alternative is that someone has to maintain the currency of the list, which means notifying the insurer when changes are necessary. It is not a recommended approach, given the possibility that names will not be added on a timely basis or may be omitted by mistake. In fact, this approach proved to be a bar to coverage for some physicians in the case of *Texas Medical Liability Trust v Zurich Insurance Co.,* 945 SW2d 839 (Tex App 1977). These physicians were denied coverage partly on the grounds that none of their names were on the schedule of additional insured persons filed with the insurance company.

It is important to note that one purpose served by the wording "blanket all vendors" or "all vendors" is to add the named vendor (or all vendors elected by the named insured on a blanket basis) as an additional insured, thereby amending the Who Is an Insured section of the policy. This interacts with another important coverage feature common to all liability coverage, the fact that the liability policy is several in nature. This means that wherever the word "insured" appears in the policy, it also includes the vendor, subject to the conditions of the preceding preamble and the endorsement wording. Thus, the policy is viewed as though it had been issued separately to the vendor and to other insureds against whom claim is made or suit is brought, except that the limits do not apply separately to each of the covered persons or organizations.

One important prerequisite for coverage under a vendors endorsement is to be specifically listed or otherwise clearly designated as an insured person under the endorsement. However, there are other conditions precedent to coverage as well. Under the ISO endorsement shown in Exhibit 12.1, vendors coverage is also contingent upon (1) bodily injury or property damage arising out of the named insured's products as shown in the schedule, (2) the products being distributed or sold in the regular course of the vendor's business, and (3) no applicable exclusions.

"In the Regular Course of"

The insuring agreement of the standard ISO vendors endorsement shown in Exhibit 12.1 and others like it requires that the product out of which the bodily injury or property damage arises must be distributed or sold "in the regular course of the vendor's business."

A case illustrating the rationale behind this language is *Hartford Accident and Indemnity Co. v Bennett,* 651 S2d 806 (Fla App 1995). A customer went to a store with the intention of buying a garden shed. While in the store he approached a smaller-scale model of the shed, which tipped over, injuring him. The store's owner sought coverage for the resulting claim as an additional insured under the shed manufacturer's liability policy. The manufacturer's insurer refused to defend or indemnify, arguing that the store owner was not an insured with regard to *models* of portable storage sheds, since the models were not "distributed or sold in the regular course of the store owner's business." An appellate court agreed with the insurer's position, stating that coverage would have applied if the injury had resulted from a full-size storage building offered by the store owner for sale to the public. However, the storage shed in this case was merely a display model that the store owner neither sold nor distributed in its regular course of business as a vendor.

What is deemed to be "in the regular course of" a vendor's business also was referenced in the *Texas Medical Liability Trust* case. Most insurers oppose the notion of covering physicians as vendors under the liability policies of hospitals because the hospital's insurers view professional liability insurance as the physician's appropriate recourse. This same line of reasoning is followed by insurers with respect to physicians as additional insured vendors under a *manufacturer's*

policy when products are recommended, handled, or sold by physicians as part of their practice. However, physicians and surgeons still frequently look to the liability policies of manufacturers when claims arise out of this "vendor-like" relationship.

The *Texas Medical Liability Trust* case was an outgrowth of the silicone breast implant class actions against the Dow Corning Company. The women constituting the plaintiff class sued the manufacturer of the implants and the physicians who performed the implant surgery. Because the typical complaint alleged that the physicians sold breast implants to the plaintiffs, the physicians contended that they were "vendors" of the manufacturer's products. In addition to the coverage problem created by the fact that the physicians' names were not on the list of scheduled vendors under the manufacturer's policy, the court determined further that the breast implants were not sold "in the regular course of" the physicians' business.

To be an additional insured under the vendors endorsement, the court ruled that not only would the physicians have to have sold the breast implants, but also that the sale of the implants would have to constitute a regular feature of the physicians' business. The undisputed evidence at trial established that the physicians in this case were selling professional services, specifically surgical procedures. The breast implant appliances at the heart of the insurance agreements were at most incidental and collateral to the professional services being rendered by the physicians.

The court also took into consideration a dictionary definition of the term "vendor": "One who offers goods for sale, especially habitually or as a means of livelihood." To be additional insured vendors, the court said, the "physicians must, in the regular course of their business, be vendors [as prescribed in the quoted definition] of ... breast implants." The court determined, however, that the physicians did not sell breast implants as a means of livelihood.

Another case interpreting what does and does not fall within "the regular course of" a vendor's business is *Mitchell v The Stop & Shop Cos.,* 672 NE2d 544 (Mass App 1996). An employee of a baking company making a delivery of bread products to a retailer was injured by a retailer's truck at or near the retailer's loading dock. The injured employee brought suit against the retailer for injuries caused by its driver's negligence. The retailer, in turn, sought defense and indemnification under the baking company's vendors endorsement. Following settlement of the claims, judgment was entered for the retailer against the baking company's insurer, which appealed.

The appeals court, in reversing the lower court's decision, held that by the terms of the vendors broad form coverage endorsement, the insurer had undertaken to defend and indemnify the retailer (vendor) only with respect to the distribution or sale of the baking company's products "in the regular course of" the vendor's business. Although the baking company's employee was injured in the course of delivering a product to the retailer, the injuries were not caused (in the court's view) by the product, nor did they arise out of "the distribution or sale in the regular course of the vendor's business of the baking company's products." Instead, the court determined that the injuries arose from the distribution in the regular course of the baking company's business of its products to the vendor. The factors that caused the accident were totally unrelated to the *vendor's* sale or distribution of the product.

The *Mitchell* court cited in support of its ruling another case that turned on precisely parallel facts, i.e., injury to a manufacturer's delivery person caused by a hazardous condition at the premises of a vendor. That decision, *Dominick's Finer Foods v American Mfrs. Mutual Insurance Co.,* 516 NE2d 544 (Ill App 1987), also held the vendors endorsement not to apply.

In *Oliver Manufacturing Co. v USF&G Insurance Co.,* 232 Cal Rptr 691 (Cal App 1986), the question was whether a vendor added to a manufacturer's policy could be covered where the product that gave rise to injury was made by an entity purchased by the manufacturer (as successor in interest) long before the injury took place and before

the endorsement was issued. The vendor maintained that the term "named insured's products" should be interpreted to include products manufactured by a predecessor corporation. The vendor also maintained that the $25 it had paid to the manufacturer for the cost of the vendor's coverage entitled it to protection.

The court, in ruling against coverage, held that the premium paid by the vendor represented coverage only for those risks arising from sales made during the current coverage period. The court also held that the vendors endorsement clearly stated that it applied "only with respect to the distribution or sale in the regular course of the vendor's business of the named insured's products." To include products manufactured by the predecessor company perhaps years earlier, the court added, would be an irrational construction of both the insured's and insurer's reasonable expectations of coverage.

Considering the fact that mergers and acquisitions are commonplace, as is the sale of a predecessor's product, the ruling in this case presents an exposure that needs to be considered very carefully. A provision in most vendors endorsements, including the current ISO vendors endorsement, that appears on the surface to possibly exclude coverage of merger and acquisition exposures, is the one that reads:

2. This insurance does not apply to any insured person or organization from whom you have acquired such products, or any ingredient, part or container, entering into, accompanying or containing such products.

The potentially problematic word in the provision is "acquired." *The American Heritage Dictionary, Second College Edition,* defines the word "acquire" to mean "to gain possession." In the typical merger or acquisition, the buyer usually gains possession of the seller's interest in the business. However, the buyer certainly does not gain possession of any products that have already been sold to the public. Instead of applying to liability inherited by virtue of a merger or acquisition, it is more likely that this provision is meant to prohibit coverage for the manufacturer or distributor of the product itself, or a component part or packaging for the product, when the manufacturer or distributor is also an insured vendor.

For example, it would apply in a situation where a retail chain supplies the manufacturer of its product with the retail chain's special packaging for the product and that packaging causes injury or damage. Coverage provided to the retailer under a vendors endorsement in the manufacturer's policy would not protect the retailer against liability arising from the packaging the retailer supplied.

Another case involving confusion as to how a blanket coverage approach functioned is *Jaftex Corp. v Aetna Casualty & Surety Co.,* 617 F2d 1062 (4th Cir 1980). Jaftex considered the issue of whether a vendor not specified on the vendors endorsement was entitled to coverage under the manufacturer's policy. The endorsement insured vendors of the manufacturer's products but did not by its terms limit coverage to particular vendors. It included a statement of premium that was to be a percentage of sales by the manufacturer to a particular vendor. The court found that this circumstance gave rise to an ambiguity as to whether all vendors were covered and considered extrinsic evidence in determining that only the particular vendor on which the premium was based was entitled to coverage.

In *Torpey v N.B. Products v George A. Caldwell Co.,* 1984–1985 CCH (Fire and Casualty) 84–202 (USDC Mass 1984), a liability policy issued to a manufacturer, which also named the distributor of the products as an insured, was held not to provide coverage to a third company that leased the manufacturer's product to a fourth company. (An employee of the fourth company was injured by the product.) The applicable vendors endorsement included any vendor among the persons insured, "but only with respect to the distribution or sale in the regular course of the vendor's business of the named insured's products." Under the circumstances of the case, the lessor of the product seeking coverage did not sell or distribute the product to the employer of the injured worker in the regular course of the lessor's business. The endorsement, therefore, did not bring the lessor within the scope of coverage of the policy.

In another instance, a vendors endorsement on a products liability insurance policy insuring a pharmaceutical firm did not provide coverage to physicians who were sued for injury to a child to whom they had administered a drug. The court held that the physicians were not "vendors" of the drug but sold only their skill and knowledge. *(Cooper Laboratories v International Surplus Lines Insurance Co.,* 802 F2d 667 (3d Cir 1986).)

Industrial Chemical & Fiberglass Corp. v The North River Insurance Co., 908 F2d 825 (11th Cir 1990), dealt with the question of whether a vendor was covered under a manufacturer's umbrella liability policy. The manufacturer's primary policy had limits of $1 million, and its umbrella policy was written for limits of $45 million. The primary policy contained a vendors endorsement, but the umbrella policy did not. In fact, the umbrella insurer maintained that its policy was exclusively reserved for its named insured (the manufacturer). However, one of the umbrella policy's provisions stated that the policy also provided coverage to "any additional insured included in the Underlying Insurances, subject to the provisions of Condition B." An attached schedule of underlying insurances listed the manufacturer's primary liability policy.

The umbrella insurer did not dispute that the primary policy was underlying insurance or that the vendor was an additional insured under that primary policy. Instead, the umbrella insurer argued that (1) its policy was never intended to provide excess coverage to vendors of the named insured's products, and (2) if coverage were intended, the vendor never gave the umbrella insurer notice that the vendor was an additional insured under the primary policy pursuant to Condition B of the umbrella policy.

Condition B of the umbrella policy provided that "[i]n the event of additional insureds being added to coverage" under the primary liability policy "during the currency" of the umbrella liability policy, "prompt notice shall be given to [the umbrella liability insurer]." The vendor was not added as an additional insured during the term of the umbrella liability policy; as a manufacturer's vendor since 1964, the vendor was already an additional insured at the inception of the umbrella liability policy.

The court, in ruling that the vendor was covered by the umbrella policy of the manufacturer, stated that nothing in the umbrella policy required specific notice of the identity of each additional insured in the underlying insurances. It is unnecessary, the court said, for a person to be described by name to be an insured under a policy, if his or her identity can be determined from the description in the policy. The notice requirement, the court added, was met by notice of additional categories or groups of insureds; in this case, notice that vendors of the named insured's products were additional insureds under the broad form vendors endorsement was sufficient.

Finally, the court also stated that the umbrella insurer's course of performance supported this construction of Condition B because the umbrella insurer never asked for the list of the names of vendors covered under the primary policy, even at the beginning of the manufacturer-vendor relationship in 1979. Condition B requires that the umbrella insurer be notified; it does not require notice from the additional insureds themselves. (See **Chapter 14** on umbrella and excess policies for additional cases and comment dealing with Condition B.)

Other Insurance Problem

The vendors that are insured on the manufacturer's policy face the same potential problem from conflicts between insurers as to whether the manufacturer's or the vendor's own policy provides primary liability coverage as is faced by other additional insureds (see **Chapter 5**). In other words, the manufacturer's insurer could assert that the vendor's own products liability insurance should contribute to the cost of defending against claims against the vendor and any resulting settlements or judgments. Unlike most other types of additional insureds, a special endorsement, Excess Provision—Vendors (CG 24 10), has long been available to deal with this potential problem. This endorsement, shown in Exhibit 12.2, may be attached to the additional insured vendor's policy to make it clear that the vendor's CGL policy is excess of insurance provided to the vendor by the manufacturer.

EXHIBIT 12.2
EXCESS PROVISION—VENDORS ENDORSEMENT (CG 24 10)

The coverage afforded the insured under this Coverage Part will be excess over any valid and collectible insurance available to the insured as an additional insured under a policy issued to a manufacturer or distributor for products manufactured, sold, handled or distributed.

The CGL other insurance provision was revised in 1997 to make coverage excess over that of any other primary policy under which the named insured has additional insured status for liability arising out of "premises or operations." When that change was introduced, the use of endorsement CG 24 10 with the CGL policy was suspended, since the purpose of the endorsement was the same as that behind the revision to the other insurance clause. The latter revision's reference to "premises or operations," however, created uncertainty as to its applicability when the additional insured coverage applies specifically to products liability. For this reason, a 1998 revision to CG 24 10 makes its use once again possible with the CGL policy, to remove any misunderstanding that coverage of the vendor's endorsement on the manufacturer's policy is primary over the vendor's CGL.

Despite the availability of the Excess Provision—Vendors endorsement, it does not see frequent use. In fact, in one of the few cases involving this issue, a wholesaler was held to be covered on a primary basis under a manufacturer's policy despite the fact that this endorsement, though available, had not been attached to the wholesaler's policy. The case is *Gamble Skogmo, Inc. v Aetna Casualty & Surety Co.,* 390 NW2d 343 (Minn App 1986). It involved a water heater manufactured by Walter Corporation. The heater incorporated a Honeywell valve. Gamble, an appliance wholesaler, purchased the water heater from Walter Corporation in the regular course of Gamble's business. The water heater was then purchased for resale by Gamble Skogmo Store, an independent business. The water heater was installed by an independent contractor, and it exploded after it was put to its intended use.

Gamble, the wholesaler, was covered under a vendors endorsement attached to Walter Corporation's liability policy. Aetna Casualty & Surety Company insured Walter, and the Travelers Insurance Company insured Gamble.

The court reviewed the respective other insurance provisions of the manufacturer's and vendor's liability policies. The court also reviewed various theories including the so-called closeness to the risk concept, which the court said posed the following three questions for consideration:

- Which policy specifically described the accident-causing instrumentality?

- Which premium is reflective of the greater contemplated exposure?

- Does one policy contemplate the risk and use the accident-causing instrumentality with greater specificity than the other policy; that is, is coverage of the risk primary in one policy and incidental in another?

(The answer to those three questions will be coverage determinative in any given set of facts relating to the other insurance issue in any case.) The court, in the final analysis, decided that the manufacturer's liability policy was primary as to the vendor. Since the Excess Provision—Vendors endorsement is readily available with standard ISO CGL forms, it is advisable that vendors request its issuance with their policies to avoid these kinds of arguments.

Coverage Limitations

The coverage provided for a vendor under the Additional Insured—Vendors (CG 20 15) endorsement (see Exhibit 12.1 on page 226) is subject to the following limitations.

1. a. Contractually assumed bodily injury or property damage liability is exclud-

ed, except for liability that the vendor would have even in the absence of the contract or agreement. An example of liability that would be incurred in the absence of the contract is when a vendor is brought into a suit merely because it distributed a product whose defect was caused solely by the manufacturer.

b. The vendor will not be covered with respect to any express warranty it makes that has not been authorized by the insured manufacturer. This provision avoids the vendor's being covered under the manufacturer's general liability policy for liability arising out of erroneous or misleading claims the vendor makes about the product.

c. There is no coverage for liability arising from any intentional physical or chemical change the vendor makes in the product.

d. The endorsement's coverage does not apply with respect to repackaging, except when purpose of the unpacking is inspection, demonstration, testing, or the substitution of parts under instruction from the manufacturer. Even then, for coverage to be effective, the products must be repackaged in the original container.

e. If the vendor has agreed to make inspections, adjustments, tests, or servicing, or if the vendor normally undertakes such tasks in connection with its distribution or sale of the product, there is no coverage for the vendor's failure to do so.

f. The vendor will have no coverage for demonstration, installation, servicing, or repair operations concerning the product away from the vendor's own premises. Unless these operations are performed in connection with the sale of the product, coverage will not apply even at the vendor's premises.

g. The vendor is not covered for products which, after distribution or sale by the named insured, have been labeled, relabeled, or used as a container, part, or ingredient of any other thing or substance by or for the vendor.

h. The vendor is not covered for injury or damage arising out of its sole negligence or the sole negligence of its employees or anyone else acting on its behalf, except with respect to activities described in coverage limitations **d.** or **f.** above, or when the vendor agrees to make, or normally undertakes to make, inspections, adjustments, tests or servicing in connection with the distribution or sale of the products. The stated exceptions—repackaging of the product; demonstration, installation, or repair; and inspection, adjustment, and testing—are arguably the only areas in which any coverage for the vendor's sole negligence could be read into the endorsement even before the sole negligence exclusion was added in 2004. The net effect of the new exclusion, therefore, seems negligible.

2. The endorsement does not apply to suppliers from whom the manufacturer has acquired products designated in the endorsement or any ingredient, part, or container entering into, accompanying, or containing those products.

Of the nine coverage limitations contained in the endorsement, the one that has undoubtedly given rise to more coverage disputes than any other is the third one (1.c.) concerning changes in the product made by the vendor. To date, insurers have not been very successful in denying coverage to vendors based on any of the preceding limitations, primarily because earlier versions of the endorsement excluded bodily injury or property damage arising out of: any physical or chemical change in the form of the product; repacking, etc.; demonstration, installation, servicing, or repair; or products that have been labeled or relabeled. Courts have ruled that this wording requires the insurer to establish a causal connection between the injury or damage and the change in the product.

Application of Endorsement Exclusions

The rationale for use of a vendors endorsement is to protect vendors from products liability claims brought against them simply because they are part of the product's distribution chain. The endorsement, as noted earlier, is not designed to address any actual negligence on the part of the vendor that has the effect of making the product dangerous or more dangerous. In keeping with this purpose, vendors endorsements exclude (1) liability resulting from physical or chemical changes made in the product by the vendor, (2) repackaging of the product by the vendor except under specified conditions associated with inspection or testing of the product, and (3) labeling or relabeling of the product by or for the vendor.

The three exclusions referred to above—and their interrelationship—have generated most of the legal disputes surrounding the vendors endorsement, including the following.

In *Mattocks v Daylin, Inc.,* 452 F Supp 512 (WD Pa 1978), aff'd 614 F2d 770 (3d Cir 1979), a pajama manufacturer purchased cotton flannelette and made pajamas from the material. A consumer was injured when a pair of the finished pajamas ignited. The insurer of the fabric manufacturer denied coverage under the vendors endorsement based on the exclusion relating to any physical or chemical change in the product made intentionally by the vendor (the pajama manufacturer). In rejecting this argument, the court held that if a change in "form" beyond the supplier's control caused the injury, then neither the supplier nor its insurer would be held responsible. However, where the change in form (i.e., from raw material into pajamas) does not cause the injury—where the injury is caused by the material itself, regardless of the form it takes—the manufacturer is responsible for any harm arising from the material.

Another argument offered by the supplier's insurer was that since the pajamas were not sold under the material supplier's label, the labeling or relabeling exclusion precluded coverage. The court rejected this argument as well because the labeling or relabeling did not cause the injury.

Sears, Roebuck and Co. v Reliance Insurance Co., 654 F2d 494 (7th Cir 1981), involved a retailer (Sears) that was named as an insured vendor under both a fabric manufacturer's and a slacks manufacturer's policy, seeking legal representation and indemnity under both policies. The injury in question arose from the burning of slacks. The products liability suit brought against Sears (for which it was seeking coverage under the manufacturers' policies) alleged that the fabric from which the slacks were made was defective, aside from any defect in the fabric, because the slacks were defectively produced and manufactured. Thus, the underlying complaint involved the potential liability of both manufacturers. Sears brought suit seeking a judgment that it was entitled to legal representation and indemnity under the vendors endorsement of both manufacturers' policies.

In considering whether the fabric manufacturer's insurer (Commercial Union) owed a defense to Sears, the court relied heavily on *Mattocks* in stating that if the mere labeling of the finished product could defeat coverage of any defect in the fabric itself, then the vendor's insurance covering the retailer "could not have been worth the piece of paper on which it was printed."

The slacks manufacturer's insurer (Reliance) argued that Sears picked out and paid for the material and directed that it be sent to the slacks manufacturer. Therefore, the insurer contended that Sears was not entitled to coverage under the vendors endorsement because the insurance did not apply (exclusion 2) to any organization from which the named insured had acquired such products or components.

In this case, the two insurers attempted to place Sears in a Catch-22 situation. On one hand, Sears would not be covered by the fabric manufacturer's policy because the fabric was changed into slacks. On the other hand, Sears would have no coverage under the slacks manufacturer's policy because Sears supplied the fabric. The court held that each of the arguments would nullify coverage intended under the endorsement. Both manufacturers' insurers were required to provide Sears with a defense.

American White Cross Laboratories v Continental Insurance Co., discussed previously, acknowledged both the *Mattocks* and the *Sears v Reliance* decisions as precedent for interpreting the labeling exclusion but reached a different decision as to coverage given the facts. Absorbent Cotton Company sold bleached and carded cotton in bulk to American White Cross Laboratories. American White Cross sterilized the large rolls of cotton and cut them into small pieces, which it packaged individually and sold to a supermarket chain. A supermarket customer who used several packages of the cotton to make a party costume was severely injured when the costume ignited. American White Cross was sued by the injured consumer for its negligent failure to put a flammability warning on the packaging it supplied for the cotton. American White Cross sought protection under a vendors endorsement naming it as an additional insured under Absorbent's liability policy.

The court held that the labeling exclusion applied and that no coverage was available to American White Cross. In reaching this decision, the court addressed *Mattocks* and *Sears v Reliance,* both of which had found the labeling exclusion not to be applicable under similar circumstances. The difference in those cases, the court explained, was that the vendors' labeling of the product was not asserted as a cause of the injury. In *American White Cross v Continental,* on the other hand, the vendor's own omission of a warning on the packaging that it designed and supplied was the premise underlying the cause of action in the suit. The court summarized the consistency of the *Mattocks* decision and its own as follows.

The *Mattocks* court held that there must be a causal nexus between the conduct of the vendor and the bodily injury before the labeling exclusion can be invoked. [These determinations] represent a reasonable interpretation of the exclusionary clauses. When, however, they are applied to the factual context presented to us, they call for an exclusion of [the vendor's] rights to indemnification because the product defect here ... asserted was that the label [the vendor] used did not warn of the inherent flammability of cotton and that this failure caused the [customer's] injuries.

Liberty Mutual Insurance Co. v Home Insurance Co., 583 F Supp 849 (USDC WD Pa 1984), involved a dispute between Liberty, as insurer for both a pajama manufacturer and a retailer, and Home, as the insurer for a fabric manufacturer. Both manufacturers' policies afforded protection to a retailer of the pajamas by means of vendors endorsements. The underlying products liability suit was for injuries sustained by a child when her pajamas caught on fire.

Liberty paid the entire amount of the judgment and defense costs associated with the suit and sought contribution from Home. Home contended that half of the judgment and defense should be borne entirely by Liberty because one of the two allegations in the suit—failure to warn of the fabric's flammable properties—was precluded from coverage by the "labeling" exclusion of the vendors endorsement (exclusion 1.g). (Home acknowledged coverage for the other allegation—that the fabric was defective—and was willing to share the judgment and defense costs with Liberty.)

The court rejected Home's argument on the grounds that: (1) the exclusion was ambiguous; (2) even if the exclusion were clearly applicable, the settlement could not fairly and accurately be apportioned between the covered and excluded claims; and (3) since allegations of failure to warn are often included in products liability suits as a matter of course, the rule of exclusion sought by Home would result in substantially less coverage in all such cases. Therefore, the entire amount of the judgment and defense costs was considered in the apportionment between the two insurers.

A vendors endorsement was held not to apply, in the case of *SDR Co. v Federal Insurance Co.,* 242 Cal Rptr 534 (1987), to a claim against a vendor where there was a nexus between injuries to a consumer and the drain cleaner sold by the vendor but no connection between the injuries and the empty bottle delivered by the bottle manufacturer to the vendor.

SDR sold a bottled liquid drain cleaner. It purchased the empty plastic bottles from Arroyo. At SDR's request and instruction, Arroyo preprinted the label and warning on the bottle. At SDR's request, Arroyo agreed to try to obtain insurance for SDR. Arroyo subsequently had SDR added to Arroyo's policy as an additional insured under a vendors limited form endorsement that was added for a flat premium charge of $25. The endorsement provided, in pertinent part, as follows.

The WHO IS INSURED provision is amended to include any person or organization designated below (herein referred to as "vendor") [SDR], as an insured, but only with respect to the distribution or sale in the regular course of the vendor's business of the named insured's [Arroyo's] products designated below subject to the following additional provisions:

9. The insurance with respect to the vendor does not apply to: ... b. bodily injury or property damage arising out of ... (iv) products which after distribution or sale by the named insured have been labeled or relabeled or used as a container, part or ingredient of any other thing or substance by or for the vendor; ....

During the policy period when the above endorsement was in effect, a consumer was injured when the acid cleaner she was pouring splattered and burned her. She sued Arroyo, which manufactured the bottle, and SDR, which made the cleaner. While Arroyo's insurer provided SDR with a defense, it refused to indemnify it because of the exclusion contained in the vendors endorsement.

In ruling for the insurer, the court stated that there was a nexus or link between the injuries sustained by the claimant, the claimed dangerous cleaner sold by SDR, and the claimed insufficient instructions on the bottle made up by SDR. As to SDR, the court said, the claim was not based on a defective bottle but was based on a defective product in the bottle or in the defective directions.

The court added that the vendors endorsement was intended to protect the vendor (SDR) against liability the vendor may incur because of a defect in the product sold to the vendor by the named insured (Arroyo). The endorsement was not intended to cover the vendor for changes in the product made by the vendor over which Arroyo had no control. Thus, there was a nexus between the injuries to the claimant and the cleaner sold by SDR. However, there was no connection between the injuries and the empty bottle as delivered by Arroyo to SDR. Therefore, coverage of the endorsement should not extend to SDR, the court ruled.

Types of Products Covered

The question of what constitutes a "product" was raised in another vendors endorsement case involving Sears. The case, *Sears, Roebuck and Co. v Employers Insurance of Wausau,* 585 F Supp 739 (DC Ill 1983), arose out of a dispute concerning an instruction manual prepared for Sears by Midwest Technical Productions on the maintenance and operation of various power tools. The manual was copyrighted by Midwest in 1974. During the preparation of the manual, all of its technical writing was handled solely by Midwest, with suggestions by various manufacturers of the tools and a review by Sears as technical adviser. Sears participated in the cover design of the manual. Sears then purchased the finished manual from Midwest for sale in its retail stores.

An injured consumer alleged that Sears had a duty to write, print, publish, and distribute an instruction manual with a reasonable degree of care and caution so as not to cause injury to the consumer, knowing that the consumer would rely on the representations made in the manual. Sears sought protection under the vendors endorsement attached to Midwest's CGL policy.

In denying responsibility to defend Sears, Midwest's insurer asserted that the underlying complaint did not involve the manual as a physical product but, rather, the intellectual content of the manual. This contention that the manual is actually two products, the court held, was not supported by the plain and unambiguous language of the policy, which made no distinction as to coverage between claims arising from physical characteristics and claims arising from intellectual content.

An argument citing the exclusion of product changes made by the vendor was also rejected by the court on the grounds that any changes made to the product before it left Midwest could not be the kind of changes contemplated in the exclusion. A further argument that the manual was only a part of the total injury-causing entity was dismissed as frivolous. Finally, the court looked to *Sears v Reliance* as a precedent in rejecting the exclusion of coverage for any organization from which the named insured had acquired any ingredient or part. The publisher's insurer was required to defend Sears in this action.

The scope of the endorsement's "change" exclusion was interpreted in a case that involved Sears in a dispute regarding two children injured by a fire in a tent sold by Sears but manufactured by another company. The trial court decision being appealed in this case found that Sears had directed the manufacturer not to take the steps necessary to make the tent fire-retardant. Nevertheless, the court affirmed summary judgment in favor of Sears (an additional insured under the tent manufacturer's vendors endorsement), holding that the "change" exclusion (exclusion 1.c) in the endorsement applied only to changes made after the product left the manufacturer's control (*Continental Casualty Co. v Sears, Roebuck and Co.,* 474 NE2d 1272 (Ill App 1985)).

Other Coverage Issues

When an entity has the bargaining power to request additional insured status, the contractual requirement should be easily understandable and broad enough to encompass the entity's needs. In the case of *General Nutrition Corp. v U.S. Fire Insurance Co.,* CA No. 3:97cv490 (USDC Va 1997), the requirement of additional insured status in the vendor's purchase order was not clear enough to encompass coverage for an allegation of trademark infringement against the vendor.

The vendor in this case purchased a line of nutrition and weight control products from a distributor. Subsequently, these products became the subject of a trademark infringement lawsuit brought by the manufacturer. The purchase order under which the vendor acquired the products obligated the distributor of the products to procure insurance as follows.

> 7. FREIGHT AND INSURANCE ... Seller agrees to carry Buyer as an additional insured under a vendor's liability insurance policy and Seller shall provide Buyer with a certificate of insurance annually evidencing adequate products liability coverage.

At the time the vendor purchased the products, the distributor was covered under a nonstandard CGL policy endorsed to provide personal and advertising injury coverage with respect to any person, organization, trustee, or estate that has obligated the named insured by written contract to provide insurance that is afforded by the policy for liability arising out of the named insured's work or product.

When the vendor sought advertising injury coverage under the distributor's policy, the distributor's insurer denied the claim. The insurer argued that the vendor's liability coverage required by the contract language quoted above was limited to bodily injury and property damage (the standard coverages typically provided by vendors endorsements) regardless of what other coverages might also be provided by the policy. The insurer argued that had the vendor wanted broader coverage, it could have required additional insured status without the restrictive modifier, "vendor's liability insurance," as contained in its purchase order agreement.

The court held that the phrase "vendor's liability insurance policy" was not adequately defined in the contract and therefore followed the general rule that ambiguities in contractual language must be construed against the drafter of the contract—in this instance, the vendor.

Summary

The common thread and underlying role of the vendors endorsement is to view the vendor as a conduit of the product and not as the instrumentality that causes the injury or damage. Having said that, the coverage provided by the vendors endorsement is not necessarily limited to vicarious liability. In many cases, both the vendor and the manufacturer are found to be partially at fault for a product injury, and standard ISO vendors endorsements have long provided that coverage. How the endorsement as revised in 2004 will be interpreted in light of the exclusion for sole negligence—a term left undefined in the endorsement—is something that only time will tell.

The fact that a person or entity is listed on the vendors endorsement does not necessarily mean that coverage will be provided. Much depends on how the wording of the endorsement modifies and interacts with the balance of the policy. In the final analysis, what counts is the actual wording of the endorsement, not what the insurer or others may say its intent is.

Chapter 12 Notes

1. There has been misunderstanding by some as to whose policy the endorsement should be attached. When a retailer or other vendor is promised vendor's insurance protection from a distributor or manufacturer, it is the insurance policy(ies) of the distributor or manufacturer that should be amended with the vendors endorsement, not the insurance of the retailer.

Chapter 13

BLANKET ADDITIONAL INSURED ENDORSEMENTS AND PROVISIONS

Many commercial general liability (CGL) insureds encounter frequent contractual demands to add other entities as insureds under their policies. Depending on the frequency of such requests, the insured can be at risk of breach of contract claims if the additional insured status is not arranged as required. For this reason, CGL policies are sometimes endorsed to provide—on an automatic basis—additional insured status to other entities that are entitled to such status by virtue of a contract or agreement with the insured. Until 1997, there was no standard endorsement available to achieve this. Therefore, such endorsements were manuscripted (either from scratch or by modifying one of the standard endorsements) or developed on a nonstandard basis by individual insurers.

For example, the endorsement used with the construction industry, Additional Insured—Owners, Lessees or Contractors (CG 20 10), became so commonly requested of contractors that some underwriters transformed it into a blanket form. An example of modifications to make the endorsement apply on a blanket basis and also to comply with the common request that the endorsement be modified to specifically state that coverage applies on a primary basis is shown in Exhibit 13.1. Note that the version shown in the exhibit is based on the 1985 edition endorsement, which included coverage for the completed operations hazard. Even though this edition of the endorsement was withdrawn from use in 1993, its wording sometimes is incorporated into blanket additional insured endorsements of some insurers. A variety of other endorsement approaches to providing blanket additional insured status have been utilized by various insureds and their insurers over the years.

EXHIBIT 13.1
EXAMPLE MODIFICATION OF CG 20 10 TO BLANKET BASIS

Name of Person or Organization:

ANY PERSON OR ORGANIZATION THAT THE INSURED HAS AGREED AND/OR IS REQUIRED BY CONTRACT TO NAME AS AN ADDITIONAL INSURED.

(If no entry appears above, information required to complete this endorsement will be shown in the Declarations as applicable to this endorsement.)

WHO IS AN INSURED (Section II) is amended to include as an insured the person or organization shown in the Schedule, but only with respect to liability arising out of "your work" for that insured by or for you.

IT IS FURTHER AGREED THAT THE INSURANCE PROVIDED BY THIS ENDORSEMENT IS PRIMARY. OTHER INSURANCE AFFORDED TO THE ADDITIONAL INSURED SHALL APPLY AS EXCESS OF, AND DOES NOT CONTRIBUTE, WITH THE INSURANCE PROVIDED BY THIS ENDORSEMENT.

Includes copyrighted information of Insurance Services Office, Inc.

EXHIBIT 13.2
EXAMPLE BLANKET AI ENDORSEMENTS

Manuscript Form 1

It is agreed that additional insureds are covered under this policy as required by written contract, but only with respect to liabilities arising out of their operations performed by or for the named insured, but excluding any negligent acts committed by such additional insured.

Manuscript Form 2

It is agreed that Coverage Part CL 100, Section II—Who Is an Insured is amended to include the following as an additional insured: Any person or organization to whom you are obligated by contract, entered into before loss, to provide insurance, but only to the extent required by such contract, notwithstanding any requirement, term or condition of any contract to which this endorsement may apply. The insurance afforded an additional insured shall be subject to all the terms, conditions, and exclusions of this policy and all endorsements attached thereto.

One of the mistakes some people make is to assume that a blanket or automatic additional insured endorsement is broad in scope. The term "blanket or automatic additional insured" should do nothing more than connote that one endorsement is to be used to encompass more than one additional insured without having to issue a separate endorsement for each such request. One should never assume anything about the scope of coverage the endorsement provides to the additional insured. It is the endorsement's language and that of the policy to which it is attached that govern coverage.

Exhibit 13.2 shows two manuscript blanket additional insured endorsements that have been issued by different insurers. Under the first, additional insureds are granted coverage only for their vicarious liability (i.e., only for liability imputed to them because of the negligence of the policy's named insured). The exclusion for liability arising out of negligent acts of the additional insured precludes coverage for the additional insured's direct liability for negligent conduct. Although eligibility as an additional insured under this first endorsement must be required by written contract, it does not matter what the contract specifies as the scope of the additional insured status, it is what this limited endorsement says. The second manuscript blanket additional insured endorsement is at the other extreme, covering as an additional insured any party that requires such status in a contract, subject only to the terms of the policy to which the endorsement is attached.

The lack of standard blanket additional insured endorsements has required many underwriters, brokers, and risk managers to manuscript endorsements such as those shown in Exhibit 13.2. This, of course, opens the door to mistakes and problems. In 1997 Insurance Services Office, Inc. (ISO), introduced two new endorsements to effect blanket additional insured status in CGL policies. This chapter examines these ISO forms as well as some of the nonstandard blanket additional insured endorsements that have been used.

Standard Automatic Insured Endorsements

As part of the 1997 endorsements revision, ISO introduced two automatic additional insured endorsements. The first, Additional Insured—Owners, Lessees or Contractors—Automatic Status When Required in Construction Agreement with You (CG 20 33), provides an owner or another contractor with additional insured status on the policy of a named insured contractor. The other, the Additional Insured—Lessor of Leased Equipment—Automatic Status When Required in Lease Agreement with You (CG 20 34) endorsement, achieves a comparable effect for the owners of equipment leased to the insured. Both of these endorsements were amended as part of the 2004 revision of forms and are discussed in these pages.

EXHIBIT 13.3
ADDITIONAL INSURED—OWNERS, LESSEES OR CONTRACTORS—AUTOMATIC STATUS WHEN REQUIRED IN CONSTRUCTION AGREEMENT WITH YOU (CG 20 33)

A. **Section II—Who Is An Insured** is amended to include as an additional insured any person or organization for whom you are performing operations when you and such person or organization have agreed in writing in a contract or agreement that such person or organization be added as an additional insured on your policy. Such person or organization is an additional insured only with respect to liability for "bodily injury", "property damage" or "personal and advertising injury" caused, in whole or in part, by:

1. Your acts or omissions; or

2. The acts or omissions of those acting on your behalf;

in the performance of your ongoing operations for the additional insured.

A person's or organization's status as an additional insured under this endorsement ends when your operations for that additional insured are completed.

B. With respect to the insurance afforded to these additional insureds, the following additional exclusions apply:

This insurance does not apply to:

1. "Bodily injury", "property damage" or "personal and advertising injury" arising out of the rendering of, or the failure to render, any professional architectural, engineering or surveying services, including:

   a. The preparing, approving, or failing to prepare or approve, maps, shop drawings, opinions, reports, surveys, field orders, change orders or drawings and specifications; or

   b. Supervisory, inspection, architectural or engineering activities.

2. "Bodily injury" or "property damage" occurring after:

   a. All work, including materials, parts or equipment furnished in connection with such work, on the project (other than service, maintenance or repairs) to be performed by or on behalf of the additional insured(s) at the location of the covered operations has been completed; or

   b. That portion of "your work" out of which the injury or damage arises has been put to its intended use by any person or organization other than another contractor or subcontractor engaged in performing operations for a principal as a part of the same project.

Copyright, ISO Properties, Inc., 2004

Automatic Additional Insured Status

The Additional Insured—Owners, Lessees or Contractors—Automatic Status When Required in Construction Agreement with You (CG 20 33) endorsement was introduced by ISO to allow contractors and subcontractors to add persons or organizations as additional insureds without being required to name such persons or organizations in the endorsement. Reference to the words "construction agreement" may also prevent its use outside the construction industry. This endorsement is reproduced in Exhibit 13.3.

Endorsement CG 20 33 provides additional insured status to "any person or organization" when the named insured has agreed in a *written* contract or agreement to include that person or organization as an insured on the policy. Like the 2004 edition of CG 20 10, which provides similar coverage to scheduled additional insureds, CG 20 33 grants coverage only with respect to the named insured's ongoing operations for the additional insured. Both endorsements also limit coverage to injury or damage that is caused in whole or in part by the named insured's acts or omissions, or the acts or omissions of those acting on the named insured's behalf in performing ongoing operations. Thus, unlike earlier editions of these endorsements, no coverage is intended to apply to the sole fault of the additional insured. The ramifications of this change in standard additional insured coverage are discussed in **Chapter 9**.

Endorsement CG 20 33 also limits the term of additional insured coverage to the time during which operations are actually being performed by the named insured. This limitation, in effect, is imposed twice—once by identifying the additional insured as an entity "for whom you are performing operations" and again with the statement: "A person's or organization's status as an additional insured under this endorsement ends when your operations for that additional insured are completed." (This wording may not automatically eliminate completed operations coverage in all cases. In those situations where property damage can be tied to operations that were not yet completed, there may still be coverage. For a more detailed discussion on this point, refer to page 178 of **Chapter 9**.)

ISO's decision to adopt the language quoted above is an acknowledgment of an important difference between scheduled and automatic additional insured status. Use of endorsement CG 20 10—or any other standard endorsement that names specific entities as additional insureds—provides insured status for the duration of that policy period but not for succeeding policy periods unless the same scheduled coverage is again endorsed onto the subsequent policy. By its very nature, however, an automatic additional insured endorsement probably will be attached to the named insured's CGL year after year, since the need for such coverage does not end

with the requirements of any individual contract or the demands of any particular additional insured. But there is the danger that someone who has qualified for automatic additional insured status under one policy term will qualify again in subsequent policy years under the automatic additional insured endorsement attached to those subsequent policies. The provision that ends insured status with the ending of the named insured's operations for the additional insured prevents this often unintended extension of coverage.

Finally, it is important to note that endorsement CG 20 33 also contains a professional services exclusion similar to the Exclusion—Engineers, Architects or Surveyors Professional Liability (CG 22 43) endorsement. The apparent rationale for this exclusion is that since the additional insured endorsement applies on an automatic basis, there is the chance that coverage could otherwise apply to contractors who are also engineers, architects, or surveyors.

Lessor of Leased Equipment Automatic Status

The Additional Insured—Lessor of Leased Equipment—Automatic Status When Required in Lease Agreement with You (CG 20 34) endorsement corresponds to the Additional Insured—Lessor of Leased Equipment (CG 20 28) endorsement in much the same way that CG 20 33 corresponds to CG 20 10. It grants automatic additional insured status to a person or organization from whom the named insured leases equipment when the named insured has agreed by contract to provide such additional insured coverage. Like endorsement CG 20 28, which provides additional insured status to *scheduled* lessors of equipment, CG 20 34 limits coverage to injury or damage caused, in whole or in part by the named insured's maintenance, operation, or use of equipment leased to the named insured by such person or organization, and specifically excludes any "occurrence" after the equipment lease expires.

Endorsement CG 20 34 also imposes a limitation on the term of insured status equivalent to that found in CG 20 33, discussed previously. It states that insured status under the endorsement "ends when [additional insured's] contract or agreement with [the named insured] for such leased equipment ends." Note that this exclusion may go beyond the one mentioned in the preceding paragraph pertaining to *occurrences* after the lease expires. With respect to both this automatic additional insured endorsement and CG 20 33 applicable to owners, lessees, and contractors, some question remains as to the effect on coverage of terminating an entity's insured status before the policy itself terminates.

A person or organization with insured status at the time of covered injury or damage is covered, even if the policy is terminated before a claim is made against the insured and tendered to the insurer. It is quite common for insurers to respond to claims for injury or damage that took place years earlier, under a long-expired policy.

Nonstandard Automatic Additional Insured Endorsements

Prior to the 1997 introduction of ISO's automatic additional insured endorsement for use by contractors, a number of different blanket or automatic additional insured endorsements had been introduced by insurers. Whether these alternative approaches will be continued after introduction of the standard endorsement remains to be seen. In any case, many of these endorsements contain provisions and limitations that are not included in the standard CG 20 10 or CG 20 33 endorsements.

Eligibility

Like ISO endorsement CG 20 33, most independently filed endorsements condition additional insured status on certain prerequisites but commonly expound on those prerequisites in more detail than the ISO endorsement. Exhibit 13.4 provides one example.

Note that the use of a certificate of insurance is a way of verifying that there has been some oral contract or agreement between the parties to make a person or organization an additional insured. (This is another example of coverage being conferred based on the issuance of a certificate of insurance, a trend that is discussed in **Chapter 20.**) The dilemma that will face insureds and insurers in such cases is the intended scope of coverage. If the certificate of insurance is unclear as to the specific additional insured endorsement to be used, or the intended scope of coverage, the courts will be forced to look to other evidence of coverage intent.

EXHIBIT 13.4
EXAMPLE MANUSCRIPT ENDORSEMENT ELIGIBILITY CRITERIA

Who Is an Insured (Section II) is amended to include as an insured any person or organization (called "Additional Insured") whom you are required to add as an Additional Insured on this policy under:

A. a written contract; or

B. an oral agreement or contract where a Certificate of Insurance showing that person or organization as an Additional Insured has been issued; but the written or oral contract or agreement must be an "insured contract," and,

  (1) currently in effect or becoming effective during the term of this policy; and

  (2) executed prior to the "bodily injury," "property damage," "personal injury," or "advertising injury."

The additional requirement that the written or oral contract or agreement must be an "insured contract" is relatively common insofar as these blanket endorsements are concerned. This provision apparently requires a reason for additional insured status, e.g., coverage to buttress a lease agreement, or a contract where the named insured assumes the tort liability of the additional insured and not simply an agreement to add someone as an additional insured. While other insurers' blanket endorsements have similar provisions to this one, most do not make the requirement that the written or oral contract be an "insured contract."

There is also a potential problem for insureds and insurers alike with provision B(2) (which also applies to other independently filed blanket endorsements) dealing with the undefined term "execution." The probable rationale for this requirement is to clarify that no protection is to be provided after injury or damage takes place in a case where there has been no expressed or implied meeting of the minds between the parties before the accident, and the only reason for the signing of the agreement is to transfer the consequences to an insurer.

The problem for insureds is that it is not unusual for contractors to commence their respective performance even before a written contract has been signed. In fact, this is quite common, particularly among owners of property or construction projects, who often require the prompt services of contractors before the contract can be formalized by signing.

Whether the contractual liability coverage is restricted to written contracts or encompasses oral and written contracts, the task of the insurer that wants to deny protection based on the failure to execute a contract before injury or damage is likely to be difficult and complex. The reason is that the undefined word "execution," as it appears in CGL policy provisions, does not necessarily mean signed and, at best, is ambiguous on this point.

Scope of Coverage

Once it is determined whether a person or organization otherwise qualifies for additional insured

status under these blanket additional insured endorsements, the next item to determine is the scope of coverage provided. Unlike the ISO endorsement, some of these endorsements will provide additional insured status when required in agreements other than construction contracts. For example, some of these confer additional insured status when required in "any written contract or agreement."

There may be both advantages and disadvantages to this approach for the named insured. The obvious advantage to the named insured is that additional insured requirements imposed by rental agreements, leases, or any other contract will automatically be complied with. The disadvantage is that it would be impossible to tailor the provisions of the endorsement such that they provide only the desired scope of coverage for any type of contract into which the named insured may enter. Often the restrictions imposed on the additional insured's coverage in these endorsements focus solely on the named insured's primary business activities and do not contemplate other activities for which the named insured may contractually agree to add other parties as additional insureds. This could result in a broader scope of coverage than the parties contemplated.

For example, blanket additional insured endorsements drafted for attachment to contractors' policies usually will be drafted with construction activities in mind. They often will not impose any restrictions on coverage provided to a lessor of premises or renter of equipment, for example. Yet, additional insured status required in these types of contracts will be effected under many of the blanket endorsements provided to contractors. If the contractor's insurance is called on to cover a loss that would not normally be contemplated by the parties, the contractor's insurance limits will be unnecessarily eroded and the contractor's insurance costs may be adversely impacted.

An example of an endorsement that contemplates a broader range of contracts than the ISO endorsement but is not as broad as those described previously is shown in Exhibit 13.5. In Example 1, note that with the addition of 1.a., additional insured status is also provided to tenants, lessees, or licensees. Provision 1.b., on the other hand, is similar to the pre-1993 ISO additional insured endorsement CG 20 10, which did not restrict coverage to ongoing operations.

Of course, some of these endorsements are more limited in coverage scope than the ISO form. Example 2 in Exhibit 13.5 shows one of these. At first blush, provision B.(1) appears to provide coverage comparable to the 1997 edition ISO automatic additional insured endorsement CG 20 33, as well as ISO endorsement CG 20 10, which seeks to limit coverage to "ongoing operations." (See **Chapter 9**.) The dilemma that will face insureds and insurers in such cases is the intended scope of coverage. If the certificate of insurance is unclear as to the specific additional insured endorsement to be used, or the intended scope of coverage, the courts will be forced to look to other evidence of coverage intent. However, provision B.(2) and specific reference to "general supervision" is a tip-off that coverage may be comparable to the owners and contractors protective (OCP) policy; or the limited ISO additional insured endorsement CG 20 09, which was withdrawn from use in 2004.

Further review of this blanket endorsement reveals that it indeed is a more limited form in light of the exclusion (similar to the one in the OCP policy) that precludes coverage for the additional insured's direct liability, except as respects general supervision.

EXHIBIT 13.5
MANUSCRIPT DELINEATION OF CONTRACT TYPES

Example 1

The insurance provided to the additional insured is limited as follows:

1. That person or organization is only an additional insured with respect to liability arising out of:

    a. Premises you own, rent, lease, or occupy or

    b. "Your work" for that additional insured by or for you.

Example 2

B. The insurance provided to the additional insured is limited to liability arising out of:

    (1) your ongoing operations performed for that additional insured, or

    (2) acts or omissions of the additional insured in connection with their general supervision of "your work."

    This insurance does not apply to:

    (3) "bodily injury" or "property damage" arising out of any act or omission of the additional insured or any of their "employees" (including temporary worker") other than the general supervision by the additional insured of your ongoing operations performed for the additional insured.

The exclusion runs counter to the *Commercial Lines Manual (CLM)* rule prescribing endorsement CG 20 10 when contractual liability coverage is being provided. The insurer of this particular endorsement apparently does not abide by that ISO rule and provides additional insureds with limited coverage potentially detrimental to both the named insured and additional insured in cases where a hold harmless agreement is in place.

If broad additional insured coverage is prescribed in a contract (e.g., coverage for the additional insured's sole fault, completed operations coverage all on a primary basis), some insurers issuing blanket additional insured endorsements will accommodate those requests. If the requests are not specifically prescribed in a contract, however, the insured receives very limited coverage. Some insurers, on the other hand, are not so accommodating, whether specific coverage requests are made in the underlying contracts or not. One such case that illustrates just how limited a blanket additional insured endorsement can be is *Continental Casualty Co. v Fina Oil & Chemical Co.,* 126 SW3d 163 (Tex App 2003).

A contractor wrote a letter to an oil company proposing to perform certain work using its equipment and providing insurance. The oil company in turn issued two purchase requisitions that comprised the work to be performed. The reverse side of the purchase orders contained terms and conditions of the sale but made no reference to the provision of insurance by the seller to the buyer. The contractor's insurance agent issued a certificate of insurance. Under the heading "additional insured," the certificated provided:

> Fina, its parent, subsidiaries and affiliated companies, and their respective employees, officers and agents shall be named as additional insured in each of the Contractor's policies, except Workers Compensation; however, such extention [sic] of coverage shall not apply with respect to any obligations for which Fina has specifically agreed to indemnify the Contractor.

The certificate also provided, under the heading "Subrogation:"

> All policies shall be endorsed to provide that underwriters and insurance companies of Contractor shall not have any right of subrogation against Fina, its parent, subsidiaries and affiliated companies, and their respective agents, employees, officers, invitees, servants, contractors, subcontractors, underwriters and insurance companies.

The suit arose following an injury to one of the contractor's employees, who alleged fault on the part of the oil company for several reasons. The same insurer had issued both the contractor's CGL policy and its workers compensation policy. After learning of the employee's lawsuit, the insurer, which had already paid medical expenses and wage loss to the employee, also filed a lien for the amount paid against the oil company. As a result of these actions, the oil company sought coverage under the contractor's insurance as an additional insured The insurer denied coverage to the oil company.

The additional insured endorsement issued by the contractor's insurer was a blanket one, stating in part:

> If you are required to add another person or organization as an additional insured on this policy under a written contract or agreement currently in effect, or becoming effective during the term of the policy, and a certificate of insurance has been issued, then Who Is an Insured (section II) is amended to include as an insured that person or organization (called "additional insured").

The insurance for that additional insured is limited as follows:

> 1. That person, or organization, is only an additional insured for its liability arising out of premises "you" own, rent, lease or occupy or for "your work" for or on behalf of the additional insured; and

2. The insurance afforded the additional insured under this endorsement does not apply to (a) punitive or exemplary damages in whatever form assessed against the additional insured and/or (b) any liability arising out of any act, error or omission of the additional insured, or any of its employees.

The contractor's insurer contended that no coverage applied to the oil company, because there was no written contract or agreement requiring the contractor to add the oil company as an additional insured. The oil company countered that its written bid from the contractor, which proposed to furnish insurance, became the written contract when it was accepted by the oil company. The court held that the issue was not merely whether there was a contract but whether such contract complied with the contract of insurance. The court decided that, from this perspective, the oil company was not an additional insured.

The insurer stated furthermore that, even if for the sake of argument the oil company were considered to be an additional insured, coverage for the contractor's employee's injury still would be excluded, because the blanket endorsement withheld coverage from the oil company for liability arising out of any act, error or omission of the oil company, or, in other words, for the oil company's own negligence. The court agreed with the insurer.

On the issue of subrogation, the insurer sought the money that was paid in connection with the employee's workers compensation claim. The oil company argued that subrogation of an insurer against its insured has been rejected in Texas. As it turned out, the subrogation waiver that was in effect between the parties was limited solely to the commercial general liability and owners and contractors protective liability coverages. The oil company, furthermore, was not named on the workers compensation policy and therefore was not an insured. The court ruled in favor of the insurer on this point, too.

Limits of Insurance

The ISO automatic additional insured endorsement does not include any provision that specifically limits the extent to which additional insured

status applies, barring only the restriction to "ongoing operations," discussed earlier. Other blanket additional insured endorsements, on the other hand, also address the matter of limits of insurance. Exhibit 13.6 provides an example.

EXHIBIT 13.6
LIMITS OF INSURANCE LIMITATION

The limits of insurance applicable to the additional insured are those specified in the written contract or agreement or in the Declarations for this policy, whichever are less. These limits of insurance are inclusive of and not in addition to the limits of insurance shown in the Declarations.

Although there are some exceptions, many contract insurance requirements specify that the required limits of insurance are minimums and not maximums. For example, most specify something like "the contractor shall purchase and maintain commercial general liability and umbrella/excess liability insurance with combined limits of not less than $5 million." Because it is impossible to quantify the liability assumed under contract, no prudent indemnitee or indemnitor would ever view the required limits to be maximums. But because of challenges by some insurers, to avoid the dispute, it is advisable for indemnitees to clarify their contracts by stating that the limits as prescribed are minimums and that all coverage and limits available to the indemnitor will apply to a loss.

However, if, for the sake of some argument, a court were still to hold that the limits of insurance in a contract are maximums, this could present a problem if a blanket additional insured provision had been issued with the previous provision where the policy provided higher limits. Assume, for example, a contract specified general liability coverage with limits of not less than $500,000 per occurrence and additional insured status, but the policy of the indemnitor were issued with a per occurrence limit of $1 million. If a court were to hold that the contract limit is the maximum, the additional insured endorsement provision above would have the effect of limiting coverage to less than the policy limits.

On the other hand, if a court were to hold that the contract amount is a minimum, the higher amount of the policy would apply to the additional insured and if that were not enough, the excess layers could be triggered.[1]

The provision of blanket additional insured provisions stating that limits are inclusive of the limits of insurance serves the purpose as the provision of the separation of insureds condition; that is, with the inclusion of additional insureds, the limits are not multiplied. The limits of insurance applicable in the policy apply to all insureds.

Application of Other Insurance

Another common approach is a provision that converts to a primary basis when the named insured requests that basis even in the absence of a written contract.

EXHIBIT 13.7
TYPICAL OTHER INSURANCE PROVISION

Coverage provided herein shall serve as excess over any other valid and collectible insurance available to the additional insured whether the other insurance is primary, excess, contingent or on any other basis unless a written contractual arrangement specifically requires this insurance to be primary.

Exclusions

The nature of exclusions applicable to these blanket additional insured endorsements can vary, but most other blanket additional insured endorsements are similar in one respect to the ISO endorsement—all exclude architects, engineers, or surveyors professional liability.

What other exclusions may apply varies, depending on the commercial general liability policy provisions in question. When the blanket additional insured endorsement corresponds to the coverage of an owners and contractors protective (OCP) policy, some additional exclusions apply; examples are bodily injury or property damage for which the additional insured is obligated to pay damages by reason of the assumption of liability in a contract or agreement, other than for damages the additional insured would have in the absence of such contract; and property damage to property owned, used, or occupied by or rented to the additional insured, or in its care, custody, or control.

Some of these endorsements also specifically state that no person or organization is considered to be an additional insured for the conduct of any current or past partnership or joint venture that is not named in the policy declarations. This is unlike any provision of the ISO endorsement. However, the ISO commercial general liability policy's provision that addresses past and current partnerships and joint ventures applies only when such entity is not shown as a named insured.

Summary

Blanket additional insured endorsements and provisions have been available on a manuscript basis for many years. Because these forms are not standardized, they may contain exclusions, limitations, or other problematic provisions not found in the standard endorsements. Thus, they require careful review.

In fact, enough coverage issues (like those raised in the *Fina* case discussed above) have been raised in recent years to remind persons and organizations desiring additional insured status to specifically prescribe the extent to which they wish to be additional insureds and request confirmation by receipt of the endorsement. A certificate of insurance reflecting additional insured status is not enough.

When a person or organization desiring additional insured status does not prescribe the scope of coverage it desires, it will not likely have strong grounds to insist on its own interpretation of what a blanket additional insured endorsement actually provides.

Certainly a certificate holder has a right to rely on the representations made on a certificate. And, as is mentioned elsewhere in this book, the insurer whose name appears on the certificate should honor the coverage that the certificate reflects; action may then be possible against the insurer's authorized representative who issued the certificate and made misrepresentations.

In 1997 ISO introduced two blanket endorsements. While they have brought some standardization to this coverage approach, they are not panaceas. They do not apply to all types of contract relationships (e.g., there is not one for premises leases) and they have some potentially problematic language of their own.

Chapter 13 Notes

1. In addition to the potential problems of breaching the contract's insurance requirement, wording such as that shown in Exhibit 13.6 may be found to tie the insurance coverage involved to the indemnity obligation. By stating that the limits of insurance are those specified in the underlying contract, the policy must be read with the contract's insurance requirements. In those situations where the insurance requirements and indemnity agreement are in the same paragraph, this could pose a problem if the indemnity agreement is held to be invalid. Even in situations where the insurance requirements and the indemnity obligation are in separate provisions of the underlying contract, this wording could be seized upon by a court to find that the insurance is there solely to fund contractual obligations. This is in addition to other problems in the way insurance requirements are worded in relation to the limits of insurance required.

UMBRELLA AND EXCESS LIABILITY INSURANCE

Much of the discussion in the preceding chapters applies to umbrella and excess liability policies. However, there are some unique aspects of umbrella coverage that require special mention. This chapter is devoted specifically to issues related to additional insured status that are unique to umbrella and excess liability policies.

This is a difficult task because umbrella and excess liability policies have not been standardized by the insurance industry.[1] Of course, not all commercial general liability (CGL) insurance policies are the same, but at least there is a benchmark—the Insurance Services Office, Inc. (ISO), forms—against which independently filed CGL forms can be compared. There is no such benchmark for umbrella and excess liability policies.

However, many umbrella policies contain the same additional insured provisions and similar policy conditions, such as those dealing with notice of cancellation and premium payment obligations. Surprisingly, there are not many court decisions dealing with additional insured issues under umbrella and excess liability policies. But there are a sufficient number of cases in this area to support certain points and conclusions. In addition, much, though not all, of the case precedent established litigating primary coverages will apply to umbrella coverage as well.

Broad Form Named Insured Provisions

One distinct advantage over primary liability forms that some umbrella policies offer named insureds is the automatic inclusion of the so-called broad form named insured provision. In contrast, a broad form named insured provision must be added to CGL policies, and since there is no standard ISO endorsement of this type, not all underwriters will accommodate such a request. The inclusion of a broad form named insured provision in the ISO CGL policy—in addition to the newly acquired organization provision—would be an improvement in the form. Yet, as discussed later, some of these broad form named insured provisions may also cause problems.

While many umbrella forms include broad form named insured provisions, not all of them do. Therefore, the inclusion of such a provision in a particular form could be viewed as an advantage. Most broad form named insured provisions are similar with respect to the entities that are specifically identified as eligible for named insured status. They typically provide such status to "all subsidiary, associated, owned, controlled, or affiliated companies," as well as newly acquired or formed organizations.

The major difference between broad form named insured provisions concerns requirements to notify the insurer of the various insured entities and the time within which notice must be received. It is generally advantageous to the named insured for the umbrella policy automatically to include all eligible entities without requiring the first named insured or someone else to notify the insurer of named insured additions. However, many such provisions are not so broad, and notice is often required. This variation defeats the purpose of having such a provision. Exhibit 14.1 shows two example broad form named insured endorsements—one with and one without a notice requirement.

EXHIBIT 14.1
EXAMPLE BROAD FORM NAMED INSURED PROVISIONS

No Notice Requirement

The Named Insured as shown in the Declarations and if such organization is a corporation also includes:

(1) Any subsidiary company of such organization, including any subsidiary company thereof:

    a. Existing at the effective date of this policy; or

    b. Acquired during the "policy period."

(2) Any other company controlled and actively managed by such organization or any such subsidiary, other than a partnership or joint venture:

    a. At the effective date of this policy; or

    b. If the control and active management thereof was acquired during the "policy period."

Notice Requirement

All subsidiary, associated, affiliated companies or owned and controlled companies as now or hereinafter constituted and of which prompt notice has been given to the Company.

Most umbrella forms require notice of newly acquired or formed organizations within 30, 60, or 90 days, but some require no notice at all. Umbrella policies requiring prompt notice are cause for some concern in that what is deemed to be prompt notice is often subjective and likely to lead to disputes. In determining what prompt notice is, insureds would be wise to err on the side of caution. While the term "prompt" is undefined and should be interpreted in favor of the insured, it is always preferable to avoid a potential coverage dispute by seeking clarification on terms such as this one.

A court decision that exemplifies the disadvantage of a broad form named insured provision requiring prompt notice of any changes is *American Motor Inns v Harbor Insurance Co.,* 590 F Supp 468 (WD Va 1984). The initial named insureds constituted a chain of 33 hotels that were listed on the policy. A serious accident took place at the site of a hotel that was not on the initial list of insured locations but that was added by endorsement after the incident. The insurer denied coverage, and the court agreed that since the site was not added until after the accident and no premium was paid for the addition until after the loss, the umbrella policy did not apply.

The court explained that the broad form named insured provision required that the parent company notify the umbrella insurer of the existence of any subsidiary to obtain coverage and that those "hereinafter constituted" would become insureds if prompt notice were given to the insurer. Once such notice is given, the court added, the insurer could also charge an additional premium.

The matter of an additional premium is another important consideration that should not be overlooked. The umbrella policy conditions should be scrutinized to determine if an additional premium also must be paid to obtain protection. While some umbrella policies preserve the right to make an additional premium charge, insurers often do not exercise this option. Whenever an insurer waives such charge, it is wise to request written confirmation, because an umbrella insurer could conceivably point to the provision as a basis for denying coverage by maintaining that it was denied the right to charge such premium. Of course, if the umbrella policy is written on a flat premium basis, the insurer will be precluded from raising such an argument. But if the umbrella policy is written subject to audit, this is an especially important caveat to keep in mind.

Reference in the *American Motor Inns* decision of a hotel location list also raises another caveat for insureds. Whenever a list of locations is made a part of the policy, it is beneficial for it to contain a statement indicating that the insured locations are listed strictly for rating purposes. If this intent is not clearly stated, insurers may attempt to construe the umbrella as if it were coverage applicable to scheduled locations only. In one case that was settled out of court, an umbrella insurer attempted to deny coverage for liability stemming from a business location that, prior to the date of the injury, had been sold by the named insured. This kind of action should be covered by CGL and umbrella liability policies. Yet, the insurer attempted to exclude coverage by maintaining that the accident site in question was no longer on the policy's list of locations.

The use of specific lists to identify locations and entities without clarifying wording is not desirable for other reasons as well. For example, builders and developers that routinely enter into various partnerships, joint ventures, limited liability companies, and other entities under which they do business face a problem. Each time a new entity is created or added, failure to have it added to the list may be argued by the insurer as a basis to deny coverage for failure to allow the opportunity to charge additional premiums or because the list used was allegedly all encompassing for purposes of the insurer's obligations.

While these arguments run counter to the concept of broad form named insured provisions, they are still raised by insurers and must be addressed. It is preferable to avoid this problem with wording acknowledging that additional entities will be added, that coverage is automatic for these new entities, and that additional premium charges will be based on audits at the end of each policy period unless the policy is written on a flat premium basis, i.e., a fixed premium. Without this clarification, insureds may be forced to litigate the issue. While the insured should win such disputes, the time and expense involved can be avoided by addressing the problem in advance.

Automatic Additional Insured Provision

Most umbrella liability policies use a different method for including additional insureds than do primary liability policies. Additional insured endorsements are typically not used. Instead, most umbrella forms include provisions that automatically include as insureds: (1) any persons or organizations that qualify as insureds in the scheduled underlying insurance, and (2) any persons or organizations that the named insured contractually agrees to include as additional insureds in its liability insurance. Exhibit 14.2 shows examples of these two provisions. (As a word of caution, not all umbrellas include such provisions, and some that do include them require that the insured notify the insurer when additional insureds are added to the primary policies.)

However, some umbrella insurers have policies that do require attachment of additional insured endorsements. They do so to allow underwriters to dictate the scope of coverage that will be provided under the policy, particularly where the underlying policy does not apply and the umbrella policy must drop down and apply as a primary policy.

Adding standard ISO endorsements to umbrella policies (with minor modifications) might eliminate a source of confusion in situations where the insurance requirements of a contract require both primary and umbrella layers of coverage. If standard ISO endorsement CG 20 10 or its equivalent were attached to a primary policy and to an umbrella policy, the scope and extent of the additional insured coverage up through the umbrella layers would be clear. However, where the umbrella policy is not endorsed with CG 20 10 or its equivalent, there may be problems if the umbrella provides additional insured coverage using the automatic additional insured provisions under discussion in this chapter.

If CG 20 10 is attached to the primary policy but not to the umbrella policy, how will umbrella coverage apply? The underlying coverage would apply to the full extent of the policy under CG 20 10, regardless of contract wording. If the umbrella policy provides following form coverage, there may be no problem. However, if the umbrella policy includes its own additional insured provisions, its interaction with the underlying layer of coverage may prove difficult to ascertain.

EXHIBIT 14.2
EXAMPLE ADDITIONAL INSURED PROVISIONS

(A) Any person, organization, trustee, or estate to whom or to which the Named Insured is obligated by virtue of a written contract to provide insurance such as is afforded by this policy, but only with respect to operations by or on behalf of the Named Insured or to the facilities of or used by the Named Insured.

(B) At the option of the Named Insured and subject to the terms of the coverage of this insurance, any additional insured, other than the Named Insured, included in the underlying policies as listed in Schedule ___, but only to the extent that insurance is provided to such additional insured thereunder.

(C) Subject to the terms and conditions of this policy, any additional insured included in the underlying insurance, but only to the extent that insurance is available to such additional insured under such underlying insurance.

(D) Any additional insured (not being the Named Insured under this policy) included in the underlying insurance, subject to the provisions in Condition B [Additional Insured], but not for broader coverage than is available to such additional insured under a policy of underlying insurance as set forth in Item ___ of the Declarations.

(E) Any person or organization for which an insured is by virtue of a written contract entered into prior to an "occurrence" to provide the kind of insurance that is afforded by this policy, but only with respect to operations by or on an insured's behalf, or to facilities an insured owns or uses, and only to the extent of the limits of liability required by such contract, but not to exceed the applicable limits of liability set forth in this policy.

(F) Any other person or organization if included as an insured under the provisions of "scheduled underlying insurance" or "unscheduled underlying insurance," but only to the extent that coverage is provided by your scheduled or unscheduled policy.

(G) At your option and subject to the terms of the coverage of this insurance, any additional insured(s) included in the underlying insurance listed in Schedule A, but only to the extent that insurance is provided for such additional insured(s) thereunder.

(H) Any persons or organization (other than you) included as an insured in the Scheduled Underlying Insurance but NOT for broader coverage than is available to them under the Scheduled Underlying Insurance.

(I) Anyone for whom you have agreed in writing to provide insurance such as is provided by this policy is an insured but only for operations performed by you or on your behalf or facilities you own or use.

(J) We'll protect any other person or organization who is a protected person under your Basic insurance, subject to the same coverage limitations as your Basic insurance.

(K) (A/B Policy Format)

Coverage A—Excess Liability. Any person or organization who is an insured in Primary Policies. However, any person or organization who is added as an insured in Primary Policies after the inception of our policy is an insured only when you agree prior to the time of an occurrence to provide such insurance as is afforded by Coverage A of this policy.

Coverage B—Umbrella Liability. At your option, any person or organization for whom you have agreed in an Insured Contract to provide such insurance as is afforded by Coverage B of this policy. However, such contract must be executed prior to the time of an occurrence.

One potential problem involves situations where the underlying insurer denies coverage under CG 20 10, which occurs frequently and often erroneously. The question then is, will the umbrella policy apply? First, if contractual liability coverage under the umbrella policy exists and the risk is encompassed by the indemnity requirements of the underlying contract, coverage will apply and there is no need to look to additional insured status. However, if the contract is held to be inapplicable for any reason, the insured must look solely to additional insured status. If the additional insured provision of the umbrella policy provides automatic additional insured status to all those additional insureds included in underlying insurance and the notice obligations have been complied with, coverage should apply on behalf of the additional insured.

If the automatic additional insured wording previously referenced also limits coverage to that required by contract, there is a problem. If the underlying contract is held to be invalid or if the indemnity obligation does not encompass the loss involved, there will be no coverage under the umbrella policy. If the umbrella provision also limits additional insured status to situations involving operations by or on behalf of the named insured, another problem arises. Some insurers will argue that "operations" means only ongoing operations as opposed to completed operations. This argument is without merit, since the term "operations" is not limited to ongoing operations.

The 1993 edition of ISO endorsement CG 20 10 was modified to limit coverage to "ongoing operations" but does not address the trigger of coverage. As discussed in **Chapter 9,** this limitation does not necessarily restrict coverage to *injury or damage that takes place* during ongoing operations. That important point, coupled with the plain meaning of the term "operations," makes it clear that the prior wording referring to "operations" and used by both ISO and many umbrella insurers includes both ongoing and completed operations, absent specific modification to the contrary.

While the common approach of not providing additional insured endorsements with umbrella liability insurance does reduce the amount of administrative effort and the possibility of an administrative breakdown, it does not solve all the problems. In particular, disputes involving other insurance clauses and circumstances where coverage of additional insureds extends far in excess of the required liability limits are two such problem areas that can result from this approach.

Because of these frequently disputed and litigated areas of coverage involving additional insureds, it would not be surprising to see an increase in the use of additional insured-related endorsements with umbrella coverage. Such endorsements could, for example, eliminate a considerable amount of litigation regarding which policy applies first.

The most common type of additional insured provision of umbrella liability policies is the one noted in (A) in Exhibit 14.2. It requires an obligation expressed in a written contract. While many contracts between parties are in writing, including those involving the transfer of liability, some are consummated on an oral basis. This raises other potential problems. For example, where two or more entities routinely conduct business, projects may overlap and work may begin before a contract is deemed to be executed or made. Establishing exactly when a contract is deemed executed or made is a problem that can be addressed contractually with wording stating that a contract is deemed to be executed or made as soon as any party to the agreement takes any step in furtherance of performance. This would activate coverage even without the formality of a signed contract.

Unfortunately, most additional insureds probably do not realize the conditional nature of their coverage because they seldom, if ever, see a copy of the policy. Even if an additional insured were to request a certified copy of the insurance policy to verify compliance with insurance specifications, it is unlikely that such a request would be fulfilled. Instead, what the additional insured is likely to receive is a certificate of insurance. The additional insured therefore must rely both on the named insured to properly arrange the required coverage and on broader and more precise contract provisions dealing with insurance requirements and indemnity provisions.[2] The provisions commonly in use today are often inadequate and the source of coverage litigation.

A written contract containing an indemnity clause but not specifically requiring additional insured status is not necessarily sufficient to effect additional insured status under provisions such as in (A) in Exhibit 14.2. Generally, it should be specifically stated if additional insured status is desired. However, a very strong implication of this intent may also be sufficient to invoke additional insured status. For example, a contractual requirement that "all insurance coverages carried by [the indemnitor] shall extend to and protect [the indemnitee] to the full amount of such coverage" is probably sufficient to effect additional insured status under such a clause. However, such wording, while it may get the job done, might require judicial determination. It is preferable for the contract to specifically require additional insured status in the umbrella program.

A great deal depends on the validity and enforceability of the contract. If the underlying contract, for example, were to be deemed unenforceable, so too might the insurance protection. A case in point is *Posey v Union Carbide Corp.,* 507 F Supp 39 (MD Tenn 1980). This case arose following the death of a steel company employee in an accident at the premises of a manufacturer. The decedent's estate collected workers compensation benefits and then filed suit against the manufacturer.

The manufacturer maintained that it had the rights of an "insured" under the steel company's umbrella liability policy because there was a written indemnity agreement between the two parties and the steel company's umbrella policy contained an additional insured provision identical to the one designated in (A) of Exhibit 14.2. The construction contract between the steel company and the manufacturer also contained a provision that required the steel company, as the indemnitor, to:

> ... indemnify and hold harmless the manufacturer from and against all claims ..., of every character whatsoever, for bodily injury ..., including death ... sustained by any person while on or about the premises of the manufacturer if or where such injury and/or death arose out of or

was in any way connected with the work ..., whether or not such injury ... and/or death was caused by, resulted from or was in any way connected with the negligence of the manufacturer.

In light of the above clause of the contract, the manufacturer maintained that it was entitled to coverage as an insured under the steel company's umbrella policy. However, the court stated that if the indemnification agreement between the steel company and manufacturer was enforceable, there might have been some merit to the manufacturer's argument. But under the Tennessee law, at least at the time of this dispute, the attempted transfer of an indemnitee's sole negligence under contract was against public policy and, hence, unenforceable. In addition, Tennessee law provided no exception to the prohibition against sole fault indemnification allowing insurance coverage for that exposure, as is the case in a number of states. Thus, the court explained, "a void agreement cannot be called an obligation" and, therefore, the manufacturer was not an insured under the steel company's umbrella liability policy.

A more sinister problem can arise where the umbrella policy limits coverage for the additional insured to the extent required in the underlying contract. This may make coverage dependent on the terms of the indemnity agreement between the parties. As a result, the additional insured coverage, in essence, is only there to fund the indemnity obligation. See the discussion of "inextricably tied" issues in **Chapter 4.**

Many states have anti-indemnity statutes on the books that preclude the assumption of another's sole fault in construction and other types of contracts. If that legislation causes the indemnity provision to be held invalid, the coverage obligation also may be extinguished. Insurers in states with such legislation can then routinely attack the enforceability of indemnity agreements to avoid coverage obligations in many fact patterns. Wording that limits coverage to contractual requirements is often a built-in defense to coverage.

In this circumstance, the indemnity agreement and the insurance coverage are inextricably tied. If the indemnity agreement is held to be invalid for any reason, eliminating the indemnity agreement also eliminates the additional insured coverage (which is dependent on the underlying contract terms). Of course, the contractual liability coverage also would not apply since it relies on the enforceability of the indemnity agreement. Thus, tying additional insured status to the indemnity agreement would effectively transform additional insured coverage (status) into contractual liability coverage.

An example of the problems encountered in this regard is the case of *Shaheed v Chicago Transit Authority,* 484 NE2d 542 (Ill App 1985). Here, the contract separated the provisions of insurance and indemnification. However, the provision containing the insurance requirements reads, in part, as follows.

> Subcontractor shall maintain insurance in the following limits and cause a so-called contractual liability and/or hold harmless endorsement to be issued by the insurance company or companies insuring all the Subcontractor's indemnity obligations under this agreement.

The court ultimately ruled that the indemnity agreement was invalid. In addition, since the insurance required was only for the indemnification obligation that was void and unenforceable, the court held that, in effect, there was no contractual obligation on the part of the indemnitor to obtain contractual liability insurance, thus voiding the insurance requirements.

The case of *City of Wilmington v North Carolina Natural Gas Corp.,* 450 SE2d 573 (NC App 1994), resulted in a similar finding by the court. The indemnity agreement used in this case also required that the indemnitee maintain contractual liability insurance for protection against liability assumed in the indemnity provisions.

Because both the indemnity and insurance requirements were in one paragraph and because the insurance was primarily required to fund the indemnity agreement, they were interdependent or inextricably tied. Thus, when the court held the indemnity agreement invalid, it nullified any hope of insurance coverage as well.

The problem is based on the purpose of the insurance coverage. If the purpose of the insurance is solely to fund the indemnity obligation, it is inextricably tied (interdependent) with the indemnity obligation. Thus, if the indemnity obligation is invalid, coverage disappears with the invalidated indemnity agreement.

A number of states with anti-indemnity legislation precluding sole fault indemnification have carved out a narrow exception to that doctrine. These states allow an indemnitor to purchase insurance that will cover the sole fault of the indemnitee; in some cases, it must be through an admitted or authorized insurer.

However, this exception is not satisfied by contractual liability coverage because that type of coverage does not apply to the indemnitee. Contractual liability coverage applies to the insured indemnitor and simply funds the obligation assumed by the indemnitor in a contract. This is the type of coverage that can be lost if the coverage is inextricably tied to an invalid indemnity agreement, as previously discussed.

The narrow exception to anti-indemnity legislation for the purchase of insurance will not apply in most cases unless the insurance purchased makes the party to be indemnified an additional insured. The courts view additional insured status differently than contractual liability coverage for purposes of applying anti-indemnity legislation.

Unlike contractual liability coverage, which covers the insured indemnitor's responsibility for funding contractually assumed liability, providing additional insured status gives the additional insured indemnitee its own rights under the policy. An indemnity provision, on the other hand, merely provides a recourse to recover from the indemnitor, irrespective of the indemnitor's insurance.

Furthermore, the additional insured is entitled to all rights under the policy, and the validity or terms of the contract, for the most part, are irrelevant in determining the scope of coverage. Once additional insured status is provided, only the terms of the policy dictate coverage, except where there are ambiguities in coverage. In those instances, the courts may look to the contract to determine the parties' intent.

This is one of the most important reasons why additional insured status and contractual liability coverage should both be involved in transferring risk. There are a variety of reasons why indemnity contracts might be held invalid. The most troublesome and likely source of problems is anti-indemnity legislation and related reasons. If the indemnity provision fails for any of these reasons, the purpose and positioning of the indemnity obligation and its relation to insurance coverage become important factors in determining if this type of coverage will apply.

Because coverage often is nullified with the indemnity obligation, it is essential that there be a back-up method of risk transfer in place. This points out the importance of additional insured status, which allows coverage to apply regardless of the validity of the indemnity agreement in most instances.

A case that exemplifies the use of additional insured status as a means of coming within the exception to anti-indemnity legislation for insurance coverage is *Getty Oil Co. and Texaco v Insurance Co. of North America*, 845 SW2d 794 (Tex 1992). In this case, both the indemnity and insurance requirements were combined in the same paragraph. To make matters worse, there was clear reference to the fact that the insurance necessary to cover the indemnity agreement was to be provided by the named insured indemnitor.

When the indemnity agreement was held invalid, the issue was whether the insurance requirements also would be held invalid, given their interdependence under the wording involved. The court held that, despite the positioning and apparent interdependence of the insurance and indemnity provisions, the fact that the indemnitee was required to be added as an additional insured altered the equation.

Additional insured status brought with it rights under a policy that were separate and apart and not a direct indemnification of the indemnity agreement obligation. The court also noted that the indemnity

provision required its own insurance and, therefore, was not dependent on the coverage contained in the additional insured provision. The key point is that without additional insured status, contractual liability coverage for liability assumed can be attacked as being provided solely to fund an indemnity obligation.

Limiting an additional insured's coverage to what the underlying contract requires also appears to be an emerging trend in manuscript additional insured endorsements. Additional insured coverage that is tied to the indemnity agreement creates a no-win situation for the insured. In many cases, it creates a win-win situation for the insurer that, in many states, can defeat its coverage obligation by attacking the enforceability of the indemnity agreement involved.

Whether the courts will go along with insurers on this point is unclear. Case law has not produced a case where the court was advised that the insurer was responsible for the wording that allowed coverage to be defeated in this manner. However, if the insurer requires that coverage be tied to the indemnity contract and then seeks to avoid its coverage obligation by attacking the enforceability of the indemnity wording, fairness and common sense dictate that the insurer be precluded from doing so.

If the occasion arose where only part of the contract were held to be unenforceable, presumably an additional insured provision would still apply but only to the extent of its enforceability. Examples of such cases, as noted in **Chapter 4,** are *Chrysler Corp. v Brencal Contractors,* 381 NW2d 814 (Mich 1985), and *Texaco v East Coast Management,* 719 F Supp 319 (D NJ 1989). The courts in both of these cases held that an otherwise void hold harmless agreement is still valid to the extent that at least part of the contract is lawfully enforceable.

Some umbrella liability policies contain not only an additional insured provision like the one in (A) of Exhibit 14.2 but also a provision like (B), (C), or (D). This double feature is likely to be viewed as advantageous by additional insureds because coverage is still possible in the absence of a written agreement to provide insurance or in the event a written contract of indemnity is otherwise void and unenforceable. Of course, the protection to the additional insured under provision (B), at least, is contingent on the named insured's consent. But no similar condition is applicable to provisions (C) or (D). It is unlikely that an insured could "unreasonably" withhold consent to include an insured in the underlying policy as an insured in the umbrella layer without incurring liability.

However, there may be times when even a double additional insured provision is not enough to avert problems with an umbrella policy. Take, for example, the case of *Old Republic Insurance Co. v Concast,* 588 F Supp 616 (SD NY 1984). The named insured of an umbrella liability policy was in the business of engineering and selling equipment, including products manufactured by others. This engineering firm entered into a contract—with a subcontractor that did not carry products liability insurance—that required the engineering firm to add the subcontractor to its policy as an "additional named insured." A certificate of insurance was issued showing that the subcontractor was an additional named insured on the engineering firm's primary liability policy but not under the umbrella policy.

Subsequently, three employees of the subcontractor were injured and brought suit against all of the parties. The engineering firm's primary insurer provided the subcontractor, as an insured, with defense, but the engineering firm's excess liability insurer refused to do the same. Three parts of the umbrella policy's Persons Insured provision were pertinent to this action, as follows.

The unqualified word "Assured" wherever used in this includes:

(c) any person, organization, trustee or estate to whom the Named Assured is obligated by virtue of a written contract or agreement to provide insurance such as is afforded by this policy, but only to the extent of such obligation and in respect of operations by or on behalf of the Named Assured or of facilities of the Named Assured or of facilities used by the Named Assured;

(d) any additional assured under this policy included in the underlying Insurances, subject to the provisions in Condition B; but not for broader coverage than is available to such additional Assured under any underlying insurances as set out in the attached schedule;

B.   ADDITIONAL ASSUREDS—

In the event of additional assureds being added to the coverage under the Underlying Insurances during the currency hereof, prompt notice shall be given to the Company hereon who shall be entitled to charge an additional premium hereon.

It was the engineering firm's contention that the subcontractor was automatically included by virtue of part (c) above to the same extent as the named insured for two reasons. First, the umbrella liability policy covered parties with whom the named insured had a contractual obligation to provide liability insurance. Second, the contract itself clearly evidenced that the engineering firm had such an obligation to the subcontractor.

The umbrella insurer maintained that the contract between these two parties, under which the engineering firm was required to provide and maintain insurance and to include protection for the subcontractor, was directed at the underlying liability policy alone. Evidence of this intention, the insurer said, was in the contract wherein the engineering firm, as named insured, promised to include the subcontractor as an additional named insured on the *policy* of the named insured rather than on the *policies* of the named insured. However, testimony of the parties, including the insurance broker, confirmed the intention of the parties that the subcontractor was to be included as an "additional named insured" on all the policies.

The named insured pointed out that to adopt the insurance company's interpretation of the contract between the two parties would be to "abandon common sense," because there was no reason why the subcontractor would contract for only limited liability coverage or why the named insured would assume a multimillion-dollar liability on behalf of the subcontractor. In the final analysis, the court ruled that the subcontractor was an additional named insured under part (c) of the umbrella policy. However, no opinion was expressed on whether notice was provided as required under part (d) of that same policy.

In another case, an additional insured was held to be covered but only after it had assumed the umbrella policy's self-insured retention. This imposition of the self-insured retention appears to have resulted from a misinterpretation of the umbrella policy since it applied the self-insured retention even though the primary policy applied to the claim. The case in question is *Maryland Casualty Co. v Chicago & North Western Transportation Co.,* 466 NE2d 1091 (Ill App 1984). It involved a dispute over whether the lessor of a premises was protected under the lessee's primary and umbrella liability policies. The court ruled that the lessee's primary liability policy was to cover the lessor as an additional insured.

The lessee's umbrella insurer argued that the lessor was not covered by the policy. The umbrella policy provided, in part, that the insurer:

> will indemnify the insured [lessee] for ultimate net loss in excess of the retained limit which the insured ... shall become legally obligated to pay as damages because of Personal Injury Liability ....

The retained limit was $10,000. Although the umbrella policy did not designate an additional insured, the policy did extend coverage to:

> any additional insured included in the underlying insurance but only to the extent that insurance is provided to such additional insured thereunder.

The lessor was just such an insured under the CGL policy. However, the court held that the coverage

of the umbrella policy only attached after the predetermined $10,000 retained limit was exhausted. The lessor, therefore, was required to expend an amount in defense or settlement of the case equal to the retained limit before the umbrella policy could apply.

Scope of Coverage

The fact that an umbrella liability policy automatically includes a certain kind of additional insured provision does not necessarily mean that protection will apply when needed. The reason is that some umbrella policies have certain "strings attached" that have the effect of making the protection of additional insureds subject to yet other conditions.

Extent of Additional Insured's Fault

The preconceived notion of some insurers under primary liability policies that an additional insured's protection is limited to its vicarious liability, despite what the endorsement says, also extends to some umbrella insurers. In one case, an umbrella insurer maintained that under an additional insured provision similar to provision (A) of Exhibit 14.2, reference to "but only with respect to operations by or on behalf of the Named Insured" precluded coverage for an additional insured when liability arose from the additional insured's sole fault.

In this case of *Florida Power & Light Co. v Penn America Insurance Co.,* 654 S2d 276 (Fla App 1995), Florida Power and Light (the Utility) was sued by an employee of a contractor, Eastern Utility Construction (Eastern). The employee was injured at the Utility's premises. Pursuant to the work project, Eastern entered into a contract with the Utility and was required to procure and maintain various kinds of liability insurance in a minimum amount of $300,000 per occurrence. Accordingly, before commencing work, Eastern obtained a CGL policy for limits of $500,000 per occurrence and a $1 million excess liability policy from Penn America. The additional insured provision of this excess policy provided insured status to the following.

> (a) any person or organization, trustee or estate to whom or to which the named insured is obligated by virtue of a written contract or permit to provide insurance such as is afforded by the terms of this policy, but only with respect to operations by or on behalf of the Named Insured or to facilities used by the Named Insured and then only to the extent of the "coverage required" by such contract and for the "limits of liability specified in such contract," but in no event for insurance not afforded by this policy nor for limits of liability in excess of the applicable limits of liability of this policy.

In his amended complaint, the injured employee of Eastern alleged that it was the Utility's negligence that led to the accident and injuries. The case was eventually settled for $2 million with the primary insurer tendering its limits of $500,000. However, the excess insurer filed a declaratory judgment action seeking a determination that its policy did not cover the Utility.

It was clear, said the court, that the Utility was an organization to whom Eastern, the named insured, was obligated by virtue of a written contract to provide insurance such as is afforded by this policy. The problem, from the court's perspective, was that the policy did not define "operations by or on behalf of the Named Insured," and the issue was whether the employee's injury claim came within the ambit of that undefined phrase of the policy.

Although there were no Florida cases that had dealt with this policy provision, the court did find persuasive cases from other jurisdictions. Two of these cases are discussed in this book: *Casualty Insurance Co. v Northbrook Property & Casualty Co.,* 501 NE2d 812 (Ill App 1986), and *McIntosh v Scottsdale Insurance Co.,* 92 F2d 251 (10th Cir 1993).

The court in the *Florida Power & Light* case held that there was no language in the additional insured provision of the policy that required fault on behalf of Eastern before the Utility could be considered an additional insured. Thus, the language

in question, similar to other cases referred to by the courts, can only be considered ambiguous at best. The court also stated that the language used by the umbrella insurer required only that the Utility's liability arise out of the operations of Eastern. It was obvious, the court added, that the injury and subsequent lawsuit arose out of some type of "operations" of Eastern. The umbrella insurer, therefore, did not utilize specific language limiting coverage to the vicarious liability situation. Because the language actually utilized was ambiguous at best, the additional insured provision was construed against its insurer.

Notice and Additional Premium

Some umbrella policies require that the insurer be given notice (either prompt or within 30, 60, or 90 days) if additional insured status is to be granted. If a loss occurs before the time period required for notice has expired, the fact that no notice was given will not preclude coverage.

Whether a requirement of prompt notice has been complied with will be a question of fact that often will require litigation to resolve. In many policy provisions requiring notice that additional insureds are being added, the insurer also reserves the right to charge an additional premium for the additional insured. Once notice is given, coverage applies, but there may be an additional premium required either following receipt of notice, particularly in cases when the umbrella coverage is written on a flat premium basis, or at the end of the policy period following a premium audit when the policy is not written "flat."

The case of *King v Employers National Insurance Co.,* 928 F2d 1438 (5th Cir 1991), discussed in detail later, exemplifies the problem of a prompt notice requirement and one of the various ways that requirement can be interpreted by the courts.

Both the condition concerning an additional premium and the notice provision could be incorporated within a provision entitled "Premium" or "Additional Insured." Examples of such umbrella policy conditions are included in Exhibit 14.3.

Note that provisions 1. and 2. in Exhibit 14.3 are essentially the same except as respects the matter of premium charges. Under provision 1., the additional premium has no relationship to the charge, if any, that may have been applicable with the underlying liability policy. However, in provision 2. the insurer appears to be precluded from charging a premium unless a charge has been made under the primary policy. Generally, one can assume that if an umbrella policy is written on a "flat" basis, i.e., not subject to audit, no premium charge should be assessed for an additional insured unless there is a specific provision in the policy that states otherwise, such as condition 3. below.

EXHIBIT 14.3
NOTICE AND ADDITIONAL PREMIUM REQUIREMENTS

1. In the event of additional insureds being added to the coverage under the underlying insurance during the policy period, prompt notice shall be given to the Company and the Company shall be entitled to charge an appropriate additional premium hereon.

2. In the event of additional insureds being added to the coverage under the underlying insurance prompt notice shall be given to the company and if an additional premium has been charged for such addition on the underlying insurance, the company shall be entitled to charge an appropriate additional premium hereon.

3. The premium for this policy is a flat premium and is not subject to adjustment except that additional premiums may be required for additional insureds....

These types of provisions are probably included in umbrella policies primarily to protect insurers from incurring substantial increases in exposure without having an opportunity to charge for them. If, for example, a named insured in the retailing business acquires a large toy manufacturer during the policy period, its potential exposure increases

dramatically. Without a provision of this type, there is the potential that coverage would be provided without appropriate compensation.

Depending on the terms of the agreement involved and the wording of the umbrella policy, most umbrella policies cover additional insureds if a contract with the named insured requires they be insureds. However, many of those policies provide coverage only to the extent required by the contract. As stated previously, this can lead to complex coverage disputes surrounding the enforceability of the indemnity provision and, thus, the insurer's coverage obligation under the contract wording. Most umbrella policies also cover additional insureds added to the underlying policy but usually do so only to the extent of the underlying policy. So, there can be situations where the contract requires less coverage than is normally provided by the umbrella or where the underlying policy is more restrictive than the umbrella policy. However, this is not the norm.

As a general rule, therefore, additional insureds added in compliance with contractual provisions do not materially increase the umbrella insurer's loss exposure beyond what would have been assumed under an indemnity agreement in the first place. Because of this, insurers usually waive the additional premium charge. Whenever this is done, the waiver should be in writing; otherwise, if a problem arises over the protection of an additional insured, an insurer may raise the issue of premium payment in an effort to avoid coverage.

A case in point is *The City of Northglenn, Colo. v Chevron, U.S.A.*, 634 F Supp 217 (DC Colo 1986). This case involved an oil company (the lessor) that leased its service station to an individual operator (the lessee). Under the lease agreement, the lessee was to obtain both primary and excess liability policies and to name the lessor as an additional insured. The lessee obtained a garage liability policy and an excess liability policy, both of which were signified in a certificate of insurance provided to the oil company.

The suit arose following leakage of gasoline in sewer lines near the service station that resulted in the evacuation of 42 families from the neighborhood. Subsequent investigation determined that the leakage had occurred from an underground line connecting the tanks to the station's dispensers. The city and some of its residents filed suit against the lessor for bodily injury and property damage caused by the leakage.

The excess policy, as issued, was a master policy that not only covered all of the lessee-dealers but also clearly named the lessor as an insured on the policy. Despite that fact, the excess liability insurer maintained that it was not the intent that the lessor be an insured because it did not pay any premiums for the protection. Instead, each lessee paid a premium for individual coverage. However, the excess liability policy was silent as to any additional premium requirements for additional insureds.

In any event, the Colorado court held against the insurer, stating that it was not a prerequisite to the status of being an insured that one undertake or perform a duty to pay premiums. Since there was no specific reference regarding the additional insured's payment of premium, the lessor, as additional insured, was not responsible for the payment of premium and coverage was not conditioned on such payment.

Another case in point is *King v Employers National Insurance Co.,* 928 F2d 1438 (5th Cir 1991). A general contractor (GC) contracted with a subcontractor (SC) to construct a sewer main. During the work, two employees were injured when a crane leased by the GC collapsed. Both employees, after collecting workers compensation benefits, filed a suit against the crane owner and its manufacturer. The compensation insurer also sought reimbursement for the benefits it had paid. However, the crane owner maintained that it was an additional insured under the policies of the GC.

At the time of this accident, the GC had three layers of general liability insurance: a primary policy with limits of $500,000, an excess policy with limits of $500,000 excess of the primary, and an umbrella policy with limits of $5 million. The primary insurer listed the crane owner as an additional insured and conceded that the owner was covered

under its policy. However, the district court ruled that the excess policy only covered named insureds and not additional insureds. While the court agreed that the umbrella policy covered the crane owner as an additional insured, the policy did not "step down" to cover the layer of insurance provided by the excess insurer. This ruling left the crane owner with a $500,000 gap in coverage.

On appeal, the crane owner conceded it was not a named insured on the excess policy. It contended it was an "other insured" under that policy because it was an additional insured in the underlying policy. The excess liability policy did not define the term "insured" but did contain the following language: "The provisions of the immediate underlying policy are incorporated as part of this policy except for ... provisions therein which are inconsistent with this policy." Thus, the crane owner argued, because the primary policy provides coverage for the crane owner, the excess policy also covers the crane owner as long as that coverage is not inconsistent with the excess policy. The court, on appeal, agreed with the crane owner. In doing so, it stated that it did not find the addition of the crane owner as an insured to be inconsistent but, instead, to be "supplemental."

However, the excess insurer argued that it was not promptly notified of the crane owner's addition as an insured. The court noted, however, that the excess policy did not require that notice of additional insureds be given. Instead, it required that prompt notice be given "for any change in *coverage* of the underlying insurance." In the Declarations page of the policy, "coverage" includes general risks such as bodily injury and property damage. Thus, said the court, the word "coverage," as used in the excess policy, referred to the nature of the risks insured against and not to the parties insured. The higher court, therefore, reversed the district court's judgment, denying the crane owner additional insured status under the excess liability policy.

The umbrella insurer also filed an appeal objecting to the district court's decision that the crane owner was an additional insured. The umbrella policy, unlike the excess policy, defined "insured" as including "any other person or organization who is an additional insured under any underlying policy of insurance." Because the crane owner was an additional insured on the underlying policy, the court held that the owner was an insured under the umbrella policy. However, the umbrella insurer argued that the following provision in its policy negated coverage for an additional insured such as the crane owner.

> *Additions.* In the event additional Insureds or additional coverages are added to the underlying insurance while this policy is in force, prompt notice shall be given to the Company and the Company shall be entitled to charge appropriate additional premium.

The umbrella insurer argued that because it did not receive "prompt notice" that the crane owner was an additional insured in the underlying policy, its umbrella policy did not cover the crane owner. The court, on the other hand, noted that the "prompt notice" provision was designed to give the insurer two options. It allows the insurer to evaluate whether to charge an additional premium or to cancel the policy upon giving 30 days' notice of its intent to do so. "These limitations in the notice provision persuade us that the provision is not a condition of coverage," the court said. Thus, failure to give the umbrella insurer prompt notice of the crane owner's addition as an insured in the underlying policy did not void coverage under the umbrella policy.

Whether a premium charge is made or not, many umbrella policies make additional insured coverage contingent on notice to the insurer. The named insured or whoever is servicing the policy on behalf of the named insured must understand these kinds of conditions to avoid breaches of conditions that may lead to coverage disputes, especially since additional insureds rarely have the opportunity to review such policies.

The decision in *King* makes good sense. Additional insureds do not have the opportunity to see these kinds of notice conditions and, therefore, have to rely on the named insured to see to it that protection is effected properly. In time of dispute, however, the additional insured should not be penalized because notice was not given by the named insured as required. Likewise, the protection should not be nullified by the named insured's oversight because it also could have the effect of creating a breach of contract on the named insured's behalf for failing to procure the protection it may have promised under contract.

The decision in *King*, while it makes sense, is not uniformly applied. As discussed earlier, requirements of prompt notice are inherently subjective, given that the facts of a particular case will dictate what is prompt in any given scenario. The problem with this subjectiveness is that it usually requires litigation to resolve.

A case holding the opposite of *King* and demonstrating the fact that different jurisdictions view this issue differently is *MND Drilling Corp. v Harold Lloyd,* 866 SW2d 29 (Tex App 1987). This case involved an umbrella policy that provided automatic additional insured status to any entity included as an additional insured in the underlying insurance. However, that additional insured protection was contingent on the named insured providing prompt notice of additional insureds added to the underlying policy and reserved the right for the insurer to charge an additional premium (as required by Condition B).

The named insured failed to provide notice when the additional insured was added to the underlying policy. However, the named insured argued it had complied with the prompt notice requirement because it had paid an additional premium based on an audit of its payroll. Nowhere was it reflected that the additional premium was for any additional insureds. The court held that there was no room for ordinary minds to differ on the facts. Prompt notice, the court held, must mean at least notice given within a reasonable time in light of the circumstances. The court then ruled that the imposition of an unrelated additional premium did not constitute prompt notice.

What was not addressed by the court was the effect of Condition B outside of the confines of the notice requirement. Condition B is not an exclusion. It is a condition precedent to coverage. The named insured in *MND* could have paid the additional premium at the time of audit, designated it as such and there would be no problems, or made it at any time subject to the caveat that if payment is made or tendered well into litigation there may be objections that a court might entertain. Failure of the named insured to designate the additional premium as being in part for the additional insured added to the underlying policy precluded the court in the *MND* case from finding that an additional premium had been paid for the additional insured.

However, because Condition B is a condition and not an exclusion, all that would have been required to comply with this condition was the payment of an additional premium, which the named insured could have paid at any time, even after the initial audit. Once the additional premium has been paid, Condition B has been complied with. The question then would be whether the payment came too late in relation to the loss and the proceedings under way.

The prudent thing for insureds to do in these situations is to tender the additional premium required immediately upon notice of a loss that involves the additional insured. That payment would create compliance with Condition B, subject to legal doctrines of reliance, estoppel, and others that could be raised if the additional premium were paid so long after the loss and well into litigation as to make it irrelevant.

Another issue that arises in this context is the insurer's duty to notify the insured that the additional premium has not been paid so as to facilitate the timely payment of that obligation. Once a claim is tendered to the insurer, the insurer knows full well that the insured is relying on coverage that would apply if the additional premium were to be paid. Failure to alert the insured of this fact could be argued as being a waiver of the insurer's right to rely on that condition to defeat coverage.

Because the term "prompt" is subjective and often requires litigation to interpret, it should be labeled as ambiguous and interpreted in favor of insureds. Provisions requiring notice as soon as practicable are easier to understand in that they take into ac-

count the fact that each factual scenario will pose its own obstacles to providing notice. While this, too, is somewhat subjective, it puts insurers on notice that they must accommodate such circumstances. Prompt notice requirements tend to cause more rigidity in the insurers' position on this issue and, in essence, promote litigation.

For an insurer to maintain that the rationale behind the notice provision also is to preclude coverage for certain entities it does not want to protect as additional insureds even if notice had been prompt also would work a hardship on named insureds that otherwise agree to add others as additional insureds—particularly since an umbrella policy is designed to cover catastrophic liability exposures. In most cases, the addition of insureds does not increase the risk since, apart from the concept of severability, the additional insured receives no greater protection than the named insured.

Finally, the umbrella underwriter has the obligation to request information about additional insureds under primary policies. If a primary policy, for example, contains a blanket additional insured endorsement, the umbrella underwriter should know that and take it into consideration, but it is up to the underwriter to obtain the facts.

Underlying Coverage Prerequisite

Another important consideration about the protection of additional insureds under umbrella policies is the scope of coverage afforded in the underlying policy. Many umbrella policies contain a specific declaration to the effect that the additional insured's protection is for coverage no broader than that provided by underlying liability insurance. Therefore, what coverage the additional insured receives from the umbrella policy commonly is less than the protection received by the policy's named insured.

Additional insureds are not always concerned about the scope of coverage provided by umbrella policies, because in many instances they assume that they will be the beneficiaries of the broader coverage usually provided by this form of excess coverage, in addition to the additional limits it makes available. This assumption is premised on the expectation insureds have regarding the broad scope of umbrella coverage in general. This expectation is difficult to overcome, given that additional insureds rarely have the opportunity to review the umbrella policy to which they have been or will be added.

An umbrella policy that is modified with a "broad as primary" endorsement certainly would be welcomed by an additional insured if it knew such an endorsement existed. On the other hand, an overly restrictive contractor's limitation endorsement would not be a desirable addition to the umbrella policy. But the existence of either of the two endorsements is not disclosed to anyone other than the policyholder in most cases.

Applicable Limits of Liability

Provisions in umbrella liability policies that automatically include as insureds those persons and organizations that are covered by the underlying liability policy are usually viewed as advantageous for both indemnitors and indemnitees. If the additional insured is added to a program of insurance that involves several layers of coverage—primary, umbrella, and excess—the additional insured is entitled to coverage under all those layers in the event a loss exceeds the primary layer of coverage. This will be the result, regardless of the amount of insurance required in the underlying contract. As was previously stated, the underlying contract can only affect contractual liability coverage.

This also would be the case where the additional insured wording limited coverage to that required by contract. However, as pointed out previously, this requirement is dangerous for the insurer and the additional insured. If the underlying contract is deemed to be invalid and the insurer's coverage obligation is defeated because the insurer required that coverage be tied to the contract, the insurer may find that it is required to provide coverage regardless of an invalid indemnity requirement.

The reason underlying the listing of specific coverages and limits in contracts usually is not to restrict the amount or scope of coverage that will be required or provided. The purpose usually is to establish a minimum limit and coverage scope that must be maintained. Giving careful consideration to the inherent risks associated with performance of the contract and establishing a minimum limit sets a benchmark for potential service providers or project bidders. It allows contractors and others that do not have in place limits of coverage larger than the minimum specified in the contract to bid without having to pay additional and sometimes prohibitive premiums to compete with larger entities. This custom and practice is evident from the fact that the contractual indemnity provisions do not usually cap indemnitors' potential liability to the amount of required insurance. The contractor's or service provider's liability under the indemnity agreement can substantially exceed its liability insurance limits.

Absent a policy provision specifying that coverage is limited to that required by the contract, additional insured status is not dependent on or limited by the underlying contract. Coverage applies based on the terms of the policy. Where the additional insured is included in a program with multiple layers of coverage absent policy wording to the contrary, all layers apply to a loss.

A layered excess liability program is designed to interact. Each layer provides an orderly transfer of the defense and/or indemnity obligation from one layer to another. If the insurers in layers above the primary policy desire to preclude their application to additional insureds, the policies must be endorsed to do so. That, in turn, would be difficult to do in a blanket approach. Instead, underwriters would have to identify each exposure on a case-by-case basis, which is simply not a common industry practice.

The argument has been made that this is not an intended result, but this argument lacks validity, because it is, in fact, an intended result. Underwriters do not preclude the application of all layers of coverage despite knowledge that they may apply in the event of a large loss involving more than one layer of the named insured's insurance program. Likewise, it is rarely the intent of an additional insured to limit its coverage to the primary layer when the exposure is much greater.

The named insured also benefits from making all layers available. If the additional insured's loss is caused by the named insured or arises out of the named insured's operations, it will be required to indemnify the additional insured in most instances. Therefore, making all layers of coverage available to the additional insured changes very little. Whether by common law indemnity obligations, contractual liability coverage, or suits against the named insured by the additional insured, all layers of coverage will likely get involved. If the insurer endorses coverage to preclude excess layers of coverage from applying to the additional insured, the named insured could end up paying the loss out of its own pocket if coverage is not otherwise available in one of the ways previously set forth, as might be the case where the indemnity clause in the contract is held to be invalid.

There are other practical reasons for making all layers of coverage available to the additional insured. In most cases, there is no additional premium charged for adding additional insureds. Even in those cases where insurers reserve the right to charge an additional premium, that cost is usually passed along in the contract price. One result is that in the event of a loss and resulting litigation, the additional insured and the named insured can present a united front instead of blaming one another and creating bad publicity. Because both are insureds under the same policy, disputes between the insureds are kept at a minimum.

Despite all of this, umbrella insurers do, in fact, argue that the additional insured's protection is limited to the minimum amount of liability limits required by the contract. For example, a contract may require that the named insured provide a liability insurance policy for limits of $1 million. If the primary policy is subject to a combined single limit of $500,000, the umbrella insurer may maintain that the additional insured's protection is limited to no more than $500,000, since the combination of the primary and the umbrella policy limits

will be equal to the $1 million limit as specified in the contract.

To overcome these kinds of arguments by umbrella insurers, contracts of prospective additional insureds sometimes specify that the amount of liability insurance to be carried shall be for "not less than" a certain specified limit.[3] Assume, for example, that the combined single limit of a CGL policy is $500,000. To get into the higher layers of another's umbrella insurance program, the specifications may not designate a CGL policy but only the coverages usual to a CGL and business auto policy, and require that the liability insurance be for no less than, say, $5 million.

A case that exemplifies this is *Valentine v Aetna Insurance Co.,* 564 F2d 292 (9th Cir 1977). A general contractor on an apartment project subcontracted the installation of equipment to a heating company. The contract required that the heating contractor procure liability insurance coverage "of not less than $300,000/$500,000 per occurrence" to protect the general contractor against liability for damages because of injuries sustained by persons.

The subcontractor named the general contractor as an additional insured on an endorsement to the subcontractor's primary liability policy, which provided coverage for limits of $100,000. This endorsement made the general contractor an additional insured "only as respects their interest as they may appear in work performed for them by" the subcontractor. This endorsement also stated that the subcontractor's liability policy was primary and that any insurance carried by the additional insured would be excess and in no way contributing. The subcontractor also maintained a follow form umbrella policy that provided limits of $1 million excess of the $100,000 primary limits. The general contractor maintained liability insurance consisting of a primary policy for limits of $200,000 and an excess liability policy for $2 million excess of the primary limits.

An employee of the subcontractor was injured on the job and brought suit against the general contractor. Since the subcontractor's insurance companies denied coverage, the general contractor looked to its own insurer for defense. The general contractor's excess insurer paid the judgment and then brought suit seeking contribution from the subcontractor's insurance companies. The lower court ultimately decided that the subcontractor's primary and excess insurance covered the general contractor. On appeal, the subcontractor's excess insurer argued that even if the subcontractor's primary and excess policies provided coverage for the accident, such coverage should have been limited to a total of $300,000, because the subcontractor agreed to procure "not less than" $300,000 coverage. However, the higher court in this case found that the contract language between the two parties did not support a restriction on the terms of the umbrella policy because the contract only set a floor—not a ceiling—on the coverage provided.

The *National Union Fire Insurance Co. v Glenview Park District,* 594 NE2d 1300 (Ill App 1992), case, discussed in **Chapter 20,** also involved the applicability of umbrella liability coverage and the appropriate limit for that part of a suit not covered by the primary policy. The umbrella insurer argued that because its named insured (the contractor) did not agree in writing with the public entity (the additional insured) to obtain excess and umbrella liability insurance, the public entity was not deemed to be an insured under the policy. The written contract between the parties included the following insurance requirement.

> The contractor shall secure and maintain in his own name with the Glenview Park District specifically noted as an additional insured, Public Liability insurance covering Bodily Injury and Property Damage with limits of not less than $1 million [per occurrence and in the aggregate].

The court found that the public entity was an insured under the policy. The contractor had agreed in writing to secure public liability insurance naming the public entity as an additional insured. The court also stated that the insurer's umbrella policy constituted public liability insurance. (The term "public liability" was used to connote what is currently referred to as "general liability" insurance. Since both public liability and general liability are generic terms that are encompassed by the kind of coverages that an umbrella policy provides, the court's opinion appears to be appropriate.)

The fact that the policy provided for greater coverage than the minimum prescribed by the contract also did not vitiate the policy's inclusion of the public entity as an additional insured. The certificate of insurance, which stated that it conveyed no right to the holder, designated the public entity as an additional insured that listed four policies of insurance. The umbrella policy with limits of $2 million was, therefore, required to respond on behalf of the additional insured.

To avoid providing more limits than requested—or paid for under the terms of a contract—the limits of insurance provided to the additional insured might be capped. One technique that has been used on occasion is to add to the umbrella policy special wording dealing with the application of limits. For example, at least one umbrella is subject to the following provision.

> The limits of liability as applicable to this policy shall be available first to the named insured. Any remaining limits will then be made available to any additional insureds covered by this policy.

Unfortunately, this wording could place the named insured (indemnitor) in breach of contract. Most contracts obligate the indemnitor, (usually the named insured) to provide additional insured status and usually for a minimum amount. Because additional insured status contemplates all coverage available under the policy, this type of restrictive wording may not be in compliance with the insurance required in many agreements used today. Insurers are aware of the requirements imposed on their insureds in providing additional insured status.

As a result, it will become increasingly difficult for insurers to avoid liability for provisions such as this one that are or should be known to place many insureds in breach of contract or that are substantially certain to do so in many cases. In the past, this was not a serious problem, because coverage litigation was not as prevalent as it is today. However, given the enormous number of coverage disputes today, particularly disputes involving additional insured status, this type of wording will become increasingly troublesome for insurers and insureds alike. Breach of contract for outright failure to provide additional insured status is discussed later.

Another technique is to specify in the additional insured endorsement, as attached to the umbrella policy or within the umbrella policy's provision dealing with additional insureds, that the additional insured is covered for an amount equal to the lesser of the limits required in the contract or the policy limit. There are at least two dangers in taking this approach. First, it is difficult to draft wording that clearly communicates the intent. For example, such clauses can sometimes be read to imply that the limit provided to the additional insured is separate and in addition to the existing policy limits. In other words, there is a risk that trying to impose this limitation could actually create ambiguities in the wording that may be interpreted by a court to actually expand coverage.

The second danger with attempting to cap the limits provided to additional insureds to the limit required in the contract is that this may conflict with the indemnity provision and result in a coverage dispute. For example, assume that a lessor includes a hold harmless agreement in its lease along with a requirement that the lessee purchase $1 million of liability coverage and include the lessor as an additional insured. Further assume that the lessee actually purchases $10 million of coverage and a situation arises wherein the lessor is found liable for $5 million as a result of the tenant's negligence.

There is no contractually imposed dollar limitation on the amount of liability transferred to the lessee by the indemnity provision. Therefore, a $1 million limitation on the coverage provided to the lessor as an additional insured would conflict with the provision of the insured's full limits that the lessor would receive through the tenant's contractual liability coverage. In such a situation, the lessor should probably receive the full limits under the tenant's contractual liability coverage if the hold harmless clause was deemed valid but only the $1 million it required if the clause was held invalid.

However, it is difficult to draft a clause that clearly conveys this intent, and it is impossible to predict how such a dispute would ultimately be resolved by a court of law.

As stated earlier in this chapter, there are a number of practical reasons why insureds want to make all layers of coverage available to additional insureds. Primary among these is that it is impossible to quantify liability assumed under contract, and additional insured status can be used to buttress that responsibility if necessary. Covering additional insureds for all layers does not prejudice the named insured, given that its liability is there in any event and thus the coverage would apply regardless of whether all layers of coverage apply directly to the named insured or are tapped when the additional insured sues the named insured. There may be situations where the named insured would not have liability for all the coverage conferred on the additional insured. However, the risk of not making all limits available to the additional insured is greater than any cost or expense in doing so routinely.

Also, as previously discussed, the technical problems involved in drafting policy wording to limit coverage for the additional insured, the potential that the named insured would be held in breach of contract for allowing such a limitation, and the extensive underwriter involvement necessary to make it work means it is unlikely that there will be any concerted effort to change the way additional insured coverage applies in this regard.

In summary, named insureds generally should not allow their insurers to cap the limits provided to additional insureds unless the named insureds negotiate a cap into the indemnity provision. To cap coverage in one respect but not the other is likely to lead to litigation.

Breach of Contract

The subject of breach of contract for failing to add another party to a liability policy as an additional insured is more fully discussed in **Chapter 21**. However, one case involving an excess liability policy is more appropriately discussed in this chapter because it also involves the issue of minimum limits.

In *Musgrove v Southland Corp.,* 898 F2d 1041 (5th Cir 1990), an electrical contractor was supposed to have added an oil refinery as an additional insured on its liability policies, but it failed to do so. When the refinery was sued and sought protection under the contractor's liability insurance program, coverage was denied. The refinery argued that the contractor's excess liability policy should have provided protection—because of the policy's automatic additional insured feature—even though the limits required would have been satisfied by the contractor's primary liability policy. The refinery that sought protection for higher limits, therefore, was unable to obtain the benefit of the contractor's excess coverage.

This case arose following the death of two employees of the electrical contractor who were performing work at the oil refinery. At the time of the accident, the contractor carried a CGL policy with limits of $1 million and an excess liability policy for an undisclosed amount. Despite contractual obligations requiring it to do so, the contractor failed to name the refinery as an additional insured on either of its liability policies until after the accident. The lower court ultimately held against coverage in light of the breach, and the refinery appealed.

The refinery argued that once its contract with the contractor was executed, the refinery automatically became an insured under the contractor's excess liability policy. It maintained that the contractor's excess liability policy should "drop down" to cover losses under $1 million in the event the contractor's primary liability policy provided no coverage. The refinery based its argument on the definition of "insured" in the excess liability policy, which included:

> any person, organization, trustee or estate to whom or to which the Named Insured is obligated by virtue of a written contract to provide insurance such as is provided by this policy.

The refinery's purchase order contract with the contractor obligated the contractor to provide comprehensive general liability insurance up to $1 million per occurrence for the contractor and the refinery. The court ruled, however, that because the excess liability policy only covered those losses in excess of $1 million, that policy did not afford the coverage that the contractor's contract with the refinery required.

However, the refinery argued that its contractor's manual—incorporated in the purchase order contract by reference—obligated the contractor to provide the refinery with coverage afforded by the excess liability policy. The pertinent manual section provided as follows.

> 2.2.1 All insurance coverages carried by the Contractor, *whether or not required hereby,* ... shall extend to and protect Company ... to the full amount of such coverage, but not less than the following shall be provided: [Emphasis added.]
>
> ... c. Comprehensive General Liability insurance ... not less than $1,000,000 per occurrence.
>
> 2.2.5 ADDITIONAL NAMED INSURED— Contractor shall cause the insurance company to name Company as an additional insured on all of the above insurance ....

According to the refinery, under the foregoing provision, the contractor's voluntary decision to obtain excess liability coverage for itself triggered an obligation to obtain the same coverage for the refinery. The court disagreed. It explained that the purchase order contract specifically limited the CGL coverage that the contractor was required to obtain for itself and the refinery to $1 million per occurrence. According to the manual, the court stated, the contract prevailed in any conflict. Thus, any effort to use manual section 2.2.1 to increase the coverage required of the contractor above the level required by the contract was without force. Alternatively, the court said, the manual could be construed to avoid conflict by reading section 2.2.1 to provide that the contractor's voluntary decision to obtain additional coverage for itself included the prerogative of obtaining additional coverage for the refinery. However, the decision to obtain the additional coverage, said the court, was strictly voluntary.

Inherent in the court's ruling is the concept underlying contractual liability coverage that the underlying contract's terms dictate the scope of coverage required. In this case, the terms of the contract simply did not require the insured to do what the refinery asserted it should have done.

The court also found that the contractor was required by contract to name the refinery as an additional insured on its primary insurance but failed to do so. The refinery argued that the contractor's primary liability policy provided the refinery with protection for this breach under the primary policy's blanket contractual liability coverage. (The refinery made this same argument with respect to the contractor's excess liability policy too. But because of the court's finding that the contractor was not required to provide excess liability coverage, the contractor did not breach its contract by failing to do so under the excess liability policy.)

The court reviewed a number of cases from other jurisdictions on whether failure to procure insurance for additional insureds is deemed to be covered by contractual liability insurance, such as the case of *Olympic, Inc. v Providence Washington Insurance Co.,* 648 P2d 1008 (Alaska 1982). It then ruled with the majority that such breach is not deemed to be within the scope of contractual liability coverage.

Excess Liability Policies

While the terms "excess liability policy" and "umbrella liability policy" are often used synonymously, they are not the same. For the purpose of this book at least, an excess liability policy is one used to provide limits in excess of an underlying liability policy (usually an umbrella liability policy). An excess liability policy is no broader than the underlying liability policy; its sole purpose is to provide additional limits. An excess liability policy, therefore, does not need a self-insured retention provision since it will not cover a loss that is uninsured by the policies below it.

While excess liability policies will drop down over reduced or exhausted underlying aggregate limits in some cases, they will not drop down and act as a primary policy when the underlying insurance does not apply. That type of drop down feature is unique to the umbrella policy.

It is important to note that while it is desirable to obtain an excess liability policy on a strictly "follow form" basis, it is usually not possible to do so. Unfortunately, many of the excess liability policies offered today state that they are follow form except with respect to certain conditions or exclusions. Generally speaking, three excess liability policy formats are in use today: true follow form, conditional follow form, and stand-alone. True follow form coverage consists of a paragraph or two stating that all coverage terms of the underlying policy are adopted and that the excess layer will follow those terms and conditions, the only exception being policy limits.

Under a conditional follow form excess policy, the terms and conditions of the underlying policy are also adopted but only to the extent that those underlying terms and conditions do not conflict with the terms of the excess policy. The format includes many of its own terms and conditions that control in the event that they conflict with the terms of the underlying policy.

A stand-alone excess policy provides coverage on its own terms and conditions. There is no follow form provision; this form of excess coverage is self-contained. In many ways, it resembles an umbrella policy without the drop down feature.

Whenever an excess liability policy contains the preamble that reads, "Except as otherwise provided by this policy ...," it is a good indication that there are exceptions, and the excess liability policy is not a true follow form even if it is referred to as such. Examples of provisions included in excess liability policies that govern the extent to which they follow form are included in Exhibit 14.4.

EXHIBIT 14.4
EXCESS POLICY FOLLOW FORM PROVISIONS

True Follow Form

This [excess liability] policy incorporates the terms and conditions of the underlying policy, number ... as issued by ... Insurance Company, except with respect to the limit of liability provision.

In the event of any conflict between the terms and conditions of this [excess liability] policy and the underlying policy, as designated above, the terms and conditions of the underlying policy shall control.

Follow Form with Exceptions

Except as otherwise provided by this policy, the insurance afforded herein shall follow the terms, conditions, definitions and exclusions of the controlling underlying liability policy designated in the declarations.

Follow Form with Exceptions

The insurance afforded by this policy is subject to the same warranties, terms, conditions and exclusions as are contained in the underlying insurance, except, unless otherwise specifically provided in this policy, any such warranties, terms, conditions or exclusions relating to premium, the obligation to investigate and defend, the amount and limits of liability, any renewal agreement.

With the exception of the stand-alone format, and even then in some cases, the Persons Insured provisions of excess liability policies, regardless of whether other provisions follow form, are not as extensive as they are with umbrella liability policies. The reason is that excess liability policies generally are meant to include those same insureds that are protected by underlying umbrella and primary liability policies.

If an excess liability policy is on a true follow form basis, it should not contain a Persons Insured provision at all. The provision of the underlying policy, instead, should be automatically incorpo-

rated by reference into the follow form. However, the fact that an excess liability policy is not a true follow form does not necessarily mean that the nature of the insureds is any less than under any follow form policy, even if the Persons Insured provision of the excess liability policy is briefer than the provision of the policy it follows or the lead policy. Two typical excess liability policy insured provisions are provided in Exhibit 14.5.

Who qualifies as an insured under a policy that is subject to provision (A) in Exhibit 14.5 depends largely on who is deemed to be an insured in the "Immediate Underlying Policy," as defined. Insofar as insureds are concerned, this provision of the excess liability policy is follow form. The fact that provision (B) in Exhibit 14.5 does not specifically refer to the insured provision of an underlying policy does not mean that the kinds of insureds necessarily are limited. Say, for example, that an umbrella policy written beneath an excess liability policy subject to provision (B) wording includes as an insured anyone to whom the named insured is obligated by virtue of a written contract to provide liability insurance. While provision (B) does not specifically state that it would encompass such additional insureds, it nonetheless would include them because it contains follow form provisions relating back to the umbrella form. The reference to the word "includes" in provision (B) means the phrase should be interpreted not as a limiting statement but as an expansive one. For example, the *American Heritage Dictionary, Second College Edition*, states that "*include* is used most appropriately before an incomplete list of components."

EXHIBIT 14.5
EXCESS LIABILITY INSURED PROVISIONS

(A) "Insured" means the Named Insured and any other insured as defined in the Immediate Underlying Policy.

(B) The word "insured" includes the Named Insured and/or any officer, director, stockholder, partner or employee of the Named Insured, while acting in his capacity as such.

What this means is that while persons who fit the titles or capacities as listed in provision (B) are unquestionably insureds for purposes of that policy, those who also are deemed insureds in underlying policies may also qualify as insureds in the excess liability policy. If this were not so, provision (B) of the excess policy would have been more appropriately worded by substituting the word "means" for the word "includes." It is not the purpose of the excess liability policy to reinvent the wheel but instead to reflect more accurately the policy's intent with less verbiage.

Additional Insureds and Other Insurance

One of the more controversial issues that involves umbrella and excess liability policies concerns the application of other insurance provisions. Much of the reason for the controversy is that most such policies contain other insurance provisions specifying that they apply on an excess basis rather than on a contributing basis. These provisions conflict whenever there is more than one such policy, and that conflict often is difficult to reconcile. This is unlike primary liability policies where the possibility of other insurance is recognized and taken into consideration in consummating an equitable apportionment of insurance limits in most cases.

Compounding the problem of other insurance provisions within umbrella and excess liability policies is the frustration that both named insureds and additional insureds experience when other insurance provisions do not result in equitable loss adjustments as anticipated by the respective parties. These problems are much like the ones that confront additional insureds under primary policies, as discussed in **Chapter 5.**

The umbrella policy's named insured may desire that an additional insured be given preferential treatment as dictated by a contract between the two parties. After all, if the protection is not provided as agreed to by the parties, the named insured may still be answerable to the additional insured. Yet, the named insured may not want to give the additional insured a free rein on all of the

limits of insurance as may be available to the named insured.

Equally as frustrating to the additional insured is the situation where, instead of obtaining a certain amount of primary protection under the named insured's umbrella policy, the additional insured's own umbrella policy also is required to contribute on a pro rata basis with the named insured's umbrella policy. What must be especially disconcerting to the additional insured is when both its primary and umbrella liability policies are taken into consideration, along with the named insured's primary and umbrella liability policies, in determining the respective parties' contribution for damages, instead of viewing the additional insured's insurance as excess of the named insured's insurance portfolio.

A case in point is *Liberty Mutual Insurance Co. v Pacific Indemnity Co.,* 579 F Supp 140 (WD Pa 1984). This case involved a store owner who maintained a CGL policy with a limit of $100,000 and an umbrella liability policy with a limit of $10 million. The other party was a cement company that had purchased a CGL policy with a limit of $100,000 and an umbrella liability policy with a limit of $5 million. Both liability policies of the cement company listed the store owner as an additional insured. While the apparent intent of the store owner's request to be an additional insured on the cement company's insurance policies was to defer the store owner's policies as a secondary source of protection, the court did not see it that way. The court instead concluded that the primary liability policies of both the store owner and the cement company stood on equal footing. As a result, both shared in the payment of damages as well as the legal costs.

Since each party contended that the other's umbrella policy was primary, the final question that had to be resolved dealt with the respective parties' excess liability policies. After taking into consideration each of the policies' other insurance provisions, the court concluded that since the policies' other insurance provisions conflicted with one another, they were to be disregarded and each was to stand on its own merits. But, because the additional insured store owner's umbrella policy limit was $10 million (and it presumably charged more for its coverage according to the court) and the named insured cement company's umbrella liability policy limit was $5 million, each of the umbrella insurers was required to pay the damages on a pro rata basis according to the limits of the respective policies.

In the final analysis, the store owner's request to be an additional insured on the cement company's liability policies no doubt fell short of the store owner's expectations. The court evidently missed the entire point for the store owner's request to be an additional insured on the liability policies of the cement company, although perhaps the rationale for additional insured protection was not explained properly. This case exemplifies how the very purpose for additional insured status can be defeated when there is a misunderstanding about the underlying intent.

This is another example of the importance of utilizing both additional insured status and contractual liability coverage. If both forms of protection are in place and the underlying contract clearly requires that the indemnitor's policy apply on a primary basis, the issue of other insurance could be resolved by relying on contractual liability coverage.

Often the question is asked, "Which form of coverage, additional insured status or contractual liability coverage, applies when both are required?" The answer is whichever form gets the job done. In the *Liberty Mutual* case, contractual liability coverage properly presented to the court could have resolved the other insurance issue by invoking contractual liability coverage and pointing out contract wording dictating which policy applies on a primary basis.

Summary

Many of the problems with additional insured status in umbrella and excess policies are identical to those that involve primary liability policies. However, the method by which additional insured status is automatically granted may create some unique problems with respect to reporting to the insurer, premium payment, and the provision of excessive limits of liability.

The provisions that automatically include additional insureds should be reviewed. If necessary, they should be amended to avoid overly demanding reporting requirements. If the parties agree to limit the application of coverage to one layer or a specific amount, then the contract must be clear that both the level of indemnity under the hold harmless agreement and the amount of insurance available to the indemnitee as an additional insured are to be capped. All potentially applicable policies would have to be endorsed accordingly.

Chapter 14 Notes

1. A tool that makes umbrella coverage analysis easier is *Commercial Liability Insurance,* published by International Risk Management Institute, Inc., Dallas, TX. It includes comparisons of more than 200 policy forms.

2. Of course, the named insured also must be aware of the additional insured's needs and ensure that such needs are provided for, if reasonable. Otherwise, the named insured might still be held answerable if the additional insured's needs are not met. Thus, those who service accounts must be cognizant of not only the needs of their clients but also the needs of others who deal with their clients.

3. A number of cases have dealt with the "not less than" certain specified limit with mixed results. In the following cases, for example, the "not less than" language clearly established a minimum—not a maximum—coverage requirement: *Lirett v Union Tex. Petroleum Corp.,* 467 S2d 29 (La App 1985) [construing Texas law]; *Maxus Exploration v*

Moran Bros., 773 SW2d 358 (Tex App 1989).

In the following cases, the "not less than" language clearly meant a minimum and a maximum, thus precluding an additional insured for enjoying the higher limits maintained by the named insured: *Forest Oil Corp. v Strata Energy,* 929 F2d 1039 (5th Cir 1991); *Rupp v American Crystal Sugar Co.,* 465 NW2d 614 (ND 1991). The rulings in these cases reflect the fact that the automatic additional insured coverage in the umbrella policies involved was limited to the contractual obligations. This form of additional insured coverage, as previously discussed, is nothing more than contractual liability coverage. As such, it can lead to many problems as discussed earlier. Clear contract wording requiring that all coverage available to the indemnitor and applicable to a loss be made available to the indemnitee would have eliminated any confusion. All layers of coverage available then would apply even with policy wording limiting coverage to contractual requirements.

Chapter 15

COMMERCIAL AUTO INSURANCE

The primary focus of this book is on additional insured status with respect to commercial general liability (CGL) and umbrella liability insurance because it is with these policies that most problems and concerns arise. However, questions also arise concerning the need for additional insured status in other types of commercial insurance. This chapter answers some of the questions regarding additional insured status and related issues in commercial auto insurance. **Chapter 16** focuses on additional insured status and workers compensation insurance, and **Chapter 18** addresses property insurance concerns.

In 1898 automobile insurance first was made available in the United States. During those early years, only the named insured (i.e., the owner of the insured auto) was covered by the policy. It was not until 1918 that an endorsement first became available to cover persons while operating the auto with the knowledge and permission of the owner and named insured.[1]

The first standard automobile policy was introduced for use in 1936. In time, the provisions specifying who was insured under the policy were structured to encompass three broad categories of insureds: (1) the named insured (owner) of the specified auto(s), (2) permissive users, and (3) any person or organization legally responsible for the use of such automobile by the owner or permissive user.[2]

The moniker "omnibus" was assigned to the provisions used to designate covered persons or organizations under early automobile policies because the policy automatically encompassed virtually anyone who could be liable for an insured vehicle. The precise definition of "insured"

was "any person using the automobile, provided the actual use thereof is with the permission of the named insured." (The term "omnibus" is a word that connotes a "vehicle designed to carry a comparatively large number of passengers."[3]) Although the current designation of Who Is an Insured is not as broad as the earlier definition, the term "omnibus clause" is still commonly used, particularly with respect to issues involving additional insured status under auto insurance policies. It has been said that with its introduction, the auto policy's omnibus clause became the focal point of more litigation than any other clause of the policy.

The problems over permissive use have centered on (1) how the policy was to apply when the permissive user—rather than the auto's owner—was at fault, (2) the application and extent of express or implied permission beyond the auto's original permittee, and (3) the meaning of the word "use." These problems are discussed in this chapter.

Severability of Interests

The 1955 edition of the automobile policy first addressed how the policy was to apply if a claim was brought against one or more of several insureds under the policy. It was then that a severability of interests provision was added to the automobile policy. The 1997 provision is shown in Exhibit 15.1. The provision is referred to as the "separation of insureds" condition in commercial general liability policies, but it is incorporated into the definition of "insured" in the current Insurance Services Office, Inc. (ISO), commercial auto policies.

EXHIBIT 15.1
1997 SEVERABILITY OF INTERESTS PROVISION

Except with respect to the Limit of Insurance, the coverage afforded applies separately to each insured who is seeking coverage or against whom a claim or "suit" is brought.

Under the severability of interests provision, each person or organization seeking protection under the policy's omnibus clause is viewed as though it had been issued a separate policy. As a result, a determination that one insured is to be without coverage for some reason (e.g., the application of an exclusion or violation of a policy condition) should not affect the availability of coverage to the other insureds. However, the limits of the policy are not cumulative no matter how many claims or suits are brought.

The purpose of the severability of interests provision, conceptually at least, is to provide each insured with the same coverage the insured would have received had each purchased a separate auto policy. By covering all additional interests under one policy, the insurer can avoid issuing separate policies to each person or organization that seeks insured status. In reality, the severability of interests provision does reduce the number of policies actually issued. However, all insureds under the policy must share the same limit of insurance.

As mentioned in **Chapter 6,** where the severability of interests provision is discussed in depth, the structure and wording of liability coverage has always inherently included the concept of severability. Among the reasons this provision was specifically written into many forms was to strengthen the intent of the policies that the obligations of the named insured and any other insureds be treated separately. Because severability of interests is inherent in the structure of liability insurance policies, there is no way to eliminate its operation other than by inserting specific language to do so.

One policy provision in which some insurers have attempted to dilute severability of interests is the employers liability exclusion. The employers liability exclusion under an automobile liability coverage form, like that found in other forms of liability insurance, excludes bodily injury to an employee of the insured arising out of and in the course of employment by the insured. If the conduct of a person designated in the policy as an additional insured should accidentally cause injury to the named insured's employee, the additional insured will have protection for a suit brought directly against it. In effect, the employers liability exclusion does not affect coverage of the additional insured in this instance, since it applies only to liability of the employer of the injured claimant. The employer should be protected against this excluded exposure under the employers liability coverage portion of a workers compensation policy, or by a stop gap endorsement (applicable in monopolistic fund states). In light of the severability of interests provision, the applicability of an exclusion to one insured (in this case, the named insured employer) does not preclude coverage for other insureds unless specifically stated to do so.

Some insurers have attempted to negate severability by rewording standard exclusions, like the employers liability exclusion, so that they apply to *all* insureds rather than to *the* insured against whom claim is made or suit is brought. One method of modifying exclusionary language to this end is to make exclusions applicable to "an insured" rather than "the insured." In the example of the employer's liability exclusion, the revised language would read as follows.

This insurance does not apply to bodily injury to an employee of *an* insured arising out of and in the course of employment by *an* [or *any*] insured.

Because the concept of severability of interests is implicit in liability insurance policies, insurers' attempts to undermine the concept with language like that quoted above can run the risk of ending in ambiguity—and a policy interpretation favorable to the insured.

Sometimes insurers will argue that an additional insured is still subject to the employers liability exclusion without any change in the exclusionary wording. This was one of the issues in *Centennial Insurance Co. v Ryder Truck Rental,* 149 F2d 378 (5th Cir 1998).

Fulfilling a promise in a truck lease and service agreement to purchase liability insurance and to hold the lessor (Ryder) harmless for injuries to it, as well as to its employees, drivers, and agents, the lessee (Scholastic) obtained a business auto policy and a commercial general liability policy and listed Ryder in the certificates of insurance for both policies as an additional insured. A disagreement ensued between Scholastic's insurer over the extent of the business auto policy's coverage when a Scholastic employee sued Ryder for injuries suffered in a fall down the ramp of the leased truck. When Ryder sought defense from Scholastic's insurer, the claim was denied based on the workers compensation and employers liability exclusions of the business auto policy.

The business auto policy (BAP) in question excluded from coverage "any obligation for which the insured or the insured's insurer may be held liable under any workers compensation, disability benefits or unemployment compensation law or any similar law" and "bodily injury to an employee of the insured arising out of and in the course of employment by the insured." The policy also included a severability of interests provision within the policy's definition of "insured."

Ryder, the additional insured, argued that the workers compensation and employers liability exclusions in Scholastic's policy were triggered only when the insured claiming coverage was being sued by one of its own employees—not in the case of one insured's employee bringing suit against another insured. The insurer countered that the severability of interests provision in no way precluded the workers compensation and employers liability exclusions from controlling when, as in this case, an employee of one insured sues another insured for injuries.

The appellate court agreed with Ryder and held that neither of the two exclusions relied on by the insurer under its BAP was applicable. In reviewing cases from other jurisdictions, the court also noted that the preponderance of pertinent cases favored Ryder's construction of the BAP.

Extent of Permission

The application and extent of express or implied permission beyond the auto's original permittee also has been a frequent source of problems. In a nutshell, when the original permittee allows another party (the second permittee) to use the auto, the question arises whether that second permittee also is an insured. Coverage often has been extended to a second permittee while using or operating an auto with the permission of the original permittee who had the permission of the named insured to grant such use. However, there have been other instances where courts have held that the right to designate additional insureds (permittees) is exclusive to the named insured and is not delegable. Another problem area involving extent of permission is when an employee who has permission to use an auto for business purposes also uses the auto for personal or unauthorized use.

Meaning of "Use"

Historically, the more common problems involving the omnibus clause concern the meaning of "use." For example, a fairly typical accident scenario is one in which a truck driver, while being directed by another party, backs into another object. The question then arises whether the person directing the backing operation is actually "using" that truck (if claim is brought against that individual or his employer). Cases of this kind have met with mixed results.

While the term "using" was not defined in early policies (and still is not defined in modern policies), it is said to include the loading and unloading of the automobile.[4] The problem was encountered in determining when the loading of a vehicle began or when the unloading process ceased. Two schools of thought developed on this issue—the completed operation rule and the coming to rest rule. As a result of these rules and the undefined term "use," a number of cases arose over the omnibus clause.

Two connected cases that typify the nature of these kinds of problems are *Wagman v American Fidelity and Casualty Co.,* 109 NE2d 592 (NY 1952), and *Bond Stores v American Fidelity and Casualty Co.,* 133 NYS2d 297 (NY Sup 1954). Wagman, an employee of Bond Stores, injured a passerby while directing the loading of a truck. The injured party sued Bond Stores, which, in turn, impleaded Wagman. Wagman sought protection under the trucker's insurance policy as a person "using" the truck (which would make Wagman an automatic additional insured). The court agreed that Wagman was an insured, holding that the trucker's insurance applied even though neither the truck's owner nor its employee was involved in the accident.

A later case, *Kennedy v Jefferson Smurfit Co.,* 688 A2d 89 (NJ 1997), held that a shipper's negligent selection of a defective pallet during loading was part of the "use" of a tractor-trailer. Thus, the shipper qualified as an additional insured under the omnibus provision of the truckers policy.

It took two 1978 endorsements to address the issue of where general liability coverage ends and auto liability coverage begins, and vice versa. At the time, the combined general liability-auto policy was a popular means of writing coverage for the two liability exposures. The endorsement to the general liability portion of the policy defined, for the first time, what the words "loading or unloading" meant with respect to an auto. (The definition as it currently appears in the CGL is virtually the same, except that it now applies to loading or unloading of an aircraft or watercraft.)

The endorsement to the auto liability portion of the policy deleted the exclusion related to loading or unloading of property and replaced it with ones virtually the same as the current "handling of property" and "movement of property by mechanical device" exclusions. The endorsement also restricted the application of the omnibus clause as respects persons moving property to or from a covered auto. That is, only the named insured's employees, a lessee or borrower, or any of their employees are insureds under the policy while moving property to or from a covered auto. (Note that the terms "loading or unloading" are nowhere to be found in the auto liability policy.) Although these changes to the CGL and BAP have dealt with these particular issues concerning permissive use, some of the other problems over such use still continue today.

Current Automobile Policies

A variety of commercial auto policies currently are available to cover the exposures faced by different types of businesses. Most insurers use standard forms drafted by ISO. In addition to the standard policies, however, a few insurers offer their own independently filed policies that resemble the standard versions.

The four standard commercial auto policies (or "coverage forms," as they are commonly called) currently available are the (1) business auto coverage form, (2) truckers coverage form, (3) motor carrier coverage form, and (4) garage coverage form.[5] The coverage forms are combined with common policy conditions to structure an auto policy.

Business Auto Coverage Form

The business auto coverage form, as it is known today, was first introduced by ISO in 1978. At the time of its introduction, the BAP, as it was known then, replaced the comprehensive auto policy and basic auto policy. The purpose of the BAP was to handle all commercial vehicle exposures other than those within the category of the truckers coverage form (which was designed primarily for businesses that conveyed property of others) or the garage form (which was designed primarily for auto dealerships, garages, and repair shops). So if a business did not come within the scope of a trucker or garage, as defined, it could be written under the business auto policy.

Part of the stated purpose of the 1978 BAP was to simplify the Persons Insured provision, as compared to the auto policies it replaced, without changing the coverage concepts. In this regard, the persons insured were categorized into three broad groups: the named insured, permissive users, and vicarious insureds. (These same three broad groups continue in current policies, although the status of persons within the groups sometimes varies, as will be pointed out later.)

Named Insured Status

The *named insured* obtains the broadest protection encompassing all of the policy's covered liability exposures. *Permissive users* are considered to be insureds so long as the user has the named insured's permission to use the owned, hired, or borrowed auto. (This assumes that both owned and hired autos are covered autos.) Included within this category are partners or executive officers of the named insured entity. However, specifically precluded from this class of permissive users are the following.

- The owner or anyone else from whom a covered auto is borrowed (unless the covered auto is a trailer connected to the named insured's owned covered auto)

- Employees for a covered auto owned by that employee or a member of his or her household

- Persons employed in an auto business, other than such business of the named insured

- Anyone other than the named insured's employees, partners, members of a limited liability company, a lessee, borrower, or any of their employees, while moving property to and from the covered auto[6]

- Any partner for a covered auto owned by such partner or a member of his or her household[7]

Within the category of *vicarious insureds* are persons or organizations who may be liable for the conduct of any insured in the preceding two categories. For example, this would provide insured status to the owner of a construction project with respect to a claim made by a third party who is injured in an accident involving a contractor's auto. This would be true even if there were no requirement in the construction contract for the contractor to add the owner as an additional insured to its auto policy.

Similarly, a lessor of premises would be provided insured status in its tenants' auto policies with respect to operation of the tenants' autos on the premises. Thus, for example, the lessor of an office building with a parking garage would be covered under the policy of its tenant if the lessor was held vicariously liable for the auto's operation in the garage.

The business auto policy was revised in 1990, 1992, 1993, and 1997. The Who Is an Insured provision from the most recent (1997) edition policy is shown in Exhibit 15.2. Most of the changes made in the provision over the years have been relatively minor. For example, exception b.(3) was expanded to add "storing" to the list of types of businesses not considered insureds in the 1992 and subsequent editions.

Probably the most important change to the Who Is an Insured provision in recent years has involved coverage of vicarious insureds. The change is illustrated in Exhibit 15.3. As can be seen, the 1978 and 1980 edition auto policies contained an exception denying insured status to the owner of a covered auto that the insured hired or borrowed, unless the auto was a trailer connected to an auto owned by the insured. Thus, this provision would deny insured status to the owner (lessor) of a vehicle leased by the named insured.[8]

In 1987 two changes in the Who Is an Insured provision took place. The exception with respect to owners of hired or borrowed autos was relocated from the paragraph pertaining to vicarious insureds to the preceding paragraph, thus making it applicable to the permissive user category of insureds (see paragraph b.(1) in Exhibit 15.2). Then, as can be seen in Exhibit 15.3, an even more expansive exception to the vicarious insured provision was added.

EXHIBIT 15.2
1997 WHO IS AN INSURED—AUTO

1. WHO IS AN INSURED

The following are "insureds":

a. You for any covered "auto".

b. Anyone else while using with your permission a covered "auto" you own, hire or borrow except:

   (1) The owner or anyone else from whom you hire or borrow a covered "auto". This exception does not apply if the covered "auto" is a "trailer" connected to a covered "auto" you own.

   (2) Your "employee" if the covered "auto" is owned by that "employee" or a member of his or her household.

   (3) Someone using a covered "auto" while he or she is working in a business of selling, servicing, repairing, parking or storing "autos" unless that business is yours.

   (4) Anyone other than your "employees," partners (if you are a partnership), members (if you are a limited liability company), or a lessee or borrower or any of their employees, while moving property to or from a covered "auto".

   (5) A partner (if you are a partnership), or a member (if you are a limited liability company) for a covered "auto" owned by him or her or a member of his or her household.

c. Anyone liable for the conduct of an "insured" described above but only to the extent of that liability.

Copyright, Insurance Services Office, Inc., 1996

Due to the incorporation of the terminology, "Anyone else *who is not otherwise excluded under paragraph b. above* ...," in the 1987 edition, the vicarious insured provision incorporated all the exceptions to the permissive insured category. The permissive user exceptions now included owners of hired or borrowed autos in addition to employees operating their own autos, those in various auto businesses, those loading or unloading a covered auto, and partners using their owned autos. Thus, the 1987 edition BAP not only excluded such owners or others as permissive users but also for their vicarious liability.

As can be seen in Exhibit 15.3, the broad exception of "anyone not otherwise excluded above"

was deleted from the vicarious insured provision in 1990. In its explanatory memorandum (CA–90–090MF) announcing the 1990 revision, ISO simply commented that this deletion of the exception was simply a return to the previous (i.e., 1978 and 1980) wording. It is true that the grant of insured status to those who may be vicariously liable in the 1990 and later edition forms is virtually identical to the 1978 and 1980 editions. Very significantly, however, it lacks the exception with respect to the owners of hired or borrowed autos. As a result, the 1990 and later edition business auto coverage forms would cover the vicarious liability of the owner of an auto that is hired or borrowed by the named insured.

EXHIBIT 15.3
HISTORICAL APPROACHES TO
VICARIOUS INSUREDS

The following are "insureds":

1978 and 1980 Approaches

Anyone liable for the conduct of an insured described above is an insured but only to the extent of that liability. However, the owner or anyone else from whom you hire or borrow a covered auto is an insured only if that auto is a trailer connected to a covered auto you own.

1987 Approach

Anyone else who is not otherwise excluded under paragraph b. above and is liable for the conduct of an "insured" but only to the extent of that liability.

1990 and Later Approach

Anyone liable for the conduct of an "insured" described above but only to the extent of that liability.

Includes copyrighted information of Insurance Services Office, Inc., with its permission.

Now that the vicarious insured category of the BAP encompasses "[a]nyone liable for the conduct of an 'insured' described above ...," the owner of a hired or borrowed auto has protection as a vicarious insured so long as its auto is being used by the named insured or a permissive user. It is important to note that this applies only to the owner's vicarious—not direct—liability.

For example, if the owner/lessor of the vehicle is found to be liable for the negligent operation or use of the vehicle by the lessee (the named insured), coverage would apply on behalf of the owner/lessor in the lessee's policy. On the other hand, if the owner/lessor was directly liable because it failed to properly maintain the vehicle, coverage would not apply because the liability did not arise from the negligence of the named insured or a permissive user.[9]

While this change may provide some coverage to owners of hired or borrowed autos, the insurance applies as excess over any other collectible insurance. The one exception is when the auto is a trailer connected to a covered auto owned by the named insured. In this case, coverage applies on a primary basis. Of course, lessors can still be provided with primary coverage by adding them as insureds with the Additional Insured—Lessor (CA 20 01) endorsement rather than relying on this automatic coverage.[10]

Application to Employees

There is much misunderstanding over how the business auto coverage form applies to employees who use their personal autos in the furtherance of their employers' business. It is quite clear that employees in these cases do not fall within the permissive use category of their employers' commercial auto policies. In fact, the reverse is true; that is, if both an employee and his or her employer are brought into a suit because of an accident caused by an employee while operating his or her own auto, primary protection of the employer is under the employee's personal auto policy. The reason is that the personal auto policy generally contains an insured provision, similar to the one in commercial auto policies, that automatically covers as an insured individuals or entities that may be held vicariously liable for the operation or use of the covered auto.

Not only are the mechanics of the personal auto policy with respect to this exposure not always understood by insureds, even insurers apparently have difficulty understanding the proper application of this coverage aspect. A case in point is *Georgia Mutual Insurance Co. v Rollins, Inc.,* 434 SE2d 581 (Ga App 1993). An employee was involved in an accident while driving his own vehicle on company business. The claimant sued both the employee and his employer. The employee asked his insurer for defense, but when the employer also asked the employee's insurer for defense, it was denied.

The employee's personal auto policy included the typical definition of "insured," as follows.

(a) With respect to the insurance for bodily injury and for property damage liability the *unqualified* word "INSURED" includes the named insured and if the named insured is an individual, his spouse, if resident of the same household, and also includes any person while using the automobile and any person or organization legally responsible for the use thereof, provided the actual use of the automobile is by the named insured.

Of course, the court ruled that the employer was an insured on a primary basis under the employee's automobile policy pursuant to this "omnibus clause."

What can be especially unfortunate in cases such as this one is when the employee's personal auto limits are inadequate to handle the defense and indemnification of both the employee and his or her employer. The employer does not have to worry because once the limits of the employee's auto policy are exhausted, the employer can look to its own commercial auto policy (employer's nonownership liability coverage) for excess protection, provided the appropriate covered auto symbol was depicted on the policy's declarations page.

Sometimes as an employment "perk," an employer will purchase excess liability insurance for the benefit of employees in the event the limits of the employee's personal insurance fall short of need. This can be accomplished by adding the Employees as Insureds (CA 99 33) endorsement to the commercial auto coverage form of the employer. Charitable, religious, and educational institutions, as well as governmental agencies, also often request such an endorsement be added to their commercial auto policies to cover authorized volunteers under the Social Service Agencies—Volunteers as Insureds (CA 99 34) endorsement.

Philosophies and opinions differ as to whether the practice of adding employees or volunteers as insureds while using their own autos (and any other nonowned autos) is advisable for the named in-

sured. On the positive side, it can provide valuable protection for an employee and thus have a positive effect on morale. However, the existence of coverage may cause plaintiffs to push for higher awards, and losses paid as a result of the coverage will affect underwriters' views of the account in the future. Underwriters will sometimes accommodate a request for this modification if they are provided some proof that employees and authorized volunteers are maintaining personal auto insurance with limits higher than the minimums required by the financial responsibility law of the state in which they are operating.

Truckers Coverage Form

Like the BAP, the first standard ISO truckers policy was introduced in 1978. The *Commercial Lines Manual (CLM)* defines a "trucker" as "a person, firm or corporation in the business of transporting goods, materials or commodities for another." This definition is broad enough to encompass public, contract, and "exempt commodity" carriers, furniture movers, as well as building supply dealers who haul sand, gravel, and other materials for others.

Not eligible for this kind of policy (but by exception, therefore, eligible under the BAP) are private carriers (i.e., those who transport their own products or materials) and public and private liveries. While it would appear that a truckers policy might be required by owner-operators of tractor-trailers who hire out their services to other truckers, such is not the case. The reason is that owner-operators are typically protected under the insurance program of the trucking firm that hires their services.

However, when these owner-operators are not engaged in transporting goods or commodities on behalf of a trucking firm, such as when they are operating without a trailer attached (bobtailing) or while their trailer is empty (deadheading), the owner-operator may need separate coverage, sometimes referred to as "bobtail liability coverage." This coverage is provided by attaching the Truckers—Insurance for Nontrucking Use (CA 23 09) endorsement to the BAP.

While the Persons Insured provision of the truckers policy consists of the same three broad categories of insureds as found with the business auto policy, the class of insureds varies within those categories because of the nature of the exposures for which the truckers policy was designed. The Who Is an Insured provision from the 1997 edition of the truckers form is shown in Exhibit 15.4.

EXHIBIT 15.4
1997 WHO IS AN INSURED—TRUCKERS

1. WHO IS AN INSURED

The following are "insureds":

a. You for any covered "auto".

b. Anyone else while using with your permission a covered "auto" you own, hire or borrow except:

   (1) The owner or anyone else from whom you hire or borrow a covered "private passenger type auto".

   (2) Your "employee" or agent if the covered "auto" is a "private passenger type auto" and is owned by that "employee" or agent or a member of his or her household.

   (3) Someone using a covered "auto" while he or she is working in a business of selling, servicing, repairing, parking or storing "autos" unless that business is yours.

   (4) Anyone other than your "employees," partners (if you are a partnership), members (if you are a limited liability company), a lessee or borrower or any of their "employees," while moving property to or from a covered "auto".

   (5) A partner (if you are a partnership), or a member (if you are a limited liability company), for a covered "private passenger type auto" owned by him or her or a member of his or her household.

c. The owner or anyone else from whom you hire or borrow a covered "auto" that is a "trailer" while the "trailer" is connected to another covered "auto" that is a power unit, or if not connected:

   (1) Is being used exclusively in your business as a "trucker"; and

   (2) Is being used pursuant to operating rights granted to you by a public authority.

d. The owner or anyone else from whom you hire or borrow a covered "auto" that is not a "trailer" while the covered "auto":

   (1) Is being used exclusively in your business as a "trucker"; and

   (2) Is being used pursuant to operating rights granted to you by a public authority.

e. Anyone liable for the conduct of an "insured" described above but only to the extent of that liability.

continued

EXHIBIT 15.4
1997 WHO IS AN INSURED—TRUCKERS (cont.)

However, none of the following is an "insured":

a. Any "trucker" or his or her agents or "employees", other than you and your "employees":

(1) If the "trucker" is subject to motor carrier insurance requirements and meets them by a means other than "auto" liability insurance.

(2) If the "trucker" is not insured for hired "autos" under an "auto" liability insurance form that insures on a primary basis the owners of the "autos" and their agents and "employees" while the "autos" are being used exclusively in the "truckers" business and pursuant to operating rights granted to the "trucker" by a public authority.

b. Any rail, water or air carrier or its "employees" or agents, other than you and your "employees", for a "trailer" if "bodily injury" or "property damage" occurs while the "trailer" is detached from a covered "auto" you are using and:

(1) Is being transported by the carrier; or

(2) Is being loaded on or unloaded from any unit of transportation by the carrier.

Named Insured Status

The named insured is given the broadest protection of any insured. Such coverage applies to the direct and vicarious liability of the named insured and, unlike the coverage of other insureds, applies to liability arising from the faulty maintenance of covered autos.

Permissive User Insureds

The truckers policy provides insured status to permissive users in the same manner as does the BAP, subject to the following important exceptions. First, not considered to be a permissive user under the truckers policy is the owner or anyone else from whom the named insured hires or borrows a covered "private passenger type auto." However, by exception to this provision, a permissive user would encompass an owner of a *commercial auto* while that auto is hired or borrowed by the named insured (trucker). For example, the owner-operator of a tractor-trailer unit that is rented or loaned to the named insured (trucker) would be a permissive insured under the truckers policy.[11]

The second exception is similar to the first. An employee or agent of the named insured who uses his or her own private passenger type auto in connection with the named insured's business is not considered to be an insured. (The named insured, of course, would be protected against its vicarious liability.) However, by exception, such an employee or agent would be an insured while using his or her *commercial auto* in connection with the named insured's business.

Finally, a partner of the named insured or a member of a limited liability company is viewed in the same light as employees of the named insured. Thus, a partner of the named insured (or a member of a limited liability company) is not considered to be an insured while using his or her "private passenger type auto" (or one owned by a household member) in furtherance of the named insured's business. But if the vehicle is of a commercial type, the partner or limited liability member is an insured within the permissive user category.

Also considered to be within the permissive user category of the truckers coverage form is anyone from whom the named insured hires or borrows a covered trailer. However, the trailer must either be (1) connected to another covered auto that is a power unit or, if it is not connected, (2) used exclusively in the named insured's business as a trucker pursuant to operating rights granted to the named insured trucker by a public authority. Unlike the BAP, coverage under the truckers policy also extends to anyone from whom the named insured hires or borrows a covered auto (other than a trailer) while it is being used exclusively in the named insured's business as a trucker pursuant to operating rights granted by a public authority.

Vicarious Insureds

Finally, like the BAP, the truckers coverage form contains a vicarious insured category that includes as an insured "anyone liable for the conduct of an 'insured' described above to the extent of that liability."

Exceptions to the Who Is an Insured Provision

By its very nature, the truckers coverage form is not meant to be an all-encompassing contract from the standpoint of additional insureds. Therefore, there are a couple of categories of persons or organizations that are beyond the intended scope of this coverage form. The first such category of persons or organizations is any "trucker," as defined, including its agents or employees (other than the named insured and its employees) if the trucker is a self-insured.

This is a protective measure against self-insured truckers that may be less cooperative than those that maintain insurance. It also helps to alleviate problems coordinating protection between one trucker's insurance and another's self-insurance program. (When both truckers are insured, the two policies' "other insurance" clauses accomplish this coordination, but an "other insurance" clause in a policy does not coordinate with a self-insurance program.)

Likewise, any trucker (other than the named insured and its employees) that does not purchase liability insurance to apply on a primary basis for

hired autos it may use in its trucking business is not an insured under the named insured trucker's policy. In other words, the trucker that is using the auto in its business (regardless of whether the auto is owned or hired) is obligated to provide primary liability coverage. That includes the obligation to provide coverage such that it is available to the owner of the hired auto and its agents or employees. Any trucker that thus fails to provide reciprocal protection to an owner of a hired vehicle is denied protection when the situation is reversed.

Another category of persons or organizations who are not considered to be permissive user insureds under the truckers coverage form is any rail, water, or air carrier if bodily injury or property damage occurs while the trailer is detached from the named insured's covered auto and is being transported, loaded, or unloaded by any rail, water, or air carrier. Without this restriction, it would be possible for an employee of such carrier to obtain insured status under the named insured's truckers coverage form.

Motor Carrier Coverage Form

The motor carrier form is the latest commercial automobile coverage form to be introduced (in 1993) by ISO. Its purpose is to be more compatible with the needs of the trucking industry in the wake of reduced regulatory authority and the dismantling of the Interstate Commerce Commission.

This new form may be used not only as an alternative to the truckers coverage form but also in place of the business auto coverage form in some instances. In fact, the motor carrier form is likely to eventually replace the truckers coverage form. One reason is that this new form encompasses more classes of operations than does the truckers form. This is evident when one compares the definitions of "motor carrier" and "trucker."

The term "motor carrier" is defined within the new coverage form to mean "a person or organization providing transportation by auto in the furtherance of a commercial enterprise." On the other hand, the definition of "trucker" in the truckers coverage form is limited to "any person or organization engaged in the business of transporting property by auto for hire."

EXHIBIT 15.5
WHO IS AN INSURED PERMISSIVE USER EXCEPTIONS
(BUSINESS AUTO, MOTOR CARRIER, TRUCKERS)

Anyone else (other than the named insured) is an insured while using, with the named insured's permission, a covered auto the named insured owns, hires, or borrows *except:*

Business Auto	Motor Carrier	Truckers
(1)The owner or anyone else from whom the named insured hires or borrows a covered auto (unless the covered auto is a trailer connected to a covered auto the named insured owns)	(1)The owner or any *employee, agent, or driver of the owner,* or anyone else from whom the named insured hires or borrows a covered auto	(1)The owner or anyone else from whom the named insured hires or borrows a covered *private passenger type* auto
(2)The named insured's employee if the covered auto is owned by that employee or a member of the employee's household	(2)The named insured's employee *or agent* if the covered auto is owned by that employee or agent or a member of their household	(2)The named insured's employee *or agent* if the covered auto is a *private passenger type* auto and is owned by that employee or agent or a member of their household
(3)Someone using a covered auto while working in an auto "business" that is not the named insured's business	(3)Same as BAP	(3)Same as BAP
(4)Anyone (other than the named insured's employees, partners, members, a lessee or borrower, or any of their employees) while moving property to or from a covered auto	(4)Same as BAP	(4)Same as BAP
(5)A partner or member of the named insured for a covered auto owned by the partner or member or a member of their household	(5)Same as BAP	(5)A partner or member of the named insured for a covered *private passenger type* auto owned by the partner or member or a member of their household

In light of the "motor carrier" definition, it is entirely possible for the motor carrier form to encompass the transportation of not only others' property, but also the insured's own property. Prior to the introduction of this form, motor carriers whose business involved transporting for themselves and others would have been required to purchase a business auto policy (for the transportation of their own property) and have the Truckers (CA 23 20) endorsement attached to handle the transportation of others' property.

While many provisions of the motor carrier coverage form are identical to the truckers coverage form, there are some exceptions, particularly with respect to the Who Is an Insured provisions. The reason, which may not be immediately obvious, is that the motor carrier form, by its nature, covers not only regulated but also nonregulated motor carrier exposures (i.e., those transporting property of others and those transporting their own property) and, therefore, must include more insureds.

Who Is an Insured

Under both the motor carrier and truckers coverage forms, anyone liable for the conduct of an insured (to the extent of that liability) is an insured along with the named insured. Likewise, under both coverage forms, certain entities are not insureds, e.g., someone working in the business of selling or servicing autos; someone other than an employee moving property to and from the covered auto; or rail, water, or air carriers for detached trailers. Beyond those provisions, both policies, insofar as the omnibus insureds are concerned, differ in a number of ways. Exhibit 15.5 illustrates the key differences of insureds among the BAP, truckers, and motor carrier coverage forms.[12]

The point to keep in mind when comparing the Who Is an Insured provisions of the motor carrier coverage form and the truckers coverage form is flexibility stemming from relaxed regulations. In other words, the truckers coverage form is structured as if all motor carrier operations were subject to exactly the same regulations, and all operations were conducted in accordance with operating rights granted by a public authority. It automatically presumes that, in all but specifically excepted cases, the liability insurance of the motor carrier under whose authority the transportation is being conducted will be primary for the benefit of owner-operators. The motor carrier form, on the other hand, makes no reference to such regulations. Like the truckers form, it does provide a means for the liability insurance of the motor carrier to be primary for the benefit of owner-operators, but this coverage arrangement can be modified by agreement between the motor carrier and owner-operators. See the comparison in Exhibit 15.6.

Garage Coverage Form

The garage coverage form is a specialized policy designed to provide insurance to commercial insureds that sell, service, or repair autos or trucks. The form combines into one policy coverage for the insured's exposure to premises, operations, products, completed operations, independent contractors, contractual, and vehicular liability. In other words, it provides the coverages of both the business auto policy and the commercial general liability policy. As a result, its Who Is an Insured provision, shown in Exhibit 15.7, combines elements of both of these policies.

All of the provisions dealing with insured status for covered autos except subparagraph (d) are identical to those in the business auto coverage form. Most important to the subject of this book is the omnibus clause granting insured status to "anyone liable for the conduct of an insured...."

As it relates to garage operations, the Who Is an Insured provision limits insured status to the named insured, the named insured's partners, members of a limited liability company, employees, directors, or shareholders, but only while acting within the scope of their duties. This provision is significantly more narrow than the CGL policy. As compared to the CGL coverage form, the garage coverage form omits the following insureds: partners' spouses, real estate managers, and newly acquired organizations. Coverage for partners' spouses and newly acquired entities is available with the attachment of the Broadened Coverage—Garages (CA 25 14) endorsement.

EXHIBIT 15.6
DIFFERENCES IN WHO IS AN INSURED
MOTOR CARRIER VERSUS TRUCKERS COVERAGE FORMS

The following entities (e.g., lessors, owners, or anyone else from whom the named insured hires or borrows a covered auto) are specifically included as insureds under the coverage forms. Keep in mind that this presumes appropriate covered auto symbols (e.g., any auto or owned autos plus hired autos) apply for leased or hired autos.

Motor Carrier Coverage Form	**Truckers Coverage Form**
The owner or anyone else from whom the named insured hires or borrows a covered trailer is an insured:	The owner or anyone else from whom the named insured hires or borrows a covered trailer is an insured:
While the trailer is connected to a covered power unit,	While the trailer is connected to a covered power unit,
or,	or,
If the trailer is not connected,	If the trailer is not connected,
While it is being used exclusively in the named insured's business	While it is being used exclusively in the named insured's business as a trucker (for hire)
	and
	While it is being used pursuant to operating rights granted to the named insured by a public authority
The lessor (including the lessor's employee, agent, or driver) of a covered power unit is an insured:	The owner or anyone else from whom the named insured hires or borrows a covered power unit is an insured:
While the power unit is leased to the named insured under a written agreement (if the written agreement does not require the lessor to hold the named insured harmless)	While the power unit is being used exclusively in the named insured's business as a trucker (i.e., motor carrier for hire)
And then	and
Only when the leased unit is used in the named insured's business as a motor carrier for hire	While it is being used pursuant to operating rights granted to the named insured by a public authority

continued

EXHIBIT 15.6
DIFFERENCES IN WHO IS AN INSURED
MOTOR CARRIER VERSUS TRUCKERS COVERAGE FORMS (cont.)

Alternatively, the following types of entities are specifically *not* included as insureds under the coverage forms. In this case keep in mind that, given the appropriate covered auto symbols, the named insured, but not the owners of the autos, e.g., would have liability coverage for injury or damage arising out of the use of the autos.

Motor Carrier Coverage Form

Anyone else (including the named insured's employee, agent, partner, or member) is not an insured:

> While using a hired, borrowed, or non-owned covered auto that is owned by that person or a member of his or her household

Any motor carrier for hire (including its agents or employees), other than the named insured and his or her employees, is not an insured:

> If the motor carrier is subject to motor carrier insurance requirements and meets them by a means other than auto liability insurance (unless the named insured has agreed to hold the for-hire motor carrier harmless under a written lease agreement)

> Or

> If the motor carrier's auto liability policy does not provide hired auto coverage on a primary basis for the owners (including their agents and employees) of leased autos

>> While such autos are leased to that motor carrier

>> and

> Used in that motor carrier's business

Truckers Coverage Form

Anyone else (including the named insured's employee, agent, partner, or member) is not an insured:

> While using a hired, borrowed, or non-owned covered *private passenger type* auto that is owned by that person or a member of his or her household

Any trucker (for hire) (including his or her agents or employees), other than the named insured and his or her employees, is not an insured:

> If the trucker is subject to motor carrier insurance requirements and meets them by a means other than auto liability insurance

> Or

> If the trucker's auto liability policy does not provide hired auto coverage on a primary basis for the owners (including their agents and employees) of hired autos

>> While such autos are being used exclusively in the trucker's business

>> and

>> Pursuant to operating rights granted to the trucker by a public authority

---

EXHIBIT 15.7
1997 WHO IS AN INSURED—GARAGE

1. **WHO IS AN INSURED**

   a. The following are "insureds" for covered "autos":

   (1) You for any covered "auto".

   (2) Anyone else while using with your permission a covered "auto" you own, hire or borrow except:

      (a) The owner or anyone else from whom you hire or borrow a covered "auto". This exception does not apply if the covered "auto" is a "trailer" connected to a covered "auto" you own.

      (b) Your "employee" if the covered "auto" is owned by that "employee" or a member of his or her household.

      (c) Someone using a covered "auto" while he or she is working in a business of selling, servicing, repairing, parking or storing "autos" unless that business is your "garage operations".

      (d) Your customers, if your business is shown in the Declarations as an "auto" dealership. However, if a customer of yours:

         (i) Has no other available insurance (whether primary, excess or contingent), they are an "insured" but only up to the compulsory or financial responsibility law limits where the covered "auto" is principally garaged.

         (ii) Has other available insurance (whether primary, excess or contingent) less than the compulsory or financial responsibility law limits where the covered "auto" is principally garaged, they are an "insured" only for the amount by which the compulsory or financial responsibility law limits exceed the limit of their other insurance.

      (e) A partner (if you are a partnership), or a member (if you are a limited liability company), for a covered "auto" owned by him or her or a member of his or her household.

   (3) Anyone liable for the conduct of an "insured" described above but only to the extent of that liability.

   b. The following are "insureds" for "garage operations" other than covered "autos":

   (1) You.

   (2) Your partners (if you are a partnership), member (if you are a limited liability company), "employees", directors or shareholders but only while acting within the scope of their duties.

Unlike the CGL coverage form, the garage coverage form does not distinguish between employees and executive officers. In distinguishing between the two, the CGL policy's fellow employee exclusion does not apply to claims against executive officers (see **Chapter 2**). The garage policy, on the other hand, apparently provides insured status to executive officers as employees. Thus, the fellow employee exclusion would likely be applicable to claims by injured employees against the executive officer of a business insured under a garage policy.

Commercial Auto Endorsements

There are a number of endorsements available for attachment to the business auto, truckers, motor carrier, and garage coverage forms that provide additional insured status or otherwise change the application of the Who Is an Insured provision. Most of these endorsements may be used with any of these forms, but a few are available only for use with the garage form. They are all briefly discussed in the following.

Endorsements for All Commercial Auto Forms

The endorsements shown in Exhibit 15.8 are available for attachment to the commercial auto forms. With the exception of the Social Service Agencies—Volunteers as Insureds (CA 99 34) endorsement, which is not applicable to the garage form, they can be attached to any of the ISO commercial auto coverage forms.

Vicarious Liability and Additional Insured Status

When it comes to commercial automobile liability insurance, there is widespread misunderstanding of how coverage applies under the omnibus clause to those who may be vicariously liable for the operation or use of a covered auto. As a result, it is not uncommon for one party to contractually require another party to provide it with additional insured status by endorsement to the auto policy.

For example, the owner of a construction project may include a clause in the construction contract requiring the contractor to name the owner as an additional insured in the contractor's auto policy by attaching an endorsement to the auto policy. Similarly, a lessor of a building might make such a requirement of its lessees.

Of course, these requirements are generally unnecessary because the omnibus clause would automatically provide insured status to a project owner or premises lessor held vicariously liable for the operation of its contractor's or lessee's vehicles.[13] As a result, there has historically been no standard endorsement in the ISO forms portfolio to add additional insureds to auto policies. Nevertheless, requests from insureds for such endorsements to comply with contract requirements come with such frequency that insurers have begun developing their own additional insured forms.

This problem grew to the point where ISO drafted and filed an endorsement in conjunction with its 1997 policy filings that will signify that protection is being provided to those persons and organizations who may be held liable for the conduct of an insured under the business auto coverage form, garage coverage form, motor carrier coverage form, and truckers coverage form.

The Designated Insured (CA 20 48) endorsement really does not change the application of the policy. It simply reaffirms the application of the omnibus clause with respect to the party designated in the endorsement's schedule. The endorsement's operative wording is shown in Exhibit 15.9.

A similar additional insured endorsement (TE 99 01 B) is available for use with the Texas business auto policy and other commercial auto forms used in that state. In addition to specifying insured status for an entity named in the endorsement—to the extent of that entity's liability for acts or omissions of the named insured—the Texas endorsement also requires notice to the additional insured when the policy is canceled.

EXHIBIT 15.8
WHO IS AN INSURED—BUSINESS AUTO POLICY EFFECT OF COMMON ENDORSEMENTS

- With the **Individual Named Insured (CA 99 17)** endorsement, members of the named insured's household become insureds for autos that are not owned by them (or members of their household) or furnished for their regular use. The endorsement is mandatory if the named insured is an individual who owns a private passenger auto. It requires no additional premium; coverage would be excess.

- With the optional **Drive Other Car Coverage—Broadened Coverage for Named Individuals (CA 99 10)** endorsement, the individuals named in the endorsement (and their spouses) become insureds while using autos they or members of their household do not own. There is a premium charge for the endorsement; coverage would be excess.

- With the optional **Employees as Insureds (CA 99 33)** endorsement, employees become insureds while they are using their own or other nonowned autos in the named insured's business or personal affairs. There is a premium charge for the endorsement; coverage would be excess. This assumes that nonowned autos are covered autos under the policy.

- With the optional **Social Service Agencies—Volunteers as Insureds (CA 99 34)** endorsement, volunteers and owners of loaned autos become insureds while using the covered auto in activities necessary to the named insured's business. There is a premium charge for the endorsement; coverage would be excess. This assumes that nonowned autos are covered autos under the policy.

- With the optional **Employee as Lessor (CA 99 47)** endorsement, employees become insureds while their owned auto is leased to the named insured. The auto is treated as an owned auto rather than a nonowned auto; therefore, coverage would be primary. There is a premium charge for the endorsement.

- The **Employee Hired Autos (CA 20 54)** endorsement expands the Who Is an Insured provision. It includes employees who rent vehicles in their own names to carry out their employers' business.

- The **Fellow Employee Coverage (CA 20 55)** endorsement and the **Fellow Employee Coverage for Designated Employees/Positions (CA 20 56)** endorsement have been introduced to delete the fellow employee exclusion in its entirety from the business auto policy or to delete this exclusion for specified employees or positions in the firm.

A question that naturally arises is what effect will there be on protection if a person or organization that seeks protection as an insured against its vicarious liability stemming from use of an automobile is not named on any endorsement? The answer should be none. The fact that a person is listed on this designated insured endorsement merely serves to clarify what already exists and is issued only to appease those who want tangible assurances that protection will be there if needed.

There is really no need to contractually require this endorsement.

Principal-Agent Relationships

A person's or organization's liability for the conduct of an insured under a commercial auto policy will depend on the facts. One cannot simply point to the omnibus clause of the policy and claim insured

---

EXHIBIT 15.9
DESIGNATED INSURED ENDORSEMENT
(CA 20 48)

Each person or organization indicated above is an "insured" for Liability Coverage, but only to the extent that person or organization qualifies as an "insured" under the Who Is An Insured provision contained in SECTION II of the Coverage Form.

Copyright, Insurance Services Office, Inc., 1996

---

status on the basis of a business relationship with an insured under the policy. A principal-agent relationship must first be established. This was one of the arguments in the case of *Progressive Casualty Co. v Brown's Crew Car of Wyo.,* 27 F Supp 2d 1288 (USDC D Wyo 1998*).*

Brown was a common carrier providing transportation services for the Union Pacific Railroad Company. CTS contracted with various transportation companies for purposes of securing transportation services for the railroad's employees and entered into a contract with the railroad to provide such services for Union Pacific's employees. That contract required CTS to:

> defend, indemnify and save harmless Union Pacific from and against any and all claims, demands, suits, losses, expenses, etc., arising out of injury or death of any person ... while in or about Transportation Company's and selected Alternate Transportation Company's vehicles or while in or about any vehicle provided by or on behalf of CTS or Transportation Company for transportation services when such injury ... results from ... the willful or negligent acts or omissions of CTS.

Brown entered into a contract with CTS to provide transportation services to Union Pacific. This contract required Brown to maintain insurance for the benefit of Union Pacific and to indemnify and hold harmless both the railroad and CTS. While Brown was transporting a railroad employee, an accident occurred in which the employee was in-

jured. The employee sued the railroad under the Federal Employers Liability Act (FELA), alleging that his injuries were due to the railroad's negligent failure to provide a safe place to work. The employee also sued Brown for negligence and claimed status as a third-party beneficiary to the CTS/Brown contract.

The question considered by the court was whether Union Pacific qualified as an insured under Brown's business auto policy. The court concluded that Brown had no employment or contractual relationship with Union Pacific on which to base a principal-agent relationship and that Union Pacific exercised no control over Brown's conduct that would create the kind of vicarious liability referred to in the BAP omnibus clause. It therefore held that the railroad was not a named insured, additional insured, or vicarious insured under Brown's BAP.

Garage Endorsements

There are a number of endorsements designed for use exclusively with the garage policy because they apply to the policy's coverage of garage operations rather than its auto liability coverage. The first such endorsement that affects the Who Is an Insured provision is the optional Broadened Coverage—Garages (CA 25 14) endorsement, which provides eight coverage extensions. Among these, the endorsement grants insured status to the spouses of the partners if the named insured is a partnership. It also provides automatic coverage for newly acquired garage businesses for 90 days.

Another optional endorsement, the Owners of Garage Premises (CA 25 09) endorsement, can be used to extend coverage to the owner/lessor of the insured's leased premises. It is essentially identical to the Additional Insured—Managers or Lessors of Premises (CG 20 11) endorsement used with the CGL coverage form. As such, it provides the lessor with additional insured status with respect to "that part of the premises leased" to the named insured. As discussed in **Chapter 7,** care should be exercised in properly describing the premises in the endorsement to avoid conflicts over the extent of the premises and the applicability of coverage thereto.

ISO has also developed and filed in its 1997 policy filings two other optional additional insured endorsements for use with the garage coverage form. The Additional Insured—Lessor of Leased Equipment (CA 20 47) endorsement is designed to provide insured status to the owner of equipment leased by the insured with respect to vicarious liability imposed on the lessor. The Additional Insured—Garages—Grantor of Franchise (CA 20 49) endorsement provides insured status to a person or organization shown in the schedule of the endorsement with respect to its liability as a grantor of a franchise to the named insured.

Summary

While most additional insured status concerns involve commercial general liability and umbrella liability insurance, there are times when individuals and entities want assurances that they have comparable protection under other forms of insurance dealing with commercial autos, statutory workers compensation, and property.

From the standpoint of commercial auto insurance, there are instances when persons or organizations have additional insured status without even realizing it. The reason is that the commercial auto policy generally is structured to automatically include as an insured anyone who has the named insured's permission to use the covered owned, hired, or borrowed auto. Furthermore, anyone who is liable for the conduct of any insured also is protected under most commercial auto policies.

However, not all those who are automatically protected as insureds under commercial auto policies necessarily accept that fact and often desire written assurances of protection. When these kinds of requests are made, endorsements are sometimes used to confirm coverage. New standard endorsements for this purpose are now available.

Of course there are also instances where insured status is needed and the policy does not automatically respond. There are a variety of standard commercial auto endorsements available to fulfill these needs.

Chapter 15 Notes

1.   Wood, Glenn L.; Lilly, Claude C., III; Malecki, Donald S.; Graves, Edward E.; and Rosenbloom, Jerry S., *Personal Risk Management and Insurance,* Vol. I, 4th ed., Malvern, PA: American Institute for Property and Liability Underwriters, 1989, p. 79.

2.   Austin, June M., "Permissive Use Under the Omnibus Clause of the Auto Policy," Employers Reinsurance Company, a written speech prepared for delivery at the Claims Conference of the Conference of Mutual Casualty Companies, May 4, 1961, Chicago.

3.   Gosnell, Maurice E., "Omnibus Clause in Automobile Insurance Policies," *Insurance Law Journal,* April 1950, p. 237.

4.   The CGL policy presents further evidence on this point. It contains a specific exclusion of auto liability to avoid overlapping with the coverage afforded by commercial auto policies. This exclusion specifically states that use of an auto includes loading and unloading. The term "loading or unloading" is also defined in the CGL.

5.   There is one other standard form—the business auto physical damage coverage form (CA 00 10)—that is not frequently used. In most respects it parallels the business auto coverage form except that it insures only physical damage to covered autos. Since it does not cover liability exposures, it is not specifically discussed in this chapter.

6.   References to members of a limited liability company as permissive insureds were added to the BAP in the 1997 policy edition.

7.   The partner, like an employee, is not an insured while using his or her own auto on

partnership business. The partner is expected to purchase personal auto insurance just as the employee is expected to do so. When a partner's auto is being used in business and either symbol 1 (any auto) or symbol 9 (non-owned autos only) of the BAP is shown in the declarations, the partnership—but not the individual partner—is an insured for liability coverage. The same goes for the other commercial auto coverage forms, which use different symbol numbers but apply coverage in the same manner.

8. Insured status could be provided on behalf of lessors by way of the Additional Insured—Lessor (CA 20 01) endorsement.

9. Insurers that desire to exclude all coverage of the owner of a hired or borrowed auto, other than a trailer connected to the named insured's covered auto, would have to leave permissive user provision b.(1) intact and re-insert the vicarious insured provision of earlier policies. (Either the 1978/1980 provision or the 1987 provision would produce the desired effect.)

10. While there are three broad categories of insureds under the BAP policy, there are a few differences in the various editions of the form. The fact that ISO has made changes to its BAP provisions does not necessarily mean that all insurers have adopted later forms or that all state regulators have approved them. Insurers that use their independently filed commercial auto policies and adopt their language, in part, from the ISO provisions may or may not grant this same liberalization of coverage.

11. Contrast this with the way coverage would apply under the 1990 and later edition business auto coverage form. Under this form, the owner-operator would not be a permissive insured, but it would be a vicarious insured if the owner-operator's power unit were rented to the named insured trucker.

12. This exhibit is adapted from "ISO Motor Carrier Coverage Form," *Commercial Auto Insurance,* June 1999, pp. XI.B.1–XI.H.16, published by International Risk Management Institute, Inc.

13. There is a remote chance that the contractor or lessee could be insured on a nonstandard auto form that does not contain an omnibus clause. This would be most likely when the insurance is purchased in the excess and surplus lines marketplace, as is sometimes the case with truckers and even some contractors. This possibility, however, could be dealt with through a contract provision requiring an additional insured endorsement only when the policy does not automatically provide insured status.

Chapter 16

WORKERS COMPENSATION INSURANCE

The standard workers compensation and employers liability insurance policy covers employers for liability imposed on them by workers compensation statutes or under common law for injuries to their employees. Since the sole purpose of the policy is to cover injuries to the insured's employees, it is not generally appropriate for one party to a contract (e.g., the owner of a construction project) to require the other party (e.g., a contractor) to provide additional insured status as is commonly done with liability insurance. If this were to occur, the additional insured would be covered for injuries to its employees under the contractor's workers compensation policy, and the contractor's insurer would require an appropriate premium for this coverage.[1]

For this reason, the insurance industry's rating manuals are very specific about who can be added as an insured to these policies. For example, General Rule III.B.1 of the National Council on Compensation Insurance (NCCI) *Basic Manual for Workers Compensation and Employers Liability Insurance* specifically states that "separate legal entities may be insured in one policy only if the same person, or group of persons, owns the majority interest in such entities."

Indemnitees have two basic concerns that relate to an indemnitor's workers compensation insurance. One concern is the responsibility imposed when independent contractors do not purchase workers compensation insurance. Under the laws of most states, an organization is responsible for providing workers compensation benefits to the employees of an independent contractor if the contractor fails to provide them.[2] This occurs most frequently when the independent contractor fails to purchase workers compensation insur-

ance. To alleviate this concern, indemnitees should simply require indemnitors to purchase workers compensation insurance and furnish proof they have done so.[3]

The second major concern relating to an indemnitor's workers compensation insurance involves the possibility of subrogation by the indemnitor's workers compensation insurer. If, for example, a contractor's employee is injured due to the negligence of the project owner, the contractor's workers compensation insurer may subrogate against the project owner to recover funds paid to or on behalf of the injured employee.

This second concern can be alleviated in several ways. One way the exposure is typically dealt with is by including an indemnification clause in the contract requiring the contractor to hold harmless the project owner. Since the employee injury exclusion in the commercial general liability (CGL) insurance policy does not apply to the contractual liability coverage, the contractor's CGL policy will respond to this transfer of liability.[4]

A second way of covering the exposure is by securing additional insured status in the contractor's liability policies. As discussed in **Chapter 6,** an additional insured is covered for liability to an injured employee of the named insured.

A third method of handling this exposure is to contractually require the indemnitor to waive rights of subrogation. With respect to workers compensation insurance, waivers of subrogation are effected by adding the Waiver of Our Right To Recover from Others (WC 00 03 13) endorsement to the policy. Insurers often charge an additional premium for this endorsement.

It should be realized that waivers of subrogation do not completely address the loss exposure. While they do preclude the contractor's workers compensation insurer from subrogating against the owner, they do not address the possibility of the contractor's employee bringing a claim against the owner. Additional insured status and contractual liability coverage of liability transferred through an indemnity clause, however, *will* respond to either suits brought by the employee or the workers compensation insurer. Therefore, a waiver of subrogation is not a substitute for indemnity clauses or additional insured status. Since waivers of subrogation are not a complete solution to the problem and an additional premium is often charged for them, a strong argument can be made for not requiring waivers of subrogation with respect to workers compensation.

There is a third concern that many indemnitees often do not recognize. Traditionally, workers compensation insurance, one of the earliest forms of no-fault coverage, has been considered the exclusive remedy for employment-related injury. Once workers compensation benefits have been paid or become payable, the employer is immune from any further obligation to pay additional sums to the injured employee. There may be situations where the indemnitor attempts to raise the exclusive remedy doctrine of workers compensation as a shield when the indemnitee seeks to enforce its indemnity agreement with the indemnitor. This can occur when the employee of the indemnitor is injured, collects workers compensation, and then sues the indemnitee for additional recovery.

In many states, the indemnitor's agreement to indemnify will not, in and of itself, act as a waiver of the employer's immunity granted by the exclusive remedy of workers compensation legislation. This can be particularly troublesome to indemnitees in the construction industry, where third-party-over actions are prevalent. Although claims of this sort can take various forms, the most typical third-party-over scenario involves injuries to a subcontractor's employee, who obtains workers compensation benefits and then files suit against the project owner and/or general contractor for damages in excess of the workers compensation benefits paid.

The project owner or general contractor in turn looks to the subcontractor who has agreed to hold them harmless to the fullest extent permitted by law. Having complied with the statutory requirements for immunity from employee injury, the subcontractor then finds itself legally obligated to pay further damages for the same injury.

Indemnitees like the owner or general contractor in the scenario described above are sometimes surprised to find that there may be difficulties in enforcing their rights under the indemnity agreement. Some workers compensation statutes bar enforcement of an indemnity agreement arising out of injury to the indemnitor's employee if the indemnitor has satisfied its statutory workers compensation obligation.

A court case involving a statute that limited indemnity agreements in this way is *Holman Erection Co. v Employers Insurance of Wausau*, 920 P2d 1125 (Or 1996). A subcontractor agreed to obtain insurance protecting the general contractor against claims for bodily injury or property damage arising out of the subcontractor's work. The subcontractor failed to arrange such insurance. The construction contract also required that the subcontractor indemnify the general contractor for liability because of injury to the subcontractor's employees. One of the subcontractor's employees was injured and sued the general contractor, who submitted the claim to the subcontractor's insurer. The claim was denied because the general contractor had not been added as an insured to the policy in compliance with the contract insurance requirements.

The subcontractor argued that the insurer was required to defend the general even though the subcontractor itself was not a party to the suit. The subcontractor contended that the suit against the general was effectively a suit against the subcontractor, given the latter's obligation to indemnify the general. Instead of raising the exclusive remedy doctrine as a shield to the indemnity action against it, the subcontractor was seeking to circumvent that shield. In this case it fell to the court to invoke the exclusive remedy doctrine, quoting the relevant Oregon statute:

> The liability of every employer who satisfies the duty required by the workers compensation

law is exclusive and in place of all other liability arising out of injuries, diseases, symptom complexes or similar conditions arising out of and in the course of employment that are sustained by subject workers, the worker's beneficiaries and anyone otherwise entitled to recover damages from the employer on account of such conditions or claims resulting therefrom, *specifically including claims for contribution or indemnity asserted by third persons from whom damages are sought on account of such conditions*, except as specifically provided otherwise in this chapter. (Emphasis added.)

In applying this shield created by the exclusive remedy doctrine, the court held that the subcontractor should not be held "directly or indirectly" liable for the employee's work-related injuries. This prohibition applied even where the employer was named in a lawsuit to recover damages pursuant to a contractual indemnity provision like the one at issue here. The court's interpretation of the statutory language quoted above meant that the subcontractor's position—that it was the real defendant in the suit against the general contractor—was without merit. If the subcontractor (employer) could not be sued in the first place once the employee recovered workers compensation benefits, how could it be the real defendant in the suit against the subcontractor's indemnitee?

To overcome the contractual risk transfer problem created by this broad application of the exclusive remedy doctrine (i.e., its application to the employer's indemnity obligations as well as its obligation directly to the injured employee), the indemnitee can require a contract provision in which the indemnitor (the party providing indemnity) waives its statutory immunity under workers compensation laws, only as to the indemnitee.

The limited waiver will help to avoid situations wherein the indemnitee attempts to enforce the indemnity agreement and the injured employee's employer (the indemnitor) argues that enforcing the indemnity agreement circumvents the sole and exclusive remedy doctrine of workers compensation. According to this argument, if the employer is forced to indemnify the indemnitee for injuries the

employee sustained on the job, the employer, in essence, is paying for an on-the-job injury, recovery for which is limited to workers compensation by statute in most states.

By obtaining a limited waiver, assuming it is not prohibited by law in the state involved, an employer obligated to indemnify the indemnitee may be precluded from raising the workers compensation shield as a potential defense in situations like those described here.

Applicable law should be consulted to determine if such waivers are valid and enforceable. Many workers compensation statutes limiting the rights of third parties to recover from the employer do not address the enforceability of waivers of statutory immunity. What is unclear in the wording of the Oregon statute quoted above is how it would apply if an employer waived its statutory immunity with respect to a specific party. Generally speaking, statutes follow two different approaches. Some specifically state that an employer's immunity can be waived if expressly provided for in a written contract. Others are silent as to express waivers, and it is by case law that statutes are interpreted to be truly an exclusive remedy—or viewed as flexible enough to hold the employer liable for contractual indemnity obligations. One example of a statute referencing an express waiver is California's labor code, which states in part:

> ... the employer shall have no liability to reimburse or hold such third person harmless, in the absence of a written agreement to do so ...

One of the issues in *Waterwiese v KBA Construction Managers,* 820 SW2d 579 (Mo 1991), was the ability of a third party to enforce its indemnity rights against the employer of an injured worker who sues the third party after collecting workers compensation benefits. The relevant portion of the Missouri workers compensation statute reads in part:

> Every employer subject to the provisions of this chapter shall be liable, irrespective of negligence, to furnish compensation under the provisions of this chapter for personal injuries

arising out of and in the course and scope of his employment, and shall be released from all other liability therefor whatsoever, whether to the employee or any other person.

In upholding the right of third parties to enforce indemnity obligations applicable to damages they were required to pay because of injury to the indemnitor's employee, the court cited *McDonnell Aircraft Corp. v Hartman-Hanks-Walsh Painting Co.*, 823 SW2d 788 (Mo 1959), which held that the term "therefor whatsoever" in the quoted passage of the Missouri statute means:

... all other liability for personal injuries or death of an employee, and does not mean liability for breach of an independent duty or obligation owed to a third party.

... Since such third parties receive no benefit from the compensation act in the absence of an express provision of the act, it does not seem proper to hold that, by implication, the act has taken from them rights which they had before.

The *Waterwise* court then concluded that:

although an employer is generally immune from civil suits because of workers compensation, the employer can contract to indemnify a third party for damages the third party is liable for.

One case in which the court struggled over the applicability of a waiver of the employer's rights is *Easter v Exxon Co.*, 699 SW2d 168 (Tenn 1985). The Tennessee court in that case stated:

We now consider the statute. After reading and rereading it, we do not believe that it could be reasonably construed to bar contractual indemnity on the basis that the statute sets forth the employer's liability and this liability cannot be extended even by agreement of the employer. If that were so, whenever an employer through contract with his employee agreed to do more for his employee than required by the workers compensation law, such contract would be illegal and unenforceable. We decline to so construe the statute and if courts from other states have so construed similar statutes, so be it, but we do not and we find no case by a Tennessee court which requires such construction.

Whether the right of an employer to waive its statutory immunity is allowed in a given state must be established before such waivers are relied on. One important element of a waiver is specificity. The waiver should be specific as to the exact code section under which statutory immunity is being waived. In some jurisdictions, even where waivers are allowed, a broadly worded waiver applicable to the entire workers compensation act may be deemed unenforceable. Whether there is a statutory requirement that a waiver be "express, clear, and unequivocal," it should be worded in that manner to avoid problems.

Borrowed Employee Situations

There is a unique type of situation where it is appropriate for one contracting party to require a type of additional insured status on the workers compensation policy of another party. This situation can arise when an employer (the "regular employer") lends, rents, or leases an employee to another employer (the "special employer" or the "alternate employer"). In such a situation, the special employer becomes responsible for providing the employee with workers compensation if there is an express or implied contract of hire between the two, the employee is engaged primarily in work for the special employer, and the special employer controls the details of the work.[5]

Obvious examples of where the lent-servant doctrine applies are with respect to temporary employment services and employee leasing concerns. In most cases, the special employers (i.e., the firm leasing its employees from the employment contractor) of employees provided on a temporary or long-term basis by such a firm have the responsibility to provide workers compensation benefits to injured employees under the law. However, many other common business practices create situations where the applicability of the lent-servant doctrine is much less clear-cut. Some examples of practices where the doctrine may or may not apply, depending on the specific facts, include the following.

- Rental of machinery, equipment, aircraft, or vehicles with operators, pilots, or drivers.

- Provision of personnel by a manufacturer to train the employees of the purchaser of machinery or equipment in the proper use, operation, or maintenance of the equipment.

- Provision of personnel by a building management company to provide janitorial, maintenance, and other services for the building owner.

- Provision of workers to a joint venture by a corporation that is one of the joint venture partners.

When these types of situations arise, disputes between the two employers and their workers compensation insurers over who is responsible for responding when an employee is injured can easily arise. Unless the potential problem is dealt with contractually and with proper modification of workers compensation policies, the outcome—as determined by applying workers compensation law—may be contrary to what the contracting parties intended.

For example, assume a contractor rents a crane with an operator and the operator is injured on the job and files a workers compensation claim with the crane rental company's insurer. The crane rental company's insurer could assert that the contractor is actually the special employer of the crane operator and is responsible for workers compensation benefits. If it is found that there was an implied contract of hire between the crane operator and the contractor, that the operator was working principally for the contractor, and that the contractor controlled the details of his or her work, the crane rental company's insurer could prevail.

In many instances like this one, the parties do not intend for the recipient of the services to become a special employer with responsibility to provide workers compensation on behalf of injured em-

ployees. The parties often assume that the regular employer of the worker will be responsible for providing workers compensation under the law, and they usually require workers compensation insurance from the regular employer to meet the financial responsibility of providing benefits. In such cases, application of the lent-servant doctrine would circumvent the intent of the parties.

The intent of the parties in such a situation can be assured by having the regular employer attach the Alternate Employer (WC 00 03 01) endorsement to its policy.[6] This endorsement (see Exhibit 16.1) resembles an additional insured endorsement. It is attached to the regular employer's policy and covers the special employer's obligation to pay workers compensation benefits (or its legal liability under tort law) to workers supplied to it by the regular employer. The remedy to the injured employee is statutory benefits in either case. The endorsement also waives any right of subrogation the insurer might otherwise have against the special employer.

For example, the contractor renting a crane with an operator could require the crane rental company to have the Alternate Employer endorsement added to its workers compensation policy. Then the crane rental company's insurer would pay benefits to the injured crane operator even if the contractor would normally be responsible for doing so as a special employer under the state's workers compensation law.

The actual endorsement contains a schedule (not shown in the exhibit) in which the alternate employer, the state of special employment, and the contract or project are to be delineated. An insured that is infrequently required to provide this endorsement can have it attached each time it is needed, with the schedule completed to apply specifically to the particular situation. For example, the special employer might be listed as "Acme Construction Company," the state as "Michigan," and the contract as "Crane rental agreement number 4325."

On the other hand, it can also be structured to apply on a blanket basis when the insured is frequently re-

---

EXHIBIT 16.1
ALTERNATE EMPLOYER ENDORSEMENT
WC 00 03 01A

This endorsement applies only with respect to bodily injury to your employees while in the course of special or temporary employment by the alternate employer in the state named in Item 2 of the Schedule. Part One (Workers Compensation Insurance) and Part Two (Employers Liability Insurance) will apply as though the alternate employer is insured. If an entry is shown in Item 3 of the Schedule, the insurance afforded by this endorsement applies only to work you perform under the contract or at the project named in the Schedule.

Under Part One (Workers Compensation Insurance) we will reimburse the alternate employer for the benefits required by the workers compensation law if we are not permitted to pay the benefits directly to the persons entitled to them.

The insurance afforded by this endorsement is not intended to satisfy the alternate employer's duty to secure its obligations under the workers compensation law. We will not file evidence of this insurance on behalf of the alternate employer with any government agency.

We will not ask any other insurer of the alternate employer to share with us a loss covered by this endorsement.

Premium will be charged for your employees while in the course of special or temporary employment by the alternate employer.

The policy may be canceled according to its terms without sending notice to the alternate employer.

Part Four (Your Duties If Injury Occurs) applies to you and the alternate employer. The alternate employer will recognize our right to defend under Parts One and Two and our right to inspect under Part Six.

Source: Alternate Employer Endorsement, WC 00 03 01A, National Council on Compensation Insurance, Effective February 15, 1989.

---

quired to provide the endorsement by carefully completing the schedule with appropriate information. For example, the special employer might be listed as "Any customer with whom the insured contractually agrees to provide this coverage," the state as "Any state listed in Item 3.A. of the Information Page," and the contract as "Any equipment rental agreement." Of course, the actual phraseology used should be tailored to meet the particular circumstances and needs of the insured.

Since the policy would cover injuries to lent employees, the payroll of the lent employees is used in calculating the regular employer's premiums just as if they were performing normal duties for the regular employer. Conversely, the payroll of borrowed employees covered under this endorse-ment should not be included with the payroll of the special employer's other employees in determining the regular employer's premium.

The fact that an alternate employer endorsement is attached to a workers compensation and employers liability policy does not necessarily mean that questions of appropriate responsibility will be avoided. In one case involving this endorsement, there still was some dispute over the endorsement and who had immunity under the workers compensation act and who did not, despite what appeared to be a well thought-out program between an employee leasing firm and a lessor. In the final analysis, the court ruled that both the lessee and lessor were coemployers and, therefore, were both entitled to immunity under the exclusive remedy provision of this state's workers compensation law. The case is *Brown v Aztec Rig Equipment,* 921 SW2d 835 (Tex App 1996).

In this case, Administaff was in the business of staff leasing. Through client service agreements, it employed the existing work force of an entity and then leased it back to carry out the client's business. Aztec was in the business of repairing and refurbishing oil and gas equipment. In this particular business relationship, Administaff agreed to lease employees to Aztec and maintain workers compensation insurance. The agreement also stipulated that Administaff was the employer for some purposes, Aztec was the employer for some purposes, and both Administaff and Aztec were coemployers for purposes of employers liability under the workers compensation law. Attached to the workers compensation policy obtained by Administaff was the Alternate Employer endorsement.

The claimant in this case was one of the leased employees who was injured while working on Aztec's premises and filed suit against both entities. At the time of his injury, he was being supervised by persons employed by Administaff but leased to Aztec to carry out Aztec's business activities. Prior to his injury, the claimant signed an employment agreement with Administaff and agreed in writing that for purposes of workers compensation insurance, he was an employee of both Administaff and the Client Company (eventually Aztec).

Both Administaff and Aztec maintained that the exclusive remedy provision barred the claimant's suit because both were coemployers and the claimant was covered by the workers compensation policy obtained by Administaff. Nonetheless, among the arguments raised by the claimant was that the Alternate Employer endorsement attached to the workers compensation policy on which Administaff was the sole named insured did not relieve Aztec from its obligations to obtain its own workers compensation insurance. The basis for the claimant's argument was the following language from this endorsement.

The insurance afforded by this endorsement is not intended to satisfy the alternate employer's

duty to secure obligations under the workers compensation law. We will not file evidence of this insurance on behalf of the alternate employer with any governmental agency.

In support of the above argument, the claimant pointed to another Texas case, *Zavala-Nava v A.C. Employment, Inc.,* 820 SW2d 14 (Tex App 1991), involving the alternative employer endorsement where a firm that leased an employee was held not to be covered under the leasing agency's workers compensation policy. However, the court's decision here was based on a "subscriber" status that is no longer applicable in Texas. Also of importance was the fact that, unlike the *Zavala-Nava* case, the alternate employer endorsement in the *Brown* case also included the typewritten addition stating that "it is agreed that this endorsement applies to all ... clients and/or subscribers of [Administaff], in its capacity as an employee leasing firm where [workers compensation] is provided by the leasing firm." The court in the *Brown* case stated that because the above quoted language was not included in the policy at issue in *Zavala-Nava,* that case was inapplicable.

The above provision quoted from the Alternate Employer endorsement stating that it is not intended to satisfy the alternate employer's duty to secure its obligations under the workers compensation law may appear to be contradicting another provision of this endorsement. This provision states that both workers compensation and employers liability coverages will apply as though the alternate employer is an insured. In actuality, the intent here is to make sure that an entity does not try to escape its obligation to purchase workers compensation insurance in cases where it may not be viewed as an alternate employer. In fact, the court in the *Brown* case also made this intent clear when it stated that "[a]s for employees not assigned by Administaff, Aztec was responsible for providing workers compensation insurance for those employees."

Landerman v Liberty Services, 637 S2d 809 (La App 1994), involved the question of whether the status of an alternate employer was the equivalent of an additional insured under various liability policies. It involved a crew member of a barge owned by McDermott that was being used to perform services for an oil field servicing company, Liberty Services, Inc. An agreement between McDermott and Liberty required both to assume all risks of liability in connection with injuries and to defend and indemnify each other for claims brought by their respective employees. This contract also required Liberty to maintain workers compensation insurance with an Alternate Employer endorsement in favor of McDermott.

On the date of the accident, Liberty not only maintained a workers compensation policy with a maritime endorsement, but also two excess maritime employers liability (EMEL) policies and a CGL policy, all of which provided additional insured status to McDermott, along with an alternate employer endorsement applicable to the WC and EMEL policies.

After the employee settled with Liberty, McDermott was the only defendant. As such, McDermott sought coverage under Liberty's CGL policy as an indemnitee. The CGL insurer accepted Liberty's obligation but also claimed that the EMEL policies provided coverage to McDermott as an alternate employer. However, the EMEL insurers denied coverage by maintaining that both the watercraft liability and protection and indemnity (P&I) exclusion endorsements precluded McDermott from coverage. The watercraft exclusion provided in pertinent part: "the indemnity granted under this policy shall not apply: 1. To liability to Captain and Crew of, and employees on Assured's owned and/or operated watercraft." Since McDermott owned the vessel, it was deemed to be an insured within the watercraft exclusion of EMEL policies and, therefore, outside of coverage.

McDermott argued, on the other hand, that "assured" was not defined in the EMEL policies and that it was only an alternate employer and not a named insured or additional insured. The court, nonetheless, ruled that if McDermott was an alternate employer, it was an assured, and an assured was subject to the EMEL policies' exclusions, including those applicable to watercraft and P&I.

It is difficult to draw conclusions on whether this decision was appropriate, since it is not possible to view all the provisions of the policies. However, the CGL insurer's decision to respond to its named insured's contractual liability obligations appeared to be appropriate even though the indemnitee (McDermott) was an alternate employer. It probably was the exception to the CGL policy's employer's liability exclusion for liability assumed by the insured under an "incidental contract" that motivated the CGL insurer to respond on behalf of its named insured and indemnitor (Liberty) to the call for protection by McDermott.

Some underwriters are reluctant to provide the Alternate Employer endorsement. Why they are unwilling to provide this endorsement is uncertain. However, the fact that, under this endorsement, workers compensation insurance becomes payable on behalf of the entity held to be responsible as the employer of the injured employee can be viewed as a "win-win" situation for the entities included under the workers compensation policy to which this endorsement is attached. In the absence of this endorsement, the insurer's obligation is solely to the policy's named insured. If that named insured is not held to be the employer, the insurer does not have to pay benefits as required by law.

In light of this reluctance of some underwriters to add the Alternate Employer endorsement, agents and brokers should seek out willing insurers to avoid problems. Likewise, it is necessary for agents, brokers, and consultants to determine if this endorsement should be prescribed. In the case of *Huval v Offshore Pipelines and B&I Welding Services & Consultants v North Star Agency and Excell Mel Underwriters,* 86 F2d 454 (5th Cir 1996), a barge repair contractor brought an action against its insurance agent for failing to procure an Alternate Employer endorsement on its workers compensation and excess maritime employer's liability policies. The court ruled against the insurance agent and apportioned 40 percent of the fault to the insurance consultant who played a significant role in obtaining the other coverages involved. The court declined to apportion all liability to the consultant, because the evidence did not establish that he undertook to procure coverage to the exclusion of the agent.

Dual Employment and Joint Employment

Dual employment and joint employment situations are similar to lent employments, but they pose some different insurance problems. Dual employment occurs when an employee is under the control of and performs services for two or more employers, and the employee's activities for each employer are separable and can be identified with one employer or the other. Joint employment occurs when an employee is under the *simultaneous* control of and performs services for two or more employers and performs similar services for both employers.[7]

For example, two physicians may decide to office together and share certain employees but otherwise keep their practices completely separate. Assume one of the employees is a receptionist who handles appointments and greets patients for both physicians. The other employee is a bookkeeper who works exclusively for one physician 3 days a week and the other physician 2 days a week. Since the physicians simultaneously control the receptionist, and the services performed for the two physicians are the same, this is likely to be a joint employment situation. On the other hand, the bookkeeper probably presents a dual employment situation since he or she works for each physician on different days and maintains different books and records for them. In such a situation, both employers may be responsible for providing workers compensation benefits to the bookkeeper.

Generally speaking, both employers are jointly and severally liable for compensation benefits in a joint employment situation. On the other hand, the employer for whom the employee was working at the time of injury is generally liable in a dual employment situation.

Properly arranging insurance to cover these types of situations can be challenging. The two employers have separate exposures under the workers compensation act, but they cannot purchase a single workers compensation policy since the two businesses are not under common ownership. This will not present a major problem when the two employers are large enough to need workers compensation insurance for employees they do not share with each other. The jointly or dually employed employees would be covered under their individual policies.

In those instances where the two employers agree that one of them will be responsible for carrying the workers compensation insurance for dual or joint employees, the organization agreeing to carry the insurance could add the alternate employer endorsement to cover the other organization. This should accomplish their intent in most circumstances, but there is a possibility that some claims, particularly those involving dual employment situations, could fall outside the scope of the alternate employer endorsement. In such a situation, the employer would have its own policy to rely on as a backup to coverage under the alternate employer endorsement.

With smaller employers such as the two physicians in the previous example, however, purchasing two separate minimum premium policies can be problematic. The optimal way for the two physicians to solve this problem is probably to form a professional corporation and have it hire the employees. This would allow the purchase of a single policy. Another approach that *may* work is for one of the employers to agree to carry the insurance on the employees and protect the other employer using the Alternate Employer endorsement. However, this endorsement is not designed for this purpose and there is a possibility, especially in a dual employment situation, that the employer who is not named as an insured could be found solely responsible for benefits to an injured employee that would not be covered under the endorsement.[8]

Employee Leasing

Employee leasing is a method by which a client's staff is provided by a leasing company. Usually, all or most employees of the client are transferred to the labor contractor and those employees are then leased back to the client. This type of arrangement is usually long-term and permanent in nature as opposed to a temporary labor service. In contrast, temporary labor services (e.g., Kelly Temporary

Services and Manpower Temporary Services) focus on solving short-term staffing problems by providing workers to fill positions on a temporary basis. The exposures and concerns presented from the use of temporary labor services are covered in the preceding discussion of borrowed servant situations.

With respect to the narrow focus of this book, the key concern arising from employee leasing situations is to arrange coverage such that the intention of the parties (i.e., the client and the labor contractor) as to who will be responsible for providing

workers compensation coverage is carried out.[9] State laws vary with respect to whether the labor contractor or client is held responsible, and the laws in a number of states are currently in a state of flux. However, the predominant position of the states is that the client firm is the employer responsible under the workers compensation law because of the degree of control it maintains over the workers. This also appears to be the preferred approach of the insurance industry, since the National Council on Compensation Insurance (NCCI) advocates this approach.[10]

EXHIBIT 16.2
EMPLOYEE LEASING ENDORSEMENTS WHEN COVERAGE IS CLIENT'S RESPONSIBILITY

Client's Policy

Labor Contractor Endorsement (WC 00 03 20)	A type of additional insured endorsement that covers the leasing contractor for any liability it may have to injured employees it leases to the client under either workers compensation law or common law. It also waives the insurer's right of subrogation against the labor contractor. The endorsement is very similar to the Alternate Employer endorsement, except it is designed specifically for employee leasing exposures.
Multiple Coordinated Policy Endorsement (WC 00 03 23)	An endorsement used in states that require a multiple coordinated policy plan. Under a multiple coordinated policy plan, the employee leasing company a each of its clients are issued, by a single insurer, separate policies that have common expiration dates. The Multiple Coordinated Policy endorsement stipulates that the policy covers only liability for bodily injury to employees leased to the insured (client) by the employee leasing company named in the endorsement. If the client has other employees, workers compensation coverage for these employees must be provided under a separate policy.

Labor Contractor's Policy

Employee Leasing Client Endorsement (WC 00 03 19)	Requires the labor contractor to provide certain information to the insurer concerning its clients and the employees it leases to them. Requires the contractor to obtain certificates of insurance from clients showing that they are providing workers compensation coverage and establishes the insurer's right to make an additional premium charge if the contractor fails to do so. When this endorsement is used, the leasing/labor contractor would have coverage for its liability to employees if the client failed to maintain coverage.
Labor Contractor Exclusion Endorsement (WC 00 03 21)	May be used as an alternative to the Employee Leasing Client endorsement to exclude coverage for employees leased to clients. Unlike the former endorsement, no coverage is provided on behalf of the labor contractor for its liability to employees if the client fails to maintain coverage.

EXHIBIT 16.3
EMPLOYEE LEASING ENDORSEMENTS WHEN COVERAGE IS LEASING CONTRACTOR'S RESPONSIBILITY

Client's Policy

Employee Leasing Client Exclusion Endorsement (WC 00 03 22)	The endorsement excludes coverage for workers leased from a leasing contractor while maintaining coverage for workers directly employed by the client.

Labor Contractor's Policy

Alternate Employer Endorsement (WC 00 03 01)	Used to cover the client for any liability it may have to injured employees it leases from the leasing contractor under either workers compensation law or common law. It also waives the insurer's right of subrogation against the client company.

The basic prerequisites for properly arranging coverage are to first determine what is permissible (or required) under the law of the particular state in which a leasing arrangement is being used and then to determine the intent of the parties as delineated in the leasing agreement. Once these basic facts are determined, it simply becomes a matter of selecting the appropriate endorsements to tailor coverage to the law or the agreement.[11]

NCCI has promulgated six endorsements specifically for use in tailoring coverage in employee leasing situations. These endorsements are summarized in Exhibits 16.2 and 16.3. As sown in the exhibits, one of the parties adds a type of additional insured endorsement (e.g., the Labor Contractor endorsement or the Alternate Employer endorsement) to its policy affirming coverage for the leased employees (whichever employer would otherwise be held responsible under the law), while the other party adds an endorsement (e.g., Employee Leasing Client Exclusion endorsement or the Labor Contractor Exclu-

sion endorsement) excluding coverage for the leased employees. This approach avoids the possibility of double coverage under the two companies' policies.

Summary

The standard workers compensation and employers liability insurance policy used in most states is designed to cover employers for liability imposed on them by statute of common law for injuries to their employees. Since the sole purpose of the policy is to cover injuries to the insured's employees, it is not generally appropriate to provide additional insured status as is commonly done with liability insurance. However, there are some unique circumstances, such as in borrowed servant situations or employee leasing, where one organization is presented with an exposure that might be best covered under the policy of another organization. Special endorsements are available to protect employers against these exposures.

Chapter 16 Notes

1. In fact, the court in the case of *Reagen's Vacuum Truck Service v Beaver Insurance Co.,* 37 Cal Rptr 2d 89 (Cal App 2 Dist 1994), held that an additional insured endorsement to a workers compensation and employers liability

policy provided coverage to an additional insured only if the additional insured were the employer of the employee who was injured. It is not the purpose of an additional insured endorsement attached to a WC/EL policy to transform the policy to one providing general liability coverage. The same rationale applied in this case also underlies the premise that employment exclusions, even if worded to apply to insureds or any insured, have application only to the employer-employee relationship. These exclusions are not intended for application to nonemployers, despite attempts to do so by some insurers.

2. All states except Alabama, California, Delaware, Iowa, and Maine require principals to provide workers compensation coverage for the employees of uninsured independent contractors. Larson, Arthur, *Larson's Workmen's Compensation Desk Edition*, Chap. 9, § 49.11, p. 9–1, Rel. 43 6/99, New York: Matthew Bender & Co., Inc.

3. For this reason, workers compensation insurers require their insureds to obtain certificates of insurance from their independent contractors. When insureds fail to obtain certificates of insurance from independent contractors, their workers compensation insurers assume that the subcontractors were not insured and charge an additional premium as if the independent contractor's employees were directly employed by their insureds. The exact procedure for this, as used in most states, is delineated in General Rule IX.C.3 of the *Basic Manual for Workers Compensation and Employers Liability Insurance*, published by the National Council for Compensation Insurance.

4. However, caution must be exercised with respect to umbrella liability policies, because it is not unusual to note exclusions for employers liability coverage even though the underlying (primary) employers liability policy is scheduled.

5. Larson, Arthur, *Larson's Workmen's Compensation Desk Edition,* § 48, p. 8–100, Rel. 43 6/99, New York: Matthew Bender & Co., Inc.

6. In California an "Additional Insured Employer" endorsement serves essentially the same purpose.

7. Larson, Arthur, *Workmen's Compensation for Occupational Injuries and Death,* Desk Edition, § 48.40, Rel. 43 6/96, New York: Matthew Bender 1993.

8. The California *Workers' Compensation Insurance Manual* deals specifically with joint employment situations and allows two or more employers to purchase a single policy to cover this exposure. In conjunction with this, an "Additional Insured Employer" endorsement is used to cover joint employment situations. That endorsement would not present the possibility of a coverage gap to one of the employers that exists under the NCCI alternate employer endorsement. Since the California rule and endorsement specifically deal with joint employment situations, however, the approach may not work for dual employments.

9. Another key concern is the application of the CGL fellow employee exclusion and insured status provided to leased workers. This is covered in detail in **Chapter 3.**

10. In the past, leasing arrangements have been used by some companies to avoid the consequences of their poor risk management practices by transferring their employees from a company with a high debit experience modifier to a new company with a unity modifier and then leasing them from the new company. It becomes difficult or even impossible for an organization to manipulate its experience modifier through leasing arrangements when the client is responsible for providing workers compensation insurance.

11. As respects state statutory requirements, California, for example, addresses employee leasing in the following manner: An employing leasing company and a client company may enter into an agreement that must be enforceable and valid whereby the leasing company provides the employees and the workers compensation coverage for those employees to the client company. Both employers are considered to have paid for compensation and afforded coverage by exclusive remedy as long as an enforceable agreement has been executed and coverage for the leased employees remains in effect for the length of employment (California Labor Code 3602(d)).

Chapter 17

PROFESSIONAL AND E&O LIABILITY INSURANCE

Many types of organizations and individuals also provide professional or quasi-professional services that present liability exposures not covered by commercial general liability (CGL) and umbrella liability policies.[1] Examples include medical practitioners, accountants, attorneys, and design professionals. These individuals and firms usually purchase professional liability insurance to cover these exposures.

Thus, the question often arises as to whether it is appropriate for others to require additional insured status under these policies. As with CGL insurance, there are a couple of broad categories of persons or organizations that may desire such coverage: those working for the professional organization as employees or independent contractors and the professional organization's clients. Each category is discussed in this chapter.

Individuals and Firms Working for the Professional

Like all other businesses, architectural, legal, medical, and other professional firms or individuals employ various people, some of whom are professionals and some of whom are not. These people may, of course, be sued individually for their actions. Most professional liability policies take an approach similar to that of the CGL policy and cover as automatic insureds the partners, principals, directors, stockholders, managers, and employees of the named insured professional firm. The better policy forms cover both current and former employees. An example of an "insured" definition effecting this

coverage in an architects and engineers professional liability policy is shown in Exhibit 17.1.

EXHIBIT 17.1
PROFESSIONAL LIABILITY "INSURED" DEFINITION

The term "the Insured" shall mean:

1. the Named Insured

2. a principal, partner, director, officer, or stockholder of the Named Insured, but only while acting in his respective capacity as such; and

3. a salaried employee of the Named Insured, but only with respect to Professional Services performed or failed to have been performed on behalf of the Named Insured in his capacity as such; and

4. a former principal, partner, director, officer, or salaried employee of the Named Insured, but only with respect to Professional Services performed or failed to have been performed on behalf of the Named Insured prior to the termination of his respective capacity.

The term "Named Insured" shall mean the proprietor, firm or organization specified in Item 1 of the Declarations.

Source: Architects & Engineers Insurance Company, Professional Liability Insurance Policy for Architects & Engineers, Form N7670 (10/89).

It should be noted that, in most professional liability policies, these people have insured status only while acting within the scope of employment for the named insured. Because professionals of all kinds sometimes undertake work in their spare time or moonlight with other organizations, it should be made clear to these people that no coverage will be provided for such activities under the named insured's professional liability policy.

In a few instances, professional liability policies do provide coverage for outside activities, most notably in police professional liability policies, via the so-called moonlighting endorsement. However, such coverage is not automatic and must be specifically added by endorsement. Therefore, if a professional firm seeks to provide coverage for an employee's/partner's outside activities, it may be available only upon special request.

Another type of relationship that invokes automatic insured status in some policies is an independent contractor relationship. Under some professional liability policies, persons "for whom the named insured is legally responsible" are provided "insured" status. This is most common with lawyers professional liability insurance due to the prevalent use of "of counsel" and other independent contractor professionals. While it is not common for hospital professional liability policies to cover medical staff (i.e., nonemployee physicians who have been granted the privilege of practicing at the hospital), such physicians are usually covered by the hospital's policy for acts in conjunction with their work on hospital credentialing and peer review committees or while working in supervisory capacities. However, they will not be covered for liabilities associated with direct patient care.

Although the ideal situation is for outside individuals (and organizations) working with insureds to have their own professional liability coverage, there may be times when these entities are uninsured or underinsured. Therefore, it is advantageous for policies to extend coverage for these individuals or organizations.

When outside professionals are retained on an independent contractor basis by a professional firm, it often is possible to add them as insureds by endorsement if the policy does not grant automatic insured status. Of course, this will be subject to the discretion of the underwriter, and an additional premium is often charged for the extension.

The Professional's Clients

It is not unusual for nonprofessional persons and organizations to request additional insured status under the liability policies of professionals. For example, contract insurance requirements sometimes require that the project owner be added to the professional insurance policy of the design professional, construction manager, architect, engineer, or surveyor. Similarly, private and public entities sometimes request additional insured status on the medical professional liability policies of physicians or nurses employed by the entity. One basis for these requests is that some people simply feel that their insurance requirements should apply to all coverages under the approach of "ask and you shall receive." Another reason is to preclude the professional liability insurer's ability to subrogate against the party asking to be an additional insured.

However, most professional liability insurers will not comply with these requests. While professional liability insurers generally want to preserve whatever subrogation rights they might have, there are at least four other principal reasons insurers routinely refuse to effect additional insured status to nonrelated parties, such as clients, under professional liability policies.

First, professional liability insurers, as a matter of policy, will not add anyone who is not an employee otherwise under the control of the named insured professional. To do so can substantially increase liability exposure and even introduce a morale hazard. In fact, this thinking is reflected in one treatise that says:

> Professional liability insurers will not extend the definition of the named insured to include a project owner or other participant in the project who is not directly employed by the design professional or otherwise under the direction or

control of the design professional in the performance of their professional services.[2]

For this reason, reinsurance agreements involving professional liability insurance may also prohibit insurers from providing additional insured status and waivers of subrogation.

The second reason insurers refuse to add unaffiliated entities as insureds is that the policy's purpose is to cover actual or alleged liability emanating from the professional's rendering or failure to render "professional services." Professionals are required to adhere to a particular standard of care, and when their conduct falls short of the mark, their insurance may apply for any damages sought. Said another way, the professional liability policy is designed to provide coverage for "members of a particular professional group from the liability arising out of a special risk such as negligence, omissions, mistakes, and error inherent in the practice of the profession."[3]

A person or entity who is not a professional engaged in the same activity as the named insured (i.e., does not have the same type of professional qualifications as the named insured) does not face the exposure insured by the policy and, therefore, would not benefit from being an insured under the policy. Professional liability policies are not designed or intended to cover ordinary negligence. For example, if a hotel employs a physician to administer to hotel guests, professional liability insurance written for the physician may not be of any value to the hotel, since the hotel's executives are not likely to be in a position to commit an act of medical malpractice. Rather, the hotel's exposure is for negligence in hiring or supervising the medical professional, which is not considered a professional liability exposure by insurers.

However, it is possible for a professional's liability for rendering or failing to render professional services to be imputed to a nonprofessional such as an employer or client, and that is the reason most organizations request additional insured status. Of course, the organization's own CGL and umbrella liability insurance would cover its exposure to vicarious liability arising from the acts of its employed or independent contractor professionals in most cases. For example, protection for liability arising from the hotel's in-house physician would apply under the standard CGL policy provisions.

Similarly, a project owner's own liability insurance would not usually exclude liability of the owner for bodily injury or property damage arising from design error committed by an architect who designed its building. The problem is that this does not achieve the goal of insulating the principal's own insurance program from loss resulting from the action or inaction of the independent contractor professionals it employs. Unfortunately, the insuring agreements of professional liability policies do not stipulate that they will cover the vicarious liability of nonprofessional employers or other parties, and most insurers simply refuse to draft specialized endorsements to effect coverage of this nature.

The third reason professional liability insurers are reluctant to add additional insureds even if they are not professionals is because some additional insureds could commit acts of professional negligence potentially within coverage of the policy. Since a professional is not recognized solely by title but instead by his or her performance, people who are not professionals by definition can, in the eyes of the law, still commit professional negligence.[4] Thus, insurers fear that by adding a nonprofessional client as an insured, they may be covering a substantial liability exposure that they have not adequately underwritten.

The fourth reason professional liability insurers usually reject requests to add others as additional insureds is to avoid covering another professional's exposure without the ability to underwrite and make an appropriate premium charge for the coverage. For example, some project owners employ architects or engineers to oversee their construction projects. Adding such a project owner as an additional insured to an architect's or engineer's policy could significantly increase the insurer's exposure, and the insurer may not even be aware of it.

While most professional liability insurers refuse to add clients as additional insureds on the policies of professionals they insure, it is sometimes possible to persuade them to do so on a limited basis. When such coverage is afforded, the endorsement is usually very restrictive. Coverage generally applies only to the vicarious liability of the additional insured (i.e., liability imputed to the additional insured solely resulting from acts of professional negligence of the named insured). Any liability resulting from the negligence, professional or otherwise, of the additional insured is typically excluded.

If a principal is held liable for the professional acts of its independent contractor professional, the principal will have remedies against that professional in many cases. And, in most cases, the professional's liability insurance will be triggered to cover these damages. Therefore, obtaining this limited scope of additional insured protection may help to protect from liability, but it generally will not be as effective as obtaining additional insured status under a CGL policy.

One case in which a client did obtain coverage for its vicarious liability as an additional insured under a professional liability policy is *Washington Sports and Entertainment v United Coastal Insurance Co.*, 7 F Supp 2d 1 (USDC DC 1998).

A project owner entered into a design-build contract requiring the architect to provide professional liability coverage. The policy issued covered the architect's liability for "negligence, error or mistake in rendering or failing to render professional services." It was written with limits of $5 million and included the project owner as an additional insured. The endorsement covered additional insureds "only for liability arising from the professional services performed by any Named Insureds on this policy and only for claims by persons or entities not insured on this policy." Additionally, the policy stated that any claim that would be excluded from coverage if brought directly against any insured was excluded as to all insureds, regardless of the insured or other party against whom the claim was brought. (This wording was intended to eliminate severability of interests as a policy condition.)

The project owner sought coverage under the architect's professional liability policy for an action brought against the project owner and architect by the Paralyzed Veterans of America (PVA). The PVA alleged that the design of the building denied access to persons in wheelchairs, in violation of the Americans With Disabilities Act (ADA). The architect's professional liability insurer refused to the defend the project owner on two grounds: (1) that the injunctive relief being sought in the underlying case did not involve "damages" as covered by the policy, and (2) that the allegations in the suit were aimed at design decisions made solely by the project owner and merely complied with by the design professionals, while the additional insured project owner was covered only for errors and omissions committed by the named insured architect.

The project owner argued that the coverage for additional insureds was not limited to vicarious liability since such a limitation was not clearly stated in the policy. It cited two court decisions in which additional insureds were provided coverage for their own negligence, although the cases cited involved general rather than professional liability policies.

The key issue, then, was whether any claims in the PVA litigation triggered the project owner's vicarious liability for the architect's actions, as opposed to the project owner's direct liability for its own acts and omissions. Under normal circumstances, the court said, the architect is liable for design decisions, including those regarding ADA compliance. The design-build agreement in question, said the court, shifted at least some responsibility for ADA decisions to the project owners, thereby making their liability for these decisions direct, not vicarious. The insurer argued that the project owner had contractually assumed liability for *all* ADA decisions, thereby negating coverage.

In the final analysis, the court did not agree with this assertion of the insurer, ruling that the policy did afford the project owner with a defense to the claims in the PVA litigation. Although the policy's coverage might not apply to each claim or to every element of relief sought by the PVA, said the court, the policy did provide coverage for some claims and for some relief. From the court's perspective, this partial coverage was sufficient to trigger a duty to defend the entire claim. Interestingly, the court stated that the underlying PVA suit, which sought "other and further relief" as the court deemed proper, was not a claim for compensatory damages in the traditional sense. Nonetheless. the court held that the claim could be viewed as a demand for compensatory damages for purposes of triggering insurance coverage. This opinion and the wording it relied on are analogous to finding a defense obligation for the allegations raised in affirmative defenses and other responses to lawsuits.

Summary

Professional liability insurance policies usually take the same approach to insuring employees, partners, stockholders, and other similarly affiliated persons as do CGL and umbrella policies. They are usually provided with automatic insured status with respect to liability arising from their duties for the named insured.

On the other hand, professional liability insurance custom and practice does not contemplate adding clients as additional insureds. Contract insurance requirements imposing this requirement usually will be either met with great resistance or breached. (The *Washington Sports* case best exemplifies the time and expense in store for insurers that make exceptions for covering the vicarious liability of additional insureds.) For this reason, they generally should not be included in contracts.

Chapter 17 Notes

1. Neither the standard CGL policy nor most umbrella policies contain a broad professional liability exclusion. The principal exclusions contained within the policies typically exclude coverage for employed medical professionals (as insureds) and contractually assumed design professional liability. Other types of professional liability are covered by the basic policy if they meet the various coverage requirements of the policy (e.g., if they involve bodily injury, property damage, or personal injury that is not expected or intended and that arises from an occurrence). The problem with relying on CGL and umbrella policies is that many professional liability losses do not involve bodily injury, property damage, or personal injury. In addition, liability insurance underwriters usually will attach a profes-

sional liability exclusion endorsement to CGL and umbrella liability policies written for professional firms.

2. Roland H. Long, L.L.M., *Law of Liability Insurance*, Sec. 12D.02, New York, NY: Matthew Bender Co., p. 12D – 7.

3. *Ibid.*

4. For example, some years ago a candy striper at a hospital administered a needle to a patient in the presence of a physician and caused irreparable harm to the patient. The court decided that the candy striper committed an act of professional negligence but was not covered under the hospital's professional liability policy because the candy striper was not a professional.

Chapter 18

COMMERCIAL PROPERTY INSURANCE[1]

In the day-to-day management of a property insurance program, requests to "name" someone other than the insured on the policy are commonplace. Usually the entity making the request has a legitimate reason for doing so, and often the request is both specific and correct as to exactly how the policy should be amended to protect its interests in covered property.

But sometimes an entity with every right to have its interests in covered property protected under the policy requests the wrong kind of endorsement, given its interest in the property. Other times the entity making the request is asking for something to which it is not entitled. Sometimes, for example, an entity that has a legitimate reason for wanting to be named as an additional insured under the insured's liability policy will, out of ignorance, "throw in" a request to be named as an additional insured under the property policy.

In part, the purpose of this chapter is to sort out what is and is not accomplished by naming someone with an interest in covered property as an additional insured, loss payee, or mortgagee under property insurance policies. A summary appears in Exhibit 18.1.

Insurable Interest

Designating an individual or entity as an additional insured, mortgagee, or loss payee on a commercial property policy gives that person or entity a claim to insurance proceeds that would otherwise belong solely to the insured. Only those who have an insurable interest in covered property can legitimately be given a claim to the insurance proceeds. Obviously, the property owner has an insurable interest in that property. Those who have loaned money to the property owner may also have an insurable interest in the covered property—in specific items pledged as collateral or, in some cases, in all of the insured's property. Persons or entities that can be held responsible for damage to the property also have an insurable interest in it, to the extent of their legal liability. For example, property leases often have provisions making the lessee responsible for any damage to the leased property. In fact, in building leases involving a sole tenant, the tenant is often required to purchase insurance covering the building.

In addition to an insurable interest for damage to the property they construct or install, subcontractors have an insurable interest to the extent they are entitled to payment for work on a given project. However, the insurable interest of subcontactors is only equal and often subordinate to the interests of the contractor or owner, particularly as to the owner after title to the property being constructed has passed to the owner. The limits of commercial property insurance purchased should take into account the extent of insurable interest possessed by all of the parties involved.

Mortgagees

A mortgagee is a person or entity that has an interest in property offered as collateral for a loan. Usually the mortgagee's interest is in real property (land and the buildings and other structures on that land) rather than personal property.

Most commercial property insurance forms include a mortgage clause that provides special protection for those designated on the declarations page or in an endorsement to the policy as mortgagees of covered buildings and structures. As an example, the Insurance Services Office, Inc. (ISO), mortgage holders provision from the Building and Personal Property form is shown in Exhibit 18.2. If a particular form does not have a built-in mortgage clause, one can be added by endorsement.

Regardless of whether the mortgage clause is built into the form or added by endorsement, the key mortgage clause provisions are quite standard from one policy to the next.

- The mortgage clause establishes that payment for covered loss or damage to buildings or structures will be made to the mortgage holder(s) shown in the declarations—not to the insured or to the insured and the mortgagee.

- The mortgage clause also establishes that coverage applies for the benefit of the mortgagee even if the insured's claim is denied because of the insured's acts, provided that the mortgagee pays any premium due on request and notifies the insurer of any change in ownership, occupancy, or substantial change in risk known to the mortgagee.

EXHIBIT 18.1
ADDITIONAL INTERESTS ENDORSEMENTS COMPARISON

Type of Endorsement	Typical Insurable Interest	Receipt of Loss Payment	Typical Notice of Cancellation	Coverage Despite Insured's Acts
Mortgage Holders Provision or Endorsement	Holds mortgage on covered building(s)	Exclusive	For cancellation by the insurer only. 30 days, except 10 days nonpay. May include 10 days' notice of nonrenewal.	Yes
Loss Payee Endorsement	Leases personal property to the insured, may also be a creditor	May be exclusive or shared with the insured	None, unless specifically requested.	No
Lenders Loss Payable Endorsement	Creditor with an interest in covered personal property.	Exclusive	For cancellation by the insurer only. 30 days, except 10 days nonpay. May include 10 days' notice of nonrenewal.	Yes
Additional Insured Endorsement	Owner of building(s) leased to the insured	Shared with the insured	None, unless specifically requested; check policy cancellation provisions.	No

Source: *Commercial Property Insurance*, Copyright © 1994, International Risk Management Institute, Inc.

EXHIBIT 18.2
ISO MORTGAGE HOLDERS PROVISION

2. Mortgage Holders

  a. The term "mortgage holder" includes trustee.

  b. We will pay for covered loss of or damage to buildings or structures to each mortgage holder shown in the Declarations in their order of precedence, as interests may appear.

  c. The mortgage holder has the right to receive loss payment even if the mortgage holder has started foreclosure or similar action on the building or structure.

  d. If we deny your claim because of your acts or because you have failed to comply with the terms of this Coverage Part, the mortgage holder will still have the right to receive loss payment if the mortgage holder:

   (1) Pays any premium due under this Coverage Part at our request if you have failed to do so;

   (2) Submits a signed, sworn statement of loss within 60 days after receiving notice from us of your failure to do so; and

   (3) Has notified us of any change in ownership, occupancy or substantial change in risk known to the mortgage holder.

   All of the terms of this Coverage Part will then apply directly to the mortgage holder.

  e. If we pay the mortgage holder for any loss or damage and deny payment to you because of your acts or because you have failed to comply with the terms of this Coverage Part:

   (1) The mortgage holder's rights under the mortgage will be transferred to us to the extent of the amount we pay; and

   (2) The mortgage holder's right to recover the full amount of the mortgage holder's claim will not be impaired.

   At our option, we may pay to the mortgage holder the whole principal on the mortgage plus any accrued interest. In this event, your mortgage and note will be transferred to us and you will pay your remaining mortgage debt to us.

  f. If we cancel this policy, we will give written notice to the mortgage holder at least:

   (1) 10 days before the effective date of cancellation if we cancel for your nonpayment of premium; or

   (2) 30 days before the effective date of cancellation if we cancel for any other reason.

  g. If we elect not to renew this policy, we will give written notice to the mortgage holder at least 10 days before the expiration date of this policy.

- Finally, the mortgage clause establishes that the mortgagee will receive written notice of policy cancellation by the insurer—usually 10 days' notice of cancellation for nonpayment of premium and 30 days' notice of cancellation for any other reason. The mortgage provision in current ISO forms goes so far as to promise the mortgagee 10 days' notice of nonrenewal—a right not even granted to the insured. Note, however, that the typical mortgage clause addresses only cancellation by the insurer; the clause is silent on notice of cancellation at the insured's request.

The loss payment aspect of the mortgage clause is not unique. Loss payee clauses can accomplish the same result if they are worded to make loss payable only to the loss payee instead of to the loss payee and the insured. Additional insured endorsements also entitle the named entity to payment for covered loss—although usually an additional insured will be included in, rather than be the exclusive recipient of, any loss payment in connection with specified property.

The notice of cancellation aspect of the mortgage clause is not unique either. Loss payee and additional insured endorsements can be written to promise prior written notice of cancellation—although notice of cancellation provisions are not standard in these types of endorsements as they are in a mortgage clause.

But continuation of coverage for the benefit of the mortgagee, even if coverage is otherwise invalidated by some act of the insured (arson, for example), is a benefit normally available only to mortgagees and to other secured creditors under a lenders loss payable endorsement (CP 12 18, Loss Payable Provisions).

Loss Payees

A loss payee is a person or entity that is entitled to all or part of the insurance proceeds in connection with the covered property in which it has an interest. Often those asking to be named as loss payees have leased some type of equipment to the in-

sured—a photocopy machine, for example. As a word of caution, however, the term is often used generically, and it is usually advisable to review the contract, type of transaction, and type of property involved to determine the extent of protection needed by the organization requiring loss payee status.

Loss Payee Endorsements

There is a loss payable endorsement for use with the ISO commercial property forms. Actually, the current ISO loss payee endorsement (CP 12 18, Loss Payable Provisions) is a combination of two prior endorsements: CF 12 18, Loss Payable Clause; and CF 12 19, Lenders Loss Payable Clause. The loss payable portion of the current ISO endorsement, like its predecessor, simply states that loss to covered property in which a designated loss payee has an interest will be adjusted with the insured and payable jointly to the insured and the loss payee.

Many insurers simply use a general change endorsement to designate a loss payee. Insurer loss payee endorsements, whether reprinted or issued on general change endorsements, may not make any mention of loss adjustment. Also, they may specify that loss to covered property in which the loss payee has an interest will be payable to the loss payee instead of to the insured and the loss payee.

Loss payee endorsements do not normally give the loss payee any rights or responsibilities under the policy other than the right to receive payment for covered loss to the property in which it has an interest. A case in point is *Northwestern National Casualty Co. v Tigner,* 520 NW2d 771 (Minn App 1994). It involved an owner of a commercial building who challenged a lower court's decision holding that the owner, who was named as a loss payee on a tenant's policy, was not entitled to recover under the tenant's property policy for damages to the building caused by the tenant when moving out. Although the insurer relied on two policy exclusions to deny coverage, the court held that it was not necessary to decide whether either exclusion barred coverage because the building owner (loss payee) did not establish that any coverage existed. Furthermore, the tenant made no claim for coverage under the policy.

Although the building owner maintained that she had a right to recover under the loss payable provisions of the policy, the court, in affirming the lower court's decision, held otherwise. It stated that there are two primary methods by which the interest of someone other than the named insured can be protected: (1) the standard mortgage clause, and (2) the loss payable clause. The court explained that the first clause constitutes an independent contract between the insurer and mortgagee, and coverage cannot be defeated by the conduct of the mortgagor. Under a loss payable clause, on the other hand, the right of the loss payee to recover can be extinguished in situations where the named insured has no right to recover.

The court explained that before the building owner could become eligible for coverage under the tenant's policy, the tenant must first be entitled to recover. However, the tenant did not make a claim for coverage. Therefore, the building owner had no right to assert a claim for damages.

These endorsements also are sometimes written to provide the loss payee with notice of cancellation.

Lenders Loss Payable Endorsements

A lenders loss payable endorsement gives a creditor of the insured the same rights and duties that a mortgage clause gives a mortgagee. In fact, the provisions of the lenders loss payable portion of the current ISO Loss Payable endorsement (reproduced in Exhibit 18.3) are nearly identical to the provisions of the ISO mortgage holders provision in the ISO Building and Personal Property form. The difference between the two is that the mortgage clause applies only to mortgagees of real property (land and the buildings and other structures on that land), whereas the lenders loss payable provisions can apply to creditors with an interest in any covered property (real or personal), provided that interest is established in a written contract.

Notice that the lender's loss payable portion of the Loss Payable Provisions endorsement can be used instead of the mortgage provision built into the ba-

sic form to recognize the interests of a mortgagee or trustee. Since the provisions of the two are virtually identical, using a lender's loss payable endorsement instead would not place the mortgagee at any particular disadvantage. As a practical matter, however, since a mortgage holders provision is built into the basic form, mortgagees and trustees whose interests are in buildings and other structures are usually designated on the Declarations page as mortgage holders, and there is no need for any endorsement. A lender's loss payable endorsement is generally used to secure special protection for creditors whose interest is in personal property rather than buildings and other structures.

Contract of Sale

The ISO Loss Payable Provisions (CP 12 18) endorsement includes a contract of sale option that, if elected, recognizes simultaneous insurable interests of a buyer and seller of covered property. The contract of sale provisions specify that loss will be adjusted with the insured but payable jointly to the insured and the designated loss payee. The contract of sale option also modifies the other insurance provision so that it applies to the loss payee as well as to the insured.

Additional Insureds

As with liability insurance, the terms "additional named insured" and "additional insured" do not have clear, well-established meanings with respect to property insurance. Even the meanings of the terms "named insured" and "insured" must be gleaned from general usage and common sense.

The term "named insured" refers to the entity or entities that are "named" as the "insured" on the declarations page or, if all the names will not fit in the "insured" blank on the declarations page, on a supplemental named insured endorsement referred to on the declarations page. The named insured is generally the party who has procured the policy and in whose name it was issued. The term "insured" can certainly be used to refer to these "named insureds" but, depending on the context, could also encompass others designated as covered under the policy.

EXHIBIT 18.3
ISO LENDER'S LOSS PAYABLE PROVISIONS

From ISO's Loss Payable Provisions Endorsement (CP 12 18):

C. Lender's Loss Payable

1. The loss payee shown in the schedule or in the declarations is a creditor, including a mortgage holder or trustee, whose interest in covered property is established by such written instruments as:

   a. Warehouse receipts;

   b. A contract for deed;

   c. Bills of lading;

   d. Financing statements; or

   e. Mortgages, deeds of trust, or security agreements.

2. For covered property in which both you and a loss payee have an insurable interest:

   a. We will pay for covered loss or damage to each loss payee in their order of precedence, as interests may appear.

   b. The loss payee has the right to receive loss payment even if the loss payee has started foreclosure or similar action on the covered property.

   c. If we deny your claim because of your acts or because you have failed to comply with the terms of the coverage part, the loss payee will still have the right to receive loss payment if the loss payee:

      (1) Pays any premium due under the coverage part at our request if you have failed to do so;

      (2) Submits a signed, sworn proof of loss within 60 days after receiving notice from us of your failure to do so; and

      (3) Has notified us of any changes in ownership, occupancy or substantial change in risk known to the loss payee.

      All of the terms of this coverage part will then apply directly to the loss payee.

   d. If we pay the loss payee for any loss or damage and deny payment to you because of your acts or because you have failed to comply with the terms of this coverage part:

      (1) The loss payee's rights will be transferred to us to the extent of the amount we pay; and

      (2) The loss payee's rights to recover the full amount of the loss payee's claim will not be impaired.

3. If we cancel this policy, we will give written notice to the loss payee at least:

   a. 10 days before the effective date of cancellation if we cancel for your nonpayment of premium; or

   b. 30 days before the effective date of cancellation if we cancel for any other reason.

4. If we elect not to renew this policy, we will give written notice to the loss payee at least 10 days before the expiration date of this policy.

The term "first named insured" was introduced in the 1986 ISO commercial forms; it has since been incorporated into many insurer and manuscript commercial property forms. As discussed in **Chapter 4,** the insured whose name is listed first on the declarations page or named insured endorsement (the "first named insured") has the authority to request changes in or cancellation of the policy on behalf of all insureds. In the event of cancellation by the insurer, prior written notice will be sent only to the mailing address of the first named insured, and any return premium will be sent to the first named insured.

Usually the term "additional insured" is used in one of two situations.

- When coverage for the benefit of the additional insured is being added after policy issuance—hence the term "additional" insured, since that name is being added to the original named insured wording

- When the additional insured does not have an insurable interest in all of the covered property but only in a particular item of property that is one of many items of property covered under the policy

In the first situation, the insurer could reissue the declarations page, but this may be unnecessary or even problematic. Another alternative would be to endorse the policy with an amended named insured list that includes the "additional" insured—but this also may be unnecessary.

Occasionally, an entity with an insurable interest in all or substantially all of the insured property may be designated in an endorsement as an additional insured. This could occur because the name was mistakenly omitted when the policy was originally issued or because the insurable interest was acquired after the policy's effective date. The most common reason for designating a person or entity as an additional insured instead of including them as a named insured in the policy declarations is that the party has an insurable interest in only a small portion of the covered property.

A request to name someone as an additional insured arises most often when the insured is the sole tenant in a building and is required by the lease to insure the building and name the building owner as an additional insured. If the commercial property policy purchased by the insured tenant covered only the leased building, it would be appropriate to show both the tenant and the building owner as named insureds in the Declarations. However, the policy typically covers other property of the tenant in which the building owner has no insurable interest. Showing the building owner as an additional insured with respect only to that particular building protects its interest in that property without otherwise involving it in the policy.

There may also be a mortgagee for the leased building that is entitled to be recognized as a mortgage holder under the policy. In this case, the insured tenant, the building owner, and the mortgagee all have valid insurable interests in that property. Normally, the tenant would be the named insured, the building owner would be shown as an additional insured with respect only to that particular building, and the mortgagee would be shown as the mortgage holder for that particular building only.

Additional Insured Endorsements

There are no standard additional insured endorsements promulgated by ISO for use with its commercial property insurance forms. An additional insured endorsement to a commercial property policy usually consists of a statement typed onto an otherwise nearly blank general change endorsement form that simply says that a given individual or entity is an additional insured. Generally, the only preprinted entries on the form are spaces labeled for insertion of the effective date, the policy number, and the names of the insurer and the insured.

Loss Payment

Naming someone as an additional insured establishes that person or entity as an insured. It is the insureds who receive the loss payment under a property insurance policy. Accordingly, it may be unnecessary to specify that an additional insured is also a loss payee.

In the event of covered loss to the property in which the additional insured has an interest, the insurer might issue any loss payment check to both the named insured and the additional insured. It would not be possible for either party to obtain the funds without the cooperation of the other.

However, where the policy has not been endorsed in a manner clarifying the interests of the parties or the underlying contract does not do so, insurers may be reluctant to disperse funds. As a result, a dispute may ensue resulting in the insurer's depositing policy proceeds into a trust account or with the court as an interpleader, pending a resolution of the dispute. For that reason, it remains preferable that additional insureds be designated as loss payees to the extent of their interest.

Notice of Cancellation

An additional insured endorsement may or may not establish that the additional insured will be provided with a specified number of days (commonly 30 days) of advance written notice of policy cancellation. If the endorsement does not grant notice of cancellation, whether the additional insured is entitled to notice of cancellation depends on the cancellation provisions of the policy. The cancellation provision in the ISO common policy conditions form establishes that only the first named insured will be notified of cancellation by the insurer. Therefore, an additional insured would not be entitled to notice of cancellation by the insurer.

An additional insured should check the language of the applicable cancellation provision (in the policy form or in the additional insured endorsement) to make sure that it would be notified of cancellation, whether by the insurer or by the named insured. ISO notice of cancellation provisions address only cancellation by the insurer. The language of some insurer forms is more favorable to the additional insured (and to all insureds other than the "first named insured") than ISO forms on this point.

No Protection from Insured's Acts

Additional insured endorsements normally do not provide the additional insured with coverage de-

spite any acts of the insured that invalidate coverage. Only mortgage clauses and lenders loss payable clauses do that.

Actually, according to current ISO commercial property language, intentional concealment or misrepresentation of a material fact by any insured voids coverage for all insureds. So an additional insured's conduct could conceivably void the named insured's coverage under some circumstances.

Subrogation

The main advantage of being an additional insured instead of a loss payee is that the insurer should not be able to subrogate against an additional insured for negligent damage to covered property. This is because insurers are generally prevented from recovering loss payments from their own insureds. A loss payee is not an insured and thus receives no protection against subrogation.

As Their Interests May Appear

The phrase "as their interests may appear" is often used in additional insured endorsements to property insurance policies. For example, an additional insured endorsement might read as follows.

> It is hereby agreed and understood that XYZ Company is added as an additional insured as their interests may appear.

This language is intended to restrict the recovery rights of the additional insured to only the proceeds in connection with the covered property in which the additional insured has a legitimate insurable interest. The same result can be accomplished by naming the party as an additional insured "with respect only to" the particular item of property in which the additional insured has an interest. ("It is hereby agreed and understood that XYZ Company is added as an additional insured with respect only to the building located at ....") In the absence of any language that limits the additional insured's recovery rights, the insurer would have to include the additional insured on all loss settlement checks issued in connection with the policy, and the insured would have to secure the additional insured's release to get the funds. The result could be a dispute similar to that referenced previously in the discussions on the desirability of making additional insureds loss payees as well. In such disputes, the insurer will likely deposit policy proceeds into a trust account or with the court.

However, the phrase "as their interests may appear" has occasionally been interpreted by the courts as limiting not just loss recovery but also immunity from subrogation. The phrase "with respect only to" could certainly be interpreted in the same way.

Immunity from subrogation is usually not a big concern for commercial property additional insureds. Additional insureds on commercial property policies are usually the owners of property that is leased to the insured. They seldom have any access to or control of the covered property, and thus they are very seldom in a position to negligently cause a loss to covered property. Furthermore, commercial property policies virtually always have a subrogation provision that allows the insured to waive recovery rights in writing prior to loss, and there is often a provision in the lease wherein the insured tenant waives any recovery rights against the building owner.

But immunity from subrogation is a very big concern for builders risk additional insureds, most of whom are contractors and subcontractors whose negligent work could cause a covered builders risk loss. The topic of builders risk subrogation is discussed later. Although builders risk additional insureds, as a group, have much greater exposures in this area than commercial property insureds as a group, the following discussion applies equally to those commercial property additional insureds who are in a position to negligently cause a covered loss.

Builders Risk Additional Insureds

Naming the general contractor and the subcontractors as insureds under the builders risk policy is one way to entitle them to an appropriate share of the insurance proceeds. Contractors and subcontractors often are, in reality, owners or creditors with a very legitimate insurable interest in the property under construction.

Ownership in a construction project typically changes during the course of the project. Although the party commissioning the construction project will ultimately be the owner of the completed building, as a general rule the percentage of ownership of the so-called owner increases gradually as payments are made to the various contractors. The project owner is seldom the sole owner of property under construction until the general contractor (at least) has been paid.

Most often, the contractor—not the owner—purchases the construction materials and is reimbursed only periodically during the construction process. Thus, it is entirely appropriate for the general contractor and the subcontractors to be named insureds under the builders risk policy. As part-owners of the insured property or as creditors of the insured to the extent of the labor and materials advanced, they should rightly have a claim to the builders risk insurance proceeds.

In terms of giving the contractor a valid claim to builders risk insurance proceeds, there is little or no difference between being the named insured, an additional insured (unlike the potential problems for doing so in a liability policy), or a loss payee. Any of these approaches should accomplish that purpose.

The advantage of including the general contractor and the subcontractors as named insureds under the builders risk policy, instead of as an additional insured or loss payee, is that it should help to prevent the builders risk insurer from attempting to recover from the general contractor or any of the subcontractors for losses allegedly caused by their negligence.

Subrogation is a particularly crucial issue in builders risk insurance because the parties to a construction contract usually intend for the builders risk insurance to be their sole remedy for covered damage caused by the negligence of any of the parties. Standard construction contracts usually require one of the parties to the contract (most often the project owner) to purchase a single builders risk policy on the project protecting the interests of the owner, contractor, and subcontractors. Furthermore, standard construction contracts contain mutual waivers of subrogation in which all parties to the construction contract agree to give up their rights of recovery against the others with respect to losses covered by the builders risk policy.

However, in the absence of clear policy provisions to the contrary, insurers generally have the right to recover for paid loss from a negligent third party. Since some builders risk losses can be the direct result of a contractor's negligence, it is understandable that insurers would prefer to retain recovery rights against building contractors. Nevertheless, industry practice is for builders risk insurers to assess the contractor's competence and the likelihood of covered losses caused by the contractor's or subcontractors' faulty workmanship as part of the builders risk underwriting process.

The quoted builders risk rate is presumed to reflect the insurer's inability to recover from the contractor. An insurer that balks at waiving subrogation rights against the contractor probably writes mostly permanent property insurance and is unfamiliar with the unique needs of the construction industry and the insurance arrangements that have been devised to respond to those needs.

Three policy provisions should prevent a builders risk insurer from subrogating against a contractor or subcontractor whose negligence is the cause of a covered loss.

- A subrogation clause allowing the insured to waive recovery rights against others in writing prior to loss.

- A named insured provision that includes the general contractor and all subcontractors as insureds.

- A waiver of subrogation endorsement in favor of the general contractor and all subcontractors.

Any one of these ought to be enough to prevent subrogation by the builders risk insurer. However, because there have been instances of attempted—and even successful—subrogation by builders risk insurers against negligent contractors or subcontractors when the policy contained one or more of these features, it is best to include all three whenever possible.

Builders Risk Policy Subrogation Provision

As discussed previously, construction contracts generally contain mutual waivers of subrogation in which all parties to the contract agree to give up any rights of recovery for loss that they might have against the other parties to the contract. It is important to realize that the effect on the builders risk coverage of including mutual waivers of subrogation in the construction contract will depend on the subrogation provisions of the builders risk policy.

The subrogation clause in virtually all commercial property policies written on existing structures grants permission for the insured to waive recovery rights against others in writing prior to loss. (This permission may be affirmatively stated, or it may be inferred from a provision that prohibits the insured from giving up recovery rights after loss.)

Unfortunately, builders risk policy subrogation provisions are not as predictable as commercial property subrogation provisions. Since there is no single standard builders risk policy in widespread use, the subrogation or waiver of recovery rights provision in each builders risk form under consideration must be examined to be sure that preloss waivers of recovery rights by the insured are allowed.

If the builders risk policy has a subrogation provision that prohibits the insured from waiving recovery rights against others, execution of a contract containing a typical mutual waiver of subrogation provision would constitute a violation of the policy conditions by the insured, and that violation might well prevent any builders risk loss recovery. On the other hand, if the subrogation provision allows preloss waivers by the insured, the insurer should recognize and honor any waiver of recovery rights provision that is included in the construction contract.

However, at least one state, California, has case law that may preclude the validity of preloss waivers.[2] The rationale given is that a right of subrogation does not exist (is incohate) until after payment is made on behalf of the insured. Therefore, the insured cannot waive what is not yet in existence. For this reason, it is wise to have the subrogation waiver specifically granted in an endorsement to the policy, at least in California.

The entire issue of subrogation is what is referred to in legal terms as an equitable remedy as opposed to a legal one. What this means basically is that the courts are free to fashion relief as much or more on what they perceive to be fair as opposed to being strictly bound to legal precedent. Because of this, it is dangerous to assume hard-and-fast rules that will apply in every fact pattern.

There is another problem in this context that should be taken into account when addressing the issue of subrogation. It is not uncommon for agents and brokers to forget to submit requests to insurers for the issuance of additional insured endorsements. Thus, the additional insured may be lulled into a false sense of security. If the additional insured status is not consummated because of an oversight on behalf of the agent or broker, the additional insured could find itself without coverage and subject to the insurer's subrogation action.

Including Contractors as Insureds

Naming all contractors and subcontractors as insureds under the builders risk policy to prevent subrogation against them is done on the assumption that an insurer cannot subrogate against an insured under the policy. While this principle has usually been upheld in court, there have been instances of insurers attempting to recover builders risk losses from a contractor or subcontractor

named as an insured under the builders risk policy. A few of these attempts have been successful.

In some cases, the courts have said that use of the phrase "as their interests may appear" in the named insured language limits the protection of the policy (both as to loss recovery and as to immunity from subrogation by the insurer) to only the specific work that the contractor or subcontractor did. This interpretation might allow the insurer to subrogate against the negligent contractor or subcontractor for resulting damage to other portions of the project. Therefore, it is recommended that the phrase "as their interests may appear" not be used in builders risk named insured provisions or endorsements.

Even where a builders risk policy covers various parties "as their interest may appear," subrogation is sometimes precluded. A case in point is *Dyson & Co. and St. Paul Fire & Marine Insurance Co. v Flood Engineers, Architects, Planners,* 523 S2d 756 (Fl App 1988).

A municipality contracted with an engineering firm to design and engineer the specifications for a sewage treatment plant. The general contractor was required to obtain a builders risk policy to protect its interests, along with the city and the engineering firm. While the general contractor did obtain the policy, it failed to have the city and engineering firm named as insureds on the policy. A fire occurred during a performance test and the general contractor was paid for the loss sustained.

Following payment by the general contractor's insurer and an assortment of related actions, both the general contractor and its insurer filed an action against the engineering firm alleging negligent design and seeking to recover for the amount paid under the builders risk policy. The engineering firm responded that the general contractor's breach of its obligation to insure the engineering firm's interests under the builders risk policy barred any action against it to recover any amounts paid under that policy.

The general contractor and its insurer argued in return that the engineering firm could not be an insured under the policy because it had no insurable interest in the covered property. They contended that the only interest the engineering firm had was that of being held free from liability for damages caused by its negligence. The contractor and its insurer argued that this was an interest encompassed by liability insurance, not first-party property coverage in the form of builders risk insurance. A trial court agreed with the engineering firm, and the general contractor appealed.

One section of the contract between the city and the general contractor read as follows.

> The Contractor shall also take out and maintain at his expense during the life of this Contract, Builders Risk Insurance satisfactory to the Owner which shall protect the Contractor, the Owner, and the Engineer as their interests may appear, for the following hazards to work....

The parties conceded that the general contractor had failed to include the engineering firm in the insurance policy. As a result, the builders risk policy covered only the general contractor and its subcontractors. The court said that if the engineering firm had been an insured under the builders risk policy as required by the contract, the general contractor and its insurer would have been precluded from seeking subrogation as long as the engineering firm had an insurable interest in the project. According to the court, the engineering firm did have an insurable interest in the project.

After reviewing a number of cases concerning subrogation under builders risk policies, the court determined that the majority view supported the engineering firm's contention that the phrase "as their interests may appear" in builders risk policies includes liability as well as property interests. The court held that where the potential risk to be insured under a builders risk policy is one of liability for damages to the construction project, such risk will constitute an "insurable interest." Although the engineering firm could not point to any tangible property interest it had in the project, such as bricks, mortar, or other equipment, it had a substantial interest in being held free from any liability arising out of its participation in the project.

Thus, the court said, the engineering firm had an insurable interest to the extent to which it might have become legally responsible for the fire loss to the property as a result of its own negligence. It therefore was held to have an insurable interest sufficient to support its right to enforce compliance with the builders risk coverage provisions of the contract. This in turn precluded enforcement of the builders risk insurer's right of subrogation, since it would have had no subrogation rights if the engineering firm had been added to the policy as required.

Waiver of Subrogation Endorsement

The ultimate precaution against subrogation by the builders risk insurer is a waiver of subrogation *endorsement* to the builders risk policy, issued by the insurer, in favor of all contractors and subcontractors. Since such an endorsement constitutes an explicit agreement on the part of the insurer not to subrogate, one might think that no insurer whose policy contained such an endorsement would dare to go into court in a subrogation attempt. Amazingly, however, there has been at least one case (*Turner Construction Co. v John B. Kelly Co.,* 442 F Supp 551 (1976)) where that occurred. A builders risk insurer, whose policy named the contractor and all subcontractors as insureds and contained a waiver of subrogation endorsement in favor of all those insured by the policy, was nevertheless allowed to subrogate against a negligent subcontractor.

The court stated that the protection of the policy extended to the subcontractor was limited by the use of the phrase "as their interests may appear" to the amount of the subcontractors' labor and materials. Further, the subrogation waiver endorsement functioned only to prevent the insurer from recovering the subcontractor's portion of the builders risk proceeds.

From this example, it would seem that to ensure that a builders risk waiver of subrogation endorsement is enforceable, the endorsement must explicitly state that the insurer relinquishes recovery rights against contractors and subcontractors working on the construction project, even if their negligence causes a covered loss and regardless of the extent of their insurable interest in the covered property.

Recent Trends

Although there is no absolute guarantee that any builders risk policy provision will prevent a builders risk insurer from attempting to subrogate against a contractor or subcontractor, the recent trend has been for courts to disallow subrogation against contractors and subcontractors, even when the builders risk policy did not contain policy provisions designed to prevent it.[3] It may be that the issue of builders risk subrogation is viewed by most insurers as having been settled by the courts in favor of the contractors. However, it would be wise not only to include the provisions discussed here but also to deal with experienced and reputable builders risk insurers that understand the intent of all parties to look to the builders risk policy as the sole remedy for covered loss.

Severability of Interests

Unlike liability insurance, property insurance policies do not contain severability of interests provisions. However, this does not mean that the coverage afforded by property policies is not several. The provisions of property policies can and do apply separately to each insured, though the concept of severability is applied differently. Drafters of property policies often attempt to dilute the concept of severability by wording exclusions or other policy provisions so that a loss caused by one insured precludes recovery of loss by another insured who may have an insurable interest.

Such an attempt was the basis of the coverage dispute in *Pink Cadillac Bar and Grill v U.S. Fidelity and Guaranty Co.*, 925 P2d 152 (Kan App 1996). The named insured business included two owners, who were corporate officers, and a silent partner. Following damage to the business establishment caused by a fire of suspicious origin, the insurer paid the bank, as mortgage holder, sums for the

cost of repairs to the building but refused to pay the silent partner and one of the officer-owners for losses associated with personal property and business interruption. The insurer's denial of coverage was based on a contention that the silent partner had either set the fire or concealed that he had it set by another person.

A trial court found that the silent partner had not intentionally set the fire but that he did conceal or misrepresent a material fact during the insurer's investigation of the claim. The court also held that the severability of interests clause of the package policy under which coverage was being sought created an ambiguity. On the basis of that ambiguity, the court ruled that the silent partner's conduct should not exclude the other owner, an innocent coinsurer, from recovering under the policy.

On appeal, the insurer argued that the trial court erred in finding an ambiguity in the insurance policy concerning severability. It contended that the severability provision pertained only to the liability portion of the package policy and did not affect application of the policy's concealment clause, which voids coverage in the case of concealment or misrepresentation of a material fact or fraud committed by "an insured." The insurer read this provision as precluding coverage for *all* insureds if any one of them was guilty of concealment or misrepresentation.

The appellate court ruled that (1) the severability clause of the policy did not apply to the claim brought under the policy's property coverage; and (2) the silent partner's concealment or misrepresentation of a material fact barred coverage for all insureds.

How other similar cases may be resolved will hinge on the fact pattern and the nature of the property policy in question. In fact, the question often arises whether coverage under a builders risk policy, which usually includes many insureds, is several even though it does not contain a severability clause. For example, if a subcontractor were to perform defective work that had to be redone, is an exclusion dealing with the cost to make good faulty work applicable to the general contractor who is responsible for a subcontractor's performance? Or is application of that exclusion limited to coverage of the negligent party who causes the uninsured loss? As would be expected, some insureds under builders risk policies feel that the exclusion should only apply to the party that caused the uninsured loss. The rationale for this position is that part of the reason for purchasing a builders risk policy is to protect insurable interests against fortuitous loss, which can include negligence of other parties. This concern is not necessarily limited to the faulty workmanship exclusion. What is sometimes referred to as the "error in design" exclusion has also been the focal point of litigation on this issue. Since builders risk policies are not standard, the resolution of this question will hinge on the specific policy provisions in effect.

An example is *Dow Chemical Co. v Royal Indemnity Co.,* 635 F2d 379 (1981), which involved the collapse of a domed building while under construction. The builders risk policy on the project excluded losses resulting from "faulty workmanship or other error, omission, or deficiency in respect to operations involving the construction, installation, repair or erection of any insured property, when attributable to or performed by the insured or any person or persons in the employment or service of the insured." Since the primary cause of the collapse was faulty workmanship on the part of the subcontractor, the coverage issue was whether the subcontractor or others performing work for the subcontractor were considered to be "in the service of the insured." The court held that the subcontractor was not in the service of the insured within the meaning of the specific policy language, and that the exclusion therefore did not apply.

A case involving a similar loss but producing a different conclusion is *Kroll Construction Co. v Great American Insurance Co.,* 594 F Supp 304 (1984). The general contractor in this case brought an action against its insurer to recover under its "all risks" builders risk policy covering an office building for costs incurred in correcting deficient waterproofing materials and/or work furnished by the subcontractor. The coverage issue was whether the policy excluded the cost of making good faulty or defective workmanship or materials of a third-party subcontractor or just that of the general contractor.

The general contractor argued that to interpret the "cost of making good" provision to exclude losses caused by a subcontractor would render the policy's coverage meaningless. The contractor also maintained that its reasonable expectation was to be protected against the consequences of a subcontractor's actions and that the insurer had a duty to specifically exclude from coverage losses resulting from the faulty or defective work of subcontractors if that was the coverage intent.

The court agreed that the policy would have been clearer if the exclusion applied specifically "regardless of to whom attributable" or "to the workmanship of subcontractors as well as the workmanship of the general contractor." However, omission of such wording was not held to be detrimental to the insurer's case, because the "faulty workmanship" exclusion applied to "the cost of making good *any* faulty or defective workmanship." (Emphasis added.) The breadth of the word "any," the court explained, made the exclusion applicable a subcontractor's workmanship as well as to the general contractor's.

Insurers attempting to subrogate against insured parties under a builders risk policy commonly maintain that coverage is limited to the insurable interest of that party or, in other words, to the extent of the work that has been performed by that party. Thus, if one insured's work produces covered damage to another insured's work, the first insured should be subject to subrogation. Builders risk insuring agreements should be carefully examined on this point. Some policies cover physical loss or damage to property of others. The "others" in this regard could be other interests involved in the project. Some policies may also cover physical loss or damage to property for which the insured may be legally responsible, including liability assumed under contract. The point is that individual policy provisions cannot be read in isolation.

Summary

While there is no standard additional insured endorsement available for use with commercial property insurance policies, there are numerous situations where the policies need to be amended to reflect the protection of persons or organizations who may have an insurable interest in the covered property. Included in this category are mortgagees and other creditors of real and personal property, as well as buyers and sellers of covered property. There are still others who desire additional insured status under property policies to prevent subrogation actions against them, such as contractors insured under builders risk policies. Whatever the motive, property policies generally can be amended to protect the insurable interests of parties who are not automatically covered by the policies.

Chapter 18 Notes

1. Most of this discussion is adapted from "Protecting the Interests of Others: Additional Insureds, Loss Payees, and Mortgages," *Commercial Property Insurance,* Dallas, TX: International Risk Management Institute, Inc.

2. *Liberty Mutual Insurance Co. v Altfillisch Construction Co.,* 70 Cal App 3d 789 (1997). For more comprehensive discussions of subrogation waivers, see *Malecki on Insurance,* Vol. 3, No. 12, p. 1; and *Contractual Risk Transfer,* Section V, "Waivers of Subrogation," Dallas, TX: International Risk Management Institute, Inc.

3. For a state-by-state survey of cases on the issue of subrogation by builders risk insurers against insured contractors, refer to "Builders Risk Subrogation," Ch. VII, *Construction Risk Management,* Dallas, TX: International Risk Management Institute, Inc.

MARINE AND AIRCRAFT INSURANCE

This chapter explains basic coverage issues surrounding additional insured status under marine and aircraft liability insurance policies. Since coverage for additional insureds is so closely associated with the use of indemnity agreements and often results in subrogation efforts, those topics will be examined as well.

A certain mystique and a reputation for being a "world unto itself" surround the subject of marine insurance. In fact, however, basic marine coverage principles are in most ways quite similar to other forms of insurance. And while actual policy language may differ significantly from that of commercial property or liability forms, marine insurance policies are subject to exactly the same rules of contract interpretation that apply to other coverage lines.

The concepts associated with additional insured status discussed in earlier chapters of this book also are relevant to marine exposures, and the rationale for requesting indemnity agreements and waivers of subrogation are the same in many cases for both marine and nonmarine exposures. Coverage disputes are sometimes resolved by reference to English law, especially when U.S. law provides no useful precedent. Otherwise, anyone familiar with insurance principles and practices in other coverage lines should have no difficulty understanding marine insurance issues as well.

The discussion of marine insurance in this chapter will focus on protection and indemnity (P&I) forms, although comprehensive general liability, marine general liability, and marine excess liability policies—and even builders risk forms—also

are mentioned as the facts of a particular coverage issue warrant. Protection and indemnity coverage is usually the most appropriate form of liability insurance for ship owners, but it is not uncommon to find CGL policies converted into coverage for marine risks approximating that of a protection and indemnity policy.

The second part of this chapter addresses additional insured status under aircraft liability insurance. This subject is somewhat less complicated than marine insurance. In fact, aircraft liability policies correspond very closely to insurance written for auto exposures, particularly with respect to the use of omnibus clauses or similar Who Is an Insured provisions.

Marine Liability Insurance

The questions to be addressed in the first part of this chapter are whether, and to what extent, parties can be added as additional insureds under marine liability insurance policies; whether having this status thwarts subrogation attempts by insurers; and in what way indemnity agreements (to the extent that they are valid and enforceable) interact with additional insured status and subrogation. Simple answers to these questions are not easy to come by, in part because marine insurance is written under a wide variety of coverage forms for an almost limitless number of ocean and inland water risks. To simplify the task as much as possible, the principles discussed in this chapter will reflect only the most common P&I coverage provisions in use in the United States.

EXHIBIT 19.1
PROTECTION AND INDEMNITY VERSUS GENERAL LIABILITY COVERAGE

It is not unusual to see a CGL policy modified by the elimination of the watercraft exclusion and other provisions in an apparent attempt to obtain equivalent or at least comparable coverage to that provided by a protection and indemnity (P&I) policy. Care must be exercised in substituting a CGL policy for a P&I policy because a number of features peculiar to each of these policies are difficult to modify. The P&I form used for this comparison is form SP–23, since it is commonly used and contains relatively broad coverage provisions. However, readers are cautioned that this comparison is only an overview. For purposes of actual coverage analysis, the specific language of the form in question should be examined closely.

P&I	CGL
Insurer "indemnifies" the insured	Insurer "pays on behalf of" the insured
Insuring agreement restricts coverage to liability, risks, events, and happenings herein set forth	Legally obligated to pay except as otherwise excluded
Does not exclude punitive damages but can by endorsement	Same
Excludes liability of insured to employees under state and federal compensation acts, except the Jones Act (the Merchant Marine Act of 1920)	Same, but also excludes the Jones Act and other employer liability exposures
Covers hospital, medical, and other expenses for which the insured is liable as necessarily incurred, subject to $200,000 maximum for burial of seamen	Coverage C—Medical Payments with significant differences relating to premises of the insured
Coverage for reparation expenses for seamen	None
Coverage for collision damage to other vessels	Same, if watercraft exclusion is deleted
Coverage for damage to other vessels, other than by collision	Same, if watercraft exclusion is deleted
Coverage for damage to property other than vessels (e.g., destruction of a crane owned by the insured because of negligent operations of the insured's own vessel)	Same with deletion of the watercraft exclusion and the care, custody, or control exclusion to cover some risks (e.g., the crane risk)
Coverage for wreck removal expenses of own vessel	Mitigating expenses are questionable, unless it involves someone else's vessel or property
Damage to cargo in the insured's care, custody, or control is covered	Not covered unless the care, custody, or control exclusion of the current CGL policy is deleted
Fines or penalties are covered	Likely covered as damages
Quarantine expenses paid	Not covered
Cargo owner's proportion of general average loss is covered	Not covered
Defense costs within limits	In addition to limits
Limited contractual coverage (i.e., to liability that the insured would have in the absence of contract)	Broad form contractual within the basic provisions but can be reduced by endorsement
Breach of contract excluded. Injury or damage otherwise covered by the policy is not excluded merely because liability for such injury or damage is assessed on a contractual theory (i.e., alleging breach of contract).* In some cases, notice to underwriters is required immediately upon knowledge of a breach involving specified conditions, such as cargo, trade, locality, towage, salvage activities, date of sailing, loading, or discharging cargo at sea.	Injury or damage otherwise covered by the policy is not excluded merely because liability for such injury or damage is assessed on a contractual theory (i.e., alleging breach of contract). Injury or damage arising out of a breach of contract is specifically excluded only for advertising injury, impaired property or property not physically injured.*
Conditions:	
Notice of loss	Same as notice of occurrence
Assignment	Same
Subrogation	Same
Other insurance is excess	Different provisions
Cancellation provisions	Different provisions

*Vandenberg v Superior Court of Sacramento County, 1999 WL 669778 (Cal August 30, 1999)
Source: Malecki on Insurance, November 1994, © Malecki Communications Company, Cincinnati, OH.

Protection and indemnity insurance protects a vessel owner against a variety of liability exposures for injury to persons or damage to property of others, including injury to the crew and damage to cargo. P&I coverage can be extended to provide collision liability coverage, applicable to physical damage to the vessel on an excess basis over coverage provided by first-party property ("hull") insurance.

There is no standard P&I coverage form, and insured exposures vary from policy to policy. One marine insurance reference characterizes typical covered risks as follows.[1]

> Loss of life, personal injury, and illness of *any* person, except employees covered under Workmen's Compensation Act (the term "any person" as used here includes the crew, passengers or other persons lawfully on board the vessel, stevedores, and any person injured on shore by the vessel); repatriation expenses; excess collision risks; damage caused otherwise than by collision; damage to docks, buoys, structures, etc.; wreck removal; cargo losses; fines and penalties; mutiny and misconduct; quarantine expenses; putting-in expenses (incurred with respect to landing injured or sick seamen and passengers); cargo's proportion of general average; pollution liabilities; expenses of investigation and defense; and expenses incurred with the express authorization of the association in the interest of the association.

The rationale for the term "protection and indemnity" is that insured marine liability exposures can be divided into two broad categories: "protection" risks encompass liability for injury and damage to property of others, and "indemnity" risks are concerned primarily with damage to cargo and fines and penalties. At one time, insurance for these two categories of exposure was handled separately. The coverages are now combined as one under the title "protection and indemnity" coverage.[2]

P&I coverage is provided for the most part by P&I clubs, which are actually mutual insurance associations owned by the vessel owners. These mutual associations operate like pools and have the authority to assess members when loss experience turns out to be worse than expected. With the exception of some pollution risks, insurance underwritten by the P&I clubs is maintained without a formal dollar limit of coverage. A smaller share of P&I insurance is underwritten by conventional insurance companies under policies that state specific limits of insurance.

A table outlining the general coverage differences between a P&I policy and a CGL policy modified to provide coverage of marine liability exposures is shown in Exhibit 19.1.

Identifying Insureds

One of the many points on which P&I forms differ significantly from one another is the way in which insured interests are identified or defined. Of particular importance to the subject of additional insured status is the issue of which persons—beyond the named insured vessel owner—are considered insureds under the policy. (Many marine insurance forms use the older British term "assured" to identify the person or persons provided coverage under the policy, often reserving the term "insured" to refer to the subject of the insurance or the perils against which insurance is being written. Except in direct quotation, this chapter preserves consistency by using the term "insured" in both senses, even where the particular policy in question may use the term "assured.")

"As Owner" Clauses

Form SP–23 (January 1956 ed.), one of the most widely used forms, refers *solely* to the assured as the *owner of the vessel*, or what is called an "as owner" clause. Normally, this means that no one is considered to be an assured other than the owner of the vessel. However, this form also recognizes that the assured (vessel owner) may have other interests that could be encompassed by this form. In those cases, this form states that:

> the Assurer [hereinafter, the insurer] shall not be liable to any greater extent than if such insured were the owner and were entitled to all

the rights of limitation which a shipowner is entitled.

This also applies to form SP–38 (1955 ed.) and probably many others. Neither of these forms appears to recognize the addition of others as insureds, unless they are considered to be owners of the vessel at the time of loss (which is possible when an person or entity qualifies under an "as owner" clause, discussed below, or when the particular P&I form is amended).

The function of a marine policy "as owner" clause is to address situations in which a person or entity other than the actual vessel owner faces liability exposures that are normally associated with vessel ownership. Under such circumstances (the chartering of a vessel, for example), the person or entity acquiring ownership exposures is considered to qualify as an insured under the P&I policy to the same extent as if that person or entity were the actual vessel owner.

There are three general types of charter: (1) A *voyage charter*, as the name suggests, lasts for a single voyage (usually one way); under this type of charter, the vessel owner retains the responsibility for navigation of the vessel. (2) A *time charter* is effective for a specified period of time, such as 6 months or a year; as in a voyage charter, the vessel owner has responsibility for the vessel's navigation. (3) In a *bareboat charter*, the charterer is responsible for operating the vessel as if it were the owner as well as for obtaining necessary insurance.

"As owner" clauses are typically thought of as broadening the P&I policy's coverage by making it possible for nonownership interests to obtain coverage for liability arising out of the operations of a vessel. But these clauses can also be interpreted as having a delimiting effect on coverage as well.

An illustration of this point is the case of *Gaspard v Offshore Crane and Equipment,* 106 F3d (5th Cir 1997). Chevron leased a cargo vessel from Secor Marine. The charter agreement between Chevron and Secor not only contained an indemnity agreement but also required Secor to purchase P&I insurance and to name Chevron as an additional insured. The policy purchased by Secor covered personal injuries occurring during the policy period and arising out of, or having relation to, the insured's chartering, brokering, towing, berthing, servicing, operating, maintenance, and/or use of vessels, including loading and/or unloading. The policy omitted the customary "as owner" language.

An employee of a drilling company working on a Chevron oil platform boarded the cargo vessel next to the platform to help unload pipe. A crane used in the off-loading operation malfunctioned, causing injury to the employee. The cause of the injury was determined to be negligence in the operation of the crane. The employee made a claim against Chevron, which in turn sought indemnity from Secor under the charter contract and by virtue of its status as an insured under the Secor P&I policy.

In the ensuing coverage litigation, a district court ruled that Secor had no obligation to indemnify Chevron and that the P&I policy did not extend to Chevron's operations as a platform owner or to operations of the platform crane. The U.S. Court of Appeals reversed this judgment, holding that inclusion of the phrase "loading and unloading" in the indemnity portion of the charter contract changed the scope of the indemnity agreement so as to make it applicable to the claim against Chevron. The court determined that Chevron had gone "out of its way" to specify that loading and unloading operations were part of the scope of the indemnification and that Chevron's own negligence would not be a bar to that indemnification. The court also held that the deletion of the "as owner" clause in the P&I policy created a genuine issue of fact as to whether the policy covered vessel-related liabilities involving Chevron's negligence in its capacity as a platform operator.

Precedent established in earlier, similar cases required some causal relationship between (1) the vessel for which P&I coverage was written and (2) the resulting injury when an "an owner" clause was in place. By omitting the "as owner" language from its policy, Secor's P&I insurer had eliminated the requirement of such a causal connection.

The court in *Gaspard* was guided by one of its own earlier decisions—*Helaire v Mobil Oil Co.,* 709 F2d 1031 (5th Cir 1983). In that case, the court had ruled that omitting the words "as owner" could expand coverage for other insured entities to include injuries inflicted as a platform operator rather than merely as the operator of the vessel.

In another case—*Clark v B&D Inspection Service,* 896 F2d 105 (5th Cir 1990)—a bareboat charterer who entered into a time charter agreement with an insured contractor was considered to be the owner of the vessel within a liability policy's watercraft exclusion. The case arose out of paint coating company's agreement to refurbish some offshore platforms for an oil company. The paint coating company entered into a time charter agreement with a marine transport company under which the latter would operate a vessel in connection with the paint coating company's duties under the oil company's contract. The paint coating company and the marine transport company agreed to name the other on its insurance policy as part of their time charter agreement.

In compliance with its agreement with the oil company, the paint coating company secured the services of a company to inspect its work. An employee of this inspection company was injured while attempting to swing onto the vessel, and litigation ensued. The liability policy issued to the paint coating company included the following additional insured provision.

> This policy includes as an additional insured, any person or organization when required to be so named but only as respects operations of the named insured.

The insurer took exception to a lower court's conclusion that the marine transport company was an additional insured under this provision, arguing that the marine transport company was not "required to be so named" and that the liability of and claims against the marine transport company were not connected to the paint coating company's operations.

The court of appeals disagreed with the insurer, stating that the marine transport company was re-quired to be named as an additional insured by virtue of its agreement with the paint coating company that each would name the other on their respective insurance policies. The record did not indicate, the court said, that the agreement between the two was an "informal arrangement."

However, the insurer went on to argue that its policy contained an exclusion for injuries arising out of the operation of any watercraft operated by an insured. None of the parties disputed that this exclusion encompassed the marine transport company's claims. An endorsement attached to the policy stated that the watercraft exclusion did not apply:

> to any watercraft, provided such watercraft is neither owned by the insured nor being used to carry persons or property for a charge.

The paint coating company's insurer argued that the marine transport company was a bareboat charterer of the vessel and therefore an owner of the vessel for the term of the charter. The marine transport company and its insurer, on the other hand, argued that marine transport company was neither an "insured" nor an "owner" within the meaning of this endorsement. The court responded, saying that there was little doubt that the marine transport company was an insured for purposes of the endorsement and watercraft exclusion. The court also stated that it was clear that the marine transport company must be treated as an owner within the meaning of the exclusion and the endorsement:

> If full possession and control of the vessel is turned over to the charterer, the contract is a demise or bareboat charter ... The charterer is regarded as the owner of the vessel for the period of the charter and is responsible for the vessel's operation ... A demise is "tantamount to, though just short of, an outright transfer of ownership."

This court also referred to a number of cases, including *Stockstill v Petty Ray Geophysical,* 888 F2d 1493 (5th Cir 1989), for the concurring opinion that a bareboat or demise charterer may be considered a vessel owner for purposes of P&I coverage.

The court concluded that the marine transport company was treated as an owner for purposes of the above watercraft exclusion and endorsement modifying that exclusion. Because the status as an owner was sufficient to defeat the endorsement, the watercraft exclusion applied to the marine transport company, the court said.

These cases illustrate coverage variations created by the absence of a P&I "as owner" clause. As noted earlier, most protection and indemnity policies contain such a clause. One widely used exception is the ASM form (1963 ed.), which automatically includes as insured entities not only the ship owner, but also any operator, manager, charterer, mortgagee, trustee, receiver, or agent of the insured vessel.

Additional Insured Status Still Has Its Advantages

Being an additional insured on a P&I policy does not always guarantee that the policy will respond in the same way as it does for the named insured. However, contracts for work involving maritime risks do not limit the insurance solely to P&I policies. It is not unusual for contracts to specify a marine liability policy or "comprehensive general liability" policy, owners and contractors protective liability policy, and umbrella liability or bumbershoot liability policy. (A bumbershoot policy is an umbrella policy that generally is written when 50 percent or more of the risks involve aviation or maritime exposures.) A marine difference-in-conditions (DIC) policy may not be specified by contract but conceivably could still apply if the named insured were to maintain one as part of its insurance portfolio.

Thus, while an entity may not qualify for coverage as an insured under the P&I policy of a vessel owner with whom it is doing business, it may still be able to obtain coverage under the vessel owner's umbrella, bumbershoot, or DIC liability policy. In fact, the additional insured under one of these poli-

cies may be better off than the named insured, since the additional insured (who does not qualify for coverage under a P&I policy) does not have to contend with any limiting conditions of coverage imposed with respect to underlying policies.

In some cases, the umbrella or bumbershoot policy is triggered solely for the protection of an additional insured, who does not qualify for P&I coverage, while the P&I policy alone may have limits sufficient to fund the named insured's liability without having to resort to the excess layer. In such cases, the excess insurer may be expected to argue that the additional insured is in fact covered "as owner" under a P&I policy, so as to delay triggering of the excess policy until the applicable underlying policy limits have been exhausted and paid.

Furthermore, it is not unusual for an entity to be made an additiona insured under "comprehensive general liability and marine insurance policies without restriction of any kind." That is a departure from the coverage provisions of most standard and manuscript additional insured endorsements. The effect is carte blanche coverage virtually equivalent to that provided a named insured.

Waiver of Subrogation versus Additional Insured Status

One reason for requesting additional insured status under a P&I policy is to avoid subrogation by a vessel owner's insurer once the insurer has paid damages allegedly caused in whole or in part by the additional insured. Some industry experts believe that a broad waiver of subrogation is a better solution— if subrogation is the only motive in asking for additional insured status. The rationale for this point of view is that additional insured status may not fully insulate a party from subrogation, while a broad subrogation waiver is clearer evidence of the intent of the parties. There are also the possible coverage limitations and deductibles of additional insured status—restrictions of which the additional insured may not even be aware until a claim is made. (The latter problems can be avoided by requiring both additional insured status and a waiver of subrogation. Additionally, contract provisions can be crafted to apply any policy deductible only to the named insured, as long as steps are taken to make certain the policy is then modified in accordance with the contract requirements.)

Neither approach by itself—additional insured status or waiver of subrogation—is an appropriate method of avoiding subrogation by a P&I insurer in every fact situation. In the case of *Wiley v Offshore Painting Contractors,* 711 F2d 602 (5th Cir 1983), one of the issues was the subrogation rights of an insurer against an additional insured. The dispute arose following injury to a seaman and two painters in an explosion on an offshore oil and gas production platform. The court held that where insurance policies (i.e., P&I and hull coverages) named Chevron (the platform owner) as an additional insured and waived all subrogation rights against Chevron with regard to vessels "that may be employed by or actually working for" Chevron, coverage was extended to Chevron to the same extent as to the named insured for operation of the vessel, *but not as owner or operator of the platform.* Thus, the waiver of subrogation did not apply to claims arising out of Chevron's negligence while acting as platform owner.[3]

Marathon Oil Co. v Mid-Continent Underwriters, 786 F2d 1301 (5th Cir 1986), is another case involving the interplay of additional insured status and subrogation under a P&I policy. Like the *Wiley* case, it involved bodily injury on an oil platform. The oil company had chartered a vessel from a boat rental company under an agreement that required additional insured status for the oil company and a waiver of any subrogation rights against it. The policy was issued in compliance with these requirements, but only while the vessel was chartered to the oil company and for claims arising out of the operation of the vessel.

A seaman was injured while working aboard the vessel as a result of the negligence of an employee of the oil company, a crane operator aboard a fixed platform. The insurance policy covered the oil company for liability incurred as an operator, owner, or charterer but not for liability arising

out of its capacity as a platform owner. However, the court in this case determined that a waiver of subrogation is not coextensive with, but is broader than, coverage under the insurance policy. In the court's words:

> When underwriters issue a policy covering an additional assured and waiving "all subrogation rights" against it, they cannot recoup from the additional assured any portion of the sums they have paid to settle a risk covered by the policy, even on the theory that the recoupment is based on the additional assured's exposure from risks not covered by the policy.

Both the *Wiley* and the *Marathon* decisions are reasonable applications of basic insurance principles. If a P&I policy is extended to cover an entity as an insured for the particular circumstances in which that entity functions "as owner," then the additional insured status should be restricted to what the P&I policy was meant to cover—not expanded to cover exposures of the additional insured outside that defined scope. By the same token, an additional insured's coverage does not necessarily apply to the same extent as the coverage afforded to the actual vessel owner (named insured). Much depends on the facts and the policy in question.

Contractual Liability Exposures and Coverages

Insurance issues surrounding contractually assumed liability and indemnity are much the same for both maritime and nonmaritime contracts. For example, an indemnitor in a maritime contract is not required to assume the liability of an indemnitee for the consequences of the indemnitee's own fault unless the contract clearly shows the unequivocal intent of the indemnitor to do so.

However, there are some important distinctions in the way contractual assumptions are addressed in P&I policies. Unlike commercial general liability, marine general liability, and umbrella and bumbershoot liability policies, P&I policies do not typically include coverage for liability assumed by the ship owner. For example, clause 29(e) of the ASM form excludes any liability:[4]

> ... for any claim for loss of life, personal injury or illness in relation to the handling of cargo where such claim arises under a contract of indemnity between the Assured and his subcontractor.

Other forms are subtler in their approach to excluding contractual liability. Form SP–23, for example, states as follows.

> [U]nless otherwise agreed by endorsement to this policy, liability hereunder shall in no event exceed that which would be imposed on the Assured by law in the absence of contract.

A case involving the application of the above language of Form SP–23 is *Landry v Oceanic Contractors,* 731 F2d 299 (5th Cir 1984). Oceanic entered into an operating agreement under which it chartered a vessel owned by Tidex. Oceanic began using the vessel to assist in performing operations on a fixed platform located in the Arabian Gulf. Under Oceanic's operating agreement, Tidex was to maintain protection and indemnity insurance in the amount of $1 million on form SP–23 or its equivalent, including other coverages. The policy that was issued listed Tidex as one of the policy's named insureds. Oceanic was included as an additional insured under a provision stating that the word "assured" includes:

> any person, organization, trustee or estate to whom or to which the 'Named Assured' is obligated by virtue of a contract or agreement to include or name as an assured, co-assured or additional assured.

A suit arose following injury to one of Oceanic's employees under the Jones Act. The case was settled in the course of the trial. Both Oceanic and Tidex funded the settlement of the case, reserving their rights to litigate the liability between themselves. The district court found Oceanic to be 70 percent liable and Tidex 30 percent liable. The vessel, while unseaworthy, was held not to be the legal cause of the injury. The court

also held that the insurance policy afforded no coverage to Oceanic, the additional insured, since the policy's insuring agreement promised to indemnify the insured for personal injury liability but limited the coverage of additional insureds to "liabilities that may be imposed against the Named Assured by law in the absence of contract." The district court construed this phrase to mean that Oceanic was covered "if it was liable vicariously, or otherwise, for liability which was imposed against Tidex by law," but that coverage was not afforded "for liability that was assumed by the named assured under contract." Because the liability of Oceanic was not predicated upon any liability of Tidex, the court found no coverage.

The court of appeals concurred with the district court's interpretation of the contract, holding that additional insureds were covered under the policy *only* for liabilities that could be imposed against the named insured (Tidex) by law. In other words, covered liability of Oceanic had to be predicated on some legal liability of Tidex. In addition, the court agreed that additional insureds under the policy had no coverage for liability imposed on the named insured by contract.

Another commonly used protection and indemnity form, SP–38, attempts to have the best of both worlds by stating that the insurer will not pay for:

> any liability assumed by the assured beyond that imposed by law; provided however that if by agreement, or otherwise, the assured's legal liability is lessened, then this Company shall receive the benefit of such lessened liability.

In effect, these exclusionary clauses resemble the exception to the contractual liability exclusion of the commercial general liability policy, by the terms of which coverage applies to the extent that liability would apply in the absence of the contract.

It is not unusual to see maritime contracts of indemnity supplemented by requests for additional insured status, just as is done in relation to nonmarine exposures. If the contractual assumption is deemed to be void and unenforceable for some reason, or simply if additional insured coverage under the endorsement is broader in scope than the indemnity agreement, then the indemnitee can rely on its additional insured status for coverage. Additional insured status "backs up" the indemnity agreement in a "belt-and-suspenders" approach to risk transfer.

Indemnitees under marine contracts may have similar motivation in requiring both indemnification and additional insured status, but the procedure for effecting this belt-and-suspenders strategy can be different in a marine context. The differences are illustrated by the case of *Tullier v Halliburton Geophysical Services, v McCalls Boat Rentals,* 81 F3d 552 (5th Cir 1996). An employee of Halliburton Geophysical Services, Inc. (HGS), slipped and fell while working on a vessel owned by McCall. The employee sued and settled with HGS and McCall. Both HGS and McCall had agreed to indemnify and defend the other party against claims brought by or on behalf of the indemnitor's employees under the time charter agreement. While the cross-indemnity provisions were identical in nature, the insurance requirements backing up these contractual assumptions differed.

HGS was required "to insure the liabilities it assumes under this Time Charter with a manuscript comprehensive general liability coverage with appropriate maritime endorsements."[5] McCall, on the other hand, agreed to provide the following.

1. P&I coverage under form SP 23 to at least the full value of the vessel with minimum limits equal to $1 million per occurrence. The policy was to be endorsed with additional insured coverage, and the "as owner" limitations additional insured status were to be deleted.

2. Comprehensive general liability policy, or its equivalent, with limits of $1 million per accident or occurrence.

3. Follow form excess liability providing a single limit of no less than $5 million per occurrence.

4. On all policies referred to, McCall (the owner) was to obtain endorsements showing that HGS was an additional insured.

5. All the required policies were to be endorsed to provide that their coverage was primary with respect to the additional insured.

Based on these contract requirements, McCall brought an action against HGS seeking defense and contractual indemnity, while HGS cross-claimed against McCall for breach of the charter agreement, because of McCall's alleged failure to provide the contractually required insurance. The district court concurred with McCall's argument that, because HGS was obligated to indemnify McCall for injuries to HGS's employee, HGS could not rely on McCall's insurance—through the additional insured provision—to fulfill its responsibility. In doing so, the district court relied on two cases: *Wilson v JOB, Inc.,* 958 F2d 653 (5th Cir 1992); and *Spell v N.L. Industries,* 618 S2d 17 (La App 1993).

On appeal, the decision of the district court was reversed. The circuit court cited a line of cases, commencing with *Ogea v Loffland Brothers Co.,* 622 F2d 186 (5th Cir 1980), which it found applicable to the contractual relationship between McCall and HGS. The circuit court held that a contracting party like McCall, which has been held harmless by the other party but has also named the indemnitor (here HGS) as an additional insured under its liability policies, must first exhaust the insurance it agreed to obtain before seeking contractual indemnity.[6]

In the *Ogea* case, Phillips was obligated to indemnify Loffland for damages paid to an employee of Phillips's contractor, regardless of fault. The contract between Loffland and Phillips also provided that Loffland was to obtain insurance naming Phillips as an additional insured for obligations incurred in relation to the contracted work—drilling operations—and to include a waiver of subrogation in favor of Phillips. The court in *Ogea* held that the indemnity provision would only apply to damages in excess of the required limit of liability and that Phillips's indemnity obligation was covered by the policy. In reaching its decision, the court stated as follows.

> Loffland claims that this action should be exclusively governed by the indemnity sections of the contract.... Loffland contends that we should not refer to any other provisions of the contract in assessing Phillips's liability.

> We cannot accept Loffland's contention. To do so would ignore the well-recognized principle under Louisiana law that the contract must be viewed as a whole. As such, Article 14 and 15 of the drilling contract must be read in conjunction with each other in order to properly interpret the meaning of the contract. By doing so, it is clear that the parties intended that Phillips would not be held liable for injuries incurred on its off-shore platform up to $500,000. The insurance to be acquired and maintained by Loffland would cover such damages. For damages in excess of $500,000, the indemnity provisions would come into effect.

Another later case following the decisions of *Ogea* and *Tullier* is *Computalog, U.S.A. v Mallard Bay Drilling*, 21 F Supp 620 (USDC ED La 1998). Because Computalog stipulated that its damages were less than the $5 million limit of insurance required by contract, and the insurance coverage stipulated in that amount was obtained by Mallard, no contractual liability was thereby triggered.

Aircraft Liability Insurance

Like marine insurance, aircraft liability insurance is provided under a variety of nonstandard coverage forms. While the largest share of the aircraft insurance market is handled by pools, individual insurers also offer the coverage, both domestically and in the London market. Marine insurance principles played an important role in the development of the earliest aviation insurance policies, aircraft being viewed by underwriters as comparable to boats in the loss exposures they present. In fact, even today, physical damage coverage on an aircraft is referred to as "hull" coverage.[7]

While many aspects of aviation insurance demonstrate a marine influence, aircraft liability insurance as it is written today bears the strongest resemblance to commercial automobile liability coverage, particularly with respect to the persons or organizations afforded insured status. The person or entities commonly qualifying as insureds under an aircraft liability policy are the named insured (the person or organization named in the policy declarations), any other person while using (e.g., an employee or agent) or riding in (e.g., a passenger) the described aircraft with the named insured's permission, and any person or organization legally responsible for the aircraft's use, provided that use is with the named insured's permission.

Given the variety of uses to which aircraft are put and the variety of individual and corporate interests that operate aircraft, particularly in general aviation, it is not surprising that individual policy definitions of who is an insured sometimes prove inadequate or inappropriate. For example, it is not unusual to see aircraft policies amended with broad named insured endorsements similar to those used with commercial general liability policies. In some cases, these broad named insured endorsements need to be tailored to address the coverage needs of specific business configurations, such as limited liability companies or general partnerships.

When additional insured status is requested in connection with commercial auto liability coverage, the motive is to protect the additional insured against any liability that may be imputed to it based on the acts of the named insured. Even though the commercial auto policy automatically includes coverage for persons facing this exposure, some additional insured interests still require an endorsement naming them specifically. Standard endorsements exist for this purpose in connection with commercial auto policies, but no similar endorsement is available with aircraft policies, probably because there is an absence of demand for it.

Additional insured status with respect to commercial auto liability insurance seldom, if ever, is requested to buttress an otherwise unenforceable or inapplicable indemnity agreement. The same is true for aircraft liability insurance. The reason for this is that the nature of the contractual risk transfer in connection with aircraft operations is limited to what an indemnitor would be held liable for even in the absence of an indemnity agreement— that is, to protect people and property from liability arising out of the ownership, maintenance, or use of aircraft.

Aircraft liability coverage for additional insureds matches this limited scope of aviation indemnity agreements; that is, coverage typically applies only with respect to the additional insured's (indemnitee's) vicarious liability, since use of the aircraft usually is limited to the named insured's operations as listed in the policy declarations and only when the aircraft is operated by pilots employed or hired by the named insured.

In addition, most aircraft liability forms, unlike automobile liability coverage forms, specifically exclude liability assumed under contract. Contractual liability for the use of aircraft is handled under the commercial general liability policy, although the aircraft liability form can be modified by endorsement, if necessary, to add coverage for certain contracts of indemnity.

Court decisions involving additional insured status under an aircraft liability insurance policy are rare. Perhaps the most common scenario for litigation involves persons or organizations claiming that they qualify for automatic insured status under the policy's definition of "insured." One such case is *RLI Insurance Co. v Drollinger,* 97 F3d 230 (8th Cir 1996), which involved an accident in which a named insured pilot was killed and his wife was injured. The insurer maintained that, while the policy covered claims for injury to passengers, coverage did not apply if the passenger is the resident spouse of the named insured. The court ruled that the policy was ambiguous on this point and that the claim therefore was covered.

Most insurers are willing to add insured persons to an aircraft liability policy on a case-by-case basis, despite the unavailability of standard language to effect such a change. Lessors of aircraft, for example, may require that insured status for them be manuscripted onto the policy, not only for physical loss of the aircraft but also for liability imputed to the lessor stemming from use of the aircraft by the lessee.

Summary

Persons and organizations requiring additional insured status under marine liability insurance do so for reasons essentially the same as for non-marine risks: to create a backup source of recovery in the event of an unenforceable indemnification agreement, to obtain direct coverage on a primary basis under an indemnitor's liability policy, and to reduce the chances of subrogation attempts against it.

However, the scope of coverage for additional insureds under a marine liability policy may be narrower than the corresponding coverage under a general or auto liability policy. For example, coverage for additional insureds under a P&I policy is very limited unless the policy is amended with an "as owner" clause that gives the additional insured the same coverage as that provided to the named insured (owner) of the vessel.

Additional insured status under marine liability policies also differs from the same feature of non-marine coverages in that it is seldom relied upon as an alternative to an unenforceable indemnity agreement. Under a marine liability policy, coverage as an additional insured applies first; the indemnitor's contractual liability coverage applies as a secondary recourse. Moreover, protection and indemnity (P&I) policies typically do not provide contractual liability insurance for contractual assumptions over and above what would apply in the absence of contract unless the underwriter endorses the policy.

Aircraft liability policies are similar in many ways to commercial auto liability insurance, particularly with respect to the coverage for those parties defined as automatic insureds. For example, both types of insurance commonly cover the named insured, permissive users, and persons or organizations legally responsible for the use of the aircraft (auto).

There is little need for creating additional insured status by endorsement to an aircraft liability policy since, like commercial auto liability forms, coverage would be limited to the additional insured's vicarious liability, and most aircraft forms automatically include coverage for persons and organizations that may be held liable for the use of aircraft.

One significant difference between aircraft liability and commercial auto insurance is the approach of the two policies to contractual liability. Liability contractually assumed with respect to the ownership, maintenance, or use of aircraft is covered under CGL policies, and the same exposure is customarily not insured in aircraft liability forms. Contractual liability having to do with the ownership, maintenance, or use of auto, on the other hand, is a covered exposure in commercial auto liability forms.

Chapter 19 Notes

1. Alex Parks, *The Law and Practice of Marine Insurance and Average*, Vol. II, p. 842.

2. Ibid., p. 843.

3. On rehearing at *Wiley,* 716 F2d 256, the court held that because Chevron was an additional insured and the policy covered a fire loss, whether it resulted from Chevron's ownership or operation of the vessel, the insurer was precluded from recovering against Chevron under the principle that an insurer may not recover from its insured.

4. Parks, p. 900.

5. This approach has not turned out well for some indemnitees under nonmarine situations, particularly where the courts have held that the if the indemnification requirement is deemed to be unenforceable, it may also nullify insurance requirements pertaining or applicable to the nullified indemnity wording. In the words of some courts, the two provisions are so "inextricably tied" that the voiding of one inevitably makes the other unenforceable. It is uncertain whether this has been an issue with marine insurance exposures. However, it has prompted considerable dispute with nonmarine risks. See, for example, "Drafting Insurance Specifications in Contracts: Avoiding 'The Inextricably Tied' Issue," *Malecki on Insurance,* Vol. 4, No. 5, March 1995.

6. Other similar cases with the same conclusion are: *Klepac v Champlin Petroleum Co.,* 842 F2d 746 (5th Cir 1988) and *Woods v Dravo Basic Materials Co.,* 887 F2d 618 (5th Cir 1989).

7. *Commercial Liability Insurance and Risk Management,* Vol. I, 3d ed., 1995, pp. 297–298.

Chapter 20

CERTIFICATES OF INSURANCE

The risk management technique of noninsurance transfer is unique in that its implementation is largely beyond the control of the organization attempting to use it. With contractual or noninsurance risk transfer, one party (the indemnitee) basically depends on a second party (the indemnitor) to arrange insurance protection on its behalf. Indemnitees can make very specific and comprehensive contractual requirements concerning the protection to be afforded, but they have very few alternatives for verifying that indemnitors have complied with them.

A factor that accentuates the potential for problems is that indemnitors often are relatively small firms without internal risk management or insurance expertise. The insurance implications of the contracts they sign are far from the most important concerns of these organizations, and they are often forgotten once contracts are executed. As a result, communication breakdowns between indemnitors, indemnitees, and the insurance agents of the indemnitors often result in failure to comply with insurance requirements (particularly when the requirements would make necessary some change in the policy, such as the addition of an endorsement).

The certificate of insurance is the primary vehicle for verification that insurance requirements have been met. However, certificates usually do not include sufficient information to verify that all of the requirements are met, particularly when they are very specific and comprehensive. Instead, certificates provide evidence that certain general types of policies are in place on the date the certificate is issued and that these policies have the limits and policy periods shown. Certificates do not guarantee that:

(1) the coverage will not be canceled,

(2) limits will not be exhausted by claims in other projects or activities in which the party providing the certificates is involved,

(3) required endorsements will be attached to the policy, or

(4) the policy has not been neutered with restrictive endorsements. Some examples of details that generally would not be revealed on a certificate are the inclusion of a cross-liability exclusion endorsement, a contractual liability limitation endorsement, or a limited additional insured endorsement.

With some justification, different people have different perceptions of the purpose and scope of certificates of insurance. To marine underwriters, from whom much of the insurance tradition and current practices in the United States are derived, certificates of insurance only provide evidence that insurance is in place. As stated in 1 Arnould, *Marine Insurance*, 138:

> It [a certificate of insurance] is not, and does not purport to be, a policy, but states that a policy covering the goods is in existence, and gives details of the vessel, voyage, subject matter and refers to the terms and conditions of the underlying policy.[1]

Most property and casualty insurance underwriters in the United States view certificates in a similar way to marine underwriters. However, many certificate holders do not believe that the purpose and use of certificates should be so limited. Many certificate holders either believe the certificate is—or attempt to turn it into—a contractual agreement between themselves and the other party's insurer. As a result, disagreements over the purpose and scope of certificates are common, and they sometimes lead to litigation.

What complicates matters is that it is difficult to predict the outcome when such arguments go before the courts. It is the purpose of this chapter to identify and address some of the key issues arising from the use of certificates as evidence that insurance is in place.

Historical Development

Certificates were probably first used by property and casualty insurers in the late 1930s and early 1940s when large corporations began including specific and detailed insurance requirements in contracts with their service providers or other companies with which they had business relationships. During this time, it also was common for entities to request written proof of insurance on an insurer's letterhead.

Prior to 1976, the year standard certificates were introduced, insurers generally developed their own certificate forms. Even though there were many different insurers, however, most such certificates were essentially identical in content. Indicative of these early forms of certificates is the one illustrated in the case of *United Pacific Insurance Co. v Meyer*, 305 F2d 107 (1962).

As concisely as possible, the certificate in this case, as well as those available during the same period, identified the following.

- The insurance company that issued the certificate

- The name and address of the named insured

- The policy number

- The limits and coverages

- The inception and expiration dates of the policies

However, these older certificates typically were not subject to any conditional language or limitations, as is usually the case with the certificates used today.

A few court decisions adverse to insurers probably provided the impetus to add conditional language to certificate forms. One such case might have been the *United Pacific* case mentioned previously. The question there was whether a general contractor's liability policy also encompassed the coverage of a subcontractor as was required by the specifications of the project owner. The court held that since the certificate issued by the insurer stated that "all operations were covered" with respect to the policy designated in the certificate, the owner had a right to rely on the apparent meaning of that language even though the policy contradicted it.

The organization known as Agency Company Organized Research Development (ACORD) is credited with introducing the first standard certificate of insurance in 1976. Currently, ACORD certificates are available to provide evidence of property and casualty insurance. These standard forms are updated by ACORD from time to time. ACORD also offers a training guide that provides suggestions for the proper issuance of certificates.

Problems with Standard Certificate Forms

An indemnitee under a contract has attempted to transfer certain liabilities and responsibilities to the other contracting party. If the other party fails to comply with its contractual obligations, the certificate holder may experience a financial loss. Therefore, most indemnitees naturally seek assurances that the contract's insurance requirements have been met, and the certificate of insurance is the insurance industry's mechanism for doing so. Unfortunately, standard insurance certificate forms used by insurers have shortcomings that often do not give the degree of assurance that certificate holders would prefer.

The parties entering into contractual agreements generally purchase the types of insurance required in the contract (e.g., workers compensation and liability insurance) as a matter of standard business practice, and it is not necessary to purchase specific insurance to meet the contractual obligation. However, it is sometimes necessary to modify the policies that are already in place to comply with special requirements made in a contract. For example, it is often necessary for one party's liability policy to be endorsed to make the other party an additional insured.

Unfortunately, it is not uncommon to overlook the need to make these types of special modifications. And, since standard certificate forms are very general in nature, they often do not provide a convenient way to indicate compliance with specialized insurance requirements made in the contract. Therefore, the certificate does not make its holder aware of the breach of contract.

Compounding this problem is the fact that certificates—at least those issued on the standard forms—do not alter the rights or obligations of the insureds or the insurer, nor do they broaden the policy's coverage. In fact, the standard ACORD form includes a specific clause, shown in Exhibit 20.1, to make this intent clear. As a result, certificate holders have no way of determining whether the contract's insurance requirements have been fully met if they accept the standard certificate form.

EXHIBIT 20.1
"FOR INFORMATION ONLY" PROVISION

This certificate is given as a matter of information only and confers no rights upon the certificate holder. This certificate does not amend, extend or alter the coverage afforded by the policies listed below.

Source: Certificate Form 25-N (1/95) ACORD Corporation, 1988.

It should be noted that this conditional language is not a legal requirement, i.e., imposed by law, in most states. California is one exception, and this state's insurance code section 384 states as follows.

A certificate of insurance or verification of insurance provided as evidence of insurance in lieu of an actual copy of the insurance policy shall contain the following statements or words to the effect of:

This certificate or verification of insurance is not an insurance policy and does not amend, extend or alter the coverage afforded by the policies listed herein. Notwithstanding any requirement, term or condition of any contract or other document with respect to which this certificate or verification of insurance may be issued or may pertain, the insurance afforded by the policies described herein is subject to all the terms, exclusions and conditions of such policies.

Certificate language may also be subject to state insurance department regulation, as is the case in New York. Circular Letter No. 8, issued by the New York State Insurance Department on June 7, 1995, requires that certificates that alter the language of the policy, or include statements that the wording of the certificate will control in the event of any inconsistency or conflict between the certificate and the policy, actually amount to policy forms. Prior to use, therefore, it is necessary to file the certificate and receive the Insurance Department's approval pursuant to the procedures set out in section 2307(b) of the New York Insurance Law. It should be noted that the ACORD certificate does not contain any of the objectionable language targeted by Circular Letter No. 8.

Even though most states do not have statutes requiring the conditional wording for certificates, most insurers require it as a condition precedent to issuing certificates. There are, of course, exceptions wherein insurers are persuaded to issue manuscript endorsements without these provisions, but these cases are probably the exception rather than the rule.

The "for information only" provision on certificates has been relied on by the courts in allowing insurers to avoid providing coverage for certificate holders when the actual terms of an insurance policy did not correspond with those indicated by a certificate. One such case is *Kaufman d/b/a 3816 Associates v Puritan Insurance Co.,* 511 NYS2d 307 (AD 2 Dept 1987).

This was a case where a landlord brought an action for breach of contract based on a former tenant's alleged promise to add the landlord as an additional insured. The certificate did not reflect the additional insured status as issued and contained the standard conditional wording to the effect that it was issued as a matter of information only and conferred no rights on the certificate holder. In denying the landlord any protection, the New York court stated that the certificate of insurance was merely a confirmation that the former tenant had acquired insurance on the premises and contents.

A similar case where the certificate of insurance was held not to confer any special rights to its holder is *Mercado v Mitchell,* 264 NW2d 532 (Wis 1978).[2] Before Mitchell could operate amusement rides on city property, the company was required to procure and produce a copy of a liability policy including the city as an additional named insured. Rather than providing a copy of the policy, however, the agent sent the city a certificate of insurance, which the city accepted. However, the actual policy did not cover a roller coaster—the source of a person's injury and subsequent suit against the city.

The city argued that the amusement company's liability insurer should have been estopped from denying coverage because the issuance of the certificate led the city to believe that the requested coverage was being provided. The court, however, upheld the insurer's coverage denial, holding that the certificate's disclaimer clearly alerted anyone relying on it that coverage was limited to the terms of the policy.

Since a certificate of insurance does not amend, extend, or alter the policies designated, it should not matter when during the policy period a certificate is issued, barring only that the limits of the policies listed may have been reduced or exhausted. However, the insurer in the case of *Dryden Central School District v Dryden Aquatic Racing Team, 195 Ad2d 790,* (NY 1993), attempted to disclaim coverage when a certificate of insurance was issued 3 months after the policy inception reciting the policy period (a claims-made policy was written for a 1-year period commencing December 31, 1989) and additional insured status.

In 1987 the school district entered into an agreement with the Dryden Aquatic Racing Team (DART), granting DART permission to use the district's pool for its program. In exchange, DART agreed to provide a CGL policy to the school district. The broker issued a certificate of insurance on March 20, 1990. However, a minor sustained injuries prior to issuance of the certificate (on February 13, 1990) when she dove into the shallow end of the pool during a DART-authorized practice. The school district first received written notice of a claim for damages and medical expenses on April 23, 1990. The parents of the minor commenced a negligence action against the school district, DART, and United States Swimming (USS) in October 1991.

The school district sought coverage as an additional insured under the CGL policy obtained by DART, maintaining that the minor's injury occurred during the policy period during an insured activity. However, the insurer denied the school district indemnity and defense based primarily on an affidavit of the broker, who said that it was never her intention, the broker firm's intention, or the insurer's intention to have the certificate of insurance extend coverage retroactively for the February 13, 1990, accident. Among the insurer's arguments was that the claim was interposed one day prior to the issuance of the certificate naming the school district as an additional insured.

The court disagreed with the insurer. It stated that the certificate referenced the policy number. Furthermore, both the accident on February 13, 1990, and the date claim was first filed (April 23, 1990) were during the policy period. The court also held that neither the policy nor the certificate could be read to limit coverage to claims made after the date of the certificate. Thus, even though the medical expense claim of March 19, 1990, was deemed to have been made against the insured under the policy, that claim, said the court, still fell within the policy period. Finally, the court stated that the fact the certificate of insurance was dated March 20, 1990, did not alter the effective dates of the policy period, and there was no evidence that the insurer ever communicated an intent to limit the school district's coverage to claims made after the issuance of the certificate.

What is not clear about this case is whether the CGL policy obtained by DART for the school district actually was issued with an endorsement naming the school district as an additional insured. If the contract in 1987 between the school district and DART required additional insured status but the policy was not modified to that effect, the insurer might have had an argument, because the certificate of insurance is not the vehicle for amending the policy. On the other hand, there is an argument that the school district that receives a certificate of insurance verifying additional insured status has the reasonable expectation that the policy is, in fact, modified to provide additional insured status. The additional insured should not be penalized. If, in fact, that policy was not endorsed, the problem should be resolved between the insurer and the broker.

It is not unusual for the person who prepares the certificate to list only the coverages and limits requested in the contract. For example, a contract that requires an indemnitor to maintain general liability coverage for not less than $1 million per occurrence may be shown on the certificate of insurance as a CGL policy with a limit of $1 million, even though the policy actually has higher liability limits. Some people maintain that the certificate holder only receives the benefit of the coverages and limits as shown on the certificate and no more. This, of course, is not true, because the certificate does not alter, extend, or amend coverage. It is for information only, and it is the policy or policies applicable to the claim that control. One of the few exceptions to when a certificate can be relied on to limit the extent of coverage is when the policy is modified so as to confer coverage based on the certificate, i.e., the certificate and policy work in tandem. This approach is discussed later in this chapter.

Sometimes attempts are made to use the certificate as a binder or, in other words, evidence that a certain policy or policies will be issued in the future. The space where the policy number is usually designated reflects an insurance company name and states that the policies are to be listed or "t/b/a" (to be announced). However, a certificate is not a binder. A certificate of insurance is merely a vehicle for verifying that certain coverages and limits are already in effect. A certificate, therefore, should not be used in the place of a binder.

However, it is not unusual for insurance companies to delay issuing policies for months after their inception dates. If a certificate holder desires proof of insurance, it would be perfectly normal to prepare a certificate even though the policies have not been issued, as long as the person who prepares the certificates has the policy numbers. Even so, there are rare occasions where policy numbers are not designated but where the insurer has agreed to provide coverage or has agreed to renew the policies, and a certificate holder demands proof of insurance before permitting a job to commence. In these cases, it would be proper to list the coverages, the insurers, and limits with a special description to the effect that insurance is available to cover the specific project in question on the date it commences, even though the certificate is issued before the inception date of the new policies. Agents, brokers, and underwriters need to have some understanding and agreement for this procedure to apply without a problem.

It is important to recall that merely referencing a coverage as being provided is not the same as specifying the scope and limits of the coverage that must be available at any given time. When a policy is looked to for protection at the time of a claim, coverage may be inapplicable for a number of reasons. For example, the limits may have been depleted in satisfying other claims or the policy may turn out to have been manuscripted or modified with restrictive endorsements that restrict coverage. The problems inherent in monitoring compliance with insurance requirements are discussed at length in **Chapter 21.**

Fictitious Insureds or Insurance

Probably the most common area in which certificates of insurance and insurance policies conflict is with respect to additional insured status. Certificate holders are often listed as additional insureds on certificates without the policy actually being endorsed to reflect that intent. An extreme case of this that often occurs is for a copy of an additional insured endorsement to be attached to the certificate but not the policy. This practice may not provide additional insured status and, thus, is sometimes called the "fictitious insured syndrome."

Sometimes this problem stems from a lack of communication. The insurance agent, for example, may have the authority to add another party to a policy as an additional insured and may issue a certificate indicating that this has been done while forgetting to ask the insurer to issue the endorsement. When the additional insured later seeks protection, the insurer denies such protection, shifting the blame elsewhere.

EXHIBIT 20.2
ACORD CERTIFICATES NOTICE PROVISION

Should any of the above described policies be canceled before the expiration date thereof, the issuing company will endeavor to mail _____ days' written notice to the certificate holder named to the left, but failure to mail such notice shall impose no obligation or liability of any kind upon the company, its agents or representatives.

Source: Certificate Form 25–N (1/95) ACORD Corporation, 1988.

This, of course, is really a matter of principal-agency liability and should not detrimentally affect the certificate holder.[3] However, concise wording in the certificate's preamble indicating that the certificate is "for information only" fosters an insurance company's opportunity to deny any protection. This provision of the ACORD form is included in Exhibit 20.2.

The insurance company maintains that it does not matter what the certificate says, it is what the policy states that counts. When such circumstances go before the courts to be resolved, the outcomes are unpredictable.

Frequently, the certificate of insurance confirms that the certificate holder is an additional insured, but the exact additional insured endorsement is not shown. It may not always be necessary to designate the appropriate endorsement form number unless more than one could be issued. For example, there have historically been two standard ISO additional insured endorsements available for owners, lessees, or contractors, one of which (CG 20 09) provided a much more limited scope of coverage than the other (CG 20 10). In such a case, it would be prudent to require that the actual form name and number be delineated on the certificate.

There have been some actual instances where a certificate of insurance has been issued confirming additional insured status without further description in circumstances where the broader endorsement, CG 20 10, should have been issued. But at the time the additional insured sought protection, the insurer produced additional insured endorsement CG 20 09 and then stated that no coverage applied for the additional insured's sole fault allegations. These are not isolated cases. To reduce the chances of problems, it would behoove those who request additional insured status to specify the specific additional insured endorsement, if possible, and for the person who prepares the certificate to make sure a specific form number is designated.

Policy Terms Control

A complex case where the policy terms—not the certificate—governed coverage is *SLA Property Management v Angelina Casualty Co.*, 856 F2d 69 (8th Cir 1988). A group of individuals and companies formed a partnership to acquire a short-line railroad on which to ship grain to market. The partnership hired a contractor to fix the tracks and rail beds. When the contractor later abandoned the project, the partnership acquired the contractor's rights under its insurance policies and filed suit against the contractor's two insurance companies.

The court ruled against the partnership because the contractor's breach and resulting damages did not constitute property damage as covered by the liability insurance. A second reason for denying coverage was based on the certificate of insurance. One of the two insurers maintained that the contractor was not its named insured. The insurer maintained that the contractor's name was listed on the certificate of insurance by mistake and that the insurer actually provided insurance to another rail company.

The court stated that the law governing this issue was clear, "The certificate is not part of the contract of, or necessary to, the insurance ... It served merely as evidence of insurance." So with a discrepancy between the insurance policy and certificate, the policy took precedence.

Another long and complex case worthy of mention is *Mercado v Mitchell, supra*, which worked to the disadvantage of the insurance broker. A minor was injured while riding on a roller coaster on church grounds. Suit was filed against the owner of the amusement rides, its insurer, and insurance agents. It was alleged that the liability policy as procured was fraudulently obtained through a conspiracy so as to provide incomplete coverage. The plaintiff also alleged that the certificate of insurance as filed by one of the insurance brokers with the city did not specifically indicate what was or was not covered. As a result, the amusement ride owner held himself out to the city as possessing a liability policy that covered all injuries and damages that could arise and result from these rides.

Under city ordinance, a license was required to operate a carnival. Part of this ordinance stipulated that no license would be granted unless the applicant filed a liability insurance policy with the additional condition that the applicant indemnify and hold harmless the city and its officers, agents, and citizens against any and all injuries and damages arising from the conduct of such carnival for which the license has been granted. However, a certificate of insurance was filed instead of a policy and was approved by the city's attorney. It stated, in part, as follows.

> This certificate of insurance neither affirmatively nor negatively amends, extends or alters the coverage afforded by any policy described herein.

The certificate also indicated that the city was an "additional named insured." However, the insurance policy stated that it only applied to the named hazards and that no coverage was provided for any hazard or operation not specifically described. Nine amusement devices were listed in the description of hazards, but the roller coaster was not among them.

The amusement company's insurer alleged that it had never agreed to provide coverage for a roller coaster, it was not asked to provide coverage for such device, and it had no knowledge that its named insured was operating a roller coaster. The plaintiff argued that the insurer should be estopped from denying coverage because the certificate of insurance as filed did not describe the devices covered and, thus, led the city to believe that, in compliance with the ordinance, all of the amusement devices were covered. The lower court, however, granted the insurer its motion for summary judgment, holding that the certificate was not fraudulent.

On appeal, the court ruled that the amusement company's insurer was not estopped from denying liability arising from the operation of the nonlisted amusement device. The decision was made, in part, based on the fact that no ambiguity could be found when both the policy and certificate of insurance were examined together. The court also stated that the certificate of insurance would clearly alert anyone relying on it to the fact that coverage was limited to the policy's terms.

The higher court also ruled that the plaintiffs had a right to sue the insurance agents. Since the plaintiffs were considered to be third-party beneficiaries, they had a standing to sue the insurance agents for failing to procure sufficient insurance to protect them, as stipulated by the ordinance, based on their allegations of conspiracy and negligence.

Certificate Controls Over Policy

A case where the certificate was held to be controlling is *Bucon, Inc. v Pennsylvania Manufacturing Association Insurance Co.,* 547 NYS2d 925 (AD 3 Dept 1989). A property owner contracted with a contractor to supply the materials and erect the roof of a building. The contractor, in turn, hired a subcontractor to erect the roof system at the site. The contract required the subcontractor to hold harmless and indemnify the contractor and the project owner against all claims arising out of the subcontractor's performance of the work. It also required the subcontractor to procure, maintain, and furnish evidence to the contractor of comprehensive general liability insurance, including coverage for the products and completed operations hazard, with the contractor as an additional insured.

Pursuant to the above requirements, the subcontractor sent a certificate of insurance to the contractor, prepared and executed by the subcontractor's insurer. The certificate attested that the insurance had been issued to the subcontractor and summarized the types of coverages and limits. However, the certificate was rejected by the contractor because it did not indicate that the contractor was an additional insured. When the subcontractor notified its insurer of this discrepancy, the insurer issued a new certificate identical to the previous one except that it added a notation that the contractor was an additional insured.

During the construction process, an employee of the subcontractor was injured and subsequently sued both the property owner and the contractor. They both sought protection under the subcontractor's liability insurance. Coverage was denied by the insurer because the policy issued to the subcontractor was never amended to include the contractor as an additional insured. The insurer further contended that the designation of the contractor as an additional insured on the certificate was a clerical error.

The court ruled that by issuing the certificate of insurance signifying the contractor as an additional insured, the insurer was estopped from denying coverage for the contractor. The uncontested evidence submitted established that the insurer was informed that the contractor had required a revised certificate and that the contractor had relied on the amended certificate in permitting the subcontractor to proceed with its work. The court also held that the contractor's reliance on the certificate was reasonable, despite the form language—emphasized by the insurer—that the certificate did not "amend, extend or otherwise alter the terms and conditions of insurance coverage contained in the policy."

The facts in this case distinguish the court's ruling from other cases that do not allow certificates to affect coverage, particularly when the certificate states that it does not alter, extend, or amend coverage. The reason is that, in this case, the insurer issued a certificate evidencing coverage and then, upon learning that the coverage the insurer represented was inadequate, reissued the certificate to reflect the coverage required by contract.

The court did not rule that the certificate in this case altered, extended, or amended coverage. Instead, the insurer, because its conduct created a justifiable reliance on coverage it stated it would issue, was estopped (precluded) from denying coverage it had represented was in place. This is much different from situations where certificates are issued without the insurer itself making representations or conducting itself in a manner that would lead the insured to rely on coverage.

Apart from the aforementioned commentary, there are unusual cases where the certificate of insurance controls over the policy. One such case is *B.T.R. East Greenbush v General Accident Co.,* 205 AD2d 791 (NY 1994). Both a property owner and general contractor on a shopping center construction project sought additional insured status under the liability policy of a steel fabricator (subcontractor) following the injury of an employee of the subcontractor.

The liability policy issued to the subcontractor was for a 1-year period commencing December 23, 1987. It was on June 17, 1988, that the subcontractor's employee was injured at the construction site. One day later, on June 18, a certificate of insurance was issued indicating the property owner and general contractor were additional insureds and reciting the policy period corresponding to the period on the policy. However, the policy was not endorsed to provide additional insured status. The trial court determined that the policy period, rather than the certificate date, controlled and granted the coverage sought.

On appeal, the insurer argued that the certificate did not confer any rights on the certificate holders and, in fact, clearly stated that it did not amend, extend, or alter the coverage provided by the policies. The insurer also argued that the certificate's issuance date supported its claim that the property owner and general contractor were not insureds under the policy on the date of the injury. However, the insurer failed to offer any extrinsic evidence of its intent that the issuance date of the certificate was controlling or that the general language of the certificate superseded the designation of the project owner and general contractor as additional insureds. The court of appeals, however, ruled in favor of the project owner and general contractor because, in the words of the court:

> The only reasonable interpretation to be given to the phrase 'ADDITIONAL INSURED' followed by plaintiffs' names is that General Accident meant to extend coverage to them under the terms of the policy....

Certificate and Policy Work in Tandem

While standard certificates generally are not intended to amend the policy, some insurers construct certificates that do effect coverage. For example, some umbrella policies issued by the London market contain a definition of insured (assured) that encompasses additional insureds (assureds). In defining what entities constitute an additional assured, a caveat is included to limit the scope of coverage provided. One such umbrella states that coverage applies to the additional assured:

> but only to the extent (subject to all other provisions of the policy) and for such limits of liability and for such coverages as the Named Assured, before loss has agreed:
>
> > i.   by certificate of insurance to provide, or to the extent which a court may hold, after loss, that the Named Assured is obligated to provide, or
> >
> > ii.   in the absence of a certificate of insurance, by contract or agreement to provide for such interest.

Under this policy wording, the certificate of insurance must be read with the policy to determine the extent of coverage afforded to the additional insured. Or, to say it another way, the policy confers coverage based on the certificate. This approach can work for and against the additional insured. If the certificate specifically identifies the project and lists the policies and their limits applicable to that project, the additional insured could be precluded from accessing layers of coverage above that required in the certificate. An example might be where the certificate specifically makes the statement that the coverages and limits, as identified, are in effect for the additional insureds (which are not necessarily all of the named insured's insurance portfolio). The certificate also describes the nature of the additional insured's interests, such as a specific lease for a certain location or for a specific job to be performed by the named insured for the additional insured, with an added statement to the effect that additional insured status is limited to the coverages listed on the certificate.

However, if, as in some cases, the certificate does not contain the previous provisos that limit coverage and merely states that a person or entity shall be held to be an additional insured with respect to "any liability arising out of work performed under the underlying contract," the picture changes dramatically. Now the certificate, which the policy acknowledges will dictate the extent of coverage, requires that the coverage provided apply to any liability. As a result, all layers of coverage affected by the certificate will be activated, regardless of specific limits listed in the certificate.

A case in point is *Great Lakes Dredge & Dock Co. v Commercial Union Assurance Co.,* 57 F Supp 2d 525 (Ill 1999). Here, the City of Chicago claimed additional insured status under the excess liability policies of a contracting firm for actual as well as potential liability arising out of damage to and flooding of the Chicago freight tunnel system. The city's contract required that the contractor carry liability insurance, be responsible for all damages the city might have to pay in consequence of any acts of the contractor in connection with the work under the contract, and be covered as an additional insured. The contract also required that the contractor maintain liability coverage for special hazards, including collapse and damage to underground utilities and any other hazards involved in the work to be performed under the contract. The contractor sought summary judgment on its request for a declaration that the city was not covered as an additional insured under any of the four umbrella policies involved.

The underlying contract obligated the contractor to obtain comprehensive general liability insurance and stipulated that "the amounts of insurance specified shall be as follows unless otherwise specified.…" The amounts listed in the contract were reflective of the primary layer of coverage only. The city requested, and the contractor agreed to provide, certificates of insurance listing the city as an additional insured. The certificates that were provided in compliance with this agreement included typical disclaimers to the effect that they were issued as a matter of information only and did not confer any rights on the certificate holder. The certificates went on to state that the city was a named additional insured "with respect to any liabilities arising out of work performed under this contract."

The umbrella policies defined "assured" to include entities:

> for which any Named Assured [i.e., the Contractor] is responsible … to add as an additional assured … but only to the extent … and for such limits of liability and for such coverages as the Named Assured, before loss, has agreed … by certificate of insurance to provide.'

So while the contract specified the coverage to be provided, it was not clear whether the limits specified were a cap or a minimum. The umbrella policies, on the other hand, provided additional insured coverage to the extent set forth in the certificate, not the contract. Therefore, the certificate (in tandem with the policies) was purported to be the document determining the scope of coverage for the additional insured.

In arguing against additional insured coverage for the city under the umbrella policies, the contractor advanced two arguments that the court recognized as cogent. The contractor pointed out that the language under which the city was covered for "any liabilities arising out of this contract" did not specify *to what extent* the city was covered. The city responded that the language should be construed broadly. Second, the contractor asked (rhetorically) why it would voluntarily obtain for the city coverage that was not required by the underlying contract. In response, the city provided expert witness testimony that the contractual insurance requirements of the underlying contract would be viewed—in light of industry custom and practice—as minimum requirements, not a cap on the coverage being requested or provided. This testimony went on to state that normal contractual provisions would make the city an additional insured for the full limits of coverage, and that obtaining coverage on that broad basis would have cost the contractor little or nothing extra.

The validity of the city's arguments with respect to cost is reinforced throughout this book. Liability policies traditionally include broad contractual liability coverage for a premium that is loaded into the rate. This is done because it is virtually impossible to quantify the liability being transferred or assumed under contract. The purpose of additional insured coverage written in conjunction with contractual liability coverage is to reinforce and back up the insured's obligations under the indemnity agreement—the belt-and-suspenders strategy. That is to say, if contractual liability coverage does not respond to the indemnity agreement, coverage still applies to the city as an additional insured. The court was charged with analyzing these issues to determine if summary judgment, ruling out additional insured coverage for the city under the umbrella policies, was proper. The court determined that summary judgment would not be proper absent a material factual dispute concerning the city's additional insured status. Looking just to the certificates and the policies, the court stated that it was difficult to determine the extent of the city's coverage. "They [the certificates and policies] are more silent than they are ambiguous," the court added. The court expressed its dilemma as follows.

What is clear is that the piling cluster contract required Great Lakes to provide certain limited coverage; Great Lakes provided this through a primary policy. Were this the limit of the city's coverage, the excess policies would not be involved. What is also clear is that under Illinois law, where a certificate states clearly (as this one does) that it is subject to the terms of the policy or policies at issue, it is so subject and can create no new rights in itself ... But the rub in this case is that while Illinois law requires that a certificate worded as the ones at issue here were is subject to the terms of the policies, the policies at issue here are made expressly subject to the certificate. And the certificate contains language that can at least arguably be construed as covering the city for "any liabilities."

However, the court declined to recognize the city's additional insured status under the contractor's excess policies. It based its decision in part on the fact that the certificate request forms contained a space for indicating the policies under which the city was an additional insured, but excess liability was not checked. The certificate, the court added, listed the coverages that the contractor was informing the city it had obtained, and excess coverage was not among them. As discussed elsewhere in this chapter, a certificate of insurance does not define or modify the terms of coverage provided by a policy evidenced in the certificate. But because the policy in this case expressly stated that the certificate would modify coverage, the court was inclined to attribute greater significance to the certificate provisions. From the court's perspective, the evidence failed to provide any basis for finding that the "any liabilities" language was a description of the amount of coverage rather than the types of liability for which coverage under the listed policies could be sought.

There is also a growing number of instances where insurers are using certificates to confer additional insured status under primary liability policies. One insurer, for example, issues an endorsement to its CGL policy entitled "Additional Insured—Certificate Holders." This endorsement states that all additional insureds so identified and included on certificates of insurance on file with the company are deemed to be additional insureds but only as respects the certificate holder's interest as it appears on the certificate of in-

surance. This approach should reduce problems commonly associated with the so-called fictitious insured syndrome. Thus, if the certificate lists someone as an additional insured, that person or entity automatically obtains additional insured status under the policy.

However, recipients of this kind of certificate must be careful that the certificate does not impose inordinate limitations on the interests of the additional insured. In other words, the additional insured status should correspond to the additional insured's coverage. This procedure also presents potential problems to the insurer, particularly when certificates are not properly categorized by underwriters when received. In addition, what happens when the certificate cannot be located by the insurer, and it is not certain whether one was ever issued or sent to the insurer? The insured may have a problem.

Another approach taken by some insurers is to attach to the primary liability policy a blanket additional insured endorsement that provides that if the named insured is required to add another person or organization as an additional insured under a written contract or agreement currently in effect or becoming effective during the term of the policy, and a certificate of insurance lists that person or organization as an additional insured, then the policy's Who Is an Insured provision is amended to include such person or organization. Such endorsements also usually describe the extent of the additional insured status, and some stipulate that the limits of liability for the additional insured are those specified in the written contract or agreement, or in the policy, whichever is the lesser. The approach of restricting the limits to those required in the underlying contract can be problematic, as discussed in this chapter.

Protection Below Expectations

The heart of the dispute in the *Great Lakes* case discussed above was generated by a lack of clarity as to the extent to which the additional insured was to be protected. Not all cases are resolved with a ruling favorable to the additional insured.

In fact, the *Great Lakes* case did not end with a finding of coverage. The ruling consisted only in a finding that there were not grounds for summary judgment to eliminate coverage as a matter of law. Despite findings in its favor, the city still faced a trial to prove its case. Similar cases, in which the dispute hinges on additional insured status, either the scope or the limits of which are not spelled out, are not difficult to find.

Assume that a city contractually requires a road builder to hold it harmless for their joint negligence and add it as an additional insured on the road builder's liability policies. The road builder submits a certificate that verifies the various coverages and limits required and indicates the city is an additional insured. The problem is that the city does not know to what extent coverage is being provided. If, for example, endorsement CG 20 09, Additional Insured—Owners, Lessors or Contractors (Form A), were to be attached, the coverage would fall short of what was requested, since the coverage provided by the endorsement in question is not as broad as the liabilities being transferred in the contractual agreement (see **Chapter 7**).

This places the additional insured in somewhat of a dilemma. It also can adversely affect the named insured, because if the protection falls short of what is prescribed, the named insured may be responsible for the difference. The rationale regarding responsibility on the part of the named insured is similar to the rationale discussed in **Chapter 14** regarding why a named insured would want to make all layers of coverage available to an additional insured. If a loss exceeds the insurance limits required, in many instances the named insured is going to be responsible for the difference. While chances are that the excess coverage available to the named insured will still respond, it remains preferable that it respond directly on behalf of the additional insured for the reasons previously discussed. It obviously is beneficial for the person who ultimately selects the additional insured endorsement to be familiar with the contract specifications as well as the insurance policy.

Matters became even more complicated during the 1980s with an outgrowth of independently filed insurance policies that, while perhaps patterned after Insurance Services Office, Inc. (ISO), forms, took on marked departures in the scope of coverage they provided. The result is that, short of obtaining an actual copy of the additional insured endorsement or a certified copy of the policy, the certificate holder must have faith that the coverage sought actually is being provided even if the certificate is not specific enough to verify the coverage. One way many additional insureds get around this problem, at least in part, is to require that they be named as additional insureds using specific editions of standard ISO commercial general liability forms and endorsements and to umbrella and excess liability coverage meeting certain requirements. By insisting on standard ISO forms, the additional insured can identify, without an actual copy of the policy, the coverage to be provided. The only things that then must be reviewed are the endorsements attached to the policy.

There are, of course, other related issues such as knowing whether policy limits are being eroded by claims and suits unrelated to the activities involving the additional insured. However, these issues, too, can sometimes be addressed contractually. The problem is that if the policy does not provide the coverage as contemplated, the certificate holder may be denied the very protection being sought.

A case in point is *National Union Fire Insurance Co. v Glenview Park District,* 594 NE2d 1300 (Ill App 1992). A contractor entered into an agreement with a park district to refurbish an ice rink. The contract required the contractor to maintain liability insurance for no less than $1 million per occurrence and to add the park district as an additional insured. The contractor produced evidence of both primary and excess liability insurance.

When an employee of the contractor was injured, his legal guardian filed suit against the park district alleging the district's negligence and violation of the Illinois Structural Work Act. When the district sought protection from the contractor's insurer, the insurer filed a declaratory judgment action seeking a determination that it was not obligated to defend or indemnify the district because the terms of its policy excluded coverage for damages arising from the negligence of the district as an additional insured. The contractor's excess liability insurer also joined in the proceedings and alleged that it, too, had no duty to indemnify because the district was not an insured under the excess policy.

The additional insured endorsement that applied to the park district reads as follows.

> The Persons Insured provision of this policy is amended to include as an Insured any Persons or organization whom the Named Insured has agreed by contract, either oral or written, prior to loss, to include as an Insured with respect to operations performed by or on behalf of the Named Insured. Such insureds included by contract shall hereinafter be referred to as Additional Insureds, and *the insurance afforded in paragraph A above shall not apply to damages arising out of the negligence of the Additional Insured(s)* .... [Emphasis added.]

While the endorsement referred to a paragraph A, no such provision was within the policy. Although this reference was awkward, according to the court, it did not affect the interpretation of the endorsement. The court ultimately held that, while the negligence exclusion of the additional insured endorsement was valid, coverage still existed for liability of the park district arising from violation of the Act. The court also ruled that the excess liability policy provided primary coverage for the district with respect to claims against it that were not covered by the primary policy. The rationale for coverage is more fully discussed in **Chapter 14,** which deals with umbrella and excess liability insurance issues.

Persons and organizations who seek additional insured status are likely to see more of these situations arise where an insurer will acknowledge the existence of an additional insured endorsement, but it will turn out to be an endorsement that is very limited in scope. As noted previously, one way to deal with this kind of situation is to specify the nature of the additional insured endorsement wording and request a copy of the endorsement with the certificate of insurance. Of course, this documentation must be reviewed, and it must be rejected if it does not satisfy the contract requirements.

A more stringent step would be to reject any certificate of insurance from an insurer that, as a matter of practice, issues such a limited additional insured endorsement without the right to review it prior to awarding work. This measure will benefit not only the additional insured but also the named insured if the latter has agreed to provide an additional insured endorsement according to certain prescribed wording; failure to fulfill such a request could result in a breach of contract and liability that is not covered by liability insurance. (See **Chapter 21,** which discusses compliance problems.)

Notice Problems

Since they rely on the insurance required of indemnitors in their contracts, indemnitees naturally desire to be informed promptly whenever the policy or policies are changed materially, not renewed, or canceled. However, insurers desire to keep their administrative burden as low as possible—and, just as importantly, avoid the possibility of breaching an agreement with another party with which they have no direct contractual relationship. For this reason, they are reluctant to agree to provide a party other than the first named insured with notice of cancellation or nonrenewal. Accordingly, the standard certificate does not obligate insurers to provide certificate holders with such notice. Contracts with more detailed insurance requirements often require notice of cancellation or changes in coverage. Even if it takes an endorsement to require that the insurer provide the additional insured with notice of cancellation, notice of changes in coverage can be provided by the named insured. While this relies heavily on the additional insured's ability to enforce contractual requirements against the named insured and the named insured's ability to pay if necessary, this is true of many responsibilities imposed on the named insured. The notice provision of the current ACORD Certificate Form 25–N (1/95) is reproduced in Exhibit 20.2.

While the certificate stipulates that the issuing insurer will endeavor to provide notice of cancellation, it does not require it to do so and does not even address nonrenewal or material changes imposed on the coverage terms. For the most part, the courts seem willing to give credence to this provision. For example, one court, in *Mountain Fuel Supply v Reliance Insurance Co.,* 933 F2d 882 (10th Cir 1991), made the following comment about it.

> The language in the notice of cancellation clause appears to be phrased so as to avoid creating any firm obligation to give notice. It states that the insuring company "will endeavor" to mail notice to the certificate holder, "but failure to mail such notice will impose no obligation or liability of any kind upon the company."

Since the issuance of a certificate does not obligate the insurer to provide the certificate holder with notice concerning material changes or an intent not to renew, a party who agrees to such conditions in a contract (e.g., an indemnitor) may ultimately be held accountable for any damages sustained by the other party resulting from lack of such notice.

Many risk management and insurance professionals have criticized this aspect of the standard certificate form. For example, industry commentator David Warren wrote that this provision is a "wimpish abdication of responsibility!" He also said, "It's the insurer's *duty* to notify the certificate holder—not something they *may* do if they can get around to it and can't find something more interesting to do."[4]

Many insurers probably fulfill their promises and notify certificate holders of policy cancellations. But if they do not send notices, whether they should have may very well be a question for the courts to decide. Of three cases on this point, two ruled in favor of the insurer.

The first case, which has been widely publicized over the years, is *U.S. Pipe and Foundry Co. v USF&G Co.,* 505 F2d 88 (5th Cir 1974). A lessee of real estate was required to purchase liability insurance and provide the lessor with a certificate of insurance. The certificate's provision concerning notice stated that the insurer "will make every effort to notify the holder ... of any material change in or cancellation ... but assumes no responsibility for failure to do so."

After the policy was renewed and another certificate issued, the insurer notified the lessee of its intention to cancel the policy but did not likewise notify the lessor (certificate holder). About 3 months after the policy was canceled, an explosion occurred on the leased property, resulting in extensive damage to adjoining property and in 1,100 lawsuits against the lessor.

The lessor subsequently sued the lessee's insurer to obtain coverage under the canceled policy. However, the trial court ruled in favor of the insurer, and the higher court, in construing the law of Alabama, affirmed the trial court's decision, providing the following reasons.

- A certificate of insurance issued to a lessor indicating that liability insurance has been acquired by the lessee does not constitute a contract between the lessor and the insurer. In other words, there was no privity between the lessor and the lessee's insurer.

- The provision of the certificate regarding notice in the event of cancellation was a mere promise, unsupported by any consideration. The court explained that while "forbearance can be a consideration," the court found none. It also stated that the 10-day notice period "was not supported by any consideration in the legal sense by way of either detriment to [the lessor] nor an advantage to the insurer."

- The certificate holder was not considered to be a third-party beneficiary on the policy. In order that the contract be for the benefit of a third party, the court said the contract must have been intended for the direct benefit of a third party, as distinguished from a mere incidental benefit to such third party.

The fact that another party, such as a certificate holder, is a third-party beneficiary may still not be enough to hold an insurer to its promise. A case in point is

Birmingham Fire Insurance Co. of Pennsylvania v Allstate Insurance Co., 349 S2d 646 (Fla 1977). A general contractor hired a subcontractor to handle the plumbing work for several buildings that were under construction. As required by ordinance, the subcontractor's insurer issued a certificate of insurance to the municipality that contained the following provision.

> It is agreed that cancellation of this policy shall not be effective as to the interest of the principal (municipality) hereinafter named until 30 days of notice of cancellation has been sent by certified mail.

When the subcontractor failed to pay its premium, the insurer sent notice of cancellation for nonpayment to the named insured subcontractor, but no notice was sent to the certificate holder (the municipality). Subsequently, an employee of the subcontractor allegedly caused a fire while using a soldering torch.

The property owner's fire insurer paid the loss and filed suit in subrogation against the subcontractor and its insurer. The subcontractor's liability insurer, however, maintained that the policy was canceled. The municipality's fire insurer argued that the policy was in force as far as the municipality was concerned because, as a certificate holder, it never received notice of cancellation. Also, as subrogee (i.e., the person who is subrogated), it was a third-party beneficiary. The Florida court, however, ruled that a third-party beneficiary has no greater rights than the named insured (the subcontractor). Since the policy was canceled, it also was considered to be terminated from the standpoint of the third-party beneficiary.

However, in another later case in a different jurisdiction, the certificate holder that did not receive proper notice, albeit in somewhat unusual circumstances, was granted protection under the policy. The case is *John Bader Lumber Co. v Employers Insurance of Wausau,* 441 NE2d 1306 (Ill App 1982). Here, the lumber company owned a parcel of property that it leased to a manufacturer. The manufacturer was to obtain the insurance for the benefit of both parties. Sometime later, the building was

damaged by fire, and a person was injured when one of the walls collapsed. Suit was filed against the lumber company (the lessor), which sought protection from the liability insurer of the manufacturer (the lessee). However, coverage was denied.

The liability insurer argued that there was evidence that the lessor and lessee had mutually agreed to terminate the lease between the time of the fire and the accident stemming from the collapsed wall. Also, under the terms of the master policy issued to the manufacturer and the certificate of insurance as issued to the lessor, coverage ceased when the manufacturer was no longer a tenant. The Illinois court, however, was not persuaded by the insurer's arguments. It stated that the certificate of insurance as issued to the lessor provided that, in the event of cancellation, 10 days' written notice of cancellation was to be provided to the insured. But instead of specifying an expiration date and occurrences that would terminate the coverage, the certificate merely stated that coverage was effective until canceled.

The court found that notice to the lessor was required by the terms of the certificate. The court also stated that the insurer could not resort to provisions of the master policy issued to the lessee to support its contentions because the lessor was never issued a copy of the policy. The court explained that the lessor, therefore, should not be held to have knowledge of significant exclusions or provisions, and these should not be considered.

Because Bader was not issued a copy of the policy, the court held he was entitled to rely on the certificate. This holding is consistent with other cases, some of which were discussed previously. This line of cases gives effect to the insured's expectation of coverage based on a reliance factor, whereby the insured relied on coverage and that reliance was justified for some reason.

Based on the aforementioned cases, it appears that insurers will not be held responsible for failure to provide notice of cancellation to certificate holders. Even a holding that there is privity of contract—because the certificate holder is an additional insured in the policy—still is not likely to change the policy's condition concerning notice, because the additional insured cannot obtain any greater rights than the named insured. And, in the event the policy covers more than one named insured, it is the first named insured, at least under current CGL forms, to whom the insurer is obligated to give notice.

There does not appear to be much a certificate holder can do about this problem. In fact, the court in the case of *Bradley Real Estate Trust v Plummer & Rowe Insurance Agency,* 609 A2d 1233 (NH 1992), said that, from the standpoint of giving notice, the disclaimers are clear. It also stated rather bluntly that:

> In effect, the certificate is a worthless document; it does no more than certify that insurance existed on the day the certificate was issued. We leave it to the legislature or to the future bargaining of the parties to rectify inequities in the notification process.

The most commonly attempted solution is to require a more affirmative notice requirement in certificates accepted from insurers. Another alternative is to require actual endorsement of the policy to provide the additional insured with cancellation notice. However, many insurers are unwilling to comply with such requests. In addition, more stringent requirements may still be unenforceable for the same reasons as discussed in the previous cases—lack of privity of contract because there is no consideration.

This also demonstrates the importance of including a clear and enforceable indemnity provision in the underlying lease or services contract. With an enforceable indemnity provision, there is still the possibility of collecting directly from the indemnitor when its insurer fails to respond on its behalf. On this score, it may behoove those on whose policies certificates are issued to directly inform certificate holders of changes in coverage or in cancellation in the event the insurer does not do so. This step could prevent the indemnitor from being accused that it breached its promise, particularly since such breaches are not generally covered by liability policies.

Adequacy of Aggregate Limits

A hotly debated subject in recent years concerns the aggregate limits of liability imposed by commercial general liability (CGL) insurance policies and how much more quickly the limits can be exhausted by claims or suits today than in the past. It is not only the increase in claims and the generous jury awards that are problematic, but also the change in how aggregate limits apply to the various coverages of primary and excess liability policies. Under the 1986 and later edition CGL forms, for example, all liability claims involving premises-operations, independent contractors, and contractual liability exposures are subject to one general aggregate limit. But each such exposure is subject to only a property damage limit that applies separately to each project or premises under the provisions of the 1973 and earlier edition CGL policies.

Prospective certificate holders who are concerned about the adequacy of aggregate limits on the policies of others may be in a position to request that the aggregate limits be some multiple of the per occurrence limit. Or, if appropriate, they should require that the insurance be written with a per location or per project aggregate limit with such separate limit reflected in the certificate. Much will depend on the bargaining power of the parties and the willingness of the insurer to comply.[5]

The concern over the availability of aggregate limits was heightened with the introduction of the claims-made CGL and umbrella policies. Certificate holders feared that by the time a claim is made against the named insured (and an additional insured and/or certificate holder), the limits, as stated in the certificate, may be seriously depleted or totally exhausted.

This may be a legitimate concern, but it also is a problem that prevails with policies written on an occurrence basis. It does not matter whether the policy on which a certificate is issued is written on a claims-made or an occurrence basis, since the limits of either type of policy can be reduced or exhausted by the time a claim is made against the additional insured, negotiated, and settled or adjudicated.

A related concern is whether the limits as requested by an additional insured or certificate holder will be available at time of need. An earlier edition of the ACORD insurance certificate contained the following statement.

> This is to certify that policies of insurance listed below have been issued to the insured named above and are in force at this time.

The probable reason that this provision was deleted in later ACORD certificates is that the statement would not be true if one or more of the policy's aggregate limits had been reduced prior to issuance of the certificate. In fact, the 1993 edition of ACORD certificate 25–S acknowledged this fact with the subtle statement that, "Limits shown may have been reduced by paid claims." A similar provision is included in the 1995 25–N edition.

Apart from the possible measures that certificate holders may be able to invoke on their own, no changes should be expected from ACORD. In fact, in response to an article about the ACORD certificate, ACORD stated that there were no plans to include a provision related to the status of aggregate limits in the certificate for the following reasons.

- It would be impossible to determine at any given time what the remaining aggregate limits are on a policy.

- Even if some kind of system were implemented to report the reduction of aggregate limits, the limits could be totally exhausted by the time a new certificate was issued.[6]

ACORD's position is that current certificates give adequate warning to holders about pitfalls of aggregates in the provision shown in Exhibit 20.3.

An ACORD representative stated that this certification has "withstood the test of time" and, considering that it makes reference to policy condi-

tions, it is broad enough to encompass aggregate limit provisions.[7] Therefore, unless certificate holders can take special precautions, they need to be aware of the caveats that come with such documents.

EXHIBIT 20.3
PRESERVATION OF POLICY
PROVISIONS CLAUSE

This is to certify that the policies of insurance listed below have been issued to the insured named above for the policy period indicated, notwithstanding any requirement, term or condition of any contract or other document with respect to which this certificate may be issued or may pertain, *the insurance afforded by the policies described herein is subject to all the terms, exclusions and conditions of such policies.* Limits as shown may have been reduced by paid claims. [Emphasis added.]

Source: Certificate Form 25–N (1/95) ACORD Corporation 1988.

Problems with Limits

The adequacy of limits is only one problem associated with the limits of coverage available. Certificate holders often request specific limits in a contract and, whether the expectation is specifically stated or not, expect that those limits will be the minimum available. If, for example, a certificate holder requested $2 million in limits in the underlying contract, and the party providing coverage had $10 million in applicable coverage, the party requiring the coverage would not expect that its coverage would be limited to the $2 million referenced in the contract. In most cases where limits are specified, they are viewed as a *minimum*, not a cap. While it is preferable that contracts state that the limits being required will be "no less than," that wording is not always used.

The limits reflected in certificates of insurance are likewise viewed as a minimum, absent wording that they will be "no more than." Disputes often arise when the loss exceeds the amount of insurance required in the underlying contract and the certificate holder seeks to recover sums excess of those required in the contract. Those providing evidence of insurance often take the position that the limits stated in the certificate are all that will be provided. However, as stated throughout this chapter, the certificate does not alter the terms of the policy or the underlying contract. Thus the certificate holder in most cases will rely on those limits as a minimum, absent some clarification to the contrary in the certificate or the underlying contract. To avoid such disputes, certificate holders are well advised to address this issue in the underlying contract and to require that the certificate also reflect that the limits shown are a minimum.

Deductibles and Self-Insured Retentions

Another area of dispute surrounding the use of certificates of insurance is the disclosure of any self-insured retentions, layers of self-insurance, and fronting arrangements. Certificates of insurance do not reflect the use of such risk financing techniques, and certificate holders as well as additional insureds are often surprised to learn that the insurance reflected in a certificate is provided not by an insurance company, but rather by one of these techniques. Problems can arise where the party providing evidence of coverage in the certificate cannot pay the sums that are documented in the certificate and provided by a layer of self-insurance. Likewise, problems can arise where additional insured endorsements are issued. Additional insured status cannot literally be provided by a layer of self insurance. This may not be a problem with fronting policies (discussed in **Chapter 4**) or where a self-insured retention is used in conjunction with an insurance policy. But it is a problem where the party providing evidence of coverage is self-insured.

The standard ACORD form certificate of insurance did not reflect any information regarding self-insured retentions until 1997. Even then, the only question asked was whether there was a deductible in the excess layers. Likewise, the certificate introduced by ISO in 2004 addresses this is-

sue only in the context of a question regarding the existence of a deductible in the excess layer of coverage. While the information requested may be adequate to disclose deductibles used in conjunction with an umbrella or excess policy, it does not inform the certificate holder of the common use of deductibles in the primary layer or the use of self-insurance, large self-insured retentions, or fronting arrangements which typically comprise the first layer of coverage and would not literally require disclosure as a deductible in the excess layer. Certificate holders and additional insureds alike are typically unaware of this blind spot.

Why certificates do not provide this information is unclear. What is clear, however, is that additional insureds and those requesting proof of insurance must request the disclosure of self-insurance, deductibles, self-insured retentions, and fronting arrangements in the underlying contract. Their use, application, and interpretation should be spelled out to avoid problems in the event of a claim or suit and the contract should require that their use be disclosed in the certificate of insurance.

Agent/Broker Liability for Issuance

Sometimes a problem will develop over the issuance of a certificate of insurance, and the question that needs to be resolved is whether the insurance representative was acting as the agent of the insurer or the named insured at the time the certificate was issued. The answer to this question is of importance because it can spell the difference between coverage and no coverage and possibly an action against the agent or broker.

A case in point, which revolved around notice under a certificate of insurance, is *Dumenric v Union Oil Co. of California,* 606 NE2d 230 (Ill App 1992). A property owner entered into an agreement with a contractor. The agreement provided that the work would begin on October 21, 1984, and that the estimated time of completion was October 21, 1985. The contractor also was to provide liability insurance with the property owner as an additional insured.

A certificate of insurance was issued by the insurance broker on October 18, 1984. The certificate was sent to and reviewed by the property owner on approximately October 24, 1984. The certificate stipulated that the property owner was an additional insured and would be given 10 days' notice of any cancellation of the policy. The certificate also stated that the policy was to run until October 21, 1985.

Suit was subsequently filed against the property owner by an employee of the contractor who allegedly was injured on December 11, 1984. When the property owner sought protection as an additional insured under the contractor's policy, the property owner was informed that the contractor's coverage had expired on November 21, 1984, before the date of the alleged injuries. The property owner also submitted an additional claim made against it by yet another employee of the contractor.

The crux of the issue in this case hinged on the relationship between the insurance broker and the insurer. It was the insurer's position that: (1) it issued a policy to the contractor only; (2) it never issued the certificate of insurance to the property owner; and (3) the broker was the agent of the contractor and not of the insurer.

The trial court found that the insurance broker was an agent, or apparent agent, of the insurer and that the broker bound the insurer to provide coverage to the property owner. The judge stated that if the broker had exceeded his authority, the insurer should proceed against the broker.

On appeal, the broker testified that he had been a practicing insurance broker since 1962 and during that time he represented numerous insurers. He considered himself an agent and a broker, sometimes acting on behalf of the insurer and sometimes on behalf of the insured. His agency agreement with the insurer authorized him to issue certificates, subject to sending copies to the insurer. He testified that he was not required to contact the insurer before issuing certificates of insurance. He simply called the underwriter or sent a copy of the certificate.

After the broker had obtained a policy for his contractor client, the insurer informed the broker that it was not going to renew the policy but agreed to extend its coverage for 1 month until November 21, 1984. He also was told by the contractor that it needed a certificate because it was going to do some work for the property owner. The broker, therefore, instructed an agency clerk to type the certificate. However, the certificate was dated October 18, 1984, and, in error, stated that it would expire on October 21, 1985, instead of October 21, 1984.

While the certificate signified that the property owner was an additional insured, the policy was never amended with an endorsement to that effect. It was stated that the insurer was experiencing substantial breakdowns of procedural systems during this time, and endorsements were not being issued after certificates of insurance were submitted.

The broker had some contact with the contractor in November 1984 but was informed that the insurance was placed with another agency. About March 6, 1985, the broker was contacted by the property owner's representative and was asked if the broker was still providing insurance for the contractor. The broker responded that he was no longer providing insurance for the contractor and wrote a letter to the property owner informing it of this fact.

The property owner also received a certificate of insurance from another insurance agency on October 29, 1984, which stated that insurance was being provided to the contractor. However, this insurance was different because it did not list the property owner as an additional insured, it did not contain a "cross-liability endorsement," and it did not address the required waiver of subrogation. The property owner, however, did not look into this certificate because it still possessed the one previously issued by the first broker.

The president of the contracting firm testified that he switched brokers in early fall of 1984 after the insurer decided not to continue liability insurance. However, the insurer's cancellation notice was sent to the contractor and the broker but not to the property owner. Both parties argued extensively and cited many cases on the issue of whether the broker was, in fact, an agent of the insurer.

The insurer also contended that the property owner did not reasonably rely on the certificate of insurance, because the property owner received a revised certificate of insurance by the new broker 5 days after the first certificate was issued by the prior broker. In substance, the insurer argued that the new certificate of insurance from the replacement broker provided duplicate coverage. The property owner, in turn, argued that it was not duplicative coverage because, among other things, it was not listed as an additional insured. The court of appeal ultimately decided that fairness required that the loss fall on the insurer rather than on the innocent insured where the insurer created the appearance of authority in a broker.

In the case of *Broderick Investment Co. v Strand Nordstrom Stailey Parker*, 794 P2d 264 (Colo App 1990), an independent insurance agency was held not bound by representations regarding the extent of coverage shown in a certificate of insurance. The agent was engaged to obtain insurance for its client, Ponderosa Timber Company. Broderick Investment Company (BIC) and Ponderosa entered into a contract to perform certain work. Under the contract, Ponderosa was obligated to provide liability insurance with limits of $1 million and to furnish a certificate of insurance before the work started. The agent submitted the certificate as requested by its client.

About 3 months after the certificate was issued, Ponderosa requested that its limits be reduced to $50,000 as a cost-saving step. BIC was not notified of this change. Some time later, an employee of Ponderosa accidentally started a fire on BIC's property, causing damage that far exceeded the $50,000 limit maintained by Ponderosa. BIC therefore brought suit against Ponderosa, its insurer, and the agent. The allegations were that the agent knew or should have known about Ponderosa's contract with BIC and that BIC would rely on the certificate. However, the record did not indicate any knowledge by the agent that performance under the contract had not been completed by the date the coverage was reduced.

BIC asserted that the certificate contained a promissory representation by the agent as to the amount of insurance in force and that there was a material issue of disputed fact as to whether the agent knew BIC would justifiably rely on the representation in the certificate. Because the agent failed to notify BIC of the reduction in coverage, BIC argued that the agent was bound by the representation in the certificate. The court, however, ruled for the agent, aligning itself with other appellate decisions that have considered the legal effect of similar provisions contained in the certificate at issue here. These provisions, the court explained, limit the certificate to an informational document only, which is subject to the terms of the policy. The court also said that the certificate has been interpreted as not creating any type of contractual relationship for the benefit of the certificate holder.

Ponderosa's right under the terms of the policy to reduce the amount of coverage was not disputed, and the certificate did not contain any representations by the agent that BIC would be notified if Ponderosa exercised its right to modify the amount of coverage. Under these circumstances, the court said, it could find no basis for application of the promissory estoppel doctrine. The court also stated that, given the express limitations in the certificate as to the ongoing accuracy of the information it contained, the agent assumed no duty to inform BIC of changes in the certificate. To find otherwise, the court held, would require that BIC establish a request to the agent that it be told of any material change in the information contained in the certificate. However, such an issue was not presented, the court said.

Suit was also filed against an insurance agency in a case discussed earlier in this chapter, *Bradley Real Estate Trust, et al., v Plummer & Rowe Insurance Agency*. In that case, a real estate trust brought suit for indemnification based on a certificate of insurance issued to a third party. The trial court granted the agent its motion to dismiss on the grounds that the real estate trust lacked a standing to sue and because the certificate imposed no duty on the part of the insurer to notify the real estate trust of the policy's cancellation.

The appeals court affirmed. It found, first of all, that the real estate trust could not maintain an indemnification action against the agent because any promise contained in the certificate was made to the trust's property manager and not to the trust. The court reasoned that the property manager, who was not a party to case, would have been the proper plaintiff. The question was raised whether the property manager was the real estate trust's agent, thereby allowing the trust to exercise the property manager's rights against the insurance agent. On this count, the court held that if there were sufficient facts to find an agency relationship, the trust might maintain the suit for indemnification against the insurance agent.

The second issue on appeal was whether the certificate of insurance created a duty to inform the property manager of the insurance policy's cancellation. The trial court held that such a duty was not created, on the basis of three clauses found in the certificate: (1) the certificate does not amend, extend, or alter the coverage afforded by the policies, (2) insurance afforded by the policies described is subject to all the terms, exclusions, and conditions of such policies, and (3) should any of the described policies be cancelled before the expiration date, the issuing company will endeavor to mail 30 days' written notice, but failure shall impose no obligation or liability of any kind upon the company, its agents, or its representatives. The appeals court held that the disclaimers of liability contained in the certificates were clear. As referenced earlier, the court also stated that the certificate in effect "was a worthless document" that did nothing more than certify that insurance existed on the day the certificate was issued.

Failure To Review the Certificate

When compared to the cost of adding an additional insured to a liability policy, the potential cost of failing to fulfill that promise can be staggering. Therefore, it is not unusual for those who have breached (or may breach) their contracts—from failing to procure a certain kind of coverage or to add a named certificate holder as an additional insured—to be faced with the realization that unless they eliminate or reduce their potential exposure

for noncompliance of their contractual obligations, they may have to retain all of the unplanned financial consequences.

One defense commonly employed by those confronted with a failure to procure coverage as promised is to maintain that the certificate holder waived the right to raise this contractual requirement by accepting a noncomplying certificate without questioning it. An example would be accepting a certificate of insurance that does not reflect the holder as an additional insured even though that was required in the contract. If the certificate holder does not point out the noncompliance and request a certificate delineating the coverages required in the contract, an argument may be made that it has waived its right to collect damages resulting from the breach at a later time.

A case in point is *Geier v Hamer Enterprises*, 589 NE2d 711 (Ill App 1992). A contractor entered into a contract with a property owner to perform certain work on a building. Included in the contract was the requirement that the contractor name the property owner as an additional insured on its policy and provide a certificate of insurance acceptable to the owner *prior* to the commencement of work.

Subsequently, an employee of the contractor filed suit against the owner for injuries sustained. The record does not indicate whether the owner ever tendered its defense to the contractor. However, the owner did file a complaint against the contractor that alleged, in part, that the contractor breached its contract by failing to procure insurance as required and sought damages in an amount equal to the financial and economic losses sustained by the owner as a result of the breach. The contractor defended by alleging that the owner waived the right to allege breach of contract by allowing the contractor to commence and complete its work without requiring that the certificate of insurance called for in the contract be provided prior to the beginning of the job. The court agreed with the contractor.

In making this decision, the court looked to an earlier Illinois case, *Whalen v K-Mart Corp.*, 519 NE2d 991 (Ill 1988), where the court also held that the general contractor and property owner had waived the right to assert the subcontractor's contractual insurance requirements. The contract in that case provided that "the subcontractor shall not commence work ... until he has obtained all insurance required ... and certificates of insurance [are] delivered to the contractor." It also provided that the subcontractor "agrees to procure at his own expense, before the commencement of work, comprehensive general liability" insurance, and the subcontractor was to "immediately and before commencing work deliver such policy or policies or certificates of insurance to the contractor."

The *Whalen* court held that both the contractor and property owner waived this condition precedent by permitting the subcontractor to commence work and by paying the subcontractor upon completion without concern for these contract requirements. The court stated as follows.

> If a [party] has intentionally relinquished a known right, either expressly or by conduct inconsistent with an intent to enforce that right, he has waived it and may not thereafter seek judicial enforcement.

In accordance with the ruling in *Whalen,* the court in *Geier* ruled that since the contractual provisions requiring the procurement of insurance were substantially similar to those in the *Whalen* case, both the contractor and property owner had intentionally relinquished their right to rely on the contractual provisions.

The position taken by the contractor and owner—which was rejected by the court—argued that the *Whalen* logic did not apply to this case because the contract language in *Whalen* prohibited the commencement of work until all insurance had been obtained. It was argued that no such prohibition was contained in the *Geier* contract. Instead, it was argued that the obligations requiring the subcontractor to maintain insurance and contract language requiring the subcontractor to provide a certificate of insurance prior to the commencement of work were separate and distinct.

The contractor and owner also argued that the subcontractor should not benefit from its own misconduct in failing to procure insurance. However, the court nonetheless ruled against the contractor and owner, citing that parties to a contract may waive provisions placed in a contract for their own benefit and, therefore, that the principle of freedom to contract was being upheld.

The fact that two courts (in one state) held that a breach of contract was waived—by permitting someone to commence work without first furnishing a certificate of insurance that was required by contract—could lead to the conclusion that waiver is a foregone conclusion if those who require certificates of insurance do not enforce the underlying contract. However, this is not so.

The result in another case within the same jurisdiction ended differently. This case is *Lavelle v Dominick's Finer Foods,* 592 NE2d 287 (Ill App 1992). This is a complex case that involved a number of different issues. A store owner hired a contractor to install a sprinkler system in the store. After the work was completed, final payment was made for the work. However, a suit was subsequently filed against the store owner by a contractor's employee, who was injured while installing the system. The complaint alleged violation of the Structural Work Act and negligence of the store owner.

The store owner filed a third-party complaint against the contractor, seeking indemnity from the contractor pursuant to a contractual indemnity agreement. The store owner also alleged that the contractor breached its contractual agreement by failing to obtain insurance naming the store owner as an additional insured. The contractor argued that both of these allegations of the store owner were expressly waived in a provision of a contract wherein the store owner, on final payment for completion of the work, waived all claims against the contractor. The contractor also maintained that the store owner impliedly waived the requirement for the contractor to provide it with insurance when the store owner failed to require the contractor to file certificates of insurance prior to allowing the contractor to begin work on the project.

The store owner maintained that the waiver provision, as read by the contractor, was quoted out of context and was applicable only to the progress of the work and compliance with the project specifications. Any other interpretation of the waiver provision, the store owner argued, would render meaningless the indemnity and insurance provisions contained in the agreement, because any claims that the store owner would have against the contractor for indemnification or breach of contract for failure to provide insurance were unlikely to arise or be discovered until after completion of the installation work.

When the lower court ruled in the contractor's favor, the store owner challenged the court's dismissal of his complaint, which alleged that the contractor failed to obtain insurance adding the store owner as an additional insured pursuant to the following provision in the addendum to the contract.

> It is extremely important and expressly understood and agreed that each Contractor shall be responsible for any and all damages to property and any and all injuries or disease or death to any one person arising directly or indirectly from, or in connection with work performed, or to be performed under this contract, including extra work. Therefore each Contractor shall purchase and maintain such insurance as will protect him from any and all claims …
>
> The Contractor shall procure insurance naming … [the store owner], its agents and employees as additional insured. The Contractor shall submit the Certificate of Insurance to the … [store owner] before commencement of the work. The … [store owner] will procure and maintain a "Builders Risk Insurance" policy.

In its complaint, the store owner alleged that the contractor failed to obtain the required "personal injury" insurance and umbrella policy to cover excess liability as provided in the contract and failed to obtain the required insurance adding the store owner as an additional insured. The store owner further alleged that if the contractor had met its contractual obligations, the store owner would have been protected as an additional insured, and the insurer would have been required to defend and indemnify the store owner in the contractor's employee's claim.

The contractor argued that the store owner impliedly waived its claim of breach of contract to procure insurance, because the store owner received a certificate of insurance from the contractor that did not indicate that the store owner was an additional insured. Nevertheless, the store owner still allowed the contractor to complete its work under the contract without requiring the contractor to procure the insurance guaranteed under the contract.

The store owner, on the other hand, contended that its acceptance of the certificate of insurance was not proof of its intent to waive the contractual provision to procure insurance. The store owner stated it was unaware that the policy referenced in the certificate did not name it as an additional insured. Further, since the store owner did not have a copy of the insurance policy issued to the contractor, it was without notice as to whether it was named in the policy as an additional insured.

The court of appeal ruled for the store owner. In doing so, it stated that the store owner's intention to waive the contract's provision requiring the contractor to procure insurance naming the store owner could not be inferred from the facts of the case. It also stated that it could not be clearly inferred from the circumstances that the store owner's failure to take any specific action showed an intent to permanently relinquish its right to be insured. Finally, the contractor did not suggest that it was in any way misled into acting in any particular way based on a reasonable belief that a waiver had occurred.

A number of cases in other jurisdictions have likewise ruled against waiver of another party's breach of contract dealing with insurance and certificates of insurance. In *Myers v Burger King Corp.,* 618 S2d 1123 (La App 1993), the property owner allowed a contractor to begin renovation work before it had obtained a certificate of insurance representing that the owner was covered by the contractor's insurance.

This conduct was held not to have waived the owner's right to claim that the contractor breached its contractual obligation to provide coverage where the owner was unaware that it was not insured until after a contractor's employee suffered injuries. The contractor admitted it failed to name the owner as an insured because he did not read the contract and because he assumed that this contract was the same as previous contracts required by the owner. In finding a breach of contract for failure to procure insurance, the court stated that a person who signs a written instrument is presumed to know its contents and cannot claim that he or she did not read or understand the document.

In *Edwards v International Business Machines Corp. and Pike-Paschen II,* 174 AD2d 863 (NY 1991), a subcontractor's employee was injured on IBM's premises and filed suit against IBM and its general contractor. The latter two parties then filed a third-party-over action against the subcontractor for indemnification. IBM also alleged that the contract further obligated the subcontractor to secure an owners and contractors protective (OCP) liability policy in IBM's name but failed to do so and was therefore liable for the resulting damages.

The subcontractor contended that IBM may have waived the obligation to obtain an OCP policy because, prior to the commencement of the work, IBM accepted certificates of insurance that did not identify IBM as an insured. The court ruled that this argument was without merit because the contract required any waivers to be in writing and none was ever executed.

In *Texaco, Inc. v East Coast Management,* 719 F Supp 319 (D NJ 1989), a contract with a contractor required that a certificate of insurance specifically quoting the contract's indemnification agreement and naming the owner as a "coinsured" be delivered to Texaco prior to commencement of work. Under the terms of the contract, "failure to keep the required insurance policies in full force and effect … shall constitute a breach … and the [owner] shall have the right to immediately cancel and terminate this agreement."

Following an action against Texaco and the denial by the contractor's insurer to provide protection, Texaco brought an action against the contractor alleging, in part, that the contractor failed to name Texaco as a "coinsured" as required by contract. The contractor replied that Texaco waived any such requirement by permitting the contractor to commence work without first demanding a certificate of insurance. Texaco countered that it was the contractor's burden to show that either (1) a certificate was issued or (2) Texaco did not demand a certificate and that, in fact, it was not produced. The court found that the contractor failed to satisfy this burden with respect to the waiver issued.

In *Howe v Lever Brothers Co.,* 851 SW2d 769 (Mo App ED 1993), the court held that neither the property owner nor the general contractor waived its contractual requirement that a subcontractor obtain insurance naming both as additional insureds when the certificates were not delivered before work began as provided by the subcontract. The subcontractor argued that the conduct of the owner and general contractor in disregarding their contractual right to obtain status as insureds under the subcontractor's policies, coupled with their permitting and encouraging the commencement of work, constituted a waiver of their rights.

The court disagreed with the subcontractor. Testimony indicated that the general contractor and subcontractor had dealt with each other on various projects in the past, and the contracts on this project included similar provisions concerning insurance. (This assumption can backfire, as it did in the *Myers v Burger King* case where the contractor did not read the contract because he assumed it was the same as in earlier work with the owner. If the contractual provisions remain the same, there may not be a problem, but one cannot always make that conclusion.) Moreover, the project was a "very dynamic, very fast-track project," where paperwork followed the commitments.

Regardless of the consequences, there will always be those who play the odds and, for whatever reason, disregard their contractual obligations or fail to ensure that the representations made in certificates truly reflect the nature of the protection being provided. Allowing a promisor to escape contractual obligations (such as the failure to procure certain insurance) because a certificate holder relied on the disclaimer required by statute in some states and case law in others, runs counter to the law governing certificates and is unfair in many instances.

A contractual obligation to provide insurance and/or a certificate should not be abrogated except in a written addendum to the contract signed by both parties. This is a provision built into most contracts and should be given effect in situations such as described previously.

Likewise, promisors should not be allowed to escape their contractual obligations in failing to procure insurance merely because the other party fails to verify, prior to the commencement of work, that the certificate conforms to the protection required. If an insurance certificate does not amend, extend, or alter the coverage of policies as listed, it likewise should not be used as a defense against a breach of contract merely because the holder does not verify or question the protection represented on these certificates.

Attempts To Solve the Problems

As can be seen from the problems previously discussed, the insurance industry has drafted standard certificate of insurance forms with a very simple goal in mind. Insurers are attempting to provide certain basic information to certificate holders without contractually obligating themselves beyond any obligations expressed in the underlying insurance policies issued to the named insured (e.g., additional insured status provided by an endorsement to the policy). Insurers have good reasons for limiting the purpose of certificates in this way.

- Many commercial insureds are required to provide evidence of insurance to hundreds or even thousands of other organizations. Keeping up with differing requirements of each (and the status of each project or activity for which they are provided) would be an overwhelming administrative burden.

- By using one standard certificate form that contains known terminology, insurers can routinely issue certificates using clerical staff without requiring lengthy review by underwriters or other trained technical staff. This approach also allows insurers to delegate certificate issuance to their agents.

- Insurers generally receive no additional compensation for issuing certificates of insurance. Extending their contractual obligations beyond what they agreed to in the insurance policies without compensating them for the additional administrative expense or additional liability may, therefore, be inequitable.

Certificate holders, on the other hand, often have in mind much more substantial goals when they require evidence that a contracting party is meeting the insurance obligations it agreed to in the contract. After all, they are relying on the insurance evidenced by the certificate to insulate them from the possibility of substantial financial harm. Therefore, they often want a guarantee that the actual scope of coverage provided complies with the terms of the contract and that they will receive notice if the coverage is canceled or not renewed.

The guarantee that indemnitees often want is far beyond the scope of the insurers' goal to provide basic information. Thus the standard ACORD certificate, which was drafted by insurers, falls short of the lofty objectives of many certificate holders.

Some certificate holders go to great lengths in their efforts to secure this guarantee of coverage. The three most common approaches to circumventing the weaknesses in the standard certificate of insurance form are as follows.

- Requiring the standard certificate to specifically incorporate the contract by reference

- Requiring certified copies of the actual insurance policies rather than a certificate

- Requiring evidence of insurance be provided on a special manuscript certificate form drafted by the certificate holder

Each of these approaches is discussed in the following pages.

Specific Designation of Contracts

A measure sometimes taken by insurance certificate holders (who may or may not be additional insureds) to strengthen the promise of insurance is to require the recital, verbatim, of the entire indemnity agreement on the certificate. This approach may very well be interpreted to extend the coverage provided on behalf of an indemnitee beyond the terms of the actual insurance policy.

A case illustrating this practice is *J.M. Corbett Co. v Insurance Co. of North America,* 357 NE2d 125 (Ill App 1976). A subcontractor was hired by a general contractor to perform certain work. The contract provided that the subcontractor would furnish insurance with a satisfactory insurer. The subcontractor procured an insurance policy and tendered the certificate of insurance, which was accepted. The certificate contained the following indemnity provision.

> It is understood and agreed that the subcontractor will indemnify and save harmless the contractor from and against any and all claims for injury or death of persons or damage to property (including costs of litigation and attorneys fees) in any matter caused by, arising from, incident to, connected with or growing out of the work to be performed under this contract, regardless of whether such claim is alleged to be caused, in whole or in part, by negligence, or otherwise, on the part of the contractor or its employees.

During the work period, a vehicle rented by the subcontractor was involved in an accident that caused property damage at the work site. The vehicle's owner filed suit against the general contractor who, in turn, looked to the subcontractor's insurer for protection. The insurer denied coverage, relying on a rented vehicle exclusion.

The general contractor argued that the subcontractor's certificate of insurance did not contain any language to the effect that the certificate was subject to the terms and conditions of the policy. The court ruled, however, that a certificate of insurance, as accompanying paper, along with riders and endorsements, must be read together with the policy to determine the scope of coverage. One of the major problems encountered by the court was that the policy excluded rented vehicles but the certificate of insurance did not. The coverage, therefore, was uncertain.

The court resolved the uncertainty by ruling in favor of the general contractor and requiring the insurer to provide coverage. In doing so, the court explained that the general contractor did not receive a copy of the policy, the policy exclusion did not apply because it conflicted with the hold harmless agreement, and the policy exclusion was not mentioned on the certificate.

It is because of the potential for holdings such as this that insurers resist requirements to add contract language to certificates. In fact, the ACORD training manual on certificates of insurance specifically recommends that wording from contracts not be quoted on certificates. Often, underwriting manuals of insurers contain similar prohibitions.

However, some certificate holders and their indemnitors are able to persuade insurers to incorporate the indemnification clause into the certificate despite these prohibitions. In such a case, the insurer is likely to require some additional qualifying language on the certificate to reduce chances of problems. For example, the insurer might add a provision such as the following to the certificate, preceding the indemnity agreement.

> Such insurance as is afforded by the policy for the contractual liability stated on this certificate applies to "bodily injury" or "property damage" with respect to which liability is assumed by the insured under the following contractual provision.

While this type of provision limits the protection the insurer must provide by the terms of the policy, it also helps to clarify the extent to which an indemnitee is protected. In other words, one of the big concerns of certificate holders is that they do not know if the liability policy in question will cover liability arising from their sole fault—assuming that the particular state has no law prohibiting such liability from being passed through indemnity clauses.

The problem with this type of wording, as discussed previously, is that it makes the contractual liability insurance and the indemnity obligation interdependent or inextricably tied. As such, there is a risk that if the indemnity obligation is struck down for assumption of sole fault or some other reason, the insurer's obligation falls as well. If this approach of incorporating indemnity wording into the certificate is followed, it is essential that the belt-and-suspenders concept be applied.

That is, contractual liability coverage must be used in conjunction with additional insured status. That way, if contractual liability coverage does not apply because the indemnity agreement is invalid or limited in scope, additional insured status may be relied on to provide protection to the additional insured. There are other problems that might arise where the practice of incorporating the indemnity agreement into the certificate is followed.

Insureds still face the prospect that the insurer will contest coverage on the grounds that the certificate does not alter, extend, or amend coverage. Insurers, on the other hand, run the risk of arguments by insureds that the insurer has waived that argument by allowing the incorporation of the indemnity agreement into the certificate. In fact, the insurer might find that by consenting to this procedure, it has waived arguments regarding other provisions of the certificate and their inability to alter, extend, or amend coverage.

In the absence of the verbatim reference of the indemnity agreement on the certificate, the indemnitee does not have complete assurance that it will be protected even if contractual liability coverage is acknowledged as being provided. Though rarely done, the contractual liability coverage of the policy could

be limited to "intermediate" contractual agreements or, in other words, to the comparative rather than the sole fault of the indemnitee. Unless a certificate is issued that reflects that broad form indemnity clauses are covered or a separate endorsement is issued to the indemnitee to verify coverage, the verbatim reference of the indemnity agreement on the certificate may be the only other way to ensure that such protection is being provided. However, this, too, is subject to the caveats previously discussed.

Specific Designation of Contract Name and Number

Instead of reciting the entire indemnitee agreement, the certificate may signify the work to be performed by job contract name and number. Depending on the circumstances, this practice may work for or against the certificate holder.

A case illustrating one potential outcome when a contract is designated by name or number on the certificate is *Mamba Engineering Co. v Jacksonville Electric Authority,* 470 S2d 758 (Fla App 1985). The project owner entered into a contract with an engineering firm to construct electric transmission lines. The engineering firm was to provide various types of insurance including an OCP policy for the project owner's benefit. Also, certificates of insurance, which were to list the type of policies to be provided, were to be filed with the project owner prior to the commencement of the work. A certificate was issued, but it did not mention the OCP policy. The project owner, nonetheless, permitted the engineering firm to commence work.

An employee of the engineering firm was injured on the job and filed suit against the project owner, who looked to the engineering firm for two reasons: (1) the contractual indemnity provision and (2) the engineering firm's failure to provide the proper insurance as required under the contract.

Summary judgment was entered in favor of the project owner based on the court's finding that the project owner had not, as a matter of law, waived its right to sue the engineering firm for its failure to provide the OCP policy. The court also noted that the certificate of insurance furnished by the engineering firm did not support an inference that the project owner knew the OCP policy had not been furnished. To the contrary, the certificate of insurance expressly referred to the job contract by name and number.

The engineering firm, therefore, was held to be accountable for resulting damages because of its breach of contract in failing to procure proper coverage. While the specific designation on the certificate of insurance of the contract name and number worked to the advantage of the certificate holder in this case, it certainly was not an advantageous measure insofar as the entity on whose behalf the certificate was issued.

Designating a specific job on a certificate in cases where the policy is to confer coverage based on the certificate may be effective if done carefully. This procedure was explained in relation to the *Great Lakes Dredge & Dock Co.* case discussed on page 349. However, an additional illustration may be warranted. Assume an endorsement is manuscripted to confer additional insured status to the extent of the limits of liability and the coverages the named insured has agreed, before loss, to provide by certificate of insurance. The certificate then lists all of the policies, numbers, periods of coverage, limits maintained, and insurers. Under description of operations, it might show who the additional insured is, the contract/purchase order number, and which of the policies, identified by numerical number or letters, is applicable. For example, if coverage is to be limited solely to that provided by the commercial general liability policy with combined single limits of $1 million, the certificate should clearly reflect that it applies only with respect to Coverage A or Coverage 1.

Apart from that approach, designating a specific job on a certificate can lead to ambiguities if the wording is given effect in interpreting coverage. For example, to what extent is coverage provided for operations related to the project but conducted off the construction site? Likewise, designating specific jobs on the certificate can lead to problems, such as those discussed previously in relation to the effect of certificates on coverage and the positions taken

by insureds and insurers in this regard. Following this procedure requires a well-thought-out approach and carefully crafted wording. Even then, there could be problems for the named insured, additional insured, and insurers involved.

Requesting a Certified Policy

To overcome some of the drawbacks of standard certificates, some parties will request certified copies of the required insurance policies instead of a certificate of insurance. Receipt of actual copies of the policies certainly gives the certificate holder an opportunity to verify that the policies meet the scope of coverage required in the underlying contract. Of course, this approach does not in and of itself overcome the potential of the policies being canceled and the insurer failing to notify the indemnitee.

Requests for certified copies of the indemnitor's insurance policies are often denied or ignored for a variety or reasons, including the following.

- The policies called for in the contract have not actually been issued to the insured at the time the contract is issued.[8] This is probably the most common reason why requests for certified copies are ignored.

- Commercial lines policies, with all of their schedules and endorsements, are so complicated to assemble that providing a complete copy is not always as simple an administrative task as it sounds.

- Insurance policies often contain confidential information (e.g., annual payroll expenditures) about the named insured. This fact is not considered at the time the contract is negotiated but comes to light later when the obligation is supposed to be performed and the named insured does not wish to disclose it.

In such cases, it is quite common for the insurer or agent to ignore the request for certified copies of the policies and instead to issue a certificate of insurance. Since many indemnitees do not have a well-organized and carefully administered program monitoring compliance with contractual insurance requirements, they often accept certificates instead of polices, without complaint. Those that do monitor and control the process often accept certificates after losing a debate on the subject.

Regardless of the reasons, the indemnitee does not, in many instances, receive copies of the policies and is thus prohibited from reviewing the actual policies to verify whether the coverages requested are actually being provided.

As can be seen in the case of *Bonner County v Panhandle Rodeo Assn., supra,* 620 P2d 1102 (Idaho 1980), this can work to the certificate holder's advantage. A county and fair association (the county) leased its fairgrounds each year to a joint venture formed by two organizations (the rodeo) for the purpose of sponsoring a rodeo. A dispute arose over the insurance coverage provided by the rodeo when the county sought defense and indemnification with respect to an action filed against the county by a woman who suffered injuries in a fall from a bleacher seat during the rodeo.

A provision of the lease that was the center of the controversy read as follows.

> The tenant shall provide and procure extended insurance liability coverage in an amount of at least $250,000 per person and $500,000 aggregate, and Third Party property coverage of $250,000, and shall present proof of the same by filing a copy of the insurance policy with the landlord at least ten (10) days prior to the rodeo performance dates. *The tenant shall hold harmless the landlord for any liability incurred as a result of the rodeo performances,* and the landlord shall have no financial responsibility for any debt or obligation incurred by the tenant. [Emphasis added.]

Pursuant to these requirements, the rodeo's insurer issued a liability policy to which was attached an additional insured endorsement that read as follows.

> It is agreed that the "persons insured" provision is amended to include as an insured any person

or organization (public or private), but only with respect to liability arising out of:

1. The ownership, maintenance or use of premises or other facilities leased, loaned or donated to the named insured;

2. The existence, maintenance, repair, construction, erection or removal of advertising signs, awnings, canopies, marquees, street banners or decorations and similar exposures by the named insured; And subject to the additional exclusions: this insurance does not apply:

   1. To any occurrence which takes place after the named insured ceases to have use of said premises, facilities or above items;

   2. To structural alterations, new construction or demolition operations performed by or on behalf of the person or organization as described above;

   3. To liability arising out of the *sole negligence of the additional insured* hereunder. [Emphasis added.]

Also attached to the policy was another endorsement that provided as follows.

> The company will pay on behalf of the insured all sums which the insured, by reason of contractual liability assumed by him under any written contract of the type designated in the schedule for this insurance, shall become legally obligated to pay as damages because of bodily injury or property damage to which this insurance applies.

The immediate endorsement also provided that the insurance did not apply "to liability of the indemnitee resulting from his sole negligence."

Even though required by the lease agreement, a copy of the insurance policy was not filed with the county. Historically, the rodeo filed a certificate of insurance but never the policy itself. That particular year, the county received a photocopy of the certificate and expressed dissatisfaction over receiving a copy instead of an original certificate. But the insurance agent brought assurances that the photocopy was a true and correct copy and that an original would be forthcoming.

Thereafter the lease was signed. Both the photocopy and the original of the certificate contained language stating that the certificate was informational only and that an underlying policy controlled the coverages and limits. However, both copies of the certificate also indicated that insurance coverage was being provided on "contractual blanket written agreements." The certificate also signified that it was being issued for the special rodeo event.

When the county turned to the rodeo's insurance, the insurer denied coverage because of the sole negligence exclusion in the policy. The county then brought suit against the rodeo and its insurer, seeking defense and indemnification of the suit brought by the injured woman. The court ruled in favor of the county and against the insurer that coverage applied for two reasons. First, the policy that contained the contractual liability exclusion for the sole fault of the indemnitee was never provided to the county. Instead, a certificate was issued that the county did not request. Second, both the policy and the certificate indicated that coverage applied for written contractual agreements.

This case illustrates how the practice of requesting certified copies of insurance policies may enhance an indemnitee's legal position when the policies are not provided. By declining to issue the certified copy of the policy, the insurer in effect forces the additional insured to rely solely on the certificate. However, in the event of a questionable claim, the additional insured could maintain that it had the reasonable expectation that the policy covered such a claim and that if it had the opportunity to see the actual insurance policy rather than being denied that right, this problem might not have arisen. The certificate holder thus would argue that it should be given the benefit of any doubt.

Manuscript Certificate Forms

Some organizations with substantial bargaining positions attempt to dictate the terms and conditions that may be included on certificates issued to them. Some even go so far as to draft their own "comprehensive" certificates and require that they be completed on behalf of those that have agreed to indemnify them. For example, it is not uncommon for construction project owners, particularly governmental entities, to attempt to require contractors to provide evidence of insurance on a special manuscript certificate form.

These manuscript certificates, of course, typically do not include the conditional language found in the ACORD form stating that the certificate does not amend, extend, or alter the coverage under the listed policies. And indeed, these certificates may be found by some courts to actually override the limitations of an insurance policy.

A case in point is *Mountain Fuel Supply v Reliance Insurance Co.,* 933 F2d 882 (10th Cir 1991). This is a complex case because it involved certificates issued over a period of years with some issued on a manuscript form while others were on a standard ACORD form. Sometimes the insurance agent for the contractor—who was to complete and return the certificates—signed the document, and at other times it was issued unsigned. Likewise, the certificates sometimes acknowledged that the certificate holder was to be recognized as a named insured on a primary basis, and at other times there was no mention of such insured status.

The issue was whether the certificate holder was an insured under the contractor's liability policies at the time of an accident. The manuscript certificate indicated that the certificate holder was an insured, but no additional insured endorsement was added to the policy. The court ultimately held that the certificate holder was, in fact, an insured under the policy. However, the court further ruled that coverage still did not apply because the accident had taken place after the expiration date designated in the certificate.

An important point about this case is the recognition by the court that there are standard and nonstandard certificates. As to the nonstandard ones, the court stated that:

> numerous companies, especially in certain industries, have a need for a more individualized certification of insurance indicating that coverage of a particular type is in place. These companies typically have their own certification form which must be completed by the hired company's insurance agent or insurance company.

For good reason, many insurance agents and brokers are reluctant to complete manuscript certificates. As a matter of good risk management practices, these agents sometimes turn to their insurance company underwriters for completion instead. But if expediency is necessary, the agents may have no other alternative but to complete such certificates.

However, when the insurance is handled by a broker instead of an agent, the certificate may require that the authorized signature be that of an insurer. Not all such manuscript certificates will necessarily be rejected by underwriters. As noted previously, much depends on what the certificate's requirements are.

One problem associated with manuscript certificate wording is that it may be interpreted against the party drafting it. Another is that if it is rejected by insurers, the indemnitee has the burden of ensuring that a satisfactory alternative is utilized. This can prove to be an elusive goal for entities involved in numerous contracts and dealing with a variety of indemnitors and insurers. Standard certificates may not be what is desired, but they may be the best alternative for some given the potential problems discussed. Those who utilize manuscript wording must take the precautions necessary to ensure that the problems addressed in this book and others are taken into account.

A Practical Look at Administration

The problem with all of these solutions to the limitations in insurance certificates is that their imple-

mentation is largely beyond the control of both the certificate holder and the indemnitor/named insured. There are no conditions in insurance policies requiring insurers to comply with special requirements for evidencing the existence of insurance coverage. These special requests generally impose much more substantial requirements on insurers than is their policy to accept. Therefore, as mentioned previously, many insurers refuse to honor these requirements when presented with them.

While the use of manuscript certificates, incorporation of the indemnity provision, or certified copies of policies may reduce the additional insured's level of uncertainty regarding the implementation of insurance requirements, they also typically lead to involved debates between the various parties. The time and effort spent debating whether such requirements will be met might be better spent in implementing other risk management programs, such as safety or loss control programs.

Of course, these requirements could also work against indemnitees if they do not follow through with an effective administrative program. For example, imagine how different the *Bonner* case (see page 368) might have gone if the insurer had provided a copy of the policy to the county and the county had failed to find and require the removal of the problematic exclusion.

Indemnitees who require that certificates (whether on a standard or manuscript form) or copies of policies be provided are strongly advised to carefully review the documents they actually receive and require correction of any problems they uncover. Otherwise, they may find themselves estopped from claiming breach of contract by the indemnitor in failing to arrange insurance as required and unable to assert a reasonable expectation of coverage from the insurance policy. Many companies do not have sufficient staff to properly review and respond to the certificates of insurance they receive. Even fewer organizations have staffs with the knowledge and time to effectively review copies of the indemnitor's actual insurance policies.

The administration of risk transfer control programs can be tedious, frustrating, and time-consuming. As demands on indemnitors and their insurers increase, more time is required by more knowledgeable staff to monitor compliance with contract provisions. It is important to consider how the indemnitee can better transfer risk and to implement whatever methods are necessary to the extent practical. What must never be forgotten is the liability exposure faced by the parties involved and the importance in addressing that liability. If additional staff is not practical, then it may be necessary to make adjustments in the priority assigned to existing staff and the functions they spend their time on. After a loss, the overriding question will simply be, "Is it covered?"

The Wrap-Up Approach

Monitoring certificates of insurance in connection with construction contracts is a difficult, sometimes impossible task. There are numerous cases, including those discussed above, where the party obligated to provide coverage failed to do so. Some of those cases result in verdicts favoring the owner or contractor that was denied the additional insured status it was promised and some do not. However, even in those cases where a failure to procure the coverage represented in the certificate results in a favorable verdict for the party that was not provided coverage, there can be problems. All too often those who fail to comply with their contractual obligation to provide insurance are unable to financially withstand the consequences of their failure. As a result, even an owner or contractor who succeeds in obtaining a judgment against the defaulting party may not be compensated.

Because an inability or failure to successfully monitor compliance can result in serious financial consequences, it is extremely important for those requesting certificates also to request additional insured status (belt-and-suspenders) and to amend their own insurance program to respond in such situations. An option gaining popularity that alters the very essence of additional insured status, a wrap-up virtually obviates the need for certificates with large construction projects. Developers, property owners, and contractors embarking on construction projects usually opt for the traditional approach to insuring their exposure. Under this approach, the owner, developer or contractor imposes insurance requirements and requires that certificates of insurance be provided to evidence compliance with those insurance requirements.

Many of the problems associated with this approach in terms of monitoring compliance with the insurance requirements are addressed in **Chapter 21** and will not be repeated here at length. However, it is important to remember that even where the coverage required in the contract is evidenced in the certificate, ensuring it will actually be provided is no easy task. As the problems discussed throughout this chapter indicate, asking for a specific endorsement, limit, or coverage feature and getting it are two different things.

As discussed in **Chapter 21,** two methods of insuring large construction projects are gaining increasing popularity. These are owner controlled and contractor controlled insurance programs, commonly referred to as wrap-ups. A brief summary of how these programs work can be found in **Chapter 21.** The characteristic of wrap-ups relevant to this discussion is that all (or most, depending on the program) of the coverage to be provided for construction is procured by the owner or contractor. Once the coverage is purchased, all parties to be involved in the project, the owner or developer, contractors, and subcontractors, are insured under the same policies. That being the case, there is no need for the owner or contractor to request or monitor certificates of insurance in order to determine if they are in compliance with contractual insurance requirements imposed. The owner or contractor procuring the coverage knows what coverage is being provided to each of the project participants. While the potential for coverage disputes remains, the problem of ensuring that each party to the project has in fact purchased coverage is mitigated substantially. The owner or contractor need not concern itself with what overly restrictive endorsements might be attached to the policies of subcontractors and others. Likewise, the limits each of those entities will have available for a given project and the ability to cancel coverage are now issues within control of the owner or contractor.

Insurers' Changing Role

Faced with increasing administrative burdens involving certificates of insurance, some insurers are directing their agents not to forward copies of "standard" insurance certificates. To save time and the expense of double handling and mailing the certificate, these insurers indicate that they will no longer accept or maintain "standard" certificates. Taking this step of course requires that the insurer define what it means by a "standard" certificate. Typically this means differentiating between one issued as a matter of routine as opposed to one that would require the underwriters prior approval. One insurer defines "standard" certificate using the following guidelines.

- Use of a current ACORD certificate form.

- No modification in the certificate. The phrase "will endeavor" in the cancellation clause cannot be amended or eliminated; no hold harmless language may be typed on the certificate; and no special items may be added, such as requiring advance written notice to the certificate holder before any material changes are made to the policy. (Precluding any modification to certificates will ensure that many of them will not qualify as standard. The insurance requirements imposed in many contracts often require modifications like those discussed here.)

- The information contained in the certificate should mirror the policy in relation to the policy period. Notations referencing that coverage applies until cancelled are not acceptable.

- The coverage, limits, and other features represented in the certificate must be less than or equal to what is actually provided in the policy.

- The cancellation clause may not exceed 30 days.

- Certificates may only be issued for those specifically named under the policy or de- fined by the language of the broad named insured or blanket insured endorsement.

Insurers imposing this new approach often require that the agent keep copies of all "standard" certificates issued by the agent and that they be made available to the insurer upon request. This then shifts the burden of administering the certificate to the agent. While this may lessen the underwriter's burden, it also may increase the insurer's potential for problems. Transferring control of the certificate to agents means a loss of control for the insurer. For example, when an agent fails to issue a certificate and then learns of a loss or claim, it might backdate its files to cover its E&O exposure. This could then deprive the insurer of any defense it might have to providing coverage, even where the facts are such that the agent's failure should have relieved the insurer of its coverage obligation. A related problem here is that E&O insurers will eventually exclude this exposure from the coverage provided to the agent. When that happens, the deep pocket will be the insurer allocating the obligation to monitor certificates to the agent.

Do's and Don'ts

It might appear—at least from the standpoint of this discussion—that insurance certificates present more pitfalls than they actually are worth. But apart from obtaining a certified copy of the policy, which usually is impractical for a variety of reasons, the only other viable document that can provide some general verification of coverages is the insurance certificate.

Unfortunately, there are more problems over certificates than there are solutions. However, some of these problems can be eliminated with proper observance and conduct by certificate holders, agents and brokers, risk managers, and insurers. The following are some of the "do's and don'ts" that are recommended to reduce problems.

- A certificate of insurance should not be viewed as a policy endorsement, particularly if the certificate contains "conditional language" to the effect that the certificate does not amend, extend, or alter coverage of the policies listed.

- Authorized agents and brokers who issue and sign certificates of insurance should make a good faith effort to see that copies are directed to the responsible underwriters. While it is not always practical to do so, it is advisable that this procedure be documented (e.g., with an accompanying memo) whenever possible.

- Insurance company underwriters should not view certificates of insurance as a nuisance. Considering the problems stemming from the use of certificates, they should be considered as important as other documents relating to insurance matters.

- Insurance agents and brokers should think twice about signing certificates in bulk for later issuance by their clients. Likewise, risk managers and other personnel who have responsibility for seeing to it that certificates must be issued should consider the possible problems emanating from this practice. This procedure can present principal-agency problems of great magnitude.

- A certificate should not list the holder as an additional insured unless the policy is endorsed to that effect. It is also suggested that the certificate designate the appropriate kind of additional insured endorsement (e.g., Additional Insured—Owners, Lessees or Contractors CG 20 10). This step may assist additional insureds in opposing insurers' arguments that a more restrictive endorsement was acceptable. While a certificate cannot alter coverage terms and the policy issued will control, it is possible that this evidence will be considered by courts in an attempt to resolve any ambiguities. Otherwise, it may be advisable to request an actual copy of the endorsement in question. If a certificate designates the holder as an additional insured but the policy is not likewise endorsed, the problem and its resolution should be limited solely to the insurer and the issuer and not affect the "innocent" certificate holder.

- In cases involving and addressing contractual liability coverage, the certificate should reflect the scope of contractual liability insurance being provided—that is, whether the policy encompasses "broad form" indemnity clauses or is limited to "comparative fault" clauses. The ACORD form is deficient in this regard because it merely signifies that contractual liability insurance is being provided without designating the nature of the coverage. However, requiring that the indemnity agreement be attached to the certificate or that the agreement be recited verbatim to ensure some broader coverage is likely to be an exercise in futility, because most underwriters either will not comply or will also add conditional language to clarify that it is the policy that will ultimately control the scope of coverage.

- Insurance agents should never sign manuscript certificates as authorized representatives without first verifying the acceptability of the certificates with insurers. This may be an impractical recommendation when time is of the essence, but agents may be doing so at their own peril. The reason is that insurers are likely to insist on the conditional language before the certificate is accepted, and this conditional language is likely to have the effect of transforming the manuscript certificate to the same level as the standard one used by the insurer.

- Insurers should make a good faith effort to see that certificate holders are properly notified of policy cancellations. However, insurers are under no obligation to notify certificate holders of any material changes in the policies, despite those frequent requests.

- Certificate holders should carefully review the documents they receive for compliance with the underlying insurance requirements. Failure to find and require correction of a clearly identifiable incongruity may make it impossible to successfully assert a claim against the indemnitor or the insurer.

While the foregoing recommendations may reduce some of the problems confronting all parties involved with insurance certificates, they certainly will not solve them all. One of these problems that appears to be irreconcilable is how to determine whether the policy coverage meets the reasonable expectations of the certificate holder. This has always been a problem, but it has been magnified in recent years by the trend toward nonstandardization of policy forms. There has been a tremendous growth in the number of independently filed policy programs, and there is no way to determine what the policies cover without analyzing them and the endorsements attached. But for the certificate holder, this is usually impractical, if not impossible, to do.

Summary

Certificates of insurance originally were introduced to verify that certain general types of coverages and limits were being provided by the insurers designated thereon for the period stipulated. Over the years, some certificate holders have attempted to make certificates do more than insurers intend for them to do. But whether the result is as expected depends on the circumstances and the court of jurisdiction.

What complicates matters is that a growing number of insurers are using independently filed policies and endorsements, and it is virtually impossible to determine the scope of coverage being provided, particularly with respect to additional insured endorsements. An additional insured, for example, may have the reasonable expectation that the coverage being provided to it corresponds to what it has specified in a contract. But until something happens, the additional insured does not know the nature of the endorsement, and by then it may be too late.

The fact is that the contract has no bearing on the scope of coverage provided to additional insureds. The contract can only affect contractual liability coverage. Only in cases where there is an ambiguity will the court interpreting additional insured coverage look outside of the policy to determine intent.

A situation of growing magnitude concerns breach of a promise to provide insurance as specified. A

party, for example, may designate an additional insured on a certificate of insurance but forget to amend the policy. In cases of this kind, the party who breaches such a promise may be answerable for resulting damages. Often, the breach falls on the shoulders of agents and brokers who issue certificates of insurance but fail to follow up on whether the policy has been amended with the additional insured endorsement to properly reflect the request.

To strengthen promises, some certificate holders will request that an entire indemnity agreement be recited verbatim on the certificate. However, a growing number of insurers are balking at such requests since it could imply that the policy will cover all of the damages and costs as transferred under those contracts. In addition, this practice runs the risk of inextricably tying the additional insured status to the indemnity agreement, which could defeat coverage if the indemnity agreement is unenforceable.

Another concern of certificate holders is over the adequacy of aggregate limits. What may be necessary—given the willingness of the insurer and insured alike—are higher multiples of aggregates written on a per location or per project basis.

Those who do not trust certificates of insurance and desire a more solid basis for confirming coverages may request certified copies of insurance policies. The flaw with this technique, however, is that the policies will rarely be received in a timely manner, if at all.

Regardless of the consequences, there will always be those who play the odds and for whatever reason disregard their contractual obligations or fail to see to it that the representations made in certificates reflect the nature of the protection actually being provided. Those who want to avoid these kinds of problems will find they have no easy task before them. It often takes considerable time to read and understand the requirements of contracts (even if the promisor or one who agrees to the contract seeks professional assistance in a timely fashion). It also is time-consuming not only to implement the requirements but also to verify that they, in fact, have been put into place.

The administration of insurance certificates is an enormous task, considering that countless certificates may be required by some entities, and the subjects discussed are only some of the many problems associated with the issuance and administration of certificates. Those authorized representatives of insurers who generally complete and sign certificates often complain that to read contracts to determine the insurance requirements and to verify the representations of certificates are too timely tasks. Perhaps so, but this is a responsibility that comes with the territory. There is no other way by which proper protection can be recommended; the exposures must be identified and evaluated. Without doing this, if a problem arises, one can be assured of involvement in legal actions that are far more time-consuming and costly.

Chapter 20 Notes

1. As cited in *Atlas Assurance Co. v Harper, Robinson Shipping Co.,* 508 F2d 1381 (9th Cir 1975).

2. This case is discussed in more detail beginning on page 347.

3. According to ACORD's certificate of insurance training guide, page 122, "A certificate should be prepared to evidence coverage for an Additional Insured only when substantiated by an endorsement to the policy."

4. Warren, David, "Create Your Own Certificate of Insurance," *The Warren Report,* Orinda, CA: David Warren, CPCU, April 1988, p. 81–85.

5. "The New CGL Aggregate and Certificates of Insurance," *The Risk Report,* Vol. IX, No. 10, Dallas, TX: International Risk Management Institute, Inc., June 1987, pp. 7–8.

6. "IIR/ACORD Clarifies Position on Aggregates," *Rough Notes,* Indianapolis, IN: Rough Notes Co., Feb. 1987, p. 32.

7. *Ibid.*

8. The insurance industry is notorious for experiencing incredibly long delays in issuing commercial lines insurance policies. It is not unusual for commercial lines policies to be issued many months after their inception.

Chapter 21

COMPLIANCE PROBLEMS

Compliance with a requirement to add an additional insured imposes an administrative burden on the named insured, its insurance representative, and its insurance company. In most cases, additional insured status must be specifically arranged in the commercial general liability (CGL) policy by attaching a specific endorsement. Some, but certainly not all, umbrella policies also require a policy amendment or at least some kind of notice to the insurer. Obviously, this requires administrative effort on the part of the named insured to request the endorsement from the insurance agent or broker. The insurance representative, in turn, must request the amendment from the insurer, and the insurer must issue the endorsement. A breakdown in this process can easily occur, resulting in a breach of contract. These kinds of breaches—based on how frequently they are litigated—occur often.

Many of the cases dealing with the breach or failure to procure insurance are discussed in this chapter. Unfortunately, the cases do not mention the reason for the breach. Some of the cases reveal that, while a promise is made to provide certain insurance, whether it is ever fulfilled is inconsequential until a claim or suit arises. It is usually too late to do anything if third-party bodily injury or property damage leading to liability results and the promised insurance has not been procured. Once such a breach resulting in liability has occurred, the question usually arises whether a liability policy covers the resultant damages.[1]

What is especially important about this subject is the consequence for failing to name another party as an additional insured. Indemnitors who have failed to comply with requirements to add others as insureds to their policies have often been held accountable for whatever damages would otherwise have been payable on behalf of indemnitees. If the belt-and-suspenders concept of providing additional insured status and contractual liability protection is followed, the risk of unindemnified loss stemming from the other party's noncompliance is minimized. Thus, if the additional insured endorsement is never issued with a primary liability policy but an enforceable contract of indemnity encompasses the claim, failure to add the party as an additional insured may be irrelevant as to that claim. However, potential problems still exist. For example, the indemnity agreement may prove to be unenforceable for a variety of reasons. Or the scope of an indemnity claim does not match the scope of the hold harmless agreement—i.e., a comparative fault indemnification addressing allegations of the indemnitee's sole fault.[2]

A case in point is *Cosimini v Atkinson-Kiewit Joint Venture,* 877 F Supp 68 (USDC RI 1995). The court held here that the insurance procurement clause did not require insurance for the indemnitee's negligence when the clause stated that "insurance shall cover performance of the above indemnity obligation, Subcontract Number … Article 14," the liability was limited to the percentage of the indemnitor's fault.

It is interesting to note that the contract in this case included classic inextricably tied wording. The indemnity obligation and insurance requirements were in the same paragraph. In addition, the insurance requirements included wording to the effect that the insurance required would cover the indemnity obligation. The indemnity obligation, in turn, indemnified the indemnitee for its sole fault. Rather than void the entire provision based on the requirement for indemnification of the indemnitee's sole fault, the court instead modified the indemnity provision to exclude that portion requiring indemnification for the indemnitee's sole fault. The court then ruled that contractual liability coverage applied only to the extent required by the contract. The parties in this case were fortunate. Had the court ruled the indemnity provision invalid instead of modifying it, the indemnity obligation and the coverage obligation, which were inextricably tied and interdependent, could have both been voided. Since the potential liability is great, the failure to keep one's promise about adding others as insureds can be very costly.

Administrative Burdens

The situation most likely to result in the named insured being held accountable for failing to maintain insurance for another party as the additional insured involves the necessity of attaching an endorsement to the named insured's policy. In other words, to comply with a request to make a party an additional insured under the named insured's policy, some amendment must be made to an already existing insurance policy. One possible reason for the failure to fulfill these requests—apart from the named insured's oversight or failure to read the contract—is that the additional insured has no way of knowing whether the endorsement has been issued because the additional insured seldom receives a copy of the policy or the endorsement.

If a certificate of insurance is requested, the additional insured at least has the opportunity to verify whether its request has been fulfilled. However, as pointed out in **Chapter 20,** the fact that a certificate lists another party as an additional insured does not necessarily mean that the policy has been amended to that effect; although there should be some accountability by the issuer of the certificate for failing to do what is reflected by the certificate. But whether the certificate of insurance turns out to be a false sense of security, the certificate at least offers the additional insured some tangible evidence that its request has been fulfilled.

Relevant Case Law

There have been a number of court cases on the failure to comply with requirements to provide additional insured status to others. While most involve construction operations, some deal with property leasing concerns. Frustration frequently results when the parties who impose contractual requirements on which they depend for protection discover that their attempts were thwarted because the other parties failed to comply with their obligations.

Lease Agreement Breaches

One of the cases most frequently cited by courts of various jurisdictions for the principle that breach of contract to procure insurance is not considered to be covered by a liability policy is *Olympic, Inc. v Providence Washington Insurance Co. of Alaska,* 648 P2d 1008 (Alaska 1982). This case dealt with two sister corporations, one of which was a real estate developer (the lessor) and the other a grocery store (the lessee). The lease agreement required, among other things, that the lessee provide liability insurance on the store premises on behalf of the lessor. The pertinent provision read as follows.

> The lessee shall provide and maintain public liability insurance in a minimum amount of three hundred thousand dollars ($300,000), naming the Lessor as an additional insured, which insurance will save the Lessor harmless from liability from any injuries or losses which may be sustained by any persons or property while in or about said premises.

The lessee obtained a liability policy, but this policy named only the lessee as an insured. The policy also contained a named insured endorsement that extended coverage to various other stores, but the lessor was not listed on this endorsement either. All parties apparently agreed that the lessee breached its obligation to procure insurance and include the lessor as an insured.

A fire broke out at the store premises, and a firefighter was killed. His estate commenced a wrongful death action against the lessor and lessee, alleging negligence in failing to install a sprinkler system and various other building code nonconformities that allegedly were the proximate cause of the firefighter's death. The lessee's insurer ultimately paid the damages of $600,000 and then sought contribution in the amount of $300,000 from the lessor's insurer. The principal question was whether the lessor's insurer was required to indemnify the lessee's insurer.

One of the primary arguments of the lessor's insurer was that the lessee's liability policy covered the breach of contract concerning failure to procure insurance. This argument was based on the policy's contractual liability exclusion. The lessor's insurer asserted that this exclusion of "liability assumed by the insured under any contract except an incidental contract" implied that the policy provided coverage against liability under any contract defined as "incidental." Since the lease covenant did come within the scope of the policy's "incidental contract" definition, it was argued, the lessee's breach gave rise to liability covered by its policy.

The Alaska court, however, did not agree with that reasoning. It explained that to be covered under a general liability policy, a contract not only must be "incidental" within the meaning of the policy but it also must be a contract in which liability was assumed. It stated that liability assumed by the insured under any contract refers to liability incurred when one promises to indemnify or hold harmless another and does not refer to the liability that results from failure to procure insurance.

Reliance Insurance Co. v Gary C. Wyatt, Inc., 540 S2d 688 (Ala 1988), involves an equipment lease. Here, a contractor (the lessee) leased a crawler crane from a rental company (the lessor) for use at a construction site. Part of the lease agreement stipulated as follows.

    (a) It is understood and agreed that the Lessee will include the interest of Essex Crane Corporation as an additional interest under their general liability and automobile insurance policies with respect to this equipment during the term of rental.

    (b) Liability of Lessee: The Lessee shall indemnify the Lessor and hold harmless against all loss, damage, expense and penalty arising from any action on account of personal injury … occasioned by the operation of any equipment during the rental period ….

The contractor had in place a CGL policy. However, it failed to have the lessor of the crane added as an additional insured. An employee of the contractor was injured by the leased crane and filed suit against the lessor, the crane's manufacturer, and his employer. The lessor, in turn, filed a cross-suit against the contractor seeking indemnity under the lease agreement and asserting a claim for breach of contract based on the contractor's failure to include the lessor of the crane as an additional insured under the policy as required by the lease.

The contractor's insurer maintained that no coverage applied to the lessor because the claim against its named insured contractor was based on breach of contract and not on an occurrence resulting in bodily injury or property damage. The Alabama court in this case explained that there is a difference between coverage under an indemnity agreement and noncoverage for breach of contract. Under the terms of the contractor's CGL policy, coverage applied for liability assumed by the insured under any contract relating to its business, i.e., an "incidental contract," so long as the liability assumed is predicated on an "occurrence" that results in bodily injury or property damage.

The question as raised by the court was whether the contractor's failure to perform its agreement to name the lessor of the crane as an additional insured under the contractor's policy constituted an "occurrence" that resulted in bodily injury or property damage. While there was no case law on which to rely in the state in question, the court did refer to the prevailing law of other states, relying on such cases as *Olympic,* discussed previously.

In the final analysis, the court ruled that the contractor's failure to procure liability insurance as required constituted a breach of contract—not an occurrence that resulted in bodily injury or property damage, which is the coverage afforded by a CGL policy. No coverage, therefore, applied to the lessor of the crane under the contractor's policy.

Construction Contract Breaches

In *Borough of Wilkinsburg v Trumbull-Denton Joint Venture and CNA,* 568 A2d 1325 (Pa Super 1990), a borough brought action against a general contractor that allegedly failed to obtain insurance for the protection of the borough. The general contractor was retained to perform some work on an interstate highway. To discharge its responsibility for handling traffic, the general contractor entered into a contract with the borough to use off-duty police officers to regulate traffic. The general contractor was required not only to maintain certain insurance but also to add the borough as an additional insured on the contractor's liability insurance. The policy was purchased, but the contractor failed to get the borough listed as an additional insured.

Following an accident, suit was filed against the borough, its police officer who was regulating traffic at the time of the accident, and the general contractor. When the borough sought protection under the general contractor's liability policy, it was discovered that the borough was not included as an additional insured. The borough, therefore, looked to its own insurer for protection. An action was later filed by the borough's insurer against the general contractor for reimbursement. The trial court in this case held in favor of the borough, and the contractor's insurer appealed.

On appeal, the general contractor maintained that it was not liable because it did not cause the accident and, therefore, was not legally responsible for the accident. However, the court said the issue was not whether the general contractor was liable for causing the accident but whether it was liable for breaching its contract. The appellate court agreed with the trial court, holding that a breach did take place.

An interesting and important issue in this case dealt with the matter of damages versus premium owed. The court explained that the damages incurred from the failure to meet the contractual requirement should not be measured by the premium the general contractor would have had to pay to cover the borough. This measurement would have been considered only if the general contractor notified the borough that the insurance could not be obtained. That was not the case here. In this case, the court held that, where a party breaches an agreement to obtain insurance, such party is liable for the full amount of the damages sustained, i.e., the amount of the award against the municipality.

The case of *Aetna Casualty & Surety Co. v Spancrete of Illinois,* 726 F Supp 204 (Ill 1989), was precipitated by an employee of a subcontractor who brought suit against the general contractor for injuries allegedly sustained at the site managed by the general contractor. The general contractor, in turn, filed a complaint against the subcontractor that involved three counts. Two of the three counts asserted the same claims against the subcontractor that the employee brought against the general contractor. In its third count, the general contractor asserted that the subcontractor breached its contract by failing to fulfill its obligation to name the general contractor as an additional insured in certain liability policies covering the subcontractor's work at the site.

The subcontractor's insurer also filed an action seeking an order that it had no duty to defend or indemnify the general contractor. The liability policy included blanket contractual liability coverage. However, the general contractor's action was not based on the subcontractor's assumption of liability; instead, it was based on the subcontractor's breach of the contract under which the subcontractor agreed to procure liability insurance naming the general contractor as an insured. As a result, the Illinois court ruled that the contractual liability coverage as afforded by the policy of the subcontractor did not apply to the general contractor's third count. Accordingly, the insurer was not obligated to indemnify the subcontractor. But the insurer nonetheless did have the duty to defend its named insured (the subcontractor) for the third count—the alleged breach of contract—and to pay attorneys' fees and costs incurred by the named insured for the entire action.

The case of *PPG Industries v Continental Heller Corp.*, 603 P2d 108 (Ariz App 1979), involved circumstances where a contractor (Heller) should have been added as an additional insured to a subcontractor's (PPG's) liability insurance, but the subcontractor failed to do so. It also dealt with the proper measure of damages in cases of breach.

This case arose after an employee of PPG was injured on the job site and filed an action against Heller. The employee alleged that Heller failed to properly maintain a stairwell that was used to descend from the job location on the roof of the building under construction. Heller's insurer defended the claim and ultimately paid a $70,000 award to the injured employee. Heller's insurer, in turn, filed a suit in subrogation against PPG alleging that: (1) PPG had entered into a contractual agreement with Heller, (2) PPG failed to include Heller as an insured for operations covered by the contract, (3) such failure to include Heller on PPG's liability insurance constituted a breach of the agreement, and (4) the insurance as requested by Heller would have protected it against claims such as the one in question.

PPG lost the decision at trial and appealed the case. The first issue on appeal was whether the primary liability insurance that Heller requested from PPG would have protected Heller in the underlying action. The subcontract agreement, in addition to listing the various coverages and limits to be provided, also stipulated, in part, the following.

(VIII) Such policy or policies shall be endorsed to include the contractor, its officers and employees as additional insureds and shall stipulate that the insurance afforded for the contractor, its officers and employees shall be primary insurance and that any insurance carried by the contractor, its officers or employees shall be excess and not contributing insurance.

Certificates of insurance shall be furnished by the Subcontractor to the Contractor before any work is commenced hereunder by the Subcontractor. The Certificates of Insurance shall provide that there will be no cancellation, reduction or modification of coverage without ten (10) days' prior written notice to the Contractor. In the event the Subcontractor does not comply with the requirements of this section, the Contractor may, at his option, provide insurance coverage to protect the Owner and Contractor and charge the Subcontractor for the cost of that insurance. The required insurance shall be subject to the approval of the Contractor, but any acceptance of insurance certificates by the Contractor shall in no way limit or relieve the Subcontractor of the duties and responsibilities assumed by him in this Subcontract Agreement.

If higher limits or other forms of insurance are required in the general contract or by the owner, Subcontractor will comply with such requirements.

PPG did admit that it did not secure an insurance policy to protect Heller and therefore breached one section of this contract. However, PPG also argued that the insurance requested still would not have protected Heller because the underlying cause of action did not result from PPG's operations. But, after reviewing other sections of the contract, looking into the meaning of "all operations," and reading pertinent sections of state statutes and Occupational Safety and Health Act (OSHA) regulations, the court found that the injury did, in fact, result from PPG's operations and not Heller's operations, as alleged by PPG's employee.

Another issue on appeal was whether Heller sustained any damages other than the additional premium it may have been required to pay for resulting loss experience. The court rejected this argument, holding that the subcontractor must pay the $70,000 along with costs and attorneys' fees, which were initially paid by Heller's insurer. PPG, the court explained, was not relieved of such liability merely because Heller took the precaution to insure itself.

The case of *Cone Brothers Contracting Co. v Ashland-Warren, Inc.*, 458 S2d 851 (Fla 1984), between a subcontractor and a general contractor, resulted in damages in excess of $183,000. The damages represented the amount for which the subcontractor was liable for failing to obtain liability insurance for the benefit of the contractor. The trial court held the subcontractor responsible for the damages stemming from breach of contract and that a statute that imposed certain restrictions on indemnification agreements in construction contracts did not apply because the contractor's cause of action grew out of breach of contract to provide certain insurance. The subcontractor appealed its case.

This case arose following two motor vehicle accidents involving a temporary barrier wall on a bridge project of the general contractor. The terms of the contract between the general contractor and subcontractor stipulated, in part, as follows.

> The Subcontractor shall provide and maintain minimum public liability and property damage insurance in companies acceptable to the Contractor, in such amounts as may be agreed upon …. The Subcontractor specifically obligates itself to indemnify and protect the Contractor and save it harmless from any and all claims, suits or liabilities for injuries to persons, including death, and from any other claims, suits or liabilities arising out of the performance of the work or in any way occasioned by any act or omission of the Subcontractor or any of its officers, agents, employees or servants or any Subcontractor or other person directly or indirectly engaged by it. *All of the insurance policies as hereinbefore provided under this section shall name the Contractor as an additional insured thereunder,* shall assume and provide for the Contractor's defense, and shall serve to indemnify and protect the Contractor and save it harmless from all claims, suits or liabilities as set forth in these Terms and Conditions or any of them.

> The Subcontractor shall furnish the Contractor with certificates evidencing that such insurance is provided and in full force and effect before starting work and at any other time when requested by the Contractor. All said certificates shall set forth on the face thereof contractual coverage as required herein. No amendment or cancellation of any of said policies shall be effective until after thirty (30) days' notice in writing to the Contractor.

> The Subcontractor shall indemnify and protect the Contractor and the Owner and save them harmless from any and all loss, damage, costs, expenses and attorneys' fees suffered or incurred on account of any breach of the aforesaid obligations and covenants, and any other provision or covenant of this contract.

After being named a defendant in the case, the contractor demanded that the subcontractor or its insurer protect it in accordance with the contract. However, the demand was rejected by the subcontractor's insurer on the basis that the general contractor was negligent and, thus, the indemnity agreement was unenforceable. The demand also was rejected because the subcontractor had not made the general contractor an additional insured on the liability policy as required by the contract. The contractor therefore was required to retain its own legal counsel to defend the lawsuits.

The contractor filed three counts against the subcontractor. The first count sought damages, costs, and interest based on *contractual indemnity.* The second count was based on *common law indemnity,* alleging that the proximate cause of the accidents was the subcontractor's negligence and that the contractor's liability was merely derivative. The third count also sought damages, costs, and interest for *breach of contract* based on the subcontractor's failure to obtain liability insurance making the contractor an insured as required by the contract.

The subcontractor answered and denied liability on the grounds that (1) the jury verdict that found the contractor partially at fault precluded its claim for contractual or common law indemnity, (2) the general contractor was negligent in administering the contract and discharging its supervisory duties, and (3) the contract failed to comply with a state statute that imposed certain restrictions on indemnification provisions of construction contracts.

On appeal, the Florida court affirmed the trial court's decision that the subcontractor was accountable to the general contractor. In doing so, the court held there was a breach, a fact that the subcontractor did not dispute. Also, the statute governing indemnification agreements in construction contracts had no application in situations involving contract provisions relating to breach or failure to procure insurance. The subcontractor, therefore, was required to pay the damages and costs that otherwise would have been covered by the liability policy.

While *Mamba Engineering Co. v Jacksonville Electric Authority,* 470 S2d 758 (Fla App 1985), was discussed in **Chapter 20** as respects insurance certificates, it also deserves discussion here since it involved failure to provide insurance as agreed to under the contract. Briefly, an electric authority (the owner) entered into a contract with a contractor for the purpose of constructing electric transmission lines. The contractor was to provide various forms of insurance, including an owners and contractors protective (OCP) liability policy, and was to file certificates of insurance specifying the types of policies to be provided. The certificates, as issued, noted the various coverages but omitted reference to the OCP policy. Following injury sustained by an employee of the contractor and suit against the owner, the owner paid damages to the claimant in excess of $1 million. The owner then filed a complaint against the contractor based on contractual indemnity and for failure to provide insurance as required by the contract.

The Florida court ultimately ruled in favor of the owner, holding that the certificate of insurance as furnished by the contractor did not support an inference that the owner knew the OCP policy had not been furnished. To the contrary, the certificate expressly referred to the construction contract by number. In addition, the certificate of insurance did not affirmatively indicate omission of any coverage as required by the contract. The court of appeal, in affirming the trial court's decision, ruled that the contractor was liable to the owner for $800,000 in damages caused by breach of contract by the contractor in not procuring the proper insurance coverage.

In *Encarnacion v Manhattan Powell, L.P.,* 685 NYS2d 227 (NY 1999), a subcontractor's employee was shot by an unknown assailant at the work site. The subcontractor had agreed to indemnify and hold harmless the project owner and general contractor from any claims arising out of the subcontractor's work. The contract also required the subcontractor to maintain liability insurance and to name the project owner and general contractor as additional insureds "as their interests may appear." The subcontractor failed to arrange the required additional insured status. When the project owner and general contractor tendered defense of the employee's claim against them to the subcontractor's insurer, the claim was denied on the basis that neither was an insured under the policy. The subcontractor ultimately was held liable for the resulting damages awarded against the owner and contractor, including defense costs.

When an agent or broker fails to arrange contractually required insurance coverages, a limited number of defenses are available to the agent or representative when an uninsured loss ensues, but these defenses are not always effective. In *Waterwiese v KBA Construction Managers,* 820 SW2d 579 (Mo 1991), a masonry subcontractor working on an office building project for the state of Missouri agreed by contract to obtain OCP liability insurance for the benefit of the project owner (the state) and the owner's construction manager, KBA. When an employee of the subcontractor was injured in the course of the project and brought suit against the state and KBA, it was discovered that the subcontractor's agent had failed to procure the OCP policy called for in the contract.

The agent advanced two arguments in defending himself against the resulting claim: (1) that the injury was caused by the construction manager's direct negligence (failure to prevent the use of non-OSHA-compliant scaffolding at the job site) and that the resulting liability would not have been covered by an OCP policy in any event; and (2) that in allowing the subcontractor's work to proceed in the absence of the contractually required coverage, the state and its construction manager waived their right to enforce the contract insurance requirement.

The court disagreed on both counts. It determined that the loss could be attributed to KBA's general supervision of the subcontractor, an exposure that specifically would have been covered by OCP liability insurance. And on the waiver issue, the court said as follows.

> The state's and KBA's actions must be so manifestly consistent with and indicative of an intention to renounce a particular right or benefit that no other reasonable explanation of their conduct is possible.

The court found no evidence that the state or KBA intended to release the subcontractor from its obligation to provide OCP liability insurance.

No Liability for Contract Breach

The fact that one party promises to add a person or organization as an insured but fails to do so will not necessarily result in a successful breach of contract suit or award of damages. Much depends on what is requested, whether that request was reasonable, and the degree to which that reasonable request was met.

In *University of Houston v Sterling Bank*, 963 SW2d 93 (Tex 1998), a landlord (the university) brought an action against a tenant (the bank) to recover for breach of a lease agreement. The case arose after a bank employee slipped on some water that had leaked from a ceiling that was under repair. The accident occurred in front of the bank but within the common area of the university premises. The employee sued the contractor that was doing the ceiling repair and the university.

The lease agreement between the university and the bank required that the bank name the university as an additional insured on its liability policy, but the bank had failed to do so. In pursuing its breach of contract claim against the bank, the university argued that if it had been provided with the required additional insured status, the bank's insurer would have defended the claim against it. On the other hand, the bank argued that its employee fell outside the area covered by its liability insurance, so that even if the university were an additional insured, the bank's insurer would have had no duty to provide a defense. Because the injury

occurred in a common area of the university premises rather than on premises leased to the bank, the court ruled that the bank's insurer would owe no duty of defense and that no contractual obligation had been breached.

Another case involving a landlord-tenant relationship in which the failure to procure additional insured status for the landlord was held not to be material is *Light v Martin*, 653 NYS2d 16 (NY 1997). An accident occurred on a driveway leading from a building's loading dock (which was a common area, not part of the tenant's leased premises). The court stated that even if the tenant had procured the contractually required additional insured status for the landlord, the landlord would have had no coverage for the claim against it. (It is interesting to contrast the *University of Houston* and *Light* rulings, with their narrow readings of causation, to the decisions of many other courts in interpreting broadly the "arising out of" wording of standard additional insured endorsements. See **Chapter 9.**)

In one construction case, *Office Structures v Home Insurance Co.*, 503 A2d 193 (Del 1985), a court found that a subcontractor was not liable to pay damages incurred by a project owner after the subcontractor failed to provide additional insured status to the owner. A key factor in this decision was that there was no enforceable hold harmless agreement in the contract.

An injured employee of a subcontractor brought suit against the project owner. The owner was defended by its insurer, which then sought reimbursement from either the subcontractor or its insurer. According to the original contractual terms, the subcontractor was required to indemnify the owner for the latter's own negligence. However, this language was eliminated from the contract.

Under another provision of the contract, the subcontractor was required to provide and maintain, at its cost and expense until completion of the work, such insurance as was required from time to time either by the owner or by applicable law. The subcontractor was also required to include the owner as a named insured.

The subcontractor's liability policy reflected the limits as required by the contract. However, the certificate of insurance, while it listed the owner as a certificate holder, did not show the owner as an insured. The subcontractor also obtained an umbrella liability policy that defined the "insured" to include the named insured, subcontractor, and others to whom the named insured was obligated under written contract or agreement to provide insurance such as was afforded by the umbrella policy.

The owner raised three basic arguments as to why it was protected by either the subcontractor or the subcontractor's insurance.

- The subcontractor did, in fact, agree to indemnify it for its own negligence.

- The contractual liability insurance obtained by the subcontractor through its primary and excess insurers provided the owner with coverage as stipulated in the contract.

- If the insurance did not apply, then the subcontractor would be the bearer of risk.

In elaborating on the first point above, the owner maintained that the subcontractor did agree to indemnify the owner for its own negligence, noting as follows:

> [That certain courts] have held that the presence of a contractual agreement that a contractor procure particular insurance suggests that both parties to the contract intended that the contractor indemnify the other party to the contract for that other party's own negligence.

The court ruled that the validity of the foregoing argument was irrelevant because both parties agreed to eliminate the sole fault portion of the indemnification agreement. The injured employee alleged joint and several negligence of the parties, but nowhere was it asserted that the owner was vicariously liable for the negligence of the other parties. Since that was the case, the court said that the owner was liable only for its own negligence.

The owner asserted next that the subcontractor's obligation to procure liability insurance constitut-

ed a "contractual liability assumed by the subcontractor" and therefore came within the scope of the primary policy's coverage. The court disagreed here, too, maintaining that breach of contract to procure insurance does not fall within the scope of contractual liability insurance.

In its next argument, the owner maintained that the subcontractor's excess liability policy should provide protection, since the owner came within the policy's definition of "insured." (The excess policy automatically included as insureds those with whom the named insured contractually agreed to provide such status.) However, the court also disagreed here, holding that since the subcontractor did not assume the liability of the owner, no coverage applied under either the primary or the excess policy.

Finally, the owner maintained that if it was not covered under the subcontractor's liability insurance, the subcontractor should be obligated to provide the protection itself. The owner pointed to the theory that one who agrees to obtain insurance but fails to do so becomes the bearer of the risk. In making this argument, the owner contended that the subcontractor's obligation to obtain insurance under the contract was separate and distinct from the contract's indemnity provision. However, the court disagreed with this argument. The court explained that the contract must be read as a whole and the subcontractor cannot be held to assume the risk when it was not liable to indemnify the owner for its own negligence in the first place.

In conclusion, the court held that neither the subcontractor nor its insurers were liable to indemnify the owner for the insurance proceeds paid and the costs and expenses incurred in the action brought by the subcontractor's employee. Furthermore, neither the construction contract nor the subcontractor's insurance provided the owner with protection against its own negligence.

Another case where there was no liability for breach, except for legal costs incurred at the hands of an insurance agency's failure to add a project owner as an additional insured, is *Hutchins v Hill Petroleum Co.,* 623 S2d 649 (La 1993). A contractor provided maintenance services under contract with a project owner for 3 years. The agreement in place during the first 2 years contained hold harmless agreements, whereas the third-year contract also required additional insured status. During the period of this third-year contract, a third-party-over action was instituted by an injured employee of the contractor against the project owner. Since the project owner was not named as an additional insured and the contractor did not provide a defense for it, the project owner did not renew its contract with the contractor.

The contractor filed a suit against its insurance agency for failing to include the project owner as an additional insured. The contractor asked for indemnity for any liability to the project owner and damages for nonrenewal of the labor contract. Because the project owner was held to be the statutory employer of the injured employee, the demand of the project owner against the contractor and the demand of the contractor's claim were history.

However, a separate trial was instituted by the contractor against its insurance agency for lost profits from nonrenewal of the project owner's contract. Although there was a factual dispute about fault, the failure to name the project owner as additional insured was found to be a legal cause of the contract's nonrenewal. The trial court found the agency 75 percent at fault and the contractor 25 percent at fault for lack of prudence. The trial court also fixed the contractor's lost profits at $100,000 and its attorneys' fees at $7,500. While the court of appeals affirmed the attorneys' fees, it reversed judgment for lost profits based on two grounds: (1) the contractor could not recover for losses beyond the scope of the insurance contract's coverage; and (2) the contractor could not prove it lost profits as a result of the nonrenewal.

An interesting side note to this case concerns the insurance agency's alleged fault. The producer denied seeing the third-year contract requiring additional insured status until after the accident. The producer also denied being instructed to name the project owner as an additional insured. The contractor and its bookkeeper, on the other hand, testified that the producer picked up a copy of the contract in question. Another employee of the contractor also testified that he had a telephone conversation in which the producer was orally instructed to add the project owner as an additional insured. This conversation purportedly took place shortly after the third contract was signed. The appeals court stated that the trial court's conclusion that the insurance agency was at fault "was not clearly wrong."

Compliance and the Wrap-Up Approach

Monitoring compliance with the insurance requirements imposed in construction contracts is a difficult—some would say impossible—task. Those imposing the requirements are often at the mercy of the very party obligated to provide the contractual protections. Even when a failure to arrange required coverage results in a favorable breach of contract verdict, there can be problems. What the cases discussed in this chapter do not show is whether the successful litigant ever got paid. All too often, those who fail to comply with their contractual obligation to provide insurance are unable to meet the legal and financial consequences of their failure to do so. As a result, even an owner or contractor who succeeds in obtaining a judgment against a defaulting party may not be compensated.

Because an inability or failure to monitor compliance successfully can result in serious financial loss, it is extremely important for those seeking additional insured status to be certain that their own insurance programs will respond when contractual requirements are not met. One method of achieving such certainty, which is gaining popularity within the construction industry, alters the very essence of named insured versus additional insured relationships. An increasing number of owners and contractors are choosing to insure construction exposures under owner-controlled or contractor-controlled insurance programs (OCIPs/ CCIPs), commonly referred to as wrap-ups. Under such programs, the owner or contractor purchases liability and property coverages necessary to insure the project, including the interests of all participating contractors and subcontractors. Typically, wrap-up programs involve workers compensation, general liability, umbrella/excess liability, and builders risk or course of construction coverage. Additional coverages, such as pollution or professional liability, may sometimes be included.

Purely in terms of monitoring compliance with insurance requirements, a wrap-up program provides an advantage over traditional construction insurance arrangements. The owner or contractor—depending on whether it is an OCIP or a CCIP—that procured the insurance knows exactly what coverages apply to it and to each of the other project participants. Concerns about overly restrictive endorsements attached to subcontractors' policies, available limits of insurance for the project, and cancellation of required coverages are reduced or eliminated.

Wrap-ups can create their own unique set of problems and concerns. As discussed in **Chapter 2,** instead of being designated as additional insureds, owners and general contractors typically share named insured status with other participating entities. In many cases, this significantly alters the application of coverage to the parties that would otherwise be additional insureds under someone else's policy; as discussed in **Chapter 4,** the rights and obligations of insureds/additional insureds on the one hand and named insureds on the other differ in several important ways. These differences require careful analysis of wrap-up coverage provisions, but once they are addressed, compliance issues become less of a concern for owners and general contractors.

The relative pros and cons of conventional versus wrap-up programs will depend in large part on the risk management capabilities of the controlling party—i.e., the owner or contractor. In some cases, the increased administrative demands of a wrap-up will be offset by the chance to eliminate the difficult tasks of monitoring compliance with dozens of insurance requirements.

Summary

Additional insured status is generally thought of as a backup to an indemnity clause. For reasons unknown, however, the indemnity clauses were not even mentioned in many of these cases. From the issues discussed in some of these cases, there is some question whether the parties to the litigation really understood that indemnity agreements, contractual liability insurance, and additional insured endorsements are supposed to work in tandem. Coverage should not be precluded simply because such an endorsement was not attached to a policy when an otherwise valid indemnity agreement and contractual liability insurance are in place.

What probably confused the situation was the way in which the complaints were worded. In some cases, for example, the issue before the court was whether the failure to name someone as an additional insured was a breach and, further, whether such breach or failure to procure the additional insured endorsement was the subject of contractual liability insurance. Unfortunately, the added existence of an indemnity agreement and its impact on the policy's potential coverage was often overlooked.

In any case, it is clear that the contractual liability coverage of a CGL policy should not be relied on to cover breaches of a contractual requirement to add another party as an insured to an insurance policy. In lieu of this, indemnitees should include a carefully drafted indemnity provision in contracts and make an effort to obtain evidence, through a statement on an insurance certificate, that they have, in fact, received additional insured status in the indemnitor's policies. Likewise, indemnitors must take seriously the insurance requirements to which they contractually agree—or face the possibility of becoming the insurer of last resort.

1. On the issue of failure to procure an additional insured endorsement as requested, the courts in every one of the cases discussed in this chapter ruled that such failure or breach is not considered to be liability assumed under contract or agreement and, hence, is not the subject of a liability policy's coverage. Despite that trend among the courts, there still is some question as to whether the opinion of the courts necessarily is correct. The rationale for that statement is based in part on the broad phraseology of modern liability policy insuring agreements and on the sometimes faulty reasoning of some courts and their reliance on outdated authority.

    It certainly is a subject that deserves some in-depth study before any meaningful conclusions can be made. In the meantime, the authors wish to make clear that they do not necessarily agree with the opinions of the courts, which have held that failure to procure certain coverage is not the subject of a liability insurance policy.

2. As mentioned throughout this book, additional insured endorsements seldom are manuscripted to correspond to the extent of contractual risk transfer. For example, the standard ISO endorsement, Additional Insured—Owners, Lessees or Contractors (CG 20 10), encompasses the additional insured's sole fault. The fact that the contractual risk transfer is enforceable may not always be enough to encompass a sole fault allegation. The scope of indemnity agreements varies, and not all encompass sole fault either by design or by operation of law. Because of that, this kind of endorsement would be necessary. However, despite the fact that with additional insured status only policy terms dictate the scope of coverage, some would argue that coverage of the endorsement should be no broader than the indemnity agreement. A contract generally is not referred to until after some event happens. By this time, it is too late to refer to the contract to determine the scope of an additional insured endorsement. The endorsement controls. Generally speaking, the only times the contract is referred to is when (1) contractual liability coverage is in question, (2) a policy provision is ambiguous and it is necessary to determine the intent of the parties, or (3) where the scope of additional insured status is to correspond to the extent of the contractual risk transfer.

A NOTE ON CGL
FORM NAMES AND EDITION DATES

It is common in the insurance industry to differentiate between various editions of the same form by the edition dates. Unfortunately, the tumultuous evolution of commercial general liability (CGL) insurance has resulted in inconsistencies in the edition dates of the latest CGL forms that can result in confusion. This issue and the names by which the various policy editions are referred to in this book are explained below.

The pre-1986 versions of the CGL policy were entitled "comprehensive general liability insurance." The last version of this form bears a 1973 edition date, and it is therefore called the 1973 CGL policy. The 1973 CGL policy is still used on occasion by some insurers.

The 1973 CGL policy was replaced by two "commercial general liability" forms in 1986 (one of these forms has a claims-made trigger and the other an occurrence trigger). These forms first went into general use in 1986, and the insurance industry, therefore, refers to both of them as the 1986 forms. However, it should be noted that the occurrence form shows November 1985 as its edition date and 1984 as its copyright date. The claims-made form shows a February 1986 edition date and a 1984 copyright date. To be consistent with industry terminology, these policies are referred to in this book as the 1986 CGL forms.

The 1986 CGL forms were revised in 1988, but the revisions did not go into general use until 1990. Because they were much less controversial than the 1986 revisions, the industry never really developed a name for these new forms. To keep the name consistent with the edition dates printed on the policies, they are referred to in this book as the 1988 CGL policies. However, it should be understood that some insurance practitioners and other publishers may refer to them as the 1990 CGL policies.

CGL forms were revised again in 1993, and these versions bear an editorial date of October 1993, although their use in some states was not implemented until 1994. They are referred to in this book as the 1993 CGL forms.

The year 1996 saw another revision of the CGL forms. This revision included important amendments to the coverage forms and several endorsements. Most states approved these forms for use in March or May of 1996. These forms are called the 1996 edition forms in this book.

A 1997 endorsement revision included mandatory endorsement changing the application of the other insurance clause for additional insureds. The CGL coverage forms were not changed in 1997, however.

The next countrywide filing of the CGL coverage form was made in 1998. It introduced a number of changes clarifying the intent of the pollution exclusion—including one that prevented coverage for additional insured project owners from eliminating coverage for a named insured contractor's off-premises operations.

In 1999 ISO filed a mandatory endorsement revising the CGL insuring agreement to address issues involved in the triggering of coverage for ongoing injury or damage once the insured becomes aware of that injury or damage.

The most recently introduced CGL coverage form bears an edition date of "10 01" and is referred to generally within the insurance industry—and in this book—as the 2001 CGL. It incorporated the 1999 insuring agreement and clarified coverage for Internet liability exposures.

In 2004 some profound changes were made to standard additional insured endorsements—princi-pally the replacement of the once-standard "aris-ing out of" language with what the insurance industry believes to be narrower "caused by" lan-guage. That change and its consequences are dealt with throughout this book in references to the "2004 ISO revision."

COMMERCIAL GENERAL LIABILITY ADDITIONAL INSURED ENDORSEMENTS

This appendix contains 33 Insurance Services Office, Inc. (ISO), endorsements that specifically address additional insured status in the CGL policies (category 20). Also included are two endorsements used with the OCP policy (CG 20 31 and CG 29 35). These endorsements and the page on which each is found are listed below.

COMMERCIAL GENERAL LIABILITY

THIS ENDORSEMENT CHANGES THE POLICY. PLEASE READ IT CAREFULLY.

ADDITIONAL INSURED – CLUB MEMBERS

This endorsement modifies insurance provided under the following:

COMMERCIAL GENERAL LIABILITY COVERAGE PART.

WHO IS AN INSURED (Section II) is amended to include as an insured any of your members, but only with respect to their liability for your activities or activities they perform on your behalf.

POLICY NUMBER: **COMMERCIAL GENERAL LIABILITY**

THIS ENDORSEMENT CHANGES THE POLICY. PLEASE READ IT CAREFULLY.

ADDITIONAL INSURED – CONCESSIONAIRES TRADING UNDER YOUR NAME

This endorsement modifies insurance provided under the following:

    COMMERCIAL GENERAL LIABILITY COVERAGE PART
    PRODUCTS/COMPLETED OPERATIONS LIABILITY COVERAGE PART

SCHEDULE

Concessionaire:

(If no entry appears above, information required to complete this endorsement will be shown in the Declarations as applicable to this endorsement.)

WHO IS AN INSURED (Section II) is amended to include as an insured the concessionaire(s) shown in the Schedule but only with respect to their liability as a concessionaire trading under your name.

COMMERCIAL GENERAL LIABILITY

THIS ENDORSEMENT CHANGES THE POLICY. PLEASE READ IT CAREFULLY.

ADDITIONAL INSURED – CONDOMINIUM UNIT OWNERS

This endorsement modifies insurance provided under the following:

COMMERCIAL GENERAL LIABILITY COVERAGE PART.

WHO IS AN INSURED (Section II) is amended to include as an insured each individual unit owner of the insured condominium, but only with respect to liability arising out of the ownership, maintenance or repair of that portion of the premises which is not reserved for that unit owner's exclusive use or occupancy.

POLICY NUMBER: **COMMERCIAL GENERAL LIABILITY**

THIS ENDORSEMENT CHANGES THE POLICY. PLEASE READ IT CAREFULLY.

ADDITIONAL INSURED – CONTROLLING INTEREST

This endorsement modifies insurance provided under the following:

COMMERCIAL GENERAL LIABILITY COVERAGE PART.

SCHEDULE

Name of Person or Organization:

(If no entry appears above, information required to complete this endorsement will be shown in the Declarations as applicable to this endorsement.)

1. WHO IS AN INSURED (Section II) is amended to include as an insured the person(s) or organization(s) shown in the Schedule, but only with respect to their liability arising out of:

   a. Their financial control of you; or

   b. Premises they own, maintain or control while you lease or occupy these premises.

2. This insurance does not apply to structural alterations, new construction and demolition operations performed by or for that person or organization.

COMMERCIAL GENERAL LIABILITY
CG 20 07 07 04

THIS ENDORSEMENT CHANGES THE POLICY. PLEASE READ IT CAREFULLY.

ADDITIONAL INSURED – ENGINEERS, ARCHITECTS, OR SURVEYORS

This endorsement modifies insurance provided under the following:

COMMERCIAL GENERAL LIABILITY COVERAGE PART

A. **Section II – Who Is An Insured** is amended to include as an additional insured any architect, engineer, or surveyor engaged by you but only with respect to liability for "bodily injury", "property damage" or "personal and advertising injury" caused, in whole or in part, by your acts or omissions or the acts or omissions of those acting on your behalf:

1. In connection with your premises; or

2. In the performance of your ongoing operations.

B. With respect to the insurance afforded to these additional insureds, the following additional exclusion applies:

This insurance does not apply to "bodily injury", "property damage" or "personal and advertising injury" arising out of the rendering of or the failure to render any professional services by or for you, including:

1. The preparing, approving, or failing to prepare or approve, maps, shop drawings, opinions, reports, surveys, field orders, change orders or drawings and specifications; or

2. Supervisory, inspection, architectural or engineering activities.

COMMERCIAL GENERAL LIABILITY

THIS ENDORSEMENT CHANGES THE POLICY. PLEASE READ IT CAREFULLY.

ADDITIONAL INSURED – USERS OF GOLFMOBILES

This endorsement modifies insurance provided under the following:

COMMERCIAL GENERAL LIABILITY COVERAGE PART.

WHO IS AN INSURED (Section II) is amended to include as an insured any person(s) using or legally responsible for the use of golfmobiles loaned or rented to others by you or any of your concessionaires but only for their liability arising out of the use of the golfmobiles.

POLICY NUMBER: COMMERCIAL GENERAL LIABILITY
                                                     CG 20 10 07 04

THIS ENDORSEMENT CHANGES THE POLICY. PLEASE READ IT CAREFULLY.

ADDITIONAL INSURED – OWNERS, LESSEES OR CONTRACTORS – SCHEDULED PERSON OR ORGANIZATION

This endorsement modifies insurance provided under the following:

COMMERCIAL GENERAL LIABILITY COVERAGE PART

SCHEDULE

Name Of Additional Insured Person(s) Or Organization(s):	Location(s) Of Covered Operations
Information required to complete this Schedule, if not shown above, will be shown in the Declarations.	

A. Section II – Who Is An Insured is amended to include as an additional insured the person(s) or organization(s) shown in the Schedule, but only with respect to liability for "bodily injury", "property damage" or "personal and advertising injury" caused, in whole or in part, by:

1. Your acts or omissions; or

2. The acts or omissions of those acting on your behalf;

in the performance of your ongoing operations for the additional insured(s) at the location(s) designated above.

B. With respect to the insurance afforded to these additional insureds, the following additional exclusions apply:

This insurance does not apply to "bodily injury" or "property damage" occurring after:

1. All work, including materials, parts or equipment furnished in connection with such work, on the project (other than service, maintenance or repairs) to be performed by or on behalf of the additional insured(s) at the location of the covered operations has been completed; or

2. That portion of "your work" out of which the injury or damage arises has been put to its intended use by any person or organization other than another contractor or subcontractor engaged in performing operations for a principal as a part of the same project.

POLICY NUMBER:

COMMERCIAL GENERAL LIABILITY
CG 20 11 01 96

THIS ENDORSEMENT CHANGES THE POLICY. PLEASE READ IT CAREFULLY.

ADDITIONAL INSURED – MANAGERS OR LESSORS OF PREMISES

This endorsement modifies insurance provided under the following:

COMMERCIAL GENERAL LIABILITY COVERAGE PART

SCHEDULE

1. Designation of Premises (Part Leased to You):
2. Name of Person or Organization (Additional Insured):
3. Additional Premium:

(If no entry appears above, the information required to complete this endorsement will be shown in the Declarations as applicable to this endorsement.)

WHO IS AN INSURED (Section **II**) is amended to include as an insured the person or organization shown in the Schedule but only with respect to liability arising out of the ownership, maintenance or use of that part of the premises leased to you and shown in the Schedule and subject to the following additional exclusions:

This insurance does not apply to:

1. Any "occurrence" which takes place after you cease to be a tenant in that premises.
2. Structural alterations, new construction or demolition operations performed by or on behalf of the person or organization shown in the Schedule.

POLICY NUMBER:

COMMERCIAL GENERAL LIABILITY
CG 20 12 07 98

THIS ENDORSEMENT CHANGES THE POLICY. PLEASE READ IT CAREFULLY.

ADDITIONAL INSURED –
STATE OR POLITICAL SUBDIVISIONS – PERMITS

This endorsement modifies insurance provided under the following:

COMMERCIAL GENERAL LIABILITY COVERAGE PART

SCHEDULE

State Or Political Subdivision:

(If no entry appears above, information required to complete this endorsement will be shown in the Declarations as applicable to this endorsement.)

Section II – Who Is An Insured is amended to include as an insured any state or political subdivision shown in the Schedule, subject to the following provisions:

1. This insurance applies only with respect to operations performed by you or on your behalf for which the state or political subdivision has issued a permit.

2. This insurance does not apply to:

    a. "Bodily injury," "property damage" or "personal and advertising injury" arising out of operations performed for the state or municipality; or

    b. "Bodily injury" or "property damage" included within the "products-completed operations hazard".

POLICY NUMBER: **COMMERCIAL GENERAL LIABILITY**

THIS ENDORSEMENT CHANGES THE POLICY. PLEASE READ IT CAREFULLY.

ADDITIONAL INSURED – STATE OR POLITICAL SUBDIVISIONS – PERMITS RELATING TO PREMISES

This endorsement modifies insurance provided under the following:

COMMERCIAL GENERAL LIABILITY COVERAGE PART.

SCHEDULE

State or Political Subdivision:

(If no entry appears above, information required to complete this endorsement will be shown in the Declarations as applicable to this endorsement.)

WHO IS AN INSURED (Section II) is amended to include as an insured any state or political subdivision shown in the Schedule, subject to the following additional provision:

This insurance applies only with respect to the following hazards for which the state or political subdivision has issued a permit in connection with premises you own, rent, or control and to which this insurance applies:

1. The existence, maintenance, repair, construction, erection, or removal of advertising signs, awnings, canopies, cellar entrances, coal holes, driveways, manholes, marquees, hoist away openings, sidewalk vaults, street banners, or decorations and similar exposures; or

2. The construction, erection, or removal of elevators; or

3. The ownership, maintenance, or use of any elevators covered by this insurance.

COMMERCIAL GENERAL LIABILITY

THIS ENDORSEMENT CHANGES THE POLICY. PLEASE READ IT CAREFULLY.

ADDITIONAL INSURED –
USERS OF TEAMS, DRAFT OR SADDLE ANIMALS

This endorsement modifies insurance provided under the following:

COMMERCIAL GENERAL LIABILITY COVERAGE PART.

WHO IS AN INSURED (Section II) is amended to include as an insured any person or organization using or legally responsible for the use of draft or saddle animals or vehicles for use with them, provided that the use is by you or by others with your permission.

POLICY NUMBER: **COMMERCIAL GENERAL LIABILITY**
                                                  CG 20 15 07 04

THIS ENDORSEMENT CHANGES THE POLICY. PLEASE READ IT CAREFULLY.

ADDITIONAL INSURED – VENDORS

This endorsement modifies insurance provided under the following:

COMMERCIAL GENERAL LIABILITY COVERAGE PART
PRODUCTS/COMPLETED OPERATIONS LIABILITY COVERAGE PART

SCHEDULE

Name Of Additional Insured Person(s) Or Organization(s) (Vendor)	Your Products

Information required to complete this Schedule, if not shown above, will be shown in the Declarations.

A. Section II – Who Is An Insured is amended to include as an additional insured any person(s) or organization(s) (referred to below as vendor) shown in the Schedule, but only with respect to "bodily injury" or "property damage" arising out of "your products" shown in the Schedule which are distributed or sold in the regular course of the vendor's business, subject to the following additional exclusions:

1. The insurance afforded the vendor does not apply to:

   a. "Bodily injury" or "property damage" for which the vendor is obligated to pay damages by reason of the assumption of liability in a contract or agreement. This exclusion does not apply to liability for damages that the vendor would have in the absence of the contract or agreement;

   b. Any express warranty unauthorized by you;

   c. Any physical or chemical change in the product made intentionally by the vendor;

   d. Repackaging, except when unpacked solely for the purpose of inspection, demonstration, testing, or the substitution of parts under instructions from the manufacturer, and then repackaged in the original container;

   e. Any failure to make such inspections, adjustments, tests or servicing as the vendor has agreed to make or normally undertakes to make in the usual course of business, in connection with the distribution or sale of the products;

   f. Demonstration, installation, servicing or repair operations, except such operations performed at the vendor's premises in connection with the sale of the product;

CG 20 15 07 04   © ISO Properties, Inc., 2004   **Page 1 of 2**

ADDITIONAL INSURED – VENDORS (cont.)

g. Products which, after distribution or sale by you, have been labeled or relabeled or used as a container, part or ingredient of any other thing or substance by or for the vendor; or

h. "Bodily injury" or "property damage" arising out of the sole negligence of the vendor for its own acts or omissions or those of its employees or anyone else acting on its behalf. However, this exclusion does not apply to:

(1) The exceptions contained in Subparagraphs **d.** or **f.**; or

(2) Such inspections, adjustments, tests or servicing as the vendor has agreed to make or normally undertakes to make in the usual course of business, in connection with the distribution or sale of the products.

2. This insurance does not apply to any insured person or organization, from whom you have acquired such products, or any ingredient, part or container, entering into, accompanying or containing such products.

 CG 20 15 07 04

COMMERCIAL GENERAL LIABILITY
CG 20 17 10 93

THIS ENDORSEMENT CHANGES THE POLICY. PLEASE READ IT CAREFULLY.

ADDITIONAL INSURED – TOWNHOUSE ASSOCIATIONS

This endorsement modifies insurance provided under the following:

COMMERCIAL GENERAL LIABILITY COVERAGE PART

WHO IS AN INSURED (Section II) is amended to include each individual townhouse owner, but only with respect to liability as a member of the townhouse association and not with respect to any liability arising out of the ownership, maintenance, use or repair of the real property to which the owner has title.

POLICY NUMBER: **COMMERCIAL GENERAL LIABILITY**

THIS ENDORSEMENT CHANGES THE POLICY. PLEASE READ IT CAREFULLY.

ADDITIONAL INSURED –
MORTGAGEE, ASSIGNEE, OR RECEIVER

This endorsement modifies insurance provided under the following:

COMMERCIAL GENERAL LIABILITY COVERAGE PART

SCHEDULE

Name of Person or Organization:

Designation of Premises:

(If no entry appears above, information required to complete this endorsement will be shown in the Declarations as applicable to this endorsement.)

1. WHO IS AN INSURED (Section II) is amended to include as an insured the person(s) or organization(s) shown in the Schedule but only with respect to their liability as mortgagee, assignee, or receiver and arising out of the ownership, maintenance, or use of the premises by you and shown in the Schedule.

2. This insurance does not apply to structural alterations, new construction and demolition operations performed by or for that person or organization.

COMMERCIAL GENERAL LIABILITY

THIS ENDORSEMENT CHANGES THE POLICY. PLEASE READ IT CAREFULLY.

ADDITIONAL INSURED – CHARITABLE INSTITUTIONS

This endorsement modifies insurance provided under the following:

COMMERCIAL GENERAL LIABILITY COVERAGE PART.

WHO IS AN INSURED (Section II) is amended to include as an insured:

1. Your members but only with respect to their liability for your activities or activities they perform on your behalf; and

2. Your trustees or members of the board of governors while acting within the scope of their duties as such on your behalf.

COMMERCIAL GENERAL LIABILITY
CG 20 21 01 96

THIS ENDORSEMENT CHANGES THE POLICY. PLEASE READ IT CAREFULLY.

ADDITIONAL INSURED – VOLUNTEER WORKERS

This endorsement modifies insurance provided under the following:

COMMERCIAL GENERAL LIABILITY COVERAGE PART

WHO IS AN INSURED (Section **II**) is amended to include as an insured any person(s) who are volunteer worker(s) for you, but only while acting at the direction of, and within the scope of their duties for you. However, none of these volunteer worker(s) are insureds for:

1. "Bodily injury" or "personal injury":

    a. To you, to your partners or members (if you are a partnership or joint venture), to your members (if you are a limited liability company), to your other volunteer worker(s) or to your "employees" arising out of and in the course of their duties for you;

    b. To the spouse, child, parent, brother or sister of your volunteer worker(s) or your "employees" as a consequence of paragraph **1.a.** above;

    c. For which there is any obligation to share damages with or repay someone else who must pay damages because of the injury described in paragraphs **1.a.** or **b.** above; or

    d. Arising out of his or her providing or failing to provide professional health care services.

2. "Property damage" to property:

    a. Owned, occupied, or used by,

    b. Rented to, in the care, custody or control of, or over which physical control is being exercised for any purpose by

    you, any of your other volunteer workers, your "employees", any partner or member (if you are a partnership or joint venture), or any member (if you are a limited liability company).

COMMERCIAL GENERAL LIABILITY
CG 20 22 10 01

THIS ENDORSEMENT CHANGES THE POLICY. PLEASE READ IT CAREFULLY.

ADDITIONAL INSURED – CHURCH MEMBERS AND OFFICERS

This endorsement modifies insurance provided under the following:

COMMERCIAL GENERAL LIABILITY COVERAGE PART

A. Paragraph **2.a., Exclusions** of **Section I – Coverage C – Medical Payments** is replaced by the following:

We will not pay expenses for "bodily injury":

a. To any insured, except church members who are not paid a fee, salary or other compensation.

B. Section II – Who Is An Insured is amended to include the following as insureds:

1. Any of your church members, but only with respect to their liability for your activities or activities they perform on your behalf.

2. Any:

a. Trustee, official or member of the board of governors of the church; or

b. Members of the clergy

but only with respect to their duties as such.

COMMERCIAL GENERAL LIABILITY
CG 20 23 10 93

THIS ENDORSEMENT CHANGES THE POLICY. PLEASE READ IT CAREFULLY.

ADDITIONAL INSURED – EXECUTORS, ADMINISTRATORS, TRUSTEES OR BENEFICIARIES

This endorsement modifies insurance provided under the following:

COMMERCIAL GENERAL LIABILITY COVERAGE PART

WHO IS AN INSURED (Section **II**) is amended to include as an insured any executor, administrator, trustee or beneficiary of your estate or living trust while acting within the scope of their duties as such.

POLICY NUMBER: **COMMERCIAL GENERAL LIABILITY**

THIS ENDORSEMENT CHANGES THE POLICY. PLEASE READ IT CAREFULLY.

ADDITIONAL INSURED – OWNERS OR OTHER INTERESTS FROM WHOM LAND HAS BEEN LEASED

This endorsement modifies insurance provided under the following:

COMMERCIAL GENERAL LIABILITY COVERAGE PART.

SCHEDULE

Designation of Premises (Part Leased to You):

Name of Person or Organization:

(If no entry appears above, information required to complete this endorsement will be shown in the Declarations as applicable to this endorsement.)

WHO IS AN INSURED (Section II) is amended to include as an insured the person or organization shown in the Schedule but only with respect to liability arising out of the ownership, maintenance or use of that part of the land leased to you and shown in the Schedule and subject to the following additional exclusions:

This insurance does not apply to:

1. Any "occurrence" which takes place after you cease to lease that land;

2. Structural alterations, new construction or demolition operations performed by or on behalf of the person or organization shown in the Schedule.

CG 20 24 11 85   Copyright, Insurance Services Office, Inc., 1984   **Page 1 of 1**

COMMERCIAL GENERAL LIABILITY

THIS ENDORSEMENT CHANGES THE POLICY. PLEASE READ IT CAREFULLY.

ADDITIONAL INSURED – ELECTIVE OR APPOINTIVE EXECUTIVE OFFICERS OF PUBLIC CORPORATIONS

This endorsement modifies insurance provided under the following:

COMMERCIAL GENERAL LIABILITY COVERAGE PART.

WHO IS AN INSURED (Section II) is amended to include as an insured any elective or appointive officer or a member of any board or commission or agency of yours while acting within the scope of their duties as such.

POLICY NUMBER:

COMMERCIAL GENERAL LIABILITY
CG 20 26 07 04

THIS ENDORSEMENT CHANGES THE POLICY. PLEASE READ IT CAREFULLY.

ADDITIONAL INSURED – DESIGNATED PERSON OR ORGANIZATION

This endorsement modifies insurance provided under the following:

COMMERCIAL GENERAL LIABILITY COVERAGE PART

SCHEDULE

Name Of Additional Insured Person(s) Or Organization(s)

Information required to complete this Schedule, if not shown above, will be shown in the Declarations.

Section II – Who Is An Insured is amended to include as an additional insured the person(s) or organization(s) shown in the Schedule, but only with respect to liability for "bodily injury", "property damage" or "personal and advertising injury" caused, in whole or in part, by your acts or omissions or the acts or omissions of those acting on your behalf:

A. In the performance of your ongoing operations; or

B. In connection with your premises owned by or rented to you.

POLICY NUMBER: COMMERCIAL GENERAL LIABILITY

THIS ENDORSEMENT CHANGES THE POLICY. PLEASE READ IT CAREFULLY.

ADDITIONAL INSURED – CO-OWNER OF INSURED PREMISES

This endorsement modifies insurance provided under the following:

COMMERCIAL GENERAL LIABILITY COVERAGE PART.

SCHEDULE

Name of Person or Organization:

Location of Premises:

(If no entry appears above, information required to complete this endorsement will be shown in the Declarations as applicable to this endorsement.)

WHO IS AN INSURED (Section II) is amended to include as an insured the person(s) or organization(s) shown in the Schedule, but only with respect to their liability as co-owner of the premises shown in the Schedule.

CG 20 27 11 85   Copyright, Insurance Services Office, Inc., 1984   **Page 1 of 1**   □

POLICY NUMBER:

COMMERCIAL GENERAL LIABILITY
CG 20 28 07 04

THIS ENDORSEMENT CHANGES THE POLICY. PLEASE READ IT CAREFULLY.

ADDITIONAL INSURED – LESSOR OF LEASED EQUIPMENT

This endorsement modifies insurance provided under the following:

COMMERCIAL GENERAL LIABILITY COVERAGE PART

SCHEDULE

Name Of Additional Insured Person(s) Or Organization(s)

Information required to complete this Schedule, if not shown above, will be shown in the Declarations.

A. **Section II – Who Is An Insured** is amended to include as an additional insured the person(s) or organization(s) shown in the Schedule, but only with respect to liability for "bodily injury", "property damage" or "personal and advertising injury" caused, in whole or in part, by your maintenance, operation or use of equipment leased to you by such person(s) or organization(s).

B. With respect to the insurance afforded to these additional insureds, this insurance does not apply to any "occurrence" which takes place after the equipment lease expires.

POLICY NUMBER: **COMMERCIAL GENERAL LIABILITY**

THIS ENDORSEMENT CHANGES THE POLICY. PLEASE READ IT CAREFULLY.

ADDITIONAL INSURED – GRANTOR OF FRANCHISE

This endorsement modifies insurance provided under the following:

COMMERCIAL GENERAL LIABILITY COVERAGE PART.

SCHEDULE

Name of Person or Organization:

(If no entry appears above, information required to complete this endorsement will be shown in the Declarations as applicable to this endorsement.)

WHO IS AN INSURED (Section II) is amended to include as an insured the person(s) or organization(s) shown in the Schedule, but only with respect to their liability as grantor of a franchise to you.

COMMERCIAL GENERAL LIABILITY
CG 20 30 01 96

THIS ENDORSEMENT CHANGES THE POLICY. PLEASE READ IT CAREFULLY.

OIL OR GAS OPERATIONS – NONOPERATING, WORKING INTERESTS

This endorsement modifies insurance provided under the following:

COMMERCIAL GENERAL LIABILITY COVERAGE PART

WHO IS AN INSURED (Section II) is amended to include as an insured, any owner, co-owner, party of joint venture, mining partner or limited liability company having a nonoperating working interest in any oil or gas lease of which you are the operator, but only with respect to their liability arising out of such nonoperating working interest.

To the extent insurance would be afforded under this endorsement, the limitation contained in the final paragraph of WHO IS AN INSURED (Section II) with respect to any partnership, joint venture or limited liability company not shown as a Named Insured in the Declarations does not apply.

COMMERCIAL GENERAL LIABILITY
CG 20 31 07 04

THIS ENDORSEMENT CHANGES THE POLICY. PLEASE READ IT CAREFULLY.

ADDITIONAL INSURED – ENGINEERS, ARCHITECTS OR SURVEYORS

This endorsement modifies insurance provided under the following:

OWNERS AND CONTRACTORS PROTECTIVE LIABILITY COVERAGE PART

A. Section II – Who Is An Insured is amended to include as an additional insured any architect, engineer or surveyor engaged by you, but only with respect to liability for "bodily injury" or "property damage" caused, in whole or in part, by your acts or omissions or the acts or omissions of those acting on your behalf:

1. In connection with your premises; or

2. In the performance of your ongoing operations.

B. With respect to the insurance afforded to these additional insureds, the following additional exclusion applies:

This insurance does not apply to "bodily injury" or "property damage" arising out of the rendering of or the failure to render any professional services by or for you, including:

1. The preparing, approving, or failing to prepare or approve, maps, shop drawings, opinions, reports, surveys, field orders, change orders or drawings and specifications; or

2. Supervisory, inspection, architectural or engineering activities.

© ISO Properties, Inc., 2004

POLICY NUMBER:

COMMERCIAL GENERAL LIABILITY
CG 20 32 07 04

THIS ENDORSEMENT CHANGES THE POLICY. PLEASE READ IT CAREFULLY.

ADDITIONAL INSURED – ENGINEERS, ARCHITECTS OR SURVEYORS NOT ENGAGED BY THE NAMED INSURED

This endorsement modifies insurance provided under the following:

COMMERCIAL GENERAL LIABILITY COVERAGE PART

SCHEDULE

Name Of Additional Insured Engineers, Architects Or Surveyors Not Engaged By The Named Insured:

Information required to complete this Schedule, if not shown above, will be shown in the Declarations.

A. Section II – Who Is An Insured is amended to include as an additional insured the architects, engineers or surveyors shown in the Schedule, but only with respect to liability for "bodily injury", "property damage" or "personal and advertising injury" caused, in whole or in part, by:

1. Your acts or omissions; or

2. The acts or omissions of those acting on your behalf;

in the performance of your ongoing operations performed by you or on your behalf.

Such architects, engineers or surveyors, while not engaged by you, are contractually required to be added as an additional insured to your policy.

B. With respect to the insurance afforded to these additional insureds, the following additional exclusion applies:

This insurance does not apply to "bodily injury", "property damage" or "personal and advertising injury" arising out of the rendering of or the failure to render any professional services, including:

1. The preparing, approving, or failing to prepare or approve maps, drawings, opinions, reports, surveys, change orders, designs or specifications; or

2. Supervisory, inspection or engineering services.

© ISO Properties, Inc., 2004

COMMERCIAL GENERAL LIABILITY
CG 20 33 07 04

THIS ENDORSEMENT CHANGES THE POLICY. PLEASE READ IT CAREFULLY.

ADDITIONAL INSURED – OWNERS, LESSEES OR CONTRACTORS – AUTOMATIC STATUS WHEN REQUIRED IN CONSTRUCTION AGREEMENT WITH YOU

This endorsement modifies insurance provided under the following:

COMMERCIAL GENERAL LIABILITY COVERAGE PART

A. **Section II – Who Is An Insured** is amended to include as an additional insured any person or organization for whom you are performing operations when you and such person or organization have agreed in writing in a contract or agreement that such person or organization be added as an additional insured on your policy. Such person or organization is an additional insured only with·respect to liability for "bodily injury", "property damage" or "personal and advertising injury" caused, in whole or in part, by:

1. Your acts or omissions; or

2. The acts or omissions of those acting on your behalf;

in the performance of your ongoing operations for the additional insured.

A person's or organization's status as an additional insured under this endorsement ends when your operations for that additional insured are completed.

B. With respect to the insurance afforded to these additional insureds, the following additional exclusions apply:

This insurance does not apply to:

1. "Bodily injury", "property damage" or "personal and advertising injury" arising out of the rendering of, or the failure to render, any professional architectural, engineering or surveying services, including:

    a. The preparing, approving, or failing to prepare or approve, maps, shop drawings, opinions, reports, surveys, field orders, change orders or drawings and specifications; or

    b. Supervisory, inspection, architectural or engineering activities.

2. "Bodily injury" or "property damage" occurring after:

    a. All work, including materials, parts or equipment furnished in connection with such work, on the project (other than service, maintenance or repairs) to be performed by or on behalf of the additional insured(s) at the location of the covered operations has been completed; or

    b. That portion of "your work" out of which the injury or damage arises has been put to its intended use by any person or organization other than another contractor or subcontractor engaged in performing operations for a principal as a part of the same project.

COMMERCIAL GENERAL LIABILITY
CG 20 34 07 04

THIS ENDORSEMENT CHANGES THE POLICY. PLEASE READ IT CAREFULLY.

ADDITIONAL INSURED – LESSOR OF LEASED EQUIPMENT – AUTOMATIC STATUS WHEN REQUIRED IN LEASE AGREEMENT WITH YOU

This endorsement modifies insurance provided under the following:

COMMERCIAL GENERAL LIABILITY COVERAGE PART

A. Who Is An Insured (Section II) is amended to include as an additional insured any person or organization from whom you lease equipment when you and such person or organization have agreed in writing in a contract or agreement that such person or organization be added as an additional insured on your policy. Such person or organization is an insured only with respect to liability for "bodily injury", "property damage" or "personal and advertising injury" caused, in whole or in part, by your maintenance, operation or use of equipment leased to you by such person or organization.

A person's or organization's status as an additional insured under this endorsement ends when their contract or agreement with you for such leased equipment ends.

B. With respect to the insurance afforded to these additional insureds, this insurance does not apply to any "occurrence" which takes place after the equipment lease expires.

COMMERCIAL GENERAL LIABILITY
CG 20 35 10 01

THIS ENDORSEMENT CHANGES THE POLICY. PLEASE READ IT CAREFULLY.

ADDITIONAL INSURED – GRANTOR OF LICENSES – AUTOMATIC STATUS WHEN REQUIRED BY LICENSOR

This endorsement modifies insurance provided under the following:

COMMERCIAL GENERAL LIABILITY COVERAGE PART

Section II – Who Is An Insured is amended to include as an insured any person(s) or organization(s) that grants licenses to you when you and such person(s) or organization(s) have agreed in writing in a contract or agreement that such person(s) or organization(s) be named as an additional insured on your policy. Such person(s) or organization(s) is an insured only with respect to their liability as grantor of licenses to you.

A person(s) or organization(s) status as an additional insured under this endorsement ends when:

1. The license granted to you by such person(s) or organization(s) expires; or

2. Your license is terminated or revoked by such person(s) or organization(s) prior to expiration of the license as stipulated by the contract or agreement.

POLICY NUMBER:

COMMERCIAL GENERAL LIABILITY
CG 20 36 10 01

THIS ENDORSEMENT CHANGES THE POLICY. PLEASE READ IT CAREFULLY.

ADDITIONAL INSURED – GRANTOR OF LICENSES

This endorsement modifies insurance provided under the following:

COMMERCIAL GENERAL LIABILITY COVERAGE PART

SCHEDULE

Name of Person(s) or Organization(s):

(If no entry appears above, information required to complete this endorsement will be shown in the Declarations as applicable to this endorsement.)

Section II – Who Is An Insured is amended to include as an insured the person(s) or organization(s) shown in the Schedule, but only with respect to their liability as grantor of a license to you.

POLICY NUMBER:

COMMERCIAL GENERAL LIABILITY
CG 20 37 07 04

THIS ENDORSEMENT CHANGES THE POLICY. PLEASE READ IT CAREFULLY.

ADDITIONAL INSURED – OWNERS, LESSEES OR CONTRACTORS – COMPLETED OPERATIONS

This endorsement modifies insurance provided under the following:

COMMERCIAL GENERAL LIABILITY COVERAGE PART

SCHEDULE

Name Of Additional Insured Person(s) Or Organization(s):	Location And Description Of Completed Operations

Information required to complete this Schedule, if not shown above, will be shown in the Declarations.

Section II – Who Is An Insured is amended to include as an additional insured the person(s) or organization(s) shown in the Schedule, but only with respect to liability for "bodily injury" or "property damage" caused, in whole or in part, by "your work" at the location designated and described in the schedule of this endorsement performed for that additional insured and included in the "products-completed operations hazard".

THIS ENDORSEMENT CHANGES THE POLICY. PLEASE READ IT CAREFULLY.

ADDITIONAL INSURED – STATE OR POLITICAL SUBDIVISIONS – PERMITS

This endorsement modifies insurance provided under the following:

OWNERS AND CONTRACTORS PROTECTIVE LIABILITY COVERAGE PART

SCHEDULE

State or Political Subdivision:

(If no entry appears above, information required to complete this endorsement will be shown in the Declarations as applicable to this endorsement.)

WHO IS AN INSURED (Section II) is amended to include as an insured any state or political subdivision shown in the Schedule, subject to the following provisions:

1. This insurance applies only with respect to operations performed by you or on your behalf for which the state or political subdivision has issued a permit.

2. This insurance does not apply to:

    a. "Bodily injury" or "property damage" arising out of operations performed for the state or municipality; or

    b. "Bodily injury" or "property damage" included within the "products-completed operations hazard."

Copyright, Insurance Services Office, Inc., 1988

MANUSCRIPT ADDITIONAL INSURED ENDORSEMENTS

The primary emphasis of this book is on additional insured coverage as provided in standard policy language, such as that prescribed by Insurance Services Offices, Inc. (ISO), for its member and subscriber insurance companies. ISO has promulgated a number of standard endorsements that address a variety of common situations in which additional insured status might be sought by one party under the general liability policy of another party. (See **Appendix B** for a selection of these ISO endorsements.) Over the past decade, a growing number of primary and umbrella liability insurers have been quietly implementing their own manuscripted versions of additional insured endorsements, either as alternatives to corresponding ISO endorsements or as ways of addressing exposures for which no standard additional insured endorsement has been developed.

Some of these endorsements can be misleading in that they resemble standard endorsements in their format or language. In fact, it is not uncommon for manuscript endorsements to include an acknowledgment that they incorporate or "include" copyrighted ISO language. Such a statement should not be taken to mean that all the coverage provisions of the endorsement correspond to standard ISO coverage.

What insureds are likely to find in a manuscript endorsement is a combination of standard ISO terminology mixed with the insurer's own wording. Such endorsements must be analyzed carefully. When standard and nonstandard policy wording interact, the result often has an effect on other policy provisions in ways that may surprise even the drafter. It is a mistake to assume that the rules by which standard wording is interpreted have no application when applying coverage under manuscript additional insured endorsements. Understanding how manuscript wording modifies other coverage provisions requires a knowledge of the meaning and intent behind the standard wording that has been altered or modified.

Since so many of these endorsements are in use, a random selection is reproduced in this appendix, without company identification, to facilitate a discussion of the range of nonstandard coverage provisions in the marketplace. Given this random selection process and the varying content of the endorsements discussed, no attempt has been made to apply a "favorable" or "unfavorable" rating to any individual endorsement. Such judgments can only be made by those implementing the endorsements, in light of the coverage being sought by the additional insured and the underwriting position of the insurer. What may be considered unacceptable to one insured may be acceptable to another, depending on the circumstances.

A point that will be repeated more than once in this appendix is that no one should assume broader—or narrower—coverage under a manuscript, blanket, or automatic additional insured endorsement. While most manuscript endorsements are typically designed to limit the insurer's exposure in comparison to a standard endorsement's coverage, that is not always the case. The old adage, "Read your policy," is perhaps even more true for nonstandard forms than for standard. Each endorsement must be read to determine if it will meet the needs of the person or entity requiring it and to determine its impact on underlying contract requirements and other policy provisions.

Many persons and organizations that request additional insured status through a contract provision do not appreciate how many different ways of arranging additional insured status there are. In any given set of circumstances, most of those additional insured requests will prove to be wrong for the particular exposures being addressed. A simple, nonspecific request to be "made an additional insured" under someone else's policy can be complied with in ways that fall far short of what the additional insured needs and thought was being required.

Many of the manuscript endorsements discussed in this chapter make reference to coverage for liability "arising out of" the named insured's operations. The term "arising out of" is used in many of the endorsements contained in this appendix; its effect on coverage will not be elaborated on here. For a complete discussion of the interpretation of this important phrase, see **Chapter 9.** Suffice it to say here that the phrase connotes a broad scope of coverage, even in endorsements whose purpose is to limit coverage with respect to certain loss exposures, such as completed operations.

EXHIBIT C.1
ADDITIONAL INSURED—OWNERS, LESSEES OR CONTRACTORS (FORM B)

This endorsement modifies insurance provided under the following:

COMMERCIAL GENERAL LIABILITY
COVERAGE PART

SCHEDULE

Name of Person or Organization:

WHO IS AN INSURED (Section II) is amended to include as an insured the Person or Organization in the Schedule, but this insurance with respect to such Person or Organization applies only to the extent that such Person or Organization is held liable for your acts or omissions arising out of and in the course of operations performed for such Person or Organization by you or your subcontractor.

The endorsement shown in Exhibit C.1 does not carry a copyright notice or any other acknowledgment that it includes copyrighted material of ISO. However, the title could lead an insured to believe that it is a version of ISO endorsement CG 20 10—the endorsement commonly sought to cover the additional insured's sole negligence and including coverage for completed operations. The fact that ISO eliminated reference to the term "Form B" from the title of CG 20 10 in 1997 may help people to recognize that endorsements with this title are not standard ISO vintage. However, until all ISO "Form B" endorsements arc taken out of circulation, insureds will be confused by endorsements like the one below.

Note that one of the objectives of the endorsement in the exhibit is to provide the additional insured with coverage only for its vicarious liability. In other words, the insurer seeks to limit coverage to liability imputed to the additional insured because of the acts or omissions of the named insured or its subcontractor. Thus, for example, a claim or suit alleging that the additional insured was independently negligent or otherwise responsible for injury or damage occurring in conjunction with operations of the named insured may not be covered. The degree of coverage, if any, may hinge on the additional insured's ability to allocate some of its liability to the conduct of the named insured and the applicable law in the jurisdiction involved.

Reference in the endorsement limiting coverage to the extent the additional insured is "held liable" reinforces this premise. In light of that language, not only the issue of vicarious liability of the additional insured but also the issue of allocation must be addressed. The latter requires a finding of what the additional insured was "held liable" for and the scope of "arising out of" wording.

Another troublesome feature of this endorsement and others like it is reference to work performed by the *named insured's* subcontractor. It would be preferable for the endorsement to state that coverage applies to liability arising out of work performed on behalf of the named insured. Reference to work performed by the named insured's subcontractor may fuel an unwarranted dispute. For example, if an owner hires a general contractor to perform some work and this contractor hires a subcontractor, is the subcontractor performing work for the owner or for the general contractor?

Also, where a contractor on behalf of a developer/owner does the construction work involved, it is not unheard of for some insurers to argue that a contractor is not, literally speaking, a "subcontractor." As a result, the argument goes, the contractor's work is not the subject of the exception to the "your work" exclusion (l) of the commercial general liability (CGL) insurance forms. Insurers attempt to support this position by pointing to the definition of the "products-completed operations hazard." That definition holds that "your work" will be deemed completed:

> ... (3) When that part of the work done at the job site has been put to its intended use by any person or organization other than another contractor or subcontractor working on the same project.

Insurers advocating this position argue that, because this part of the definition differentiates between contractors and subcontractors, omission of the word "contractor" from the exception of "your work" exclusion (l) is intended to limit application of the exclusion to subcontractors in the true sense of the word. At best, such a reading creates an ambiguity, given that the term "subcontractor" is not a defined policy term.

As a result, extrinsic evidence may be allowed by the courts to determine the scope of coverage. Among the documents that might be looked to are construction contracts that often require the following.

1. The owner/developer's approval of all subcontractors

2. That the contract is assignable to the owner/developer in the event any contract is terminated

3. That agreements between the contractor and subcontractor protect the rights of the owner/developer with respect to work performed by the subcontractors

4. That subcontractors be afforded the same rights and remedies against the owner/developer as the contractor

---

EXHIBIT C.2
ADDITIONAL INSURED—WHERE REQUIRED UNDER CONTRACT OR AGREEMENT

This endorsement modifies insurance provided under the following:

COMMERCIAL GENERAL LIABILITY COVERAGE FORM

Section II—Who Is An Insured is amended to add:

Any person or organization who you become obligated to include as an additional insured under this policy, as a result of any contract or agreement you enter into, excluding contracts or agreements for professional services, which requires you to furnish insurance to that person or organization of the type provided by this policy, but only with respect to liability arising out of your operations or premises owned by or rented to you. However, the insurance provided will not exceed the lesser of:

1. The coverage and/or limits of this policy, or

2. The coverage and/or limits required by said contract or agreement.

The apparent attempt of the endorsement shown in Exhibit C.2 is to provide blanket additional insured coverage, subject to the existence of a requirement to that effect in a contract or agreement. That intent is made clear given that there is no schedule for inserting the additional insured's name. The endorsement states that coverage can be no greater than what the policy provides but could be less, depending on what the contract stipulates.

For example, if the risk assumed in the indemnity portion of the contract excludes the additional insured's comparative fault, that may be the extent of the coverage provided the additional insured even though the policy would otherwise provide broader protection to the indemnitee (additional insured). Such would be the result if the contract did not have separate insurance requirements apart from the indemnity obligation or where the insurance requirements only require limited coverage, which is an unlikely event. Another scenario where this could pose a problem to the additional insured involves insurance requirements that specify a specific sum of coverage, thus capping the limits available to the additional insured.

Insurers constantly strive to devise wording that will provide additional insureds with coverage that corresponds closely with the degree of contractual liability being transferred. However, such efforts often make the additional insured's insurance coverage appear to be solely for the purpose of funding the indemnity agreement. This results in what is referred to in **Chapter 4** as the "inextricably tied" problem. Insurers engaged in this exercise rationalize that it is unfair for them to provide an additional insured with coverage that is broader than the protection the additional insured (indemnitee) is attempting to obtain under an "insured contract."

Additional insureds counter this argument by stating that the degree of risk transferred in the indemnity portion of the contract is not fully representative of their intent in that regard. The reason is that indemnity agreements, particularly those involving construction contracts, are not always capable of reflecting the full degree of risk the additional insured (indemnitee) seeks to transfer. Because of this potential for problems, additional insureds argue that they use their bargaining power and value of the contract to require additional insured status providing coverage broader than the indemnity obligation. This, the additional insured argues, is the true intent regarding the scope of coverage being bargained for.

Under the wording of the endorsement shown in Exhibit C.2, the additional insured indemnitee may get what it wants by properly wording the insurance requirements, separate and apart from any obligation on the part of the named insured to indemnify the additional insured. If a contract were to require the named insured to maintain "not less than" $500,000 CGL limits and the named insured maintains primary policy limits of $1 million, it appears that the full policy limits would be available to the additional insured under this endorsement.

A problem with this endorsement is that one needs to read the contract to determine the extent to which an additional insured is covered. As mentioned throughout this book, the additional insured endorsement (or provision) and the policy to which it is attached should be the controlling documents to determine additional insured status. It should not be necessary to consult other documents unless there is a problem interpreting the additional insured endorsement or provision. The wording of this endorsement departs from that approach.

Another problem with this endorsement, from the perspective of an insurer, is that there is no stipulation that the contract or agreement needs to be in writing. Oral agreements can get an insurer in trouble because they can promote collusion, i.e., where the named insured and additional insured maintain after a loss or claim that they agreed to additional insured status.

The endorsement shown in Exhibit C.3 states that additional insured status must be required in a written contract or agreement and that such status must be reflected in a certificate of insurance. Coverage applies to exposures involving work performed by the named insured or on its behalf and also for liability arising out of the premises hazard, i.e., the realty the named insured owns, rents, leases, or occupies. From the standpoint of coverage for liability arising out of work performed for the additional insured by the named insured or its behalf, coverage is broad enough to encompass the additional insured's liability. Also, based on the wording of this endorsement, coverage applies to work in progress and after it has been completed.

The applicable limits of additional insured coverage hinge on the underlying contract requiring additional insured status and the policy to which the endorsement is attached. The lesser of those two amounts controls. The problem with this approach, again, is that one needs to refer to the contract even in the absence of a dispute. Given the growing sophistication of indemnitees and their lawyers with respect to the drafting of insurance requirements in contracts, policy limits will likely be the lesser of the two amounts. The amount required in the contract will usually be more than what the policy provides.

EXHIBIT C.3
BLANKET ADDITIONAL INSURED ENDORSEMENT

This endorsement modifies insurance provided under the following:

COMMERCIAL GENERAL LIABILITY COVERAGE PART

WHO IS AN INSURED (Section II) is amended to include as an insured any person or organization (called additional insured) whom you are required to add as an additional insured on this policy under a written contract or agreement currently in effect or becoming effective during the term of this policy provided that a certificate of insurance showing that person or organization as an additional insured has been issued.

The insurance provided to the additional insured is limited as follows:

1. That person or organization is only an additional insured with respect to liability arising out of:

    a. Premises you own, rent, lease or occupy or

    b. "Your work" for that additional insured by or for you.

2. The limits of insurance applicable to the additional insured are those specified in the written contract or agreement or in the Declarations for this policy, whichever are less. These limits of insurance are inclusive of and not in addition to the limits of insurance shown in the Declarations.

The insurance provided to the additional insured does not apply to "bodily injury," "property damage," "personal injury" or "advertising injury" arising out of an architect's, engineer's, or surveyor's rendering of or failure to render any professional services including:

1. The preparing, approving, or failing to prepare or approve maps, drawings, opinions, reports, surveys, change orders, designs or specifications; and

2. Supervisory, inspection, or engineering services.

Because this endorsement provides blanket or automatic additional insured coverage that does not require scheduling each additional insured, it excludes the professionals identified in the last part of the endorsement. This professional services exclusion is meant as a safeguard for situations where underwriters are unable to attach a professional services exclusion each time the exposure arises. That safeguard is often necessary, given that this endorsement automatically includes additional insured status whenever required by contract.

There is no mention in this or most other manuscript endorsements as to the application of coverage in relation to other insurance, despite the fact that one of the reasons for requiring additional insured status is to obtain primary protection under the liability policy of the named insured. The CGL policies of some additional insureds are modified with the Other Insurance Condition endorsement. That endorsement, introduced by ISO in 1997 for occurrence (CG 00 55) and claims-made (CG 00 56) policies, was incorporated into the policy provisions in 1998. If the additional insured's policy contains this revised language, it does not matter that an additional insured endorsement does not mention the application of other insurance. The additional insured's own CGL policy will apply excess of the policy providing additional insured status. However, if the additional insured's policy reflects pre-1977 language and the additional insured endorsement does not address this issue, a dispute as to which policy is primary is likely. (Similar endorsement wording can be made applicable to umbrella excess liability policies.)

A potential for coverage disputes in this endorsement is the reference to a certificate of insurance and the requirement that the certificate list the additional insured. Generally speaking, and as discussed in **Chapter 20**, certificates do not alter, extend, or amend coverage. However, that rule might be challenged where, as here, the policy itself references the certificate. The endorsement in Exhibit C.3 specifically requires that a certificate of insurance evidence an intent to provide additional insured status. As a result, that intent is in essence made a part of the policy to which the endorsement is attached. Because of this, it could be argued that other descriptions of coverage and limits contained in the certificate are incorporated into the policy.

The endorsement reproduced in Exhibit C.4 acknowledges that it includes copyrighted material of ISO. As previously stated, this wording should serve as a warning to compare the endorsement's language with standard additional insured wording to pinpoint any differences between the two.

This endorsement requires that the additional insured be scheduled in the policy rather than providing coverage automatically as may be required by contract. Note that to qualify for additional insured status, the person or organization must be identified in the endorsement or the policy Declarations and the obligation to add the additional insured must be evidenced by a written contract and verified by way of a certificate of insurance.

Apart from those requirements, the additional insured's coverage is virtually identical to that provided under ISO's Additional Insured—Owners, Lessees, or Contractors (CG 20 10) endorsement, 11–85 edition. Coverage applies to the additional insured's sole fault and encompasses liability after operations have been completed.

This endorsement, like the one in Exhibit C.3, includes a professional services exclusion to preclude additional insured status to architects, engineers, and surveyors. Given that this endorsement requires the scheduling of additional insureds, it is difficult to understand the rationale for this exclusionary provision. Perhaps it is a "fail-safe" procedure in the event underwriters overlook the need for the professional services exclusion—a problem that was discussed earlier.

Unless an additional insured specifies in its written contract that the endorsement is to be primary and the additional insured's own policy is to apply on an excess basis, the coverage of this endorsement will apply excess of the additional insured's coverage. If the additional insured's CGL policy contains current (post-1997) other insurance language stating that the policy applies excess over any other policy where such named insured is covered as an additional insured, a dispute may arise between the two insurers. The criterion for applying coverage under the policy to which the additional insured is added will be whether the written contract stipulates that coverage of the additional insured endorsement is to be primary. This point is becoming less of a problem with the growing sophistication of additional insureds.

Like some of the other manuscript endorsements shown in this appendix, this endorsement requires reference to the underlying contract to determine coverage. This is something that could be a problem if the contract is held to be unenforceable. Persons and organizations seek additional insured status, among other reasons, to ensure that they are protected by the indemnitor's (named insured's) policy. If the contract is unenforceable, that fail-safe mechanism might be eliminated where coverage is contingent on a contract requirement.

As was the case with the endorsement shown in Exhibit C.3, this endorsement also requires that the additional insured be shown on a certificate of insurance. With that requirement come all the problems (or benefits, depending on the facts and perspective) that were discussed earlier.

EXHIBIT C.4
ADDITIONAL INSURED—OWNERS, LESSEES OR CONTRACTORS (FORM B)

This endorsement modifies insurance provided under the following:

COMMERCIAL GENERAL LIABILITY COVERAGE PART

SCHEDULE

Name of Person or Organization

Any person, organization, partnership or joint venture listed on a Certificate of Insurance on file with us, for which you have agreed in a written contract to provide liability insurance.

(If no entry appears above, information required to complete this endorsement will be shown in the Declarations as applicable to this endorsement.)

WHO IS AN INSURED (Section II) is amended to include as an insured the person or organization shown in the Schedule, but only with respect to liability arising out of "your work" performed for that insured by you or on your behalf.

If the additional insured is an architect, engineer or surveyor, we won't cover "bodily injury," "property damage," or "personal injury" that results from the performance or failure to perform any "professional services" for you or on your behalf. "Professional services" include but are not limited to the following:

1. The preparing, approving, or failure to approve maps, drawings, opinions, reports, surveys, change orders, designs or specifications; and

2. Supervisory, engineering, surveying or inspection services.

The following is added to Section IV—COMMERCIAL GENERAL LIABILITY CONDITIONS, Subsection 4. Other Insurance

Insurance provided by this endorsement is excess over other valid and collectible insurance available to the additional insured, whether primary, excess, contingent or any other basis.

However, we will consider the insurance provided by this endorsement to be primary insurance and any other insurance provided to the additional insured shall be in excess and not contribute with the insurance provided by this policy, only if your contract with the additional insured requires this insurance to be primary.

All other terms of your policy remain unchanged.

EXHIBIT C.5
CONTRACTOR'S BLANKET ADDITIONAL INSURED ENDORSEMENT

This endorsement modifies insurance provided under the following:

COMMERCIAL GENERAL LIABILITY COVERAGE PART

A. WHO IS AN INSURED (Section II) is amended to include as an insured any person or organization (called additional insured) whom you are required to add as an additional insured on this policy under:

1. A written contract or agreement; or

2. An oral contract or agreement where a certificate of insurance showing that person or organization as an additional insured has been issued; but the written or oral contract or agreement must be:

    a. Currently in effect or becoming effective during the term of this policy; and

    b. Executed prior to the "bodily injury," "property damage," "personal injury," or "advertising injury."

B. The insurance provided to the additional insured is limited as follows:

1. That person or organization is only an additional insured with respect to liability arising out of:

    a. Your premises;

    b. "Your work" for that additional insured; or

    c. Acts or omissions of the additional insured in connection with the general supervision of "your work."

2. The Limits of Insurance applicable to the additional insured are those specified in the written contract or agreement or in the Declarations for this policy, whichever is less. These Limits of Insurance are inclusive of and not in addition to the Limits of Insurance shown in the Declarations.

3. Except when required by contract or agreement, the coverage provided to the additional insured by this endorsement does not apply to:

    a. "Bodily injury" or "property damage" occurring after:

        (1) All work on the project (other than service, maintenance or repairs) to be performed by or on behalf of the additional insured at the site of the covered operations has been completed; or

continued

EXHIBIT C.5
CONTRACTOR'S BLANKET ADDITIONAL INSURED ENDORSEMENT (cont.)

    (2) That portion of "your work" out of which the injury or damage arises has been put to its intended use by any person or organization other than another contractor or subcontractor engaged in performing operations for a principal as part of the same project.

  b. "Bodily injury" or "property damage" arising out of acts or omissions of the additional insured other than in connection with the general supervision of "your work."

4. The insurance provided to the additional insured does not apply to "bodily injury," "property damage," "personal injury," or "advertising injury" arising out of an architect's, engineer's, or surveyor's rendering of or failure to render any professional services including:

  a. The preparing, approving, or failure to prepare or approve maps, drawings, opinions, reports, surveys, change orders, design or specifications; and

  b. Supervisory, inspection, or engineering services.

5. Any coverage provided under this endorsement to an additional insured shall be excess over any other valid and collectible insurance available to the additional insured whether primary, excess, contingent or on any other basis unless a contract specifically requires that this insurance be primary.

As the title of the endorsement in Exhibit C.5 connotes, it is to be used to add contractors as additional insureds on an automatic basis when required by a written contract or agreement or by an oral contract or agreement. However, intent to add an additional insured by virtue of an oral contract must be reflected through the issuance of a certificate of insurance. Also, the written or oral contract or agreement must either be currently in effect or become effective during the policy period and be executed prior to the injury or damage. This latter requirement is common to contractual liability insurance but not to additional insured status. It is a requirement to be heeded, because the point at which a contract is executed is not always easy to determine. The less clear the answer to that question, the better the chance of a dispute with the insurer. It would behoove those who draft contracts to insert a clause, in conformity with applicable law, if any, to the effect that the contract or agreement be considered executed at the time performance begins. With oral contracts, this condition is not as much of a problem, since performance of the contract, usually self-evident, is a form of execution.

Note that part B of this endorsement may restrict the additional insured's coverage to the equivalent of an owners or contractors protective (OCP) liability policy. This could be a serious limitation, depending on what is required in the contract. For example, if the contractual assumption of the named insured (indemnitor) entails the comparative fault of the additional insured (indemnitee), this endorsement may fall short of the coverage required. The only coverage the additional insured obtains for its sole fault has to do with its general supervision of the named insured's work.

However, this limitation has no application where the underlying contract or agreement requires such coverage. (See paragraph 3 of the endorsement.) This is a subtle and interesting feature requiring close scrutiny of the indemnity provisions and insurance requirements of the underlying contract. Where the underlying contract imposes a requirement for these coverages by way of an indemnity agreement without insurance requirements, the "inextricably tied" issue discussed in **Chapter 4** is again relevant. Where the contract contains sepa-

---

EXHIBIT C.6
AUTOMATIC ADDITIONAL INSURED—OWNERS, LESSEES OR CONTRACTORS

This endorsement modifies insurance provided under the following:

COMMERCIAL GENERAL LIABILITY COVERAGE PART

1. WHO IS AN INSURED (Section II) is amended to include as an insured any person or organization (called "Additional Insured") whom you are required to add as an Additional Insured on this policy under:

    A. a written contract; or

    B. an oral agreement or contract where a Certificate of Insurance showing that person or organization as an Additional Insured has been issued; but the written or oral contract or agreement must be an "insured contract" and,

        (a) currently in effect or becoming effective during the term of this policy, and

        (b) executed prior to the "bodily injury," "property damage," "personal injury," or "advertising injury."

2. With respect to the insurance afforded this Additional Insured, the following additional provisions apply:

    A. The coverage afforded to such person or organization shall continue for a period of thirty (30) days after the effective date of the applicable "work" or until the end of the policy period, whichever is earlier. However, if you report to us within this period the name of the person or organization, as well as the nature of the work involved, the coverage afforded under this coverage form to such person or organization shall continue until the expiration of this policy.

    B. The insurance provided to the Additional Insured is limited to liability arising out of:

        (a) your ongoing operations performed for that Additional Insured, or

        (b) acts or omissions of the Additional Insured in connection with their general supervision of "your work."

    C. The Limits of Insurance applicable to the Additional Insured are those specified in the written contract or agreement or in the Declarations of this policy, whichever are less. These Limits of Insurance are inclusive of and not in addition to the Limits of Insurance shown in the Declarations.

    D. Exclusions b., j., k., and l. under Coverage A., Bodily Injury and Property Damage Liability (Section I Coverages) do not apply.

continued

EXHIBIT C.6
AUTOMATIC ADDITIONAL INSURED—
OWNERS, LESSEES OR CONTRACTORS (cont.)

E. Additional Exclusions. This insurance does not apply to:

(1) "Bodily injury" or "property damage" for which the Additional Insured is obligated to pay damages by reason of the assumption of liability in a contract or agreement. This exclusion does not apply to liability for damages that the Additional Insured would have in the absence of the contract or agreement.

(2) "Bodily injury" or "property damage" occurring after:

(a) All work, including materials, parts or equipment furnished in connection with such work on the project (other than service, maintenance or repairs) to be performed by or on behalf of the Additional Insured at the site of the covered operations has been completed; or

(b) that portion of "your work" out of which the injury or damage arises has been put to its intended use by any person or organization other than another contractor or subcontractor engaged in performing operations for a principal as part of the same project as listed in the Schedule.

(3) "Bodily injury" or "property damage" arising out of any act or omission of the Additional Insured or any of their "employees" (including "temporary worker"), other than the general supervision by the Additional Insured of your ongoing operations performed for the Additional Insured.

(4) "Property damage" to:

(a) property owned, used or occupied by or rented to the Additional Insured;

(b) property in the care, custody or control of the Additional Insured or over which the Additional Insured is for any purpose exercising physical control; or

(c) any work, including materials, parts or equipment furnished in connection with such work, which is performed for the Additional Insured by you.

(5) "Bodily injury," "property damage," "personal injury" or "advertising injury" arising out of an architect's, engineer's, or surveyor's rendering of or failure to render any professional services including:

(a) the preparing, approving, or failing to approve maps, drawings, opinions, reports, surveys, change orders, design or specifications; and

(b) supervisory, inspection, or engineering services.

Coverage provided herein shall serve as excess over any other valid and collectible insurance available to the Additional Insured whether the other insurance is primary, excess, contingent or on any other basis unless a written contractual arrangement specifically requires this insurance to be primary.

rate insurance requirements calling for coverage encompassing completed operations and sole fault, the limitation of coverage in part B of the endorsement would not apply.

The limits of insurance applicable to the additional insured depend on those specified in the written contract and the policy to which the endorsement is attached. While the endorsement provides *coverage* with respect to either oral or written contracts, it is silent on the issue of *limits* in relation to oral contracts. Because the endorsement requires a certificate of insurance to evidence additional insured status where oral contracts are involved, the certificate may also state what the limits are to be. However, allowing a policy to be amended by the certificate could pose problems.

The additional insured's coverage under this endorsement, as explained in paragraph 5, is excess, unless the contract or agreement requires the insurance to apply on a primary basis. As is becoming commonplace—primarily with blanket additional insured endorsements—this endorsement specifically excludes additional insured status for architects, engineers, or surveyors.

The endorsement reflected in Exhibit C.6 is unusually long and to some extent confusing. Like some of the other endorsements in this appendix, it provides coverage contingent on a written contract or an oral contract evidenced by a certificate of insurance. Like the endorsement shown in Exhibit C.5, this endorsement addresses contracts currently in effect or becoming effective during the policy period and executed prior to the injury or damage. One area of potential confusion created by this endorsement is that the written or oral contract or agreement requiring additional insured status must be an "insured contract," as defined in the policy. But under part E of the endorsement, liability assumed under contract or agreement is excluded, other than for liability that the additional insured would have in the absence of the contract or agreement.

A coverage limitation in this endorsement that may trouble insureds is the deletion of broad form property damage coverage under part 2D and 2E(4)—coverage for property damage to any work performed by the named insured for the additional insured. There is, for example, no coverage typically provided by exception to exclusion j of a CGL policy, for damage to property while being constructed, other than that particular part out of which damage arises.

This endorsement also raises the issues related to oral contracts, coverage evidenced by certificates of insurance, and a failure to address limits in relation to oral contracts, all of which were discussed earlier for other endorsements.

Overall, the apparent intent of this endorsement is to give the additional insured as little coverage as possible and to place that coverage on an excess basis, unless primary coverage is required by contract. This endorsement may fall short of providing the coverage required by contract, making matters difficult for the named insured who agrees to provide additional insured status, subject to certain stipulations. On the other hand, this endorsement would comply with additional insured requirements that do not specify any particular scope of coverage. For that reason it serves as a prime example of why additional insured requirements should be specific. If an additional insured wants broad coverage but does not specifically request it, the coverage provided by this endorsement is in full compliance with insurance requirements.

CASE INDEX

TOPICAL INDEX